THE COMPLETE
BOOK OF THE DOG

Editorial Adviser David Macdonald MA DPhil

Contributors

Ronald S Anderson BVMS PhD MRCVS
W F Butler BVSc PhD FRCVS
Andrew Edney BA BVetMed MRCVS
Terry McHaffie MBE
Peter Messent MA DPhil
Valerie Riley BVSc MRCVS
James Serpell BSc PhD
M J R Stockman MRCVS
Catherine Sutton
Malcolm B Willis BSc PhD
Stephen Wright
Charles Wyant

THE COMPLETE BOOK OF THE DOG

Pelham Books
LONDON

First published in Great Britain by
PELHAM BOOKS LTD, 44 Bedford Square,
London WC1B 3DP
1985

Designed and produced by
The Rainbird Publishing Group Ltd
40 Park Street, London W1Y 4DE

© The Rainbird Publishing Group Ltd, 1985

Editor: Lizzie Boyd
Art Editor: Sally Smallwood

British Library Cataloguing in Publication Data

The Complete Book of the Dog
1. Dogs
I. Macdonald, David W.
636.7   SF426

ISBN 0-7207-1606-3

Text set by Servis Filmsetting Ltd, Manchester
Illustrations originated by Bridge Graphics Ltd, Hull
Printed and bound by Arnoldo Mondadori Editore, Verona, Italy

CONTENTS

FOREWORD

This book is not only about dogs, all dogs, whether purebred or not, but also about their owners. Man and dog are inseparable – the result of a unique relationship that has evolved and endured for thousands of years.

When parenthood is contemplated, people generally have at least a sketchy idea of how to care for their child, guide it in its infancy, support it during its schooling and set it on the path to adulthood. It is easy to become a dog owner without appreciating what the responsibilities are and how much continuous care is necessary. A dog does not become a well-behaved, trusted and trusting member of a family without the owner making a considerable effort. Unlike a child, a dog does not grasp the significance of every unspoken word or gesture, nor is he always able to convey to his owner his moods, anxieties and needs. Understanding between dog and owner is a two-way process but even the most loving owner knows moments of helplessness when his charge's behaviour is totally inexplicable.

It is this gap that *The Complete Book of the Dog*, with its team of distinguished contributors, attempts to bridge. Each is an authority in a particular field of dog study and shares with the reader his or her profound knowledge.

The book begins with a history of the dog, from Paleolithic times to the present. Although this may not appear to be essential knowledge, it does throw light on why dogs are as they are, and how the friendship between us developed. Thereafter, the book follows the dog from the moment when a young puppy leaves his mother for a world dominated by man. This canine 'Dr Spock' is full of practical advice on routine care, on basic training and how to help a dog fit into his new environment. His psychology is explored and the reasons for his sometimes perplexing behaviour explained. His anatomy and sensory make-up are made clear in easily understood diagrams. The essential aspects of exercise, diet and sexual activities, all of which make a happy and contented dog, are fully discussed. Not least, there is a valuable section on the love that must be given to a dog during his declining years.

Despite the mutual understanding that develops between owner and dog, he is unable to inform us of any pains he may be suffering. The health and fitness section helps to overcome this problem by pinpointing symptoms and suggests suitable veterinary treatment and its probable outcome.

Finally, there is a compendium of recognized pure breeds, giving details of their characteristics, temperament and suitability for intending owners.

6

EVOLUTION & DEVELOPMENT OF THE DOMESTIC DOG

The origin of the domestic dog has long been the subject of controversy. It is difficult to believe that animals as different as Pugs and Greyhounds, Chihuahuas and St Bernards are all descended from a single common ancestor. Even Charles Darwin, father of modern evolutionary theory, was so bemused by the sheer variety of domestic breeds that he readily accepted the idea of mixed descent from several different wild species. During the 1950s the Austrian ethologist Konrad Lorenz narrowed the field by arguing that all dogs could be divided into two types, one derived primarily from the wolf (*Canis lupus*) and the other primarily from the golden jackal (*Canis aureus*). Other authorities rejected both jackals and wolves as possible progenitors and proposed instead a hypothetical wild-dog ancestor (*Canis ferus*) which had since become extinct.

The solid, square-limbed Pug and the dainty, graceful Italian Greyhound are as different as chalk and cheese, yet both are descended from the wolf

Today the picture has become considerably clearer as the result of much careful research. Detailed studies of anatomy have virtually eliminated the golden jackal from anything but a minor contribution to canine ancestry; the bones of its skull and the size and structure of its teeth differ markedly from those of the dog. In contrast, the skull and tooth remains of early domestic dogs have been found to be similar to and, in some cases, nearly identical to those of small wolves.

Research on comparative behaviour patterns has also provided convincing evidence of wolf ancestry. In one study it was found that of a total of ninety different behaviour patterns recorded in domestic dogs, only nineteen were absent in wolves and that those missing were all comparatively minor activities which probably do occur in wolves but have never actually been observed. Conversely, all the behaviour patterns observed in wolves but not in dogs arose in special hunting contexts which domestic dogs do not normally encounter. Based on available evidence it is probable that all modern dog breeds are indeed descended from the wolf, most probably one of the smaller subspecies which today inhabit parts of southern Asia.

Canis ferus, the hypothetical wild ancestor proposed by some authorities, never gained many adherents, mainly because no fossil remains have ever been unearthed to confirm its existence. Indeed, the invention of this apparently mythical beast as an alternative to the wolf and jackal may have arisen largely from prejudice. Since time immemorial, Europeans have traditionally, and erroneously, regarded jackals as miserable, cowardly scavengers, and the unfortunate wolf has been unfairly branded as a symbol of diabolical cunning and ferocity – the proverbial bane of innocent little girls in red riding hoods.

The first domestication

The earliest domestication of the wolf probably took place either in southern Europe or Asia Minor. A fragment of jawbone, recovered from a Paleolithic site in West Germany and thought to be about 14,000 years old, may prove to be the oldest known remains of a domestic dog. The jaw is relatively short compared to that of a wolf, and consequently the teeth are more crowded together. Both these attributes are typical of early dogs and probably reflect changes in the quality of the animals' diet as a result of domestication. Other important finds include bone fragments from Iraq and the entire skeleton of a four- to five-month-old puppy which was buried together with its human owner some 12,000 years ago in northern Israel. These and other discoveries indicate that the wolf was domesticated before any other animal species.

Although no record has survived of the precise events which led to the eventual domestication of wolves, a variety of imaginative reconstructions have been written on the subject. Most of these see domestication as the deliberate outcome of human ingenuity: our ancestors perceived the potential value of wolves for hunting and guarding, for scavenging or for consumption and therefore took the necessary steps towards domesticating them. There is little evidence that our prehistoric forebears were gifted with such insight, and it is more likely that the enduring partnership between man and beast was initially the product of chance rather than design.

The people who inhabited Europe and the Near East during the Paleolithic period (c.14,000–12,000 years ago) lived entirely by hunting and foraging for food on a day-to-day basis. In this respect they were similar to the few hunting and foraging cultures that survive in remote areas of the world to this day. A common feature of such societies is their habit of capturing and raising young wild animals as pets. Such pets are generally baby birds or mammals brought home alive from hunting forays and usually adopted by the women in the settlement, who may even suckle young mammals at the breast like orphaned children. At this stage the adopted animal acquires a special status within the community; it may be given a personal name and be treated like a member of the family, and when it dies it may be mourned and buried formally. Ordinarily, the killing and eating of such pets is taboo.

Aboriginal pet-keeping of this type is no better understood than pet-keeping in Western societies. However, it is thought to originate from the so-called 'cute response' – the almost reflex, protective and parental reaction that human and animal infants seem to excite in most adults. Whatever its origin and function, the pet-keeping tendency probably played a major part in the process of wolf domestication. During the first few months of their lives, wolf pups are as appealing or 'cute' as dog pups, and it is more than likely that our Stone Age ancestors occasionally succumbed to their charms and made pets of these animals. The widespread belief that wolves are utterly savage and untameable is entirely erroneous. In fact, if they are obtained at the age of three to seven weeks and raised in the company of people, wolves become almost as affectionate and friendly towards people as domestic dogs.

A pet female wolf during Paleolithic times might have owed its primary allegiance to humans, but would also have been capable of responding in a normal social and sexual manner to wild wolves it encountered near its human foster settlement. Provided it mated successfully with a male of the same species, such a wolf could, at least in theory, become the ancestor of a domestic line. A number of other mammals subjected to the same treatment might have behaved in a similar way, and this raises the question of why Stone Age Man domesticated wolves long before any other species. One possible explanation is that wolves were already predisposed to life in partnership with humans.

A bond of similarity

Like human hunting and foraging societies, wolf packs are generally small, containing on average from ten to twenty closely related individuals. These packs also specialize in the co-operative hunting of large game animals, as did our ancestors at the time of wolf domestication. Life within closely knit social groups of this kind depends upon a relatively sophisticated system of communication and a high level of mutual understanding between group members. Through a constant exchange of signals individuals express their intentions and emotional states to others; serious conflict is thereby avoided, and the group is able to function as a single co-operative unit. The wolf has only a limited range of vocal signals, but is nevertheless among the most visually expressive of all canids, able to convey a wide range of clear and unambiguous messages through subtle changes in its attitude, posture and facial expressions. Much of human communication is also on the level of non-verbal signals and, in a sense, the two species possess a common language of gesture and nuance which can be used as the basis for a co-operative relationship.

Like humans, wolves are most active during the daytime, and they also resemble humans in being intelligent, playful and emotionally responsive. They are clean animals, and although they prefer a meat diet, they can subsist for long periods on carrion and vegetable material. These various factors created a bond of similarity between people and wolves and made possible their co-existence in a combined social group.

The structure of a wolf pack is maintained by dominance hierarchies. The highest-ranking male in the pack is generally the focal point of group activities, and the internal stability of the pack rests on recognition by lower-ranking animals of this individual's dominant status. When wolves are reared in the company of people, the habit of deferring to socially dominant individuals is easily transferred to humans, thus enabling wolves (and dogs) to adjust to their necessarily subordinate role within human society. Deference to people is more difficult to entrain in less hierarchical animals such as cats, and this fact may help to explain why early on the wolf was singled out for domestication.

These, then, were the basic ingredients for a recipe which culminated in wolf domestication: (1) human pet-keeping tendencies or, more precisely, the human habit of generalizing social and parental responses to include members of other species; (2) the natural tameability of young wolves and their willingness to accept human domination; and (3) the extraordinary behavioural and ecological similarities between wolves and hunting peoples which enabled these two species to live harmoniously together. Gradually, through trial and error, domestic wolves acquired important economic functions, such as hunting and guarding, within human society, but it is unlikely that such practical considerations played any major part in their original domestication.

A question of timing
Irrespective of whether wolves were domesticated accidentally or deliberately, there still remains the question of timing. There is no way of knowing exactly how long ago people began keeping wolves as pets; even if bones of pet wolves were found in early archeological sites, they would be indistinguishable from those of wild wolves killed for food or pelts. In all probability, the practice of capturing and taming young wild animals is as ancient as hunting itself, and yet there are no obvious signs of wolf domestication until the end of the Paleolithic period. The critical factor may well have been climate.

The domestication of the wolf coincided with the end of the last Ice Age, a period of rapid climatic change which began roughly 14,000 years ago. At the time much of Europe and Asia was covered by plains of tundra-like vegetation which supported vast herds of large mammals, such as bison, reindeer, mammoth, and a variety of wild sheep, goats and horses which supplied man with an abundant and ready source of food. The grazing herds were constantly on the move, migrating north and south with the seasons, and obliging the hunters to be equally mobile and nomadic. When the glaciers finally began to retreat, the rich Ice Age fauna on which people had depended also disappeared and with it the traditional nomadic life style.

Wolves and feral dogs feed their puppies in a standing position. Most domesticated dogs lie on their sides while the litter suckles

The few cultures that survived, diversified and instead of depending on a few species of large mammals, they began to eat a wider range of foods, including fish, shellfish and a high proportion of vegetable matter. Because they no longer depended on migrating herds, people settled for the first time in permanent villages. It was this shift from nomadism to settled village life which probably acted as the catalyst for wolf domestication.

Although Stone Age peoples and wolves had much in common, they also differed in one important respect. When a woman bears a child, she is normally able to resume her usual activities within a short time after giving birth. If she needs to travel, she carries the infant along with her other possessions. The situation for wolves is rather different. Wolf mothers give birth in semi-permanent dens, and the pups are not fully mobile until they are four or five months old. The mother must therefore remain within daily commuting distance of the den for about a third of a year before she can move on.

Even if the nomadic Ice Age people had made a habit of capturing and rearing wolf pups, the normal parental routines of a pet wolf would have been disrupted by the restless life style of its human foster family. The wolf mother would have been forced to desert its owners or to abandon its pups before they were old enough to fend for themselves. In neither case would subsequent domestication have been feasible. However, once people began to live in permanent settlements, this conflict of interests was immediately resolved, and domestication became not only possible but virtually inevitable.

The evolution of the dog

Within the last 14,000 years – a comparatively short period in evolutionary terms – the domestic wolf has been transformed into a bewildering array of different breeds, races and local varieties of dog – far more than is found in any other domestic animal species. Roughly 180 distinct dog breeds are currently recognized by the American Kennel Club, 160 by the English Kennel Club, and the total number of true-breeding types throughout the world has been estimated at anything from 400 to 800.

Several factors were responsible for the explosive evolution of new canine varieties. During the period which followed domestication, pet wolves lived among many small, sedentary and isolated tribal societies where mating with unrelated individuals would have been rare. Inbreeding is known for promoting rapid genetic divergence between animal populations. Genetically, wolves are also highly variable and this tendency would have expressed itself under the abnormally protected environment of domestication.

Jack Russell Terriers have been around for more than a century and a half, immensely popular in Britain as sporting and pet dogs, yet they are still not recognized as a breed

Pet owners also played a major part in promoting diversity. By killing, driving away and generally discouraging individuals with undesirable characteristics, our ancestors perhaps unconsciously selected the dogs they preferred. Animals which displayed attractive or desirable attributes, such as useful or appealing behaviour and unusual physical peculiarities, may have been preferentially treated. As a result of receiving better care and food, these favoured individuals would have been healthier and better able to produce and raise pups similar to themselves. Each village, tribe or region might have shown different preferences: some would favour large dogs, others small; some would have appreciated long hair, others short. This capricious selection procedure, combined with the random expression of novel genetic traits, would gradually produce many local varieties of dog, each as distinctive and unique as the different cultures in which they originated. It is from these early prototypes that all domestic dog breeds were ultimately derived.

Many attempts have been made to retrace the 'family trees' of modern dogs by comparing them with the subfossil remains of their archaic predecessors. All such reconstructions are based on superficial similarities and must remain speculative. Our knowledge of the early history of domestic breeds is as fragmentary as the bone remains on which it is based. Archeological finds from Neolithic and Bronze Age sites show that prehistoric dogs came in a considerable variety of shapes and sizes, but it is not known whether these variations reflect regional differences between populations or individual differences within them. They provide no evidence of unbroken lines of genetic descent between Stone Age dogs and any modern breed.

The first breed to be accurately represented in ancient art was the African Basenji. These dogs were evidently used for hunting in predynastic Egypt more than 6000 years ago. Somewhat later other breeds were portrayed in Egyptian frescoes, including Mastiffs, Greyhounds and Salukis, a range of nondescript hounds, and a curious short-legged creature resembling a piebald Dachshund. Early Mastiffs were remarkably similar to the modern breed of the same name, and they were great favourites with the Babylonians and Assyrians during the third and fourth millennia BC; their courage and ferocity were much admired, and they were realistically depicted on the walls of tombs and palaces.

The ruling classes of ancient Greece and Rome were also enthusiastic about their dogs, particularly various sporting breeds. Much of their literature was devoted to the special talents and uses of hunting dogs, but the descriptions were neither detailed nor illustrated. As a result, we know that they possessed many different breeds or regional varieties, but we have no clear idea of what they looked like. Artistic representations include a number of heavily built Mastiff-like breeds, Greyhounds, Toy or Maltese dogs resembling small Spitz, and a variety of other large and small hounds.

The evolution of domestic dogs remains largely obscure until the end of the fourteenth century, when Gaston de Foix, a French nobleman, published a treatise on hunting in which the sporting dogs of the period were finally named, described and illustrated. Six breeds are mentioned in this compendium: the Mastiff, the Alan Viautre (a kind of Bloodhound), the Alan Gentil (a form of Deerhound), the Levrier (a Greyhound), the Chien Courant (a prototype Foxhound), and the Chien Oysel (a small hawking dog somewhere between a Poodle and a Spaniel in appearance). The care, breeding and use of dogs was almost exclusively an aristocratic pastime in those days, and remained so until the nineteenth century. The emphasis was on sporting breeds, although new and unusual varieties were also prized. This taste for the bizarre was provided for by explorers and merchants who returned from voyages to the New World, China and the Indies with a number of exotic breeds which were soon assimilated into European high society. Out of this fertile mixture of native and foreign varieties our modern breeds of dogs emerged.

Ancient dogs depicted in drawings and sculptures as long ago as 6000 BC are unmistakable prototypes of many of today's breeds. From left to right are the Pharaoh Hound, Greyhound, Saluki, Mastiff, and the Basenji

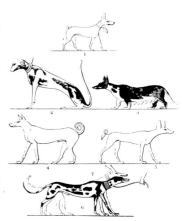

Egyptian frescoes from 4000 BC and Babylonian and Assyrian bas-reliefs from the same period illustrate the popular dogs of the era. Most are hounds and resemble the earlier Greyhounds, Salukis, Basenjis and Mastiffs. A short-legged, long-bodied hound, with prick ears, is not dissimilar to the Dachshund

GENETICS & HEREDITY

The body and organs of a dog are made up of millions of minute cells, each a nucleus containing small thread-like structures called chromosomes. These number seventy-eight, regardless of the breed, as they do in the wolf. Other species have different numbers of chromosomes.

The genes which influence the physical make-up, character, behaviour, health and well-being of the dog are found on the chromosomes. They themselves are long molecules of deoxyribonucleic acid (DNA) linked in two strands rather like the sides of a ladder, with the rungs being chemical bases known as adenine, thymine, cytosine and guanine. A gene is believed to be a portion of the double-stranded DNA, consisting of several hundred base pairs; it is the arrangement of these base pairs which determines the action or potential action of that particular gene. A single chromosome may contain hundreds, even thousands of genes.

Genes have the ability to replicate themselves, effectively unchanged, and the ability to control or influence certain biochemical functions that bring about particular effects in the organism. All the genes in a particular cell do not necessarily function, or they function at a certain stage of life only; the consequences of such actions may be crucial to animal breeders.

It would be more accurate to speak of the seventy-eight chromosomes in the dog as thirty-nine pairs, since the actual units differ in size and shape, and two of each type can be located in a cell. A pair of chromosomes is called a homologous pair; one member of each pair comes from the sire and one member from the dam; therefore one half in each of the thirty-nine chromosome pairs was inherited from the father and the other half from the mother. One parent may appear to have been more influential than the other, but both will in reality have contributed equally to the genetic make-up of their offspring.

In males, one of the homologous pairs is unequal, being made up of a large chromosome (called X) and a smaller one (called Y). This unequal XY set is the determinant of sex, or rather of the male sex, since females carry two paired X chromosomes. All females are thus XX and transmit only an X to all their offspring, while males are XY and can transmit either an X – in which case the offspring is female – or a Y – in which case a male progeny results.

During normal growth, cells multiply by one cell duplicating itself to become two, two becoming four, etc. When one cell becomes two by splitting each of the chromosomes into two identical ones, one set of seventy-eight goes to one end of the cell and the other set moves to the opposite end before splitting away to form the second cell. This process, known as mitosis, goes on constantly during the growth process. During the formation of germ cells (ova and sperm) a different process, known as meiosis, is needed if the chromosome number is to be maintained in the species. At fertilization, sperm – or ova – are formed with only one member of each homologous pair of thirty-nine chromosomes in each sperm (or ovum), resulting in a zygote (fertilized egg) with the correct seventy-eight chromosomes.

The Mendelian Laws

Basic laws governing biological inheritance were discovered in the 1860s by Gregor Mendel, the Austrian monk who gave his name to the principles which hold good to this day, though our understanding of the underlying mechanisms has altered. A particular gene controlling a specific function is always found at a particular point or locus on a certain chromosome. As the chromosomes come in pairs there can only be two of any particular gene in an animal, one on the chromosome from the sire and one from the dam. The gene at a locus may

Alleles of the S series		
Allele	Consequence	Breeds
S Solid	No white markings (referred to as self coloured)	All breeds with no white spots or markings
s^i Irish spotting	White markings around neck, on chest and feet	Boxer, Basenji, Boston Terrier
s^P Piebald	Extensive white, uneven patches	Beagle, Fox Terrier, Foxhound, Basset Hound
s^w Extreme-white spotting	Almost all-white, occasional coloured patch over one eye or on one ear	Bull Terrier, Pyrenean Mountain Dog, Samoyed, Sealyham Terrier

Some breeds carry several of these alleles. Other breeds carry only one, eg S, and all members of that breed are homozygous for that allele

Some genes may have a series of alleles, though any particular dog can only carry two at the most. The S series has several alleles; their dominance is shown (*opposite*) in descending order; the breeds listed are samples only

control a specific function, but differing versions (alleles) of the gene may influence this function. If a dog carries two identical alleles it is said to be homozygous at that locus; with two different alleles it is heterozygous. Some alleles are relatively powerful (dominant) and can influence the outward expression of a feature even when present on only one chromosome; others must be present on both chromosomes (recessive) to have any effect. In the science of genetics letters are used to distinguish genes, capitals indicating dominant genes and lower case recessive versions.

Many characteristics, particularly coat colour, are inherited in a relatively simple fashion, others are more complex. Some genes act in apparent isolation, while others are influenced by the presence or absence of genes at some other locus. The B/b series which determines black and chocolate coat colour is influenced by the so-called extension series of which two versions, E and e, exist in the Labrador Retriever breed. The dominant E allows black pigment to form over the whole body, assuming the animal carries black, but the recessive allele e prevents it and causes pigment to be tan or yellow except on the nose and pads. Therefore, in order to be black, a dog requires not only the B allele but also at least one E allele. A BB dog which also carried ee would have yellow coat colour because the B series cannot function in the presence of the ee combination.

Hemophilia

The X and Y chromosomes are known as the sex chromosomes, all others as autosomes. Genes carried on autosomes can occur in either sex, but genes carried on the sex chromosomes are transmitted in conjunction with sexual status. A gene carried on a Y chromosome could not appear in a female which only has XX. Few, if any, important genes are carried on the male, largely inert Y chromosome, but a major problem, hemophilia A, is found on the X chromosome. This disease, found in man as well as in the dog, is brought about by the failure of blood to clot or to clot quickly enough. It is the end product of a complex series of reactions, controlled by particular genes or factors. Hemophilia A occurs when factor VIII is impaired.

All male offspring obtain their father's Y chromosome and all get one of their mother's X chromosomes. If she is a carrier of the defective X^h allele, male puppies will be hemophiliac and suffer in varying degrees from mild to severe symptoms. Many will die of internal hemorrhaging.

All female offspring inherit their father's normal X^H allele, but while half will get a normal X^H from the mother, the other half will inherit the defective X^h and be carriers like their dams. In due course they will transmit hemophilia to their sons even when mated to quite innocent sires. Although sons carry only one X^h they become hemophiliac because there is no masking X^H on the Y chromosome. Female offspring can theoretically become hemophiliac if a

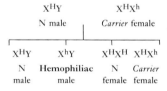

Factor VIII functions through a gene on the X chromosome. A normal male is X^HY, a normal female X^HX^H, with H indicating the normal, dominant allele. In a female with X^HX^h, the recessive allele h causes Factor VIII to fail; while appearing normal, she is in fact a carrier and will be capable of bearing hemophiliac progeny

carrier female is mated to an affected male, but as few such males survive to breeding age, and even fewer are bred from, the condition is rarely seen in bitches. Other inherited bleeding diseases are generally autosomal.

Merle

In some instances the heterozygote (carrying two different alleles) overrules the homozygote with two identical alleles where dominance is incomplete. A classic example is the colour factor or merle gene found in some Collie breeds. Most dog breeds and indeed most Collies carry the alleles mm and show no trace of blue; however, some Collies are Mm in genetic structure and have the characteristic dappled coat of normal and bluish pigmentation. A dog inheriting the MM state is not merle but nearly all-white; it is also frequently deaf, with related eye defects. Mating merle (Mm) to merle (Mm) is rarely practised as it may result in MM animals; most merles come from Mm to mm matings in which the genotype MM cannot be produced.

Inherited eye diseases

Some alleles act in such a way as to bring about variable effects, depending on several factors, including the rest of the animal's genetic make-up. One recessive gene causes the condition known as Collie Eye Anomaly (CEA), seen in sheepdog breeds such as the Rough Collie, Shetland Sheepdog and, to a lesser extent, the Border Collie. Dogs carrying the combination cea cea exhibit the disease, which may vary from total blindness with detached retinas to almost unimpaired vision but with an abnormal eye picture when seen through an ophthalmoscope. The normal dog (CEA CEA) and the carrier (CEA cea) will have correct vision.

Another type of inherited disorder is caused by incomplete penetrance, in which a particular gene, usually dominant, fails to express its presence in the phenotype, as in Centralized Progressive Retinal Atrophy (CPRA) in Labradors. This eye disease is thought to be so dominant that the presence of only one allele, CP, will cause impaired vision. In most cases CP CP and CP cp animals are affected and only cp cp animals have unimpaired vision. However, in some 20 per cent the CP cp heterozygote appears phenotypically normal, and the gene is therefore said to show 80 per cent penetrance.

Inherited defects

From time to time defects appear in all dog breeds. Although there is no evidence to show that dogs are more prone to defects than other species, certain defects are more prevalent in the dog and in particular in certain breeds. Most, though not all, defects are inherited, some occurring early in life when the conscientious breeder would cull the litter. Others do not manifest themselves until later. Congenital defects are those obvious at birth or soon after, but not all inherited defects are congenital nor are all congenital defects inherited.

Potential dog owners should be aware of the kind of defects known to exist in a particular breed, and dogs should be purchased from breeders using combative schemes against particular diseases. The British Veterinary Association and the Kennel Club operate eye schemes (BVA/KC schemes) for testing against defects such as Progressive Retinal Atrophy (PRA).

Some defects are more aesthetic than pathological. Certain coat colours and types which are biologically sound may be frowned upon in the show ring. It would be illogical to buy a show dog with an unacceptable coat type or colour, but in a pet dog both may be irrelevant.

Hip dysplasia

Certain canine defects are inherited in a more complex manner by the joint action of many genes together with environmental influences. Hip dysplasia, a defect also known in man, cattle and cats, is common in the dog. An affected dog will be born with apparently normal hips, but as the dog becomes older the ball and socket joint of the hip ceases to fit properly. The inherited defect may vary from a mild case with no obvious ill effects to severe crippling.

The variation seen in hip status is controlled by many genes (polygenic) which act in an additive fashion: the more hip dysplasia genes a dog has, the worse will be its hip status. However, the action of some genes depends more on combinations of specific genes than on numbers, and environmental factors can have an adverse effect upon hip status. Rapid growth in early life and certain forms of exercise, in particular high jumping or scaling, can accelerate hip dysplasia. The condition is more prevalent in large breeds of dog and largely unknown in tiny breeds. However, there are great differences between breeds, and deliberate attempts have been made to select against the condition. Estimates of the additive genetic component vary from 25 to 45 per cent, but they depend on the method of assessment, the breed and the country of study. In some European countries, notably Scandinavia and Switzerland, compulsory schemes have been introduced to fight hip dysplasia, while optional schemes exist in the United States and Britain. Methods of assessment rely upon X-rays of the hips taken after the age of one year (two years in the United States). In some countries, hips are graded, usually into five different categories; the British Veterinary Association scores hip status numerically on a scale from 0 to 54, with lower scores being better.

Complex inherited traits

Not all polygenic characters can be classified into grades; some, such as epilepsy, are all-or-nothing traits in that the dog is either normal or abnormal. Such traits, known as threshold traits, are difficult to work with but can respond to selection. Anyone purchasing a dog in a breed in which polygenic defects are common should ensure that parental stock are evaluated. It would, for example, be foolish to purchase breeds like German Shepherd Dogs, Labradors, Golden Retrievers or the giant breeds like Newfoundlands and St Bernards without seeking hip scores from the British Veterinary Association/German Shepherd Dog League or their equivalent in other countries.

A dog is acquired for its virtues rather than for its defects, but virtues are different things to different owners. Sound character is the most important trait of any dog whether it is acquired as a family pet or as a potential show or working dog. In working breeds it should be possible to obtain a dog of sound character and working ability as well as beautiful looks, but in some breeds working and show strains have tended to diverge, polarizing in two quite different looking animals.

Most of the aspects governing so-called beauty, character and working ability are inherited. They are, with a few exceptions such as coat colour, largely polygenic in their mode of control. The dog is the result of genetic make-up and environmental influences. The latter may start in the womb of the mother and be carried on throughout the first years of life. A black dog will be a black dog regardless of nutrition, but a genetically large dog will achieve its potential only if it is correctly reared. A dog of inherently sound character may end up aggressive or afraid of particular influences if it is not correctly socialized in puppyhood, and if the owner fails to establish a human pack order.

Breeding and selection

Polygenic characters tend to follow a pattern in which most individuals under study fall around the centre or mean, with fewer at the two extremes. Taking wither height as an example, there are few really small animals of a particular breed and few really large ones, with most around the middle height. The number of genes which, with environmental influences, control height may be unknown, but selection can still be undertaken; many breeds have been altered or 'improved' without breeders knowing the number of genes involved.

A breeder seeking to improve or increase a particular trait must first identify those members of the breed which excel in that trait and then mate extreme examples. Progress depends on two features. One, called the selection differential, is the extent to which the selected group (parents) exceeds their population mean; the other, called the heritability, is the extent to which the character under examination is inherited in an additive fashion. If a trait is not highly inherited, even intense selection will give little response; in contrast a highly inherited trait will not be altered if minimal selection is made for it.

Most breeds have been altered over the years, some out of all recognition, such as the Bulldog, and at the same time new breeds, like the Rottweiler and the Dobermann, have been created. Selection for particular features under genetic control has been instrumental in both instances, and new breeds have involved cross-breeding followed by selection for a specific type. Not all selection has been desirable, and the show ring has encouraged exaggeration in some aspects. There is, for example, little doubt that selection for particular eye shapes has resulted in inturned eyelids (entropion) in breeds like the Chow Chow and Bloodhound, and selection for broad heads in Boxers and Newfoundlands has resulted in additional incisor teeth in the upper jaws. Extra teeth may be a minor issue, but entropion is painful and necessitates surgery. Exaggerated shapes have led to spinal abnormalities in some breeds and to respiratory problems, heart disease, bone problems, etc., in others.

Altering one part of a dog may result in correlated changes in another part. Reducing wither height and body weight, for example, is likely to bring about a reduction in litter size. In general, but excluding giant breeds, there is a tendency for larger taller breeds to produce large litters, but for litter size to be associated positively with mortality.

Breeding of dogs should be done only after considerable study, and before attempting to change a breed by selection, the dog should be considered as a whole. Improving hip status is laudable, but if done in isolation it might result in retardation in other aspects.

Breeding systems

The first stage of any breeding programme is selecting the dog, the second deciding which dog to mate to which. Cross-breeding is the most effective for farm livestock, but dog-breeding is greatly influenced by pedigree. In pure breeding, mating is between unrelated animals of the same breed (outbred) or with closely related animals of the same breed (inbred). It is commonly but erroneously thought that all dog breeds are highly inbred, with consequent character failings. While a purebred animal is more inbred than a crossbred, not all purebreds are highly inbred. Taking 0 per cent as a totally outbred dog and 100 per cent as purely inbred (brother/sister matings for many generations), many dog breeds would have average inbreeding levels of 4–5 per cent and below. In numerically small breeds, the levels may reach 12–14 per cent, equivalent to having the same grandparent on both sides of a pedigree.

Inbreeding is a powerful tool for fixing certain features and is almost always undertaken in the establishment of breeds of any species. However, it does bring to the surface hidden defects, usually recessive, and at high levels (in excess of 20–30 per cent) can bring about serious problems usually affecting viability traits. Experiments with Beagles have shown that at extreme inbreeding levels some 75 per cent of all pups die before ten days old; high inbreeding in a Foxhound colony led to reduced litter size largely due to reduced sperm count in the males. Similar problems would be expected in other breeds. On the plus side, inbreeding can increase uniformity when combined with selection, and it has minimal effect on traits which are highly inherited in an additive fashion. However, inbreeding is best left to experienced breeders with knowledge of their breed and its pedigrees. Novice breeders often mate dogs on the evidence of their pedigrees, but this is an unwise policy: a pedigree is only as good as the dog which bears it.

Retrieve is an inherent trait in such gundog breeds as Labradors and Spaniels

WORKING DOGS

Since joining forces with humanity some 12,000–14,000 years ago, dogs have altered dramatically not only in physical appearance but also in the variety of uses to which they have been put. At different times and in different localities, dogs have been employed for hunting and fishing, guarding and guiding, herding, and fighting, bull and bear-baiting, drawing sledges and travois, turning spits and detecting truffles and for racing and clowning. They have also been used as a source of meat, wool and companionship, as receptacles for waste disposal, as weapons of war and as objects of religious worship.

Terriers, bred to hunt rodents, make trustworthy companion dogs

Few of these uses would have made sense to the people who first domesticated wolves. The number of useful roles which dogs can play in societies of subsistence hunters and gatherers is fairly limited, and the newly domesticated wolves of the late Paleolithic period would have been physically and temperamentally unsuited to many of the specialized tasks that their descendants perform so skilfully. Nevertheless, the life styles of wolves and Stone Age humans shared much common ground; while tame wolves are neither particularly obedient nor easily trained, they are doubtless efficient at carrying out wolfish tasks, and some of these natural abilities and habits would have been potentially useful to their human masters.

Toy dogs of diminutive size are known as lap dogs

Dogs as Scavengers

Throughout many of the poorer regions of the world, feral or stray dogs play an important role as urban scavengers. Some authorities have suggested that this useful habit may have been the original reason for domestication of the wolf. There is evidence for and against this suggestion. It is known that wolf domestication coincided with the first appearance of village settlements and with a relatively sudden increase in human population density. Both these circumstances would have resulted inevitably in the accumulation of organic waste in the vicinity of human habitation, and this, in turn, would have created potential health hazards. Our ancestors stood to benefit from encouraging other species to clear up the mess, but humans have an almost universal aversion to scavenging animals of any kind. This attitude embraces not only wild animals, such as rats, jackals, hyenas and vultures, but also scavenging domestic dogs like the 'pariahs' which abound throughout Asia and North Africa. Animals which feed on carrion and ordure are commonly infected with various parasitic diseases, some of which can be transmitted to people through physical contact.

Working dogs like Siberian Huskies are built for stamina, like hounds for the hunt

The Islamic perception of dogs as 'unclean' may be a simple cultural device for keeping potential sources of infection at arm's length.

The dog's ability to survive off the waste products of human culture has helped it to survive where it would otherwise have perished, but its scavenging behaviour could have done little to improve its reputation.

Ancient Watch Dogs

Most domestic dogs bark when alarmed or excited, and some react to the slightest disturbance with a veritable storm of hysterical yapping. By comparison, the barking of wolves is subdued and infrequent, occurring only in moments of intense excitement or in response to threatening intrusions, usually by other wolves, into the home range or territory. The difference in barking incidents between dogs and wolves is largely the product of genetic changes. It would seem that artificial selection by man has had the effect of reducing the level of stimulation needed to evoke defensive behaviour in most domestic breeds. Deliberately or unconsciously dogs have been bred to overreact to suspected threats and, judging from the exaggerated responses of some breeds, the process of selection must have been intensive. Recent research by criminologists in Britain has shown that the sound of a barking dog inside a house remains one of the most effective defences against burglary.

Special breeds of guard dog have been in existence for thousands of years. The prosperous citizens of ancient Babylonia and Assyria kept large and reputedly savage Mastiffs to counteract urban crime. By way of encouragement, they were given suitably bellicose names such as *Hesitate Not*, *Biter of the Adversary* and *Expeller of the Sinful*. The same people had the habit of burying tiny terracotta figurines of Mastiffs under the doorways of their houses, presumably as a kind of magical deterrent to evil spirits and burglars. Even earlier than this, dogs acquired a reputation as guardians of livestock. In Sumerian texts of about 5000 BC the dog-headed goddess *Bau* (whose name is probably derived from the sound of a dog's bark) was described as a protector of flocks. Similarly, the symbol of royalty in early dynastic Egypt, the so-called 'Sceptre of the Pharaohs', was a shepherd's crook, the handle of which was shaped like a dog's head. Early sheepdogs probably did little in the way of livestock herding, their primary role being as protectors of the flock from thieves and predators. Ironically, the principal antagonist in this respect was their own ancestor, the wolf. In parts of Europe and Asia where simple pastoral economies are maintained to this day, ancient breeds of flock-guarding sheepdogs are still in use. They include the Tibetan Mastiff, a notoriously ferocious breed from the Himalayas and Mongolia; the Komondor and Kuvasz from the plains of Hungary; the Bergomasco and Maremma from the mountains of Italy, and the well-known Pyrenean Mountain Dog. All are large, heavily built animals with thick coats to protect them from the elements; the fur is generally white, a colour thought to be least alarming to sheep. Typically they are reared in close company with sheep so that they grow up regarding the members of the flock as social companions.

Although specialized guard dogs came into their own with the advent of prosperous urban civilizations, ordinary household dogs were probably valued as early-warning devices long before this. Hunting and nomadic peoples, fearful of animal marauders (and malevolent spiritual beings), would appreciate the vigilance and alarmist behaviour of their dogs. The dog's natural animosity towards strangers would also be a considerable asset during hostilities between neighbouring groups.

Dogs as Hunting Partners

In Paleolithic Europe and Asia Minor, people and wolves probably hunted similar types of game, chiefly species of large-hoofed animals. There is a popular notion that man's earliest economic use for the domestic wolf was as a hunting partner. Opinions differ as to the origin of this primitive hunting association, one being that the original domestication of wolves evolved from an older symbiotic exploitation of wild wolves by human hunters; Stone Age hunters might have taken advantage of the superior running and tracking abilities of wolf packs by following them to the kill and then depriving them of most of the carcass. Aboriginal hunters in central Australia have been observed occasionally exploiting packs of wild Dingos in precisely this fashion, although the practice has not resulted in their domestication (or redomestication).

Conversely, it could be argued that the deliberate location and pursuit of hunting wolf packs would have been more arduous and less rewarding for our ancestors than hunting independently. Wolves often hunt over enormous distances, and the majority of these expeditions fail to culminate in successful kills. Paleolithic hunters may have robbed wolves of their prey from time to time on an opportunistic basis, but on balance it is unlikely that they would have adopted this style of hunting as a way of life. Unfortunately, archeological records shed little light on the question of whether Stone Age people made use of tame or domestic wolves for hunting, and whether their efficiency as hunters was enhanced as a result. The oldest indisputable evidence of dogs being used for hunting comes from predynastic Egypt some 6000 years ago, at least 6000 years after the original domestication. The dogs depicted in the art of the period were almost indistinguishable from the modern Basenji, a breed still used for hunting in parts of central Africa. The fact that a special breed of hunting dog was already in existence at this time confirms that hunting was one of the earliest recorded economic functions of domestic dogs, but it does not tell us when the practice began or how widespread it was in Antiquity.

The evidence from contemporary hunting societies is equally ambiguous. There are no wild *Canis* species in South America, and many of the hunting tribes in the southern part of the Amazon Basin never encountered dogs until the arrival of Europeans. In many cases, they regard dogs as useless or even dangerous, but this attitude does not appear to affect their hunting success. However, in northern Amazonia, Venezuela and Guyana, the majority of Indians believe that they can hunt effectively only with canine assistance, and consequently they value good hunting dogs above most other possessions.

The same attitude is found in Australia. Aboriginal tribes in the arid interior used to keep dogs and tame Dingos in large numbers and evidently regarded them with affection, but they did not employ them for hunting, and the dogs apparently showed little inclination to participate. In contrast, the Aborigines of northeastern Australia used to capture and tame wild Dingo pups to assist them in hunting. According to the nineteenth-century Swedish explorer Lumholtz, these animals, though somewhat unreliable, were indispensable for hunting certain types of game. He described how a hunting Dingo 'sometimes refuses to go any farther, and its owner has then to carry it on his shoulders, a luxury of which it is very fond'. Lumholtz's observations provide evidence that simple hunting societies were quite capable of taming and using wild dogs for hunting. Unfortunately, there is no way of knowing whether Paleolithic people made similar use of wild wolves. The Dingo itself is probably derived from domestic dogs brought to Australia thousands of years ago by settlers from South-East Asia. Although it has since reverted to a wild state, the tradition of using it for hunting may have survived intact from these early times.

Hunting with dogs is widespread among African hunter societies, such as the Pygmies of Zaïre and Cameroon, the Dorobo of Kenya and the !Kung San Bushmen of Botswana. The dogs are usually employed for hunting small antelope and warthog. The latter has an unusual defensive strategy: when pursued by carnivores it races to its burrow and reverses down it so that only the formidable bony head and tusks protrude from the entrance. In this position it is invulnerable to attack by most predators, but not to a combined assault by men and dogs hunting together. The dogs keep the warthog *in situ* until the hunters arrive to dispatch the animal with spears.

The introduction of hunting dogs around the turn of this century has revolutionized the basic economy of the Andaman Islands in the Indian Ocean. Formerly, the Andamese subsisted largely on shellfish, but by 1960 they had evolved a flourishing hunting economy based largely on the capture of wild pig. Like their warthog relatives, the wild pigs of Asia stand at bay to defend themselves when attacked; ordinarily, this tactic would drive off all but the largest packs of dogs, but when men and dogs hunt together the same behaviour is virtually suicidal.

It would appear that the value of dogs as hunting aids depends on the local situation and the types of game. Certain species which tend to stand at bay or to take refuge in burrows or streams when pursued would stand little chance if hunted by dogs accompanied by humans. Other species which take to their heels and attempt to outdistance canine pursuers would probably have been unsuitable game. Stone Age dogs would either have become exhausted or would have left the hunters far behind.

Dogs as a Food Source

Mammals such as goats, sheep, pigs and cattle owe much of their success and popularity as domestic species to the fact that they or their products are edible and can be farmed on a commercially viable basis. Few people would regard the domestic dog in the same light, despite the fact that dog meat is edible and was or still is eaten in various parts of the world. The general reluctance to accept the idea of an early gastronomic relationship between man and dog may not be entirely the product of Western squeamishness. Wolves are primarily carnivorous, and grow and reproduce best on a diet of meat; had our ancestors wished to farm them for food, they would have been obliged to catch and kill other species to feed them on.

In spite of this obvious economic restriction, dogs were formerly raised for food on something approaching a commercial scale in certain regions of the globe, notably southern China, Polynesia and Central America. This form of exploitation probably originated as a means of coping with chronic shortages of animal protein from more conventional sources and people were forced to fall back on dog-eating as a last resort. Significantly, cannibalism was also widely practised in some of these areas, possibly for the same reason. Elsewhere, dogs were also eaten from time to time, but almost invariably the practice had important ritual connotations.

Domestic dogs treat people as members of their own species and by so doing compel people to regard them as part-human and to grant them privileges and rights which would normally be reserved for people. For this reason, dog-eating is taboo in many cultures and viewed as a form of cannibalism. Yet ironically, the dog's affinity for humans may under certain circumstances provide a reason for eating it. Among certain North American Indian tribes, dogs were sacrificed and offered as food at ceremonies designed to cement political friendships; since the Indians were extremely fond of their dogs, the act of killing and offering them as food represented the supreme sacrifice, the ultimate and morally binding gesture of friendship.

In a number of other cultures, dog flesh was eaten as a prelude to warfare on the assumption that warriors would absorb the courage, nimbleness and sagacity of the animals. The eating of dogs had even greater symbolic significance in societies where dogs were revered as spiritual allies or totems. Within totemic cults it is believed that the flesh of the totem, eaten at the appropriate time and with correct ceremony, has magical rejuvenating qualities. The eating of dogs or wolves as part of religious or devotional ceremonies is possibly as ancient as totemism itself. Later the ritual probably acquired secondary importance compared with dog meat as a source of protein sustenance, and with shortages of alternative foods, the secondary role took precedence and evolved into the intensive use of dogs as food items. This trend finally culminated in special edible dog breeds, such as the Chow Chow and the native dogs of Polynesia, which were able to survive and reproduce on a largely vegetarian diet.

The Dog as Deity

In some societies the dog acquired a complex religious role. Probably the best known example is the ancient Egyptian jackal-headed god Anubis, often depicted as dog or even wolf-headed. Among other things Anubis presided over the process of embalming or mummification, by which means the ancient Egyptians sought to ensure resurrection and eternal life for the deceased. In the guise of embalmer, Anubis played a central role in the cycle of death and rebirth, providing the key to the next world and guiding the souls of the departed on their final journey.

The concept of the dog as a spiritual intermediary between this world and the next is extraordinarily widespread. It recurs over and over again in myths, legends and religious beliefs in areas as far apart as Africa, New Zealand and North America. The same general theme predominates: that the help and guidance of the dog is needed for a smooth transition from death to afterlife. It is not known why this association between dogs and death evolved independently in so many different cultures, but most authorities link it to the dog's (and jackal's) habit of consuming carrion. There could, however, be another less macabre interpretation.

The Egyptian god Anubis, presiding over the embalming of bodies for the afterlife, is depicted in ancient papyrus scrolls as having human form, with the head of a golden jackal or dog

Greyfriars Bobby

In Western cultures the dog is the proverbial symbol of fidelity, a reputation it has acquired by its habit of remaining faithful to one owner regardless of circumstances. One of the best known examples of this phenomenon was provided by a Skye Terrier called Greyfriars Bobby, which in 1858 joined his master's funeral procession and then remained in the vicinity of his grave in Greyfriars churchyard in Edinburgh until his own death fourteen years later. According to one account, Bobby also died lying stretched across his master's resting place and by special permission the grave was allowed to be opened, and the faithful little creature was interred beside him who he had loved so well. A statue and drinking fountain were later erected opposite the main gates of the churchyard in memory of Bobby.

The story of Greyfriars Bobby is far from unique. European folklore recounts similar anecdotes, and as early as the first century AD the Roman writer Pliny described several comparable incidents, one of which created such a stir in Rome that it was inscribed in the National Records. In this case the dog belonged to a condemned slave, and according to Pliny it

'. . . could not be driven away from him in prison and when he had been flung out on the steps of lamentation would not leave his body, uttering sorrowful howls to the vast concourse of the Roman public around, and when one of them threw it food it carried it to the mouth of its dead master, also when his corpse had been thrown into the Tiber it swam to it and tried to keep it afloat, a great crowd streaming out to view the animal's loyalty.'

If such an incident could produce a profound impression on the normally ruthless Roman populace, it is not difficult to imagine the superstitious awe and reverence it might have inspired in people belonging to earlier and less sophisticated cultures. For them, the animal's behaviour would have conveyed not only a deep sense of loss but also an apparent desire to recall the dead person to life or to join him in death. Assuming a belief in some form of spiritual continuity after death, these people could have concluded that the dog's services were needed in the next world. Such an idea could gradually have developed into religious cults and practices in which the dog as a sacred entity came to represent a mediator between life and death as well as a spiritual guide and protector in the world beyond the grave. This theory would help to explain the ancient custom of burying people with their dogs. Archeologists have unearthed vast numbers of joint dog-human mortuaries from pre-Columbian locations in North and South America, and from Neolithic and Bronze Age sites in Japan, China, Europe, the Near East and North Africa. The oldest of these graves was found at a site called Ein Mallaha in northern Israel. It contained the remains of an elderly human and a five-month-old puppy who had been buried together 12,000 years ago. Perhaps in recognition of the bond which had joined them in life, the dead person's hand had been placed on the puppy's shoulder – a timeless and eloquent gesture of friendship.

Dogs as Companions

The discovery at Ein Mallaha provides remarkably early evidence of the dog's symbolic association with death. It also demonstrates the importance primitive man attached to one of the dog's outstanding qualities: its single-minded loyalty and devotion to human beings. It seems likely that Stone Age people, like their descendants, valued the emotional rewards of dog ownership as much, if not more than, the economic benefits.

The use of dogs and other animals solely for companionship is not confined to modern affluent societies. The keeping of dogs as pets is widespread among relatively simple hunting and foraging societies. The Comanche Indians of North America possessed only two domestic animals, the dog and the horse. Horses were an indispensable part of the Comanche economy, yet the Indians regarded them entirely as useful objects. In contrast, dogs served little if any economic function, yet they were treasured as pets; warriors pampered them, carried them on horseback to prevent them from getting sore feet, and regarded the loss of one dog as far worse than the loss of several horses.

Even in societies where dogs were economically important, their role as companions was frequently acknowledged. In Polynesia, where dogs were often eaten, it was common for particular puppies to be adopted and raised as pets by the inhabitants; usually such companion dogs were exempt from slaughter. In spite of so much evidence it is only since the 1970s that scientists have begun to research and evaluate the reasons why the companionship of dogs is so important to the mental and physical health of highly industrialized societies (see *The Faithful Friend*).

German Shepherd Dogs are highly efficient guard dogs, of their home territory and, professionally trained, of security installations

Modern Working Dogs

In purely economic terms, the domestic dog is probably less important today than in the past. Despite this, different kinds of working dog serve a greater variety of useful roles in modern society than before. Diversification is largely due to a better understanding of animal husbandry and to the mechanisms of genetic inheritance since the nineteenth century. These have made possible the systematic selective breeding of dogs in order to emphasize particular canine attributes and skills. Nowhere is this process more apparent than among sporting breeds; while the medieval huntsman had to choose from only four or five breeds of hunting dog, the modern field sportsman can choose from a vast array of hounds, setters, pointers, retrievers and terriers, each of which has been selectively bred to excel at one specialist aspect of hunting.

Man's best friend is intensely loyal, as a trusted companion (*above*) and as an untiring herder of sheep (*below*)

Selective breeding has also greatly improved dogs for herding livestock. Most dogs display a wolfish tendency to stalk, chase and drive large game animals, but in breeds like the Border Collie, certain elements of hunting behaviour have been encouraged at the expense of others so as to produce a dog which can safely be used for controlling flocks of sheep.

Selectively-bred working dogs still need careful training before they can perform their particular task adequately. Recent advances in our knowledge of animal behaviour and animal learning have made the job of dog trainers easier and more effective. Systematic training procedures, in conjunction with natural and artificially selected abilities and talents, have greatly altered the role of modern working dogs. Guide dogs for the blind (see page 24) is one outstanding example of the blend of careful selection and training in action, and similar programmes are being successfully applied to hearing dogs for the deaf, and to dogs intended as aids to the physically handicapped.

New uses for domestic dogs are constantly being discovered. One novel use, which has recently received some attention, is the possibility of employing dogs to detect ovulation in cattle. The success of artificial insemination techniques depends to a large extent on the ability to discern when a cow is ovulating and therefore capable of conceiving. Present methods of detection are expensive and not always accurate; bulls perceive the correct timing by scent, and recent tests have shown that dogs with their sensitive noses are capable of the same level of discernment.

GUIDE DOGS FOR THE BLIND

The sight of a guide dog leading its blind master or mistress through the bustle of busy streets is a source of pleasure and admiration. In and out of crowds, through stores and markets, boarding buses and trains, owner and dog stride out confidently together. Theirs is a partnership shared by thousands of blind men and women throughout the world. It is not new. Records survive of dogs being used as guide-companions in Pompeii and in thirteenth-century China. Today they may be seen in Norway and New Zealand, on Fifth Avenue and on Gorky Street.

Without its distinctive harness, usually white, there is nothing to distinguish the trained guide from any other dog. Outside working hours, it romps as freely in the park as any other pet dog, and is just as skilled at turning an appealing eye to any visitor who might offer a tidbit. But it *is* special. A guide dog is the eyes of its owner, the trusted companion, and the link with the outside world.

A potential guide dog must possess certain qualities. It should be intelligent and even-tempered, displaying neither nervousness nor indifference to sudden noises and obstacles. It must be strong and healthy, obedient yet capable of exercising judgment. Only a few breeds fulfill these conditions; in Britain, where the Guide Dogs for the Blind Association was established in 1934, German Shepherd Dogs were long the preferred breed, but today about half of the trained guide dogs are Labradors. Crosses between Labradors and Golden Retrievers have also proved successful, and the Association maintains carefully selected bitches and stud dogs for breeding. Most guide dogs are bitches which are less domineering than males, and both sexes are neutered before intensive training begins.

In most countries guide dogs begin life as the result of a careful breeding programme. From birth they are given specialist care; even as tiny puppies they are handled gently for a few minutes each day to accustom them to stress. At six to eight weeks old the puppies are placed with selected foster families who will rear them in their homes. The walkers teach the puppies to be well behaved and socially acceptable. As one of an ordinary family, the puppy will join in holidays, accompany the puppy walker on shopping expeditions to busy stores and become accustomed to the sights and sounds of city traffic. These varied experiences will prepare the puppy for its future work.

The puppy will stay with the foster family until it is ready to begin serious training; for Labradors and Labrador-Retriever crosses, this usually occurs in their twelfth month. At this point they are returned to the training centre. German Shepherds, Golden Retrievers and other breeds may take longer to mature. For a young dog, the transition is a perplexing time. Life in kennels is very much more spartan than the home comforts he or she has been used to, but the majority quickly adjust to pack life. Others respond only slowly to the reassurances of the handlers, and a few are unable to settle; they are returned to their puppy walkers or found pet homes, as they lack the ability to adapt which every guide dog must have. It requires a great deal of self-confidence to walk through strange streets and to pass potentially aggressive dogs.

Training guide dogs

Once at the training centre, work begins in quiet areas. On long, straight walks to the park the dog is taught to trot ahead, not to walk at heel. Any attempt by the dog to anticipate a turn leads to the route being altered, to terminate at a different destination. At the end of the walk there will still be the pleasure of a game or a romp. In this way the dog learns that by accepting directions its walks will always be rewarded, and each outing becomes an exciting mystery tour.

Training a guide dog takes months of practice before dog and instructor become a team. Learning to lead includes coping with traffic, sitting at road kerbs, refusing to go ahead in sight of a moving vehicle, and avoiding obstacles (*opposite*). Approaching an obstruction, the guide dog is taught, first to sit, then to find an alternative route round the obstacle before returning safely to the pavement

When the dog has begun to think ahead and anticipate, the next stage, the kerb drill, is introduced. The dog is taught to indicate each road by stopping at the pavement edge. This will give its future blind owner warning of a step down and the chance to listen carefully for traffic. The guide dog is not always able to cope with modern traffic. The responsibility for choosing a safe time to cross rests with its master, and guide-dog users are advised by the training schools to obtain sighted help at busy road junctions.

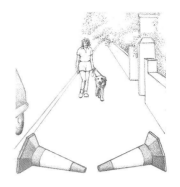

With time, training becomes more intensive, quiet side roads giving way to suburban areas, with people, prams and shopping trolleys cluttering the pavements. Guide-dog trainers refuse to pass through gaps too small for their height and width, and slowly, by constant repetition, the dog learns to choose that path which will allow for its companion's bulk. Eventually it will forget that a choice ever existed and will automatically take the clear space. Artificial obstacle courses are set up within the grounds of the training school, where the dog learns to avoid them before being faced with increasingly difficult hazards on the road. At times it will have to leave the pavement to negotiate major obstructions, or to retrace its steps to get round a temporary barricade.

In town, it learns to tackle public transport, lifts, revolving doors, stores, escalators and pedestrian crossings. With practice and yet more practice the dog becomes foot-perfect. Visits to the park and the country become rewards for hard work in conditions chosen to test it to the full. Finally, all the potential errors a blind person might make are re-created. The trainer dons a blindfold, and only after successful guided walks through town conditions will he be satisfied that the dog is fully trained and safe to be handed over to its new owner.

The ultimate partnership

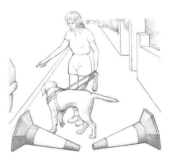

The choice of the dog's future master or mistress will already have been made, with compatibility, size, walking speed and work load having been taken into account, togther with other physical, temperamental and social factors. The new owner must attend the training school for a four-week residential course to learn how to care for and use the dog. Under professional guidance, owner and guide dog learn to adjust to each other without outside distractions.

The training course is a concentrated repeat of the dog's training. Quiet walks, on which owner and dog come to know and understand each other, give way to busier areas. Short outings stretch to periods of up to two hours' duration. Throughout, the trainer is on hand to encourage, instruct and cajole. The unit, as owner and dog are described, must learn from mistakes and experience, like mother and toddler. A child must fall before it can learn to walk; the trainer's job is to ensure that the 'falls' in city streets full of traffic and other hazards are not too dangerous. For the owner, the course is demanding and nerve wracking. He or she may never before have walked without holding someone's arm or have ventured beyond their immediate neighbourhood. It takes a great deal of courage, after years of dependency, to pick up the harness handle and give the very first command 'Forward'.

Over the weeks a bond between owner and dog is forged which will last for years. Although there are doubts and moments of despair, mistakes grow fewer, and mutual confidence shows in the visible pride and enjoyment man and dog have in each other. Ownership of a guide dog means more than having the freedom to go anywhere at will. It enables a blind person to take his or her equal place among family and friends, join in social activities and gain a large measure of independence to such an extent that the blind owner can become the one to offer help instead of receiving it. The blind mother may offer to collect her

neighbour's children from school or help with shopping in times of sickness. A husband will not need the wife's guidance to go to the barber's. Young people can attend classes, social gatherings and youth clubs on their own.

After years of being dependent and met with sympathy and social embarrassment, the blind person as a guide-dog user becomes the object of envy as the possessor of something beautiful and enviable. The dog becomes an ice-breaker, and people who would not know how to start a conversation with a blind person can do so with a simple query about the dog's age, name or breed. The dog returns its owner to society.

It is not the white harness that makes a guide dog special, for only special dogs are good enough to wear one. Once owner and dog become one unit, their progress is checked and maintained with regular aftercare visits and health checks. The average working life of a guide dog is eight to nine years; it is then retired as an ordinary pet animal, often into the same household, and replaced with a young guide dog. In Britain, the high costs of training and keeping guide dogs are met entirely by charity. This in itself bears testimony to the high regard in which guide dogs, the best of man's best friends, are held.

POLICE & SEARCH DOGS

Highly trained dogs are used by police forces throughout the world, for patrol duties and crowd control. They are trained to track and pursue suspects and taught how to arrest law breakers. Police and security dogs patrolling building sites and vital installations are generally more effective in the prevention of crime than sophisticated burglar alarms.

Increasing drug abuse and acts of terrorism throughout the world have prompted police and other law enforcement agencies in many countries to examine critically the methods and systems employed to combat these evils. The Royal Air Force Police of Britain, with many years of experience in the use of police dogs, are leading the world in training dogs to detect narcotics, arms, ammunition, and explosives.

Since the late 1960s, when a German Shepherd Dog and a Labrador were first successfully trained and employed as drug detectors, the Royal Air Force Police have undertaken the training of servicemen from other forces and countries in this specialized role. As terrorist activity throughout the world became an almost daily occurrence, successful trials established that dogs, and in particular German Shepherds, could be reliably trained to detect explosives. Subsequent training was extended to include the detection of arms and ammunition. Today, Royal Air Force Police search dogs, or sniffers as they are affectionately termed, are in service with the Royal Navy, the United States Navy and Air Force, and Her Majesty's Customs and Excise, and search-dog handlers have been trained for many other countries.

Police dog breeds

Any good working dog is potentially suitable for search work. Most commonly used are German Shepherds, Labradors, and other gundog breeds such as German Shorthaired Pointers, Irish Water Spaniels, Flat-coated and Golden Retrievers, and English Springer Spaniels. There is a popular, but erroneous, theory that a drug dog becomes addicted to the drugs which it is trained to detect. Neither are 'bomb' dogs addicted to gelignite or TNT. The only addiction utilized in search-dog training is the dog's desire to retrieve. That

Police dogs are trained for varied duties, depending on their natural abilities. The German Shepherd Dog, though not by nature a retriever, has a strongly developed aptitude for obedience and can be trained to apprehend without injury

desire provides both the incentive and the drive necessary to train the dog. Although the actual conditioning process is simple, great patience and understanding is required in building up concentration and agility in a potential search dog, which will have to adjust to many environments, such as airports and aircraft, docklands and cargo ships, freight sheds with a multiplicity of cargo, private accommodation, and open fields and hedgerows.

Breed qualities

Dogs selected for intense and painstaking training in the search field must display certain qualities before they can be accepted. Although certain breeds lend themselves to such duties, success depends upon selection of individual dogs within the breeds. Any potential dog must have had a sound environmental education, with less emphasis on obedience training and more on developing a bold, friendly and well-adjusted animal. In order to fulfil the requirements for detection work, a dog must have moderate to low body sensitivity, which means it takes knocks well, and moderate voice sensitivity, responding to various voice tones. It must also possess strong hunting and retrieving instincts, combined with boldness, physical strength, and potential agility.

Search dogs track by scent, and in highly intelligent breeds like Labrador Retrievers, this characteristic can be directed towards sniffing out narcotics and explosives

Certain inherited characteristics make certain breeds ideal for search-dog training. The German Shepherd Dog, for example, fits in every way the image of a police dog, having medium body sensitivity. It is a popular breed from which correct selection can be made, and it is highly receptive to training. Retrieving is an acquired behaviour pattern in the German Shepherd.

The Labrador Retriever is another successful search dog which normally causes no apprehension to the public. It has highly developed olfactory instincts, moderate to low body sensitivity and a more independent nature than the German Shepherd. Retrieving is an instinctive behaviour pattern, and the Labrador usually has well-developed hunting instincts.

Individual characteristics of certain gundog breeds also have a bearing on selection for search-dog training. The Hunter, for example, should display determination to search without a visual incentive, and while it may not retrieve, it should have the desire to pick up. Similarly the Retriever should distinguish itself by its determination to fetch, and though it may require a visual incentive it should be eager to carry and be possessive with the prey.

Training search dogs

As in all aspects of dog training, the training of search dogs, irrespective of the selected scents they are required to search for, must be based on firm yet sympathetic understanding of the workings of the canine mind. The success of specialized training lies in creating the correct incentive, harnessing the drive and channelling it to a useful end. Coupled with a sympathetic and thoughtful handler, the result is a highly effective team ready and able to assist the various law enforcement agencies in their fight against crime.

Dogs which are accepted for police-search duties undergo a fifteen-week course. During training the team spirit is forged between the animals and their handlers, based on patience, determination, integrity and affection on both sides. The outstanding factor is patience. All search dogs undergo a routine monthly veterinary inspection; from the age of seven years, when they are nearing the end of their working lives, they receive a thorough six-monthly inspection to ensure that they are still in good health and able to carry out their duties. At about eight years of age a search dog is retired, the handler usually buying the dog, which has justly earned a quiet retirement.

Gift dogs

All dogs trained and used by the Royal Air Force Police have been donated by the public, many dogs coming from leading show kennels. It is indicative of the high standards at these kennels, specializing largely in producing show stock, that first-class working dogs can emerge.

High standards for potential canine recruits are set by the Royal Air Force Police. Each year the Service require some fifty trained dogs. To reach this figure two hundred dogs will be tested, approximately half of that number will enter training, and of these less than half again will qualify. The recruited gift dogs – German Shepherds and Gundogs – are all pedigrees aged between ten months and two and a half years. Potential gift dogs are examined by expert inspectors in their own homes. Such inspection is the first hurdle in this unique recruiting programme, which aims to keep the worldwide police-dog strength of the Royal Air Force at around 800. After a dog's pedigree and age have been established, a strict acceptance test is carried out covering the animal's build, movements and general health. Sadly, even the finest family pet can sometimes prove unacceptable when judged against the high standards required.

RACING DOGS

Dog racing exists in several forms, each suited to the strength, temperament and original purpose of the particular breed. With the exception of sled-dog racing and agility competitions, the principle is to provide a substitute quarry, and for this reason the most commonly raced breeds are the sighthounds, of which the Greyhound is the best known.

Greyhound racing

The sport of Greyhound racing originated in the United States early this century and has become popular throughout the world. It came to Britain in 1926, when a dog called *Mistley* crossed the line ahead of the others in the very first race, at Belle Vue, Manchester. A governing body, the National Greyhound Racing Club, was formed, which licenses approved stadiums and maintains a register of the dogs. All dogs raced on recognized tracks must run under their registered name and must be trained by a licensed trainer.

These rules and other precautions protect the public from malpractice. On unlicensed or flapping tracks, numerous in the Midlands and the North of England, racing is more devious. The same dog may run at different tracks under several pseudonyms and may be trained by its owner, limiting the degree of control the stadium can exercise. The Greyhound is primarily a betting medium, and it may suit its owner better for it to lose than to win. Many dogs are run below their best form in order to keep 'a bit in hand' – just before the summer holidays or Christmas, winning times can improve dramatically.

Races take place on an oval track, and six dogs run at a time. The distances vary from 300-yard (274 m) sprints to 900-yard (823 m) marathons. Since the early days, times have improved greatly, and modern Greyhound stars achieve speeds of up to 40 mph (64 km/h).

Whippet racing

This form of racing is traditionally associated with the mining communities in England and was widespread before the Greyhound boom. A straight track was divided into taped lanes, and instead of emerging from traps the whippets were thrown into the race by handlers known as slippers. There was no moving lure, with each dog racing to seize a sack or towel, waved beyond the finishing line by its owner. Today this style of running, called rag racing, exists only in the Potteries in the North of England.

Modern whippet racing is a thriving and popular amateur sport with little gambling or foul play. Handicapping may be on time or, more commonly, by weight when a one yard (1 m) advantage for every pound ($\frac{1}{2}$ kg) of weight difference is given to the lighter dogs. Scaled-down versions of greyhound traps are used, and the whippets chase a lure of rags wound in on an electric pulley. The distance varies from 140–200 yards (128–183 m), but whippets are equally at home on a greyhound track over 300 yards (274 m). Bitches are usually preferred to dogs of the same weight.

Whippet racing is popular throughout the world. In most countries it is confined to pedigree whippets, but in Britain the traditional, specially bred racing strain is more numerous.

Lurcher meetings

The lurcher, a type of dog rather than a specific breed, is sometimes defined as a gypsy or poaching dog. Usually the result of crossing Greyhounds with Terriers and sheepdogs, lurchers are enjoying a considerable vogue at the present, and competitive racing is a feature at most of the lurcher shows which are staged in the summer months. Racing is to a lure, as in Whippet racing, and dogs are set loose by their owners. This results in rather uneven starts, which is proabably no bad thing, as most lurchers have had little or no schooling. Up to ten dogs may be run at the same time. Lurchers are by definition supposed to run within their capabilities to enable them to turn quickly on a hare, and racing is not a valid test. It also tends to make them hard-mouthed and spoil them for their proper hunting work.

Hound trailing

This is the only racing based on scent and is confined to the fells of northern England. The highly specialized hounds, of Foxhound origin, follow the line or drag of an extremely odorous sack that has been pulled over several miles of moorland. The course, up to 10 miles (16 km) long, is laid out around a valley so that the hounds are in sight of the spectators most of the time. Once the hounds return to the valley floor and are in view of their owners they are 'ragged' like Whippets to produce a finishing burst. Betting on trail hounds can be heavy, but race meetings are governed by strict rules laid down by the various associations.

Sled-dog racing

This is primarily a North American sport although supporters of the Husky breeds in other parts of the world also practise it. Teams of Huskies pull lightweight racing sleds (or wheeled buggies in warmer climates) over trails of varying lengths. Races may be as short as 10 miles (16 km) or as long as the 1169 miles (1881 km) Iditarod race between Anchorage and Nome.

For the shorter distances, the teams are largely crossbred Huskies with Border Collie, Setter, Greyhound or Coon Hound blood to give speed. The true Huskies are at their best in protracted endurance events. Teams of up to sixteen dogs are driven by the 'musher' and can achieve an average speed of 20 mph (32 km/h); the record for the Iditarods race is fourteen days, more than 80 miles (129 km) a day.

A DOG
IN THE FAMILY

A DOG IN THE FAMILY

Before acquiring a puppy, the prospective dog owner usually ponders a number of options in order to arrive at the sort of dog which would suit his or her particular life style. The first stage in the elimination process ought to be the very simple, but all-important question 'Am I the type of person who can cope with a dog?' As one major canine charity in Britain says on a car-sticker: A dog is for life, not just for Christmas. The thought of owning a young faithful dog, eager to join the family on long walks across summer fields, can be persuasive, but that is only one of several aspects: a young dog grows old; youthful health will probably deteriorate; the rolling fields with grazing sheep have warning notices that dogs must be kept on a lead; and the sunshine of summer becomes the sleet of winter.

Dog ownership entails more than the pleasant company of a faithful friend. It carries with it certain responsibilities, and a number of factors must be considered in order to balance the equation. Basically, these factors relate to economic circumstances and to the availability of time, space, and energy.

Financial Considerations
Apart from the initial outlay on buying a puppy, or dog, and the basic equipment, there are recurring costs which will considerably affect the household budget, depending on the size and breed of dog. The largest is without doubt feeding; it is unrealistic to suppose that even a miniature dog can be fed a nutritionally balanced diet from table scraps, and a large dog will make an appreciable difference to the weekly food bill.

Veterinary fees must also be taken into account. It is essential that a newly acquired dog be inoculated against distemper, hard pad, hepatitis and parvovirus, followed by annual booster vaccinations. With luck, visits to the veterinary clinic will be few for the young dog, barring accidents, but middle and old age bring inevitable problems requiring medical attention. Several pet-insurance schemes exist which for an annual premium cover the majority of veterinary fees. Boarding kennels may be an occasional or regular expenditure during holidays or illnesses in the family. Fees are usually charged on a daily rate, varying with the size of the dog. In addition, long-coated dogs may need clipping and stripping once or twice a year.

In Britain, all dog owners are obliged by law to obtain a licence. At present, this negligible amount is under review, and it seems possible that increased licences may be issued by local authorities.

Time for the Family Pet
As a member of the household, the family dog is entitled to a certain amount of regular attention, especially as a puppy and again in old age. He needs feeding and exercising every day, frequent grooming with comb and brush, with an occasional bath and care of nails and teeth.

Time must be set aside for the basic training of a puppy, for playing with the young dog and stimulating the activities of the middle-aged, and for caring for the older, perhaps ailing dog.

Some people seem to think that the possession of a large garden absolves them from exercising the family dog on all but the few occasions when plenty of time is available. As soon as they are let out of the kitchen door, most dogs make a nuisance of themselves by disturbing the entire neighbourhood for about ten minutes first thing in the morning or late at night by chasing the birds and the neighbour's cat, or by rushing madly up and down barking at the dog next door. For the rest of the time they lie curled up on the back porch or, worse still, whine and yelp in an attempt to get back indoors. A dog needs organized exercise on a regular basis virtually every day. Obviously there will be times when it is impossible to get him out for a constitutional, but provided that it does not happen too often, he will forgive. Neither does the exercise have to be of the same duration every day; some owners make a rod for their own backs by sticking so rigidly to the daily routine that the dog becomes master.

In general, the bigger breeds need more exercise than the smaller ones; this is a generalization, and some very large breeds such as the St Bernard do not relish the sort of terrain and distance which would delight a Border Collie. The required amount of exercise should be discussed not only with the breeder but also with owners of single dogs of the same type. Breeders can have a different viewpoint because two or three dogs exercised together can run off steam in much shorter time than one on its own. The question of exercise takes priority in the selection list because it is often the most time-consuming factor. Where available time is in relatively short supply, the chosen dog should be of a type which does not demand too much exercise.

Dogs with long coats obviously need more grooming than short-coated dogs. At the same time, longer-haired breeds require different amounts of time and effort; the beautiful tresses of the graceful Afghan Hound, for example, will tangle irretrievably if neglected for more than two or three days while the much harsher coat of the Keeshond can do without the brush and comb routine for a couple of weeks provided that grooming is then literally skindeep.

Most dogs shed their dead hairs more or less continuously. Long hairs do not necessarily cause greater problems in respect of clearing up; hairs from short-coated dogs penetrate carpets and furnishing fabrics and defy both vacuum cleaner and brush. The only breeds which do not cause such aggravation are those which do not moult, such as Poodles and Bedlington Terriers, whose coats are stripped regularly at dog parlours. Some people are allergic to dog hairs and coat dust; anyone with a known history of allergies, such as asthma and eczematous skin lesions, should consult a doctor as to the possibilities of complications resulting from the purchase of a dog.

Feeding costs are undoubtedly the most important part of the financial equation, while the time factor is minimal in respect of commercially prepared foods. However, cans and dog packs have to be bought and carried home, which takes time and has to be remembered along with other shopping.

Additional Considerations

Unless the dog has his living quarters in an outside kennel, the house will almost certainly show his presence. Hairs are not the only evidence. If he has a temporarily upset stomach he may not manage to reach the garden before he is sick or has diarrhoea, both catastrophes on unpatterned carpets.

Garden fences, other boundaries and gates should be sound enough to prevent the dog from escaping into neighbouring gardens and into the road.

Above and beyond all other considerations, the potential owner must have a genuine desire for the companionship of a dog and the willingness to expend care, affection, and loyalty long after the 'cute' puppy stage is past. Every year thousands and thousands of perfectly healthy animals are rejected as unwanted for one reason or another, many of them having to be painlessly destroyed by welfare societies or private veterinary practitioners. In 1982 alone more than 1000 Old English Sheepdogs passed through the hands of the breed club's 'Rescue' organization when owners discovered too late that the television commercial's cuddly dog required constant grooming of the coat.

Coat grooming varies from breed to breed. Silky, long-haired dogs like the Afghan Hound (*top*) need thorough brushing every few days to avoid matting; the long but harsh coat of the Keeshond (*bottom*) needs less frequent attention

Choice of Dog

Having made the decision to acquire a dog, a number of other questions must be settled before the actual purchase. The most important concern age, breed status, size, temperament, and sex.

Puppy or adult dog

There is obviously a minimum age for removing a puppy from its mother and its first environment, though these are not necessarily one and the same. As a rule, pups are entirely dependent on their mother's milk for the first two to three weeks, and partially for another similar period (see also page 110). If mother and pups are healthy, a breeder would consider allowing the pups to leave their first home at the age of six weeks, but the vast majority of breeders prefer eight weeks as the ideal time for the litter to be dispersed. Some pups are deliberately retained for longer than this, usually because a breeder of show stock needs more time to determine the true potential of individual pups.

The most important factor influencing the decision about dispersal time is the so-called socialization period. Animal behaviourists consider that the period between six weeks and three months is the ideal time for a puppy to learn to adapt to a rapidly changing world. Leaving home and entering a totally new environment is as bewildering to a young canine as going to school or play-group is to a child. It has been established that puppies raised in relative isolation, with their mother as the centre of their lives, and only the breeder representing the human race, are much better able to accept new human contact if it occurs in that vital six- to thirteen-week period. Beyond that, puppies may revert almost to the wild if they are denied the socialization period at the effective time.

Acquiring a puppy at the age of about eight weeks means that it will have the best opportunity to adapt to the peculiarities of its new environment, which include humans and other animals in the household, as well as the house rules which will determine its future life. It also means that the new owner will be responsible for much of the rearing process, the character building and the house training, all demanding certain skills and special responsibilities. In addition, the owner commits himself to ensure that the puppy develops normally and remains healthy by dealing with such vital matters as worming, and protective vaccinations.

On the other hand a dog can be acquired at a later age, as an older puppy or as an adult. Some breeders 'run on' youngsters until their show, breeding, or training potential can be assessed. A potential purchaser of such a dog should satisfy him or herself as to the true reasons why older pups are eventually offered for sale. It is entirely possible that what is a defect as far as the breeder is concerned may not be a drawback to the pet owner, but the factor should be considered dispassionately before a decision is made.

Acquiring an adult dog often turns out to be a success, but again the reasons for its availability should be thoroughly explored (see also page 42). One disadvantage may be that the adult dog usually has its character firmly formed, and bad habits will be more difficult to eradicate than to avoid. On the other hand, many people deliberately obtain adult dogs, taking advantage of the fact that the puppy problems have been dealt with by somebody else.

Purebred or mongrel

Possibly the single most contentious factor in discussing what type of dog should be acquired is its ancestry. The only common factor for all purebred dogs is that both parents come from the same breed, and even this is not an accurate guide, as some may be bred without regard to a definite programme, while others may be closely bred from parents of different but similar strains.

A mongrel, a term which is sometimes used as a disparagement, can be the product of two purebred parents of different breeds, in which case the offspring is referred to as crossbred. Alternatively, the ancestry may include a kaleidoscopic array of mixed breeds; such mongrels are often jocularly known as 'Heinz' varieties. The term purebred is preferable to pedigree because the latter can have connotations of pampered show dogs or imply Kennel Club registration. While all Kennel Club registered dogs are purebred, there is no necessity for an owner to register a dog in order to prove that it is purebred.

The advantages of choosing a purebred dog include the fact that a source of supply can be found with relative ease. The various breeds all have clubs which will advise on purchase and handling. Virtually all purebred pups were conceived deliberately and will therefore have been reared, before birth and after, to reasonable standards; they will not vary from their ancestors, except minimally in size and coat type, and within the limitations that temperament is partly controlled by inheritance, they can be expected to behave to the breed pattern. In addition, the sire of a litter is, except in a tiny percentage of cases, totally identifiable and can, if required, be seen and handled so that the purchaser can get some idea of likely temperament.

The main disadvantages of the purebred dog can be attributed to the very fact that it is purebred. The emergence of a breed of dog which will breed 'true' is the result of a long selection process, and when the particular type is fixed in its characteristics and continues to produce generations of closely similar dogs, a new breed can be said to have been produced. Because closely similar dogs are thereafter used in a breeding programme, the chances of finding not only the desired attributes in many specimens but also any undesirable characteristics or faults are increased. This is the reason why inherited defects occasionally occur in purebred dogs. Conscientious breeders, aware of an inherited defect emerging in the breed, do their best to eradicate it, but the warning signs may not be obvious; they may be missed or on occasions deliberately ignored.

In Britain, the Kennel Club and the British Veterinary Association have together devised methods of assisting breeders to tackle the more prevalent defects. A potential purchaser of a particular breed is advised to make enquiries from the local veterinary practice as to the known presence or absence of hereditary defects, such as hip dysplasia (structural defect of the hip-joint) or progressive retinal atrophy and hereditary cataract (diseases affecting the eyes). This does not imply that purebred dogs invariably inherit some defect, but certain breeds, including several of the more popular ones, seem more prone than others. All large breeds with the exception of racing Greyhounds may inherit hip dysplasia, for example, and several breeds, irrespective of size, inherit generalized or central PRA. It is expensive to breed and rear strong, healthy puppies, and some breeders are under pressure to try to keep alive some of the less robust members of a purebred litter. Many breeders cull those puppies which do not appear perfect, especially in the case of breeds which have large litters, such as Labrador Retrievers and Great Danes. Culling is less common with breeds having small litters, such as the tiny Chihuahua, which may produce only one puppy and rarely more than four or five; the breeder consequently has more incentive to keep the pups alive.

Another, slight disadvantage of the purebred dogs lies with the owner rather than with the dog. Certain breeds attract a certain type of owner on a status-symbol basis: the Afghan Hound complements the tall, elegant couple; the German Shepherd Dog appeals as a protector to nervous people, who may not consider the possible complications of handling a powerful, intelligent creature.

The mongrel is often considered by its devotees as more intelligent and healthy than the purebred dog, but there is little evidence to prove this one way or another. It may well be that because mongrels are difficult to sell or give away, only the biggest and strongest looking are, in many cases, retained at birth. Inherited defects are more likely to appear in crossbreds than in unrecognizable mongrels because of their closeness to the pure strains from which they originate. Defects do occur in mongrels, but to a lesser degree, probably because of the culling which takes place at birth.

Mongrels of any sort are accidents. Few pet owners set out to breed a litter deliberately, and often the fact that the family bitch is expecting is only discovered when the pregnancy is far advanced or even virtually completed. The identity of the sire is often shrouded in mystery, and there may well be more than one sire to a single litter, as the bitch ovulates over a period of days and may have been mated several times as she roamed unchecked. Although it is obviously possible to see the mother of a mongrel pup and study her size, type, and temperament, the fact that she herself is the product of various canine characteristics means that she may give birth to pups which bear little or no relation to her or to each other. This coupled with doubts as to the character, background, or identity of the father makes it impossible to establish the future development and temperament of each individual pup. Records exist of matings between male Great Danes and female Dachshunds, and similar extraordinary couplings frequently occur. Mongrel puppies can, of course, be highly acceptable, but a prospective purchaser must approach the matter with an open mind and a readiness to accept surprises. These may well prove very satisfactory, but will always be unpredictable in the true nature of all surprises.

Large or small

Bigger dogs need more exercise than small ones; they also need more food, bigger beds, larger collars, stronger leads, and probably stronger owners. In addition, and for practical reasons, they are better suited to houses than apartments, unless at street level. During a debilitating or paralysing illness a large dog may have to be carried into the garden or to the car, a procedure difficult enough without the added complication of a flight of stairs or a lift temporarily out of action.

The size of the family car may be unsuited to a fully grown large dog, and the owner may be incapable of carrying it on public transport systems. Very large breeds, such as the Irish Wolfhound and the St Bernard, usually have a shorter lifespan than smaller dogs, and while these facts are only generalizations they must be taken into account before a purchase.

At the other end of the scale are the Yorkshire Terriers and other miniature members of the Toy group. Although many of them are fearless little dogs, their very size can be a danger at times; tiny puppies can be damaged by unsteady feet or by being lifted and carried clumsily.

Temperament

There are as many dog temperaments as there are breeds, and this applies equally to the mongrel and to the purebred, though in the mongrel temperament is less predictable because of the ancestral jigsaw. Only

Puppies will chew at anything – slippers and gloves, and mail and newspapers on the doormat; in the garden, they nip off flower heads and tangle with tempting branches

generalizations are possible because of the multiplicity of breeds, but the characteristics broadly follow the divisions established by the English Kennel Club. Even so there is considerable variation even between members of the same groups. See also Pedigree Breeds, page 176.

Hound dogs are first and foremost hunters of prey of one sort or another, independent, generally complacent in their relationship with humans, but not great guard dogs.

Gundogs comprise pointers, flushers and retrievers and are with only rare exceptions friendly and good house pets. However, it is debatable whether the popular Labrador and Golden Retrievers should be confined to suburban houses; they need plenty of exercise as they have a tendency to run to fat.

Terriers are quick-moving, volatile, and tend to nip. They range from medium to small, and the smaller they are the more they yap. They make good house protectors and ideal family pets, especially with children.

The Utility group, though composed of such different types as the Bulldog, Chow Chow, Poodle and Tibetan Terrier, shares the temperament found in characteristic companion dogs. With the possible exception of the Dalmatian they will bark loud and long in protection of their homes; they may bite an intruder, but usually accept strangers once they have been properly introduced.

The Working group contains the largest number of breeds, which can roughly be divided into the three categories of guarding, herding, and sledging, although some combine more than one of the characteristics. The natural skills and instincts of several breeds have been channelled into their employment as police dogs, military dogs, and guide dogs for the blind. Guard and herd dogs have an inbuilt, highly developed sense of protection, and although they make good house dogs they should never be presumed upon – any animal which has to depend on its ability to dominate cattle and sheep by speed of movement and the occasional quick nip must be expected to act before it is hurt itself. Any dog with a special working ability needs to exercise that ability, and if this is not possible a substitute occupation, such as obedience, agility and working competitions, must be found to stretch the dog's intelligence. Failure to occupy the mind may lead to boredom and destructiveness.

The massive St Bernard and the only slightly smaller Newfoundland do not fit into the three main categories, both being rescue dogs, the former in snow, the latter in water, and with gentler temperaments than others in the group.

The Toy dogs are somewhat misleadingly named, though the common characteristic is smallness of size, the largest being the Cavalier King Charles Spaniel. Temperamentally they are courageous and faithful to their owners, on occasion quite belligerent as in the tiny Chihuahua. Too often Toy dogs are treated as soft and allowed to become pampered and overfed.

Male or female

A major decision hinges on the sex of the family dog-to-be, whether a purebred or a mongrel, and irrespective of its age, appearance and probable temperament. Although the term dog is usually taken to describe an animal of either sex, in biological terms dog is synonymous with male, bitch with female.

Dogs are interested in the opposite sex most of the time; bitches have certain periods (see Reproduction, page 120), usually at six-monthly intervals, when they are on the look out for a mate. These periods when the bitch is said to be 'on heat' or 'in season' explain the most important difference between the two sexes and the sort of temperament they are likely to exhibit. Obviously male dogs are not permanently aroused, but they are more likely to have a roaming instinct, may be more aggressive and possibly slightly more difficult to persuade to concentrate on basic training. Packs of dogs could formerly be seen meandering through city streets on the chance of finding a welcoming bitch; this is now a rare sight, but gangs of uncontrolled dogs can still be a menace, especially in city centres. The majority of these packs are males and while the individual is often a reasonably well-behaved animal, he may act like a hooligan in company with others of his ilk. Most bitches tend to have a gentler temperament; they are more content to stay close to home, and are generally easier to train.

These characteristics are generalizations and apply more to breeds which display natural dominance; in small and submissive breeds, including many of the Toys, there is hardly any temperament difference between the sexes.

Neutering

Either sex can be neutered. At the present time it is more common for bitches to be spayed or sterilized by an operation which removes the sex organs than to have the male castrated by the surgical removal of the testicles. This seems a strange preference among dog owners – and contrary to neutering operations performed on cats – because spaying involves incising the abdomen, a rather more serious and considerably more expensive operation than castration.

Owners often worry that the removal of sex organs will lead to a change in the animal's character; this is rarely the case, although the less desirable aspects of male behaviour, libido and aggression, usually disappear, and the bitch naturally no longer comes into season. All neutered animals have a tendency to obesity; it is a common but erroneous belief that this is due to the neutering operation. In fact, neutered dogs of either sex become overweight through their owners' mistake in giving more food than can be converted into energy. After a neutering operation, food intake should be reduced and exercise increased.

The bitch can be spayed as a puppy, but most veterinary surgeons advise a delay until the bitch is physically and mentally mature, at three to four months after the first (or subsequent) oestrus. The popular idea that allowing a bitch to have a litter before she is spayed 'is good for her' is not borne out by fact and merely increases the number of puppies which have to be found homes. The similar suggestion that a dog should be allowed to mate a bitch in order to 'cool him off' before castration is equally misplaced. Copulation is not essential for the well-being of the dog; the majority never experience it and do not appear to suffer any frustration as a result.

Buying a Puppy

Ideally a purebred puppy should be purchased directly from the breeder so that the mother can be present to be seen, talked to and studied. It is also possible to buy purebred puppies from dealers and pet shops, but in both cases it is highly likely that the puppies have been obtained from a variety of sources. They may have travelled long distances from their home and may well have come into close contact with puppies from other litters and had time to pick up any germs. The stress of being removed from the comfort of the maternal home tests the most resilient of puppies and is compounded by transportation in a noisy train or van, the company of many strange, equally frightened pups, temperature and food changes, and a motley of human faces and voices.

For the prospective buyer, the best advice is to find a reliable breeder within a reasonable radius of home. The local veterinary practice often knows of local breeders, and this has the advantage that something will be known about the quality and the health of the pups. In addition, many small breeders advertise in the local press, to announce the sale of a forthcoming litter. There are also several weekly and monthly magazines and periodicals devoted to the world of mainly purebred dogs. They discuss exhibiting, training and breeding, and virtually every breed has its separate column; advertisements give details of pups for sale and addresses of secretaries of breed clubs. Major dog shows are excellent places for checking on a particular breed, in respect of appearance and temperament, and the major breeders.

The next step is to find a breeder who has or will shortly have puppies for sale and to make arrangements to see the litter and discuss price. If everything goes smoothly, it then becomes a question of selecting an individual puppy of the chosen sex and possibly colour, and waiting patiently until the pups are old enough to leave home, at the age of six or preferably eight weeks. The waiting time can be used to gather together the necessary basic equipment.

Check points for health

All puppies, whether purebred or mongrels, have instant appeal, easily stirring the protective instincts. Even so, the purchase of a puppy should be ruled by common sense, not sentimentality; in most cases it involves considerable expense and long-term commitment, and there is no point in taking on an animal which is unhealthy from the beginning. The basic signs of good – or poor – health are fairly easy to assess, and by sticking consistently to a check list, even the first-time buyer should be able to pick a healthy puppy from the litter.

Ask to see the whole litter running about in a small space, preferably in good natural light. Most pups will get up from sleep when a new face appears and behave actively, chasing each other and jumping up to be fondled. They will also probably empty both bladders and bowels, affording the buyer a chance of checking that motions are reasonably formed, with no evidence of violent diarrhoea. While the pups are running about, pay particular notice to any obvious signs of lameness, and to any pup which does not bother to get up. It may only mean that he is tired from racing about a few minutes earlier, but it could also be a sign of ill-health. Guard against emotions of sympathy and urges to protect and care for the little wretch. An aloof character who does not join in a family game may indeed be unsociable, to other dogs and to people in general.

Study all the puppies; if one or more members of the litter are showing signs of illness, it is best to avoid them all and leave as quickly and tactfully as possible. Disinfect footwear before visiting another kennel.

If the first impression is favourable, ask to pick up one or two pups for closer inspection, choosing first members of the preferred sex. Handling a puppy

Litter mates enjoy a cheerful romp; an indifferent puppy may be tired or ailing, or by nature unsociable

39

imparts information about its physical shape and possible temperament. A well-adjusted puppy will allow itself to be picked up and handled without panicking or cowering in fear; it should be alert and respond to sudden noises without whimpering or growling, return a gaze steadily and resume its former activities cheerfully on being set down again.

As regards physical shape, the buyer will probably have some mental picture of the expected if not the actual measured weight. If the puppy handles heavy, all well and good, but if it is lighter than expected, suspicions may be aroused, irrespective of whether the puppy is a Chihuahua or a Great Dane.

The light puppy may have a large round abdomen or belly, with the skin stretched tight, but feel bony on the back and ribs. This can be a sign of infestation with roundworms, which are extremely common even in well cared-for litters. The parasites can be expelled very early in life with repeated treatments, and this should have been done already in properly run establishments. The new owner will have to continue the treatment later, but no pups showing such obvious signs should be offered for sale.

Check that the eyes are well open and bright, showing no discharge or signs of discomfort, or of having been rubbed or scratched. At the same time check that the insides of the ears are clean and odour-free, and that the hairs round the edges are clean – the lower edges are favourite hiding places for tiny lice; tell-tale signs that small ears have strayed into the food bowl have usually been removed by ever-hungry litter mates.

The rest of the coat should also be checked; fleas favour the area along the back and especially the part just in front of the tail; actual fleas may be difficult to spot, but little black specks among the hairs may well be flea droppings. The coat itself should be shiny and clean, and there should be no distinct bare patches in areas which are otherwise well haired. The skin of the abdomen should be clean and whitish-pink, except in pigmented areas, free from spots, pustules or scabs. The area just below the anal opening should be clean; if it is dirty it could be a sign of an upset alimentary system.

Occasionally puppies have hernias, either at the navel or in the groin; those at the navel are usually tiny and rarely cause problems in later life. Hernias in the groin can be more dangerous, and if they are large enough to be spotted by a prospective purchaser, they are almost certainly too big for comfort; reject the puppy. Handling a puppy gives a good impression of the body, which should have a moderate layer of fat under the skin, and the latter should be loose enough to be picked up in folds.

It is commonly thought that a healthy dog always has a cold, slightly moist nose, and while it would generally be true that any pup with such a nose would be healthy, it does not necessarily follow that the odd warm nose indicates sickness. There should be no discharge from the nose, and the breath should smell sweet. Except when a puppy has been wrestling with his litter mates just before examination, his breathing should be easy. Study the character and rate of the respirations, and if breathing gives the impression of being laboured, something is more than likely wrong.

It can be difficult for a novice to assess the soundness of the skeleton of the dog. In general, it should be well balanced and conform to the breed standard, the back straight or slightly sloping with no obvious irregularities in the backbone curvature; the ribs should be well sprung, the forequarters straight, and the hindquarters well angulated at the knee (or stifle) joints. The head should be in proportion to the rest of the body, with level mouth, neither over nor undershot.

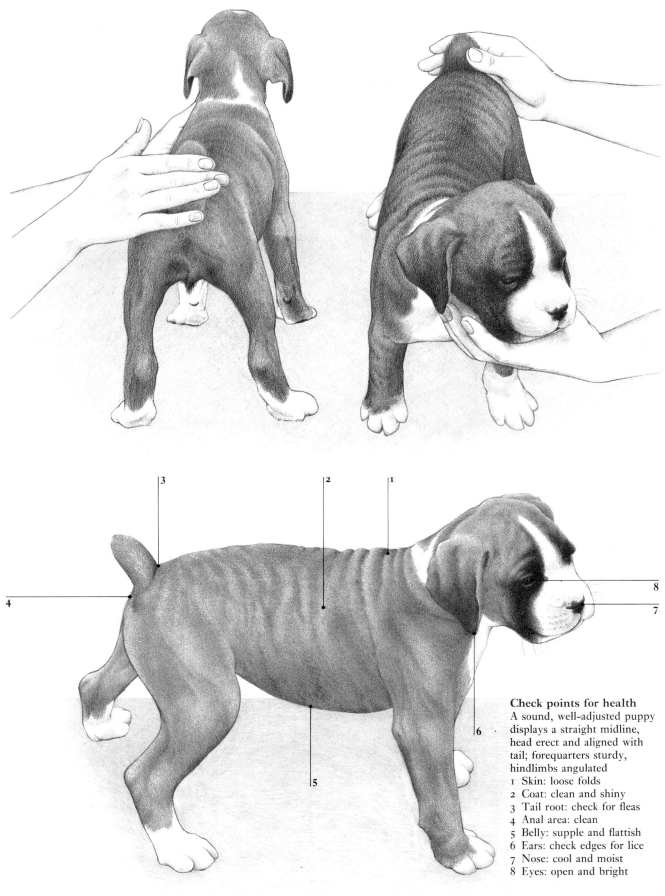

Check points for health
A sound, well-adjusted puppy
displays a straight midline,
head erect and aligned with
tail; forequarters sturdy,
hindlimbs angulated
1 Skin: loose folds
2 Coat: clean and shiny
3 Tail root: check for fleas
4 Anal area: clean
5 Belly: supple and flattish
6 Ears: check edges for lice
7 Nose: cool and moist
8 Eyes: open and bright

Some large breeds have more than their fair share of bony malformations, such as hip dysplasia; the prospective buyer would be aware of such propensities and factors from studying the breed in advance. It is advisable to obtain veterinary advice on the purchase of a breed known to have skeletal problems or other inherited defects.

The purchaser is entitled to adequate time in which to study the puppy and to obtain professional advice. With luck, the dog will be a member of the household for anything up to fifteen or sixteen years, and nothing is gained by rushing the choice. It is possible to have a veterinary surgeon check a puppy before purchase, but this may be difficult if the breeder lives a long way away. Reputable breeders will replace a puppy – or the money – if something is fundamentally wrong, and the defect is of a nature for which they can be held morally responsible. In Britain, the Sale of Goods Act applies to puppies under certain circumstances, but as these are not well defined it may be necessary to obtain the advice of a solicitor.

At the same time, the breeder has the right to refuse to sell a puppy to a buyer who does not appear to have a suitable temperament as a dog owner or who does not seem prepared to shoulder the responsibilities of ownership.

Once negotiations have been successfully completed, choice and price of puppy agreed, and collection date fixed, the breeder will issue a signed pedigree certificate, and a registration card or signed transfer form from the English Kennel Club. On collection, the reliable breeder will also provide a feeding chart, assurance that the puppy has been wormed at least twice, and advice on general care during the first few weeks.

Buying an Adult Dog

For one reason or another, it may be preferable to purchase an adult, trained dog rather than a puppy. Most breeds have some form of rescue system which tries to accommodate any dog which has to be found a new home. This may be because the original owners have moved abroad or into accommodation where dogs are not allowed, because family circumstances have irrevocably changed; or because the owner had failed to realize the full demands of dog ownership and felt incapable of keeping the animal. Whatever the reason, the fault rarely lies with the dog, and he or she will almost certainly relish a caring home. Breed rescue services can be found through the breed clubs, and these in turn can be traced through the English Kennel Club or the canine press.

In addition, a large number of rescue homes are run by welfare societies, which often have a great variety of waifs and strays on offer. Buying a dog from a rescue home requires a level head unswayed by sympathy; follow the same check list for signs of health and disease as in the puppy. Most homes will supply all available details about the dog, and with luck these will include the true reason as to why the dog is changing hands. If it is reputed to be destructive in the house, this may simply be because it was bored through too little exercise or too little human company, or both. Such a behaviour problem may be curable, but the dog must be taken on with the knowledge of such problems.

It is also important to find out about the animal's behaviour with young children, and with other dogs, and whether it is obedient or wilful. Its feeding, grooming and exercising requirements should be assessed, any known veterinary problems evaluated, and vaccination record, including certificated proof of vaccination if available, ascertained. Finally, be particularly wary and careful of a dog which has been rehomed several times; it may have been unlucky with previous owners, but the odds are against it.

The basic equipment for a new puppy (*below*) includes a bed of some sort. A strong cardboard box (1), with a bedding of dry newspaper which should be changed daily, is by far the best choice in the early stages; it can be replaced by a proper bed when the puppy has cut his teeth. Feeding and water bowls (2) are other essentials; those made from stainless steel or heavy ceramic are less likely to be knocked over; like the tools (3) used for preparing the puppy's meals, they should be washed separately

Slippers left lying around are for chewing, a strong rubber ring (4) strictly for throwing and fetching. Keep a washing bowl (5) and a cast-off towel for the puppy's exclusive use, and a rug (6) on which to dry off small muddy feet. The first lead (7) should be lightweight, made of leather, fabric or metal, with a clip-on bolt for attaching it to a narrow puppy collar (8); check collars (9) should be reserved for training lessons. The law requires all dogs to wear a name tag (10) or some other means of identification

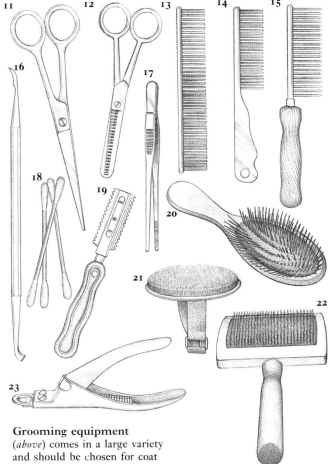

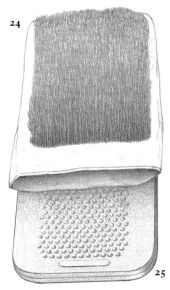

Grooming equipment (*above*) comes in a large variety and should be chosen for coat type. Long-bladed scissors (11) are suitable for trimming overgrown hair between the pads, and round-tipped scissors (12) for thinning hairs on the inner ear flaps. Metal combs (13, 14 and 15) have fine, medium or coarse teeth; they come in various sizes, with or without handles.

Descalers (16) should never be used on puppy teeth, but can be useful for removing tartar on older dogs. Tweezers (17) and cottonbuds (18) come in handy for removing grass seeds and bits of grit between toes; a stripping knife (19) is essential for preparing show dogs and for thinning out thick coats.

There is a choice of brushes, such as an all-purpose rubber-backed bristle brush (20), the so-called terrier palm or dandy pad (21) with adjustable strap, and a stripping brush (22) for wiry and close-haired coats. Nail clippers (23) should be used with caution to avoid cutting into the quick

A grooming or hound glove removes dead hairs and also acts as a polisher of the coat; it is made from horsehair (24) or from rubber (25)

Preparing the Home

Before the puppy is collected from the breeder, a few preparations should be taken in hand to await his arrival. Garden fences and gates should be made secure, and swimming pools and garden ponds covered over until the puppy has come to realize the potential danger they represent. Garden pesticides should be stored out of reach of children and animals. In the home, take care to move tempting objects out of reach of an inquisitive puppy; he will chew anything lying around, especially leather and rubber objects. Loose, trailing electric wires and flexes can cause serious accidents; leather gloves and slippers will be chewed to ribbons in a short while as will practically everything at floor level, including newspapers and mail on the front door mat. Tidiness becomes an essential household task with a puppy around.

Although a young puppy will spend much of his time sleeping, he will also want to play and should be encouraged to do so. A few toys are useful, provided that they are so large that they cannot be swallowed; squeaky toys may be too excitable. Avoid toys made from nylon and plastic, which are easily chewed by small teeth and on which the puppy may choke.

Feeding utensils

For the first few weeks, little equipment is necessary apart from feeding and water bowls, some kind of bedding, and a few grooming aids. The breeder will have detailed the sort of food the puppy is already eating, and a small stock can be laid in; a vast quantity can be a mistake when the puppy discovers there is no longer a need to dash to the trough. He may have to be persuaded before he adjusts to the new regime.

A dog must have his own food and water bowls, which should be kept apart from human utensils, even to the extent of using different washing-up bowls. Dogs are not unhygienic, but certain disease conditions (the zoonoses) can be passed from animals to man. Food and water bowls come in plastic, metal and heavy pottery. Large breeds have hearty appetites and need large bowls, and all types should be capable of withstanding proper sterilization by boiling; cheap plastic may warp into shapes unsuited for fluids. Metal bowls often attract the professional 'chewer', and plastic seems at times to hold fatal attractions; it has been known to disappear down the canine gullet, causing vomiting or uncomfortable impaction at the other end of the alimentary system. Pottery bowls should be heavy and slippery so that they cannot be picked up and dropped; choose a shape which cannot be easily overturned.

Bedding

A vast range of dog baskets and beds is available, varying from the strictly utilitarian to the frankly ostentatious. Owners may want to demonstrate their love for their pets by lavishing all manner of luxuries on them, but the majority of dogs want only a place of their own where they can feel secure and comfortable. Provided that they are protected from draughts many dogs hardly notice the room temperature, although this obviously depends on the amount of coat; a thick-coated Golden Retriever will feel the cold less acutely than a short-coated Bedlington Terrier, and a dog which has just had his coat extensively clipped or stripped will appreciate warmth on a cold night.

The first bed for a new puppy must be regarded as dispensable, and for this purpose a cardboard box lined with an old blanket is the most practical and economical. Alternatively, choose a type of bed which can easily be disinfected and cleaned. Cardboard boxes can be burnt, canvas sling bottoms on metal

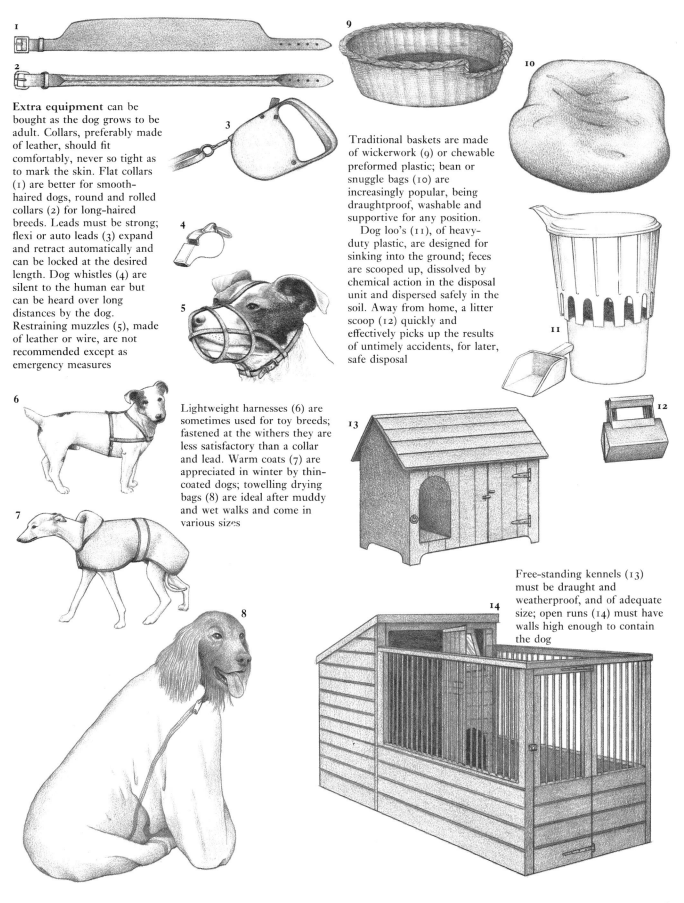

Extra equipment can be bought as the dog grows to be adult. Collars, preferably made of leather, should fit comfortably, never so tight as to mark the skin. Flat collars (1) are better for smooth-haired dogs, round and rolled collars (2) for long-haired breeds. Leads must be strong; flexi or auto leads (3) expand and retract automatically and can be locked at the desired length. Dog whistles (4) are silent to the human ear but can be heard over long distances by the dog. Restraining muzzles (5), made of leather or wire, are not recommended except as emergency measures

Lightweight harnesses (6) are sometimes used for toy breeds; fastened at the withers they are less satisfactory than a collar and lead. Warm coats (7) are appreciated in winter by thin-coated dogs; towelling drying bags (8) are ideal after muddy and wet walks and come in various sizes

Traditional baskets are made of wickerwork (9) or chewable preformed plastic; bean or snuggle bags (10) are increasingly popular, being draughtproof, washable and supportive for any position.

Dog loo's (11), of heavy-duty plastic, are designed for sinking into the ground; feces are scooped up, dissolved by chemical action in the disposal unit and dispersed safely in the soil. Away from home, a litter scoop (12) quickly and effectively picks up the results of untimely accidents, for later, safe disposal

Free-standing kennels (13) must be draught and weatherproof, and of adequate size; open runs (14) must have walls high enough to contain the dog

frames can be washed, but wicker baskets are difficult to clean after even a mild attack of vomiting or diarrhoea and they are perfect for cutting the second set of teeth on! Delay investing in an expensive basket or bed until the puppy is past the chewing stage.

Grooming equipment

All dogs need regular and thorough grooming, and this should have been started before the new puppy is collected so that the process has become routine. Some owners turn grooming into a game, but it is all too easy to allow the dog to win, and grooming can then become a constant battle of wills. All kinds of tools and equipment are available, including a range of brushes, combs, and clippers (see page 43). A hound glove, which almost acts like a polisher, is suitable for smooth coats, while longer coats need a strong-handled bristle or wire brush, and a long-tined metal comb. Dogs get wet and muddy on rainy walks. They should be dried and rubbed down with a cast-off, thick towel after they have had a good shake, preferably in the garden.

Hairy dogs have their own built-in cushions and probably will not feel the lack of a blanket in their beds, but short-coated types, especially large, heavy breeds like the Mastiff and the Great Dane, tend to rub the sharp angles like elbows or haunches. Ideally their beds should be cushioned with thick rugs, preferably manmade which, though expensive, can go in the washing-machine time and again.

Collars and name tags

The first collar should be lightweight and inexpensive; it will eventually have to be exchanged for a larger size and will probably be chewed by its wearer. Leather, either flat or rolled, is preferable to plastic, and the collar should be fitted so that it cannot slip over the puppy's ears if he pulls back against it; the type of collar which forms a noose round the neck can be alarming for a puppy if the collar is pulled up tight, and it tends to fall off if left loose. Get the puppy accustomed to wearing the collar by fitting it for an hour or two at a time; after a while a lightweight lead can be attached to the collar and the puppy walked in the garden. Leather leads are satisfactory but easier to chew than metal ones; the latter should be of good-quality stainless steel or they will rust.

In Britain, the law decrees that all dogs must have a means of identification attached to their collars; this can be a plastic or metal disc, or a small screw cap container with a paper insert. The owner's name, address, and telephone number should be inscribed on either type; it is inadvisable to inscribe the dog's name as this might help a thief to entice him away. It is also possible to tattoo a dog, either in the ear or preferably in the inside of the thigh, with indelible dye as an identification method.

Outdoor kennels

Most new owners will probably want to keep the pet dog indoors, but there is nothing against housing a dog outside provided that the kennel accommodation is draughtproof, has a source of warmth, and can be easily and properly cleaned. An outdoor kennel should preferably have a run, fenced in securely from the rest of the garden and high enough to prevent the dog from jumping over it. Fresh water must be available at all times, and the kennel should have proper sleeping accommodation. Thick-coated breeds do not need thick bedding, but shorter-coated types will be grateful for a comforting blanket.

However, most owners feel that a family dog should live in the house, where it can participate in family life and be better able to carry out the role of protector of the property.

Bringing the Puppy Home

If possible, arrange to collect the puppy at the start of a weekend when the whole family will be around and have time to settle in the new arrival. Mid-morning is a good time for collection so that the puppy can be fed its midday meal after the journey. The removal from pack life among brothers and sisters can be upsetting for any puppy, and the transition should be made as smooth and calm as possible. Arrange for two people to collect the puppy so that one can hold it on the lap, wrapped loosely in a blanket. An old towel can be brought along to catch bladder leakages or vomiting.

On arrival home, the puppy will react to the unusual happenings with an urgent need to relieve himself, and he should be taken straight to the garden before being introduced to the house. Give the puppy his meal, following the breeder's diet sheet; it will be most appetizing if warmed to body temperature.

Young puppies spend much of their time sleeping; children should be taught to let sleeping dogs lie. By the time he is removed from the litter, the puppy will have seen few people apart from the breeder, and it is essential for his equilibrium that he is given time to acclimatize to his new family and surroundings. He should therefore not be exposed to a multitude of admiring faces at the outset, nor should he be lifted up and patted continuously.

A tiny puppy must be held as carefully as a baby, in the crook of the arm, with one hand supporting the hindquarters and the base of the spine, the other the forelimbs and the head

Initially, and until the puppy is house trained, the kitchen is the most suitable living quarter; he is bound to make a mess on the floor, and linoleum or plastic tiles are easier to clean than carpets. The first night in his new home can be a traumatic experience, eased if the puppy is snug and warm. Settle him in his box, with a bedding of dry newspapers or an old blanket, and if he is left on his own in the kitchen be sure to cover the floor with newspaper. He can also be confined in a deeper box or tea chest, which serves a dual purpose: he will sleep longer in the comfortable den than if he can run around on the kitchen floor, and he will also control himself better because, like other animals, he dislikes fouling his bed. However, six hours is the maximum length of time he can be left on his own at night.

In many instances it may be kinder and give a greater sense of security if the puppy can spend the first few nights close to its new owners. He can be taken, in his box, to the bedroom until he is familiar with the house and its occupants. This course does not necessarily establish a pattern for the future; as the puppy adapts to a new life style, he will accept a few hours of solitude during the day, and eventually these can extend to nights in his bed in the kitchen.

Until the puppy has accepted the home as his own, he should not be left except for very short periods of up to 30 minutes. A sense of security and trust is essential for his future development, and this cannot be achieved in isolation; he will react by crying or by chewing everything within reach, faults which can be difficult to eradicate later.

Until the puppy has completed his vaccination course, he is at his most vulnerable to the infectious and contagious conditions to which the dog is prone; some of these can be carried on clothing and footwear, and visits by other people should be restricted. The puppy should not be taken outside the house and garden, and it should not be allowed contact with strange dogs.

Begin calling the puppy by his chosen name at once; ideally, it should be short and clearly enunciated in an even voice. Praise the puppy as he responds and gradually use different intonations for pleasure and displeasure.

1

2

3

4

Toilet training must begin as soon as the puppy has been installed in his new home. When he awakes from sleep and after a meal, pick him up and carry him outside (1)

Do not leave him unattended or he will wander off without realizing what is wanted (2). Tell him to 'be clean' or 'busy' and stay with him until he has performed satisfactorily

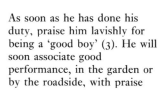

As soon as he has done his duty, praise him lavishly for being a 'good boy' (3). He will soon associate good performance, in the garden or by the roadside, with praise

Soon he will approach the door of his own accord when the need arises (4). Lacking a garden, he can be encouraged to perform on newspaper or in a box of sawdust

If he has an accident indoors, scold him at once with NO and point to the offending mess; if he persists in being naughty, tap him on the rump with a roll of newspaper. On walks, tell-tale signs of rapid circling and sniffing indicate imminent action: move him into the gutter or on to rough grass, or jerk the lead and carry on walking until a suitable place can be reached

House Training

Once the first hours of exploration are over, routine must start, with priority given to house training. This may not be the most important part of training in a dog's life, but it is vital to get the message across in a positive fashion from the very beginning. A puppy can be expected to empty its bladder as soon as it wakes from sleep, and as soon as it has been fed; it may also pass feces simultaneously. If these happenings can be anticipated and the puppy put out into the garden – or on to a piece of newspaper if no garden is available – mistakes will be infrequent, and the puppy will learn what is wanted. Watch out for warning signs usually characterized by rapid wanderings and circlings; there is only a short interval between indication and performance.

The owner must respond at once, take the puppy outside and *stay with it* until it has performed. This is the time to introduce the first command, which may be 'outside', 'be clean', 'go on', or 'be a good boy/girl'. Every time the puppy does what is required, be lavish with praise. Eventually the puppy will associate outside performance with praise, and the phrase with performance. House training a puppy takes patience and perseverance, especially if the puppy is acquired during wintry weather, but the longer it is delayed, the more difficult it becomes. As the puppy grows, the intervals between indication and performance become longer, and the adult dog can go for several hours during the day, and for most of the night, without elimination.

Normally, a puppy can control itself reliably by the age of four to six months, and by eight months it will last throughout the night provided that it is put outside last thing at night and first thing in the morning.

Worming and Vaccination

A puppy collected at about eight weeks of age will have been wormed for common roundworms by the breeder, but it is advisable to check that this has been done. In the majority of cases, roundworms are passed on by the dam to her unborn young, and reputable breeders treat the pups at the age of three weeks, with a second dose later. As the puppy grows, it should be given further worming treatment, and the veterinary surgeon is the best person to advise on dosage and frequency.

Some veterinary practices deal with all species of animals, others specialize in horses or farm animals, but almost all deal with dogs. Local practices are listed in telephone directories, at police stations, and at pet shops; the best recommendations are probably from other dog owners, and especially from competent breeders.

Every puppy requires vaccination, but the actual regime may vary because of individual circumstances. These include such factors as the level of immunity in the pup's mother, a level which she passes on in her first milk; and prevalent disease problems in a particular locality. Obtain the advice of the chosen veterinarian as to how and when the puppy should be inoculated. The dog is heir to a number of diseases, most of which can be fatal and all of which are at best unpleasant. Most, such as distemper, hepatitis, parvovirus and rabies are caused by viruses. Two forms of the bacterial disease leptospirosis affect the liver and kidneys, and one of them is the cause of Weil's disease in humans. Fortunately all serious diseases have been the subject of highly effective research, and vaccines have been produced to counter them.

Rabies, the most deadly canine disease, is almost invariably fatal when transmitted to humans; it is known as hydrophobia, literally 'fear of water'. The symptoms of rabies in man are horrifying; in dogs the signs vary, but the end result is always death. Britain is fortunate in being one of the few countries in the Western World where rabies does not occur. This is partly due to her island position and partly due to her strict quarantine regulations. Vaccination against rabies is only permissible in animals coming into the country through quarantine, or known to be going to a country whose laws insist on vaccination against the disease. Quarantine for all dogs and cats entering the United Kingdom is essential; anyone who tries to circumvent the regulations by illegally smuggling animals through is an enemy of humans and animals and is justly punished with heavy fines and/or imprisonment. Any dog imported from abroad must spend six obligatory months in Ministry-approved quarantine kennels. An owner who cannot face such lengthy separation has no other choice than leaving the dog behind.

In Britain, anti-rabies vaccines are unnecessary for the normal home population of dogs, and a great deal can be done to protect them against other serious diseases. At around eight weeks, the puppy should be inoculated with the first combined vaccine against distemper, hepatitis and the two forms of leptospirosis. This will in large measure give protection against the first two, and forms the first half of a two-phase course against the latter. The second half of the course is repeated at the age of twelve weeks to deal with those puppies whose mothers gave them a high level of immunity to distemper and hepatitis, and to complete the leptospira course. The first dose of parvo-virus vaccine may also be given to protect puppies who had lost their maternal immunity.

A final dose of parvovirus vaccine at eighteen weeks is now considered the correct timing for catching those puppies which failed to react satisfactorily to the earlier dose because of the level of protection from the dam. The initial vaccination course is comparatively expensive but is also a sensible protection of a costly and loved puppy. In any case, this lengthy programme will never need repeating *in toto*, though it is recommended that the dog is taken for an annual visit to the veterinary surgery for booster injections.

Basic Training

Once the programme of vaccination is completed, the puppy is ready for the outside world. Before that he can be accustomed to a light collar and lead in the garden and learn to walk to heel without pulling or lagging behind. In the beginning the training exercises should be of short duration, partly because the young puppy is unable to concentrate for any length of time, and partly because his bones are not yet fully formed, and the muscles still need toning up. For most pups a 15–20 minute walk is an adventure, perhaps even a frightening experience, with traffic thundering by and humans towering above a small, immature puppy.

The lead represents authority; it should be attached securely to the collar and held in such a manner that it comes under the dog's chin; if it loops over the head it will push the nose downwards and frighten the pup. Check or choke chains are not recommended for basic training exercises; the pull of the chain can easily frighten the puppy, and nasty accidents are known to occur from a loose chain caught on an obstruction and strangling the panicky animal.

The first walks should be short and pleasurable; it is less important that the puppy walks perfectly at heel than he learns to accept traffic and crowds and comes to associate a walk with a treat. When he is accustomed to collar and lead for the walk, he can be let off the lead in a safe open space, far away from busy roads where traffic bustle will not distract his attention and where the owner will not have to worry if the puppy decides to be wilful and refuse to return.

The true turning point of all obedience training is the puppy's response to the command 'Come'. Until he comes when called no progress can be made with the other basic steps of 'Sit', 'Stay', and 'Wait'. The average puppy resents being kept under control; the moment he is let off the lead he feels free and does not easily surrender that freedom. The best place to commence 'recall' training is in the garden, or in a small fenced area. Avoid places where there is a chance of the puppy escaping on to a road; the owner will panic, raise his voice, and make a mistake through a hasty move. The puppy, which senses that the handler has lost his confidence, will take off in fright, and training is automatically set back.

Let the puppy off the lead; do not call him back immediately, but let him run off the first exuberance of freedom. When he slows down and his attention is not distracted, call him by name in a pleasant but firm voice, and follow the name with the single command 'Come'. Determine from the start the command words to be used for particular actions and stick to them; 'Come' one moment and 'Here' the next only serves to confuse the puppy. Most pups will respond by taking a step or two towards the voice which is when a praising 'Good boy' is in its place to let the puppy know that he has done the right thing so far. At the same time, step away from him, patting one leg to show him where to come, and exaggerate praise for correct and prompt interpretation by the puppy. If, on the other hand, the speed of recall is slow or if the puppy comes half-way and then darts off again, ignore him and walk off, out of sight if possible. The pup will follow out of curiosity, and if that ruse fails, bend down and pretend to find something interesting on the ground. When the puppy eventually arrives do not make the mistake of grabbing him at the collar and securing him with the lead, even if it has taken half an hour to get him within range. Pat him on the head, tell him how well he has behaved, and let him go off again. If every time he returns he is put on the lead, he will soon see the drawbacks to such a deal, and the next day's exercise will take twice as long.

That first step may take a long time and require a great deal of patience, but once the battle is won, and the puppy is confident that it is worth responding

A young dog which has mastered the principles of basic training must also learn to accept his own company and await his master's return without barking or jumping up. He can be tethered high for short spells or the lead fastened in a low position to allow him to lie down

Walking to heel is the first step of training the puppy. Attach a light lead to his collar, place him on the left side, with lead in the right hand (1). Call him by name, followed by 'heel' and be ready to step forward at once with the left leg. If he fails to follow, jerk the lead firmly (2) and repeat the exercise several times

The sit command becomes the second stage of basic training. Place the left hand on the pup's hindquarters and press him firmly into a sitting position, using his name and 'sit' at the same time (3). It will take more than a few exercises and much patience, but eventually he will sit on the command only, especially if he is rewarded with a tidbit

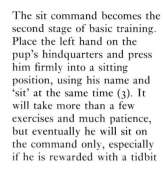

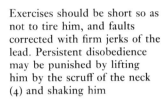

Exercises should be short so as not to tire him, and faults corrected with firm jerks of the lead. Persistent disobedience may be punished by lifting him by the scruff of the neck (4) and shaking him

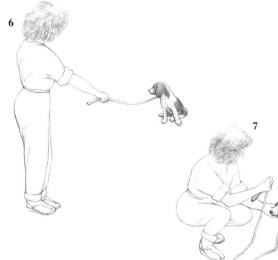

When the puppy has learned to sit on command, teach him to 'stay'. Raise the lead above his head (5) and walk slowly round him in a circle, repeating the command 'stay'. Initially he will get up or turn round for a look; each time this happens, jerk on the lead and return him to the sit before starting again.

Recall or wait-and-come is an extension of stay, with the puppy in the sit-stay position a lead's length away (6). Call his name and 'come', jerking the lead if he hesitates. When he does come, command 'sit' and crouch down to his level, praising him lavishly (7)

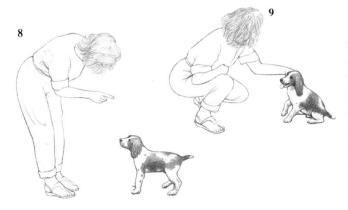

Down and stay can be taught only when the puppy obeys the basic commands instantly, on and off the lead. Have him in the sit or down position, remove the lead and walk out of sight, repeating his name and 'stay'. If he is still in the down or sit position on returning, praise him profusely; if he has moved or jumps up, withhold praise and walk away from him again

Jumping up in greeting or for attention can be an endearing trait to the owner, but not everybody appreciates muddy paws, and the habit is best discouraged from the start. At the first attempt to jump up on the owner's return, say a stern NO (8) and command 'down'. If he stays down, crouch to him (9), smiling and telling him gently what a good boy he is

because of praise or a tidbit, other basic exercises are that much easier. Repeat the recall command until he obeys unerringly, before trying it out in an open space. Never scold or punish the puppy if he fails to respond at once, and never let the exercise become so protracted that he becomes bored. Always finish a training period with a game so that he looks forward to the next session.

At heel
Basic training goes hand in hand with the first proper walks, which should be short and often, with a little heelwork introduced straightaway. Most professional dog trainers maintain that a dog should walk on the left-hand side of his owner, with the neck about level with the owner's leg. This is because most people are right-handed; hunters generally carry their guns under the right arm, and a dog on the same side would receive a few knocks from the gun as it came up to aim. It is immaterial to the dog whether it is taught to walk to heel on the right or the left side, but it would be confusing in obedience trials and when the dog is walked by somebody accustomed to the left-hand dog.

The lead is customarily carried with the loop at the end over the right wrist or grasped in the right hand; the left hand can be used for taking up the slack and checking a forward pull. No dog, young or old, should be allowed to pull on his lead; most dogs can pull more strongly than their owners and the ensuing tug-of-war results in an owner with sore shoulder muscles and a dog gasping for breath. Give the command 'Heel' and step off at a reasonable, purposeful pace, the lead held loosely in the right hand; pat the left leg encouragingly and give a small jerk to the lead to get the puppy's attention.

Once the puppy has learnt to obey the basic commands, it is a good idea for owner and dog to join a training class, where he can be taught more advanced programmes in the company of other dogs and handlers. Training classes are advertised in the local press and at veterinary surgeries; they are generally inexpensive and offer good opportunities for getting the puppy used to canine company, and for the owner to establish friendships with other dog lovers.

The reason for training a dog is simple; he must be taught his place in life and his position in the household. An untrained dog gets into mischief, and the more intelligent, the more mischief he will dream up. Untrained dogs cause road accidents, frighten or bite legitimate callers, chase sheep, trespass on private land and create annoyance in the neighbourhood with their constant barking and roaming. At worst they end up being destroyed or discarded as strays. The fault lies not with the dog but with the owner; basically there are no bad dogs, only irresponsible owners.

The Adolescent Dog
With the passing weeks the young puppy naturally grows into a young adult. As a generalization, one year of a dog's life is taken to be equivalent to seven human years, although a six-month-old pup of medium size is probably nearer the physical age of a ten to twelve-year-old child, and in a state of early puberty; in some cases a bitch may soon come on heat. The larger the breed, the later the onset of physical and sexual maturity. Bones grow in length from areas known as growth plates; while growth is still taking place the plates are said to be open, and as the period of growth comes to an end, the plates are said to close. This closure takes place as early as seven months in a dog the size of a Miniature Dachshund, but does not happen until fourteen or fifteen months in an Irish Wolfhound. A bitch puppy in the smaller breeds may come on heat at six months, while many of the giants will be eighteen months old before it occurs.

Garden boundaries should be sound enough to prevent the young and adult dog from escaping. Otherwise, he can have comparative freedom tethered to a strong line stretched between two trees and the lead attached to it. This should be long enough to allow him to reach the shade; a double knot in the line will prevent him from being caught up in the lead

A bitch can be mated and become pregnant at her first heat, and precautions must be taken against unwanted pregnancies. Most breeders advocate against breeding from a bitch as early as this on the grounds that it may stunt growth. At the other end of her life, the bitch does not cease producing eggs from the ovaries; she will continue to come on heat and be capable of mating and bearing puppies into what would be considered late middle and even old age in the human. Occurrences of twelve-year-old bitches whelping naturally, though with small litters, are not rare.

The male dog is often ready and willing to mate at six months, and it would be unwise to rely on his inexperience and youth if he gains access to a suitable bitch; even his own mother is not safe from amorous attentions. At the other end of the scale, dogs have sired litters well into their teens, which possibly accounts for the phrase that 'there's life in the old dog yet'. Generally, if pups are not wanted, they must be prevented; no benefit, but sometimes harm, is derived from letting a young bitch have a litter, or allowing a sexually overeager male to mate in order to cool him down. Dog breeding is time-consuming, costly, and fraught with complications, and best left to professional breeders (see also Reproduction and Mating, page 120).

A bitch can be prevented from mating through neutering or contraceptive pills and injections. She can also be confined while she is on heat, and the best place is often a reliable boarding kennel. If, in spite of such precautions, a female and male dog are caught in 'incriminating circumstances', pregnancy can be prevented with a hormone injection within the first day or so after mating. This must be regarded strictly as an emergency measure; any upset of the hormone balance may lead to problems in the uterus.

Car Travels & Holidays

Most puppies suffer from car sickness until they become used to the unusual nature of the motion. Often the result is vomiting, probably caused by fright as well as the actual movement. Drugs are available to control either cause, but it is much better from the start to get the dog to associate car travel with pleasure. This can be achieved gradually by having the puppy in the stationary car, feeding him a tidbit or a proper meal, for instance, and then turning the engine on without actually moving off. Once he is accustomed to the engine noise, make the first journeys short, perhaps to a destination where he can have a walk or a game. Avoid taking the dog on a car journey until at least three hours have elapsed since his last feed.

Until the dog becomes a seasoned traveller, it is recommended that another member of the household be present, to soothe him and clear up any mess from car sickness. The small puppy can be held on the lap or placed in a travel box; the back seat is the most appropriate place, and ideally the outside world and moving traffic should be outside his field of vision. Most adult dogs find the well between front and back seats the most comfortable position where they can brace themselves against sudden jerks; they should be secured with a light leather lead attached to one of the car seats' lower structures. Rails can also be erected above the rear seats to prevent the dog from jumping into the front and from being thrown at emergency stops.

Small toy breeds are easily thrown off balance and may be better confined to a travel cage or basket placed on the floor or the front passenger seat, where the dog can be reassured by the closeness of the owner.

The arrival of a dog will obviously entail changes in the household routine. Somebody must take him for early-morning walks, irrespective of inclination

Travelling by car can become a pleasure rather than anxiety if the puppy is gradually acclimatized to a moving vehicle. Sit with him in the stationary car and let him explore its interior. Eventually switch on the engine and follow this with short trips until he gets used to both the noise and the movement

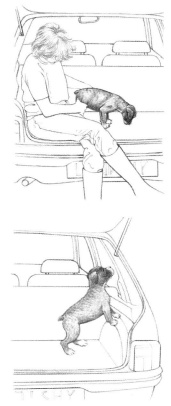

Travelling cages are useful on long journeys and are recommended for transporting show dogs. Toy and miniature breeds fit comfortably in portable carriers which are sturdy enough to remain upright. Large breeds are better restrained behind a detachable boot or rear-seat grille

and weather; the house cannot be left untenanted for the whole day because the dog must be let out, fed, watered and, most important of all, given companionship and love. One of the most significant changes concerns holidays and whether or not the dog should be included. Holidays abroad in a way present no problem because a dog cannot be taken outside Britain or Eire even on a day trip or boat journey unless on the return he goes through six months' expensive quarantine.

On holidays in the British Isles, it is often possible to take a dog along, but before booking into a hotel or guest house, find out if a dog is permitted; it will never be allowed in dining rooms, and a young puppy or a nervous dog may cause havoc if left behind in the rooms while the rest of the family dines.

Regulations at caravan and camp sites vary from place to place; even where dogs are allowed, they must obviously be under proper control and prevented from making a nuisance of themselves among other campers and holiday-makers. Some beaches are closed to dogs.

Dogs are permitted on British Rail when accompanied by their owners; unless they are guide dogs for the blind or of lap-dog size they are charged at the rate of children's tickets and are not allowed on to seats. They are also allowed on underground systems, but must be carried up and down escalators. Bus and coach travel companies have different regulations, and it is advisable to check in advance whether they convey accompanied dogs, and at what cost.

Boarding Kennels

If the dog is to be excluded from the holiday it must be accommodated for the duration with a sympathetic friend or a boarding kennel. By law, boarding kennels in Britain must be licensed by the Local Authority. They are regularly inspected to see that they comply with the requirements of the Boarding Establishments Act, and in theory licensed premises should be satisfactory as regards hygiene, comfort, and safety. Even so, it is advisable to discuss potential holiday homes with other dog owners and listen to their experiences; the local veterinary surgeon usually has a list of kennels in the area, and while he will not recommend one at the expense of another, the mere fact that a name appears on the practice list can usually be taken as an inference that it is reasonable.

Having made a choice of a boarding kennel, make an appointment to view it. If the kennel does not welcome such inspection, opt for another place which does. A properly run kennel will insist on an up-to-date certificate of the dog's vaccination and will need information about particular diets, bitches coming into heat, or chronic infirmities and medications.

A good boarding kennel can be invaluable, and it will soon be apparent if the dog was well cared for and enjoyed his holiday; there may be other occasions when he will have to go back, during family illnesses or bereavements. A boarding kennel may be expensive – and early booking is essential for the major holiday seasons – but the cost is well worth the knowledge that the family pet is secure and cared for.

The Dog & the Law

In Britain, several Acts of Parliament govern the keeping of a dog. There is a legal obligation on the owner to obtain a licence for any dog over six months old and to ensure that it carries an identification disc. The Animals Act of 1971 makes the owner responsible for any damage caused by a dog, or any other animal, to a person or property. This includes damage to livestock and farm animals, and under certain circumstances a farmer is legally entitled to shoot a dog seen to be worrying sheep. Under the same law, the owner may be held responsible for any injury caused to a road user by a straying dog.

A vicious dog attacking and biting people or other dogs may be brought under a court order, and if the owner fails to control the dog in future, the court has the powers to enforce the destruction of the dog. Stray dogs should be taken to the local police station, which is obliged to house and feed the animal for seven days; it will then be handed over to a home for strays, or destroyed. If the owner is traced, the police are entitled to recover all costs incurred.

Various local bye-laws exist which require dogs to be kept on the lead in public parks and on highways and which impose fines for fouling pavements and other public amenities.

Boarding kennels and pet shops are only allowed to operate under local licences. The importation of dogs is subject to strict government rules, and infringements carry heavy fines. The Guard Dog Act of 1975 is intended to control the use of guard dogs and requires that they must at all times be under proper control except when actually secured. A notice to the effect that a guard dog is on duty must be clearly displayed on the outside of the premises; the Act does not apply to pet dogs kept in the owner's house.

Most insurance policies covering household contents include coverage of damage or nuisance caused by a dog, but it is advisable to check with the insurers that this is so. In addition, it is possible and highly prudent to take out insurance against veterinary fees. It is easy to budget for routine vaccinations and deliberate operations such as neutering, but unexpected accidents, protracted illnesses and complicated surgery can account for heavy expenditure. Several insurance firms offer adequate and reasonable pet policies.

A Second Dog

Many owners never realize just how much fun and companionship the only dog, like the only child, is missing. Whenever possible there should be two dogs in any household, for the simple reason of giving more pleasure to the two-footed and four-footed members of the family.

Even in a single-dog household there may come a time when the idea of a second dog merits consideration. As a dog matures and passes into middle age it becomes increasingly difficult to keep it active and interested; the introduction of a new puppy, preferably of the same breed, may give it a new lease of life. The actual timing must always vary with individual circumstances, and only the owner can determine whether the resident dog will react favourably to a newcomer. It is obviously important that no preferential treatment is given to either dog, and though the older one may initially suffer pangs of jealousy he will usually end up by making friends with the newcomer.

The two dogs should not be left alone for any length of time until they have established a good relationship, and a boisterous young puppy should not be allowed to exhaust the older dog. The addition of a second dog to the household may lessen the pain of the inevitable parting when the life of the older dog comes to its natural conclusion.

Bathing

Bath time can leave the home looking like a battlefield, and the larger the dog, the more serious the ravages. Some canine authorities maintain that regular grooming with comb and brush is enough to keep a dog clean, but dogs do get muddy and smelly and attract parasites which need treatment with a medicated shampoo specially formulated for dogs. Small dogs can fairly easily be bathed in a bowl or

the kitchen sink; larger dogs must be persuaded into the bath. Start the procedure by assembling all necessary equipment: a non-slip mat in the bath, shower spray, shampoo, jug and plenty of rough towels. As it is inevitable that the owner gets almost as wet as the dog, wear a waterproof overall or do a near-strip. Run a couple of inches of tepid-warm water into the bath, and lift in the struggling animal (1)

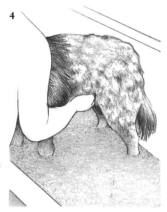

Plug the ears with cottonwool and wet the coat thoroughly, starting from the back and working towards the head (2). Make sure that the coat on the underside and on the chest is soaked through and take care to keep water – and shampoo – out of the eyes. Keep up a gentle patter of words, calling him often by name and soothing his anxiety

Apply the shampoo (3), over the rump parts first, working the suds thoroughly into the coat and massaging it down to the skin; work upwards towards the head, adding more shampoo as necessary to form a good lather; avoid shampoo in the ears. When back and sides have been done, wash the undersides equally thoroughly (4), followed by the legs and finally the tail

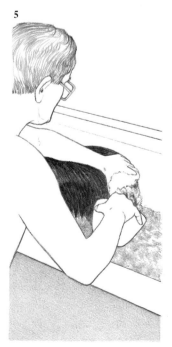

Rinse off the suds with plenty of lukewarm water from a jug or a spray, alternately with squeezing the shampoo out of the coat until it feels perfectly clean. The whole process may have to be repeated if the dog is very muddy

Squeeze as much water as possible from the coat and empty the bath before lifting the dog out and wrapping him in a towel. Watch out for the showers of water he will deposit all over as he shakes himself, and be ready with a second and third towel. Dry him thoroughly, especially in the armpits and the groin; some dogs do not mind a hairdryer, others object violently. Make sure he is dry before letting him outside

Routine Grooming

Grooming is an essential part of caring for the family dog and should be undertaken on a daily or weekly basis, depending on the breed, its daily exercise, and on the weather. Brushing and combing keep the coat clean and fresh-smelling, remove dead hairs which may lead to skin diseases, and reveal and remove any unwelcome presence of parasites. Apart from practical considerations, regular grooming also cements the emotional bond between dog and owner, and if it becomes routine from early puppyhood it evolves into mutual pleasure rather than a battle of wills.

Smooth and short-haired dogs are obviously easier and quicker to groom than long-haired types. Use a hard bristle or wire brush, or a hound glove, over all parts of the body, on top and underneath, brushing from the rear to the head,

Brushing and combing, as part of regular grooming and after a bath, should be skindeep. Miniature and smaller breeds are easiest groomed on a table top covered with an old blanket, towel or newspapers, while large and giant dogs are better dealt with at ground level. Any position that is comfortable is suitable; sitting, the dog can be gripped between the legs, and this bodily contact tends to calm a nervous dog.

Begin with the stomach, working with firm, short strokes, brushing the hairs upwards right from the roots, with flicking movements of the wrist (1). Use the brush also to loosen tangled and dead hair. Move on to grooming the forelegs (2) and follow the brush with a comb in order to remove dead hairs and to give a smooth finish to the coat (3)

Groom the inner sides of the hindquarters in the same way as the forelegs, then roll the dog over on to his stomach. Start on the back, working from the tail end towards the head, brushing and flicking the hairs up and out (4) and following with the comb. Hold the coat taut by gripping in the left hand the skin just behind the area being groomed (5). As the sides and back are being brushed and finished with the comb, brush a side tack down along the outside of fore and hindlegs (6), still gripping the skin above

Care of the Coat

Next groom the 'trousers' on fore and hindlegs, holding the tail to one side (7), brushing down and out right down to the feet and lifting the leg up as necessary (8). Be firm but gentle, avoiding twisting the limbs. Lift each foot in turn and brush carefully around the pads (9) before finishing each leg and foot with the comb. Brush the tail thoroughly, working from root to tip and comb out all dead hairs

Brush carefully round the neck and ears, holding each ear firmly while grooming the area beneath it (10), but keep brush and comb away from the face itself. Tease out any tangles on the ears with the fingers and examine the edges for possible parasites (11) – the long, drooping ears on Spaniels and similar types should be brushed carefully on both sides and finished off with a fine comb. Finally brush and comb the sides of the head, gripping the ruff firmly (12)

Lastly groom the mane beneath the head, taking each brush stroke the full length and holding the head up by the chin (13). Finish off with the comb (14) and a quick top-brushing with a palm pad or hound glove to lay the coat in its natural wave. Such thorough grooming will maintain a harsh-coated breed like the Keeshond (15) in good condition for a couple of weeks; silky-haired types like the Afghan, Setters and many Toy breeds need weekly attention, pinning up long-layered coats in order to reach the undercoat

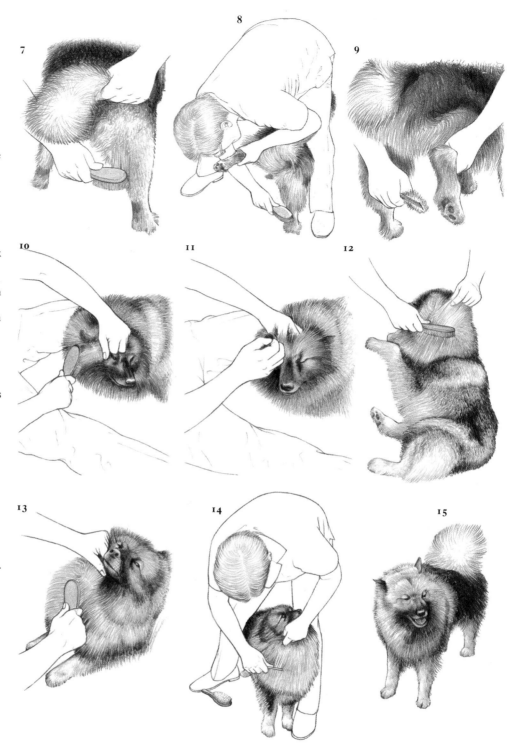

first against and secondly with the lie of the hairs. Long-coated dogs need more thorough grooming, sometimes every day, to tease out tangles and to prevent matting; the thick coat of some breeds, especially the Old English Sheepdog, otherwise becomes so entangled that knots of hair must be clipped off.

Miniature and toy breeds can be lifted on to a table top of comfortable height, while larger dogs are easier to groom at floor level. In any case, provide a non-slip surface of newspapers, an old blanket or rubber mat to catch dirt and other debris. At the same time, check the pads for grass seeds and small stones and grit, inspect the nails, with particular attention to the dew claws, and the anal area; wipe ears and eyes clean of dirt and discharge.

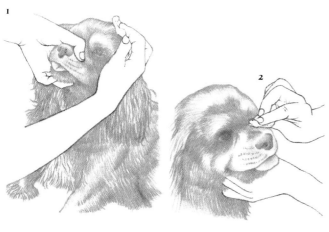

Grooming of the head must be gentle but thorough and done every few days. Many dogs secrete mucous which becomes encrusted in the facial hairs. Examine the eyes daily, holding the muzzle closed with a grip round the lower jaw (1), and wipe round each eye with moist cottonwool (2), removing any stains, loose hairs and eyelashes; use a fresh swab for each eye. Never poke into the eye itself; obvious discomfort and discharge need veterinary attention

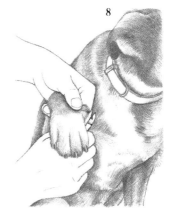

Teeth care is often neglected, leading to tartar encrustation which in severe cases needs descaling or surgical removal. Open the mouth of an obstinate dog by holding the lower jaw firmly with one hand, at the same time blocking the nostrils (3). Inspect the teeth, with special attention to the molars (4), then brush the teeth well with toothpaste (5); special dog pastes and cleaning aids are available, but ordinary dentifrice will do

Care of the feet is part of the grooming routine. Trim excessive hair growth between the toes with round-tipped scissors (6) and attend to overgrown nails. Sharp guillotine clippers are the best tool (7), but care must be taken to avoid the quick or bleeding results; the quick is difficult to see on dark-pigmented nails, and it is safest just to trim off oversharp points. Some breeds retain dew claws on the inside of the leg (8); they tend to grow round and into the flesh unless regularly trimmed

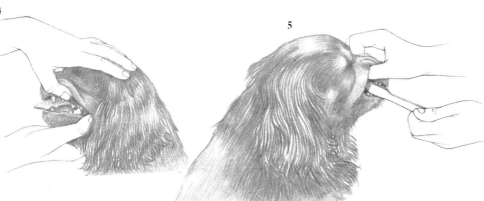

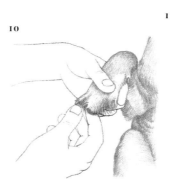

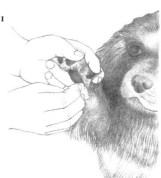

Grass seeds, and especially barley awns, attach themselves between toes and pads; use tweezers to pull them out (9) before they set up an infection. Examine the space between the toes for grit and small stones, holding the foot firmly in one hand (10). Inspect the undersides of the pads in the same way and remove embedded mud with moist cottonbuds (11)

UNDERSTANDING YOUR DOG

BEHAVIOUR PATTERNS

It is the nature of dogs' behaviour and their adaptability to man's life style which have made them so popular, not only as pets but also as working animals in many varied and important fields. The ability of two such different species, man and dog, to live and work together in harmony is less surprising than it might at first appear. Basically, the behaviour of both species has many parallels which have been exploited in vastly different cultures through thousands of years. In pre-historic times, man and wolf were often competitors in so far as both lived in groups, existed by hunting though with a supplementary diet of vegetable matter, and both had near worldwide distributions. Even if the analogy stops short here, certain common features clearly underlie the remarkable bond which today exists between man and dog.

Perhaps the most important feature of the dog's behaviour is its highly social nature. Naturally a pack animal, a dog notices and responds to the signals of other individuals. The complex communication system includes scent, sound, touch, and visual displays. Under the right circumstances, and depending on upbringing coupled with innate behaviour, dogs will socialize with their own species, with humans, and with cats and other small animals. The behavioural development of the dog generally follows a predictable pattern from which comparisons with the behaviour of the human species can be drawn.

Newborn puppies spend their waking hours seeking food and warmth from the mother. The head of the blind and deaf pup moves rhythmically from side to side in search of a teat; the sucking instinct is so strong that in the first few days a pup may try to suck a sibling's ear or tail. Unable to stand, the pup hauls itself forwards and regains its balance with the righting reflex

Birth to Two Weeks

A newborn puppy displays only a very few basic behaviour reflexes which are well suited to the immediate needs for food and warmth, both of which are provided by the mother. It is born blind and deaf, and it probably also lacks the ability to smell. It does have some sense of taste, based on the tongue receptors, and is also sensitive to cold, touch, and pain. Ninety per cent of its time is spent sleeping, and most of the remainder on sucking its mother or trying to gain access to a nipple.

At this age the puppy is unable to stand; the two hindlegs are very weak, but the puppy can move along by hauling itself forward with its forelegs, almost as if it were swimming. On wakening, a puppy will at once try to locate its mother; it crawls, not in a straight line but on a zigzag track, and if it fails to contact the mother after a short distance, it will turn and set off in a new direction. However, as soon as the puppy encounters something soft and warm, it will burrow and snuggle up for warmth if it is tired.

Maternal instincts cause the dam to retrieve a puppy which has strayed away from her warmth (1). She must also stimulate urination and defecation by gently licking the pup's inguinal region (2). Hand-reared puppies must be wiped with a warm and damp cloth to mimic the mother's normal behaviour

The tiny puppy shows certain protective responses to painful stimuli and to exposure to cold. It will immediately withdraw a limb if it encounters pain from any source and will 'mew' in distress if left out in the cold. This urgently requires a response since young puppies, unlike adults, are unable to maintain their body temperature for any length of time, and this can quickly fall below the critical level without warmth from their mother or some other source. In the cold, a pup starts to cry out, but strangely the mother does not always respond to the sound alone, although she will retrieve a pup she sees crawling away from her. On occasions a puppy may even be squashed by the mother's body despite giving cries of distress.

The behavioural repertoire of young puppies is extremely limited; they depend on their mother for food, warmth, and even to trigger elimination of the body wastes. After the age of two weeks, simple reflex responses gradually diminish, and new more complex behaviours begin to appear.

Puppies develop rapidly. At two weeks, the eyes have opened (1), and in another two weeks, vision and focus are clear and distinct (2). The puppies start to walk rather than crawl, and they move backwards as well as forwards (3). At the beginning of the fourth week, they are active for longer periods and begin to play with each other (4) and with their mother

Two to Three Weeks

The growth of the puppies is very rapid, and by the second week several of the sensory abilities become active. The eyes open between ten and fifteen days, and by the age of four weeks vision is almost as good as in adult dogs. Hearing, too, begins to become effective at about two or three weeks, and the development of the sense of smell follows a similar time course.

Behaviour also starts to change at this time. Although the mother may still lick her pups to stimulate elimination, they can now do this of their own accord, and by the fourth week the automatic reflex has completely disappeared. As the brain and nervous system develop, the puppies' general co-ordination improves rapidly; they respond to noises and can drink liquids from a bowl in addition to suckling the mother; they also start to try walking rather than crawling. At this stage they also begin to demonstrate signs of learning ability and will, for example, make associations between a punishment and the behaviour which preceded it and they may avoid a repeat painful experience. By the end of the third week, the pups are just beginning to play with each other, and this heralds the start of the next and the most significant phase of their behaviour development.

Three to Thirteen Weeks

This period is often known as the socialization phase because it is the time when many adult behaviour patterns can be irreversibly established. At the start of the fourth week, a puppy will weigh about seven times its weight at birth, and the sensory and nervous systems have matured rapidly. The puppies begin to play and interact with each other and with their mother; they start to explore their surroundings and gradually move further away from the vicinity of the mother. Motor skills also improve rapidly as the puppies start to run, manipulate objects, follow things with their eyes, and scent trails by nose.

The possibilities for social behaviour begin with the development of facial expressions and body language, including tail wagging. As they grow older, puppies play more and more with each other and spend less time with their mother. They also depend less on her for milk, and her lactation generally ceases by the tenth week in natural circumstances, although before then many pups will have been adopted. Most breeders recommend that the best period to adopt a pet dog is at the age of seven to eight weeks. This is a crucial time for socializing the puppies towards humans and for developing social skills and bonds, after they have acquired sufficient experience of the canine species.

If a puppy has no human contact in its first three months, it subsequently becomes wild, intractable, and almost impossible to train and socialize towards people. In contrast, a puppy taken from its litter mates at a very early age – five weeks for example – and given little contact with other dogs will often as an adult fail to react normally to other canines. It may display lack of interest, fear or aggression towards other dogs and is often unable to mate successfully.

At three to four weeks, puppies are extremely inquisitive and will attempt to solicit responses from animals around them. As they grow older, this social investigative tendency declines and is generally replaced by uncertainty and finally wariness, sometimes combined with fear or aggression. Six to eight weeks is the best age for introducing a puppy to people, other dogs and other pet animals, although later introductions should present few problems for dogs that have had a range of social experiences.

Socialization phase starts around the third or fourth week. The puppies begin to explore; they grasp and chew on the odd stick (1) and follow by scent and sight foreign objects like a rabbit (2, 3, 4). Individual characteristics emerge, displayed in tail wagging and facial expressions (5)

Juvenile puppies quickly acquire adult behaviour. They explore further afield (1) and engage in sexual play (2) although yet unable to mate. The female urinates in a squatting position (3) though on occasion she may adopt the flex-raise posture. As she reaches puberty, she signals her interest in the opposite sex by presenting her genital area, tail held to one side (4). The male dog passes from puberty to adulthood when he begins to urinate with one hindleg raised (5)

Thirteen Weeks to Adulthood

By the age of thirteen weeks, all the adult behaviours are present. The puppy's movements, which are already well co-ordinated, continue to improve, and the areas for exploration grow larger as the puppy investigates further from home base. Already capable of associating specific occasions with specific behaviours, the growing puppy can be trained in a variety of skills. Training ability does not improve during this juvenile phase; indeed, as the puppy grows older, its ability to learn may sometimes decline.

The end of the juvenile phase is marked by the onset of puberty. Even young puppies display adult sexual behaviour, especially during play, but like play fighting it is not serious as they are still infertile and incapable of reproduction. Male dogs reach sexual maturity at about seven or eight months, but it is a slow maturation, not a sudden onset. When a male dog begins to urinate with one hindleg raised, adulthood may be said to have arrived, although the production of fertile sperm forms the true definition.

For the female dog, adulthood is sudden in behaviour terms and is signalled by her first oestrous cycle. One day she will be indifferent to the advances of a male dog, and the next be prepared to accept him, displaying typical female receptive behaviour. The time of the first heat or oestrus varies, but usually occurs between six and nine months of age. Bitches then come into heat twice yearly, in contrast to the annual cycle of the wolf. This heightened fecundity is a result of man's domestication of the dog.

Communication by Smell

Humans cannot truly understand the dog since canine perception of surroundings and methods of communication differ so greatly. Vision is poorer, and hearing is better, but the sense of smell more than anything else separates dogs from humans. Estimates put dogs' abilities at 100 to 100 million times better than the human sense of smell. They have about fourteen times the area of cells in the nose, and the part of the brain responsive to smell is proportionally far larger than in humans.

In behaviour terms, the importance of smell is obvious to any observer. When two dogs meet, they will at once sniff each other's muzzles, inguinal and anal areas. Odour communication manifests itself in other ways: male dogs, for example, urinate far more frequently than is necessary to satisfy a physiological need. It is widely assumed that a dog marks out a territory with urine deposits, but there is little evidence of domestic dogs establishing a territory outside the home. When a dog leaves its scent mark, including the so-called dry marks, it communicates with other dogs, but the nature of the message is a mystery. The frequency of scent marking in many species is greater among socially dominant individuals, and this is probably also true of the domestic dog.

Female dogs also mark with their urine; this behaviour is often cyclical and hormone-based, and may only occur at one phase of the oestrous cycle. Spayed bitches in particular often assume the 'flex-raise' posture, with one hindleg raised and the other flexed, while a stream of urine is directed against some object on the ground. Male and female urine differ, and some chemical constituent in female urine clearly changes with the oestrous cycle, hence the attractiveness of her urine to male dogs during her receptive phase.

It is more than probable that dogs can discern other individuals from urine markings – the equivalent of fingerprints – left by previous dogs; their interest is evident in persistent sniffing on their walks. The difference in composition between male and female urine is tiny in relation to the main constituents of urea and water. The reason why bitches are more likely than males to cause scorch marks on grass is that the volume of liquid is much higher per urination and usually directed at a flat surface, while males urinate in small, if frequent amounts and commonly against vertical objects.

Smell is also communicated through feces, although the meaning of this signal is unknown. Both feral dogs and wolves tend to deposit their scats in

Dog greets dog with inquisitive sniffing of the muzzles (1). They proceed, in a general friendly manner, to inspect their respective inguinal areas (2) and finally the anal regions (3). Scent is the dog's most powerful means of communication: he trails by nose, sniffing (4) for marks left by previous passers-by. The male marks a route or territory with urine (5)

relatively prominent positions, along tracks and at the boundaries of their territories. In pet dogs, toilet training supersedes such instincts, and whatever communication is conveyed by fecal deposits, the dog's reaction seems less obvious than that to urine. In addition to fecal matter, dogs produce a smelly secretion in their anal sacs; it ranges in consistency from an almost clear liquid to a thick dark paste, which may be deposited along with the feces, or separately when the sac contents may be expelled for up to half a metre. Dogs are sometimes seen rubbing their backsides along the ground in a sitting position, and this is thought by some authorities to coincide with anal sac marking. The behavioural interpretation of this secretion remains unexplained, but suggestions have included some sort of alarm function, and a means of communicating individual differences. At the same time, it is common for dogs with impacted anal sacs to rub their backsides on the ground.

Some dogs apparently enjoy a roll in strong-smelling substances, such as dog feces, cow pats, general garbage, and tobacco. Such behaviour could be an attempt to gain extra status with other dogs through giving off a strong odour. Alternatively it might be a device to confuse potential prey since the dog's own odour could be disguised by the overlay of a different, strong scent.

Another common behaviour, which is related to scent marking, is the 'scraping' often observed in dogs which have just defecated or urinated, although they scrape at other times, too. It occurs in both sexes though more commonly in males. The only sweat glands in a dog's skin lie between the toes, and scraping could be a means of leaving the sweat scent on the ground, though this has never been proved. Scraping may also be a visual mark, as it leaves a distinctive pattern in both grass and soil.

Odour marking has various interpretations and may be used to confuse individual scent. Much to the owner's displeasure, a dog may cover himself with the odours of a dead bird (1), rotting fish, or animal excretions. Less offensive are the habitual scraping movements (2) in which many dogs engage after elimination. The sitting position in which a dog rubs its rump along the ground may coincide with anal sac marking, but may also indicate inflammation of the sacs or the presence of worms (3)

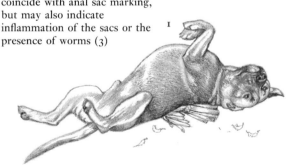

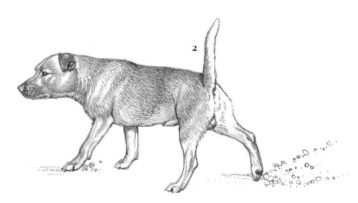

Communication by Sound

The hearing of dogs is strongly developed, and they can detect sounds of high frequencies, up to about 35 kilohertz compared with the maximum of 20 in humans. This is why some dog whistles are inaudible to the human ear. Dogs use sounds to communicate with each other, through barks, howls, growls, and whimpering or whining.

Barking is the sound most commonly associated with dogs, but strangely this is only rarely heard in the wolf. Almost certainly man selected for barking during the period of domestication so that the sound would warn him of intruders and other potential threats. It is not certain what a dog communicates to other dogs through barking, but it probably indicates a state of alertness or excitement which will often spread to other dogs in the neighbourhood, which will also start to bark.

Howling is the sound associated with wolves and is less seldom heard from dogs. It is very much a communal sound, quickly being taken up by other dogs within earshot and could help social cohesion in a group or pack. Howling can occur in several situations, for example the baying of dogs during and after a chase, and the calls of a lone individual making contact with others which take up the howl.

There is little doubt about the meaning of a growling dog: it threatens to fight or attack, and should be avoided. This is in direct contrast to the whining or whimpering sound. In young puppies it is essentially a distress call, but in adult dogs its function is more varied. Some dogs have learnt that by whining, their owners will give them sympathy, which in turn reinforces such behaviour. Dogs seldom whine in the presence of other dogs, but may do so as part of appeasement or submission to a threatening dog.

Sound language, though chiefly confined to four major groups, is distinctive, to human and canine perception. Barking (1) warns of intruders or threats to the dog's home territory, while howling (2) is an intergroup sound in the pack. Growling (3) is unquestionably a sign of aggression and impending attack, in direct contrast to the whimpering or whining dog (4), which begs for protection or attention

Body Language

Visual body language plays a vital role in communication between dogs, and between dogs and humans. Their colour discrimination is at best poor, and although they lack the ability to see detail, they are sensitive to movement; their vision is quite sufficient to register the meaning of social gestures and body postures of other dogs. While sounds are important over larger distances, as is communication by scent which can maintain its message for days and even weeks, body language is the most varied means of communication when dogs are at close quarters. Sometimes body language may combine with other communication means: the raised-leg urination of male dogs is probably a visual clue to onlookers, in addition to the long-term function of the scent mark. Body language is complex and still not fully understood by animal behaviourists. Dogs use their faces, ears, mouths, tails, and whole body for gestures and signals, both independently and in combination.

Eye contact is important. Dominant individuals will stare at other dogs, while submissive ones avert their gaze. It is inadvisable to stare fixedly at a dominant or aggressive dog, although it may be a useful means of control with other dogs which will usually look away and become submissive. The ears convey much about a dog's feelings in such breeds as Corgis, German Shepherds, several Terriers, and others whose ear shape allows movement. Erect ears indicate a confident and alert dog, which could be either friendly or aggressive. Ears held back flat against the head may mean fear or submission.

The mouth and lips also indicate mood; bared teeth may mean aggression or fear, while submissive dogs display the so-called 'submissive grin'. Tail carriage is yet another mood indicator: a tail held between the legs shows submission, held high it indicates confidence, and a wagging tail excitement.

Body gestures and postures contribute to canine communication. It has evolved as mutual understanding between dogs, and human interpretation

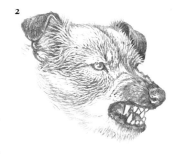

Facial expressions are clearly defined. The timid dog, ears held flat and mouth closed, displays a submissive grin (1). Erect ears and bared teeth (2) indicate aggression or fear

Body postures combine with other gestures to indicate mood. The submissive dog (1) typically adopts an almost crouching position, with ears held back and down, eyes averted, and tail between legs. Even the fur lies flat, and in extreme submission he will roll on his back and display the belly to his protagonist (3). The dominant dog takes up an aggressive stance (2), making himself look as bulky as possible, and with head and tail held high. Raised hackles along the back and shoulders, and bared teeth (4), are an offensive threat

must always contain some element of judgment and guesswork. Dogs are relatively limited in their degree of body expressions. Firstly, they have less facial musculature than humans; secondly, they have forelegs rather than arms and therefore lack that degree of fine movement central for gestures which the latter possess. Thirdly, dogs are restricted to a stance on all four legs for most of the time, and this also limits the potentials for body communication.

Posture differences are therefore subtle and may at times be difficult to comprehend for human observers. Essentially, dog postures vary along just four continua. In the first place, the body's centre of gravity can be directed well forward or well back. Secondly, dogs can stand up, crouch, lie down, or roll over; and thirdly, they can raise or lower the hairs on part of the body, especially on the back of the neck and shoulders, to make themselves look larger or smaller. In the fourth place, a dog can vary the posture of display directed towards another dog, facing him frontally, away from or sideways. These body postures are always combined with facial expressions, tail carriage, and possibly odours; one gesture may quickly merge into another.

Many basic body postures are more or less ritualized and their functions understood, by dogs and by humans. A dog which is displaying aggression or is frightened will try to look larger by raising the hair or hackles on its neck and shoulders. If it is about to attack, it will take up a forward stance, often with ears raised, although in other respects defensive, fear, and attack postures are very similar. A fearful dog will tend towards retreat and adopt a backward stance, tail down, lips bared, and ears held back. However, it may rapidly change to attack, especially if cornered. There is thus a continuum of postures and behaviours, often with only slight gradations between them, and a dog may quickly move from giving one signal to giving another.

Some body language signals involve specific postures. Dogs at play, for example, use a number of ritual behaviours, including mock fighting, chasing, and mock prey catching; by their stance they indicate that they are about to play and are not going to engage in genuine combat. The 'play bow' is the most ritualized of these stances, and a study of several breeds has shown that the angle of the body, with the front dropped to the ground and hindquarters raised, was almost identical every time this behaviour was displayed; the exact angle is even similar between breeds. Dogs engage in play as frequently as humans; one possible explanation for this could be practice for real-life situations and the exercise of muscles. The continuation of play into adulthood may in part result from domestication.

Other ritual behaviours are seen during courtship. The male will move around in front of the female, trying to gain her attention through jumps and other displays. If she shows interest, they will spar with their forelegs, and the female will next adopt the standing receptive posture (see page 66). The male's behaviour is triggered by odours from her urine and vaginal area. The raised-leg urination by male dogs is another posture associated with odour release. It is done more often when another dog is in sight and suggests that the signal is visual and more than just the deposit of a scent mark.

Invitation to play follows a strict ritual. It starts with the 'play bow', where the instigator drops on his forelimbs and engages in eye contact (1). This is followed by tail wagging, exaggerated bouncing and opened mouth (2) until the playmate takes up the chase (3); the decurved tail and laughing face of the pursued are typical of playful flight. The chase ends with a mock fight (4), the 'prey' held on the ground, unharmed, but attempting to push off his captor by straightening his legs

Social Behaviour

Mutual communication underlies the social behaviour of the dog as no species can live in a group unless the individuals are able to react to each other's status, feelings, and moods. Social behaviour is more readily apparent for the wolf, the dog's ancestor, with clear-cut relationships, defined territory, a relatively stable pack, and dominance rankings including a leading or 'alpha' male and female, and subordinates. Communication between individuals enables the pack to function as a cohesive whole.

This basic pattern becomes complicated for the domesticated dog which must relate to its own species, its human owner, and perhaps to other species, such as cats and rabbits. Domestication appears to have changed the social structure to some extent. Feral dogs, which return to breed outside man's influence, show something of the social cohesion of the wolf, although they tend to live in small groups or as solitary individuals. The territory over which they range is often tiny in comparison with that of the wolf pack, although larger than for a typical pet dog.

Social relationships are complex for the pet dog. It forms a close bond with its owner and the two develop a mutual communication system, but a pet dog must also respond to its owner's behaviour, as well as maintaining communication dog to dog. This can greatly influence some of a dog's inherent behaviours. A male dog may be permitted to scent-mark the garden as part of its territory, as well as the route of a walk, but at the same time it must learn not to mark within the house. On a walk, the problem of social relationships again arises since the dog shares that route with several other dogs, though not usually at the same time of day.

Social ranking may cause difficulties within the home. The owner must be dominant over the dog, otherwise various behaviour problems ensue. Dominance is not always easy to establish because the dog must be trained to respond to human rather than canine social cues. In a wolf or feral dog pack, the dominant or alpha individual will, where necessary, use physical means to maintain its position should any lower ranking individual challenge it. As humans are larger than dogs and control most aspects of their lives, such as feeding and exercising, dominance by the owner can usually be established and maintained. Most problems arise when a dog fails to realize that the owner is displeased; this chiefly occurs when an owner is incapable of asserting effective dominance, or when discipline is wrongly timed in relation to the relevant behaviour.

Social ranking is essential for the cohesion of pack life, in the wild and in the household with two or more dogs. The chosen leader, the so-called alpha individual, quickly rebuffs any challenge by a subordinate to his established authority, grasping him by the scruff of the neck and forcing him to the ground until the rebel rolls over on his back in total submission. In general, dominance is maintained by body signals, eye stare and scent marking

Training and Intelligence

Details of basic and advanced training are described on pages 51 and 76–83, but the fundamental principles are highly relevant to canine behaviour. The basis of training is to reward or punish a dog in order to increase or decrease the incidence of a particular behaviour. Stimuli may be coupled with reward so that the dog will later respond to the stimulus alone. In this way many behaviours can be modified through training.

Many owners argue about the intelligence of their dogs, or that of dogs versus cats. Human intelligence and its meaning is still the subject of argument amongst psychologists, and extending the concept to dogs is fraught with further uncertainties. If intelligence is defined as the ability to perform IQ tests, clearly dogs cannot be compared with humans. Another definition for intelligence as 'the mental pattern or framework which a person or animal uses to tackle a problem, based on its physical abilities and upbringing' lacks substance because suitable tests and physical capabilities are not comparable.

It is more constructive to consider the achievement by dogs of certain feats, such as bringing home the morning newspaper, opening a door, or performing agility tasks. Achievements of this kind may appear to indicate a high degree of intelligence, but they should be perceived against the behaviour qualities of the breed concerned and dog behaviour in general. For some dogs, retrieval is entirely natural, and an extension of this by training or reward can easily explain the collection of a newspaper. A dog may learn to turn a door handle purely by chance and will subsequently do it repeatedly. Careful and intensive training will enable many dogs to perform highly skilled tasks, such as agility trials and guiding the blind and the deaf.

There is no proof of thought processes occurring in canines. Philosophers, starting with Aristotle, conclude that the uniqueness of genuine language is what separates humans from other animals. While dogs communicate with one another, the complexity of the system does not constitute a spoken language. Dogs are nevertheless sentient beings and as such deserve respect for the mental qualities and feelings they display.

Many owners attribute human emotions to their dogs, and most view them as family members, not as animals (see The Faithful Friend, page 84). However, such perception is probably untenable and alternative explanations are usually possible. Dogs are capable of displaying intelligence to the satisfaction of their owners; their heightened sensory abilities may give rise to an apparent sixth sense which commands respect for their own type of mental skill.

Canine Aggression

This behaviour is an important component of a dog's overall behaviour and can cause problems to owner and non-owner alike. In itself aggression is not a problem but can be seen as such when it happens in the wrong place and at the wrong time. It is also much misunderstood, chiefly because it is not a single behaviour but can be separated into many types, with different causes and manifestations.

Some types of aggression can be regarded as natural. Canine maternal aggression is normal because a mother is expected to protect her offspring; its appearance is thought to depend on the level of hormones circulating in the blood which alter rapidly at parturition. Territorial aggression is also seen as desirable, and many owners complain if a guard dog turns out to be indifferent or welcoming to intruders. However, most dogs show some type of territorial aggression in their home, garden, or car, even if this takes the form of barking

Canine Aggression

Canine aggression is often an expression of inherent behaviour. Maternal instincts will cause a threatened bitch to rise above her litter in an attack attitude (1), and most dogs will display territorial aggression, usually by barking, at approaches to their home boundaries (2). Competitive aggression may occur where two dogs share the same food bowl (3), and manifests itself where dominance is at stake (4). Controlled aggression forms an essential part of the training programme for security dogs (5), while spontaneous aggression is a reflex response to accidental or deliberately inflicted pain (6)

rather than physical attacks. Problems may arise when a child unknowingly approaches a dog on its own and frightens it; the natural response to fear is attack if the dog is unable to retreat. A similar reflex aggression may occur in response to pain, for example when a dog is accidentally stepped on or injured in a road accident.

Several types of aggression are normally seen only between two or more dogs. One is competitive fighting, over a food bowl or toy, a second relates to dominance hierarchy. Under normal circumstances the dominant and subordinate dogs manage comfortably, knowing their own positions in the household. However, if the dominant dog ages or becomes ill, the subordinate may attempt to take over, and fighting may result. The owner can inadvertently antagonize further the dominant or prospective dominant dog by the natural human support of the underdog. Another type of aggression between dogs, known as 'intermale aggression', is typified by male dogs which attack other males, but not females. This behaviour appears to depend on the presence in the blood of male sex hormone – testosterone; studies have shown that castration or hormone treatment will usually cure it.

Prey catching and chasing are instinctive behaviours in many breeds and cannot be termed aggression, although it can become so with training. Sporting and working dogs are widely trained by the police, army and security forces; they are generally taught to grip the arm of the pursued until human assistance arrives, and to attack only on the command of the handler. Abnormal aggression is usually due to hereditary or medical reasons; a tiny minority of dogs show spontaneous aggression for no obvious reason; it may be caused by a brain tumour and occasionally by hereditary predisposition in certain individuals in a few breeds.

Behaviour Problems

Increased knowledge about dog behaviour has led to the emergence in America, Britain, and other European countries of animal psychologists who treat dogs for behaviour problems. The most common type is aggression, and the complex nature of this necessitates that diagnosis and treatment must be tailored to each individual case. There is an important distinction between the genuine canine behaviour problem and an owner's perception of the expected nature of a dog's behaviour. Some owners may expect too much from their dogs, as another species living within the family cannot be expected to behave perfectly in human terms. A bored dog will almost certainly chew something, and a dog which is thought to bark too much is essentially performing the guard function for which it has been selected.

For other owners there are genuine behaviour problems which almost anyone would accept as such. These include spontaneous aggression towards family members, destruction while the owner is absent, and persistent soiling in the house. Fortunately, the reported successes of dog psychologists are high and depend on a combination of special training programmes for the dog, advice to the owner, and sometimes accompanying drug treatment. The question of dominance in the household can be a potential problem; the owner must be dominant over the dog for an optimal relationship. Where the opposite is the case, a male dog may demonstrate its dominance by marking objects in the house, or by threatening some family members.

After the general category of aggression, the second most common behaviour problem is separation or isolation anxiety as displayed by the dog which whines or is destructive in the home when the owner is away. The causes of such behaviour are often complex, but one common factor seems to be a very close attachment between dog and owner. The dog will show great excitement on the return of the owner, jumping up and rushing wildly around in circles. It will often have attempted various ruses to persuade the owner not to leave in the first place, by lying in front of the exit door, whining when it thinks its master is about to leave, or rushing out of the door when he does leave and refusing to go back indoors, or trying to jump into the car. With a dog that is destructive while left alone, the owner may be tempted to punish the dog on his return. In practice this is counter-productive as the dog's happiness at being reunited with its owner is greater than any chastisement received. The correct therapy for such cases can be complicated and usually involves attempts to reduce attachment, and new signals to the dog on departure, clearly differentiating them from those which triggered off destruction.

The behaviour of the pet dog cannot be considered in isolation, without taking into account the behaviour of the owner, which is what in many cases causes the so-called canine behaviour problems. A dog's natural behaviour should always be respected. Man has in many ways moulded canine behaviour to suit some of his needs and must accept responsibility for the welfare of dogs and their requirements. Some behaviour problems appear more frequently in certain breeds, but the behavioural generalities already discussed and illustrated are applicable across all breeds.

All behaviour is the combined product of heredity and the effects of an animal's environment, and while the two can never be completely separated, man controls both factors to some extent. All dogs behave in the same general manner, and their natural behaviour is well suited to the environment of man who should use his knowledge to bring up his dog properly and appreciate and understand the dog as a true companion.

OBEDIENCE TRIALS

Training of a dog extends beyond the basic principles (see page 51); intense programmes eventually produce guide dogs for the blind and the deaf, police and guard dogs, hunting and shepherding dogs. In all cases success depends on instant obedience to the handler, and obedience competitions are staged throughout the world. German Shepherd Dogs and Border Collies are the preferred breeds for obedience trials, but any family pet can be trained, at home or at local training classes, to obey commands and thus become a better integrated and more disciplined member of the family.

Ideally, advanced training should begin at an early age, on the basis that it is easier to prevent than to correct faults. The sessions should be short, no longer than 10 minutes at a time, and each step should be taught thoroughly and slowly, by lengthy repetition if necessary, before progressing to the next lesson. Most dogs are more than eager to learn and willing to please their masters who in turn must display patience and understanding, of the dogs' and their own temperaments. It is important to use clear and short commands in a level voice, to refrain from all forms for punishment, and to be lavish with praise. The only necessary equipment is a training or choke collar, a long leather lead fitted with a bolt-action clip – and patience. Training is an on-going operation, from early puppyhood and as long as the dog remains active.

At obedience trials, a dog must have earned maximum points at usually three separate novice classes before it can be entered for advanced trials.

Walking at heel is most easily mastered by practising left-hand circles. With the choke collar fitted comfortably, the slip knot to the side or on top, adopt a stationary position with the dog on the left side (1); let him wander wide and bring him back to heel with a jerk of the lead. Spoken commands are unnecessary

Complete the circle, coming to a standstill in the same position at which the exercise began, with the dog close to heel on the left side, and the lead slack. Repeat the lesson several times until heelwork is perfect, then walk straight ahead and reverse the lesson to right-hand circles

Step forward (2), with the lead on the slack. Correct any attempt by the dog to move forward with a zip on the lead and return to the stationary position before recommencing the exercise until the dog has learnt to move on a slack lead and in the correct position

Anticipate a right-hand turn by the dog by thrusting the left leg forward (3), forcing him to change direction. Begin the left-hand turn, with the dog on a tight lead, and using exaggerated foot movements (4)

Continue the left-hand turn (5), with the dog close at heel, checked by the collar. Keep the strides at a steady walking pace while guiding him round the left leg

The sit and the wait position can be taught as two separate or as one combined exercise. For the sit, have the dog on the lead, walk forward a few paces and call him by name to attract his attention (1). Drop both hands into the groin in the 'come' position and step slowly backwards, with the aim of making him turn frontal to the handler and to move forwards on recall (2). Adjust the lead to raise the head slightly, command 'sit' and at the same time press the rear of the dog into a sitting position with the free hand (3)

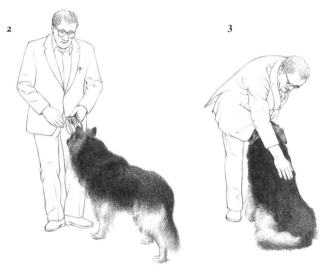

The wait position can follow when the dog has mastered the sit command. With the dog sitting in front, the lead running over his head (1), step backwards away from him, at the same time using the command 'wait'

Repeat the exercise, eventually indicating the wait command merely with a jerk of the lead (2), until the dog will remain sitting when the handler moves backwards. Reward him with praise each time he behaves correctly

Gradually extend the sit and wait exercise to a full lead's length, walking backwards in a straight line (3). If the dog gets up and starts moving forwards, return to the sit-in-front position and repeat the exercise from the beginning. When he remains sitting, begin a left-hand circle round him

Keeping the lead taut above his head, complete the circle round the dog (4), walking steadily and issuing no commands. Repeat the exercise no more than two or three times in each training session until the dog remains motionless and waiting even when the handler is out of his line of vision

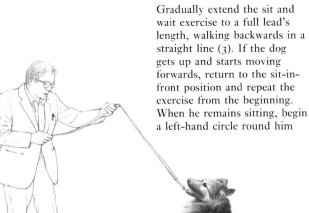

Obedience Trials

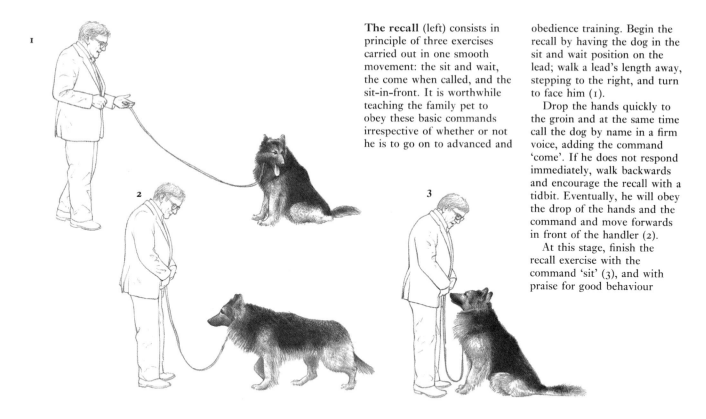

The recall (left) consists in principle of three exercises carried out in one smooth movement: the sit and wait, the come when called, and the sit-in-front. It is worthwhile teaching the family pet to obey these basic commands irrespective of whether or not he is to go on to advanced and obedience training. Begin the recall by having the dog in the sit and wait position on the lead; walk a lead's length away, stepping to the right, and turn to face him (1).

Drop the hands quickly to the groin and at the same time call the dog by name in a firm voice, adding the command 'come'. If he does not respond immediately, walk backwards and encourage the recall with a tidbit. Eventually, he will obey the drop of the hands and the command and move forwards in front of the handler (2).

At this stage, finish the recall exercise with the command 'sit' (3), and with praise for good behaviour

Sit at heel (right) is part of advanced training and useful for teaching kerb drill and for entering and leaving a car. Walk at a normal pace, with the dog close to heel by the left leg, and the lead gathered loosely in the right hand (1).

Lift the hand and the lead to tighten the collar slightly, come to a halt and issue the command 'sit', at the same time pressing down firmly on the dog's hindquarters with the free hand (2). After a few seconds, command 'heel' and progress forward (3). In time there will be no need to use the lead or the hand

After perseverance, both training lead and commands become superfluous, and the dog will automatically know the correct movement. If the handler always steps away with the right leg (4), the dog interprets this as 'stay and wait'

For forward progress, always step out with the left leg (5). To the dog, this movement is synonymous with the unspoken command 'heel'. Proper footwork by the handler enables the dog to distinguish between wait and heel without being told

Stay (right) is an important exercise in the obedience ring and equally useful for teaching the pet dog discipline. Ideally he should be used to being left tied up for short spells, without barking or making a nuisance of himself. The stay exercise can follow the sit, on the lead to begin with and off the lead later (1). The handler walks away, repeating the command 'stay'; with each session, the distance is increased until the handler eventually disappears out of sight while the dog remains still (2). It is important for the dog's confidence that the handler returns within a few minutes (3)

The finish (above and right) is the final part of the recall exercise in obedience competitions. The dog finishes in the heel position on the handler's left side, having completed a full circle right or left. Begin the exercise with the dog in the heel position by the left leg, and the lead held in the right hand (1), looping the slack behind the right leg.

Give the command 'heel', at the same time taking a step back with the right leg and transferring the lead to the left hand (2); this has the effect of tightening the lead and bringing the dog forward. Encourage him round to the left, guiding him if necessary with the right hand (3).

As the dog comes into the left turn, take a step forward (4) and tuck his head round the left leg. To complete the finish the dog will on command sit straight on the handler's left side (5).

Repeat the finish exercise time and again, with plenty of praise; eventually the dog will be proficient enough for the handler simply to hold the looped lead in front while the dog completes the tight circle with the lead playing out round the handler's legs.

For a right-hand finish, start as before with the dog in the sit position on the left, but with the slack lead in the left hand. Command 'close' and take a step backwards with the left leg, thereby bringing the dog into a left circle. As the left leg is brought forward again, the dog will come to heel on the right side

Obedience Trials

Deportment is essential for the higher classes of obedience trials where the dog is off the lead and has to execute turns at 45 or 180 degrees with nothing to guide him except the handler's body movements. The left hand and the left foot are always nearest to the dog and important for direct communication. Hold the lead lightly in the left hand (1), give a slight movement to the collar, point the left foot in the desired direction, and give the 'heel' command

Timing is all-important: lead, foot, and voice must occur simultaneously, a split second before beginning a right turn. It needs much practice, at a slow pace, and initially without the dog so that the handler can perfect his own deportment and precise footwork. Give commands and signals as the right foot hits the ground, pointing the way immediately with the left foot as this comes forward on the next step (2)

Left turns executed without audible commands require the same precision of deportment and timing (3). In training sessions, use the same three aids as for all other exercises: lead, foot, and command. With the dog in the sit position on the left, bring the left foot forward, pointing it sharply to the left

Hand signals (4) are equally important: as the handler brings his body into the turn, the right arm swings forward simultaneously with the movement of the left foot, swings back as the right foot steps through on the next pace, and returns to the side for the halt

A play toy is invaluable as a training aid for more advanced exercises and for relaxing tension. A dog should be taught to play as well as to work, and a knotted rag or a rubber ball for throwing and teasing often becomes a loved toy for joyful games during and after training sessions

The retrieve is not a natural instinct in many dogs and must be taught through training. It is compulsory in the obedience ring, and novices usually have to retrieve a dumb-bell in the prescribed sequence. Training should begin at an early age, by first showing the dog the article to be fetched (1). In nine cases out of ten, he will refuse the command to 'hold it'; press the upper lips into his mouth to force it open (2) and quickly pop the dumb-bell in. Place one hand under his chin and lift his head (3), telling him what a good boy he is

The next command to be taught is 'give' before he starts to chew or drop the article. Much patience is needed, but a dog will never be any good until he learns to release instantly on request. Even a puppy can lock his jaw tightly on the article; a finger placed in the side of his mouth, behind the article, will eventually make him release it. Only when he has learnt to hold and give, can the throwing exercise begin. At the start do not throw but place the dumb-bell two normal paces in front (4). Move the right foot forward (5), commanding 'fetch' at the same time

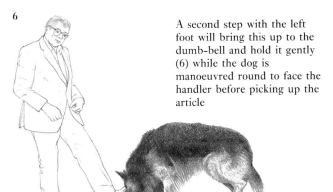

A second step with the left foot will bring this up to the dumb-bell and hold it gently (6) while the dog is manoeuvred round to face the handler before picking up the article

The final phase of the retrieve is the hands dropped in the recall position (7) and the urgent call of his name as soon as the dumb-bell has been picked up. He will return to the sit-in-front position and release the article on the command 'give'. In competitions, the retrieve is done off the lead; during training, faults are easier to correct with the aid of a check collar and lead

Obedience Trials

Scent retrieve is also known as nose work; it depends for success on perfect retrieve and perfect recall, and is equally essential for obedience, gun, and working dogs. At obedience trials, where the object is to find one particular article among others, tests are divided into three groups, ranging from the elementary to the decidedly difficult. The rules state that in none of the tests can commands or signals be given without incurring penalty

Nose work can start as a game with the play rag. Once the dog is confident at picking it up and bringing it back on the recall, teach him to take scent by rubbing a similar cloth on the hands (1), throwing it a distance, and letting the dog sniff the palm (2), at the same time commanding 'find'

Test A is considered the barometer for judging basic training and for gauging a dog's potentials in the obedience ring. He must find, from a number of different articles, the knotted rag bearing the handler's scent. The articles, which can be laid out in any pattern, should be not less than 2ft (60cm) and not more than 3ft (90cm) apart. The test is a natural progression from play with the toy rag, retrieving it from a hiding place

Test B is a follow-up to the elementary scent discrimination, with the dog having to retrieve an article scented by the handler from a number of identical, sterile articles provided by the judge. One decoy bears the scent of a trial steward. The object can be any material as long as it is retrievable

Test C is the most difficult as the article to be retrieved bears the judge's, not the handler's scent; it is placed among other identical objects which include two decoys. Usually the scent trail follows a straight line, but occasionally it is circular, which many dogs are reluctant to work. They can be taught by extending a short, straight line, first to a square, then to two semicircles and finally to a full circle with the scented rag in the middle. The rag is approximately 6–8in (15–20cm) square and varies from lightweight silk to heavy felt, sometimes weighted

Practise retrieve by hiding the scented rag under cardboard tents or among other objects. Alternatively, peg them to a line, lay the rag between them, and let him sniff it out (3)

The send away test illustrates a dog's obedience as well as his self-confidence. In the ring he will be required to move straight to a marked-out area, drop to the down at a particular spot and remain there until the recall. Practise this in a confined area with the aid of a carpet square or blanket he knows as his own, setting it always in the same place and putting him on it in the down position (1), on the lead in the initial stages

The 'look straight' command is important in the send away test. Cover the dog's eyes briefly with the hands, then straighten them out so that they act as blinkers (2). The dog can now see straight ahead only

The recall from the down position (3) is the same as from the sit in Test A. At the heel command, the dog should return at once to the position by the handler's left side

In distance control, the dog must obey six different commands as decreed by the judge. Points are lost if, at the end, the dog is forward by more than one body length. Train with the sit to the down (1): lift the left foot, place it on the lead and command 'down'. From the down to the sit (2), slide the right foot towards the front paws, pull the lead back and command 'sit'. The sit to the stand (3) is executed on a tight lead in the left hand while the left foot slides under the dog to the command 'stand'. The other three commands are the stand to the sit, the stand to the down, and the down to the stand

Advanced heelwork should be attempted only when obedience to distance control is perfect. Initially, teach the various positions with the aid of the lead, hand and foot signals, as well as commands, progressing from one position to the next when the dog is perfect and confident. Eventually he will learn to stay put in a given position while the handler walks away (1), always moving off with the right foot first as in the basic stay exercise

At the start, walk round the dog and come to a stop on the right-hand side. Both can now continue forward together before the next command is issued. Gradually increase the circle to an oval and eventually move further away. Command 'sit', followed by some heelwork, then give the command 'down' (2). This exercise is incorporated in the heelwork, but always at a normal pace, with the dog's attention focused on the handler

The movement of the handler's right foot should be sufficient signal for the dog to resume the sit position (3) by the time the handler has returned for the pick-up on the dog's right-hand side

THE FAITHFUL FRIEND

Man's best friend can become a status symbol, indicating a certain social standing and the owner's extrovert nature

Western literature abounds with canine references, and the dog has been portrayed in sculpture and paintings since ancient times, almost invariably shown as a loyal companion of man. In the field of science, on the other hand, researchers have almost totally ignored the role of the dog – and other pet animals – whether the object under study was child development, or therapy for the old or mentally ill. This neglect is all the more strange as famous scientists have commented on the human–dog relationship, including Charles Darwin in his book *The Expression of Emotions in Man and Animals*, first published in 1872. Early this century, Sigmund Freud reported that his pet Chow was frequently present during psychoanalysis sessions with his patients, and more recently, Nobel Prize winner Konrad Lorenz wrote of the human–dog relationship in his two books *Man Meets Dog* and *King Solomon's Ring*.

In the last few decades, scientists have begun to pay serious attention to this form of psychiatry, the impulse being generally attributed to a practising New York psychiatrist, Boris Levinson. In 1961 he presented a paper on 'the dog as co-therapist', in which he cited case histories where he believed the presence of his pet dog during psychiatric consultations had hastened the patients' recovery. Dr Levinson examined the relationship further in two books about the relationship between people and pets, and emphasized in particular the benefit children derive from the companionship with a dog. Since then, much new research material has seen the light of day which seems to prove that dogs are valuable not only to growing children, but also have psychological benefits for adults and especially for the elderly and housebound.

Our attitude to dogs, both historically and in the present, is often ambivalent. At one moment the dog is depicted as man's best friend, the next it becomes a derogatory comparison, as in references to 'running dog lackeys', 'a dog's life' or 'going to the dogs'. The anthropologist, Edmund Leach, has described the dog as 'lying between culture and nature'. This conflict affects our attitude, which variously attributes human qualities to dogs and variously views them strictly as animals. For most of the time, an owner treats the dog as a loved friend and companion, conferring on it honorary human status; however, this status can be withdrawn on occasions of emotional stress when the owner becomes angry with the dog because it cannot respond like a human.

Companions and Confidants

The most common reason given for owning a dog is companionship. This in itself is open to many interpretations, but recent studies have begun to tease out its most important facets. Most owners see their pet dog first and foremost as a member of the family. Researchers at the University of Pennsylvania have found that ninety-eight per cent of dog and cat owners talked to their pet every day, and that more than eighty per cent talked to them as they would to a person; twenty-eight per cent confided in their pets, or talked to them about events of the day.

Dogs are obviously not humans, but one possible explanation for this apparently irrational behaviour could be our ambiguous posture towards them. In many respects dogs are better than people – they are reliable in their behaviour and their love, and their soft coat is pleasant to stroke and touch. We can confide in them when worried and know that they will hold their silence. However, we can also cease to treat them as human beings at will and describe them as curs or in other derogatory terms.

For the most part, the human view of dogs prevails, and it is interesting to consider some recent findings of a survey of American dog owners. In more

Friend and confidant is one of the most valued aspects of ownership – a dog never disagrees nor betrays a secret

than half of the cases, the dog slept at least sometimes on the bed of a family member, and nearly all owners had a photograph of their dog, usually in a pose which indicated a close relationship, with the owner touching the animal and with the heads of the two close together, as in a parent and child relationship.

Mutual communication

The general view of dogs is as intimate human companions, and the bond between owner and dog is very strong indeed. The import of this can usefully be considered on a biological basis: people treat dogs for most of the time as humans, and dogs reciprocate by accepting humans as their masters and companions. This attitude can be attributed to their wolf ancestry as highly social pack animals; the social nature has been reinforced during domestication so that dogs integrate into a human family as if it were their own pack.

A close relationship with the dog is today perpetuated in pictures as faithfully as in ancient sculptures and frescoes

People interpret much canine communication in human rather than dog terms and believe they understand them, even if this is not always true. Dogs are indeed highly expressive, and their social language is correctly interpreted by their owners on sufficient occasions to reinforce the bond. In turn, dogs are able to understand people well enough to obey simple commands and behave in an adaptable manner which suits the particular owner. Therefore, even if the 'languages' are different, there is sufficient common ground for communication to function. Being social species, both man and dog are highly responsive to language cues, and these form the basis for the strong bond between the two.

While companionship is the main reason people give for owning a dog, another reason admitted or inferred is the benefit to self-esteem. The common saying that an owner looks like his dog may seem a little far fetched and not readily provable or disprovable. What is more certain is that some owners use their dog as a projection of their own personalities, whether consciously or unconsciously. Undoubtedly some owners will buy an elegant dog, such as an Afghan Hound or a Shih Tzu, to reflect elegance in themselves, and others will purchase a Bulldog or Dobermann to portray resolution or pugnacity. For others, the self-esteem factor is much less obvious or important, but exists nevertheless and can be regarded as a source of strength from owning a dog. This is most evident with blind owners of guide dogs. Studies have found that blind owners claim an increase in social contacts and a heightening of their status with the normal sighted through dog ownership, and that they derive as much benefit from this as from the practical guiding by the dog.

Trusted and trusting, the dog has become part of the human family and often takes the place of a child

The manner in which a dog can facilitate a conversation between the owner and a stranger has been called the 'social lubricant' effect and has been investigated in the ordinary dog owner. Dr Peter Messent studied owners who walked the same route through a London park, once with and once without their dog, scoring the reactions of passers-by. Without the dog, the subjects were ignored, but accompanied by their dog people often looked at dog *and* owner, sometimes patting the dog and, on a few occasions, even speaking to the owner. Such friendly behaviour would never occur without the dog.

As a go-between, the dog can break down many social barriers and initiate new and lasting friendships

The ability of the dog to act as an ice breaker with others can be very important for single people, especially the elderly. A Swedish survey found that seventy-nine per cent of owners in the case of city dwellers believed that their dogs had been instrumental in establishing friendships, the figure dropping to fifty-two per cent for country dwellers. In a study in Britain on the personality of dog owners versus non-owners, Dr James Serpell's most significant finding was that female dog owners considered themselves more attractive than did female non-owners. The fact that other people responded to them when they were accompanied by their dogs was probably interpreted as a greater attractiveness in themselves, an interpretation which in itself constitutes one component of self-esteem. It is interesting that the same effect was not noted in male dog-owners, a reflection perhaps of the present male-dominated society.

Society can influence people's attitude to dogs. This becomes evident when comparing dog owners in cities with those in urban areas. While the level of dog ownership is higher in the country, it is the city dwellers who generally demonstrate a closer relationship with their dogs. Country dwellers may adopt a more utilitarian viewpoint, with the dog being one of several types of animals with which they co-exist. For the city dweller, the dog may represent almost the only near-human link with the animal world.

Children and Dogs

Dog ownership is higher in households with children than in those without, and the dog would seem to play an important role. In his early writings, Dr Levinson suggested several benefits of dogs, believing firstly that they acted as friends to children or even sibling substitutes for the only child, and secondly that they were a source of play and learning which could help the child's development. The dog would also be a common focus of interest and conversation between parents and children, and it could make the child aware of responsibility to animals, and the facts of life such as body functions and sex. Finally, since dogs have short lives, grief over the death of the dog could help a child to cope with subsequent grief at the loss of a close relative.

Surprisingly few studies have been conducted on pets and children, but those completed largely support Levinson's views. The French researcher, Professor Hubert Montagner, has studied young children aged two to six years, using video observation techniques. He found much touching of the dog by the children, and nine times out of ten the child and not the dog initiated any lengthy periods of body contacts, with only children touching more. Studies at Vienna University of older children, aged eleven to sixteen, revealed significant differences between those owning pets and those without. The former group was likely to be more popular at school and to have more friends visiting them at home; ownership of a pet probably helped to teach children the skills of non-verbal communication, and this was one factor in their popularity.

Ownership of pets as a child can substantially affect adult attitudes, and differences are apparent even with very young children. A survey of attitudes to dogs and cats amongst school children aged five to seventeen years in Glasgow revealed that eighty-seven per cent liked dogs, as against sixty per cent who liked cats. Younger children tended to have slightly more positive attitudes, but ownership was the determining factor, with ninety-seven per cent of children who formerly or currently owned a dog liking them as against seventy-three per cent for those who had never had a pet.

The cultural impact of past pet ownership on present and future ownership had already been shown by Dr Serpell. For example, only a small minority of owners had had no pet during their childhood, and almost half with experience of childhood pets had one as an adult. Perhaps more striking was the loyalty shown to their childhood pets with nearly all having the same type of pet with which they had grown up.

Growing up with a pet of some kind is much more common than growing up without one. The idea of a dog completing the family seems to be a prevalent concept given that dog ownership is higher for families with children than for couples or single people of comparable age without children. An American

Sleeping together epitomizes mutual trust and cements the strong bond between human and the faithful friend

study of the behaviour of dog-owning families found that the dog could be an important 'go-between' within the family, as well as performing particular roles for different members. For the men, it was noticeable that some would touch their dog repeatedly, something they would never do in public with another person. The children played with the dog, and some used it as a confidant in times of trouble. Frequently adults would engage in playful wrestling bouts, tugs or fetch games with the dog, but generally there was more variation in the behaviour of the parents; some were close to their dog and would often touch it, talk to it, or start a game, while others were almost indifferent. The latter behaviour is apparent with several dog owners and almost always occurs when the dog is primarily the partner's pet and not their own.

In Britain, a questionnaire survey was conducted among dog-owning foster families on the assumption that such families, previously vetted and found well-functioning by the social services, would prove especially knowledgeable on the human–dog relationship. On analysis, it appeared that all members of the family, adults, natural and foster children, derived benefit from the companionship of the dog, but that the extent and the nature of the benefit varied. Foster children were reported to gain most; accepting and being accepted by the dog as a companion helped their relationships with other members of the family. While this probably reflected the sociological problems many foster children experience, the parents were at the same time aware of the help they could derive from the social therapy of the dog.

The Dog as Health Therapist

It is the health benefits a dog may give to the ordinary owner which has attracted the greatest interest recently. This was stimulated by a study in the United States of ninety-two patients recovering from coronary artery disease. Researchers found that of all the possible factors which might be associated with remaining alive one year later, pet ownership was the most significant, excluding the severity of the heart attack itself. It could be argued that this effect is due to people taking more exercise with a dog in the home, but people with other pets, which did not need to be exercised, were also more likely to be alive after one year. One likely explanation is related to mental stress. Most people prefer ordered lives, and disruption to routine, such as retirement or hospitalization, are thought to be stressful, at least in part because of the difficulties in establishing new routines. The presence of a dog or other pet offers opportunities for developing a new life style. Animals have even more regular habits than humans and expect their owners to get up at the same time in the mornings and feed them at clearly established intervals.

An additional explanation for the health benefits derived from dogs has been studied experimentally. This theory holds that pets, including dogs, have a direct physiological effect on humans. In a pilot experiment, the blood pressure of adults stroking and talking to pet dogs was measured and proved to be no different from when they were resting quietly alone, and it might even fall in the presence of the dog. This contrasts strongly with what happens when people engage in human conversations, when blood pressure almost always rises. In a separate study, the mere presence of a pet dog in the room was found to cause a lowering in blood pressure of children aged between nine and sixteen years.

The mechanism by which the stress reduction might work is still unclear and may have several components: the soft coat of a dog is pleasant to stroke, and warm; people often stroke their dogs almost without being aware of it, something which has been termed the 'idle touch', very different from people

The only child often treats the dog as the longed-for sister or brother, developing in this way a protective instinct towards smaller and helpless beings

For the older person on his own, the trusting companion often constitutes the most compelling reason for a continued, orderly existence

The faithful friend believes the bond between him and owner too strong ever to be broken

At the prospect of a temporary parting, he will plead with limpid eyes and begging posture not to be left behind

The hopeful expression gives way to dejection as the door closes, though the pricked ears still express a forlorn hope of a change of mind

consciously touching each other. The effect appears to be reciprocal since the blood pressure of the dog is known to fall when it is being stroked. It has further been suggested that the presence of calm animals, unconcerned with any dangers from their environment, has been a sign for relaxation and safety to man for most if not all of his evolutionary history. Set in a modern-home context, the sight of a contented dog may fulfil the same role and explain why a dog can reduce stress and make people feel secure.

The Dog as Protector

Feeling secure induces a sense not only of emotional but also of physical well-being. Protection is the second commonest reason owners give for keeping a dog. A barking dog defending a house is obviously a deterrent to burglars, and the size of dog is relatively unimportant; a prospective burglar will be scared off by the noise. It has even been suggested that a pack of dog food placed strategically at a front window or a tape of a barking dog can be effective in themselves. Surprisingly, no documented studies exist of the effectiveness of dogs at preventing burglaries; nonetheless it is accepted that they do, and dogs are recommended by police authorities as effective aids to protection.

For personal as opposed to property protection, the elderly may have the most to gain, being more vulnerable and frequently living alone. In many ways the elderly form a special group regarding dog ownership since their numbers are increasing, and they are more likely to feel lonely and suffer emotional isolation. The traditional extended family has declined and been replaced by the nuclear family where different generations usually live apart. Despite the obvious benefits, pet ownership is lower among older than younger age groups, possibly because older people worry over the well-being of their dogs if their own health declines, and because they see more disadvantages from dog ownership than do younger people. Perhaps most importantly, they fear the loss of their dog and their own resulting grief.

The Parting of Friends

The grief at the loss of a dog is experienced by all owners, and for the elderly particularly it can be a devastating blow. In some circumstances, elderly and single people may develop an obsessive relationship with their dog which to them seems their only genuine friend; in certain cases large amounts of money are left in the owners' wills for the dogs' upkeep. Such behaviour may seem bizarre to non-owners, but understandable to other lonely dog lovers.

When a loved dog dies, grief can be intense, and cases of pathological extended mourning have been reported by psychiatrists. Some owners may grieve over their dog for a year or longer, a timespan comparable to that following the death of a close relative. However, there are several differences between the two mourning processes. Various ceremonies and routines attend a human death and these may in themselves help the bereaved to cope with the grief, aided by emotional support from friends. No graveside rituals pertain to the death of a dog, but often the most upsetting aspect is the lack of understanding by other people. Dog owners are often so embarrassed at their own strong feelings over the loss of their pet that they have difficulty in talking about it (see also The Declining Years, page 129).

The Dog in Society

The importance of pets has begun to be realized by politicans; in the USA, bills protecting the right to own a pet have been passed in some States, and a Senate bill now prohibits bans on pets for the elderly and handicapped in federally assisted housing. In France and Sweden the right to own a dog is part of the constitution.

Part of the stimulus for protecting some rights of dog owners has come from a realization of the potential of pets in the therapy of old people in health care institutions, for certain types of mentally ill people, and for criminals in prisons. The introduction of a pet, either as a visitor or as a permanent resident, has produced dramatic changes in the social behaviour of some people in all three groups. One well-documented study was conducted in Australia, where a former guide dog, a Labrador called *Honey*, was introduced on to a geriatric ward of a Melbourne hospital. Interviews with staff and patients before and three months after Honey's arrival showed several beneficial effects in the areas of emotional well-being and physical activity; for the staff none of the prior misgivings about a dog had materialized.

Resident pets and pet-visiting schemes have become widespread in America, and some have started in Britain and other countries. An American psychiatrist has evaluated their effects, and highlighted the increase in play and laughter among patients. It is suggested that laughter can reduce stress and pain and instil a feeling of elation as a genuine physiological effect, which via neuroendocrine pathways affects the chemistry of the brain itself.

Pet therapy with the mentally handicapped and with prisoners is still in its pioneering stage. The number of pets allowed on to wards in mental hospitals is increasing, and the trend seems likely to continue. In many ways this is a return to former therapy; in the nineteenth century and even earlier, most hospitals for the mentally ill had many types of animals, as shown for example in records of the York Retreat in England in 1792, and at Gheel in Belgium as long ago as the ninth century.

So far the USA is the only country where prisons have used pets in a constructive manner for the rehabilitation of selected criminals. In one women's penitentiary, maximum-security prisoners train dogs for use as therapy or assistance for physically disabled people. Reportedly the involvement has a highly favourable impact on the prisoners' behaviour.

Friend and Companion

The relationship of owners with their dogs is as complex, individual and fascinating as human partnerships, with some key points to which most or all owners can relate. The dog is first a companion and friend, at the same time similar to and different from a human being. A dog is reliable, affectionate and gives a sense of constancy and routine to life, all roles less easily fulfilled by humans. At the same time the dog is something to care for, putting the owner in the role of parent to child in some respects, and as an equal in others. A dog is a stimulus for laughter and for play, the latter behaviour being one that adults perform more easily with a dog than with another person.

The physical characteristics of dogs are pleasant, they are usually soft to touch, warm, and never answer back. They are a stimulus for exercise and keep their owners active. They give protection and impart a feeling of security. They can improve self-esteem, and may have the ability to reduce stress. All these features can be provided at times by another person, by a dog constantly.

Humans are able to form a strong emotional bond with a dog, and the dog with the human. That perhaps is the key to the whole relationship and why it is so successful. Rudyard Kipling said it in another way in *The Power of the Dog*:
'Brothers and Sisters, I bid you beware of giving your heart to a dog to tear'.

The eagerly awaited return is anticipated long before the human ear can pick up any sounds. Pricked ears, alert eyes and expectant stance indicate the approach of well-known footsteps

Close to the door, quivering with excitement (above), the tail wags furiously in joy at the return of the master, the resumption of ordinary life, and the prospect of a game as reward for having been a good boy and protected the home

IT'S A DOG'S LIFE

ANATOMY OF THE DOG

The anatomy of the dog – and that of its feral ancestors, the wolf and the jackal – is designed for a life-style as a hunter of prey. As a quadrupedal mammal the dog walks and runs on its toes; the structure of limbs and musculature enables the wild dog to run untiringly for long periods, and teeth and jaw muscles are designed for catching, holding and rending the prey. Heart and lungs are large, while the digestive tract is relatively very much shorter when compared to that of herbivorous animals. The reproductive tract of the female is designed to carry several young, which are helpless when born.

Selective breeding has produced many different breeds of dog, but despite the diversity of external appearance, the anatomy remains essentially the same, modified chiefly only in size or shape. Many features of the anatomy of dog and human are almost identical, the similarities being most obvious in the limbs.

The Skeletal System

The skeleton is formed from a highly specialized substance known as bone, a complex of living cells embedded in a material formed mainly from a compound calcium-phosphorus salt reinforced by a meshwork of protein fibres. Throughout an animal's life, bone is constantly being removed, reformed and remodelled in order to perform its several functions. Besides supporting the body weight, bone provides rigid points for muscle attachment and for a system of levers which, when activated by muscles, effect movement of the body. Bone also protects soft structures, such as the heart and lungs, and provides some calcium for bodily needs. It is the source of bone marrow in which new red and white blood cells are formed.

Bone may be affected by hormones, mechanical stresses and tensions, injury, and dietary excesses and deficiencies of, for example, protein, minerals and vitamins. In the limbs of young animals, bones increase in length at growth plates (growing points) at either end of the bone; these ossify and disappear when the animal is fully grown.

The skull is complex, but can be divided into three main parts: cranium, face, and mandible. The cranium or braincase encloses the cavity for the brain and extends backwards from just behind the eyes to the back of the skull. Most of it is covered by the large muscles which the dog uses for chewing. The most superficial region of the cranium, between the eyes, overlies an air space or sinus, on the floor of which is the cranial limit of the brain. The cranium and the face in front of it are linked on either side by two cheek bones, the front or cranial end of which helps to form the socket (orbit) for the eye-ball, while the caudal end carries the joint surface for the mandible. The large hole in the cranium just behind this joint is the site of the ear drum.

The face consists of the nose, hard palate and teeth. The internal nasal cavity is divided into a right and left chamber by a flexible midline partition, the nasal septum, while the chambers themselves are packed with long paper-thin bone scrolls; the bone forming the floor of the chambers is also the hard palate of the mouth. The upper teeth are firmly fixed in bony sockets at the junction of the hard palate and the face. The mandible hinges with the skull on either side of the cheek bone and has a horizontal and vertical portion. The horizontal part carries the lower teeth. Strong chewing muscles are attached to the vertical part and can close the jaw powerfully using this part of the jaw as a lever.

Vertebrae, ribs and sternum

The spinal column in all breeds of dog contains seven cervical (neck) vertebrae, thirteen thoracic vertebrae, seven lumbar vertebrae, the sacrum and a varying

Key to diagram opposite:

1 Cranium
2 Cheek bone
3 Sinus
4 Orbit
5 Facial bones
6 Lower jaw joint
7 Teeth
8 Mandible
9 Ear drum
10 Scapula
11 Shoulder joint
12 Humerus
13 Elbow joint
14 Phalanges
15 Metacarpal bones
16 Carpal bones
17 Radius
18 Ulna
19 Sternum
20 Costal cartilages
21 Os penis
22 Patella
23 Phalanges
24 Metatarsus
25 Tarsal bones
26 Tibia
27 Fibula
28 Femur
29 Coccygeal vertebrae
30 Pelvic girdle
31 Lumbar vertebrae
32 Thoracic vertebrae
33 Cervical vertebrae
34 Axis
35 Atlas

number of coccygeal (tail) vertebrae. When all the vertebrae are aligned together, a wide central canal is formed inside the spinal column which extends from head to tail. Within this canal runs the major nerve trunk of the body, the spinal cord. The first cervical vertebra is known as the atlas, the second as the axis; the head nods on the atlas and rotates on the axis. The dog has thirteen pairs of ribs. The upper end of each pair forms a movable joint with the thoracic vertebra while the lower end of each pair is continued by a costal (rib-like) cartilage. The first nine pairs of costal cartilages are attached to the sternum (breast bone) and move on their upper and lower joints during breathing.

The limbs

Moving down the limb from shoulder to paw, each forelimb consists of the scapula (shoulder blade), the humerus (upper arm bone), the ulna and radius (forearm bones), and the carpus (wrist bone). The region from carpus to digits is called the forepaw and contains several carpal bones, five metacarpal bones (palm of the hand) and five digits or fingers, the bones of which are known as phalanges. Digit one, the thumb, has two phalanges, digits two to five have three phalanges. The final phalanx on each digit carries the claw.

Certain parts of the skeleton lie close to the surface of the body and are thinly clothed with muscle or skin. These regions can be seen or felt as bony protuberances under the skin, even in dark-coated and thick-haired animals.

Such identifiable areas assist veterinary surgeons in locating deep-seated structures: the heart lies between ribs 3 and 6; its position can be accurately projected by counting from rib 13 forwards

Skeleton of the dog

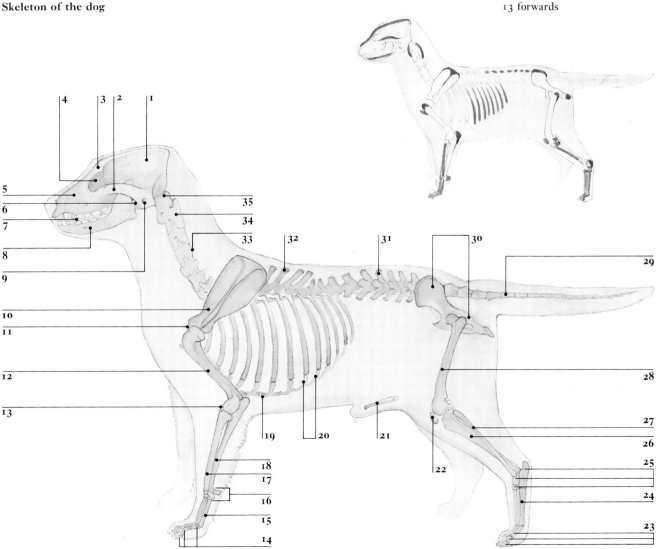

93

The hindlimb consists of the hip bone, properly known as the pelvis and the pelvic girdle. It is attached firmly to the left and right side of the sacrum and forms a rigid connection with the spinal column. The pelvic girdle protects the soft urinary and reproductive organs, while the pelvis itself carries the sockets for the heads of the left and right femurs or thigh bones. The patella (knee cap) lies at the front of the lower end of the femur. Below the femur are the tibia and the fibula (shin bones). Several tarsal bones comprise the tarsus or hock, corresponding to the ankle, above the metatarsal bones of the instep. The region from tarsus to digits is called the hind paw which has only four digits, digit one, the big toe, being absent. Each digit has three phalanges.

Separate from the main skeleton of the male dog is a rod-shaped bone called the os penis, lying within the body of the penis.

Joints, Muscles & Movement

Most joints permit movement between two or more bones, though some, such as the joints between the bones of the skull, are immovable. The opposing bone surfaces are covered with a thin bluish-white layer of cartilage which is almost frictionless and has a shock-absorbing action during joint-movement. The bones forming the joints are held firmly together by strong bands of white fibrous tissue known as ligaments, and each joint is enclosed in a cuff-like membrane, the joint capsule. The inner lining of this capsule produces a thick viscous fluid called synovia (joint oil) which lubricates joint-movement.

The major joints of fore and hindlimb correspond with those in the human arm and leg, each foreleg being made up of the shoulder, elbow and carpal (wrist) joints. The hindleg joints consist of the hip, stifle (knee), tarsal or hock (ankle) joints. The various joints between metacarpals, metatarsals and phalanges are equivalent to human finger and toe joints.

Shoulder and hip joints are ball-and-socket joints with potentials for a wide range of movement, while the elbow joint is a hinge which allows flexion and extension only. The hip joint has very free movement because of its construction; it may be defective from birth (see Hip dysplasia, page 144).

The stifle joint is the most complex; the patella (kneecap) slides on a groove at the lower end of the femur as the joint moves and increases the leverage of the cranial thigh muscles. Inside the joint are two mobile cartilage pads, and two strong cruciate, or cross-shaped, ligaments; severe lameness in active dogs is commonly caused by a rupture of a ligament following a fall.

Tendon tissue attaches muscle to bone, and the movement of joints occurs by the contraction and relaxation of muscles when stimulated by nerves. Smooth, controlled movement is brought about by the contraction of one group of muscles and the simultaneous relaxation of an opposing group. Movements that bend a joint are known as flexing, those straightening a joint as extending.

Strong muscles, not bony joints, attach the dog's forelimb to a wide area of neck and thorax and enable the limb to take long strides as the scapula, shoulder joint and humerus glide backwards and forwards over the thorax wall. The forelimbs are mainly supportive, carrying about two-thirds of the dog's total weight; most propulsive power is provided by the hindlimbs.

The Respiratory System

The function of the respiratory system is to provide the body with a constant supply of oxygen from the atmosphere, and to eliminate from the body the waste carbon dioxide gas. It consists of the nose, mouth, larynx, the trachea, the bronchi and the lungs.

The vertebral canal (1), enclosing the spinal cord (2), is made up of a number of vertebrae each joined to the next by a flexible pad, the so-called intervertebral disc consisting of outer fibrous layers (3) and an inner gelatinous area (4). If the spine is flexed too vigorously, especially in an older, long-backed dog, a prolapsed or 'slipped' disc may occur as the soft centre bursts up into the spinal canal (5), causing serious injury

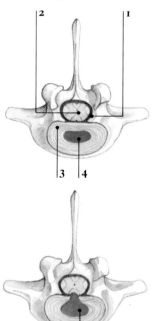

In the head the air passage (the nose) lies dorsal to the food passage (the mouth), but in the neck the air passage (larynx and trachea) lies ventral to the food passage (oesophagus or gullet), so that at the back of the throat, the region called the pharynx, the directions that food and air must take cross each other. Swallowing without food or fluid falling into the larynx is made possible by movements of the soft palate and the larynx, as is the continuous channel for air during uninterrupted breathing.

The respiratory system

A midline longitudinal section of the head illustrates the arrangement of air passages in relation to food passages

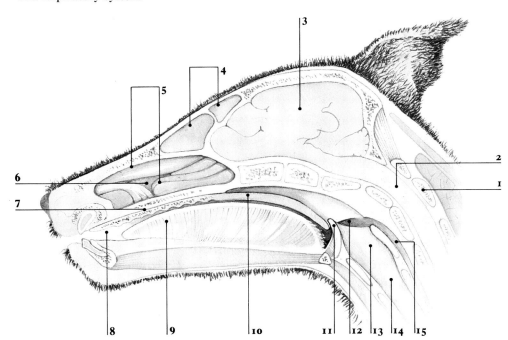

Key:
1 Cervical vertebrae
2 Spinal cord
3 Brain
4 Sinus
5 Scroll-like bones
6 Nasal cavity
7 Hard palate
8 Mouth cavity
9 Tongue
10 Soft palate
11 Epiglottis
12 Pharynx
13 Larynx
14 Oesophagus
15 Trachea

Nose and mouth are separated by the hard palate and its continuation, the soft palate, a movable muscular shelf which merges on either side into the walls of the pharynx. The soft palate is so long that its edge cannot normally be viewed; there is no uvula and mouth and nose cavities can communicate freely. The palate can be raised up to block off the rear exit from the nasal chambers during swallowing and lowered to close the back of the mouth cavity during nose-breathing; it can also be held in the half-way position during mouth-breathing (panting) so that both nose and mouth cavity have free connection to the pharynx and larynx opening.

The larynx at the upper end of the trachea is formed of curved cartilage plates that can move on each other. It keeps the commencement of the air passage open during all movements of the head and neck. During quiet respiration, air is inhaled through the nostrils and is warmed and humidified in the nasal chambers. It then passes over the soft palate directly into the open larynx with the epiglottis raised on the upper side of the soft palate. At the start of swallowing, the epiglottis is pushed back over the laryngeal entrance, and the palate raises up, closing off the nasal passages and opening up the back of the mouth so that food or liquid can pass over the larynx into the opened oesophagus. The larynx can close its internal cavity momentarily as an added protection against food materials being inhaled. During mouth-breathing, the epiglottis lies forward on the tongue; the palate is lifted and air passes freely through the mouth into the larynx.

The Respiratory System

A complex arrangement of major thoracic and abdominal organs constitutes the various internal systems. The positions differ between the sexes as shown in this diagram of the male (viewed on the left side) and that of the female (*opposite*)

Key:
1 Rectum
2 Ureter
3 Kidney
4 Spleen
5 Position of diaphragm
6 Aorta
7 Outline of lung
8 Atria of heart
9 Ventricles of heart
10 Liver
11 Stomach
12 Small intestine
13 Penis
14 Testicle
15 Vas deferens in spermatic cord
16 Bladder

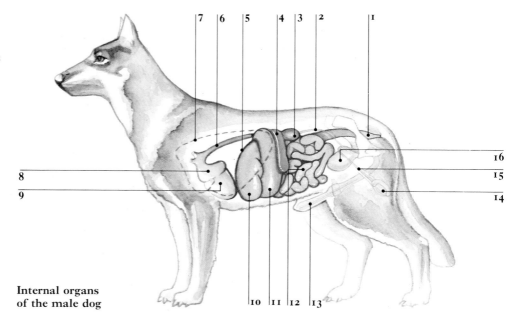

Internal organs of the male dog

Trachea, bronchi and lungs

The trachea, a flexible tube with a series of springy cartilagenous rings down its total length, can resist compression, but stretches and bends with any movement of the neck. It divides into a right and left main bronchus in the thorax at approximately rib five. The bronchi immediately enter the right and left lung, where they branch and rebranch until they become tiny tubes, less than 1 mm in diameter, and terminate in millions of tiny bubble-like air spaces or alveoli. These form the mass of the lung and give it a soft sponge-like texture.

The inside of the thorax is a sealed cavity. The walls are formed by the ribs, with breathing muscles between each rib, and the roof and floor by the vertebrae and sternum. It is separated from the abdomen by the diaphragm, a large muscular sheet and the main breathing muscle. Dividing the thoracic cavity into right and left sides is a midline partition in which the heart and major blood vessels, and the oesophagus are found; each cavity is completely occupied by a lung, covered with pleura.

The Circulatory System

The circulation is the body's transport system, conveying nutrients, water, minerals, blood chemicals and defender cells in the blood stream to every part of the body. All these substances are carried in the blood which owes its colour to billions of red oxygen-carrying cells. White cells, involved in the body's defence, are also present in blood but in far fewer numbers. The fluid component of blood contains proteins, some of which are involved in blood-clotting, as well as glucose, carbon dioxide, inorganic salts, and organic compounds such as vitamins, hormones and fats.

The function of the heart is to propel the blood round the body at sufficient velocity and pressure to ensure that all tissues constantly receive the substances they require for efficient function, an on-going process called general circulation. At the same time the heart must pump blood round the lungs so that the red cells can pick up fresh oxygen and so that carbon dioxide can be eliminated. This is called the pulmonary (lung) circulation.

The heart lies approximately between ribs three and six and a little to the left of the midline. In a slim-chested dog like the Whippet, the heart beat can be

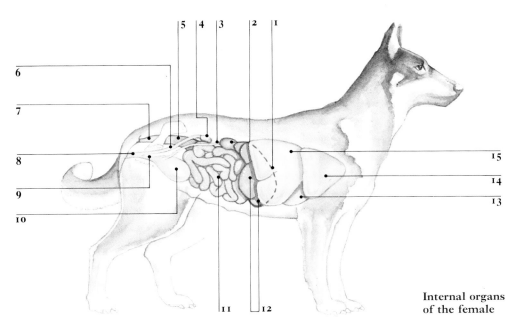

Internal organs
of the female

Abdominal and thoracic organs
of the bitch, viewed on the
right side

Key:
1 Outline of diaphragm
2 Kidney
3 Ureter
4 Ovary
5 Descending colon
6 Uterus
7 Rectum
8 Vagina
9 Urethra
10 Bladder
11 Small intestine
12 Lobes of liver
13 Heart
14 Cranial lobe of lung
15 Caudal lobe of lung

seen as a regular movement or flutter of the chest wall where the apex of the heart touches the inside of the chest wall. The heart is similar in construction to that of the human, consisting of two compartments or pumps divided down the middle by a muscular wall, the septum. Each compartment contains two chambers, the atrium, into which blood flows, and the ventricle, which propels blood into the arteries. Each chamber is guarded by a one-way valve, which prevents the backflow of blood. If any of the valves is faulty, blood may leak in the reverse direction; this can be common in older dogs, and a faulty valve causes extra strain on the heart and inefficient re-oxygenation of the blood in the lungs.

The right atrium and ventricle pump blood through the pulmonary circulation, picking up oxygen in the lungs; the oxygen-rich blood is then conveyed back to the left atrium and ventricle from which it is propelled into the aorta and distributed throughout the body by a network of arteries. The heart beat can be heard as a 'lup-dup', 'lup-dup' sound through the chest wall, corresponding to the closure times of the two pairs of valves.

The heart beat can be heard clearest at the spot between ribs 5 and 6

Arteries and veins
Thick-walled elastic vessels, the arteries, convey blood away from the heart. During every heart beat the walls of the larger arteries expand to receive the new delivery of blood, and then recoil; where an artery crosses a bone, the movement of the arterial wall can be felt as the pulse. In the dog this is best felt about half-way down on the inner surface of the thigh in the midline.

Arteries branch and rebranch, becoming smaller until they form a huge network of microscopic vessels or capillaries. These allow nutrients to pass through their walls to the tissues, then join and rejoin to become thin-walled vessels of increasing size, the veins.

The main arteries are the aorta, from the heart; the right and left common carotid arteries, to the head; the brachial and femoral arteries, to the forelimbs and hindlimbs respectively; and the pulmonary arteries, to the lungs.

Veins convey blood towards the heart; they are wider and with thinner walls than the arteries, lying in certain parts of the body in superficial positions where they can be prone to damage, especially cuts; at the same time they are

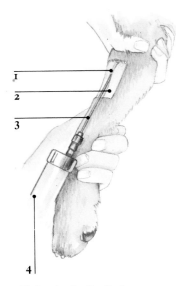

Veins in the forelimb are superficial and the best site for intravenous injections. Pressure applied to a vein (1), above a clipped and sterilized patch of skin (2), forces it to swell and become accessible to the hypodermic needle (3) as the syringe is depressed (4)

Anal sacs (1) on either side of the anus (3) secrete a fluid through the duct opening (2). Impaction of the sacs can be painful (see also page 155)

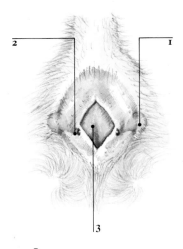

accessible to the veterinarian for intravenous injections. Blood escapes in spurts from a cut artery, but flows steadily from a cut vein; the volume of blood lost over a period of time can be great unless the hemorrhage is stemmed.

The main veins include the cranial and caudal vena cava, to the heart; the right and left jugular veins, from the head; the cephalic and brachial veins, from the forelimbs; the saphenous and femoral veins from the hindlimbs; and the right and left pulmonary veins, from the lungs.

The Urinary & Genital Systems

In dog and bitch, the urinary system consists of a pair of kidneys and ureters, the bladder, and the urethra. Urine is manufactured in the kidneys, passes through the ureters to the bladder and is eventually evacuated through the urethra. Each kidney is a bean-shaped organ, dark reddish-blue in colour and situated on the roof of the abdomen either side of the aorta. It consists of millions of pinpoint-sized filtering units through which the circulating blood passes. Waste products and excess salts and water in the blood pass through these into long, microscopically narrow tubules which convey the fluid to the point on the kidney where the ureter arises. During its passage the fluid is altered until it enters the ureters as urine, the production of which is a continuous process.

The ureters are muscular tubes which convey the urine into the dorsal surface of the bladder, a highly distensible, muscular, balloon-shaped sac which narrows to a neck in the pelvis and is continued as the urethra.

In the male dog, the urethra is narrow and curves round the near edge of the pelvic floor, passing forward into the penis. The urethra of the bitch is short and wider and opens into the floor of the vagina.

The kidneys play a large part in the regulation of water and salts in the blood and in the body tissues, rapidly altering, for example, the concentration and volume of urine in response to body requirements. Another major function of the kidneys is the removal from the blood of soluble nitrogenous waste products derived from the digestion of protein. The kidneys can also eliminate from the blood many foreign chemicals such as drugs.

The female reproductive system

The reproductive organs of the bitch consist of the paired ovaries and oviducts, the uterus, vagina, vestibule and vulva. The right and left ovaries, suspended by ligaments from the roof of the abdomen, produce ova and the female hormone, oestrogen. During pregnancy they produce another hormone, progesterone. Ova are released during oestrus and pass via the oviducts or fallopian tubes into the uterus. When a bitch is spayed, the ovaries and oviducts up to the cervix are removed.

The uterus, consisting of two long, muscular horns, terminates at the cervix as a thick muscular ring which closes completely in pregnancy; the foetuses are arranged in a row in both horns. The vagina passes through the pelvis, its caudal continuation being the vestibule, which is directed downwards to the vulva, the external opening of the genital passage.

The male reproductive system

This consists of the testicles, spermatic cord, vas deferens, prostate, urethra and penis, the former three being paired. The testicles, in the scrotum, produce spermatozoa as well as the male hormone, testosterone. The thick spermatic cord, running from each testicle into the abdomen, is made up of a large artery,

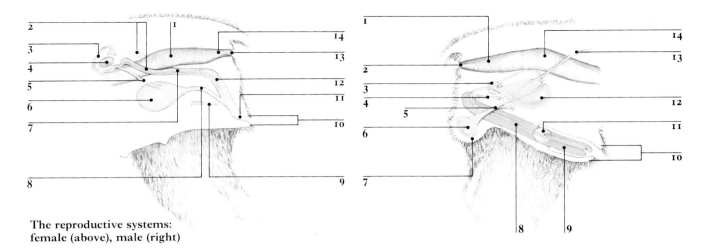

The reproductive systems:
female (above), male (right)

vein, and nerve, a slip of muscle, and the vas deferens. The latter conveys spermatozoa from the testicle to the urethra which acts as a common channel for urine and semen. The bi-lobed prostrate gland, encircling the urethra, produces the bulk of the seminal fluid in which the spermatozoa are carried.

The penis is formed of spongy erectile tissue with the urethra running through the centre. The free part of the penis has a bulbous portion. During erection and mating, this portion enlarges, locking it in the vagina of the bitch, in the so-called tie. Animals risk injury if they are pulled apart when tied.

The Digestive System

The digestive organs include the teeth, mouth, pharynx, alimentary canal, and accessory organs. Like other mammals, dogs possess two sets of teeth. The milk or puppy teeth, small and sharp, are fewer than the adult ones. The permanent teeth have usually appeared by the age of six months, with the canine (fang) teeth erupting in the fifth month. The dog has forty-two teeth, twenty in the upper jaw and twenty-two in the lower. The right and left upper jaw each has three incisors, one canine tooth, four premolars and two molars; the right and left lower jaws possess the same number of incisors, canines and premolars, but have three molars.

The incisor teeth act as nippers; the canines can hold firmly on to prey because of two powerful muscles which act to close the jaws. The roots of the canine teeth are extremely long which increases their strength. Food is held and carried by the two premolar teeth, while the molars are designed to slice and crush food, but not to chew it.

Food is reduced to small lumps by the action of the tongue and teeth and lubricated by saliva produced from four pairs of salivary glands. It is then passed through the pharynx, over the closed laryngeal entrance, and into the alimentary canal, where digestion takes place.

The remains of the digested food move into the colon or large intestine. At the junction of the small intestine and the colon is a blind-ending sac, the caecum. Some water is absorbed back into the body from the substances in the large intestine, leaving behind the soft solid mass of feces which enters the rectum and is voided through the anus.

The digestive juices in the stomach and small intestine contain enzymes which break food down into simple chemicals, soluble in water; the main food breakdown takes place in the small intestine, consisting of duodenum, jejunum and ileum. The large pancreas also produces digestive juices.

Female organs, left side:
1 Colon
2 Uterine horn (right)
3 Fallopian tube
4 Ovary
5 Ureter
6 Bladder
7 Cervix
8 Urethra
9 Pubic bone
10 Vulva
11 Vestibule
12 Vagina
13 Anus
14 Rectum

Male organs, right side:
1 Rectum
2 Anus
3 Prostate
4 Pubic bone
5 Spermatic cord
6 Testicle
7 Scrotum
8 Urethra
9 Penis
10 Prepuce
11 Bulbous part of penis
12 Bladder
13 Ureter
14 Colon

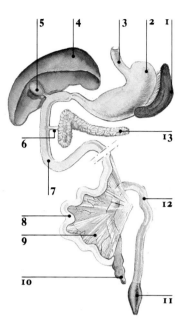

The digestive system shown in schematic form. The spleen (1), though attached to the wall of the stomach (2), is concerned with the body's defences and not digestion, which begins in the oesophagus (3). This lies behind the liver (4), which secretes bile into the gall bladder (5). Bile and juices through the duct (6) from the pancreas (13) aid food breakdown in the small intestine, starting with the duodenum (7) and going through the jejunum and ileum (8) attached by the mesentery (9) to the abdominal wall.

Digestion is complete by the time the contents of the small intestine reach the caecum (10), waste products being expelled through the rectum (11) after bacterial decomposition in the final part of the alimentary tract, the colon or large intestine (12)

Bile, which is involved with fat digestion, is emptied from the liver into the duodenum. The liver is an important gland and processes most of the products of digestion, transforming them into chemicals used for body building and repairs, bodily defences, energy, and chemicals for storage.

The Endocrine System

The endocrine system functions through chemical messages, called hormones, carried in the bloodstream. They are produced by endocrine cells and grouped in glands, or contained in organs with additional functions. The pancreas, for example, produces the hormone insulin and also manufactures digestive juices. A hormone may have widespread effects on several tissues or it may influence a specific process or organ. Imbalance of hormone levels leads to abnormality in an animal's development and function. Not all hormones are essential, but lack of cortisone, insulin, and parathormone eventually leads to death.

The major endocrine organs include the pituitary gland at the base of the brain, and the two thyroid glands at either side of the trachea; parathyroids are tiny glands embedded in each thyroid gland. Two adrenal glands cranial to the kidneys produce corticosteroid and an adrenaline compound. The endocrine cells in the pancreas produce insulin, lack of which results in *Diabetes mellitus*.

The sex hormones from the ovaries control the female reproductive cycle in conjunction with the pituitary hormones. They are also responsible for the production of the secondary sexual characteristics in the young bitch. Male hormone produced in the testicle is responsible for the secondary sexual characteristics of the male. It also controls the production of spermatozoa.

Hormones are produced by endocrine cells of which the master gland is the pituitary (1). Parathyroids (2) maintain the level of mineral salts, while the adrenals (3), cranial to the kidneys (4), control sugar, minerals, and water, and produce cortisone. Sex hormones are contained in the ovaries (5) in the bitch, and in the testicles (6) in the male. The pancreas (7) produces insulin; hormones in the thyroid glands (8) affect energy

The endocrine glands

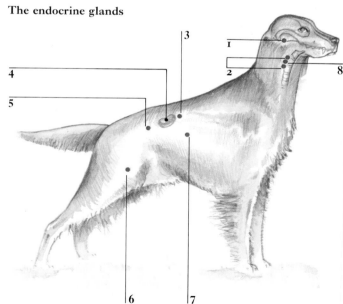

The Nervous System

Information about the external and internal environment of the body is continuously received, analyzed and processed by the brain and spinal cord, known collectively as the central nervous system. The nerves, which enter and leave the brain, and the spinal cord throughout its length are the routes along which messages, in the form of electrical impulses, travel. Sense organs throughout the body collect information about their environment, such as outside temperature, mechanical pressure, blood levels of oxygen and carbon dioxide; they code this information and send it via sensory nerves to the spinal

The central nervous system

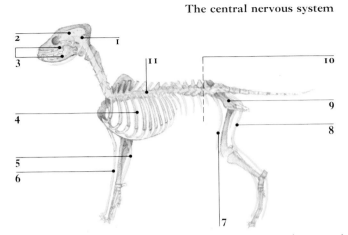

The brain, made up of the cerebellum (1) and cerebral hemispheres (2), is the seat of the 12 cranial nerves (3). Others, such as intercostal nerves (4) and the ulnar (5) and radial nerves (6), arise from the spinal cord. Major nerves in the hindlimbs, such as the femoral (7), sciatic (8) and obdurator (9), also emerge from the spine, which terminates at the sacral and tail structures (10), whose nerves are continued in the vertebral canal

cord and brain where motor nerves convey instructions to an organ or tissue.

Twelve pairs of major nerves in the head arise from the brain and emerge through holes in the skull to reach their target organs such as muzzle, eyeball, teeth or tongue. Nerves to the rest of the body arise in pairs from the spinal cord, and exit from the vertebral column through spaces between one vertebra and the next.

Skin & Associated Structures

The skin is a large organ which, among other functions, protects the body against injury, invading bacteria and toxic substances. It also plays a large part in maintaining correct fluid balance in the body, by on the one hand preventing water loss in the tissues and on the other preventing excess water from entering the body through the waterproof finish to skin and hair. Skin is formed of three layers: an outer protective and horny layer, a thin middle layer which grows actively to produce the horny layer, and a deep layer providing nourishment to the outer layers known collectively as the epidermis; the inner layer, the dermis, contains nerves, blood vessels, glands and fibres.

The hair covering the dog's body is dense in most places, with sparse growth over the abdomen, the inner thighs and inside the ears (see also Senses of the Dog, page 102). Sebaceous glands in the skin are concerned with the texture and sheen of the coat, and other, modified glands are found inside the ears, round the anus and in the foot pads. The end of the nose is hairless, and so are the four pads on each foot; they act as shock absorbers and are covered with a thick horny skin. The claws are formed from thick horn adherent to dermal tissues endowed with blood vessels and nerves; if the claws are clipped too short, bleeding results.

Both male and female dog usually have five pairs of mammary glands or nipples; in the male they are associated with rudimentary glandular tissue only. In the female, the amount of mammary tissue depends upon her stage of reproductive life.

THE SENSES OF THE DOG

The dog is very aware of its environment through its senses of sight, hearing, smell and taste. The more general senses of touch, temperature, pain and hunger, among others, are also important sources of external and internal awareness. Some sensations probably do not reach consciousness though they play an important part in the functions of the dog.

Some senses are of value in appreciating distant stimuli. Both man and dog can normally see movements at the end of the garden, or hear a dog barking in the next street, but appreciation of other stimuli must involve direct physical contact: food cannot be tasted unless it is in contact with the tongue and other parts of the mouth. The different types of sensation have been arranged in three categories as those associated with body surface, internal organs, and with muscles and joints.

Skin Sensations

Receptors for thermal stimuli (warmth and cold) are present throughout the skin, but are not as well-developed in the dog as in the human. Receptors sense changes in the environmental temperature and allow the animal to seek an equable situation or to lower or raise its body temperature as necessary either by panting or shivering, or by erecting its hair coat or taking exercise.

Touch sensation is appreciated by 'bare' areas of skin between the hair follicles as well as by the hairs themselves. Since the effect is brought about by mechanical disturbance, these receptors are sometimes called mechano-receptors. The skin between the hairs is sensitive to slight stretching and to pressure, but most sensations are received by raised spots known as touch pads which respond to direct mechanical stimulation. The skin over most of the body surface is protected by a dense layer of hairs, and the hair follicles are well

Three-dimensional section through the skin

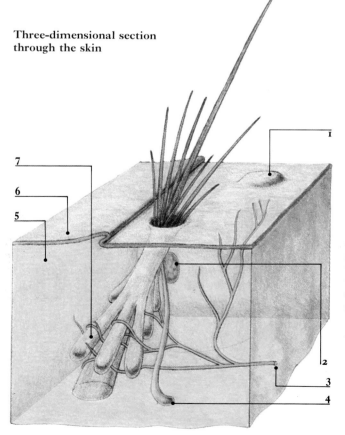

The skin consists of the outer horny epidermis and the inner dermis containing hair follicles, nerves, blood vessels and skin glands. The nerves supply sensory fibres to the hair follicles, the dermis, epidermis and touch pads. Sebaceous glands secrete a substance which helps to keep the coat waterproof; sweat glands only marginally affect thermoregulation

Key:
1 Touch pad
2 Sebaceous gland
3 Cutaneous (skin) nerve
4 Sweat gland
5 Dermis
6 Epidermis
7 Hair follicles

innervated with sensory nerve fibres. When hairs are displaced by touch or by air movements, nerve impulses are set up which are short-lived as the sensory endings quickly adapt; the sensation does not persist even if the hairs continue to be touched, unless movement continues.

Mechanoreceptors function only at near to normal body temperature. If the skin temperature falls below about 50°F (10°C) they gradually become inactive; numbness eventually sets in if the skin temperature drops further. It is evident that in the extremities, such as the feet, both sensory and motor functions occur at low temperatures: the Husky stands and moves about on ice, feeling the terrain underfoot with feet that are close to 32°F (0°C).

Within the coat some of the guard hairs are exceptionally well furnished with nerve endings and are more sensitive than other hairs to displacement. They are not easily distinguishable from the other guard hairs, but other hairs, found mainly on the head, are very obvious. Commonly called whiskers, these hairs are not only very sensitive to touch but can also be moved around to some degree because they are embedded in the muscles of the face, which can be moved voluntarily.

Whiskers occur around the muzzle and elsewhere on the body; they are especially well furnished with sensory nerve fibres and can be moved voluntarily

Vision

The eye responds to the distant stimulus of light which enters through the transparent parts and activates the sensory cells in the depths or fundus of the eye. The light rays must be focused as a clear image on to the sensory cells, not as a diffuse jumble of light and dark areas. Correct focusing involves refraction or bending of the light rays such as occurs in a camera. As refraction can only occur where there is a change in density of the material through which light passes, it mainly takes place at the outer surface of the eye where it meets the air; much less refraction occurs within the eye itself because the transparent media are of nearly the same density.

The eye has a tough outer coat, the near-opaque white sclera; at the front or anterior pole it becomes almost completely transparent and is known as the cornea. The size of the cornea is important and is proportionately larger in dogs than in humans, making it possible for more light to enter and therefore for the animal to see better in poor light. Once the light rays have met the corneal surface they are refracted, pass through the cornea, and enter a fluid-filled space called the anterior chamber.

If all the light that passed into the eye on a bright day were to be focused on to the sensory cells they might be damaged, and the stimulus would probably be painful. In order to protect the light-sensitive cells, a membrane called the iris is attached on the inside of the eye round the edge of the cornea. It has a central aperture or pupil which can expand in size from a tiny opening to one which has a diameter nearly that of the cornea itself. The pupil can therefore regulate the amount of light which enters the eye, and its movement, brought about by muscle action, is due either to the light stimulus or to emotion such as fear. Constriction of the pupil can increase the depth of focus as well as the acuteness of the image by functioning like the hole of a pinhole camera. In twilight the fully dilated pupil collects all the light possible and, though focusing may be less good, changes in light can be recognized: a cat can be seen unless it sits still.

Once the light has passed through the anterior chamber and the pupil, it passes through a shallow posterior chamber also filled with aqueous fluid. This is secreted under pressure and is responsible for keeping the eye tense and round and for helping to supply nutrient substances to the cornea and the lens. The aqueous-filled chambers are closed off by the lens. This is a transparent

Vision

Oblique section of head at the level of the orbit, showing the various components of the eye itself, the surrounding musculature and nerves

Key:
1 Tapetum lucidum
2 Pigmented fundus
3 Lens capsule
4 Lens
5 Iris
6 Anterior chamber
7 Pupil
8 Posterior chamber
9 Cornea
10 Suspensory ligament
11 Fat
12 Orbit
13 Eye muscle
14 Optic nerve
15 Brain
16 Bone

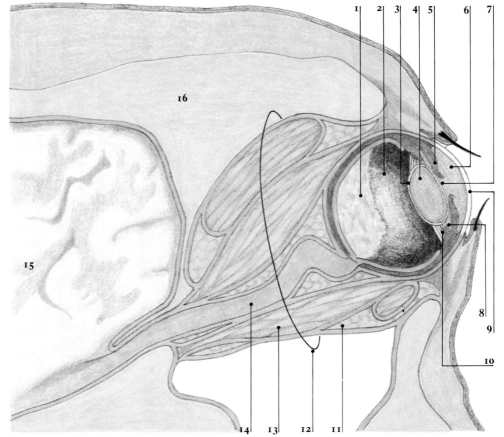

The eye of the dog

putty-like mass, easily moulded into a lens shape by the surrounding elastic capsule, attached by fine suspensory ligaments to the inside wall of the eye, just behind the iris at the ciliary processes. Muscle fibres form a ring around the ciliary region.

Because of fluid pressure within the eye, the capsule of the lens is normally under tension, and somewhat flattened. When the muscular ring contracts, tension is released and the capsule moulds the lens into a rounder shape, causing its focus to change. This change is known as accommodation; while young humans can accommodate very well, the process is much less active in the dog and its eyes are therefore much less suited for near vision.

Having been slightly refracted again at the lens, the light rays go deeper, passing through the gelatinous mass called the vitreous body. Little refraction occurs here and the focused rays impinge on the inner, sensory layer of the eye, the retina. This consists of several cell layers, and the light-sensitive layer is, strangely, furthest away from the source of light and nearer the sclera. Light must therefore pass through the thickness of the retina to reach the sensory cells, known because of their shapes as rods and cones. In the human eye, the cells of the central area of the retina, where fine detail can be appreciated, are all cones; they are associated with sharp vision and also with colour vision. A mixture of rods and cones occurs in the peripheral areas of the human retina; vision here is less acute, colour vision occurs only in good light, and in poor light only the peripheral area functions, the central area being blind.

It follows that where rods are numerous vision is less acute, colour is poorly differentiated and 'night vision' is possible. The central area of dog retina contains, in contrast to that of humans, a mixture of rods and cones, and the dog is therefore unable to see fine detail and incapable of little, if any true colour vision though all wavelengths will stimulate the retina.

Stereoscopic and binocular vision

The image focused on to the retina is inverted, but as objects are 'seen' the right way up, some mechanism for re-inversion must occur. Once rods and cones have been stimulated, they pass information on to a chain of nerve cells in the inner layers of the retina. Processes from these cells pass towards the posterior pole and converge on the off-centre optic nerve; as no sensory cells are found where the fibres exit, this region is the blind spot. The optic nerve leads to the underside of the brain where, in primitive vertebrates such as fish, all the fibres cross over to enter the opposite side of the brain. In humans, half the fibres remain on the same side. This arrangement may be responsible for stereoscopic vision where the left side of the brain receives information from the left half of each eye and interprets it in three dimensions, righting the image. In the dog only about one-quarter of the fibres remain on the same side, and stereoscopic vision may be much less than in humans.

For stereoscopic vision to occur, binocular vision must also be present. This happens when the visual fields of the two eyes overlap and is maximal when both eyes face forwards, minimal when they face sideways, as in rabbits. The eyes of the dog face somewhere between these extremes, with the optical axes lying between 20° and 50° of each other so that binocular vision is possible in an area in front of the dog.

The retina is loosely attached to the outer layers of the eye and held in place partly by intra-ocular pressure provided for by the continuous secretion of aqueous fluid from the ciliary region. To prevent excess pressure, the fluid drains off into the channel formed round the eye at the junction of cornea and iris. If pressure rises too high (glaucoma), the retina may become damaged, resulting in blurred vision or blindness. Between the sclera and the retina lies the choroid layer, which is largely responsible for the nutrition of the eye.

Tapetum lucidum

The choroid contains numerous darkly pigmented cells. At its anterior end it forms the coloured iris and acts as a curtain to prevent light from passing the wrong way through the sclera into the eye. Together with a special layer of cells just outside the sensory retina, the choroid also prevents reflection of light back on to the rods and cones except in an area round and particularly above the optic nerve. Here, the dark choroidal cells change their contents into rod-like crystals, which reflect light back towards the adjacent rods and cones.

This reflective area is called the *tapetum lucidum* (bright curtain) and is responsible for the eye shine observed when a light is shone into a dog's eyes at night. Its true function is to re-stimulate the retina so that movements can be seen more easily, and it is responsible for the cat being able to see in about one-sixth of the minimal illumination the human eye requires; the effect must be similar in dogs. This secondary stimulation of the retina is likely to reduce further the sharpness of vision, but also to increase night vision.

The eye responds to stimuli other than light. Pressure on the eye, for example, will be felt as such but will also be noticed as a patch of light. Pain can be felt, and this is the main type of sensation found on the cornea. The cornea is not supplied with blood vessels; it receives its nutriments from the aqueous fluid and from the lacrimal fluid bathing the eye.

The nasolacrimal duct

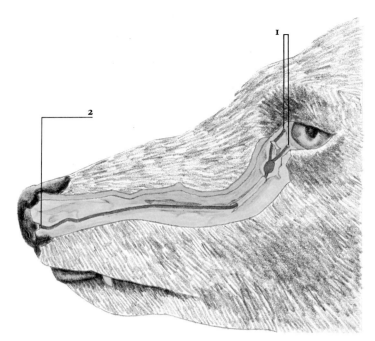

The eye is continually bathed with a layer of lacrimal (tear) fluid secreted from a gland above the eye. The fluid drains away through a small opening at the inner angle of each eyelid (1), into the naso-lacrimal duct (2) and eventually into the nostrils

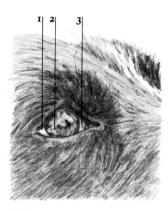

White sclera (1) appears as a continuation of the wall of the eye in the outer angle of upper and lower eyelids. The third eyelid (3) can be seen at the inner angle, near the iris (2)

Eyelids

Although the eye is a tough organ, upper and lower eyelids, and lashes, help to protect it from damage, closing reflexly if the eye is threatened. The dog has an additional 'third' eyelid, or nictitating membrane, which lies under the inner angle of the eyelids. It cannot be moved voluntarily but when the eye is pulled deeper into the socket by muscle action, the membrane is pushed across the eye.

A dog can move its eyes independently of the head which means that the animal can keep a moving object focussed on to the central area of the retina without too much head movement. Eye movements are brought about by action of muscles which run from the wall of the socket (orbit) to the eyeball; the arrangement of these muscles makes possible all movements of the eye, and in addition extra muscles can pull the eye deeper to provide extra protection.

Some breeds appear to rely on sight more than others; the Greyhound, for example, is more visually orientated than the Terrier, which relies on the sense of smell. This does not mean that one breed has better sight or sense of smell than another but that it uses that sense in preference.

None of the senses remains unchanged through life. In the puppy, the eyelids are secondarily closed until about two weeks of age, and it is therefore not surprising that other ocular structures and functions are not fully developed – the eyes only become fully functional by about six weeks. With age changes occur, and the lens commonly becomes harder and sclerosed.

Hearing & Balance

The ear on the outside of the dog's head is in reality a sound-collecting funnel known as the pinna and forms part of the external ear. The deeper part of the funnel is not easily seen, though it can be felt, and is attached to the bony skull low down at the back of the head.

The external ear leads down to the middle ear, a cavity in one of the skull bones and closed off from the external ear by a thin, semi-transparent tympanic membrane or eardrum. The cavity is also connected to the pharynx, at the back of the nose, by a narrow auditory tube which is normally closed but can be opened by swallowing in order to equalize pressure on each side of the tympanic membrane. Within the cavity is a chain of small bones (ossicles), named malleus, incus and stapes from their shapes of hammer, anvil and stirrup.

On the inside wall of the cavity, nearer to the brain, are two openings leading into a system of fluid-filled bony tubes forming the inner ear. Part of the system, the cochlea, is coiled like a snail shell; it starts at the vestibule, a large chamber, which in the opposite direction leads into three bony semi-circular canals, associated with the balance mechanism.

Mammals generally rely on the sense of smell more than on that of hearing, but the dog can still hear sound waves ranging from 20 to about 40,000 hertz (cycles per second). This upper limit is considerably higher than the human limit of about 20,000 hertz and is responsible for the dog's ability to hear high-pitched sounds inaudible to the human ear. The dog may also be more efficient in locating the direction of sound waves because the pinna is highly mobile and each ear can be moved independently in the direction of the sound source without necessarily moving the head. In all mammals, the two ears are a finite distance apart and unless the sound source is directly in front or behind, it will arrive at one ear later than at the other; turning the head will alter this and the direction can be determined.

Sound waves travel down the tube of the external ear and impinge on the tympanic membrane, causing it to vibrate. Any movement of the membrane in turn makes the ossicles vibrate. By the time the movement has reached stapes the force is increased and exerts pressure on the fluid within the cochlea; the pressure is released by the membrane between the middle and the inner ear bulging outwards.

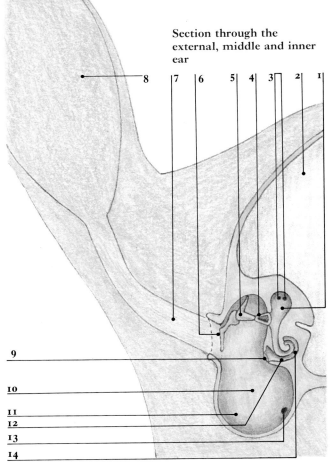

Section through the external, middle and inner ear

The tympanic membrane, to which the malleus is attached, separates the external ear from the middle ear. The stapes is attached to the membrane covering the vestibular window. The cochlear part of the inner ear is concerned with hearing, the vestibular part with balance

Key:
1 Vestibule; 2 Cranial cavity; 3 Openings into canals leading to inner ear; 4 Stapes; 5 Incus; 6 Malleus; 7 Ear canal; 8 Pinna; 9 Cochlear window; 10 Middle ear cavity; 11 Tympanic bulla; 12 Spiral lamina; 13 Opening of auditory tube to pharynx; 14 Part of cochlear canal

In sniffing, smells are wafted through the incisive duct (1) to the vomeronasal organ (2), and stimulated by a nerve (3) joining the olfactory nerve fibers (4) in the area nearest to the cranial cavity (5)

Section through the nasal cavity on the right side

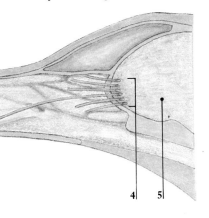

The bony canals of the cochlea contain a narrower system of membranous tubes known as the cochlear duct. Suspended in the cochlea, its soft wall is moved by sound waves, but although one side of the wall contains special sensory cells which respond to sound vibrations, this in itself will not differentiate sound of different frequencies. The wall is wider and less tense at the blind tip of the coiled tube than at the vestibular end, and a particular frequency may cause a particular part of the wall to resonate and stimulate local sensory cells. The nerve impulses so generated are transmitted to the brain via the cochlear nerve and interpreted as sound.

Balance

The inner ear functions not only as the organ of hearing, but also helps to maintain balance. The cochlear duct is connected by a narrow tube to the vestibular system which includes three fluid-filled, semi-circular canals and two other dilated chambers or sacs. When the head is turned, fluid moves and stimulates sensory cells which send information via the vestibular nerve to the brain. Here the motion is interpreted and appropriate muscular activity ensues to maintain balance, to hold the head in the correct position, or to move the eyes as necessary. Movement of the head in any direction can be recognized because the three semi-circular canals and ducts are at right angles to each other; any disturbance of the vestibular system can lead to a nervous disorder in which the eyes are in constant involuntary movement (nystagmus). The fluid-filled sacs in the vestibule contain sensors which respond to gravity and linear motion.

When a running dog turns, the head turns first. This stimulates the vestibular system before the body has had time to fall, and the animal adjusts its muscles to prevent falling. Motion sickness occurs when the vestibular system is stimulated without the normal muscular activity present.

Sensations from Internal Organs

Some sensory organs which receive the distant stimuli of light and sound are at least partly on the outside of the body unlike the so-called enteroceptors or internal sensory organs. The organ responsible for the sense of smell or olfaction is found deep inside the head.

Smell

Receptors for the sense of smell occur in the upper, innermost part of each nasal cavity. Minute particles of odoriferous substances are deposited on these receptors, particularly when sniffing, and in some manner not yet understood cause the cells to initiate impulses in the olfactory nerves which are interpreted by the brain as being due to a particular 'smell'.

The dog, like most mammals but unlike apes and their relatives, has an acute sense of smell. This is at least partly due to the fact that the lining of the nasal cavity, being folded, has a large surface area where numerous receptors can be accommodated. The sense of smell allows the dog not only to find acceptable food, but also to reject unsuitable material. It is also concerned with socially important odours, which may be individually identifiable, and aids identification of the opposite sex. The odour that arises from an animal is complex in origin, but clearly comes from body secretions, including those of skin glands and the specialized glands near the anus of dogs.

The forked tongue of a snake is used to sample the air by flicking it in and out of the mouth. When withdrawn into the mouth the animal inserts the forked tips into two openings in the roof of the mouth, which lead into blind tubes, known as vomeronasal organs. They are stimulated by a nerve which joins the olfactory nerve, and are used by the snake as olfactory organs. Most mammals have similar organs. When a dog and bitch meet, they will investigate the genital areas with their muzzles and then flutter the tips of their tongues.

Taste

Taste is a complex sensation involving firstly responses to substances which humans identify as salt, acid, bitter and sweet, and secondly responses to touch, temperature and pain. In addition the sense of smell is an important part of the sense of taste because scent particles from food in the mouth are passed up into the back of the nasal cavities where they stimulate the olfactory area.

The main site of taste receptors or taste buds is the upper surface of the tongue, though they also occur in the throat. The tongue is roughened by papillae, some of which resemble microscopic button mushrooms and are known as fungiform papillae; it is on these that most taste receptors are found.

Pain and Other Sensations

Sensation from organs in the chest is minimal. The heart can feel pain when deprived of oxygen, and the smooth membrane or pleura covering the lungs can also give rise to pain sensation when diseased, but the lungs themselves are insensitive to pain and may be diseased for a long time without any symptoms. The larger air passages such as the trachea and the main bronchi are sensitive and irritation causes reflex coughing.

Organs within the chest, abdomen and pelvis are called viscera; sensation arising from the abdominal organs is spoken of as visceral, but much of this does not reach conscious levels. Receptors on the lining of the stomach register acidity or alkalinity (the pH factor) of the contents. This may not reach conscious levels, but is concerned with the control of stomach movements. In common with the rest of the alimentary, urinary and genital systems, receptors in the muscle layer of the stomach are excited by distension and by muscle contraction. Over-distension or strong contraction may cause pain, but this is due to stretching of the outer covering, the peritoneum, as pain receptors are not present in the organs themselves. The gut can also distinguish between gas and solid matter, and in the urethra, receptors can recognize fluid flow.

Receptors in muscles and joints, known as proprioceptors, are important because they enable the animal to control its movement and stance efficiently. Special receptors, called spindle receptors from their shape, occur in muscles; they are responsive to the degree and speed of muscle stretch as in a 'knee jerk' when sudden stretching of the thigh muscles by a tap on the kneecap tendon results in involuntary contraction of the muscle and straightening of the knee. Pain receptors are probably also present in muscles; in tendons, other receptors cause muscles to relax if too much strain is put on them.

Limb position sensors occur in joints; the most important is the receptor which signals the position of a limb and the angle between the bones at a joint. This allows the dog to consciously recognize the position of a limb in space and to move it blindly, to scratch an ear for example. Many of the sensory mechanisms in the dog have effects similar to those in humans. Some are simple sensations (touch), while others involve combined sensations (nausea); some are associated with the outer part of the body, others with internal structures. The sensation of pain often appears to come from a site on the body surface, at some distance from its true origin; this is called referred pain and diagnosis of its origin can be difficult.

Dogs can taste sour (acid) food over the whole tongue; sweet taste (*striped*) occurs at the sides and tip, salt (*blue*) along the sides and at the base of the tongue. Water taste (*green*) occurs only at the tip. Individual dogs vary in their appreciation of taste, which can be altered by learning

FOOD & FEEDING

Although dogs are classed as carnivores, they would not have attained their remarkable integration into human society if they had relied on meat as their sole source of nourishment. By showing the same adaptability and flexibility in their eating patterns as in other behavioural respects – herding, guarding and retrieving – dogs adapted from an early stage in their domestication so that, unlike cats, they did not have to depend on a near exclusive diet of meat. In a nutritional sense dogs are almost as omnivorous as their human companions, but their inherent carnivore behaviour has been an important facet of their development. The instinct to chase and bring down game with speed and control has played a major part in their hunting and sporting relationship with man, and it has progressed from these activities to the sophisticated levels of Guide Dogs for the Blind or Hearing Dogs for the Deaf.

Today, relatively few breeds have the opportunity or even the ability to hunt, kill and devour the flesh of their prey. Their remarkable adaptability has lent itself to the development of breeds with other characteristics, each with its own appeal, but few of which would equip any modern breed to return to a free-living carnivorous life style, although many mongrels readily do so.

Dogs are therefore almost totally dependent on their owners or keepers to supply them with food in the quantity, regularlity, and nutritional quality which will ensure growth, maintenance and reproduction throughout their relatively long lives. Together with cats, dogs are in this respect almost unique among domesticated animals; cattle, sheep, pigs, and poultry may be as dependent on man for their daily feed, but rarely attain their allotted life-span. It is a hard fact of farming economics that as soon as cost exceeds productivity, life expectancy becomes short.

The relative longevity of companion animals and the absence of a cost/productivity constraint on their feeding puts them in a nutritional category more akin to that of man. One of the unwelcome consequences of this similarity is sharing with man some of the degenerative conditions of middle and old age, such as obesity, arthritis, diabetes, cardiac disease and cancer. It may even be that this shared susceptibility to comparable diseases may be another link in the human–dog bond.

The objective of feeding dogs is the maintenance of health and well-being during all stages of their natural life-span, an objective which can be focused and quantified by applying it to the various stages of the life-cycle.

Birth to Weaning

Bitch milk, the sole food of puppies for the first few weeks of life, differs significantly from cow's milk as shown in the table.

With the exception of lactose (milk sugar), the milk provided for a puppy by its mother has about twice as much of the major nutrients as cow's milk and the latter is inadequate as a substitute. In order to obtain the same amount of nourishment, a puppy would have to consume twice as much cow's milk as bitch milk to meet its needs, and the result would be a serious impairment to growth and development, excessive fluid and lactose intake, and continuous and severe diarrhoea. If for any reason suckling puppies require supplementary feeding, they should be given a proprietary bitch-milk substitute. There is little justification for the commonly held belief that goat's milk, which differs little from cow's milk, is a suitable substitute.

A novice breeder may be concerned about the amount of milk a litter of puppies is getting from their dam. While it is important to know this, in practice it is not so difficult to judge, because a well-fed litter is usually quiet and lies

Types of milk
(250ml/⅓pt approx)

	BITCH %	COW %
Protein	7.1	3.4
Fat	8.3	3.7
Lactose	3.8	4.8
Calcium	0.23	0.12
Phosphorus	0.16	0.10
Energy (kcalories)	160.23	95.00

sleeping heaped on each other or their mother for much of the time, particularly after a period of suckling. An underfed litter is much less restful, keeping up a plaintive and unhappy crying in their unavailing quest to fill their little bellies. It is important to recognize this state of affairs at an early stage because it may be a sign of a sudden drop in milk secretion by the bitch due to one of several possible causes, such as inflammation of the mammary gland (mastitis) or of the womb (metritis), both of which require immediate veterinary attention. If one or two weaker puppies of an otherwise well-fed litter seems to be getting less than their fair share, the owner must make sure that they are given preferential treatment, by ensuring an opportunity of suckling the mother, or by supplementing with a proprietary milk replacer.

As the pups grow older and stronger, the bitch will leave them for longer periods, so beginning the natural process of weaning. The puppies can then be offered small amounts of a good-quality commercial puppy food or any other complete food mixed to a gruel with a little boiled, warm water or warm milk. All of these foods are best warmed to blood heat, initially in order to start the puppies on solid foods. Even older animals appreciate warm rather than cold food if their appetite is impaired.

Hand-rearing a puppy demands much devoted care: frequent and small meals of an appropriate milk substitute should be administered through a miniature bottle, the puppy held almost upright, and the tiny body supported and warmed in the palm of the hand

Weaning
Many breeders have their own recipes for weaning puppies from their mother's milk. In general, weaning starts at three to four weeks when puppies are gradually introduced to milk-sloppy baby food. Weaning is usually complete at five to six weeks, when the pups are able to eat and drink on their own.

Most responsible breeders will issue a puppy's new owner with a diet sheet listing the types of food on which a puppy has been weaned. It is sensible to follow the breeder's instructions for at least a few days after bringing the puppy home, before gradually changing over to a new regime and diet over several days. An expert opinion about a suitable diet is always worth seeking on the first visit to the local veterinary surgeon. As puppies grow older the food should be made firmer, with less added water or milk, and the quantity steadily increased.

Feeding frequency
A newborn puppy spends much of its time suckling from its mother, but as the natural weaning process approaches, the bitch permits fewer and fewer suckling periods. The puppies are therefore forced to fill in the lengthening 'hungry gaps' by recourse to solid food. When the pups are fully weaned they should be fed about four times during a fourteen to sixteen hour period. There are no rigid time factors for reducing the feeding frequency with age, but a decrease in meal times becomes a natural progression as the puppy matures and its obvious need and enthusiasm for first one, then another of the regular feeds gradually diminishes.

The adult is usually fed once or twice a day; as a generalization, smaller breeds should be given two meals and larger breeds one only. This is because smaller breeds have a higher energy requirement than larger dogs in relation to body weight. However, if a small and a large dog live together in the same household, it is only fair to give the large dog a token meal at the same time as his diminutive friend is being fed.

The Growing Puppy
The period from weaning to maturity is, nutritionally, one of the most important times in the dog's lifetime, equalled only by the lactation period in

Weaned puppies quickly learn to cope with competition from litter mates and will fight for the last scrap in a shared food bowl

the nursing bitch. In relation to body weight, a growing puppy has two to three times the requirements for the essential nutrients which it will have as an adult. During the crucial growth period, the puppy is building new bone, muscles, nervous tissue, indeed all the body components, as well as maintaining and replacing energy and tissues for day to day existence and wear and tear. This remarkable process, whereby non-living components of food are transformed by the digestion into pulsating, living, breathing body cells, is one of the more underrated miracles of biology.

The levels of essential nutrients, such as protein, fat, calcium, phosphorus, and vitamins, needed by a growing puppy have been researched and proved in many nutritional studies. A balanced diet of all the essential nutrients is particularly important during the growth period. This is when the inherited potential for growth and development is realized, or not, in the transformation of food into bone and muscle; serious imbalance of one or more of the major nutrients or vitamins during growth can result in failure to achieve the true physique and conformation of the breed. An imbalance can result from a deficiency or, more commonly, from an excess of an essential nutrient, particularly if this is one of those involved in bone growth, such as calcium, phosphorus, or vitamins A and D.

Hazards of the all-meat diet
Because the dog is classed as a carnivore and meat is part of its natural food, a misapprehension persists that muscle meat will provide for all or most of its nutritional needs. Even in its wild state, the dog did not live exclusively on muscle meat; where the prey was small enough, the whole animal would be consumed, which provided the optimum balance of protein, minerals, and vitamins from the muscle, bones, liver, kidneys and stomach contents.

A diet of muscle meat alone is almost totally deficient in the calcium essential for normal bone development and is also deficient or imbalanced in a number of other essential nutrients. Such a diet, unless supplemented with calcium, phosphorus and vitamins, can result in poor growth, misshapen long bones, enlarged and painful joints, reluctance to move and even spontaneous fractures, particularly in young growing dogs of large and giant breeds.

The amount of calcium and phosphorus needed to supplement meat is relatively small; a pinch (2 grams) of raw bone to every 4 oz (100 g) of meat provides the right balance, or the recommended amount of a proprietary calcium/phosphorus supplement.

Excess supplementation
Probably more abnormalities of growth and development in puppies are due to excessive use of the many vitamin and mineral supplements available than to nutritional deficiencies. Again, growing dogs of the large and giant breeds are the most vulnerable; already programmed by selective breeding over many generations for fast bone growth, the balance in these breeds between the rate of bone growth and the ability to lay down the calcium and phosphorus which gives the bone its strength and rigidity is highly delicate.

It is natural for the owner of a new puppy of a giant breed to want it to grow into a giant among giants, and feed it accordingly. This tendency should be resisted. Steady growth on a standard diet will provide for a much sounder skeleton, and the eventual size of the adult will probably be as great as that of a youngster which has been 'forced' on a diet enriched with a motley of supplements; the freedom from bony abnormalities will certainly be greater.

Stomach upsets in puppies

Almost all puppies, like other young mammals, have an inveterate curiosity about their surroundings. This manifests itself particularly in the attempted consumption of inedible materials, such as coal, gravel, sticks, socks, slippers, furniture, etc. Incredibly, most puppies survive such experiences, though toxic household cleaners and garden pesticides, weedkillers and antifreeze for the car are common hazards which have proved too much for even the most iron-stomached puppy. If a puppy is thought to have had access to poisonous material, it should be taken immediately to the veterinarian, together with the container of the offending material.

The odd instance of vomiting recently ingested rubbish is par for the course for most puppies, and other material may simply pass through the gut and be evacuated with the normal bowel movements. By and large, if an object is sufficiently small to be swallowed it stands a good chance of passing safely through the intestines, but objects such as needles and splinters of wood or bone may penetrate the gut wall and require surgical removal.

Occasional loose bowel motions are, like occasional vomiting, almost a normal feature of puppyhood, but persistent diarrhoea coupled with loss of appetite or general condition requires veterinary attention. Loose bowel motions without loss of condition or appetite may on the other hand be due to some simple dietary constituent which the puppy is not digesting properly. Milk is one such component. Although milk is the puppy's natural food during the first few weeks of life, the ability to digest milk sugar (lactose) decreases as it grows older. Many animals can digest the lactose in milk satisfactorily, even as adults, but in a few instances this ability seems to decrease to so low a level that the lactose passes through the intestine largely undigested and causes fluid bowel motions. The problem of soft bowel motions in an otherwise healthy young dog may be solved by withdrawing milk from its diet.

Feeding behaviour and management

For most dogs, particularly when young and active, meal time is the major event of the day. Many dogs have retained the natural primitive instinct to compete for available food, an instinct which in the wild may mean the difference between survival and death. Some dogs will behave in an aggressive or defensive manner when approached at feeding time; in a puppy such behaviour may be amusing, but in the adult it is, at the least, undesirable and at worst risky, particularly to young children.

Undesirable feeding behaviour should be prevented from developing at an early stage, by deliberately approaching the puppy while it is feeding, patting or moving the bowl around, rewarding the puppy for permitting approaches and chastizing it if it objects. In this way, the puppy will grow up confident that its food will not be taken away and does not need to be defended. At the same time, a degree of defensive behaviour to food can have practical aspects in a household with two or more dogs: a finicky or fussy eater who picks at its food and walks away when fed on its own will often discover a new and healthy appetite faced with a canine companion about to empty the food bowl.

The Adult Dog

Although adulthood is considered as a relatively stable period from the nutritional aspect, some less obvious, slow or cyclical changes do affect feeding behaviour. The young dog, for example, does not suddenly change from frivolous puppyhood to staid maturity at the moment of reaching adult body

A young puppy on his own should be weaned from an aggressive defence of his food bowl. Temporary removal of the food and direct physical contact during feeding will help to teach him 'table manners'

development. A number of breeds, the Irish Setter being a prime example, remain energetically playful for a year or two longer, and this youthful behaviour is reflected in greater food requirements than in later life. In bitches, the biannual heat, or oestrus, may affect food intake, and for all dogs the season of the year often influences their energy expenditure and consequent food requirement; at winter temperatures, dogs in unheated housing require significantly more food than in summer.

Obesity

About thirty per cent of dogs are overweight in the opinion of veterinary surgeons. Obesity is by far the most common disease in the dog population, and according to one survey there would appear to be a tendency for obese dogs to have obese owners. Some breeds are more predisposed to obesity than others, with Labradors, Beagles, Poodles, and Dachshunds leading the field; Setters, Greyhounds, Afghans and Great Danes are rarely seen to be overweight. In all breeds, neutering of either sex increases the likelihood of obesity.

Obesity is usually due to the owner overfeeding the dog. Just like obese people who frequently protest that they eat little or nothing, the owner of an obese dog will maintain that the dog is getting only a small amount of food. This may well be true, as an obese dog, once it has attained its steady state of overweight, probably requires less food to maintain its heavy body weight and sluggish behaviour than it needed when it was lean and active. Dogs which are bored compensate with food, and busy owners assuage their guilt complexes with frequent snacks and choice tidbits from the table. Some dogs are known to be dining out, paying surreptitious visits to kindly neighbours.

There is not actuarial evidence that obesity significantly curtails life expectancy for the dog, but it is almost certainly true. The obese dog is more prone to diseases of the skin, heart, joints and lungs, to diabetes and to heat exhaustion; it is a high-risk patient for any surgical procedure under anaesthesia due to the technical problems of locating anything in the mass of fat which not only lies under the skin, but also envelopes the organs of the abdominal cavity. Apart from the increased risk factors for the obese dog, the quality of its life is impaired and it becomes listless, slow-moving and disinterested in its surroundings, and a poorer companion.

The cure for obesity – in dog as in man – is to reduce energy intake to less than energy output. In order to meet the deficit between income (intake) and expenditure (output), the obese dog must mobilize its capital of energy reserves stored as fat; this inevitably reduces them. The principle is simple, the practice difficult, and it is often a good idea to seek the help and advice of a veterinarian. He will review the dog's diet and advise on its modification; specially formulated obesity diets are available and have been used successfully.

The Breeding Bitch

Although most pedigree dogs are bred by professional breeders, the owner of an individual pet bitch may wish to breed from her, perhaps only once, to ensure succession or companionship for the existing animal, or just for the experience and satisfaction. Before embarking on such a course, two major responsibilities must be fully appreciated: the care of the bitch and puppies over the period of pregnancy and lactation, and the disposal of the puppies to good homes. Timing of the pregnancy must also be considered; it would be foolish to have a bitch mated three months before a planned family holiday. A bitch with a litter of pups requires a great deal of attention and commitment and cannot be

Scavenging is instinctive in many dogs, and left to their own devices they will steal any food lying around; the more crafty ones make foraging expeditions outside of the home

fostered off to boarding kennels or neighbours, however friendly. A pregnancy requires careful planning to ensure that time and facilities are adequate to the undertaking; to ensure a healthy litter, special nutritional considerations must be given to the bitch during and after the gestation period.

Mating and pregnancy

Provided the bitch is normally fed on a sound, balanced diet and is generally in good condition, no special dietary changes are required before mating. If she is obese, she should be slimmed to the appropriate weight and dimensions.

The gestation period is about nine weeks, and for the first six weeks of pregnancy the daily diet needs little change or supplements apart from possible minor modifications necessary to maintain stable condition and body weight. During this period, the foetuses are so small as to have only a negligible effect on the bitch's resources – the weight of each foetus of a Beagle bitch is less than half an ounce (ten grams) after six weeks' gestation.

During the last three weeks the food intake may be increased by about ten per cent each week, so that in the last week the bitch may be receiving about forty per cent more than in early pregnancy. These increments are broad guidelines which may be modified up or down according to body condition, breed, temperament, and (unquantifiable) number of puppies. Regardless of the amount of increase, food in the last two weeks should be given in two or possibly three meals per day. By this time the developing uterus and its contents of rapidly growing foetuses, foetal fluids and membranes will be occupying a large proportion of the abdominal cavity, and several small daily meals are easier to accommodate and digest than one large meal.

During the last day or two before whelping, a bitch may well go off her food, but provided she seems otherwise healthy, this is nothing to worry about.

The nursing bitch

A bitch with suckling puppies requires at least three times her normal food ration for the first two or three weeks in order to meet the demands of her puppies and her own increased metabolic requirements. Immediately after whelping she should be offered frequent small meals with plenty of fluid while the uterus is returning to its normal size. Food requirements and intake will quickly increase if sufficient opportunity and appetizing food is given. Any sudden decrease in food intake during the first week or so after whelping should be treated with concern as it may be an early sign of inflammation of the mammary glands or of the womb. These conditions require immediate veterinary attention as they threaten the survival of the litter.

Despite the enormous demands the puppies make, it is quite possible to maintain the bitch in good condition during the nursing period. As long as the food is soundly balanced and nutritionally complete, mineral and vitamin supplements are unnecessary. Any of the proprietary complete dog foods, if fed in correct amounts, will meet the bitch's needs. Most foods by reputable manufacturers have been subjected to trials involving bitches of various breeds, the same food being given from before mating until after weaning, with the puppies reared to six months in some cases in order to gain practical evidence of their adequacy.

Some bitches will become bored with the same food fed three or four times a day, and their interest should be kept up by providing a variety of different foods. Obtain veterinary advice before giving vitamin or mineral supplements and do not exceed the dose rates on the label.

Hand-rearing puppies

Occasionally a bitch is unable to suckle one or all of her puppies, either due to illness or loss of milk. Provided the puppies are otherwise healthy they may survive if given dedicated and near-continuous attention; for at least the first week they are incapable of doing anything for themselves, and all bodily functions must be stimulated by hand. Correct temperature, best achieved in an incubator, is of the utmost importance (see also page 127).

If all these various demands can be met, it is possible for hand-reared puppies to survive. Food, which must be formulated as near as possible to bitch's milk, should be given at approximately four-hour intervals, warmed to body heat and administered by a small syringe, miniature feeding bottle or an intra-gastric tube.

Types of Food

The feeding of dogs has changed radically since the early 1950s. Prior to that dogs were chiefly fed on butchers' scraps, table leftovers, or meat from the knacker's yard. However, changes in legislation relating to knacker meat, reduction in the availability of cheap butchers' scraps and table leftovers, and the tremendous increase in supermarket shopping have all combined to make such feeding methods less feasible or attractive. Dog owners have turned to foods manufactured and marketed exclusively for the feeding of dogs.

Prepared foods

These foods are available in three basic forms: canned, semi-moist, and dry. Frozen foods and sausages are also available, but generally less common. The main characteristics and a typical analysis of canned, semi-moist, and dry foods are shown in the table opposite.

A wide variety of prepared pet foods is available from pet shops and supermarkets; the choice is influenced by the colour, texture, smell and price of the food, and by the reputation of the manufacturer and the dog's reaction. Increasingly, nutrient information is included on labels, and it always pays to read this carefully. Some foods are formulated to meet all the dog's nutritional requirements (complete foods), others are designed to be fed with other foods (complementary foods).

Proprietary pet foods usually give feeding guidelines for breeds of particular size and weight, and the foods have often undergone extensive nutritional testing to gain practical experience of their use. More detailed information is usually available from manufacturers if required.

The basic role of a complete dog food is to provide in a balanced and palatable form all the nutrients required for the maintenance of health. Nutritionally, this is more demanding than that of any human food, as no convenience food attempts to provide a complete source of nourishment over a prolonged period. In practice, most dogs are rarely fed exclusively on prepared foods, but nutritional safety margins are such that an imbalance would be unlikely in a regime based on good-quality prepared foods as the main nutrient source.

Canned foods

Canned or tinned foods are distinguished from semi-moist and dry types by their higher palatability, moist and meaty texture and by their content of cooked, fresh materials. Most contain added minerals and vitamins to balance those occurring naturally in the meat. They may or may not contain cereal which, if present, gives a higher energy content and usually alters the texture to a more loaf-like appearance. Canned foods which do not contain cereal should be mixed with a biscuit or other carbohydrate source, otherwise their relatively

	CANNED	SEMI-MOIST	DRY (complete)
Appearance	Soft, meaty	Firmer, some look like ground or cubed meat	Hard, particulate, various shapes & sizes
Smell	Meaty, fishy	Little	Little
Ingredients	Meat & meat products, fish, cereal, vegetable protein, vitamins & minerals	Meat, poultry or fish meals; cereals, fat, vegetable protein, vitamins & minerals	Cereals, meat, poultry or fish meals; fat, vitamins & minerals
Preservation	Heat sterilized; sealed containers	Heat sterilized, with preservatives	Heat treatment; too dry for bacterial growth
Palatability	● ● ●	● ●	●
Cost per meal	● ● ●	● ●	●
Nutritional completeness	Most meet the nutritional requirements of adult dogs. Some also meet requirements for growth and reproduction		
Typical analysis in %			
Moisture	80	25	8
Protein	8	19	21
Fat	5	9	8
Carbohydrate	4	40	55
Calcium	0.4	0.8	1.1
Phosphorus	0.3	0.8	0.9
Energy: kJ/kg	3906	13020	15120
kcal/100g	93	310	360

high protein content is used wastefully as an energy source; the most important function of animal protein is the building and/or replacement of body tissues.

The protein content of canned food, when expressed as a percentage of the total nutrients (other than water), is usually higher than that of dry and semi-moist foods. In the table above, protein represents about forty per cent of the total nutrients other than water, while the proportion of protein in relation to other nutrients in semi-moist and dry foods is about twenty-five and twenty-three per cent respectively. However, the quality of protein is as important as the quantity. Less is needed of high-quality than of low-quality protein, and nutritional evaluation of proprietary foods ensures that the ingredients meet the dog's needs in both respects. In addition to traditional animal proteins, high-quality vegetable protein is included in many canned foods.

Semi-moist foods
Specialized processing and preservation enable these foods to be maintained at a higher moisture content, twenty to twenty-five per cent, and a softer texture than dry foods, without the necessity for processing at high temperatures and packaging in sealed cans. Nutritionally, semi-moist foods are often formulated to provide all the nutrient requirements without other supplementary foods. Because of their higher calorie and lower water content, they should be fed in smaller amounts than canned foods, and dogs will require significantly more drinking water when receiving semi-moist or dry foods.

Dry foods
In Britain, the main type of dry food is a baked or expanded cereal-based 'mixer', used as a complementary food with canned foods or with other meat. It is primarily a high-energy source (as carbohydrate) as well as a useful source of protein, some vitamins and minerals, and dietary fibre. Complete dry foods contain a substantial amount of animal protein, such as meat, fish, or poultry. They also have added fat, vitamins and minerals to meet nutritional requirements and may be fed dry or moistened with warm water, or milk for puppies. Non-complete or complementary biscuits or meals are predominantly

cereal, though they may have added protein or minerals to provide an economical energy source when mixed with fresh or canned meat.

Home-made foods

Dogs can be fed nutritious and highly palatable diets if their owners are prepared to expend the necessary time, money and care. Many dogs are fed on the same diet as their owners, and for the particularly discerning there are cookery books with canine recipes. In all cases, the diet must be nutritionally balanced and contain basic nutrients, vitamins and minerals.

With the exception of vitamin C (ascorbic acid), a dog requires the same major and minor nutrients as man: protein, fat, minerals, trace elements, and vitamins. Provided that correct amounts are present in the diet, no useful purpose is served by giving more. Over-supplementation with vitamins and minerals is probably a greater cause of nutrient imbalance and disease in companion animals than is insufficiency of any of them.

Vegetarian foods

Provided that the diet contains a generous supply of animal proteins, such as eggs, milk and cheese, dogs can be maintained in good health on a vegetarian diet of cereals and other vegetable matter. However, such diets are bulky and high in fibre, with a lower dry-matter digestibility than a meat-based diet. The quantity and frequency may have to be increased, with a corresponding increase in quantity and frequency of bowel motions.

Protein

Butchers' scrap meat tends to have a high fat content, and a significant amount of trimming may be necessary. Scrap fish and liver may be difficult to come by in sufficient amounts, but are excellent protein sources. Cooked eggs and cheese are also generally well accepted and are useful protein sources; milk and milk powder should be used in only limited amounts as they cause loose bowel motions. Dried beans and peas make a useful protein contribution, but have a relatively low palatability and a well-deserved reputation for causing flatulence.

Fat

This is readily and cheaply available in butchers' scrap meat and is an essential nutrient in itself, as well as a vehicle for fat-soluble vitamins. Poly-unsaturated vegetable oils, such as corn, soya bean, safflower or cottonseed oils, also provide the essential fatty acids and are readily accepted mixed in with the food. Fat is a rich energy source, and a high-fat diet will reduce the intake of other essential nutrients; it should therefore be used in moderation, particularly for growing puppies and nursing bitches.

Carbohydrate

Dogs readily accept carbohydrate-rich foods, such as bread, boiled potatoes, rice and pasta, though the bland taste of the foods may require enhancement with others of animal origin to improve palatability. Bread and potatoes also make some contribution to protein intake, but the contribution of rice and pasta, especially when highly refined, is relatively low; they should never provide a major proportion of the diet.

Vitamins

Most vitamins are naturally contained in a mixed diet of meat, liver, fish, eggs, milk and cereals. However, prolonged cooking destroys some vitamins, notably vitamin A and B_1 (thiamin). The cooking water should be fed with the other constituents to preserve the vitamins and minerals leached out into it.

Minerals

Natural sources of calcium and phosphorus include milk or milk powder, cheese, whole eggs, sterilized bonemeal and ground bone. Other minerals and trace elements are provided in sufficiency by a mixture of various foods. Green and root vegetables provide a useful and relatively cheap source of vitamins, protein and vegetable fibre. However, their palatability is relatively low, and dogs may be put off their meals if vegetables are included in large amounts.

Water

Although not a nutrient, water is the most important single component of the diet. A deficiency of water will cause disease and death more quickly than the lack of any other nutrient. Dogs have been known to survive for many weeks without food, but life expectancy is numbered in days in the absence of water. The amount of drinking water required varies according to the size of dog, type of food and environmental temperature. These variations are best met by permitting free access to fresh drinking water at all times, or at least three times a day.

A dog weighing about 31 lb (14 kg) will normally require 1.8 pints (1 litre) of water per day. If it is fed on dry food, virtually all of this water must be taken in as drinking water; with moist food, such as canned food or cooked meat with about seventy-five per cent water, substantially less water needs to be drunk to make up the total requirement. In hot weather, or after prolonged or strenuous exercise, water requirement may be twice the normal. Sea water should not be drunk, but if it does happen, an abundant supply of fresh water must be given, particularly before and during a long car journey. Dogs have died of salt poisoning after a day at the seaside lapping at the waves and then being confined in a hot car on the journey home.

Feeding guide for adult dogs

The following guidelines, based on prepared complete dog foods, are approximations. The daily requirements for individuals differ widely; the needs of a 60 lb (27 kg) Bulldog will be quite different from those of a Greyhound of similar weight. However, it is fairly easy to ascertain if an adult dog is being fed too much or too little and to adjust the amount accordingly.

	TOY BREEDS less than 10 lb (4.5 kg) eg Yorkshire Terrier, Toy Poodle, Chihuahua	SMALL BREEDS 10–20 lb (4.5–9 kg) eg West Highland Terrier, Beagle, Cavalier King Charles Spaniel	MEDIUM BREEDS 20–50 lb (9–23 kg) eg Airedale Terrier, Basset Hound, English Springer Spaniel	LARGE BREEDS 50–75 lb (23–34 kg) eg German Shepherd Dog, Labrador, Irish/ English Setter	GIANT BREEDS 75–140 lb (34–64 kg) eg Great Dane, Irish Wolfhound, Newfoundland
Approximate daily calorie needs	200–400 kcalories	400–700 kcalories	700–1400 kcalories	1400–1900 kcalories	1900–3000 kcalories
Canned dog food (395–400 g cans) with mixer biscuit, fed in proportions of 2:1 by volume	$\frac{1}{4}$–$\frac{1}{2}$ can	$\frac{1}{2}$–1 can	1–1$\frac{1}{2}$ cans	1$\frac{1}{2}$–2$\frac{1}{2}$ cans	2$\frac{1}{2}$–3$\frac{1}{2}$ cans
Semi-moist dog food (grams)	65–130 g	130–225 g	225–450 g	450–600 g	600–950 g
Dry dog food (grams)	55–110 g	110–190 g	190–380 g	380–530 g	530–830 g

MATING & REPRODUCTION

Some understanding of the canine 'facts of life' is helpful to most dog owners, either to promote or prevent the reproductive process, or simply to answer candid questions from children. Relatively few owners take the deliberate decision to breed from their bitch, but the recurring periods of heat or being in season pose questions about management, control, neutering, and mating.

Sexual Cycle of the Bitch

The pattern of sexual activity varies greatly among animals, frequent short periods of intense sexual activity being normal in some domestic species such as cows and sheep, while the dog (bitch) usually only has two periods of sexual activity in a year; occasionally there is only one or as many as three. Such a period is generally described as the bitch being in heat or in season; the physiological term is *oestrus*, from the Latin and meaning a gadfly and therefore frenzy. The bitch will permit mating to take place only when she is in season.

The physiological and behavioural changes which take place during the oestrous cycle of the bitch are controlled by the cyclical release of hormones acting on the ovaries and causing the release of the sex hormones, oestrogen and progesterone. Surgical removal of the ovaries (spaying or neutering) abolishes these cyclical changes and prevents mating and conception. They can also be prevented by the administration of synthetic hormones – the canine equivalent of the contraceptive pill – which interfere with the normal sequence of events leading up to oestrus.

Puberty

The sex glands become functional, and the first heat period may occur, from the age of six months in the smaller breeds to twelve months or more in large and giant breeds. The timing of heat periods is to some extent influenced by the season of the year, the majority occurring during spring and autumn. It is advisable to note the dates of a bitch's heat periods in the household diary; boarding kennels usually enquire if a bitch is likely to come into season soon, necessitating appropriate arrangements, and on a family holiday a bitch in heat may be difficult to control. With two or more bitches in the household, heat periods may become synchronized, but there are plenty of exceptions.

The oestrous phases

At the beginning of the heat period, known as the pro-oestrous phase, the lips of the sexual orifice, the vulva, begin to swell and become more obvious, and the bitch will lick the region frequently. The swelling is followed in two to four days by a bloody discharge, and drops of blood may be the first obvious sign.

The pro-oestrous phase may last for eight to ten days during which time the bitch is often restless and excitable; she may drink water and urinate more frequently; even a perfectly house-trained bitch will occasionally have an accident indoors. She may also become more finicky with her food. Her attractiveness to male dogs will increase, but she will not permit mating to take place. Towards the end of this phase, the vulval discharge becomes less blood-stained, often quite clear, and the lips of the vulva become tense and hot, hence the description, in heat. This marks the beginning of the oestrous phase, when mating can and will take place, given the chance.

The combined length of the pro-oestrous and oestrous phases when the bitch is in heat or in season is usually about three weeks, with oestrus lasting on average nine days, but having a range of three to twenty-one days. Mating is permitted by the bitch only during the oestrous phase; she will sometimes adopt a position with arched back and if stroked over this area will stand quite still, tail held to the side, exposing her enlarged vulva. Great care must be taken at this time to prevent her from running outdoors to ardent suitors lying in wait. She should be confined to the garden under close supervision, and if she is small enough she can be carried to an exercise area at a distance from the house so as to avoid the tell-tale urine deposits round the house by which males are attracted.

False pregnancy

Assuming that mating has not taken place, the period after oestrus (metoestrus) is characterized by a steady reduction in the vulval swelling and discharge, a return to more normal behaviour and a loss of attractiveness to male dogs. This would be the beginning of pregnancy if mating had taken place, and many bitches undergo a false or pseudo-pregnancy. During this period, they may show many of the physical, physiological and psychological signs of pregnancy, with abdominal swelling, enlargement of the milk or mammary glands, and even milk secretion. Maternal instincts of collecting and nursing soft toys and of tearing up the bed are evident; a bitch may adopt other young animals such as the puppies of another bitch, kittens, or young rabbits. Pseudo-pregnancy invariably subsides, but may persist until the end of the normal period of pregnancy, sixty-three days. The condition can be diminished by plenty of exercise and mild laxatives, or, failing all else, hormone treatment.

At the end of metoestrus, a period of sexual quiescence (anoestrus) ensues during which there is no mutual sexual interest between bitch and male dog; the vulval lips will have reduced markedly in size, and there should be no discharge. It is a matter for concern and veterinary attention if discharge does remain or recommences shortly after the end of the heat period, particularly if the bitch starts to drink frequently, show abdominal enlargement, or go off her food.

Mating

In the wild, a mature female will almost certainly be mated, perhaps several times, when she comes in heat and will then progress through pregnancy and the rearing of her young. In the companion animal, mating should only be allowed after very careful consideration. First-time breeders should consult their veterinary surgeon, who will give comprehensive advice; most breed clubs are also helpful and often know of suitable stud dogs.

Bitches will continue to have heat periods until they are quite old, though their fertility and fecundity diminish after five or six years of age. They do not experience anything comparable to the human menopause. The frequency of breeding from a bitch is dependent on litter size and the health of the bitch, and although she can in theory manage to produce two litters annually, most breeders would consider one litter a year enough.

Before embarking on the mating procedure, a number of important factors should be carefully considered, including the following:

Pros and cons of mating

There is no evidence for the popular view that having a litter is 'good' for a bitch, and that if not permitted the bitch is more likely to contract certain illnesses. Although the normal course of pregnancy, giving birth and suckling are not harmful, the potential risks to the bitch are obviously increased during this time. With small and flat-faced breeds, whelping problems are not uncommon, and veterinary advice should certainly be obtained before mating such a bitch. Her general health condition and age should also be considered; a five-year old maiden bitch is at greater risk than a two-year old.

Costs

Preparation of suitable facilities, such as a whelping box for the bitch and her litter, extra feeding for the pregnant and nursing mother, special feeding for the pups, veterinary fees, and advertising the puppies for sale, all add up to substantial costs. The sale of the puppies may not cover these expenditures.

Space and facilities

A suitable space must be set aside for whelping and for nursing of the puppies. It may be possible to provide a space in the familiar surroundings of the home, but if a garage or outdoor shed is considered for the event, it is essential that it is clean, dry, warm and light, and that the bitch becomes accustomed to it as her personal quarters well in advance of whelping. The puppies will need an adequate and secure space in which to run around for six to eight weeks before they are ready to go to their new homes. It is as well to remember that they will not be house-trained and become progressively more boisterous.

Time factors

Looking after a bitch before, during and after whelping involves a considerable outlay in time. When whelping is due, the bitch should not be left unobserved and alone for longer than one hour at a time. She will need to be fed three or four times a day when suckling the pups (see also page 115), and the rearing and cleaning of the puppies is even more time-consuming. Added to this is interviewing of prospective owners. If these duties can be distributed among the family, the load is much lightened and can be a rewarding experience.

Crossbred litters

A purebred bitch will not be spoiled for future breeding if she is inadvertently mated by a mongrel or crossbred dog. Apart from the fact that the pregnancy is probably unwanted (see below), the bitch's potential to produce purebred puppies to a future pedigree sire is not impaired. A problem does arise if a small bitch is mated by a large male; whelping may be difficult if the puppies are relatively large compared to the bitch. Veterinary advice should be taken immediately if such a mating has occurred.

Unwanted pregnancies

If a bitch gets out while in season and is out of sight for any length of time, there is a good chance that she has been mated. If pregnancy by an unknown sire is to be terminated, as it should be, the sooner veterinary attention is obtained the better, preferably within twenty-four hours. The longer the delay, the less effectively can conception be prevented and pregnancy terminated.

Homes for the puppies

Most bitches have their puppies about sixty-three days (nine weeks) after mating, and they will be ready to go to their new homes six to eight weeks after birth. Ideally, a few potential owners should be lined up before mating, and throughout pregnancy and lactation, news of the impending happy event and enquiries for good homes for the puppies spread as wide as possible. If necessary, begin advertising in local papers when the puppies are two to three weeks old; if the bitch is an unusual breed, advertising in the national press, the dog media and breed-club broadsheets will probably pay off.

Interviews with prospective owners are essential to ensure that the puppies will go to good homes. Most will be happy to discuss the type of environment they will provide, and there is no obligation on the part of the breeder to dispose of a puppy into an environment which seems unsuitable.

Veterinary care

It is important, especially for the first-time breeder, to contact the local veterinarian, when a decision has been taken to mate a bitch. Apart from advice, he will be able to suggest appropriate breeders and will be forewarned of the impending pregnancy should his services be needed. After conception, and when pregnancy has been confirmed, it is advisable to have at least one antenatal examination, followed by a postnatal check of the bitch and puppies, and possibly tail-docking and attention to dew claws.

Choice of sire

For the serious breeder, the sire is a crucial choice involving close study of the pedigrees. The private owner and amateur breeder should seek advice from the breeder of the bitch or from the appropriate breed club. Once a suitable sire has been located, early contact should be made with the owner so as to study the dog and arrange approximate dates.

There is a great advantage in choosing a proven stud dog which is kept for that purpose and which has a record of siring strong puppies of good temperament. The look and behaviour of the dog should be acceptable to the owner of the bitch before a contract to proceed is agreed upon. An experienced sire is particularly important for the bitch at her first mating; this should take place at the premises of the stud-dog owner, and the actual arrangements are best left in his hands.

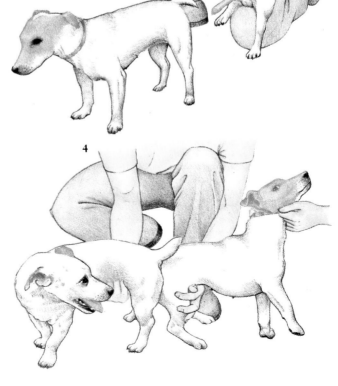

Mating between two willing partners begins with the ritualistic sniffing (1) of the genital areas. At deliberate breeding, the two dogs should be allowed time to become acquainted and in a receptive mood. Ideally, an experienced stud dog should be chosen to mate a maiden bitch, and for the young, inexperienced male an accomplished brood bitch makes the best partner; she will adopt the typical receptive stance, tail held to one side, but the young sire may need assistance (2) to begin the mating process

The tie is achieved when the male has fully penetrated the bitch (3). It may last for anything up to 45 minutes, and during that time the bitch should be held steady from the front to prevent her becoming restless and injuring the dog.

At some stage during the tie, the male dog will swing up and round so that the two dogs, while still locked in the tie, face in opposite directions (4). No attempt should be made to separate them, but the bitch will still need support

The usual time for mating is between the tenth and the fourteenth day after the first sign of heat, just after the end of the pro-oestrous phase. However, breeds and individuals vary, and the advice of the stud-dog owner should be taken. One mating does not necessarily result in conception, and most breeders mate their bitches with the stud dog on two separate and consecutive days.

The time of year must also be considered. It will probably be at least sixteen weeks after mating before the last of the puppies is disposed of, and the timing of mating should take into account holidays or other events, particularly during the last nine or ten weeks. A bitch coming in season and mated in mid-March will be whelping in mid-May, and the puppies cannot be dispersed to their new homes before early or mid-July. While this is an ideal time of year to breed from the bitch, it is less perfect from the owner's point of view; the height of the summer season does not encourage the sale of puppies. The timing of the bitch's sexual cycle obviously dictates breeding arrangements, but it may be possible to change the timing by oestrus suppressants.

The stud fee is by prior arrangement with the owner of the stud dog. If the bitch is a good specimen from good stock, the stud-dog owner may wish to negotiate for the pick of the litter as part of the fee.

The tie

The bitch is normally taken to the stud dog; an experienced sire is more relaxed and in command of the situation in familiar surroundings. The bitch in season may be apprehensive, even unnaturally aggressive, and her mouth is often softly taped to prevent her from biting her suitor or handler. The two dogs may be left together for a short while before mating provided that they do not fight.

The mechanics of mating between dog and bitch differ from that of other animals. After mounting the bitch, the dog inserts his penis into her vagina and ejaculates the semen, but the continuing enlargement of the penis coupled with muscular constriction of the bitch's vagina results in the penis being held securely in the vagina, the so-called tie. While their genitalia are still locked, the dog dismounts and swings round so that dog and bitch face in opposite directions; they may remain in this rather strange position for anything from five to forty-five minutes when mating is completed. This position is thought to assist in fertilization, and no attempt should be made to separate the two dogs as this may injure their genitalia. After mating, dog and bitch should be allowed a period of quiet rest in separate quarters.

Conception & Pregnancy

Fertilization of the ova released from the bitch's ovary happens about seventy-two hours after mating, and implantation into the lining of the uterus occurs about twenty-one days after mating.

For the first five or six weeks after mating, there is little change in the appearance or behaviour of the pregnant bitch. Depending on the number of foetuses in the uterus and the conformation of the bitch, some abdominal enlargement may be seen from the fifth week onwards. About the same time the teats may start to show some enlargement, and the milk or mammary glands usually begin to enlarge about the seventh or eighth week.

The pregnant bitch should be provided with quiet, draught-free maternity quarters where she can be carefully watched with the minimum of disturbance. A suitable whelping box can be made of chipboard, varnished to make it impermeable, or timber, with three high sides and a lower front. The size of the box depends on the size of the bitch, but it should be large enough to allow her

The bitch in late pregnancy

The bitch about to whelp

Pregnancy is rarely visually apparent during the first half of the gestation period, though changes may occur in temperament and appetite, with a decreasing interest in exercise and a corresponding need for affection. By the fifth or sixth week, physical signs of pregnancy are generally obvious: the mammary glands begin to swell, and the abdomen to show enlargement, especially when viewed from the rear. However, large breeds carrying only small litters may display no clear signs of pregnancy until shortly before delivery

As parturition approaches, the mammary glands become swollen and turgid, sometimes secreting milk. The abdominal swelling takes on a pear shape as the ligaments round the pelvic girdle loosen in preparation for the birth. Signs of imminent whelping include loss of appetite, a drop in temperature and increased restlessness and agitation, often accompanied by frenzied nest preparations. Slight muscle tremors give way to contractions, which vary in frequency and intensity

ample room for turning round without stepping on her puppies, which may number eight or ten; remember also that the box may have to accommodate puppies and bitch for up to six weeks. The height of the front should be low enough for the bitch to step over it, but high enough to prevent the puppies from following her example; an adjustable front is useful. Newspaper makes excellent bedding, being clean, warm, readily available, cheap and disposable.

During pregnancy the bitch should take her usual exercise and not be allowed to put on a lot of fat, although she will clearly become heavier with the developing uterus and growing foetuses. During the last week or two, she should be only gently exercised and discouraged from jumping and moving up and down staircases. Regular and gentle grooming should be maintained, the coat kept free of fleas and other parasites, and the hair clipped short at the rear end and round the teats. At about the sixth week of pregnancy, the bitch should be wormed under veterinary supervision.

Whelping

The average pregnancy is sixty-three days but may range from fifty-nine to sixty-five days. Bitches of the smaller breeds tend to whelp earlier than the larger breeds. One of the signs that whelping is imminent is refusal of food and possible vomiting; she will probably be restless, making frequent visits to the whelping box and tearing up the paper to make a nest. There may also be a slight mucous discharge from the vulva.

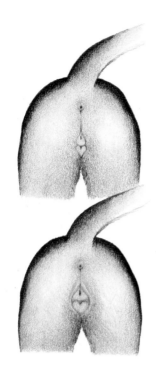

The external sex organs of the bitch are normally dark pink and constricted (top). During pregnancy and notably just prior to whelping, the vulva dilates and swells, becomes bright dark pink in colour and may discharge a clear or pale pink, odourless fluid from the vagina

If no such signs occur after about sixty-three days, the bitch may have been undergoing a convincing pseudo-pregnancy, or she may simply be a day or two longer than the average gestation. Provided that she remains fit and well, she may be left for a couple of days longer, but if any signs of illness develop, veterinary attention should be sought immediately.

The first stage of labour is usually marked by an increased restlessness. The bitch may seek out company and may lick vigorously at her vulva, but there is no obvious straining. During this period the musculature of the birth canal is relaxing, and contractions of the uterus beginning. This stage can last for six to twelve hours, but may extend to as much as thirty-six hours in a maiden bitch; she should be supervised, frequently but unobtrusively.

In the second stage of labour, the first foetus and its membranes are pushed into the birth canal by uterine contractions; this stimulates the bitch to strain, contracting her abdominal muscles to expel the foetus. A fluid-filled sac appears at the opening of the vulva, and the bitch may rupture this with her teeth, releasing and lapping up the fluid. The water bag is followed by a second, tougher membrane, the amnion, which precedes the foetus's head or, less commonly, its hindquarters.

At normal whelping, the bitch often resents interference and assistance from her owner, but if the first puppy has not been successfully delivered within one hour of the water breaking, veterinary attention should be sought. If the puppy is delivered hindquarters first, the head may be obstructing the birth canal and pressing on the umbilical cord, depriving the pup of its blood supply, with fatal results. After the puppy is expelled, the bitch will normally tear the membranes enveloping the puppy and bite through the umbilical cord still attached to the placenta. Her vigorous licking will stimulate the puppy into breathing of its own accord, but if for any reason the bitch does not do this, the puppy will die unless it is freed from the sac and its breathing started.

The placenta or afterbirth, the attachment between the membranes and the bitch's uterus, is usually expelled after each puppy and is normally eaten by the bitch. During whelping the fluids expelled from the vagina are usually dark green in colour. This is quite normal and is caused by the breakdown of pigments in the attachment of the foetal membranes to the uterus. The intervals between births of the pups are variable, depending on the numbers in the litter, and range from fifteen to sixty minutes. However, if more than two hours of straining are unproductive, the veterinarian should be summoned. Whelping may take twenty-four hours or more, but two to eight hours are more usual.

The puppies should be left with the bitch while she continues whelping, but if she is not taking time to lick them clean, they may be gently dried off with a warm towel. Newborn puppies have no mechanism for retaining their body heat, and unless they are kept warm their temperature will rapidly decrease. The recommended air temperature for a newborn litter is 80°F (26°C), but if this cannot be achieved, local heat can be provided with insulated hotwater bottles. The heat from the dam's body is the best source of warmth, and as long as the box is draught-free, the recommended air temperature is unnecessary.

Caesarian section

If after prolonged labour, the bitch is unable to expel one or more of the puppies, veterinary assistance should be obtained. Under certain circumstances, the veterinarian may decide to remove the puppies by Caesarian section – in certain breeds, such as the Bulldog, production of puppies by Caesarian method has become the rule rather than the exception.

Whelping usually begins with the appearance of the water bag; the bitch will rupture this and lick up the fluid, and shortly afterwards the first puppy should arrive. An inexperienced dam may need a little help at the start, though she generally objects to interference. In a normal birth, a puppy is delivered head first (1), enclosed in a membranous sac

The bitch immediately bites open the bag containing the puppy; at her first whelping, she may be unsure of the procedure, and the puppy should be placed close by her (2) so that she can tear the bag open

Once the pup is freed from the membranes, the mother will lick him dry all over with vigorous flicks of the tongue (3). It is essential that she clears the mouth and nasal passages first so that the puppy can start breathing on his own

The next puppy may be so imminent that the bitch will have no time to lick the first one properly; it should be wiped gently dry with a towel and returned to the warmth of the mother's body (4) while she delivers the next pup.

Normally, the birth of each puppy is followed by the placenta which the dam will eat. As the pups are born, cleaned and begin to breathe, they should be placed by a nipple

The nursing bitch

Normally the bitch should provide for all the needs of the puppies during their first three weeks: food, drink, warmth, hygiene and discipline. Cosmetic requirements, such as the removal of dew claws or tail-docking in some breeds, should be carried out between the age of three and six days of age, preferably by the veterinarian. By the age of ten days, the puppies' eyes will be open, and they will be exploring the world with increasing curiosity. At three weeks, they will begin to take solid food, and the dam will be leaving them for progressively longer periods. By the time the pups are six to eight weeks old they should be totally independent of the dam and ready to go to their new homes.

Motherless puppies

Occasionally a bitch is unable to rear her puppies, either through rejection, illness or death. This can be disastrous for the survival of the puppies, especially with a large litter, and a high degree of devoted care becomes essential. A foster mother is not always available, and hand-rearing is the only other alternative.

   Newborn puppies are totally dependent for their two vital requirements of food and warmth. They also require stimulation to evacuate their bladder and bowel contents. Normally the mother would stimulate the processes in the elimination canals with her tongue; similar stimuli can be achieved by the foster

The umbilical cord (5) is usually severed by the dam. If she fails to do this, the cord should be cut, with sterilized scissors, as far away as possible from the pup's stomach

mother with swabs of moist cotton wool wiped gently over the appropriate areas several times a day.

Correct, steady temperature is of paramount importance and must be maintained at around 88°F (31°C), decreasing to about 75°F (24°C) at the age of four weeks. This is best achieved in an incubator, though thoroughly insulated heating pads can be installed in the nursing box.

Feeding must be done by hand (see also page 110), using a small syringe or miniature bottle fitted with a rubber teat. Specially formulated milk for puppies is the only alternative to bitch's milk; it should be fed at blood heat, every four hours in any twenty-four hour period and made up fresh every day.

Birth Control

The majority of owners do not want to breed from their bitches and resort to one of three alternatives to prevent reproduction. They either exercise strict control over the bitch twice a year during the dangerous ten to twenty day period when mating might take place; or they have her surgically sterilized. Alternatively, hormonal pills can be given to suppress the occurrence of oestrus temporarily. Veterinary advice should be taken on which of these alternatives is appropriate.

Control of the bitch during her heat periods may be relatively simple if she is always exercised on a lead or kept in secure quarters to which no other dog has access. For a bitch which normally enjoys the freedom of a garden that is not dog-proof, fairly radical changes in her lifestyle must be introduced to prevent a misalliance or accidental mating.

Surgical sterilization is a permanent solution to the problem of preventing conception, and one which is adopted by many owners. Surgical removal of the ovaries and uterus of the bitch, though a major operation involving abdominal surgery, is regularly and safely carried out by veterinary surgeons. The operation can be carried out at any time after the first heat period as long as the animal is not in heat at the time.

An owner who wishes to retain the option to breed from a bitch, but at the same time wants to minimize the inconvenience of oestrus, may have the bitch treated with hormone-containing pills (progestagens). These synthetic hormones mimic the action of the naturally occurring sex hormone progesterone and suppress the secretion of the oestrogen which is essential for oestrus to occur. Hormone pills are obtainable only through a veterinary surgeon, who will advise on their use.

Male Sexual Function

Unlike the bitch, the male dog is capable of mating at any time after puberty and is usually highly sensitive to the presence of a bitch in oestrus. Some males in rural areas will travel long distances on the off-chance of an assignation with an oestrous female, and the sexual cycles of neighbouring females may well have an influence on the management of the male dog.

Surgical sterilization or castration may be carried out on males, though it is less frequent than in females. The removal of the testicles, which is a relatively minor operation compared to the removal of the female sexual organs, prevents the male from fertilizing a bitch in heat. Sterilization may also be carried out to suppress undesirable behavioural characteristics, but is not invariably successful in this respect.

THE DECLINING YEARS

Whatever the life expectancy of a dog, it is certainly less than that of its owner. In a household with a tradition of keeping dogs, the owner's life will usually represent several dog lifespans, and at some stage it becomes necessary to part company; with dogs as with humans, death is part of life.

A dog's lifespan is difficult to determine. If effective life is seen to begin at birth, the chances of a dog surviving into adulthood would be slim as neo-natal deaths account for anything up to fifty per cent of canine deaths. After the first seventy-two hours of life a puppy's survival chances improve, and after weaning they become better still. As most owners acquire their dogs as puppies of six to eight weeks, this can for practical purposes be assumed to be the beginning of their lives. A representation graph of a dog's lifespan would start at 100 per cent puppies alive on day one, falling rapidly as puppies die during their first few days; the graph would then begin to level out, possibly dropping slightly around the stressful time of weaning and relocation. It would then move gradually towards a steady level, showing barely anything except losses from unusual illnesses and accidents until the age of eight to ten years when the survivors would begin to show the effects of ageing. The line would fall more steeply, but some dogs would live for twenty or more years.

It is difficult, almost impossible, to establish the average lifespan of a dog. If it is assumed to be ten years plus, a four and a half year old dog could be expected to live for another six years; it may well live for another ten years or it may die the next day. The effects of ageing are variable. Just as there is a range of apparent lifespan, there is a good deal of difference in the effects the years have on individuals; some dogs begin to show signs of old age as young as three to four years, while others may remain extraordinarily active even after the age of fifteen or sixteen years. As a general rule, very large dogs are fairly short-lived, rarely exceeding seven or eight years. Smaller dogs, especially some Terriers, often remain healthy up to, and occasionally beyond, the age of twenty years. Tiny miniature dogs are not normally so fortunate. These factors would suggest an optimum size for a dog, above and below which its longevity may be prejudiced. This attractive hypothesis awaits further research, but it seems likely that a dog of around 22–26 lb (10–12 kg) has the best chance of a long healthy life.

Reliable information on the longevity of companion animals, particularly dogs and cats, is not readily available as they rarely die peacefully in their sleep, having lived out their normal lifespans. Although most owners would wish a natural termination to the lives of their pets, the great majority are humanely destroyed. Literally meaning ideal or gentle death, euthanasia prevents the misery of most terminal illnesses; it is a privilege to terminate pain and suffering when life no longer holds a reasonable prospect of a fulfilling existence. If euthanasia is abused or denied when clearly indicated, companion animals get a poor return for the boundless affection they give their owners.

Although the ultimate decision must rest with the owner, veterinary advice is needed in all but the most obvious cases so that the maximum benefit can be gained without unnecessary suffering. The time at which euthanasia becomes essential is easier to identify where there has been a good and steady relationship between the owner and the veterinarian throughout the dog's life. The veterinarian can distinguish between pathological changes which may respond to treatment, and the process of ageing which will eventually take its natural course. Certain changes, such as heart or kidney failure, may not be cured, but the dog may be able to lead a reasonably normal life with a few dietary changes to its everyday routine.

The Ageing Process

The most obvious sign of ageing is a progressive reduction in general activity and alertness. The usual puppy boisterousness is lost with maturity, though it can remain in some dogs for a surprisingly long time. Much of the lively activity of older dogs is a response to environmental influences, particularly those generated by the owner. A steady decline in spontaneous activity usually begins with maturity, and when a dog slows down responses to its owner or formerly interesting stimuli, it can be assumed that if nothing else is wrong, the ageing process has begun.

With declining levels of activity and unchanged or increased dietary intake the excess energy (calories) is stored as fat, and the dog becomes obese. A recent survey has shown that about thirty per cent of all dogs in Britain are obviously obese. Overweight results, among other things, in difficulty in movement, mainly because of the additional load on the joints, particularly on the hips and the stifle. There is also an additional load on the circulatory and respiratory systems, showing as laboured breathing after any kind of exertion; an accumulation of body fat without doubt reduces the lifespan of dogs as it does of humans and only dietary adjustments can reverse the situation.

Poor vision

Deteriorating eyesight is often the only early sign of ageing. Other senses, such as smell and hearing, may also decline, but lack of visual acuity is more obvious. Once the ability to see reaches the point where the dog cannot readily recognize familiar objects, clinical examination is necessary to determine those conditions which can be treated and those which must be accepted as the inevitable passage of time. Most dogs show a remarkable degree of adaptation when their senses begin to fail, especially so when they are in familiar surroundings; if the furniture is kept unchanged in its place, most dogs with failing eyesight, or even totally blind, are able to navigate themselves nimbly around obstacles. This ability is particularly evident when several dogs share the household. It is often difficult to identify which dog has little or no vision, and it is not impossible that a group of dogs could use some as yet undiscovered means of communication.

Weight loss

While obesity may be a problem in many older, formerly active dogs, inefficient absorption and conversion of food may result in progressive loss of weight. As the closely related senses of taste and smell become poorer, appetite is often lost and contributes to further weight reduction, sometimes combined with clinical conditions of the mouth, particularly dental deposits and inflammation of the gums (gingivitis). A combination of poor sensory perception and physical discomfort on eating are common causes for a decrease in food intake and weight loss in ageing dogs. Poor digestion and absorption should be countered with easily digested food, preferably in small but frequent meals.

Bland, tasteless and odourless food fails to stimulate the low powers of the senses, but the appetite may be provoked by adding special favourites to the food; almost any food can be tried, but highly palatable items with a fairly penetrating odour, such as liver, rabbit or oily fish like pilchards or sardines, may be used to good effect. Some dogs respond to proprietary canned puppy foods or a good-quality cat food, especially a rabbit variety. Others, especially those with sore mouths, may appreciate ice cream or honey; creamed and other soft cheeses are concentrated sources of nutrients and often very acceptable.

Food warmed to blood heat is attractive to most dogs as it releases the odours,

stimulating the appetite; it is also the body temperature of the prey a dog would eat in the wild. Food from the refrigerator should be allowed to reach room temperature before it is fed; warmed-up food should be disposed of, not returned to the refrigerator. Most dogs of any age prefer food wet rather than dry; canned foods can be fed wetter by the addition of warm gravy.

Digestive problems

Old age also brings digestive problems with opposite effects. Motility of the gut may slow down, decreasing the rate of passage of food to the extent that severe constipation results. Tackled in the early stages, constipation is usually alleviated by increasing the bulk of the fecal mass in the gut with agar-type preparations or bran in some form, mixed with the daily food allowance if the appetite is reasonably good. The poor palatability of bran can normally be overcome by introducing it gradually in increasing amounts over a period of one to two weeks, by warming the mixture and by feeding it wet.

Medicinal liquid paraffin is also useful for easing the passage of hard fecal matter and is virtually harmless unless used in very large amounts, when it may interfere with the absorption of some nutrients. At worst the motions become greasy and stick to the dog's rear end; if the lack of movement in the gut is complete it may not have any beneficial effect at all. On no account should human laxatives be used, and castor oil especially has no place in the treatment of dogs. Drugs should be used only on veterinary direction.

Where gut motility is retained but absorption is incomplete, the passage of fecal material is likely to be accelerated. Undigested material moves further down the digestive tract than normally, and fermentation can occur, accompanied by flatulence resulting from gas-forming micro organisms in the lower reaches of the gut. Poor water reabsorption results from ineffective lower bowel activity combined with a faster transit time through the gut, and fecal watery matter causes diarrhoea.

Mechanical agents, such as kaolin, kaolin and chalk mixtures, aluminium hydroxide gels and sterculia gum preparations, slow down the passage of material through the gut; they also tend to absorb water and therefore give more structure to fecal matter. Dehydrated instant potato powder added to the food sometimes has a similar effect. Drinking water should never be withheld; such action will not produce less fluid feces, but increases the chances of severe dehydration, always a likely result of diarrhoea. Occasionally natural yoghourt has a spectacularly beneficial effect as it repopulates the lower gut with beneficial micro organisms.

Greying Hairs

As dogs get older, their coats usually become duller, coarser and more brittle. Greying of the hair, especially around the muzzle, can be seen at an early age in some breeds, notably Labradors, and in others with strong black coat coloration. It is not harmful in any way, simply a sign of ageing. Sometimes flecks of dandruff and excessive hair shedding are apparent; conscientious attention to grooming with brush and comb, and regular bathing in an appropriate shampoo will normally keep such problems at bay.

Some non-specific coat problems where hair has become prematurely dull and brittle in spite of proper grooming and adequate diet may respond to additional fat in the form of corn oil; up to 1 fluid oz (30 ml) daily for a 22–33 lb (10–15 kg) dog is often effective. Such supplementation should not be given to a dog with digestive uncertainties, and only on the advice of a veterinarian.

Stiffening of joints

Articular and muscular degeneration, even without the burden of obesity, can progress from impairment of movement to difficulty in moving at all in a short period. Any obvious pain or persistent discomfort needs veterinary attention; treatments are available for most joint and muscle problems associated with ageing, but if left too long may prove unrewarding.

Terminal Diseases

Veterinary attention must be sought if simple measures bring no improvement in absorptive bowel function. Profound digestive changes result from various conditions common in older dogs, including liver and kidney disease, lack of digestive enzymes associated with pancreatic failure, and small intestine disease. These all require a proper diagnosis so that appropriate treatment can begin; failure to obtain professional advice in time can be fatal.

The same principle applies to developing tumours. Any unusual swelling which is visible or palpable requires veterinary examination and advice before it grows to be an inoperable tumour. It is a strong human trait to block the mind to unpalatable news, but this selfish attitude can prejudice the life of a dog who trusts in the care of his owner. Many tumours are treatable, some with good prospects of prolonged recovery if brought to the attention of the veterinary surgeon in time.

Euthanasia

The deliberate and humane ending of the life of a pet animal is undoubtedly a task for the veterinarian. The usual method is by an injection of a barbiturate or comparable drug; in itself this is a straightforward technique, but the situation is one charged with emotion.

The injection of an overdose of barbiturate effectively takes anaesthesia to the point of no return. A concentrated solution is injected directly into a vein, usually in the foreleg; deep anaesthesia is rapidly achieved and deepens gently to a peaceful death. Premedication can alleviate any apprehension a dog may exhibit as a result of its owner's agitated state. The last gasps are reflex actions in a dog already deeply unconscious, but often cause anxiety in owners, who interpret them as signs of the dog regaining consciousness. Ideally, barbiturates should be injected into a vein, but in very old or debilitated dogs with poor circulation the veins may be difficult to locate; injections into body cavities, chiefly the abdomen, have a similar effect except that larger amounts are needed.

The greatest kindness an owner can show a dog which has been loved and cared for throughout its life is a humane ending by means of an injection, by a veterinarian, preferably the one who has attended the dog regularly. Veterinarians deal with such situations practically every day, and handled sympathetically the owner will be grateful for his help through a difficult time.

No veterinarian will recommend euthanasia without having considered carefully and objectively each individual case. Advanced terminal disease may be so obvious or injuries so extensive that immediate termination of life is the only act of kindness which can be performed, but generally the veterinarian will know from experience when to hasten and when to delay the final act.

Most dog owners realize that their animals need to be released from life when this becomes a burden. They also need time to prepare themselves for parting with their animals. A sudden severance of the human/dog bond can be as traumatic, sometimes more so, as human bereavement. Euthanasia can be carried out in the owner's home or at a veterinary clinic. For the owner, it may be easier at home, but for the dog and the veterinarian the procedure is better carried out at the surgery.

Some owners prefer to stay with their animals to the end, as some measure of comfort and to reassure themselves that the correct procedure is carried out. If the owner remains calm, he may well be a help, but even slight agitation is quickly transmitted to the animal and can make matters more difficult.

Burial

The rupture of the bond between man and his dog is a time of grief and sadness. As with human bereavement, it is accompanied by certain formalities. The act of euthanasia, carried out with sympathy and understanding by the veterinary surgeon, is all the same not charitable and requires financial payment by the bereaved. Disposal of the body also falls on the owner. Some owners may prefer to inter their dogs in the garden, but this is by no means always possible. The veterinary surgeon may be able to advise on the proximity of dog cemeteries, or he may be willing to arrange for cremation at the owner's expense. Neither the veterinarian nor the local authority are responsible for the disposal of the body.

Coping with bereavement

Only recently has an appreciation of the loss of a pet animal been considered as a genuine form of bereavement. The effects on the bereaved frequently follow the same pattern as when human attachments are severed. A proper understanding of death and grief helps the owner to cope with the situation and allows the veterinarian to give positive support and guidance towards a continuing fulfilment of the human/companion animal relationship. The sequence of events in human bereavement ranges through denial, anger and depression, followed eventually by resolution and ideally by the development of a new attachment.

Sadly, society has no universally recognized outlet for the emotions to allow the equivalent of mourning. What is genuine grief over a great loss is often seen by outsiders as excessively maudlin and self-indulgent behaviour. Yet some degree of mourning is necessary to keep the sequence of events moving forward. Arrested mourning can stop this progress at any point and result in prolonged anger, resentment, depression or, in extreme cases, denial that the animal is dead. It is not unknown for owners to burden themselves with undeserved blame. The worst cases often follow what is known as double mourning, where an unresolved bereavement experience is suppressed only to be dramatically precipitated at a later date by what might be a relatively trivial set-back.

Many veterinarians work hard to ease the loss of a pet animal to their clients. Such losses are always borne better in multi-pet households, particularly when the animals are at different stages of their lifespan. In single-pet households, it is common for an owner to go through a 'denial phase of mourning', that no animal can ever replace the one just lost. Sometimes anger is directed against the veterinarian, particularly if the death is unexpected. More often the owner looks around for someone or something to blame and may often blame himself, self-accusation frequently leading to depression. The average person can cope with bereavement with support from family and friends as well as professional advisers. Time heals, and when the depression begins to lighten, the time has come for the introduction of a new companion. Introspective thoughts are diverted from the mourning process to establishing a new human/animal relationship with its promises of an infinitely rewarding future.

HEALTH
AND
FITNESS

HEALTH AND FITNESS

Good health rarely comes naturally, but must be nurtured and maintained from puppyhood and throughout the dog's life. A sensible and balanced diet, regular exercise and grooming, coupled with regular vaccinations and veterinary check-ups are the obvious responsibilities of the owner.

Just as with humans, each stage of a dog's life brings potential illnesses; they may be inherited, result from accidental injury, or be the inevitable processes of ageing. Veterinary advice should be sought sooner rather than later in order to have the problem diagnosed and treatment started.

Most dogs suffer the odd bout of vomiting and diarrhoea and have days when they seem off-colour and listless. The body's natural defences usually resolve minor problems, and the general state of good health is apparent in alertness, bright eyes, and a clean, good-textured coat; a cold nose is not necessarily a healthy sign, neither is a warm nose always a warning of illness.

The normal temperature of a dog is 101.5°F (38.6°C), but goes up during the day and after any sort of activity. It should be taken with a rectal thermometer, smeared with a little Vaseline and inserted into the rectum for three minutes. A sudden rise in temperature may indicate infectious disease and occurs with heat stroke. Abnormally high and low temperatures are signs of near-collapse and need immediate veterinary help.

Pulse rate varies with the breeds, the lowest occurring in giant breeds; it also differs with age, exercise and general state of health, from 80 to 120 beats per minute. The best site for feeling the pulse is over an artery near the skin surface; the inside of the thigh is ideal. The dog must be at complete rest when the pulse is taken.

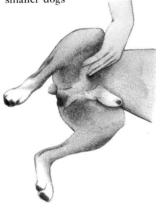

Pulse rate is counted on the artery in the groin; usually 80–120 beats per minute, it is at the higher end of the scale in smaller dogs

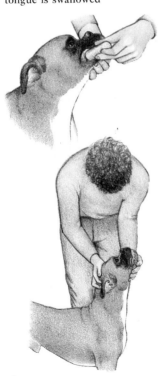

Liquid medicine trickled into the pouch of the mouth is readily absorbed. Hold the mouth closed until a tablet placed at the back of the tongue is swallowed

Nursing Care

Sick dogs instinctively seek a hideout in which to rest and recuperate from whatever troubles them. Nursing a sick animal requires patience and devotion, without too much fuss and overhandling. The bed should be clean and comfortable, out of draughts and in a room with equitable temperature. Fresh water should be available at all times. Food needs to be tempting and easily digestible; it is best fed in small amounts, if necessary by hand, until a normal diet can be resumed.

Fractures of the limbs when encased in plaster should be covered with a sock and a plastic bag tied in place with a bandage, never an elastic rubber band. Bandages on wounds can be difficult to keep in place and out of reach of the dog's paws or mouth. Elastoplast wound round the bandage is often effective; alternatively it may be necessary to fix an Elizabethan collar, fashioned from a plastic bucket, round the neck to prevent the dog from licking the wound.

Post-operative treatment

In serious and complicated cases dogs may need hospitalization and professional nursing, but often the patient will return to its home once the anaesthetic has worn off. During recovery it should be kept warm and comfortable; temporary incontinence must be accepted and cleaned up at once. The veterinary surgeon will issue specific instructions for post-surgical care, but in general violent exercise and excitement must be avoided; food should be given in small tempting amounts, and fluids may be enriched with glucose or honey.

Administration of medicines

The veterinarian's instructions must be followed implicitly; medicine should be given in correct doses, at the correct time, and for as long as directed. Human medicines should not be given to animals, except on professional advice.

Medicine can be in the form of tablets, liquids, or injections. Most dogs are notoriously suspicious of medicine and are capable of keeping tablets in the tightly shut mouth and obstinately refusing to swallow. They can usually be fooled by enclosing the tablet in some favourite tidbit of soft chocolate, meat or cheese. Alternatively, with the aid of a helper, the dog's jaws can be opened from the front and the tablet placed at the back of the throat; it will automatically go down the food pipe with the first swallow. Crushed tablets mixed in with food are unsatisfactory; they may remain uneaten.

Liquid medicine is best given through a small bottle – minute amounts can be mixed with warm water to make up the volume. The mouth should not be opened, but the pouch on the side pulled down and the medicine poured into it. With the head kept steady and slightly raised, the liquid will trickle down into the throat.

Injections, which may be essential for diabetic dogs, require a little practice with a hypodermic needle, glass or disposable, into an orange until the owner feels confident in its use. For the actual injection, back a large dog into a corner or lift a small animal on to a table. Pick up the loose skin at the back of the neck between thumb and forefinger, insert the needle firmly and quickly and depress the plunger. All non-disposable syringes and needles should be sterilized.

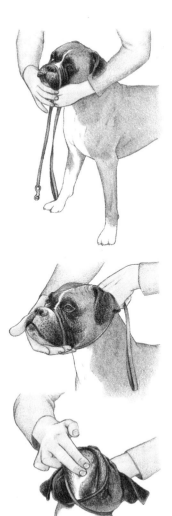

Accidents & First Aid

Dogs are liable to the same types of accidents as their owners. Traffic accidents, which can often be fatal, are common where dogs are allowed to roam free, posing hazards for themselves as well as for motorists, cyclists and pedestrians. In the countryside, potential dangers include barbed-wire fences, hidden traps, boggy ground, broken glass, exposed tree roots, and vicious animals.

In home surroundings, dogs must be protected from the potential dangers of badly insulated electrical equipment and wires, overturned pans of boiling liquids, sharp and pointed objects lying around and unprotected balconies and windows which might tempt a high jump. Power tools and sharp garden equipment can be the cause of serious physical injury, and many garden chemicals are poisonous.

The majority of accidents require immediate professional help. If possible, establish contact by telephone with the local veterinary practice warning the surgeon of the nature of the emergency. In general, first aid consists in removing the influences or circumstances which are causing the accident, without harming the animal. Making sure that the dog has a patent air passage is of paramount importance. Switch off any electric current before touching an electrocuted dog. Bleeding (see page 138) should be attended to, but avoid tourniquets except in dire emergencies. The dog should be made comfortable and brought under shelter. In a traffic accident, a badly injured dog may be in a state of shock and try to bite its rescuers in a reflex action; a scarf, large handkerchief, or a necktie should be tied temporarily round the muzzle before further action is taken. Lift the animal gently on to a blanket or jacket and get it to the veterinary practice as quickly as possible.

A temporary muzzle, fashioned from a leather lead, can be tied round an injured dog to prevent reflex biting. An unconscious victim of a traffic accident must be handled with the greatest care, lifted on to a blanket, placed on its side, and rushed to the nearest veterinary surgery

Bee Stings
Sudden pain and swelling, usually round the mouth, neck or forelimbs, and often with the bee (or wasp) close by, are generally the only signs of bee stings. Boisterous and inquisitive breeds, particularly Boxers, are the most likely to be affected. Sometimes the sting remains visible in the centre of the swelling and can be removed with a pair of forceps and a low-power lens.

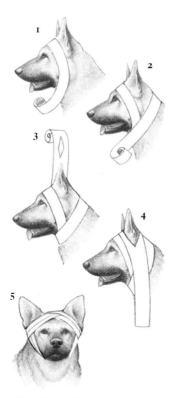

Bleeding of a serious nature must be stemmed until proper help is obtained. Cover a head wound with a cold compress and strips of bandage round the head and neck, cutting slits for the ears

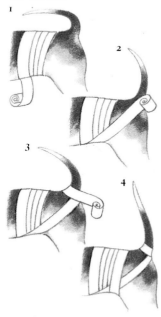

A deep wound to the abdomen can result in severe blood loss. Secure the bandage temporarily to the tail; later it can be held in place and out of reach of the paws with a dog coat

Cold compress applications of cottonwool or lint soaked in water are all that is normally needed. The excessive swelling and severe allergic reaction which sometimes follow insect stings in humans are unusual in a dog, but if it appears to be in any kind of distress or if there is a hint of obstruction of the air passage, immediate veterinary attention is crucial. Should the swelling persist for several hours the dog must be examined by a veterinarian. Multiple stings following the disturbance of a hive or swarm can be dangerous and require veterinary attention as shock and collapse is the usual outcome.

Bites

Dogs tolerate a bite wound quite well, although it frequently becomes infected and forms an abscess. Bites may be puncture wounds where infected material from the teeth is brought quite deeply into the tissues through a small wound. This soon closes while micro organisms proliferate below. Bites frequently occur about the head and the neck; on the ears, a tear may result in considerable bleeding, and the dog will shake the head and scatter blood around. Blood clots should not be removed from torn ear tips as this tends to delay healing.

Wounds on the flank can be serious if the chest is penetrated. Infection can enter the thoracic cavity as well as air, which is a serious handicap to breathing. When a large dog, particularly a Greyhound, bites, it frequently tears with one side of the mouth, anchoring with the teeth on the other side; a puncture wound in one site may therefore be associated with a tear elsewhere, and careful examination is essential, particularly with heavy-coated dogs.

All wounds should be treated initially by cleaning them of debris, except for ear tips, bathing them with cottonwool and warm water. If necessary, the site should be clipped free of hairs. All bite wounds which break the skin surface should be examined by a veterinarian, who will judge if antibiotic treatment is advisable and clean out the area thoroughly.

Bleeding

A hemorrhage from anywhere, and especially from the body's natural openings, is always a matter for concern. Even a tiny amount can appear alarming and while the loss of a small amount of blood is not life-threatening in itself, it is important to establish if blood is still being lost, where it is coming from and from which animal if after a dog fight. It is normal for bitches in season to pass blood, and blood-stained fluid also accompanies whelping; the fluid may also be coloured with the brown and green material which is formed by the breakdown of blood at the placenta.

Small cuts, broken claws, cut pads and bite wounds normally stop bleeding after a few minutes. If blood continues to flow, and particularly if it is obviously being *pumped* out, and coming from a severed artery, immediate professional attention is needed. A compress made from clean material such as cottonwool, lint or an old sheet, should be soaked in cold water and applied with enough pressure to stop bleeding, but without restricting the circulation until professional help can be obtained. Tourniquets are not advisable in anything but the direst emergencies and even then should only be applied on veterinary advice. Some breeds, such as the Boxer, seem to bleed more easily and for a longer period than others.

Severe bleeding can be fatal if a dog is involved in a serious road accident or a savage fight or has cut himself on rusty wire fences or farm machinery. The injured animal should be moved gently to a warm, dry environment and pressure-bandaging applied to obvious bleeding points. Allow the dog to drink fluids (*not* alcohol of any kind) but withhold solid food, as an anaesthetic or radiography will probably be needed later. Establish contact with the local veterinary practice at once, and in the case of a severely injured animal forewarn him of the imminent arrival of an emergency.

Bruises

A bruise or contusion occurs when small blood vessels are ruptured near the surface of the skin. They are almost invariably the result of a dog meeting some powerful force, particularly a motor vehicle. Bruises in themselves are not serious, but if the impact was violent, other injuries will be likely, and the dog needs to be examined by a veterinary surgeon in all but the most trivial cases. Bruises are difficult, sometimes almost impossible, to see in dark-skinned and long-haired dogs. In very hairy dogs, extensive clipping of the coat may be necessary to determine the extent of bruising.

Burns

In spite of fireguards and keeping pans of boiling fluids out of reach, burns will occasionally occur. A minor burn can be treated with a proprietary burns ointment after all the hair has been trimmed away, and the area gently cleaned with cold water. Serious burns require urgent veterinary treatment as they are always accompanied by shock. The burn itself will probably become infected, and the pain normally associated with burns will be prolonged. As a first-aid measure, apply cold water gently but thoroughly to the burn area.

Collapse

A dog may collapse for a variety of reasons, the commonest being heart failure although heat stroke and hemorrhage will have the same effect. Strokes, the failure of oxygen supply to part of the brain, are not common in dogs, but prolonged convulsions may lead to collapse afterwards; traffic accidents and other violent episodes may have similar effects. Whatever the reason for collapse, it is important and probably vital that veterinary help is sought immediately. With obvious environmental influences, such as strong sun or a smoke-filled atmosphere, the dog must be removed from the threat without delay. Fresh air is usually enough to bring a dog round if it is found in a room with boiler fumes – it is not always appreciated that the supply of oxygen is at its lowest near the ground in such circumstances.

With all types of collapse it is crucial to maintain an effective air passage, for even where there is adequate air supply, the dog's life may be endangered by an inability to ventilate the lungs. Any accumulation of mucus should be cleared from the throat with a clean cloth and the tongue should be pulled forward. It is unwise to allow a dog to lie on one side for any more then fifteen to twenty minutes as congestion of the lungs may lead to pneumonia. A dog which has collapsed should not be restrained, but efforts should be made to prevent self-injury if an animal is throwing itself about a room; if necessary erect a small padded area (see also Poisoning).

Coma

This is a state beyond collapse, when consciousness is lost completely, and the dog responds to no kind of stimulus. First-aid action is the same as for any other collapse, but the degree of urgency in obtaining professional help is even greater. It may be necessary to stimulate breathing by compression of the chest wall every ten seconds, with the dog's tongue held forward. If the dog has vomited, care must be taken to prevent this from being inhaled, and the air passage must be kept clear. If coma or collapse is caused by an electrical accident, switch off the current before touching the animal.

Convulsions

Convulsion may be due to poisoning (see also Cyanide, Lead, Metaldehyde, and Paraquat Poisoning), but more commonly to a form of epilepsy or infectious

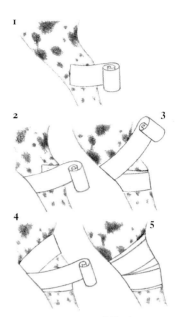

Leg injuries are difficult to bandage; bind them firmly as illustrated above, not so tight as to interfere with blood circulation. Secure the bandage with adhesive tape; tourniquets should *never* be applied

Coma and collapse call for speedy first aid. Pull forward the tongue of an unconscious dog and stimulate respiration with firm compressions of the chest wall at 10-second intervals

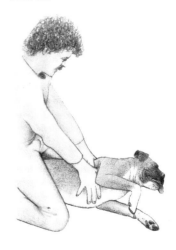

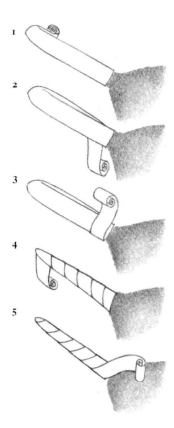

Tail wounds usually continue to bleed due to further injury. Clip hair away from the wound area, clean it thoroughly, and use a narrow bandage to cover the whole of the tail, finishing at the tail root. Change the dressing daily

disease (see Distemper and Infectious Canine Hepatitis). Conditions such as heart failure and diabetes also show various degrees of seizure in many cases.

Establishing the cause of convulsions is not a job for the unqualified, but the owner can collect any obvious evidence which may help the veterinarian to arrive at an accurate diagnosis. Any material which may have been eaten, such as flaking paint, slug bait, rat poison, or a dead animal with which the dog may have been in contact, should be brought along, together with vaccination history and records of previous illnesses. It can be frightening to watch a dog having convulsions, but it is probably unconscious during most seizures. It is important to move the affected animal into a darkened, quiet room, avoiding too much restraint. Maintain a fresh air passage, prevent the dog from inhaling fluid or vomit and do not let a dog lie on one side for more than fifteen to twenty minutes (see Collapse). Urgent veterinary attention is essential.

Cyanide Poisoning
Prussic acid, sodium or potassium cyanide are occasionally used to poison garden pests and as such become a potential danger for dogs. Affected animals show severe breathing difficulties and dilated pupils, followed by a period of over-excitement leading to convulsions, coma and death. The characteristic smell of almonds is sometimes detectable, particularly if the dog has vomited. Urgent veterinary assistance is essential.

Fish Hooks
Fish hooks lodged in the body may cause considerable distress or none at all. They are most commonly lodged in the mouth through the tongue, or worse down the oesophagus (gullet); a piece of line attached pinpoints the problem, but pulling on the line almost always worsens the situation. Occasionally fish hooks may be swallowed completely and finish up in the stomach or beyond. A radiographic examination is usually necessary to locate the hook and effect surgical removal.

If the hook is visible, in the dog's lips, ears or feet, it may be possible to expose the sharp end by pushing the hook forward and cutting off the tip with a pair of pliers before removing the remaining piece, taking care to prevent either part of the hook from becoming a foreign body somewhere else.

Foreign Bodies
Objects may become lodged in a variety of sites, most commonly in the digestive tract, anywhere from the mouth to the anus. Rounded pebbles are frequently taken into the stomach, where they may remain for several weeks, the evidence being periodic vomiting. More usually severe vomiting occurs, with none or very watery motions being passed. Pieces of bone may become lodged in the gut, often at the entrance to the stomach, or in the rectum. Dogs will eat almost anything, and many, especially Labradors, seem able to pass the most extraordinary objects without any damage. Some objects do seem to cause serious difficulties as they often become stuck, such as stockings and tights, rubber teats, large fruit stones, rubber toys and balls. Wrapping cling film is known to be injurious when swallowed.

Fractures: see Muscular & Skeletal Diseases

Grass Seeds
The awns of grasses, such as wild barley, may penetrate almost any part of a dog, those with long barbs causing serious problems as they only move forwards like fish hooks. Grass awns can penetrate the ears, eyes, feet and anal sacs, even the rectum; local irritation may be intense, particularly deep in the ear or in the eye, and the seeds may also introduce infection and abscesses. Sudden irritation, infection underrunning the skin or a persistent abscess may all be due

to a grass awn which has tracked its way below the surface. Location and removal of the awn is a skilful job, and usually one for the veterinary surgeon.

Heat Stroke

Most dogs can withstand the same temperature extremes as man and many breeds are considerably hardier than that. Even so, the first hot summer's day is often too much for the less robust, and if denied access to a cool area, dogs may collapse with heat stroke. The obese dog is most likely to be affected as a heavy layer of body fat tends to insulate the dog and prevents it from controlling body temperature as efficiently as leaner specimens. Dogs confined to cars left by thoughtless owners in direct sunlight very soon reach temperatures which they are unable to tolerate, and many experience great distress. Death is the inevitable result of prolonged exposure to high environmental temperatures. Immediate removal to a cool environment with adequate access to fresh air, and oxygen if it is available, improves the condition of the great majority of dogs with heat stroke. Ice packs or even cold water enemas may be needed, but veterinary attention should be sought without delay (see also Collapse).

Interdigital cysts or small abscesses between the toes can be induced to rupture and discharge the pus with repeat applications of hot fomentation. Leave the burst cyst exposed to the air

Interdigital Cysts

These are small abscesses between the toes and occur in all types of dog, but most frequently in Terriers, particularly West Highlands and Cairns. They may obstinately resist all forms of treatment and may have to be removed surgically. Once foreign material, such as grass seeds, has been eliminated as a cause, the general health of the dog must be considered, as these foci of infection are most common in dogs suffering from general debility.

Lead Poisoning

The most common cause of lead poisoning in dogs is from ingestion of flaking lead-based paint. The cores of golf balls sometimes contain a very toxic, lead-based fluid, and old linoleum may have lead compounds in it. Lead affects dogs with vomiting and diarrhoea, and enough abdominal pain to depress the dog's appetite. The classic sign of a blue line along the gums is sometimes evident in more chronic cases. Other signs are disturbances of the nervous system, with fits, hysteria and some degree of paralysis. Some dogs may become over-sensitive to an external stimulus. If treatment is started in time, results are often good, but urgency is essential as the most effective treatment is the use of compounds which inactivate (chelate) and excrete the remaining lead.

Metaldehyde Poisoning

Metaldehyde is used extensively to combat the slugs which cause havoc in many gardens, though newer formulations are largely non-poisonous to pets. As it is mixed with bran, metaldehyde becomes palatable and attractive to dogs (and cats). The signs of poisoning are salivation, some vomiting and a variety of nervous disorders, including overreaction to all stimuli (hyperaesthesia), leading to inco-ordination, a degree of paralysis, prostration and convulsions. Death may follow from respiratory arrest. The most effective treatment usually includes general anaesthesia and veterinary help must be obtained at once.

Lead poisoning in its chronic stages shows as a blue line along the gum. It is usually accompanied by disturbances to the nervous system

Paraquat Poisoning

Paraquat is widely used as a contact weedkiller and is extremely poisonous. The toxic effects of vomiting and breathing difficulties are similar to those in humans. The dog may show blueness of the mucous membranes of the eyes and mouth, and often there is exudation into the lungs some time after ingestion, with an effect resembling self-drowning. Death is usually the result of drinking a concentrated solution of paraquat. If a dog is known to have taken in such a poison, a veterinarian may be able to pump the stomach empty, but time is of the essence, and if distressing signs appear, euthanasia is probably indicated.

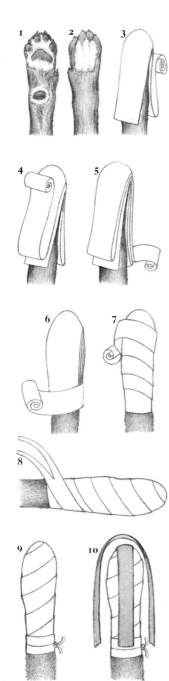

Feet injuries, to the paws, pads, or toes, must be protected from potential infection. Place cotton wool between the toes, cover the wound with lint and several layers of bandage, winding it firmly and securing it well above the wound. Keep the bandage in place with adhesive tape; a sock can be pulled over the bandage as protection

Poisoning: see entries under Cyanide, Lead, Metaldehyde, Paraquat and Warfarin. See also Diseases of the Alimentary System

Snake Bites

In Britain snake bites are rare as the only poisonous snake is the adder or viper. Even this animal will take off when disturbed. Snake bites may be seen to happen, or a dog may be observed to be in sudden pain with a swelling round its face or forelegs, sometimes with marks of a snake bite, though these are not easy to distinguish from rat bites. In either case, urgent veterinary attention is needed.

Adder bites are rarely fatal to healthy dogs, but those from venomous snakes can be quite fearsome and need urgent veterinary help.

Stings: see Bee Stings

Toad Venom Poisoning

Unlike frogs, toads defend themselves by secreting a venomous substance (Bufotoxin) through the skin. Some species have particularly noxious secretions, but those in Britain normally cause only local irritation. More serious results arise if part of the toad is actually eaten.

Usually a dog may pick a toad up in its mouth and subsequently show signs of heavy salivation and attempts at vomiting. If much venom is absorbed, convulsions and collapse with heart failure may follow, but this rarely occurs with European toad species. If a dog shows signs of having been in contact with toad venom, the mouth must be carefully washed out as soon as possible. Most dogs recover quickly, but if more generalized signs, such as collapse or convulsions, occur, it becomes a veterinary emergency.

Warfarin Poisoning

This poison, widely used to kill rats and mice, acts by the inhibition of blood clotting. Dogs can be poisoned by eating the bait, but the most usual route is via the ingestion of a poisoned rodent. Affected dogs usually collapse with acute abdominal pain and breathing difficulty, the mucous membranes inside the mouth become very pale, and the body temperature drops to a dangerously low level. A heavy dose of Warfarin will rapidly kill even a healthy dog. The need for anticoagulant and supportive treatment, usually vitamin K injections, is very urgent, but cases treated early enough have a good chance of recovery.

Wounds

Injuries which break the surface of the skin are quite common in dogs, particularly those which, like most Terriers, lead an adventurous life. Most wounds are around the head, neck and extremities of the limbs. Damage to the ears and tail is also fairly frequent (see also Bites).

The first priority is to stop any bleeding (see page 138), the next to clean the area, clipping away matted hair (avoid touching the edges of the ears or they will bleed profusely). Disinfectants should be used sparingly as they may cause more damage to the tissues. Bandaging of almost any part of a dog requires special skills, and the amateur application of bandages often results in dangerous constriction of the limbs or the arrest of breathing if applied to the head. All but the most trivial injuries should be examined and treated by a veterinarian as soon as possible.

Muscular & Skeletal Diseases

Arthritis

Joint degeneration may be a result of deterioration with age, physical damage or infectious disease. Where changes occur in the cartilage which forms the articular part of the joint they are usually degenerative rather than inflammatory. Inflammatory changes occur with generalized infections or when one or two joints only are affected by an injury. The more inflammation the more pain with movement. Infection and injury, although more painful, may often result in eventual healing. With degenerative changes there is usually less inflammation, but more limitation of movement.

Antibiotics are extensively used in the treatment of joint infections so as to prevent changes which will permanently incapacitate the dog. Joint damage usually needs radiographic examination for a proper diagnosis and evaluation of the extent of damage. The commonest joints to show pathological changes are the stifle and the hip in the hindleg, and the shoulder and carpus in the foreleg.

Some hip problems can be resolved by completely excising the head of the femur where it sits in the hip socket; certain cases need an artificial hip joint, but others manage without any femoral head at all. All joint diseases, except for the mildest sprain, show symptoms of pain, swelling, local heat or restricted movement.

Disc protrusion into the spinal canal may result in partial or complete paralysis of the hind limbs. It may follow serious injury, but is also common in certain long-backed breeds, such as the Dachshund

Disc Protrusion

The cartilaginous discs, with pulpy centres, between each vertebra in the spinal column may become displaced, or rupture and protrude into the spinal canal, exerting pressure on the spinal cord. Depending on the amount of displacement and consequent pressure on the spinal cord, and on the position in the back where it occurs, pain is present to some degree; loss of use and feeling may occur and if rupture of the disc is complete, paralysis is more likely, usually accompanied by urinary and fecal incontinence. Cases stand a better chance of recovery if some sensation is retained in the limbs; at the same time dogs with complete paralysis but in no pain may be very alert and cheerful.

Disc protrusion involving the upper part of the spine is usually extremely painful, particularly so when the neck is the seat of the trouble, as all four limbs may be affected. The dog may be unable to move its neck at all because of intense pain. Disc protrusion often follows injury such as a road accident, but may also occur after a sudden unco-ordinated movement.

The condition may take months to clear up and much devoted nursing is needed. It is impossible to predict the outcome at the early stages, but even totally paralysed cases can recover in time. Operations can be performed on suitable cases; results are variable, but the prospects are often good.

Fractures

Any bone in the body can be broken, but if the animal is healthy quite strong forces are usually involved in fractures. Bones lacking mineral deposit may break spontaneously, or with very little outside influence. Such conditions occur most frequently in dogs fed on muscle meat alone.

Fractures of the limbs are a common result of traffic accidents and similar trauma. The forelimb may break in the mid humerus, at the point of the elbow, and at the bottom of the radius and ulna just above the carpus. The hindlimb is often broken at the lower end of the femur; the smaller the end fragment, the more difficult is healing of the fracture. The head of the femur may be snapped off, resulting in considerable pain. The tibia below the knee joint and the point of the hock are other common sites. The pelvis is often broken in traffic accidents, but, like the jaw, usually heals surprisingly well.

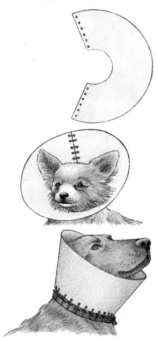

An Elizabethan collar is useful to prevent a dog from biting and tearing bandages, or licking open wounds. Fashion a funnel from stiff cardboard, with a circle cut out to fit the dog's neck; staple or lace the two edges together. Alternatively, remove the base of a soft plastic bucket, pull it over the dog's head, and lace it to the collar

Less promising are fractures of the spine as the spinal cord is likely to suffer irreparable damage; paralysis is a common result, although the bone may well heal. Modern techniques of pinning and plating, as well as long-established standing methods such as plastering, can deal with most fractured bones.

Hip Dysplasia

The hip is a relatively simple ball and socket joint, prone to inherited faulty development (dysplasia) in some breeds, resulting in various degrees of malfunction. The socket may be inadequate and too shallow for the head of the femur, the head of the femur may be misshapen, and bony outgrowths can develop round the joint itself.

Radiography is needed to assess the degree of dysplasia, but the extent of the damage to the joint may be quite disproportionate to the clinical picture. Dogs with apparently only slightly misshapen hip joints may be severely lame and in a good deal of pain. Others with extensive pathological changes may be sound for most of the time and be in no pain at all. Vigorous efforts are being made to reduce the incidence of inherited hip dysplasia, which is most prevalent in large breeds, particularly the German Shepherd Dog. Potential owners should always seek puppies from stock known to be sound. The English Kennel Club maintains a register of hip dysplasia score (see also page 15).

Various surgical procedures are used to alleviate the condition. They include removal of the femoral head and the use of artificial hip joints.

Rubber Jaw: see Diseases of the Urinary System

Scottie Cramp

Cramp occurs in dogs such as racing Greyhounds because of muscle fatigue, but a different condition seems to be peculiar to Scottish Terriers. It shows as a stiffening of the legs, usually the forelimbs; the condition appears to be inherited, but affects only young dogs, mainly under eighteen months old. As the dog ages, Scottie Cramp disappears and with patience the situation will resolve itself. Breeding from affected individuals is inadvisable. Treatment to alleviate the symptoms may be needed if the dog is unable to walk.

Swimmers

This curious condition is seen in some puppies about one to two weeks old. They are unable to walk properly but 'swim' around on their undersides, propelled by limbs held in a near-horizontal plane. The condition may affect any breed, but a particularly severe form involving irreversible brain damage has been observed in Irish Setters. A similar condition, found in some Labrador litters, appears to be more like unco-ordinated growth, with the body growing too rapidly for the legs to support it adequately. If the puppies continue to feed, relieve themselves and do not sustain any injuries, they usually recover.

Tetany

Tetanus infection, causing tetany in dogs and other mammals, is relatively rare in dogs. The organism involved, *Clostridium tetani*, normally lives in the gut of many species, particularly horses, and its presence is widespread in the soil. Farm dogs are the most likely to be exposed to Tetanus infection. The organism may proliferate in deep wounds or where oxygen is in short supply. Puncture wounds are the commonest route of entry for the organism, which produces a toxin causing the animal to go into rigid spasms. Although an affected dog does not usually eat, it does not seem to be affected with 'lockjaw', though the pull on the muscles round the head can give the appearance of a sardonic grin (*risus sardonicus*).

Death may follow if the muscles controlling respiration are in continuous spasm. Vigorous therapy can be successful if begun in time.

Diseases of the Alimentary System

Allergy: see Skin Diseases

Anorexia and Inappetance

Inappetance is simply poor appetite; anorexia, complete lack of appetite. The condition of *anorexia nervosa*, a mental disturbance, does not appear to occur in dogs. A day or so without food will not harm a healthy dog, and most are able to survive without food for quite long periods, provided that they drink water. A dog which does not eat for more than thirty-six hours should be examined by a veterinarian once it has been established that it is not finding food elsewhere, as no dog can maintain its body weight without eating something. An owner is often unaware that someone else may be feeding the dog, or that it may be supplementing its diet by hunting, by scavenging in dustbins, or by stealing food left out for birds. Heavy engorgement when an opportunity arises may be followed by a period of anorexia, but usually a dog which overeats will do so again as soon as its stomach will accommodate more food.

Inappetance is a matter of degree. Some owners believe that their dogs do not eat enough, although the healthy state of the animal indicates that it is getting adequate nourishment. Other dogs, especially toy breeds, are temperamental feeders, often because owners allow them to establish a dominant position in the household, with clearly expressed views on when and what they want to be fed. This type of spoilt behaviour may be so far-reaching that the dogs have to be fed by hand.

Various strategies can be employed to encourage reluctant feeders and can be useful in the short term if no other abnormalities are evident. However, a poor appetite with progressive loss of body weight should be investigated by a veterinarian. To overcome temporary lack of appetite, give small, frequent meals and remove uneaten food after fifteen minutes. Feed wet (canned) food made moister by the addition of water or gravy and flavour it with known favourites. Food warmed to blood heat (99–100°F/37–38°C) often stimulates the appetite as does a competitive situation with other animals in the household.

Botulism

Serious cases of food poisoning sometimes result from a toxin produced by a micro organism known as *Clostridium botulinum*. This potent toxin is usually fatal in humans, while dogs and cats are considerably more resistant. The organism and the toxin, found in decaying carcases, are easily destroyed by heat; cooking and food processing protect humans and pet animals. However, the cases which do occur are usually a result of eating unprocessed knacker meat and carrion. The result is pronounced stiffness, vomiting with collapse, paralysis and other nervous signs. Recovery is possible with urgent attention.

Canine Parvovirus

In 1978 a new communicable disease swept the world. The virus disease is related to Feline Infectious Enteritis and is believed to have derived from it by mutation. Highly infectious and affecting dogs of all ages, it had a particularly severe effect on puppies at weaning time. The organs mainly affected were the heart and the bowel; heart changes resulted in many sudden deaths, often in healthy looking puppies, at the time their new owners took possession. More frequently, profound changes in the gut lead to vomiting and diarrhoea with a good deal of blood, the lining of the gut being totally destroyed in the worst cases. Dogs collapsed and died within a short time after the onset of symptoms. Some cases recovered after intensive care and fluid therapy.

In the early stages of Canine Parvovirus it was discovered that killed vaccine for the related feline disease gave *some* protection for dogs. Canine-derived vaccines are now available and give more reliable protection, although many individuals take longer to build up immunity than others. Vaccination against Canine Parvovirus disease must be included in the programme to protect young puppies, followed by annual booster injections to maintain immunity.

Colitis

The colon in the lower bowel is primarily concerned with reabsorption of water as the products of digestion move down the alimentary tract. Any influence which leaves water within the bowel will contribute to the water content of the dog's motions, which can vary from slightly wet feces to frank diarrhoea if the colon becomes inflamed. Any blood present is usually fresh, staining the motions red, and often there is straining, discomfort and a degree of pain. Motions may contain mucus, with little evidence of unabsorbed fat.

Veterinary examination is necessary to establish the several clinical conditions. Boxers appear to have a predisposition to two types of ulcerative colitis: Histiocytic Ulcerative Colitis, which does not respond well to treatment; and Idiopathic Ulcerative Colitis, which may recover with appropriate treatment. Dietary treatment has little effect on lower bowel conditions; the underlying cause for colitis must be established.

Constipation

Dogs vary greatly in the frequency of passing stools, and in their consistency. Passing feces three or more times daily is not unusual, nor is defecation once every thirty-six or even forty-eight hours. The consistency of normal feces can vary from soft, unformed motions to quite hard material.

Constipation becomes established when there is clear difficulty in passing the stools. The usual pattern of evacuation may alter, so that a dog normally passing motions once or twice daily may suddenly fail to do so for several days and show signs of straining with some discomfort or pain. The feces passed may be much harder than usual and of small volume only, with a good deal of mucus and traces of blood. Constipation may follow a bout of acute diarrhoea and a general loss of gut motility may be due to age or a radical change of diet. Most dogs enjoy a bone to chew at, but a surplus can cause the rectum to become impacted, as can overcooked bones which splinter easily.

Dogs sometimes have difficulty in passing feces when they also have a problem digesting fat (see Pancreatic Failure), and greasy motions tend to stick to the rear. Oily laxatives should be avoided and steps should be taken to aid fat digestion. Otherwise medicinal liquid paraffin may be given at the prescribed rate; it should be stopped once normal defecation has been restored.

With poor gut motility associated with old age, bran may be added to the food, and perhaps made more palatable with agar preparations such as sterculia gum or petrolagar. Veterinary advice is needed if difficulty in defecation persists. Deeper-seated problems, such as enlarged prostate glands, can cause constipation, and laxatives should not be given for any length of time except under veterinary direction.

Copper Toxicosis

Like most metals, copper is toxic, but in normal circumstances poisoning is rare. However, some Bedlington Terriers may inherit an inability to eliminate copper via the liver. Consequently levels of copper in the blood stream rise steadily until signs of toxicity are evident. The disease may be accompanied by depression, lethargy, loss of appetite and vomiting; diagnosis can only be confirmed with blood tests. Hepatitis (inflammation) and cirrhosis (fibrosis) of the liver follow. Treatment consists of restricting copper intake: most proprietary foods have relatively modest levels of copper and are a more reliable way of controlling copper intake than made-up diets.

Dehydration

Deprived of water a dog becomes dehydrated. Water is constantly being lost from the body via saliva, urine, feces, and by way of the expelled breath. In spite of a widely held belief, dogs also lose fluid through their skin, although their ability to sweat is limited.

Dogs can survive for quite long periods without solid food, but only for a short while without water. Drinking water should always be readily available, unless veterinary advice has been given to withhold it. It should be clean and reasonably fresh. A good deal of water is absorbed from food, and most dogs prefer wet foods to dry and adjust their water balance very accurately provided that drinking water is always available.

Increased water loss, due to evaporation in hot, dry weather and to vomiting and diarrhoea, speeds up the rate at which a dog becomes dehydrated. If vomiting and diarrhoea persist, the resulting dehydration can soon become life-threatening and is particularly dangerous to young puppies and very old dogs.

Excessive urination where water is not replaced, such as can occur in salt poisoning, is also likely to lead to death. Acute dehydration results in collapse; early attention by a veterinarian to administer fluids by injection is essential.

Diarrhoea

Like vomiting or blood in the urine, diarrhoea is not a disease in itself but a clinical sign of illness (see also Colitis, Gastro-enteritis and Pancreatic Failure). Diarrhoea is an increase in the fluidity and frequency of feces caused by a variety of conditions. All but the most transient bouts require proper veterinary investigation. Where diarrhoea and vomiting are continuous, particularly in puppies, professional help is needed urgently as collapse can follow.

The commonest causes of diarrhoea result from eating garbage and from sudden changes of diet. All dietary changes, particularly when the type of food is altered from dry to soft and moist, or canned, should be made over several days. Inflammatory conditions of the digestive tract are usually associated with infectious disease, such as Canine Parvovirus and Distemper.

Some dogs are unable to digest milk sugar (Lactose) adquately due to a relative lack of the necessary enzyme Lactase. Lactose remains unchanged as it moves down the gut, drawing more fluid into the bowel and eventually fermenting in the presence of bacteria. The diarrhoea which results usually stops soon after milk is withdrawn from the diet. It is useful to withhold milk temporarily from the diet of dogs with diarrhoea of unknown cause.

Routine treatment for non-specific diarrhoea normally consists in withholding solid food for twenty-four hours and thereafter gradually increasing small amounts of any concentrated, easily digested food until the dog is back to its normal diet. Some dogs seem unable to tolerate certain foods, such as liver, which should be eliminated from the diet.

Dysphagia

Difficulty or pain on swallowing is a serious matter. If it occurs suddenly it may be due to a foreign object lodged in the mouth, pharynx or oesophagus. If the onset is gradual, it may be caused by a tumour or enlarged tonsils.

Balls, pebbles, sticks of wood and bones are the most likely foreign objects. Pieces of bone usually have to be quite large and sharp to become fixed; fish or chicken bones are the most offending, but flat pieces with projecting wings can be serious if jammed at the entrance to the stomach or where the oesophagus passes near the heart. It is not rare for a dog to break off a piece of bone so that it becomes stuck across the roof of the mouth.

As most dogs vomit readily, foreign material is usually rapidly expelled.

However, if a dog shows willingness to eat but is unable to swallow properly, and if there is pain or severe retching afterwards, a veterinary examination is needed. No more food should be given as the dog may have to be anaesthetized.

Fat Malabsorption

If fat is not digested and absorbed it passes down the digestive tract and appears as an unpleasant mass in the feces. Malabsorption of fat can be due to insufficient bile, often because of obstruction of the bile duct. It is more likely that the pancreas is unable to provide enough enzymes to digest the fat, but urgent attention is needed in either case. Bilary duct obstruction is relatively rare, but may need surgery; Pancreatic Failure is common, especially in German Shepherd Dogs/Alsatians, and tests will establish if it is the reason for poor fat absorption.

If the pancreas provides too few digestive enzymes, they must be given by mouth for the rest of the dog's life as the pancreas does not regenerate. Meals should be provided on a little and often basis and fat in an easily digested form; coconut oil is often better digested than other fats.

Food Poisoning

A sudden illness, especially when accompanied by vomiting and diarrhoea, is often blamed on 'something the dog has eaten' (see also Botulism). Establishing the cause may be difficult. Food poisoning occurs through contamination of food with Salmonellae or Staphylococci bacteria which proliferate or produce toxins. Some fungal infections are also highly toxic, and food may be contaminated with other toxic material such as pesticides (see Accidents & First Aid). In general, dogs are resistant to slightly contaminated material, and cooking destroys potentially injurious micro organisms. Canning has the same effect, and canned food has been sterilized to reduce the chances of food poisoning to a low level. In suspected food poisoning, samples of the food eaten should be taken to the veterinarian.

Gastritis

Inflammation of the stomach shows as poor appetite and usually vomiting. Gastritis may also be due to infectious disease, especially Canine Parvovirus, Distemper, or Infectious Canine Hepatitis. Bacterial infections, such as Salmonella, can have the same effect, although the inflammation extends further down the gut causing Gastro-enteritis.

Foreign material may irritate the lining of the stomach and cause gastritis. Dogs are inclined to eat all types of garbage and carrion, and it is not unusual for such material to be regurgitated. The odd vomiting episode is normal, but persistent vomiting, if blood is present and if there is obvious pain or discomfort afterwards, needs professional help.

Gastric Dilation/Torsion

In certain types of dogs gas accumulates in the stomach so that it dilates to such an extent as to become a threat to life. Breeds usually affected by the disease, sometimes known as bloat, are particularly Bloodhounds, Great Danes, Irish Wolfhounds and Irish Setters. Other breeds, such as Basset Hounds and Boxers, are also affected, and it may also occur in Dachshunds and Pekingese.

Dogs with gastric dilation usually make unsuccessful attempts to vomit and show an obvious, tight distension of the abdominal wall. If the condition is not resolved, the stomach may twist on its axis (torsion), trapping the gas and cutting off the blood supply to essential organs. A complete twist of the gut (volvulus) is life-threatening and needs urgent veterinary attention.

Gastric Dilation is usually related to greedy feeders getting excited at meal times, with a tendency to overeat and to swallow air. Breeds likely to be affected

Gastric dilation occurs in dogs which swallow air as they gulp down their food. The effect can be minimized by raising the feeding bowl above floor level

should be fed smaller meals more frequently and outside periods of activity. A food bowl raised on to a low table is said to reduce the amount of air swallowed during feeding.

Gastro-enteritis

This general term for inflammation of the digestive tract is almost always associated with vomiting and diarrhoea; in severe cases blood may also be lost. It is not a specific condition, but can be a result of infectious disease (see Canine Parvovirus and Distemper).

Gastro-enteritis commonly results from eating garbage, seen particularly in Labradors. Most poisons have a similar effect (see Poisoning), and so has overfeeding or sudden changes of the feeding regime. The condition may be an extension of gastritis.

The most serious effects of gastro-enteritis are a depletion of essential nutrients; very little is absorbed during severe vomiting and diarrhoea, and in addition dogs soon become seriously dehydrated, followed eventually by collapse, and death if fluid loss is continuous. All but the most transient cases, and particularly young animals, need urgent veterinary attention.

Histiocytic Ulcerative Colitis: see Colitis

Hypervitaminosis

Vitamins are essential for proper body functions, but excesses are in no way beneficial. Over supplementation of water-soluble vitamins – C and the B complex – is not likely to be harmful, but the fat-soluble vitamins A and D are stored in the liver and excesses can be cumulative. Over supplementation usually occurs through cod liver oil, vitamin tablets or from large amounts of food rich in vitamin A, such as liver; bone changes may result with deposition of bone in the soft tissues. Bone deformities are occasionally seen in the long bones of giant dogs such as Great Danes when cod liver oil has been given to dogs critically short of essential minerals in their diet. Far from improving bone structure an excessive intake of vitamin D depletes the skeleton as more calcium is absorbed than can be excreted.

Hypervitaminosis is easily avoided with a balanced diet and no unnecessary supplementation; where hypervitaminosis is suspected, urgent veterinary attention is essential.

Idiopathic Ulcerative Colitis: see Colitis

Infectious Canine Hepatitis (ICH)

Sometimes called Infectious Viral Hepatitis and formerly known as Rubarth's Disease (see also Blue Eye), this is a specific virus disease of the liver. It is highly infectious, and unless dogs are protected by vaccination they usually succumb to the disease. Young dogs are most at risk, although dogs of all ages may contract ICH, characterized by high fever with prostration, sometimes increased thirst accompanied by vomiting, abdominal pain, and diarrhoea, often with violent hemorrhage in the gut. The extent of blood loss usually indicates the possibility of successful treatment. With intensive care many cases recover completely, others may die within a few hours. The disease normally runs its course within a week, leading either to death or recovery.

Jaundice

Liver failure or an obstruction in the excretion of bile can be caused by the accumulation of bile salts in the bloodstream and tissues. It shows as a yellow, sometimes almost orange discoloration of the skin, the mucous membranes in the mouth and of the whites of the eyes. Jaundice is difficult to detect in dogs well covered in hair, or with heavily pigmented skin, but is usually obvious in the mouth; it is almost always a serious sign of some underlying illness.

Gastro-enteritis is common among scavenging dogs. Infectious materials should be kept out of harm's way, and garbage cans tightly closed

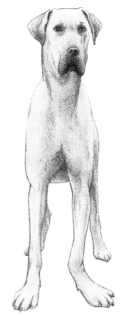

Hypervitaminosis results from excessive doses of cumulative vitamins, notably A and D. In extreme cases, the condition can lead to bone deformities and possibly liver damage

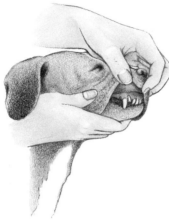

Jaundice is a symptom of underlying disease. The typical yellow coloration can be difficult to detect except in the mucous membranes of the eyes and the mouth

Pancreatic failure, due to severe inflammation, is extremely painful. The dog adopts a typical half-crouching or 'praying' posture

Jaundice is often a result of infection with Leptospira bacteria (see Leptospirosis). Dogs can be vaccinated against the two commonest Leptospira infections, both of which can affect man; humans and dogs usually contract Leptospirosis from rat contamination of water or food supplies. Jaundice can also result from toxicity with fungal contamination of foodstuffs, paraquat used as a weedkiller, or phenol used as a disinfectant.

Obesity

When body fat accumulates to such an extent that it affects body function, a dog can be said to be obese. A recent survey has shown that about twenty-five per cent of dogs in Britain are obese. The results are reduced life expectancy due to the serious effects on the circulatory system and the joints. Fat dogs are poor surgical and anaesthetic risks; they appear to age more rapidly than leaner individuals, and they become distressed on hot days as heat is retained by the insulating effects of body fat.

With a balanced diet no dog need become obese. Prepared or canned foods, fed as recommended and mixed sparingly with calorie-rich cereals, will avoid obesity. Dogs' energy needs differ widely between individuals, and in the final analysis the owner must be the best judge and assess the correct amount of food.

Once a dog has become obese, it requires great discipline to manage a slimming programme. Good results can be achieved by feeding a calculated amount of food to the exclusion of everything else, except for drinking water. If the dog is weighed at weekly intervals and a reduction of twenty per cent is made in the daily food allowance when there is no loss of weight, a good result can usually be achieved within twelve weeks. Otherwise weight reduction may have to be carried out under veterinary supervision and may involve hospitalization.

Pancreatic Failure

Inflammation of the pancreas, in the forward part of the abdomen, is usually acutely painful. The dog may stand with forequarters held low to the ground, hind parts normal in the so-called praying attitude. Attempts to move the dog are usually met with resentment because of the severe pain. Expert treatment is urgently needed or death quickly follows.

More chronic and less severe inflammation or degeneration of the pancreas leads to loss of its function in digestion. The pancreas produces enzymes for the process of digestion, particularly of fats, proteins and some carbohydrates, and with pancreatic failure the absorption of nutrients is poor. The dog may have an insatiable appetite but still be very thin, with a harsh, dry and scaly coat. The feces are foul-smelling, pale and often putty-coloured, and fat is passed in partly digested or undigested form. Carbohydrates ferment along the digestive tract, producing offensive-smelling flatus and strange digestive noises from within the abdomen. Degenerative disease commonly occurs in German Shepherd Dogs (Alsatians).

The condition must be distinguished from other bowel conditions, but once established, enzyme replacement therapy in the form of tablets is often very effective. The treatment must be maintained for the rest of the dog's life.

Poisoning

Unless a dog has been seen to ingest a poison (see Accidents & First Aid) in sufficiently large amounts to put the matter beyond doubt, the diagnosis of poisoning requires expert investigation. Dogs are fairly resilient and often readily vomit any noxious material they have eaten. Unfortunately all the signs of poisoning – vomiting, diarrhoea, convulsions, collapse, coma and death, as well as symptoms of nervous disorders, including dilated or constricted pupils, continuous eye movements, inco-ordination and paralysis – can be associated with other conditions. Any of these signs demands immediate contact with the local veterinary practice. If poisoning is suspected any evidence which might point to the ingestion of a toxic agent should be brought along.

Vomiting should be induced with a salt solution only if the dog has been seen to swallow a known, non-corrosive poison.

Vitamin Deficiency

Although this is unusual, one important group of vitamins, the B complex, is destroyed through overcooked food. Unless it is replaced with, for example, brewers' yeast, deficiency occurs as B vitamins cannot be stored in the body. The important vitamin B_1 (thiamin) is easily destroyed by heat as well as by an enzyme in raw fish. Deficiency of the vitamin causes loss of appetite, which worsens the situation, and a variety of neurological disorders may result. Administration of B vitamins by injection rapidly reverses the situation, but an adequate diet must be given to prevent recurrence.

Vitamin A deficiency may result in growth deformities and is especially associated with serious eye problems. The chief source of the vitamin is animal liver and generally the probability of deficiency is low. A regular diet of properly formulated or prepared foods should prevent vitamin and mineral deficiencies.

Vitamin Excess: see Hypervitaminosis

Vomiting (see also Travel Sickness, Gastritis, Gastro-enteritis)

Many dogs are careless feeders and frequently ingest potentially harmful materials. They also frequently overeat. In both instances they commonly and readily vomit, without much ill effect; unrestrained they may well eat the material again. They also eat fibrous grass as a prelude to vomiting, probably to give them something easier to return.

Vomiting should not be confused with regurgitation, which occurs in some bitches following stimulus from the puppies when they are hungry.

Persistent vomiting is a serious sign and needs further investigation, particularly if blood is present. Continuous vomiting, accompanied by diarrhoea, weakens a dog rapidly as it is depleted of nutrients and fluid. It may be an indication of infectious disease, such as Canine Parvovirus, the ingestion of noxious material, or the presence of a foreign body. Food should be withheld from a vomiting dog for half a day or so, and only small but frequent amounts of fluid, preferably with dissolved glucose, should be provided. Tiny amounts of easily digestible food may then be introduced, but if the dog continues to vomit, veterinary assistance is required.

Weight Loss

A gradual loss of weight may accompany chronic illness, while lack of appetite and continuous vomiting or diarrhoea cause rapid weight losses. Marked changes always require investigation, with checks on the adequacy and quantity of the diet.

Severely and continuously underweight dogs may be hyperactive – as happens in some German Shepherd Dogs. They may require medical treatment in addition to large amounts of concentrated foods.

A common reason for underweight bitches is a failure to provide them with enough food while they are rearing litters of puppies. A lactating bitch usually needs at least three times the amount of food she requires for normal maintenance of health. Working dogs, herding or shepherding, also need high levels of wholesome food; they usually have to be fed several times daily.

Coarse grass is a natural emetic for dogs with a mild stomach upset

Weight watching is no problem with small dogs which can be placed directly on the scales. Large dogs are easiest weighed with their owners, and the weight of the latter deducted

Diseases of the Circulatory & Respiratory Systems

Anemia

In practical terms anemia means loss of whole blood or a lack of some of the blood components – either red blood cells or the pigment hemoglobin, a substance which transports oxygen to the tissues and gives blood its colour.

Loss of whole blood can follow any injury which severs enough blood vessels to cause significant hemorrhage. Chronic parasitism can have a similar effect by depriving the dog of blood over a long period. Loss of blood pigment may follow infectious disease or toxicity.

The colour of the mucous membranes inside the mouth or paleness of the skin is not a reliable guide to an anemic state in a dog. Severe anemia does not necessarily show as pallor; marked paleness is not necessarily a sign of anemia, but could be due to severe shock where a large proportion of the blood has shifted away from the surface areas.

Anemia may follow certain dietary deficiencies if iron, vitamins B_{12} or B_6 necessary for blood manufacture are in short supply. Such occurrences are rare on an adequate diet, and the presence – or absence – of the anemic state is a matter for blood tests and diagnosis by a veterinarian.

Bleeding: see Accidents & First Aid

Bordetella Infection: see Kennel Cough

Bronchitis: see Coughing

Canine Parvovirus: see Diseases of the Alimentary System

Cardiac Failure

Heart problems usually relate to either valve disease or deterioration in the heart muscle. Both make the heart less efficient in maintaining circulation, with consequent congestion due to accumulation of abdominal fluid in severe cases. Some dogs develop a characteristic dry cough on exercise. Hot summer days mean added stress on dogs with faulty heart function, and fainting and collapse can easily occur if the dog stays in the sun, especially if the dog is also obese (see also Accidents & First Aid, and Obesity).

Some infectious diseases result in deterioration of the heart muscle, but heart valve deterioration is usually associated with age, although the two diseases may occur simultaneously. Drugs are available for many heart conditions and suspected cases need veterinary attention sooner rather than later. With proper treatment and revised life style they need not be fatal.

Parasitism caused by heart worm (*Dirofilaria immitis*) can bring serious heart disorders. The parasite is widespread in the United States and in tropical areas of Asia and Africa. A mosquito is needed to complete the life-cycle of heart worms. Treatment and prevention are specialized areas of medicine, sometimes requiring surgical intervention.

Coughing

A dog may cough to dislodge material such as mucus, grit, pollen, grass seeds, or fumes of some irritant material from the respiratory system. More commonly coughs are a result of local inflammation caused by micro organisms (see Distemper and Kennel Cough). Chronic circulatory congestion also produces a cough, known as a heart cough, after exertion.

Inflammation may occur anywhere in the respiratory tract. Laryngitis is common, particularly if a dog has been confined for a long period and has barked continuously. An inflamed trachea usually produces a harsh, persistent cough. Other inflammatory conditions can affect the lungs (pneumonia), the bronchi (bronchitis), and the layers of tissue between chest wall and lungs (pleurisy). Coughing can also be caused by parasitism.

Treatment of anything but a mild transient cough needs professional help in diagnosing the cause, eliminating infection, and helping the body to combat inflammation. Soothing medicines and soft foods such as honey and ice-cream play a useful part.

Endocarditis

When the heart muscle becomes inflamed it is known as endocarditis and is usually the result of bacterial infection. It is accompanied by high temperature, and the dog may be in a state of collapse (see Cardiac Failure).

Infectious Canine Hepatitis: see Diseases of the Alimentary System

Kennel Cough

This condition occurs characteristically in a dog recently returned from a boarding kennel. The harsh unproductive cough may be more or less continuous, and is exacerbated by excitement. The dog does not usually show any signs of illness except for a slight fever and poor appetite. However, secondary bacteria disease can lead to pneumonia or generalized infection.

Kennel cough is caused by *Bordetella* bacteria, as well as a number of viruses. Protection is available through vaccination and it is sensible to immunize dogs likely to be kennelled.

Laryngitis: see Coughing
Pleurisy: see Coughing
Pneumonia: see Coughing

Tracheitis

Inflammation of the windpipe can result from Bordetella infection (see Kennel Cough) or from parasitic infestation with a particular type of worm. Endoscopy techniques, by which cavities can be examined through a lighted tube, allow such conditions to be diagnosed and located. Inhalation of irritant gases, such as ammonia, can cause severe tracheitis. Removal from the source of irritation and supportive treatment are usually rewarding.

Diseases of the Skin & External Features

Abscess

This is the equivalent of a boil or carbuncle, and usually the result of micro organisms being introduced into or under the skin. Bacteria that normally live in the skin may proliferate in favourable circumstances. Abscesses in the gut or liver are difficult to detect, although the effects may make the dog very ill. Professional help is needed for a proper diagnosis. An abscess produces swelling, inflammation and local heat, and the contents become a thick liquid or semi-liquid, foul-smelling, often blood-stained mass.

Tooth abscesses in the upper jaw often show themselves initially as a swollen or weeping eye; the offending tooth must be extracted so that the pus can drain away

Bite wounds often produce abscesses as the teeth can introduce infected material through only a small tear of the skin. With little aeration of the wound, bacteria rapidly proliferate. Bite wounds can be difficult to locate in dark-skinned, long-haired dogs, and it is not always easy to distinguish between the bite wound and the site of the abscess. See also Accidents & First Aid.

Pus may track in any direction and emerge elsewhere as a fistula, or channel between the surface and another site, often a cavity such as the rectum, anal sac, or vagina. Fistulae may also form between internal structures, where their presence is difficult to detect, or they may emerge through the skin round the mouth or, more commonly, the anus, particularly in German Shepherd Dogs. Extensive surgical correction is often necessary.

An abscess may form at the root of a tooth, with pus being unable to drain away if the abscess is in the upper jaw. A weeping eruption may be present just below the eye and can easily be mistaken for an eye condition; as pus must drain downwards, the offending tooth may have to be removed.

Abscesses are treated by cleaning the area, particularly fight wounds, and removing hair, pus, and soil, grit or oil, which can contaminate the area. The dog's natural defences can be aided with local heat applied as lint soaked in hot water. This should be repeated every two to three hours during the day, and as soon as the abscess has come to a point, every effort should be made to evacuate the pus, which must be allowed to drain downwards. Failing this, the abscess must be lanced by a veterinary surgeon.

Cleaning of the area and local heat should be continued after an abscess has erupted as the exit quickly closes over, trapping any pus left inside the abscess. Any persistent or obviously painful swelling needs veterinary attention as it may contain a grass awn or piece of fish hook (see also Accidents & First Aid).

Acne

This skin condition of human puberty does not occur in dogs, but similar small abscesses are occasionally found around the mouth of a dog of any age. They are usually the result of the dog's exploration of deep cover, an encounter with a hedgehog or similar obstruction. Treatment is as for other abscesses, and care must be taken to ensure that no thorns or spines remain. Delayed healing or suspected infection under the skin (furunculosis), especially in Spaniels, need professional attention.

Adenoma

An adenoma is a tumour growing from glandular tissue. The most common and visible adenomas, though some occur internally, are found in the skin and around the anus. Skin adenomas are chiefly the result of sebaceous glands (see Cysts), and can usually be removed without any complication. Distinguishing adenomas from cysts is a task for the veterinarian, who must judge when surgical removal is needed. If left, they tend to ulcerate.

Adenomas around the anus (see also Anal Sacs) are more serious. They arise from tiny perianal glands and are usually slow-growing, although they may ulcerate and become irritating. Hormone-dependent, they are usually more common in older male dogs; if caught in the early stages, hormone treatment and castration are often effective.

Allergy (see also Dermatitis)

Allergy is a reaction to an environmental material, usually protein, which has invaded the body. The commonest allergies are seen as skin reactions or as digestive disturbances. The allergies – external sources causing allergy – can result in contact dermatitis of the type often seen in West Highland White Terriers. This breed seems to react to a large number of substances which come into contact with its skin; care is necessary in choosing bedding material.

A developing allergy is complex and more consequential than irritation, intolerance or inability to digest foods. It does not develop immediately, but begins as a period of sensitization. The identification of the substance which causes the reaction requires much detective work based on a process of elimination. Household cleaners, synthetic fibres in floor coverings and clothing, and aerosol sprays may be responsible for the occasional allergic reaction in dogs.

Food-induced allergies are relatively unusual, accounting for only one per cent of all canine allergies. The detection of the food substances which provoke an allergic reaction needs patience and relies for effectiveness on a strict regime of test feeding. The dog is put on to a basic test diet, continued over five days, of simple protein sources such as all fish or all chicken. All other foods, including vitamins, minerals and other supplements, must be excluded; drinking water is the only permitted addition. The commonest food allergens are beef, wheat, and milk protein, and these should be introduced in turn and the effect observed. If the allergic skin reaction persists on the basic diet, it may not be necessary to look beyond that, if it is an allergy at all.

Usually only small amounts of the allergen are needed to trigger an effect, and once it has been identified the offending substance must be permanently omitted from the dog's diet. Fortunately allergies in dogs are normally confined to one substance.

With contact or inhaled allergies it is usually necessary to remove the dog from its usual environment so that the signs can recede. If the condition remains after exhausting all likely allergens, professional help and probably hospitalization will be needed.

Alopecia

This skin condition shows as complete loss of hair right down to the hair follicles and is the equivalent of human baldness. Hair will not grow again where the follicles have become completely inactive, unlike ordinary hair-shedding where the hair breaks off but the follicles produce new hairs. Odd patches of alopecia, particularly in ageing dogs, are not a cause for anxiety, but extensive areas of complete hair loss are frequently associated with hormonal disturbances and indicate the need for veterinary examination. Extensive patches arranged symmetrically across the body could be an indication of thyroid of adrenal gland disturbance, or in males a tumour of the testis.

Alopecia or patches of baldness may be a natural sign of age. Large, symmetrical areas (*shown in red*) can be symptoms of disturbed hormone balance

Anal Sacs

Sometimes known as anal glands, these should not be confused with the tiny perianal glands which may develop into tumours (see Adenoma). Anal sacs are the two pockets on either side and below the anus; they are also found in cats and foxes and are the source of the powerful odour of the skunk. The secretion from these sacs contain a viscid, fatty substance with a pungent, penetrating and sickly smell. Recent research has shown that the fluid changes in consistency through the year and when a bitch is in oestrus, and normal secretions are part of the communication system between dogs. Anal sacs are often evacuated forcibly in stressful situations, as when a nervous dog is handled by a stranger.

Anal sacs sometimes become impacted with their own secretion, causing first irritation, then pain. The dog pays more attention to its rear end, at the start gnawing away at the area around the tail root. The owner suspects the presence of fleas, which may well be correct, but the dog's behaviour is also characteristic of anal sac inflammation.

Anal sac impaction should be suspected when a dog rubs its rear along the ground or attempts to chew at the tail root area

In the second stage, the dog scrapes its anus along the ground, often interpreted as evidence of worm infestation; this is rarely the reason for such characteristic behaviour, although worms may also be present. In clipped breeds, anal sac impaction may occur after a grooming, presumably because small lengths of hair block the anal ducts. More rarely and more painfully, a grass awn may have a similar effect.

Evacuation of the anal sacs is a relatively simple, if smelly procedure, but it should not be carried out unless there are signs of impaction. Unnecessary emptying of anal sacs is likely to result in chronic inflammation and increase the chances of further impactions. Anal sacs are best expressed by the veterinarian who can establish the reasons for impaction. Most anal sac conditions are related to chronic low-grade infections which need additional treatment, in extreme cases involving removal of the anal sacs.

Blindness

Breakdowns in vision are commonly due to injury, ageing, infections, disease, or inherited factors. See also Cataract, Collie Eye Anomaly, Conjunctivitis, Eye Diseases, and Progressive Retinal Atrophy.

The effects of failing eyesight may not be readily apparent as the dog easily adapts to changing circumstances. Much depends on whether vision is distorted or lessened. Distorted vision is likely to result from changes at the front of the eye, particularly lens dislocation, when the dog sees objects in a different place and may bump into them. Even so it may adapt to the location of familiar furniture, and distorted vision may not be immediately obvious to the owner. The process of lessening visual acuity is usually gradual, and often due to age. Dogs with little or no eyesight can negotiate obstructions in their household with apparent ease.

Injuries to the eye stem mainly from road accidents and fights; they are generally unsightly or the eye is held so tightly closed that the extent of the problem is difficult to establish. On occasions the eye may be dislocated completely from its socket, especially in breeds with protruding eyes, such as Pekingese and Pugs. The eye can sometimes be replaced with prompt veterinary attention, although it will almost certainly suffer some damage, but often removal of the eye is the only course of action. The dog may be more comfortable with the eye removed, the result being no worse than blindness in one eye. Dogs recover remarkably quickly, and the level of pain experienced with most eye conditions seems to be much less than in comparable human situations.

Blood blister: see Hematoma

Blue Eye

This term aptly describes a well-defined condition of the normally transparent cornea. The condition is associated with a specific virus infection (see Infectious Canine Hepatitis) or occurs after the use of certain live vaccines in some susceptible breeds, particularly but not exclusively in Afghan Hounds. Only about twenty per cent of infected animals are affected, and the condition usually resolves itself in a few days. In some cases the condition persists and may become permanent. Any discoloration or clouding of the eye is a matter for veterinary examination.

Cataract

In order to transmit and focus light on to the retina, the lens must be transparent. Degenerative changes may result in a cataract when the lens becomes opaque and visible as a cloudy reflective area deep in the eye. Usually both eyes are affected, and as less light passes on to the retina, vision is much reduced. Reflex constriction of the pupil when a light is shone on it is greatly lessened. Dogs with poor vision manage to cope well in most circumstances (see Blindness).

Cataracts are often associated with other eye diseases, particularly in cases of inflammation; they may also occur as complications or simply with general changes of age, especially in Labradors and Poodles.

Once inflammatory conditions have been controlled, there is little prospect of dissolution of cataracts, and surgical removal of all or part of a cataract may be necessary. However, dogs still have effective vision with the lens removed, provided there are no extensive degenerative changes of other structures.

Collie Eye Anomaly

Rough and Smooth-Coated Collies are prone to what is thought to be faulty development of the retina. Most structures at the back of the eye are affected, and the result may vary between mildly defective sight and total blindness. The condition is almost certainly inherited.

Cataracts can be common in aged dogs when the lens becomes opaque. Bilateral cataracts (*above*) affect both eyes and occur in many diabetic dogs

Conjunctivitis

The lining (conjunctiva) of the inner side of the eyelids and the outer layer of the eye itself, up to the transparent cornea, may become inflamed because of local irritation. Airborne irritants, such as pollen, aerosol sprays and grass seed, are the most likely causes. Eye damage following a fight or road accident can also result in inflammation of the conjunctiva. In addition a variety of micro organisms, from viruses and bacteria to fungal infections, can cause inflammatory changes. Allergies also show themselves as local eye inflammation, usually with considerable tear production and swelling.

Amateur treatment for eye conditions can be risky and is best confined to gently clearing away obvious discharge, taking great care to avoid further injury to the eye. It is sometimes possible to remove an obvious foreign object from the eye, but great care is needed with barbed grass seeds, the commonest object to invade the eye.

Cysts

The most common cysts are found in the skin as glands producing sebum, a fatty substance which helps to give texture to the skin. Sebaceous cysts can occur on any part of the body, but mainly along the back or around the neck; they often rupture and secrete a cheesy–fatty, thick fluid. Kept clean they do not normally become infected, but are likely to recur; infected cysts effectively become abscesses. Sebaceous cysts are usually harmless, but if they become irritant or enlarged, they may need surgical excision. Any swelling which grows progressively larger should be examined by the veterinarian, as occasionally tumours (see Adenoma) occur.

Deafness

With age, hearing may become impaired, though some sounds are more easily heard than others. Deafness although progressive is not necessarily consistent, and sound perception may be better at certain times than others, a fact not always appreciated by an owner of a dog which appears to be 'conveniently' deaf on occasions. Eyesight also deteriorates with age, but may do so independently of hearing. Other cases of deafness are probably inherited and present from birth, particularly in dogs without any skin pigment (albinos). Bull Terriers sometimes show this trait.

Deafness occasionally results from poisoning with carbon monoxide, and some degree of deafness is due to accumulations of wax or other secretions in the ear canal. It is unwise to probe inside the ear, and cleaning and deep examination should be left to the veterinarian.

Most sounds can be felt as vibrations even by profoundly deaf dogs, and hearing facilities are difficult to test, especially as a dog may choose not to react to a sound it can actually hear.

Demodectic Mange

The condition sometimes known as Follicular or Red Mange is the result of a proliferation of the mite *Demodex folliculorum*. This parasite lives within the hair follicles and is probably found in most dogs. How the mites become so numerous as to cause skin changes, and how they are transmitted to other dogs, is not fully understood. Transmission is thought to occur only early in life, either because the skin is lacking in physical defences or because an immune mechanism has yet to develop. Clinical signs usually appear if the dog is debilitated due to poor nutrition (see also Autoimmune Disease).

Demodectic mange is usually more unsightly than irritating and often becomes infected. Changes occur in the skin as a thickening which becomes waxy, scaly, and wrinkled like elephant hide. With infection, small patches may

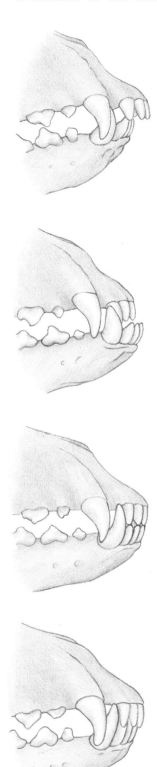

enlarge and coalesce, pustules form, and the skin has a characteristic musty smell. At this stage, the effect on the dog's general health is more profound, and the condition becomes less amenable to treatment. Demodectic mange chiefly occurs in dogs under one year old, although the skin changes may persist for years or be permanent if hair follicles are destroyed.

Dental Diseases

Most canine dental disease is a result of deposits on the teeth. Second in occurrence is inflammation of the gums (see Periodontal Disease). Teeth may be misshapen, break off or not fit properly; the 'bite' should just overlap so as to give a scissors effect rather than meeting like a pair of pincers. A faulty bite also results from the upper or lower jaw projecting forward too much or too little (overshot and undershot respectively).

Teeth may lose patches of enamel while they develop; the resulting so-called distemper teeth may be an aftermath of any serious disease in puppyhood. Although such teeth are unsightly, they do not cause the dog much inconvenience.

Dogs develop temporary (milk) teeth soon after birth; they are replaced by permanent teeth by the age of six months. A temporary tooth may still be present alongside the canine tooth for a considerable period after it would normally be lost, but this does not distort the mouth. However, food debris may become lodged between the temporary and permanent tooth, and the former is best extracted. Although temporary teeth have only the shallowest of roots, they can remain securely in place and extraction is under light anaesthesia.

Deposits on teeth are common. They begin as plaque, a thin deposit of cells visible only with appropriate staining techniques. Bacteria, dead cells from inside the mouth, and other debris become solidified and calcified through saliva. This visible, solid deposit is known as Dental Calculus, Scale, or Tartar, and forms first at the base of the tooth. It can reach quite large proportions, larger than the tooth itself, and may cause irritation of the gums (see Gingivitis); infective material trapped between the calculus and the gum contributes to periodontal disease. Calculus may also act as a mechanical obstruction to jaw movements, preventing the dog from eating properly or closing its mouth.

Dental deposits may form rapidly; most frequently encountered in old age, they can also be seen on temporary teeth. Eventually the gums recede to such an extent that the whole tooth may be shed.

Advanced techniques using ultra-sound are employed to remove dental deposits under general anaesthesia. After descaling, the teeth are cleaned and polished to slow down the rate of subsequent deposition, but prevention of calculus formation is more difficult than might be expected. Hard abrasive foods, such as biscuits and bones, may help to prevent or slow down build-up, but regular cleaning with a toothbrush and a weak solution of hydrogen peroxide is probably just as effective.

Dogs rarely get caries (cavities) in their teeth. When these do occur they can be filled with dental amalgam, but more usually the affected tooth is removed.

Dermatitis

The term describes simple inflammation of the skin and allied structures; with a proliferation of bacteria it becomes infective dermatitis. Parasitism, allergy, contact with irritants, food intolerance or deficiency, heat stroke, and a large number of other conditions may lead to dermatitis.

Skin problems are usually obvious. They take a long time to investigate and to clear up as restorative changes are slow, and diagnosis of the problem can be difficult and prolonged.

Dental diseases are chiefly confined to deposits on the teeth and inflammation of the gum. They are more likely on overshot and undershot jaws (*top two ill.*). In other instances, the teeth meet like pincers (*centre*) rather than scissors (*bottom*)

Dry Eye

The eye is normally lubricated with tears from the lacrymal gland which drain from the eye through ducts (see Lacrymal Duct Blockage). Excessive tear production or poor drainage results in discharge from the eye. Insufficient tear formation to lubricate the eye gives rise to a condition called Kerato-conjunctivitis Sicca or dry eye. The normally healthy moistness of the eye is replaced with a thick, sticky discharge, and local inflammation may lead to ulceration and permanent opacity of the cornea.

Early treatment is needed to keep the eye moist and stimulate tear secretion. In severe or persistent cases, surgery is sometimes advised. This involves transplantation of a duct from a salivary gland (the parotid) to lubricate the eye and is usually effective.

Ear Diseases

Three main areas of the ear are subject to disorders. The outer, visible part, including the earflap and canal as far as it can be seen, often sustains injuries. Cuts on the flap tend to bleed freely and provoke head shaking, resulting in more bleeding (see page 138). Blood blisters may form in the ear flap (see Hematoma).

Inflammation of the ear canal up to the ear drum is known as Otitis externa and can result from parasitic mite infestation (*Otodectes cyanotis*). It is often accompanied by excessive accumulations of wax which, in Poodles especially, may get trapped in the mass of hair within the ear. While soothing creams, olive or almond oil may be gently applied to the visible part of the ear, it is very unwise to introduce anything into the main ear canal itself. The temptation to poke cotton buds into the ear must be resisted as the result is almost invariably a worse mess than before. Professional help is required as it is for disorders deeper in the ear, beyond the ear drum.

Middle-ear disease (Otitis media) is always a serious matter; it is usually painful, disorienting, and the dog may lose his balance as well as his hearing. Dogs hold their heads on one side, and a purulent discharge may pass through the ear drum or seep out elsewhere; urgent attention is needed.

Eczema

This outmoded term is used, incorrectly, to describe any inflammatory non-parasitic skin condition. See Allergy and Dermatitis.

Ectropion

The position of the edge of the eyelid, with its attached eyelashes, in its relation to the eyeball is of importance to certain eye conditions. If the eyelid is turned out too much, it exposes a piece of the delicate conjunctiva, an occurrence which may appear appealing in breeds such as Bloodhounds and St Bernards, but soreness is likely if the eyelid turns out too much. Corrective surgery consists of removing a small crescentic piece from the affected eyelid, usually the lower one. It is a delicate operation which may need modification.

Entropion

When the eyelid turns inwards, the eyelashes make contact with the eyeball and cause inflammation and irritation. The condition is more common and more of a nuisance to the dog than Ectropion, especially in Chows and other breeds where a diamond-shaped eye is considered a desirable characteristic.

Surgical correction is more necessary with in-turning than with out-turning of eyelids because of the damage to the globe of the eye and the likelihood of impaired vision. A crescentic piece is removed from the outside of the eyelid, and it may take more than one operation to achieve the necessary result. Both upper and lower eyelids may be affected.

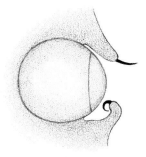

Entropion may affect either or both the upper and lower eyelids, with ingrowing eyelashes brushing against the cornea

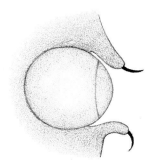

Ectropion is an eyelid defect in several breeds; the lower eyelid turns outwards and exposes the conjunctiva

Eye Diseases

A large number of conditions affect the dog's eyes and range from retinal changes to problems associated with the structure at the front of the eye. Deeper changes are rarely immediately obvious; the effects are mainly in a degree of vision difficulty, apparent as reduced visual acuity or disturbed vision (see Blindness, Blue Eye, Cataract, and Progressive Retinal Atrophy). Distorted vision presents many difficulties as the dog may see objects in a different place and fail to avoid obstructions. Professional attention is necessary.

The front chamber and outer covering of the eye is subject to injury and penetration by foreign bodies. Occasionally there is hemorrhage into the front chamber following an accident, resulting in a 'curtain' of blood in front of the lens. Although most cases resolve, urgent attention is needed to prevent blindness. Most eye injuries and infections cause inflammation and discharge, with the eye firmly closed. Veterinary examination is urgent; food should be withheld as the dog will probably have to be anaesthetized before the extent of the damage can be explored. Severe inflammation of the outer eye surface is known as Keratitis and can arise from injury or infectious disease. Occasionally, ulceration follows which may take a long time to treat successfully; if left rupture of part of the eye may result.

Keratitis should not be confused with protrusion of the third eyelid, although that condition may be an accompanying factor. The third eyelid (Membrana nictitans) acts as an additional protection for the eye; when the eye is closed, the third eyelid automatically moves across. If the eye is inflamed and partly closed, the third eyelid often shows as a 'shutter' across part of the globe.

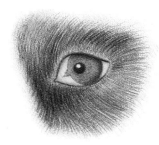

The third eyelid may be accidentally damaged, with a torn-off piece lying across the globe of the eye

Eyelid Diseases

Eyelids are usually inflamed when the eye is infected or injured. Allergies also cause swelling. The effect, on exposure to the allergen (see Allergy), may be sudden. Any of the three eyelids may be injured; it is not rare to see a piece of the third eyelid torn away and lying across the eye surface. A small gland in the third eyelid often becomes enlarged, causing the eyelid to appear prominent, sometimes turning outwards. Surgery is often needed to correct this condition and is usually effective. See also Ectropion and Entropion.

Facial Paralysis: see Diseases of the Nervous System

Fleas: see Parasites

Follicular Mange: see Demodectic Mange

Furunculosis: see Acne

Gingivitis

Inflammation of the gums can result from heavy deposits on the teeth (see Dental Diseases) or general infections in the mouth (Leptospirosis). Sometimes objects like pieces of wood or fragments of bone may become lodged between the teeth and cause local gum inflammation. Other causes are conditions which affect the whole animal, particularly kidney failure and lead poisoning. If inflammatory conditions become purulent infections, there may be enough pain to prevent eating; a highly offensive odour indicates the need for veterinary attention.

Gingivitis shows as swollen and inflamed gums. It may be due to mouth infection or to calculus on the teeth

Glossitis

Inflammation of the tongue may be accompanied by gingivitis or generalized inflammation (see Stomatitis). Glossitis on its own may be caused by penetrating or encircling objects, such as needles, fish hooks, pieces of bone or metal, and constricting material such as rubber bands and pieces of thread and fishing line. Lacerations of the tongue can occur as a result of a traffic accident or when a puppy becomes involved with metal objects. The tongue heals rapidly, and horrific-looking injuries often do well after surgical intervention.

The other common cause of glossitis results from swelling of the salivary glands, usually because the ducts are blocked. The swellings may become large and look unsightly, but response to treatment is usually favourable.

Hair Shedding

Dogs shed some hair more or less continuously, heaviest in spring and autumn when the new coat is grown. Regular grooming will help to keep the coat in good condition with the minimum of excess hair shedding. Some dogs shed large amounts of hair without apparently thinning the coat. This aberrant form of moulting is possibly due to hormonal disturbances (see Hypothyroidism) or to inadequate intakes of essential fatty acids or zinc. Environmental factors, such as the even temperatures of centrally heated rooms, may also be a factor.

Thorough bathing with a dog shampoo containing zinc, and a little corn oil, usually improves most non-specific hair-shedding conditions. Moving the dog's living quarters into a cooler room may also help. If such measures prove ineffective, the dog's hormonal state will need clinical investigation.

Halitosis

Bad breath or halitosis may be due to infective conditions in the mouth, or more generalized illness. Mouth infection is usually associated with dental deposits, gingivitis and periodontal disease, all of which require skilled attention. Bad breath can also be a symptom of a more complicated disease, such as chronic gastritis and kidney failure.

A dog's breath may be highly offensive from eating rotting material or its own feces (copraphagia). Careful investigation may be necessary to distinguish between local infection, generalized disease, and the transient passage of offensive material.

Harvest mites: see Parasites

Hematoma

A blood blister or hematoma occurs when small blood vessels accumulate as a local swelling under the skin and break. There is usually no pain or inflammation, but the swelling is unsightly and may press on other organs. The commonest site for a hematoma is in the ear flap, often as the result of physical injury. A small round swelling may quickly increase to fill the whole of the ear flap. If the hematoma is left to resorb, the ear becomes crumpled in appearance, like a 'cauliflower' ear in man. Surgery is used to drain the blood blister and to stitch the ear to retain its shape. Draining the blood is not normally effective as the root cause of the hematoma may be inflammation of the ear canal.

Most other hematomas resorb in a reasonably short time depending on size; they are not usually painful.

Hernia

This is a rupture of one body cavity into another or into a space under the skin, seen most commonly in dogs at the umbilicus or navel. If the small opening at the umbilicus does not close at the time of birth, some of the fat normally located just inside the abdomen may protrude and show as a small painless swelling. It rarely causes any problems, but occasionally umbilical hernias are large enough to contain vital organs such as the bowel, which may become trapped and its blood supply threatened. The swelling is painful, irreducible, and needs surgery without delay.

Another common hernia is in the groin; in bitches it may contain the uterus in pregnancy. Other hernias may result from severe blows such as in traffic accidents. The abdominal contents may be pushed into the chest by way of a

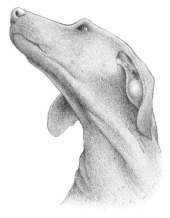

Hematoma in the ear flap can be due to heavy scratching; the blood blister may swell to fill the whole flap and then requires surgical intervention

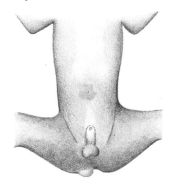

Hernias at the navel are generally trouble free, but inguinal and perineal hernias can cause serious ruptures and displacement of internal organs

diaphragmatic or hiatus hernia. Professional advice is needed with all hernias, and radiography may be the only way to establish an accurate diagnosis and the extent of the internal disarray. Extensive surgery is almost always necessary to repair damage caused by external forces.

Perineal hernia may cause the abdominal contents to be pushed into the perineal region just below the anus. This seems to occur in closely docked dogs, possibly because the musculature round the tail is too weak to maintain the integrity of the perineum.

Hyperkeratosis

Infectious disease, such as the hardpad manifestation of canine distemper, can show as a thickening of the surface of the skin, hyperkeratosis. Thickening also occurs around the nose and occasionally corn-like swellings appear at the points of the elbows, where bones are near the surface of the skin.

Excessive flaking of the skin, with drandruff or scurf over the entire body, may be related to marginal zinc intake, particularly when cereal food makes up a disproportionate part of the diet. Improved diet, frequent bathing and possibly zinc supplementation usually resolve the condition.

Keratisis: see Eye Diseases
Kerato-conjunctivitis Sicca: see Dry Eye
Lacrymal Duct Blockage

The lacrymal ducts drain most of the tears which lubricate the eyes. Drainage, through a small opening at the inner corner of each eye, may become obstructed either because the duct is too narrow to accommodate tear production or as a result of an inflammatory condition. Some of the tears produced evaporate, but the remainder flow down and stain the dog's face. On light-coloured dogs, particularly Poodles, the stains look unsightly, but are not harmful in any way.

Surgical clearance of the blocked duct under a general anaesthetic is often necessary, followed by treatment to reduce inflammatory changes in the lacrymal duct.

Lick Granuloma

This term describes chronically inflamed skin which eventually ulcerates, on the foreleg usually just above the toes. It is frequently seen in Labradors, though not confined to that breed, and in other short-haired dogs, active by nature and left to feel bored. The likely cause is a minor skin injury which is gradually opened up by the dog by continuous licking. The area becomes itchy and is not given a chance to heal.

Efforts should be made to prevent the dog from licking the granuloma, but the irritation remains for quite a time. Bandaging will not always deter a determined dog, but an Elizabethan-collar arrangement is usually effective if cumbersome. Persistent or extensive granulomas are best removed by cryosurgery, a technique in which the tissues are frozen, using a special probe.

Lice: see Parasites
Mammary Tumours: see Diseases of the Reproductive System
Nasal Discharge

Any fluid from the nose of a dog is a matter for concern. Local infections are the most obvious cause; Kennel Cough may have secondary bacterial infection resulting in a purulent or mucous nasal discharge, and Distemper may have similar symptoms, with heavy encrusting of the nose itself. Other virus infections are characterized by clearer discharges.

Discharge from only one side may be due to injury or a foreign body, such as a grass awn, which has penetrated the nasal chambers. A simple but persistent nasal discharge may require much investigation to establish the cause.

Hyperkeratosis may be a symptom of distemper infection and shows as a thickening of the skin round the nose and as corny swellings at the elbows

Lacrymal duct blockage, an inflammation which stains the facial hairs, is more unsightly than harmful

Lick granuloma, usually on the foreleg, can result from a skin lesion becoming inflamed from continuous licking

Nettle Rash

A sudden allergic reaction, urticaria, may show in the appearance of the skin. The first sign is usually a swelling of the eyelids, which may progress to a puffy enlargement of the whole head and neck. Blisters may appear, and the skin may look pitted. Sometimes the skin can be lifted or a depression made in it which remains unchanged for a long time. Urticarial or Nettle Rash reaction may follow inhalation or ingestion of any substance to which the dog has become sensitized; it can also follow an insect sting.

In many cases the allergic reaction recedes as quickly as it appears. In others it may persist, and occasionally it interferes with breathing or heart function. All but the most transient reactions need expert advice.

Otitis

Inflammation of the ear is known as Otitis, as Otitis externa when the ear canal up to the ear drum is inflamed, and as Otitis media when it concerns the inner ear parts (see also Ear Diseases). Many if not most cases of Otitis externa start with a proliferation of an ear mite (*Otodectes cyanotis*), and complications may be caused by an excessive accumulation of ear wax.

In addition, bacterial or fungal infection may make the whole ear a purulent mess. Breeds with a good deal of hair in the ear canal, such as Poodles, or with heavy ear flaps, such as Spaniels, are especially prone to infection of the ears due to poor aeration; they become an ideal medium for bacterial growth.

Foreign bodies, particularly grass awns, are the cause of many other instances of Otitis externa. Home treatment probably causes as many problems as it helps, and the temptation to poke solid objects, such as cotton buds, into the ear must be resisted. At most only that part of the ear which is clearly visible should be cleaned; a few drops of warm olive oil will loosen any wax.

Otitis media usually shows as inco-ordination, circling, overbalancing after head shaking, some pain particularly on handling, and sometimes an unpleasant discharge. This is an urgent matter for the veterinarian.

Periodontal Disease

The area of the gum which surrounds the base of each tooth is called the periodontum. Inflammatory disease is commonly seen at this site, often associated with dental deposits and gingivitis. Advanced cases show recession of the gum margin, loosening and eventually shedding of the tooth. Treatment consists in cleaning up mouth infections and in improved dental hygiene.

Progressive Retinal Atrophy

Usually referred to as PRA, this is an inherited condition more prevalent in certain breeds, particularly the Miniature and Toy Poodle, and the Briard, than in others. There are several types of retinal atrophy; general deterioration of the retina usually afflicts Poodles, and central deterioration is seen in some Briards, Labradors and Collies.

The generalized form of retinal atrophy may first be seen as 'night blindness', as that part of the eye most used to see light intensity deteriorates first. Central retinal atrophy does not usually progress to blindness and, unlike generalized atrophy of the retina, vision may be much better at the peripherals than in the centre. Vision in dull light may be better than in bright daylight.

The changes are irreversible, and as yet no treatment is available to arrest the progression of the condition. However, other changes within the eye, such as cataracts, may need treatment. Vigorous attempts are being made by breed societies and veterinary associations to try to reduce the extent of PRA, the object being to identify clinical cases and encourage breeding from stock certified to be sound.

Progressive Retinal Atrophy or night blindness is an inherited, incurable eye disease. In normal vision, light is reflected on to the retina (*above*), but with PRA the receptor cells gradually waste away (*below*)

Ringworm

Two types of fungal infection may grow on dogs' hair and skin, causing ringworm. They have nothing to do with worms, are not usually circular and are not at all common in dogs. More than half of the cases seen are caused by a fungus, *Microsporium* spp., which is more at home on cats and which fluoresces under ultraviolet light. Other species of ringworm fungus need more complex tests to establish a diagnosis.

Treatment is usually effective if slow. Fungicidal drugs by mouth and topical applications diligently applied eventually bring results as the hairs are broken off, not usually destroyed. The risk of passing canine ringworm to humans is minimal if a reasonable standard of hygiene is maintained. The condition affects debilitated individuals; nutrition should be improved.

Sarcoptic Mange: see Demodectic Mange

Seborrhoea

Seborrhoea is a common skin disease in Cocker Spaniels. The skin becomes greasy and flecked with dandruff

A dog's skin produces a wax-like, greasy secretion which lubricates the coat. An overproduction of the sebum produced by the sebaceous glands, or an accumulation of waxy secretions in association with scaliness of the skin, leads to seborrhoea. Skin and coat appear greasy, dull and scurfy and have a characteristic mouse-like smell. Some Terriers are commonly affected but seborrhoea is most frequently seen in Cocker Spaniels, probably due to hormonal disturbance. The best treatment is anti-sebum shampoos.

Stomatitis

Inflammation of the whole mouth (Stomatitis) may accompany generalized infections (see Gingivitis, Glossitis, Periodontal Disease). It may also be a result of an electrical burn or of a dog taking in irritant material by mouth. Stomatitis is a frequent accompaniment of advanced kidney disease.

Severe inflammation of the mouth requires urgent treatment as the dog will have great difficulty taking in food or water. Once established, infections in the mouth can become obstinately resistant to treatment; foreign bodies should be removed and irritant chemicals diluted with water. Live power supply near a dog with electrical burns must be switched off.

Ticks: see Parasites

Tonsillitis

Inflammation of the tonsils is usually associated with infection, general or localized. A dog with tonsillitis clearly has a sore throat, and the area behind the tongue is inflamed, sometimes ulcerated. There is loss of appetite, inability to swallow, a good deal of retching, and often high fever.

Tonsillitis usually responds well to antibiotic therapy; any generalized disease must be treated at the same time. Occasionally tonsils are the seat of more chronic infection; the focus for this and the tonsils must be removed.

Umbilical Hernia: see Hernia

Urticaria: see Nettle Rash

Warts

Small outgrowths on the skin can be a nuisance in two ways. In old dogs, the tips of the warts may be knocked or chewed off, causing bleeding. Warts inside the mouth, usually in younger dogs, may proliferate to the extent that they interfere with eating. Warts (papillomata) are nearly always related to a specific virus infection, but can progress to bacterial infection. Viral warts may disappear quickly, others may have to be removed by surgery and secondary infection treated with antibiotics. In most cases, external warts are easily removed under local anaesthesia, but they are likely to recur.

Zinc Deficiency: see Hyperkeratosis

Diseases of the Nervous System

Chorea

Involuntary regular muscle twitching is a serious sign, usually indicating a complication of distemper or related infectious disease. Tremors characteristically occur around the head and shoulders, often appearing worse when the dog is asleep. Unfortunately Chorea often begins a couple of weeks after apparent recovery, then progresses to generalized muscular spasms and culminates in fits. The dog is in a poor state which usually requires euthanasia to stop further suffering.

Occasionally, twitching remains limited to a single group of muscles, on top of the head, and may even regress altogether. Whatever the course of the illness, professional attention is urgent as soon as such signs are noticed.

Convulsions: see Accidents & First Aid

Distemper

Canine Distemper is a most miserable, often fatal affliction, caused by a virus still prevalent in Europe, although a highly effective vaccine is available. The disease, which is highly infectious, is usually seen in young dogs, but can affect individuals of any age. It is often fatal, but not immediately so, and an afflicted dog may endure a long illness, seem to recover only to succumb to complications several weeks later.

The classic signs of Distemper, not always immediately apparent, include thick discharge from eyes and nose with heavy encrustation, and persistent coughing. There is usually a fever with some vomiting and diarrhoea, and the disease may progress to pneumonia and death. With good nursing care and supportive therapy, the dog may recover completely; however, others appearing to make a good recovery become afflicted with nervous muscle twitches (see Chorea).

Vaccination will prevent almost all cases of Canine Distemper. The timing of injections and annual boosters is a matter for the veterinarian, based on the disease pattern in the locality.

Encephalitis

The brain may become inflamed, usually as a result of a viral infection, and lead to encephalitis. With this goes a variety of serious nervous symptoms, particularly seizures, inco-ordination, and aggression with infections such as rabies. The dog may lose consciousness and show obvious signs of eye defects and much pain around the head.

A similar chronic condition, occurring in older dogs, is called Old Dog Encephalitis (see below). All cases of encephalitis require urgent veterinary attention.

Facial Paralysis

The maintaining of muscle tone and power of contraction depend on the integrity of those nerves which innovate each muscle group. If nerves are damaged extensively, all power and tone is lost in the related muscle group. The motor nerve for the face is the VIIth (facial) nerve; occasionally it is severed in a serious accident, but loss of power is often due to interference with nerve conduction by extension of severe inflammation of the middle ear. The result is a general sagging of the face on the affected side; the dog cannot take up food and drools a good deal of saliva.

Old Dog Encephalitis

It is often difficult to distinguish the process of ageing from pathological changes of certain diseases. Chronic inflammation of the brain (Encephalitis) can develop very slowly from middle to old age. Dogs become less mentally alert and may lose some of the habits they have acquired over the years. They may become depressed, appear completely unaware of their surroundings for certain periods and reasonably normal the rest of the time. Like very old people, they are unable to concentrate for very long. At advanced stages the dog may have difficulty balancing, it will hold its head on one side, and move around in circles. Many cases respond to treatment with cortico-steroid drugs, though improvement is usually short-lived.

Paralysis

Damage to the nerves which control limb movement results in some loss of function, or paralysis (see Facial Paralysis). Infections such as Distemper and Rabies may lead to some degree of limb paralysis. Lead poisoning usually shows as nervous signs which may include hindlimb paralysis.

Other main causes of paralysis are disc protrusion and injury caused by violent accidents. Damage to the spinal cord is usually irreparable and complete loss of control of the hind, or all four, limbs, after a violent episode is a grave sign. If the nerves to the forelimb are severed, as sometimes happens after a blow near the first rib, the dog may drag its foreleg and cause extensive ulceration, often requiring limb amputation. Partial paralysis (paresis) may with diligent nursing respond to treatment.

Rabies

In countries such as Britain, where rabies is absent, it is difficult to grasp the extent and effect of this disease. Rabies is an infectious virus disease affecting all warm-blooded animals, including man. Normally only animals which live by biting their prey spread the disease, but in almost all species, including humans, rabies comes to a dead end in every sense. Mercifully, human deaths are rare in Europe and North America, but other parts of the world, notably Africa and India, are much less fortunate.

The main vector of rabies differs around the world and includes bats, raccoon, skunk, mongoose and red fox, but dogs are the most likely to pass rabies to humans. It is possible to protect dogs against rabies where the disease is rife, and to give humans effective vaccination protection even after being exposed to rabies, provided this is done without delay.

In dogs, the disease runs its course in about ten days, although it may be several months before clinical signs develop – hence the six-month quarantine in most rabies-free countries. The first indication of the disease is usually a change of temperament: friendly dogs may become aggressive, and very active dogs subdued. Characteristically the bark rises in pitch. The main signs which follow involve the nervous system; the widely held view that rabid dogs career around the countryside biting everything in their path is only true of a minority of cases. Many pass rapidly to a paralytic phase, so-called 'dumb rabies', where they become paralysed and unable to close their jaws. Eventually they die from respiratory failure.

Because of the health risks to the public, suspected rabies should be notified immediately, to the local veterinary surgeon and to the police.

Tetany: see Muscular & Skeletal Diseases

Diseases of the Reproductive System

Birth Difficulties

Often called dystocia, whelping problems are not uncommon, particularly in smaller breeds and those with broad heads and a narrow pelvis. Difficulty may arise from abnormalities associated with the mother, others may relate to the puppies. The bitch may lack muscle power in the womb (inertia), or there may be an obstruction in the birth canal. Inertia may result from a lengthy period of labour followed by exhaustion, or the uterus may be unable to contract.

Obstruction can be caused by constriction due to scar tissue, by a fractured pelvis which has healed irregularly, or by faulty development of the skeleton which has reduced the space available for the puppies' exit. More than one influence may have an effect on the progress of whelping. The same goes for difficulties originating with the puppies. These may happen because of maternal influences acting against the birth as when the puppies are too large for their passage or are wrongly positioned in the birth canal.

Sometimes even slight oversize is too much for the available power of uterine contraction to overcome, as can occur with the first puppy born to a young bitch, or to a large one delivered after long labour. The presence of the puppy in the birth canal usually stimulates contractions, but if the puppy is tiny the stimulus may be inadequate for proper contractions to take place. Sometimes Caesarian operations are performed, usually with good results.

See also Mating and Reproduction, pages 120–28.

Eclampsia: see Lactational Tetany

Endometritis

Sometimes the uterus becomes inflamed as a result of bacterial or other infection. General illness, usually with a vaginal discharge, follows an abortion, and resorption of foetuses can occur in pregnant bitches. Such bitches do not usually conceive, and infertility in a kennel may indicate the presence of uterine infection. Most cases of infective endometritis respond well to antibiotic treatment; failing this the uterus may have to be removed.

Infection of the uterus quickly supervenes if any part of a puppy, membranes or placenta are retained after the bitch has whelped.

A more chronic condition can affect older bitches when the internal layers of the uterus degenerate and eventually form a foul-smelling, purulent, but virtually sterile mass in the cavity. The condition is known as Pyometra (see page 169) and usually shows its presence after a bitch has been in oestrus.

False Pregnancy

Left to their own devices, bitches in oestrus would nearly all get mated and most would become pregnant. To prepare for pregnancy, most bitches produce milk after each oestrus, whether they have been mated or not. In addition, all the other signs of pregnancy may be apparent in some without any puppies being present in the womb. A bitch with this condition, known as false pregnancy, may eat more for her 'phantom' litter and put on so much weight as to add to the illusion of pregnancy. As the time for the 'birth' approaches the bitch may prepare her bed by tearing up the bedding, and she will jealously guard small animate or inanimate objects which could be mistaken for puppies; squeaky toys especially evoke a dramatic response.

Initially the bitch must be examined to determine if the pregnancy is false; the veterinarian will advise on treatment of a phantom pregnancy. Such cases usually resolve themselves, but severe psychological disturbances will need more than palliative treatment. If the bitch is obviously ill or if the condition becomes progressively more severe with each oestrus, the symptoms could point to Endometritis or Pyometra.

False pregnancy is often convincing, and the bitch displays typical maternal instincts, including enlarged mammary glands, and a passion for soft toys

Infantile Vulva

Occasionally the external sex organs of a bitch fail to develop and the vulva remains infantile. The vulva may be too small to permit mating and may interfere with the passing of urine. Urinary incontinence may accompany the condition, which is often associated with hormonal disturbances, particularly if a bitch has been spayed before she is mature. Most cases respond well to hormone therapy, which must be continued for the rest of the bitch's life.

Lactational Tetany

Lactation puts heavy demands on a bitch, with some litters weighing as much as the mother at peak lactation. Demand is at its greatest when the puppies are around three weeks old, before they begin to take significant amounts of food other than that provided by the dam.

Some bitches are unable to maintain enough calcium to meet their own needs. This is particularly so with smaller breeds, notably Chihuahua and Dachshund bitches. The condition may be further complicated by low blood-sugar levels, perhaps due to inadequate food and mineral intake, or to hormonal disturbance involving the parathyroid glands.

The signs of lactational tetany, sometimes inaptly called milk fever or eclampsia, are usually obvious. Within three weeks of giving birth, the bitch begins to pant and become restless, crying out and looking apprehensive. This progresses to muscle spasms which become frequent, followed by collapse and eventually death in severe cases. An adequate diet does not always prevent the condition, but most cases respond well to injections of calcium solution, usually given with glucose. The veterinary surgeon should be contacted at the onset of any symptoms, and alerted if a bitch with a history of lactational tetany is used for breeding.

Mammary Tumours

Any swelling of the mammary glands is a matter for further investigation as many tumours are invasive and grow rapidly. Not all lumps are tumours, but expert advice is needed for accurate diagnosis, which may involve a biopsy. Most canine mammary tumours are hormone-dependent, and spaying is usually advisable when a tumour is removed. Spaying (ovario-hysterectomy) is a useful means of preventing mammary tumours, which are comparatively rare in neutered bitches.

Mastitis

Inflammation of the mammary glands during lactation can be a serious threat to a litter of puppies. What milk is available may also be infected with micro organisms and unsafe for puppies; considerable pain, swelling and inflammation make the bitch reluctant in any case to allow suckling, and the lives of the puppies are doubly threatened.

Mastitis can occur at other times, particularly during false pregnancy if mammary development causes lactation without any puppies. It may also follow after weaning of the puppies. Mastitis may be so severe as to cause septicaemia (blood poisoning), with high body temperature, vomiting and eventual prostration. Such cases often develop an abscess in the mammary tissue. The disease is usually treated with antibiotics, but early attention is essential to avoid serious illness in the bitch and her litter.

Misalliance

Bitches in oestrus sometimes get mated against their owners' wishes. The odour generated by the discharges and urine of a bitch in heat are attractive to all male dogs in the locality, and half-hearted attempts at keeping them out will not defeat the determined male. The ardour is not confined to male dogs; a bitch in oestrus often behaves quite differently than at other times, and a normally obedient bitch may ignore its home and owner to seek out a male. Although mating is usually a fairly lengthy process, conception can occur in the space of only five minutes.

Pregnancy can be prevented by the effective and irreversible process of spaying, and by the administration of hormones. These must be carefully used, given only to healthy bitches and preferably within forty-eight hours of mating. Hormone treatment usually prolongs oestrus and should not be used more than once during any one oestrous period.

See also Mating and Reproduction, pages 120–28.

Prostate Disease

Enlargement of the prostate gland occurs in ageing dogs. It may respond, at least temporarily, to female hormone administration, and to castration. Tumours of the prostate gland may also recede following castration, but many such tumours are invasive and grow rapidly, with poor prospects for recovery. Infection of the prostate produces similar clinical signs, but these often respond well to antibiotic treatment.

As the prostate gland is located at the exit to the bladder and beneath the rectum, enlargement is usually accompanied by urinary incontinence. The enlarged gland can also press on and obstruct the rectum, and constipation, continual straining, and frequent urination are other symptoms.

Pyometra

The collection of pus-like material in the uterus, usually one to two months after oestrus, is a common occurrence in older bitches. Although the uterine contents are thick and foul-smelling, some being passed by way of the vulva in most cases, there is a surprising lack of infectious organisms. The disease is generally a sign of age, comparable to the prostate condition in males.

The onset of pyometra is often insidious, with the bitch becoming progressively more ill after each oestrus. The abdomen distends, particularly if the vulval discharge is slight, and there is evidence of greatly increased thirst, vomiting, and urination resulting from circulating toxins causing kidney failure. In almost all cases the only satisfactory treatment is the removal of the uterus and ovaries. The severity of the symptoms is not always reflected in the appearance of the uterus and vice versa; there is often a marked improvement in the dog's health once she has recovered from this major operation.

Uterine Inertia: see Birth Difficulties

Vulval Discharge

Most bitches are meticulous in keeping the vulval area clean, and any persistent discharge may be an indication of profound internal changes. The discharges which accompany oestrus are clear, viscid or bloodstained, depending on the stage of the oestrous cycle. Any discharges which continue for several days beyond the usual three weeks of oestrus are a warning sign and need closer attention. The blood often associated with cystitis (page 170) usually stains the frequently passed urine, but not necessarily at every urination. A foul-smelling discharge is almost always a sign of uterine infection or the degenerative changes of pyometra (above).

Whelping is accompanied by the passage of a good deal of fluid, some of which may be stained brown or green, and contain some blood. The passing of such fluid may be the first indication that a bitch is pregnant.

Diseases of the Urinary System

Bladder Stones

Solids can appear in the urine for a variety of reasons and at locations from the kidney, down the ureter to the bladder; they may also form in the bladder and pass down the urethra to be voided as urination. They range from sandy (sabulous) material to large concretions of urinary calculi or stones and may become lodged at any point in the urinary system. Stones are apparent within the bladder itself; occasionally they remain in the kidney or in the urethra, particularly in males, and are then unable to pass beyond the *os penis*.

Solids in the urine usually grow around a tiny nucleus of material; eventually they become large single stones or a collection of smaller ones, causing local inflammation and some degree of obstruction, partial or complete. Further inflammation results, with discomfort or pain and more urinary stasis, which again increases the size of the solids. Dogs with bladder stones characteristically pass small, frequent amounts of urine as if unable to completely evacuate their bladders. There is often evidence of blood in the urine (see Hematuria) and there may be pain or obvious difficulties on urination. In small dogs, such as Miniature Dachshunds, or dogs as large as Corgis, it may be possible to feel calculi in the bladder, or to hear them rattle when gently moved.

Urinary calculi can sometimes be dispersed by dietary means, but veterinary help is always urgently needed. Surgical removal, although a major operation into the bladder or urethra, is not too difficult, but preventing a recurrence is often the most problematic aspect of post-operative treatment. Urinary tract infection must be eliminated, and every effort should be made to prevent solids from coming out of solution. Some calculi (phosphate) are more soluble in acid urine, others (oxalate and urate) in alkaline urine, and attempts to alter the acidity/alkalinity of the urine may be advisable, under veterinary guidance.

Another preventive measure consists in keeping the urine dilute. This can be achieved by feeding canned food wetter with the addition of water, possibly with added salt to stimulate thirst and increased water intake.

Calculi

Calculi are stones which result from solids coming out of solution in abnormal situations. Although calculi can occur in the gut, gall bladder, and salivary ducts, the most common sites are in the urinary system (see Bladder Stones). Another common site for calculi is the urethra of male dogs as it passes through a channel in the *os penis*. A stone may become too large to pass through the restricted outlet, and surgical intervention becomes an emergency.

Cystitis

Inflammation of the bladder is usually the result of bacterial infection. The female urinary tract affords an easier entry for bacteria than in males, and cystitis is therefore more common in bitches. The effects of an inflamed bladder are frequent passing of small amounts of often blood stained, rather foul-smelling urine. Cystitis is almost always present when calculi form in the urinary tract, and the symptoms are similar (see Bladder Stones). The animal may have difficulty in passing urine, usually because of pain. All cases of cystitis need urgent attention, particularly where there is urinary retention.

Other causes of cystitis are bladder tumours, which are relatively rare, and injuries following traffic accidents. In the latter case, blood is usually evident in the urine (see Hematuria), but provided infection can be prevented and the injuries are not great, prospects of recovery are usually good. Radiography is needed to assess the extent of the damage. Techniques which introduce air into the bladder and the application of dyes to show the passage of urine through the urinary tract are widely used in the investigation of bladder disorders.

Treatment with antibiotics is lengthy and urine samples must be taken for several weeks.

Dysuria: see Urinary Retention

Hematuria

Blood in the urine is usually the result of physical injury, urinary calculi or infectious disease. In bitches the blood passed during oestrus or otherwise arising from the womb needs to be distinguished from blood arising in the urinary system.

Hematuria accompanies some forms of poisoning; it can also be a manifestation of cystitis and not immediately obvious because blood in the urine is often broken down and merely seen as discoloration. Diagnostic tests are necessary to determine the cause of hematuria.

Kidney Failure

The infectious disease leptospirosis (see page 175) can cause chronic kidney failure, and although vaccination has reduced the incidence of the infection, kidney disease is still a frequent cause of serious illness in adult dogs. Acute kidney failure is equally serious; with prompt treatment the prospects of recovery are reasonably good, but with age chronic disease may occur in damaged kidney tissue. Acute kidney failure is usually characterized by a sudden rise in temperature, accompanied by severe, often continuous vomiting. Thirst is usually increased, with profuse or no urination. The latter symptom is serious and indicates that the kidney has stopped functioning.

Although chronic kidney failure tends to be progressive, a large proportion of the kidney tissue must be out of action before signs of the disease develop. Once kidney function is inadequate, the dog is unable to conserve water by concentrating its urine, and large amounts of very dilute urine are passed. The dog tries to avoid dehydration by drinking more fluid, resulting in a cycle of increased thirst (polydypsia) and increased urination (polyuria).

The kidney is the route whereby the end-products of protein digestion are excreted and with reduced function these accumulate in the circulation and result in a form of self-intoxication known as uremia. Other complications include the loss of protein, minerals, and vitamins via damaged kidney tissue.

Once diagnostic tests have established the presence and extent of kidney failure (Chronic Nephritis), treatment is directed towards making the most efficient use of the remaining tissue. Part of this involves protein restriction, feeding only small amounts of those proteins most useful to the dog. Properly compensated cases may live reasonably normal lives for quite long periods.

Nephritis: see Kidney Failure

Rubber jaw

Some dogs with advanced kidney failure lose so much of essential minerals that their skeletons become seriously demineralized. This is especially apparent in the jaw, where the bones eventually consist of little more than fibrous material and become easily pliable. It is a serious problem needing expert attention.

Uremia: see Kidney Failure

Urinary Retention

Retention of urine sometimes occurs in dogs prevented from reasonably frequent opportunities to pass urine. It can also occur in overprotective bitches with newly born litters and may lead to retention cystitis (see Cystitis). It may be necessary to remove a puppy from the whelping box so as to coax the bitch out to relieve herself. Complete blockage or severe pain on urination (dysuria) can lead to serious urinary retention. The former occurs chiefly in males with urethral calculi (see Calculi), although bitches can also suffer.

Parasites

Ascarids: see Roundworms
Demodectic Mange: see Diseases of the Skin
Dermatitis: see Diseases of the Skin

Fleas

External parasites bring a series of minor problems. Dogs with a heavy infestation scratch for long periods and bite at all accessible parts of their bodies. On short-haired dogs, fleas can often be seen as they scuttle and jump. As fleas live on blood, a heavy infestation can lead to anemia in puppies, though they are usually affected by other signs of ill-health.

Fleas are some of the most persistent parasites, infesting the coat along the back and round the head. Flea collars and aerosol insecticides control adults but not eggs and larvae

Flea droppings are the usual evidence of infestation. Flea dirt, which is really dried blood, looks like specs of soot and is more easily seen in light-coloured dogs. Infestations reach their heights at the end of a hot, humid summer, and a so-called plague of parasites resistant to control measures are merely following their usual pattern. Some dogs are particularly sensitive to the flea droppings and show allergic reaction to the excreta of only a small number (see Allergy).

There is a common belief that dog fleas do not bite humans. Dogs may be infested with dog, cat, human or rabbit fleas, and while dog fleas prefer the company of dogs, they are not averse to humans. Some owners regard flea infestation as some kind of social stigma, more alarming than serious canine diseases. The best pedigree dog attracts fleas, the only crime is with the owner who does nothing to control them.

Flea control is complicated by the fact that fleas lay their eggs off the host animal; larvae can emerge within a few days in warm weather and the whole life cycle may take only a week or two. A further complication is that the flea is needed for an intermediate stage in the development of canine tapeworm, and proper control must include treatment against internal parasites.

Fleas can be controlled with flea collars used as directed, and combined with a high standard of grooming and hygiene. One easily forgotten aspect of flea control is keeping the dog's bedding and all carpets scrupulously clean.

Harvest Mites

These parasites proliferate in certain localities in Britain. The larvae of *Trombicula autumnale*, the harvest mite, appear as small reddish-orange specks on the feet of dogs. Just visible in good light, they cause severe irritation between the toes, their only indication being the dog's continual attention to its feet by licking, chewing, and biting.

Harvest mites are fairly easily controlled with careful use of medicated shampoos containing insecticidal agents. Only if secondary infection is introduced does other medical treatment become necessary.

Harvest mites are minute but can be seen as red flecks among the dog's toes. Unless eradicated they can lead to chronic irritation

Lice

Heavy infestation of these parasites shows as marked irritation, particularly around the head and neck; some types of lice live on blood and can cause anemia in young puppies. Lice are just visible, but more easily controlled than parasites, such as fleas, which spend part of their cycle away from the dog. Repeat applications of medicated shampoo are effective in most cases.

Roundworms

The common internal parasite, *Toxocara canis,* is one species of roundworms belonging to a group called Ascarids. Other mammals are infested with their own particular Ascarids.

The eggs of roundworms are passed from the dog in the motions and can remain active for long periods in the soil or sticking around the animal's anus; some are swallowed and hatch into larvae in the intestine, where they continue their life cycle. Eggs invade the muscle tissues; they remain dormant until a bitch becomes pregnant, when they migrate to the developing foetus in the womb. Many puppies are born with roundworms or absorb the parasites from the bitch's milk.

A heavy infestation can mean significant loss of nutrients and result in stunted growth or anemia. Vomiting of whole worms is common, and occasionally the gut may be perforated or completely obstructed, endangering the puppy's life. Older dogs harbour far fewer adult roundworms.

Roundworms are comparatively easy to eradicate in the mature form. Worming agents, preferably obtained from the veterinarian, will deal with developing and adult worms but will not affect immature or dormant stages. Worming of puppies should begin as early as three weeks and be repeated at two-week intervals until the age of six months and thereafter every six months.

Laboratory examination of fecal samples will identify the type of worms present and indicate the most suitable treatment. If this is carried out regularly, the effect of roundworms in dogs can be reduced to negligible levels.

The public health aspects of roundworms are worthy of attention. Larvae from fecal material left in the open may be transmitted to children; worms do not reach maturity in the human body, but heavy infestations may result in liver enlargement and obstruct the smaller blood vessels causing local inflammatory reaction. All dog owners should ensure that their dogs defecate in appropriate places, that scrupulous hygiene standards are maintained, and that puppies and bitches are regularly wormed.

Tapeworms

Like most parasites, tapeworms do not usually cause much inconvenience to their canine hosts unless infestation is heavy. However, dogs are better without tapeworms, and steps should be taken to eliminate them.

In addition there is the public health hazard of Hydatid disease, which forms cysts in the lungs and liver of farm animals as well as humans. One group of canine tapeworm, *Echinococcus* sp., use farm animals as an intermediate host and pass as adult to a dog. Problems arise chiefly from infested farm dogs, where they have access to uncooked meat or unburied sheep carcases.

Poor canine health is sometimes attributed to worm infestation, but proper examination of the dog's feces is necessary to establish the presence and type of internal parasites and appropriate treatment. Infected dogs sometimes pass live segments of the adult worm, which attach themselves round the rear of the dog and may be seen to be mobile. However, tiny segments are invisible.

Ticks

The main characteristic of these skin parasites is their ugly appearance. The brown dog tick, prevalent in North America and the carrier of several serious infectious diseases, is unknown in Britain.

The ticks, which dogs in Britain pick up from long grass where farm animals graze, are creamy-white. They will jump on to a passing dog and attach themselves with their strong sucking mouths to the dog, especially around the head and neck. Here they suck on the animal's blood, growing purple-black in colour and in size so large that they can easily be mistaken for cysts.

Eventually a tick drops off after eating several times its own weight in blood; heavy infestations may cause anemia in your puppies. Ticks are difficult to remove as they cling by their mouth parts to the dog, and attempts to dislodge them often result in leaving the head embedded in the skin; this nearly always results in an abscess. Dousing the tick with medicated shampoo or surgical spirit will usually kill it or make it loosen its grip enough to pick if off.

Trombicula Infestation: see Harvest Mites

Lice spend their entire life cycle of two to four weeks on the dog, favouring especially hairy places round the head and the ears

Ticks are ugly, creamy-white parasites which attach themselves to the neck or head of a passing dog and gorge on his blood until purple-red and distended. Unless destroyed, the female lays hundreds of eggs, which hatch in a few weeks

Miscellaneous Diseases

Autoimmune Disease

Some dogs appear to have a faulty immune system and consequently an immune response to their own proteins. Normally the system in a newly weaned puppy recognizes the proteins which go to make up its own body and refrains from reacting with an immune response to the components of its own blood, for example. The dog develops a complex defence against invading foreign proteins, such as infective micro organisms, and at the same time the mechanisms prevent a dog from digesting itself.

The end result of a series of complex multiple reactions is autoimmune disease. This can appear as anemia with cell breakdown or as a whole variety of skin changes. Although there are many other autoimmune conditions (not including AIDS, Autoimmune Deficiency Disease Syndrome, a disease of man), skin and blood changes predominate. A form of rheumatoid arthritis in dogs is also believed to be an autoimmune disease. The elucidation of a complicated series of actions and reactions requires expert skills and thorough investigation.

Brucellosis

Brucella canis is a micro organism which is related to but not identical to the organism which causes Undulant Fever in man and contagious abortion in cattle. The organism is widespread in North America, unusual in Europe, and rare in Britain; it can affect humans, but the disease is mild and transient. Most problems with canine infection are reproductive; males become infertile because of inflammation of the testicles, and bitches abort. The condition usually occurs in breeding kennels; where bitches fail to conceive or where many dead or weak puppies are born, an incidence of *Brucella canis* should be suspected.

Canicola Fever: see Leptospirosis

Diabetes

Diabetes mellitus is a disorder of the system which controls the sugar level in blood and tissues. The hormone insulin, the key to this control, is lacking. Mature Dachshunds and Poodles seem to be particularly prone to diabetes; they eat well, but lose weight drastically and suffer from constant thirst, with large volumes of urine being passed. The circulatory level of glucose remains high for a long period after a meal as insufficient insulin is available to take it out of circulation. Glucose then overflows into the urine, and this tends to draw water into the urine, making it dilute and of great volume. The consequent need to maintain bodily water balance results in the excessive thirst exhibited by diabetic dogs.

Diabetic dogs can often be stabilized with routine insulin injections given by the owners. Once stabilized all but the most brittle cases of diabetes can lead happy lives for several years. It is commonly, but erroneously, thought that carbohydrate should be withheld from diabetics. Current research supports the view that moderate amounts may be beneficial and certain high-fibre diets seem to help human diabetics. Canned food, which is more likely to be standardized, has some advantages in feeding diabetic dogs. The dog's daily routine should be as stable as possible, particularly with regard to energy intake and output; meals should be small and frequent, given always at regular intervals. Exercise need not be restricted, but it should be consistent and suited to the dog's capabilities; bitches should ideally be spayed.

Although diligent treatment can be very rewarding for the owners of diabetic dogs, the condition is progressive in most cases, a fact which must be faced at the outset.

Hypothyroidism

The thyroid gland in the throat produces hormones which control the activity of many body functions. A lack of thyroid hormones (hypothyroidism) shows itself in a general lowering of physical activity, usually accompanied by wastage of the thyroid gland; tumour tissue may be present. Hypothyroid dogs are lethargic and easily fatigued although they may be only half-way through a normal lifespan; if affected early in life they remain dwarfs. The skin becomes dry, often with extensive, symmetrical hair loss (see Alopecia), sometimes accompanied by thickening and dark pigmentation of the skin. Fertility is low and some bitches may appear not to come into season.

The signs of thyroid disease must be distinguished from other disorders, and hormone tests are needed to make a proper diagnosis. After careful assessment, thyroid hormones can be given by mouth, and in most cases the effect is beneficial, although treatment is needed for the rest of the dog's life.

Leptospirosis

Two species of Leptospira bacteria commonly affect dogs. *Leptospira canicola* results in the infection known as Canicola Fever and is spread through urine. It commonly causes kidney disease, which initially may not be serious but which may reduce kidney tissue to such an extent that kidney failure may occur with age. The other common infection is *Leptospira icterohaemorrhagiae*, associated with infection, hemorrhages and jaundice. Dogs are usually infected by contamination of food, or by rat urine.

Vaccination against the two Leptospira bacteria has fortunately reduced, but not yet eliminated these infections.

Thyroid Disease: see Hypothyroidism

Toxoplasmosis

This microscopic parasite living within cells is easily confused with Toxocara, the common roundworm but the two are quite different. The organism causing Toxoplasmosis is ubiquitous in warm-blooded animals and does not usually cause serious problems, although abortion can occasionally be attributed to Toxoplasma infection. Some dogs may have nervous symptoms similar to those in distemper. Blood tests are necessary to confirm the diagnosis, and a favourable response to chemotherapy can usually be expected. The risk of infection can be greatly reduced with effective heat treatment of all foods.

Travel Sickness

Motion sickness can be as incapacitating in dogs as in humans. The dog will salivate profusely and vomit, sometimes continuously, and may after a long journey end up in a state of dehydration and collapse.

Most dogs grow out of travel sickness in time and come to enjoy car journeys. Although anti-emetic and tranquillizer drugs can suppress motion sickness, it is unwise to dose a dog before every journey. Suitable medication for extended holiday travel can usually be obtained from a veterinarian.

Dogs can be accustomed to car travel over a period. Initially the dog can be put in a stationary car, then gradually taken on shorter and longer trips until it feels comfortable in a moving vehicle.

PEDIGREE
BREEDS

DOG SHOWS

Dog shows take place in nearly every country in the world, and the interchange of judges from one country to another is common practice. The great majority of international show judges have had vast experience, and their opinion is eagerly sought wherever they go.

In order to show a pedigree or purebred dog in any country, it must be registered with the national Kennel Club. This is done by the breeder of the puppy, and when it is sold to a new owner, the ownership is transferred at the particular Kennel Club. If a dog is sold abroad, its original registration must be registered again with the Kennel Club of its adopted country. Fees vary from country to country.

Due to quarantine regulations in Britain dogs from abroad cannot be exhibited until they have served a six months' quarantine period in a Ministry-recognized kennel. The same regulations prevent dogs from Britain being shown on the Continent or overseas unless the owner is prepared to face six months' quarantine on their return to Britain. This is both costly and time-consuming, considering the comparatively short life of a dog, and while British judges take part in shows abroad, British dogs do not unless they take up residence in that particular country. Although it would be interesting for owners of British show dogs to compete with top dogs in other countries, it would be foolhardy to relax the very necessary quarantine laws which have kept rabies out of Britain so far.

The English Kennel Club lists purebred dogs in one of six groups: Gundog, Hound, Terrier, Toy, Utility, and Working Groups. The American Kennel Club (universally known by its initials: AKC) has recently decided to divide the Working Group into the Working Group and the Herding Group, giving America seven separate groups. Scandinavia has eight groups, and in countries governed by the F.C.I. (*Fédération Cynologique Internationale*) there are even more groups, some countries having up to ten. Australia have announced their intention to follow America and split the Working Group; it may well be that some adjustment of this unwieldy Group may in time have to be made in Britain.

Breed Standards issued by the various Kennel Clubs are the guidelines to which judges work. They may in some cases vary slightly from country to country, but it is the duty of all judges to make themselves acquainted with the Breed Standards in the country where they are judging. Very high standards prevail throughout the world. Some breeds are more popular in one country than in another, but the toughest competition is always to be found in America, Australia, Scandinavia and Britain.

Championship dogs representing five of the groups under which pure breeds are classified by the English Kennel Club. Gundogs: Flat coated Retrievers (*right*); Utility Group: Schipperke (*below left*); Hound Group: Long-haired Miniature Dachshund (*below right*); Toy Group: Pug (*bottom left*); and Working Group: Rottweiler (*bottom right*)

Breed standards emphasize specific coat colours and markings as in the Beagle (*below*), Boston Terrier (*centre*), Lhasa Apso (*bottom*), Old English Sheepdog (*right*), and Cavalier King Charles Spaniel (*bottom right*)

Coat types sometimes indicate the origin of breeds and the use to which these were once put. Long warm coats are common in Asiatic breeds like the Pekingese (*right*); dense and wiry hair protect sporting types like the Brittany Spaniel (*below left*), and the Norwich Terrier (*below right*). The harsh coat and ruff of the Dutch barge dog, the Keeshond (*bottom left*), confirms his origin in the Northern Hemisphere as clearly as the short and sleek hair of the Rhodesian Ridgeback (*bottom right*) places him in the Southern

Self-esteem is typical of all Terriers, like the Irish Terriers (*below*), the Cairns (*right*) and their relatives, the West Highland Whites (*bottom left*). Quiet dignity is displayed by the Papillon (*centre right*) and Miniature Pinscher (*bottom*)

Gundogs include such opposite breeds as the smooth-coated Hungarian Vizsla (*right*), which combines the roles of pointer, setter and retriever, and the hair-to-the-ground American Cocker Spaniel (*bottom left*), which is now almost exclusively bred as a show dog. The elegant English Setter (*bottom right*) is a family and a keen sporting dog. The French Bulldog (*centre left*), though listed in the Utility Group, has given up bull-baiting and settled for life as a house pet, while the massive Newfoundland (*centre right*) continues to be a working dog

Posture indicates temperament. The Airedale Terrier (*right*) carries himself as proudly as the Smooth Fox Terrier (*bottom*) stands his ground.

The Bernese Mountain Dog (*below*) shows reserve, the Italian Greyhound (*centre*) gentleness, and the Norfolk Terrier utter friendliness

Show Dogs

A great deal of care attends the preparation of a show dog, and especially of a long-coated breed. For the serious competitor, a show dog starts with the choice of sire for the bitch, and once the puppies have arrived their progress is carefully supervised, every detail and particularly any special breed features being taken into account. With luck one or perhaps two puppies seem good enough to progress for show prospects.

Training should start at a very early age, gently at first and just enough to let the puppy know what the future may hold, never so much as to make the puppy bored. Careful rearing, feeding, and exercising, depending on the breed, is essential for all puppies, but especially so for potential show stock. Without a balanced diet, no puppy will develop properly, and this applies more so to larger breeds, where it is imperative that they make the correct bone and substance.

By the time a puppy is six months old, the age in all countries at which it can be shown, it should be conversant with show training and ready for its first event. Once embarked on a show career, avoid the mistake of overshowing the new hope. Many promising puppies have been ruined in this way; they easily become 'show-sick' and refuse to give of their best on demand.

Coated breeds must be well-trimmed and immaculately presented if they are to compete favourably, and all presentation should be done outside the ring. Handling techniques vary with the breeds; the art is best mastered by watching the experts and practising in the quiet of home surroundings.

Losing gracefully is another art to be mastered. Never blame the dog for a fault or mishap which should have been taken care of by the trainer. Dog showing has much to commend it, new friendships to be made, interests to develop, and at the end of the day the enjoyment of a companion dog, with or without any prizes.

Pedigree Dogs

For a dog to be registered with a country's national Kennel Club, it must have a proven pedigree, which in effect means that it must be purebred, from parents of the same breed which are themselves purebred. In Britain, the English Kennel Club has been in existence for well over one hundred years and maintains records of thousands of purebred dogs. It is the authority which lays down the rules under which dog shows, field and working trials are held every year. The Kennel Club also promotes the annual Crufts Show which culminates with one dog being awarded the Best in Show prize. For a dog to qualify for Crufts, it must have won Championship status or been awarded a Challenge Certificate or Reserve Challenge Certificate or won a qualifying class in a breed class, all during the year previous to the Crufts Show. A dog that has won a five-point Green Star under Irish Kennel Club rules during the previous year may also qualify. In the USA, the American Kennel Club, which celebrated its 100th anniversary in 1984, is the governing authority responsible for the records of purebred dogs, and it too controls dogshows, and field and working trials.

Breed standards are compiled by a country's national Kennel Club in conjunction with Breed Clubs. The breed standards give detailed descriptions of the breeds with regard to conformation, general appearance, particular characteristics of the breed, texture, length and colour of coat, and weight and size. They can vary slightly from country to country.

Breed Standards

In the following pages the English Kennel Club has been referred to as the UK Kennel Club

International practice has been adhered to in the breed standards in that the height and weight of the male dog, when different from the bitch, are given first

Standards may stipulate both height and weight, sometimes either, and sometimes neither

If the breed standards of the UK and AKC vary, both are given, those of the UK being first

If the English or American Kennel Clubs do not have a standard for a particular breed, this is noted.

Hound Group

This is composed of those hounds which hunt by scent and those which hunt by sight, the so-called sighthounds or gazehounds. Hound lovers are adamant that no other breed of dog gives so much excitement, pleasure and sport in return for very little, be it a pack or a single hound. They are always referred to as hounds as distinct from dogs.

Most hounds accept domesticated life well and make excellent companion and show dogs. Usually tough and hardy, they repay sensible care and reasonable exercise with many years of pleasure and true companionship.

AFGHAN HOUND
UK and AKC Standards
Height   27–29in (69–73cm)
             Bitches 2–3in (5–8cm) less
Weight AKC 60lb (27.2kg)
             50lb (22.7kg)
Origin/history In one form or another the Afghan Hound has been known in the Middle East and eastwards for thousands of years, but the first was brought to Britain from Seistan Province, Iran, and exhibited at the Kennel Club Show in 1907. The Afghan arrived in the United States in about 1926, almost entirely via Britain.
Characteristics To be truly typical the Afghan must have the inscrutable Oriental expression and look at and through you. A stylish dog of royal bearing that carries his head proudly. Skull long with prominent occiput. Foreface long with punishing jaws. Near triangular eyes, dark rather than golden. Back strong and level, of moderate length. Powerful quarters. Tail not too short, with characteristic ring at end. Silky coat long and fine on ribs, fore and hindquarters and flanks; along saddle hair should be short. All colours acceptable.
Temperament Aloof and dignified, yet happy and kind.
Drawbacks Needs frequent grooming and daily exercise.

AMERICAN FOXHOUND
No UK Kennel Club Standards
AKC Standards
Height 22–25in (56–64cm)
Origin/history The American Foxhound belongs to the same family as the English Foxhound and records show that Lord Fairfax, who had settled in Virginia, imported hounds from England in 1738. The tendency is for the American Foxhound to be a little taller than his English cousin, but this can depend greatly on the country being hunted both in America and England.
Characteristics As English Foxhound.

BASENJI
UK and AKC Standards
Height   17in (43cm)
         16in (40cm)
Weight 24lb (11kg)
         22lb (10kg)
Origin/history Originally from Central Africa and used to hunt and destroy vermin, the first Basenji reached England in 1895 and America in 1941. In 1943 a Standard was published by the English Basenji Club. The Basenji Club of America was formed in 1942.
Characteristics A lightly built, finely boned, graceful and aristocratic-looking dog noted for its inability to bark; its vocal noise has been described as a mixture of a chortle and a yodel. Wrinkled forehead gives him a worried expression; pricked ears should be slightly hooded and set well forward on top of head. Eyes dark and diamond shaped. Deep brisket runs up into a definite waist. Tail tightly curled over the spine and lies close to thigh. Coat short, sleek and fine. Colour, pure bright red, pure black, or black and tan, all with white feet, chest and tail tips.
Temperament A happy dog, anxious to please; very good with children.
Drawbacks Can sometimes be a little sharp with strangers.

BASSET GRIFFON VENDEEN
UK Kennel Club Standards
Height – Smaller variety 13–15in (33–38cm)
             Larger variety 15–17in (38–43cm)
No AKC Standards
Origin/history This Basset is bred in the Vendée in southwest France for the special job of coursing hares. The countryside there is crisscrossed with hedges, and roads that become impassable in winter, so that hunting has to be on foot. A good scent hound, with a very pleasing voice.
Characteristics Long bodied with roomy chest. Short legs large and strong. Domed head and long folded ears. Coat harsh and not too long. Colour, white self or with combination of lemon, orange, tricolour or grizzle markings.
Temperament Happy extrovert, independent but willing to please, and a good house dog.
Drawbacks Being active requires adequate exercise.

BASSET HOUND
UK and AKC Standards
Height 13–15in (33–38cm)
Origin/history Of ancient lineage and used, in his native France, as far back as the 16th century to hunt badgers and wolves. First shown in Paris in 1863. Arrived in United States in 1863 and shown in 1884. First shown in England in 1875.
Characteristics Short-legged, of considerable power. Well-proportioned lean head with skin loose enough to wrinkle freely when drawn forward. Ears long and pendulous. Eyes brown with a lovely calm expression. Breastbone slightly prominent, but chest not narrow or unduly deep. Back rather broad, and level. Quarters with well-bent stifles. Coat smooth, short and close. Colour, usually black, white and tan, or lemon and white, all recognized hound colours acceptable. Tail long, set high and carried well up, curving gently but not gay. Rich melodious voice.
Temperament Mild and kindly temperament, neither sharp nor timid, and capable of great endurance in the field.
Drawbacks Needs good exercise to keep him happy and fit.

BEAGLE (see page 180)
UK Kennel Club Standards
Height 13–16in (33–40cm)
AKC Standards
Height up to 13in (33cm)
             over 13in (33cm), but not exceeding 15in (38cm)
Origin/history Essentially British, the Beagle is one of the oldest of all pure-bred hounds even if his history is vague. A popular Hound with many monarchs and frequently mentioned in early literature, such as Chaucer's 14th-century *Canterbury Tales*. Queen Elizabeth I had a pack of pocket Beagles said to be less than 10in (25cm) high.
Characteristics A merry hound whose essential function is to hunt hares. Sturdy and compactly built, it conveys an impression of quality without coarseness. Head fairly long, slightly domed and free from frown and excessive wrinkle. Eyes large, hazel or brown, widely spaced. Topline straight and level. Chest deep to below elbow. Ribs well sprung. Well-bent stifles. Coat short, dense and weatherproof. Colour, any recognized hound colour other than liver. Tail carried gaily, not curled, tip of stern white.

Temperament Happy, intelligent and friendly hound, full of fun and stamina. Makes a good companion.
Drawbacks Highly active and needs adequate exercise.

BLACK AND TAN COONHOUND
No UK Kennel Club Standards
AKC Standards
Height 25–27in (64–69cm)
23–25in (58–64cm)
Origin/history The Black and Tan Hound has been developed in America especially for hunting raccoons. Its ancestors include the Talbot Hound, the Bloodhound, and the Black and Tan Virginia Foxhound. The Coonhound works his trail with skill and determination, although not particularly fast.
Characteristics A working dog able to withstand the rigours of winter, the heat of summer and the difficult terrain over which it is required to work. Known for its deep voice when tracking quarry. Head cleanly modelled, with medium stop. Neck muscular. Back level, powerful and strong, with visible slope from withers to rump. Quarters well boned and muscled. Coat short, dense to withstand rough going. Colour, coal black with rich tan markings.
Temperament Alert, powerful and agile hound. Primarily a working dog.
Drawbacks Not very suitable as a family companion dog.

BLOODHOUND
UK and AKC Standards
Height 25–27in (64–69cm)
23–25in (58–64cm)
Weight 90–110lb (41–50kg)
80–100lb (36–45kg)
Origin/history There is little evidence to prove how far back the origin of the Bloodhound extends, but it is a direct descendant of the old Celtic hound. It is of the purest hound blood, hence its name, and its reputation for tracking by scent is unrivalled. First used to track down man in the 14th century and now used, on occasions, to track down criminals. He hunts his quarry with great enthusiasm, but does not attack.
Characteristics Extremely powerful and stands over more ground than is usual with other hounds. Skin is thin and loose, particularly about the head and neck, where it should hang in deep folds. Expression noble and dignified, characterized by solemnity, wisdom and power. Gait elastic, swinging and free. Head narrow in proportion to length. Ribs well sprung, and chest forms a deep keel between the forelegs. Colours, are black and tan, liver and tan, and red. Tail long, set on high and carried scimitar fashion.
Temperament Affectionate, quarrelsome with neither companions nor other dogs. By nature somewhat reserved and solemn, but always gently dignified.
Drawbacks Being large, requires plenty of space for exercising and living quarters.

BORZOI
UK and AKC Standards
Height 29in (73cm)
27in (69cm)
Weight AKC 75–105lb (34–47.6kg)
15–20lb (6.8–9kg)
Origin/history In Russian, Borzoi means swift, a fitting name for this hound which has been used in Russia since the 17th century for coursing wolves, hares and other game. The breed came to England about 1875, and was first brought to America in 1889.
Characteristics A graceful, aristocratic and elegant dog possessing courage, muscular power and great speed. Head long and lean. Ears small and fine. Eyes dark, almond shaped and slanting. Deep, rather narrow brisket. Ribs well sprung and flexible. Back rises in graceful arch from near the shoulder with well-balanced fall-away. Loins broad and powerful. Coat long and silky, short and smooth on head, ears and front legs. Profuse frill on neck. Colours, any solid or colour combination is acceptable.
Temperament Courageous, but docile with strangers, makes a good companion.
Drawbacks Requires sensible and regular exercise and regular grooming.

DACHSHUNDS (see page 179)
UK Kennel Club Standards

Long-haired	Middle weight, up to	18lb (8kg)
		17lb (7.7kg)
	Heavy weight, over	18lb (8kg)
		17lb (7.7kg)
	Miniature, not exceeding	11lb (5kg)
Smooth-haired	Dogs not exceeding	25lb (11kg)
	Bitches not exceeding	23lb (10.4kg)
	Miniatures not exceeding	11lb (5kg)
Wire-haired		20–22lb (9–10kg)
		18–20lb (8–9kg)

AKC Standards
Miniature Dachshunds do not have separate classes, but are a division of the Open Class for under 10lb (4.5kg), and 12 months or more old.
Origin/history Native to Germany, Dachshunds were originally used to follow badgers to earth and known as badger dogs (Ger. *Dachshund*). They first appeared in Britain when Prince Edward of Saxe-Weimar presented some to Queen Victoria. The first Dachshund exhibited in Britain was at Birmingham in 1870, and the British Dachshund Club has the distinction of being the oldest breed club in the world. The English Kennel Club recognized the breed in 1874; the Dachshund Club of America was formed in 1895. In Germany the Dachshund is known as 'Teckel', the leading organization – the Teckel Club – was founded in 1888.
Characteristics Body short-legged, compact, and long but sinewy and well muscled, with defiant head carriage. Head long and conical, skull neither too broad nor too narrow. Eyes dark. Neck long and muscular, showing no dewlap. Breast bone prominent with depressions on both sides. Hindquarters full and broad with round rump. Colours, black and tan, dark brown with lighter shades, dark red, light red, dappled, tiger marked or brindle. Coat in Long-haired, soft, straight or slightly waved, of shining colour, feathering behind legs and tail should form a flag. Smooth-haired, short, dense and smooth, but strong. Wire-haired, body completely covered with even, short, harsh coat and undercoat, beard on chin, eyebrows bushy, and hair on ears almost smooth.
Temperament Clever, lively, bold and highly intelligent, strong, hardy and game despite their small size. Excellent and devoted companion dogs.
Drawbacks None discernible.

DEERHOUND
UK and AKC Standards
Height Dogs not less than 30in (76cm)
Bitches not less than 28in (71cm)
Weight 85lb (38.5kg)
65lb (29.5kg)
Origin/history Native to Scotland, the Deerhound, one of the oldest British breeds, is used to pursue and kill deer, hunting by sight, not by scent. Classified in 1860, four Deerhounds from the Royal Kennels were exhibited at

Islington, London in 1869.

Characteristics A graceful, dignified dog. Head broadest at ears, tapering slightly to the dark eyes, with muzzle tapering more decidedly to the nose. Neck long. Body like that of a Greyhound, but larger overall. Chest deep rather than broad. Quarters drooping, broad and powerful. Hair on body, neck and quarters harsh and wiry, softer on head, breast and belly. Coat shaggy, but not too dense. Colour, dark blue-grey, darker and/or lighter grey brindle, yellow, dandy-red and red-fawn also acceptable.

Temperament Quiet and dignified. Combination of indomitable courage, great strength and speed necessary to cope with large deer.

Drawbacks Unsuitable as a pet in a small flat; plenty of exercise necessary.

ELKHOUND
UK and AKC Standards
Height 20½in (52cm)
19½in (49cm)
Weight 50lb (22.7kg)
43lb (19.5kg)

Origin/history This breed originates in Norway and for centuries has been used to guard and defend farms and livestock against wolves and bears. A typical Spitz dog, it is a great hunter of elk, and devoted to his master. First considered for showing in 1877, the year that the Norwegian Hunters' Association held its first show.

Characteristics Hardy sporting dog, of bold and virile nature with good scenting powers. Compact and proportionately short body. Head broad between ears, clearly marked though not large stop. Ears set high, firm and pricked. Eyes dark brown. Back wide and straight from neck to stern, chest wide and deep. Quarters firm and powerful. Coat thick and abundant, coarse and weather-resistant. Colour, various shades of grey with black tips to the longer outer coat. Tail set high and tightly curled over back.

Temperament Friendly and intelligent with great energy and independence of character.

Drawbacks Coat needs frequent grooming.

FINNISH SPITZ
UK Kennel Club Standards
Height 17½in (44cm)
15½in (39cm)
Weight 31–36lb (14–16kg) approx.
23–29lb (10–13kg) approx.
No AKC Standards

Origin/history The national breed of Finland, the Finnish Spitz has been bred for hundreds of years as a hunter of forest birds. The breed was introduced to England in 1927.

Characteristics Dog considerably larger and carries more coat than the bitch. Head medium sized and clean cut. Pronounced stop. Narrow muzzle. Ears cocked and pointed. Eyes dark. Body almost square in outline. Back straight and strong. Chest deep. Coat on head and front of legs short and close; on body and back of legs longish, semi-erect or erect. Colour, reddish-brown or red-gold on the back; all other parts in lighter shades. Tail plumed and curved vigorously from its root into a complete arch.

Temperament Intelligent and courageous, tempered with caution. Eager to hunt and makes a good companion.

Drawbacks Can be a little reserved with strangers.

FOXHOUND
UK and AKC Standards
No size or weight given

Origin/history Legend has it that in 1213 King John made a request to the Mayor of Bristol that 40 Foxhounds be sent to him for hunting. Evidence exists that the Foxhound has been used in England since the end of the 17th century. The breed was developed from the old, now extinct, Southern Hounds, the Talbots and the St Huberts. Masters of different packs bred to a type to suit their own personal requirements and the characteristics of the country over which they hunted. In Britain, Foxhounds are not entered at Kennel Club Shows but have their own shows, governed by the Association of Masters of Foxhounds.

Characteristics Medium-sized well-proportioned hound with pendent ears. Skull broad. Neck long but not thick. Body deep with plenty of heart room. Back broad and well ribbed. Quarters full and of great muscular proportions. Smooth coat of various hound colours, usually tricoloured.

Temperament Very active; excellent hunting ability; enjoys pack life.

Drawbacks Unsuitable as a family companion.

GREYHOUND
UK and AKC Standards
Height UK 28–30in (71–76cm)
27–28in (69–71cm)
Weight AKC 65–70lb (29.5–31.8kg)
60–65lb (27.2–29.5kg)

Origin/history Our first knowledge of the Greyhound comes from the Tomb of Amten, in the Valley of the Nile, where carvings in three separate scenes show dogs of unmistakable Greyhound type. The tomb is thought by Egyptologists to belong to the period of 2900–2751 BC. King Solomon refers to the Greyhound in the Old Testament. It must, therefore, be one of the oldest of all dogs and during the thousands of years that he has been associated with the sport of coursing he has barely changed. It is claimed that the Greyhound can reach up to 50m/ph (80.5km/ph) on a straight track.

Characteristics Strongly built, upstanding dog of generous proportions, muscular power and symmetrical formation. Long head and neck with clean well-laid shoulders, deep chest and capacious body. Ears small. Eyes dark and bright. Arched loins finishing in powerful quarters. Coat is fine and close. Colour, black, white, red, blue, fawn, fallow, brindle, or any of the colours broken with white. Tail long, set on rather low and slightly curved.

Temperament An individualist, kind and affectionate. Possesses remarkable stamina, and his long-reaching stride enables him to cover ground at great speed.

Drawbacks Must have plenty of free running exercise.

HAMILTON STOVARE
UK Kennel Club Standards
Height 19½–23½in (49–60cm)
18–22½in (46–57cm)
No AKC Standards

Origin/history This is the most popular Hound in Sweden and bred by Count Hamilton from the English Foxhound, the Holstein Hound, the Hanoverian Haidbracke and the Courlander Hound. Used in Sweden for game hunting.

Characteristics Handsome upstanding hound of striking colouring. Well proportioned and giving an impression of great strength and stamina. Head longish with a slightly arched and moderately broad skull. Neck long. Back straight and powerful. Croup slightly inclined, long and broad. Quarters strong and parallel. Free striding and long reaching with high action. Coat consists of two layers: strongly weather-resistant upper coat close to body; undercoat short, close and soft. Colour, tan with black saddle and white markings.

Temperament Very active, free striding and long reaching dog. Excellent hunter, of amiable disposition.
Drawbacks Requires plenty of correct exercise.

IBIZAN HOUND
UK and AKC Standards
Height 23½–28in (59–71cm)
      22½–27in (56–69cm)
Origin/history The Ibizan Hound has been bred pure on the island of Ibiza in the Balearic group and in the coastal regions of Majorca, Valencia, Catalonia, and Provence. It is similar in shape to the Greyhound type as depicted in mural paintings of ancient Egypt. A valued hunter and retriever of small furred game.
Characteristics An agile hound with the ability to jump great heights without take-off. Tall, narrow and finely built with large erect ears set high. Eyes slanting, pale amber. Long flat skull with prominent occipital bone. Neck long, lean and slightly arched. Level back, sloping slightly from pinbones to rump. Gait a suspended trot of long far-reaching strides. Coat smooth or rough, always hard, close and dense. Colour, white, chestnut, lion solid, or any combination of these. Tail long.
Temperament Kind and loyal to his family but cautious with strangers.
Drawbacks Needs plenty of exercise; enjoys pack life.

IRISH WOLFHOUND
UK and AKC Standards
Height (minimum) 31in (78cm)
                28in (71cm)
Weight (minimum) 120lb (54kg)
                90lb (41kg)
Origin/history The largest of existing breeds, the Irish Wolfhound was formerly used by Irish kings to hunt wolves. The breed almost disappeared with the extinction of the wolf in Ireland, but was reintroduced by a Captain Graham, who founded the Irish Wolfhound Club in 1885. The English Kennel Club admitted the breed to its register in 1897.
Characteristics Of great size and commanding appearance. Muscular, strongly though gracefully built; movements easy and active. Head and neck carried high. Ears small and Greyhound-like. Eyes, dark. Chest deep. Breast wide. Back rather long; belly well drawn up. Coat rough and hard on body, legs and head, wiry and long over eyes and beneath jaw. Recognized colours are grey, brindle, red, black, pure white, fawn, or any colour that appears in the Deerhound. Tail long, slightly curved, moderately thick and hairy.
Temperament Gentle nature, dignified and loyal; makes a wonderful companion.
Drawbacks As a pet needs adequate space for exercise and living quarters.

OTTERHOUND
UK and AKC Standards
Height   24–27in (61–69cm)
           Bitches smaller
Weight AKC 75–115lb (34–52.2kg)
            65–100lb (29.5–45kg)
Origin/history An ancient hound of uncertain origin but probably a product of the 19th century derived from Welsh Harriers and Southern Hounds. Hunts by scents, in water and on land. Only in recent years has the Otterhound appeared on show benches in England. In America they were first shown in 1907 in Claremont, Oklahoma.
Characteristics Shaggy-coated hound, fast and untiring in water. Majestic head, strong body and loose, long-striding action. Chest deep with well-sprung oval ribcage. Level

topline and broad back. Quarters very strong. Feet webbed. Outer coat long and harsh, undercoat dense and waterproof. Colour, any recognized hound colour.
Temperament Even tempered and amiable; considerable stamina and outstanding hunter.
Drawbacks Unsuitable as a house dog because of size and hunting instincts.

PHARAOH HOUND
UK Kennel Club Standards
Height 22–25in (56–64cm)
      21–24in (53–61cm)
No AKC Standards
Origin/history The Pharaoh Hound is thought to have reached Gozo and Malta with the Phoenicians. Of very great antiquity, it resembles the Hounds depicted in Egyptian sculpture. By instinct a hunter, by scent and sight, using his large ears to a marked degree when working close.
Characteristics Noble of bearing, with clean-cut lines, graceful yet powerful. Very fast with free easy movements and alert expression. Skull long and lean. Eyes oval and deep amber. Body lithe with almost straight topline. Slight slope from croup to root of tail. Deep brisket. Strong and well-muscled quarters. Coat short and glossy. Colour, chestnut or rich tan with white markings. Tail set high, carried high and curved when agitated.
Temperament Intelligent and alert, graceful, affectionate and playful.
Drawbacks Extremely active and requires plenty of regular exercise; hunting instinct strong.

RHODESIAN RIDGEBACK (see page 181)
UK and AKC Standards
Height 25–27 in (64–69cm)
       24–26in (61–66cm)
Weight 80lb (36.3kg)
       70lb (31.8kg)
Origin/history Native of South Africa and sometimes referred to as the African Lion Hound. Its origin is shrouded in mystery but it is probably a cross with the Bloodhound. Brought to Rhodesia (now Zambia) with early settlers and used to hunt big game, particularly lions. First seen in England in the show ring in 1932 and admitted to the American Kennel Club register in 1955.
Characteristics Strong, muscular and active dog. Peculiarity of the breed is a ridge on the back formed by hair growing in opposite direction to the rest of the coat; must contain two identical crowns only, opposite each other. Skull flat and rather broad between ears. Chest not too wide but deep and capacious. Back powerful, loins strong. Coat, short and dense, sleek and glossy. Colour, light to red wheaten. Tail tapering, slight upward curve.
Temperament Courageous and excellent guard dog, very loyal to his own family.
Drawbacks A strong dog needing careful training and handling when young, and plenty of exercise.

SALUKI
UK and AKC Standards
Height 23–28in (58–71cm)
      Bitches proportionally less
Origin/history The Saluki is said to be as old as the earliest known civilization. Known as a distinct breed as long ago as 328 BC, it is the coursing dog of the Arabs and used mainly for hunting gazelle. First brought to England in 1840 and officially recognized by the English Kennel Club in 1927.
Characteristics Overall appearance is of grace and symme-

try and of great speed and endurance. Expression dignified and gentle. Head long and narrow. Ears silky, long and pendent. Eyes dark and gentle. Back fairly broad. Strong hip bones set wide apart. Coat smooth, soft and silky in texture. Colour, white, cream, fawn, golden, red, grizzle or tan, tricolour, black and tan, or variations of these colours. Tail set low, long, feathered and carried in a curve.
Temperament Affectionate hound without being demonstrative. Good guard dog though not generally aggressive.
Drawbacks Requires plenty of exercise.

WHIPPET
UK Kennel Club Standards
Height 18½in (47cm)
      17½mn (44cm)
AKC Standards
Height 19–22in (48–56cm)
      18–21in (46–53cm)
Origin/history A small replica of the Greyhound, the Whippet was evolved in England some one hundred years ago, and Whippet racing became popular at the turn of the 19th century. The breed was officially recognized by the English Kennel Club in 1890.
Characteristics General impression is of beautifully balanced muscular power and strength, like a thoroughbred horse in action. Head long and lean, flat on top. Ears small and rose-shaped. Eyes bright and alert. Neck long and muscular, elegantly arched. Chest very deep with plenty of heart room. Back showing definite arch but not humped over loin. Quarters strong and broad across thighs. Coat fine, short and close. Colour, any, solid or mixed. Tail long and tapering, carried in gentle upward curve when agitated.
Temperament Happy, intelligent and affectionate as a companion; because of size can be accommodated comfortably in most households.
Drawbacks None discernible.

Gundog Group

In this group all breeds have their particular use in the field of sport, as well as being popular show dogs and companions. At work in open fields, a gundog is happy and keen and in complete harmony with his master. Pointers and Setters have the job of locating game by ranging the ground in front of the rifles; retrievers, as their name implies, retrieve the game and should be just as efficient in water as on the land. Spaniels are versatile gundogs; the remainder of this group are excellent utility workers in the field. All make devoted companions, with pleasing temperaments and able to adapt to family conditions. Many have achieved top honours at shows.

GERMAN SHORTHAIRED POINTER
UK and AKC Standards
Height 23–25in (58–64cm)
      21–23in (53–58cm)
Weight 55–70lb (25–31.8kg)
      45–60lb (20.4–27.2kg)
Origin/history Descended from the Spanish Pointer. In the 17th century German sportsmen succeeded in producing a bird-dog that would point, retrieve, trail and be a family companion. This they achieved by introducing Bloodhound and Foxhound blood, and later English Pointer blood. The GSP was first registered in America in 1930 and in the UK in 1951.
Characteristics Furrow between eyes less deep and occiput less pronounced than in the Pointer. Nose solid brown. Eyes medium size, in shades of brown to tone with the coat, short, flat and coarse. Colour solid liver, liver and white spotted or ticked, liver and white ticked, black and white.
Temperament Keen working and watch dog with excellent nose, equally good on land and on water. Also makes a loyal and devoted companion.
Drawbacks Unsuitable for sedentary or restricted life.

GERMAN WIREHAIRED POINTER
UK and AKC Standards
Height   23½–25½in (60–65cm)
            Not less than 22in (56cm)
Weight UK 55–70½lb (25–32kg)
            45–59½lb (20.5–27kg)
Origin/history The most popular shooting dog in Germany and evolved there from the best Pointers regardless of type and coat. Based on the German Shorthaired Pointer, the coat is the most important feature and other breeds were used to perfect it. Officially recognized for Championship Show status in the US in 1959, recognized by the English Kennel Club at Championship Shows from 1986.
Characteristics Head of medium length, with dark hazel, bright and intelligent eyes. Eyebrows bushy. Muzzle long, strong and bearded. Chest deep rather than wide. Coat very harsh, medium length and abundant, with close-fitting undercoat. Tail should be docked by half its length. Colour solid liver, liver and white spotted, liver and white spotted and ticked, liver and white ticked, black and white.
Temperament Highly intelligent and friendly, an excellent companion and all-round shooting dog.
Drawbacks Requires plenty of controlled exercise to maintain fitness.

HUNGARIAN VIZSLA (see page 183)
UK and AKC Standards
Height 22½–25in (57–64cm)
      21–23½in (53–60cm)
Weight UK 48½–66lb (22–30kg)
Origin/history The only shooting dog originating in Hungary and the National dog of Hungarian sportsmen. A 14th-

century manuscript of early Hungarian codes illustrates a dog later identified as a Vizsla. Between the two world wars the breed almost died out and only survived because of a few loyal supporters. After the Russian occupation in 1945 many Hungarians fleeing to Austria took their dogs with them. It combines the duties of Pointer, Setter and Retriever.

Characteristics A medium-sized dog of distinguished appearance, robust but not too heavily boned. Head gaunt and noble, eyes slightly darker than coat. Chest moderately broad and deep, with prominent breast bone. Short back and well-muscled body. Coat short and straight, dense and coarse. Colour russet gold. Tail one-third docked.

Temperament Steady and dependable. Makes a good house dog as well as a sporting companion.

Drawbacks An active dog needing daily exercise.

LARGE MUNSTERLANDER
UK Kennel Club Standards
Height 24in (61cm)
       23in (58cm)
Weight 55–65lb (25–29.5kg)
       55lb (25kg)
No AKC Standards

Origin/history The youngest of the pointing/retrieving gundog breeds although his ancestors are as ancient as those of other German gundogs. A club was formed in Munster in 1919, the first show was held in 1921, and it is said that the twenty-three black and white dogs entered are the ancestors of the modern dogs. It was first imported into Britain in 1972.

Characteristics A multipurpose gundog, alert and energetic and ideal for rough shooters. Head solid black, though white blaze, snip or star allowed. Eyes dark brown, showing no haw. Strong, muscular body, strong back, short-coupled, slightly higher at shoulder. Free, long-striding and springy gait. Docking of tail optional. Coat long and dense, neither curly nor coarse, well feathered on front and hind legs, and on underside of tail. Body colour is white with black patches, flecked, ticked or a combination.

Temperament Keen worker easily trained; loyal, affectionate and trustworthy.

Drawbacks Needs plenty of exercise.

POINTER
UK Kennel Club Standards
Height 25–27in (64–69cm)
      24–26in (61–66cm)
AKC Standards
Height 25–28in (64–71cm)
      23–26in (58–66cm)
Weight 55–75lb (25–34kg)
      45–65lb (20.4–29.5kg)

Origin/history The first Pointers appeared in Britain about 1650 and were used in conjunction with Greyhounds for hare coursing – the Pointer would find the hare and the Greyhound would chase it. Origins are obscure, but it is thought that the Pointer came from Spain and was developed in England. Around 1730 the Duke of Kingston crossed the Spanish Pointer with the French Hound, and towards the end of the 18th century it was crossed with the Foxhound to help improve stamina and conformation.

Characteristics The head is unique, with a somewhat concave muzzle ending on a level with the nostrils and giving a dishfaced expression. Tail long and tapering and in movement lashing from side to side. Fine, short coat is hard and evenly distributed, perfectly smooth and straight. Usual colours are lemon and white, orange and white, liver and white, black and white. Self colours and tricolours are also correct.

Temperament Excellent working gundog whose job it is to search out the game ahead of the guns. Makes a good companion, appreciating regular free exercise.

Drawbacks Daily exercise is essential for good health.

RETRIEVER, CHESAPEAKE BAY
No UK Kennel Club Standards
AKC Standards
Height 23–26in (58–66cm)
      21–24in (53–61cm)
Weight 65–75lb (29.5–34kg)
      55–65lb (25–29.5kg)

Origin/history This breed originated in America, from English stock. In 1807 an English brig was wrecked off the coast of Maryland and the crew were rescued by the American ship *Canton*. Two Newfoundland puppies on board were used for breeding; their descendants were crossed with Curly and Flat Coated Retrievers plus the Otterhound, and in 1885 the breed evolved and was used for retrieving wild duck from the icy waters of Chesapeake Bay. The American Chesapeake Bay Retriever Club was founded in 1918.

Characteristics Well-proportioned, strong body. Skull broad and round with medium stop. Eyes large, yellowish and set wide apart. Hindquarters extremely powerful for swimming. Back short and well coupled. Coat thick and short, oily and water-resistant, no trace of curl permissible. Any colour from dark brown to faded tan.

Temperament A courageous dog with willingness to work and a love of water.

Drawbacks A lazy life is not acceptable.

RETRIEVER, CURLY COATED
UK Kennel Club Standards
Height 25–27in (65–69cm)
Weight 70–80lb (31.8–36.3kg)
No AKC Standards

Origin/history One of the oldest of the retrieving breeds and a cross product of the Irish Water Spaniel, Poodle and Labrador. First exhibited at the Birmingham Show in 1860, and in 1889 specimens were exported to New Zealand, and to the United States about 1907, but at present low in popularity. The Curly Coated Retriever Club was formed in 1896 but ceased to exist for some years; the present Curly Retriever Club of England was founded in 1933.

Characteristics Strong, intelligent dog with great endurance and a love of water. Long, well-proportioned head with clear, firm lines. Eyes black or brown. Good depth of brisket, well-sprung ribs and shortish in loin. Coat a distinctive feature and should be a mass of crisp, small curls; colour, black or liver.

Temperament A lovable companion and good guard dog.

Drawbacks Needs suitable space and exercise.

RETRIEVER, FLAT COATED (see page 179)
UK and AKC Standards
Weight 60–70lb (27.2–31.8kg)

Origin/history Thought to have evolved from the Newfoundland and the Labrador. Originally known as the Wavy Coated Retriever, though probably blood lines from the Irish Setter and Gordon Setter were introduced to produce this elegant dog. The earliest specimen appeared at the Birmingham Show in 1860.

Characteristics Bright and active, of medium size and exhibiting power without lumber. Head long and elegantly moulded, with flat skull and dark brown to hazel eyes. Chest deep and fairly broad, with well-defined brisket. Back short, square and well ribbed. Dense and flat coat of silky texture; colour, black or liver.

Temperament A happy intelligent dog making a good companion in the home and in the field.
Drawbacks Must have regular exercise to keep it fit and happy and prevent boredom.

RETRIEVER, GOLDEN
UK Kennel Club Standards
Height 22–24in (56–61cm)
20–22in (51–56cm)
Weight 70–80lb (31.8–36.3kg)
60–70lb (27.2–31.8kg)
AKC Standards
Height 23–24in (58–61cm)
21½–22½in (54–57cm)
Weight 65–75lb (29.5–34kg)
60–70lb (27.2–31.8kg)
Origin/history The true origin of this lovely breed was accepted as recently as 1952. In the last century a yellow Wavy Coated Retriever was mated to a Tweed Water Spaniel. From this mating came four yellow puppies which became the ancestors of all Golden Retrievers. In 1918 the Golden Retriever Club was formed in England.
Characteristics A symmetrical, active and powerful dog with body well balanced, short-coupled and deep-sprung ribs. Broad skull and clean muscular neck. Dark kindly eyes. Coat flat or wavy with good feathering, any shade of gold or cream but not red nor mahogany; dense water-resistant undercoat.
Temperament Very popular for its charming character; equally excellent as a good working dog and as a devoted companion. Much used as a guide dog for the blind.
Drawbacks Requires regular exercise and grooming to maintain good condition.

RETRIEVER, LABRADOR
UK Kennel Club Standards
Height 22–22½in (56–57cm)
21½–22in (54–56cm)
AKC Standards
Height 22½–24½in (57–62cm)
21½–23½in (54–60cm)
Weight 60–75lb (27.2–34kg)
55–70lb (25–31.8kg)
Origin/history Originally known as the St John's breed, it originated in Newfoundland, where Labradors were used by local fishermen to retrieve and drag in the ends of fishing nets to the men on shore. Their dense, waterproof coats were impervious to the icy waters of the St Lawrence River, Canada. Retrievers by nature, the breed excels as gundogs.
Characteristics Strongly built, short-coupled and very active. Broad skull, broad and deep through chest and ribs. Strong hindquarters. Eyes brown or hazel. Distinctive coat should be short and dense without wave and have weather-resistant undercoat; colours, black, yellow or chocolate. Tail like an otter's in appearance.
Temperament Highly versatile and keen to please his master. Excellent with children, and as guide for the blind. Also used to sniff out drugs and explosives. Generally long-lived, robust and healthy.
Drawbacks Has a tendency to overweight if allowed too many tidbits. Needs regular exercise.

SETTER, ENGLISH (see page 183)
UK and AKC Standards
Height 25½–27in (65–69cm)
24–25½in (61–65cm)
Weight 60–66lb (27.2–30kg)
55–61½lb (25–28kg)

Origin/history The history of the English Setter goes back 500 years, but the modern strain was greatly influenced by a Mr Edward Laverack, who in 1825 acquired two pure English Setters and started a breeding programme. Later in the 19th century, a Mr Purcell Llewellin continued the development by breeding Laverack stock with setter stock for hunting the moors in the North of England.
Characteristics Of medium height, clean in outline, elegant in appearance and movement. Skull equals muzzle in length. Eyes bright, mild and intelligent, dark hazel colour. Moderate length of body, back short and level, chest deep. Coat slightly wavy, long and silky; colours, black and white, lemon and white, liver and white, or black, white and tan. Tail, feathered, in line with back.
Temperament Happy and friendly dog with a keen game sense; well mannered and faithful. Suited to family life and ideal with children.
Drawbacks Plenty and regular exercise is essential as is daily grooming.

SETTER, GORDON
UK and AKC Standards
Height 26in (66cm)
24½in (62cm)
Weight 65lb (29.5kg)
56lb (25.4kg)
Origin/history This is the largest and heaviest of the Setter family, first bred at Gordon Castle in Banffshire, Scotland. It is generally accepted that the Gordon's ancestors include the Bloodhound, Collie and other Setters, with perhaps some of the old Spaniel blood. The British Gordon Setter Club was formed in 1927.
Characteristics Elegant and of aristocratic appearance, the body is of moderate length, deep in brisket. Head deep rather than broad. Eyes dark brown and bright. Coat short and fine on head and legs, elsewhere moderately long and practically free from curl or wave, feathering on upper part of ears, back of hind legs, on belly and chest. Colour, deep shining coal black with rich chestnut markings. Tail fairly short and should not reach hocks.
Temperament Steady, quiet, friendly and loyal. Exceptional galloping qualities as a sporting dog.
Drawbacks Loves and needs country environment.

SETTER, IRISH
UK Kennel Club Standards
No size stipulated, overall balance being stressed.
AKC Standards
Height 27in (68cm)
25in (64cm)
Weight 70lb (31.8kg)
60lb (27.2kg)
Origin/history As the name implies, the breed originated in Ireland and was probably crossed with Irish Water Spaniels, Gordon and English Setters, Spaniels and Pointers. The Irish ancestors were red and white rather than self coloured, but in 1876 the Ulster Irish Setter Club ruled that all-red dogs should be known as Irish Setters.
Characteristics Must be racy, with muscular and slightly arched loins. Head long and lean, not narrow or snipy. Eyes dark brown or dark hazel, kindly in expression. Chest deep, rather narrow in front. Coat short and fine on head, front of legs and tips of ears, elsewhere of moderate length, flat and free from curl or wave. Feathering on upper parts of ears, back of legs, belly, chest and throat; colour, rich chestnut with no trace of black.
Temperament Highly active and at times rather excitable.

Properly trained, he is a keen and tireless worker.
Drawbacks Plenty of exercise is essential.

COCKER SPANIEL, AMERICAN (see page 183)
UK and AKC Standards
Height 15in (38cm)
14in (35cm)
Origin/history The large Spaniel family includes the Cocker, a name which properly covers two distinct breeds. In the United States the Cocker has been developed along different lines from the older English Cocker. American breeders created smaller dogs with shorter backs and a different head shape in which the muzzle is shortened and has a more defined stop than on the English Cocker. The coat is also longer. By such breeding the American and English Cocker became so different that the breeds were separated in 1943.
Characteristics Sturdy body, powerful quarters and strong, well-boned legs. Height at withers should approximate the length from withers to set on line of tail. Finely chiselled head with rounded skull; eyes dark, round. Coat dense, silky, flat or slightly wavy. Colours, black, black and tan, or any solid colour; parti-colours must be two or more definite colours, in clearly defined markings.
Temperament Happy disposition with no suggestion of timidity; good family pet.
Drawbacks Coat, often reaching the ground on show dogs, must have daily attention to keep it in good order.

SPANIEL, BRITTANY (see page 181)
No UK Kennel Club Standards
AKC Standards
Height 17½–20½in (44–52cm)
Weight 30–40lb (13.6–18kg)
Origin/history This French breed has been known in Europe for centuries and might more probably be known as a Setter. First shown at the Paris Dog Show in 1900, it has been recognized by the American Kennel Club since 1931 and is one of America's most popular working gundogs.
Characteristics Compact, closely knit dog of medium size, leggy and able to cover a great deal of ground. Muzzle about two-thirds the length of skull. Eyes well protected by heavy expressive eyebrows. Back short and straight. Chest deep, reaching the elbow. Naturally tailless or not over 4in (10cm) long. Coat dense, flat or wavy but never curly; light feathering. Colour, dark orange and white or liver and white; some ticking is desirable.
Temperament Strong vigorous dog, quick of movement. Easily trained as a retriever and proved a capable gundog.
Drawbacks Highly active dog requiring correct exercise.

SPANIEL, CLUMBER
UK and AKC Standards
Weight 55–70lb (25–31.8kg)
45–60lb (20.4–27.2kg)
Origin/history Quite different from other members of the Spaniel group, the ancestry of the breed is not quite clear. It probably came to England from Europe and was developed by crossing large Spaniels with St Hubert's Hounds or Bassets. The name is from Clumber Park, the seat of the Duke of Newcastle, in Nottingham, England, where it was originally developed at the end of the 19th century.
Characteristics A massive Spaniel and with the rolling gait characteristic of the breed. Large square head, of medium length; heavy brows with deep stop. Eyes deep amber. Body long and heavy boned. Back straight and broad. Abundant coat, close, silky and straight, well-feathered on legs. Colour, plain white with lemon markings.

Temperament Very steady, reliable and quiet dog, often referred to as 'an old man's gundog' because it moves at a more leisurely pace than Springers or Cockers.
Drawbacks Being a heavy dog, he requires adequate space.

SPANIEL, COCKER
UK and AKC Standards
Height 15½–16in (39–41cm)
15–15½in (38–39cm)
Weight 28–32lb (12.7–14.5kg)
Origin/history: One of the oldest Spaniel breeds and thought to have originated in Spain as long ago as the 14th century. Early Spaniels were used for hunting quail and partridge and were known by various names including 'cocker' or 'cocking spaniel'. Accepted on the register of the English Kennel Club in 1892, and in 1902 the Cocker Spaniel Club was formed. Field trials for the breed in America were started in 1924. Sometimes known as the English Cocker Spaniel, the American Kennel Club recognized it as a separate breed from the American Cocker Spaniel in 1943.
Characteristics A cheerful, sturdy and well-balanced sporting dog that should cover the ground well. Body immensely strong with well-sprung ribs, legs straight. Firm topline gently sloping to tail. Square muzzle, distinct stop. Eyes hazel or brown, gentle and liquid. Coat flat and silky in texture. Docked tail set on slightly lower than back line. Colour various, solid, bicolours and tricolours; in self colours no white allowed except on chest.
Temperament A happy, merry and kind disposition makes him ideal as a house dog and family pet.
Drawbacks Nervousness occasionally exhibited, reputedly more often in Golden Cockers.

SPANIEL, ENGLISH SPRINGER
UK and AKC Standards
Height 20in (51cm)
Weight 50lb (22.7kg)
Origin/history Recognized as the oldest of British sporting gundogs this Spaniel is the root from which all Land Spaniels, with the exception of Clumbers, have been evolved. The Springer is probably the best all-round gundog in the family as he excels in water and can find game as well as flush it out and retrieve it. Recognized by the English Kennel Club in 1902.
Characteristics A symmetrical, compact and active dog built for endurance. Skull of medium length, fairly broad and slightly rounded. Eyes dark hazel and merry. Body strong, loins muscular with slight arch. Chest deep and well developed. Coat close, straight and weather-resistant. Colour, any recognized Land Spaniel colour acceptable, but liver/white, black/white, or either of these colours with tan markings preferred.
Temperament Happy, friendly dog making an excellent companion in the home or in the shooting field.
Drawbacks Needs regular exercise to keep him fit and to stop him getting bored.

SPANIEL, FIELD
UK and AKC Standards
Height 18in (46cm)
Weight 35–50½lb (16–23kg)
Origin/history The Field Spaniel was developed in Britain to suit sportsmen who wanted a heavier Spaniel than the Cocker. This was almost fatal to the breed because the Field became so low to the ground, of so great a length, and so sluggish of nature that he was unsuited to his job. Fortunately such breeding excesses were abandoned, and in the last fifty years a much more workmanlike Field has been produced,

with a corresponding uplift in popularity.

Characteristics Well-balanced and noble sporting dog combining beauty and utility. Distinctive head shape, long and lean, giving an impression of good breeding and character. Eyes small, brown, deep hazel or near black. Body, moderate length and well ribbed. Chest deep and well developed. Coat flat or slightly waved, never curled. Colour, self-coloured black, liver, golden liver, mahogany red, roan, or any of these with tan over eyes, on cheeks, feet and pasterns.

Temperament Courageous gundog in the field, docile in the home and loving and loyal companion.

Drawbacks Takes time to mature and needs considerate handling during this time.

SPANIEL, IRISH WATER
UK and AKC Standards
Height 21–23in (53–58cm)
          20–22in (51–56cm)

Origin/history As the name implies, the Irish Water Spaniel, of ancient lineage, was developed in Ireland. The tallest member of the Spaniel family and particularly good at retrieving in water, the coat being naturally water-resistant.

Characteristics Strongly built and compact, very intelligent, eager, and bred for work in all types of shooting. Face should be smooth, and high-domed skull covered with long curls. Muzzle squarish, eyes small, brown and alert. Back short, broad and level, barrel-shaped in appearance. Coat composed of dense, tight and crisp ringlets free from woolliness. Tail short and straight, covered up to 3–4in (7–10cm) below root with close curls, the remainder with straight fine hairs. Colour, rich dark liver.

Temperament Very loyal and devoted to his master and family. A good sense of humour.

Drawbacks Coat needs careful attention.

SPANIEL, SUSSEX
UK and AKC Standards
Height 15–16in (38–40cm)
Weight 45lb (20.4kg)
           40lb (18kg)

Origin/history This breed derived its names from Sussex, England, where, at the end of the 18th century, it was developed especially for working through dense undergrowth. Not as quick a worker as the Springer or Cocker he is inclined to give tongue or bark on scent. The first Sussex competed at the Crystal Palace Show in London in 1862.

Characteristics Strongly built, with a characteristic rolling gait. Skull wide with pronounced stop. Eyes large and hazel. Knees large and strong. Chest deep and well developed; deep in back ribs. Abundant coat, flat with no tendency to curl. Tail set low, not carried above level of back. Colour, rich golden liver, shading to gold at tips.

Temperament Energetic dog with placid temperament. Makes an excellent household pet.

Drawbacks Needs firm handling in training to make the most of his character.

SPANIEL, WELSH SPRINGER
UK and AKC Standards
Height 19in (48cm)
          18in (46cm)

Origin/history Used in Wales as a working gundog for several hundred years, but not accepted by the English Kennel Club until 1902. Smaller than the English Springer and larger than the Cocker he is a faithful and persistent worker.

Characteristics A compact and active dog built for endurance. Head slightly domed, with clearly defined stop

and well-chiselled below hazel eyes. Body short, but strong and muscular with well-sprung ribs. Tail well set on and never carried above level of back. Coat straight or flat, of good silky texture. Colour, rich red and white only.

Temperament Gentle and cheerful, with the will to please.

Drawbacks Needs careful handling; harsh treatment upsets his gentle nature.

WEIMARANER
UK and AKC Standards
Height 24–27in (61–69cm)
          22–25in (56–64cm)

Origin/history Originally a large-game dog, the Weimaraner, often nicknamed the grey ghost because of his colour, probably came from the same stock that produced other German hunting breeds, such as Bloodhounds. With the demise of big-game hunting in Germany, the Weimaraner was used on various types of game birds and, because of his soft mouth, as a water retriever. In 1929 an American sportsman, Howard Knight, took a pair of these dogs to United States, and the American Weimaraner Club was formed. The breed did not reach Britain until the 1950s.

Characteristics A medium-sized dog with easy, co-ordinated movement. Head moderately long and aristocratic, with moderate stop. Ears long and lobular, set high. Eyes amber or blue/grey. Grey nose, lips and gums of pinkish flesh shade. Well-developed deep chest. Coat short, smooth and sleek. Colour, silvery grey; shades of mouse or roe grey admissible. Tail docked at a length to just cover the scrotum in dogs and vulva in bitches.

Temperament Friendly disposition, obedient and easily trained. Makes a very acceptable and protective companion.

Drawbacks An energetic dog needing correct exercise.

Terrier Group

There is a large diversity of type in this group which could almost be subdivided into four different sections: long-legged Terriers; short-legged Terriers; Bull Terriers; and special Terriers. Long-legged Terriers would include all breeds measuring 14in (35 cm) upwards, from the highest point of the withers to the ground. Short-legged Terriers, although measuring 14in (35 cm) and less and built on a smaller frame, lack nothing of the gay and fearless Terrier temperament. Bull Breeds display the different characters of the Staffordshire Bull Terrier, the American Staffordshire Terrier, the Bull, and the Miniature Bull Terriers. Special Terriers would include the Dandie Dinmont Terrier and the Skye Terrier. All Terriers of whatever type have proved their worth as ideal companions for all age groups, and as top-class show dogs.

AIREDALE (see page 184)
UK and AKC Standards
Height 23–24in (58–61cm)
22–23in (56–58cm)
Origin/history Known as the King of Terriers, the Airedale originated in the latter part of the 19th century in Yorkshire, England. Thought to have evolved from the English Terrier and the Otterhound it is the largest of the Terrier Group. First classes for Airedales were given at the Airedale Agricultural Society Show in Yorkshire in 1879. Originally bred for going to earth after badgers and otters, it was later employed, notably in Germany, as guard, frontier, police and war dog.
Characteristics Keen of expression and quick of movement. Typical terrier, evident in proud carriage of ears and tail, and dark, alert eyes. Skull long and flat, not too broad between ears. Ears V-shaped with side carriage. Neck clean and muscular. Back short, strong and straight. Chest deep but not broad. Coat hard, dense, and wiry. Colour, head and ears tan; legs to thighs and elbows, tan; body black or dark grizzle. Tail set high and carried gaily.
Temperament Affectionate, highly intelligent and gay-spirited, with true Terrier character.
Drawbacks Coat needs constant grooming.

AMERICAN STAFFORDSHIRE TERRIER
No UK Kennel Club Standards
AKC Standards
Height 18–19in (46–48cm)
17–18in (43–46cm)
Origin/history Like the Staffordshire Bull Terrier, this breed is the product of the old Bulldog/Terrier cross and also an ancestor of the white and coloured Bull Terrier. It was bred mainly for dog fights until these were outlawed. The Staffordshire Terrier was recognized by the American Kennel Club in 1935 with the name revised to American Staffordshire Terrier in 1972. Heavier than the Staffordshire Bull Terrier it is considered a different breed in the US.
Characteristics Great strength, unusual for the size, with soundness, balance and courage. Head medium length with pronounced cheek bones and muscles. Well-sprung ribs, deep in rear. Chest deep and broad. Front legs set wide apart, feet compact. Tail rather short, set on low. Gait springy. Coat short, close, stiff to the touch. Colour, any colour, solid, parti or patched permissible.
Temperament Great courage and strength combined with high intelligence. Affectionate with his family and friends.
Drawbacks A strong dog needing firm handling.

AUSTRALIAN TERRIER
UK and AKC Standards
Height 10in (25cm)
Weight 10–11lb (4.5kg)
Origin/history The Fox, Cairn and Scottish Terriers which British immigrants brought to Australia with them were crossed with the Sydney Silkie Terrier to produce the Australian Terrier. First exhibited in Melbourne in 1885 it was introduced to England in 1903, gained Kennel Club recognition in 1933 and was admitted to the American Kennel Club Register in 1960.
Characteristics Essentially a working terrier, alert and active. Sturdy and low set, rather long in proportion to height. Muzzle strong and powerful. Ears small, set high and usually pricked. Eyes dark, small with keen expression. Gait free, springy and forceful. Coat harsh, straight and dense, with short soft undercoat. Colour, blue, steel, or dark grey-blue, with rich tan on face, ears, underbody, lower legs and feet. Tail docked.
Temperament Active and happy small terrier.
Drawbacks Coat requires regular grooming

BEDLINGTON TERRIER
UK and AKC Standards
Height 16in (40cm)
Weight 18–23lb (8–10.4kg)
Origin/history The Bedlington takes its name from the mining village of Bedlington in Northumberland, England, where he was originally used as a ratter. The soft top-knot suggests a relationship with the Dandie Dinmont Terrier.
Characteristics Graceful, lithe and muscular dog. Pear-shaped head. Skull narrow, but deep and rounded. Ears low set, close to head. Eyes small and bright. Body flexible, flat ribbed and deep through the brisket. Back roached, loin markedly arched. Coat a distinctive feature, thick and linty standing well out from the skin, but not twisting. Colour, blue, blue and tan, liver or sandy. Tail thick and tapering, set low and gently curved.
Temperament Charming companion, makes an excellent pet, fond of home comforts.
Drawbacks Loves gallops at great speed and requires occasional opportunity for this.

BORDER TERRIER
UK and AKC Standards
Weight 13–15½lb (6–7kg)
11½–14lb (5–6kg)
Origin/history As the name suggests the Border Terrier comes from the Border Counties of Scotland and England. Essentially a working terrier and used for going to ground after fox. The breed was recognized by the English Kennel Club in 1920, the year the Border Terrier Club was formed.
Characteristics Combines activity with gameness. Head characteristic, like that of an otter – moderately broad in skull with a short strong muzzle. Eyes dark with keen expression. Small V-shaped ears. Body deep and narrow, fairly long; ribs carried well back. Hindquarters racy. The skin must be thick. Coat harsh and dense, with close undercoat, should be tidied only, not stripped. Colour, red, wheaten, grizzel and tan, or blue and tan.
Temperament Courageous in work; intensely loyal as a companion, and gentle with children.
Drawbacks Independent of mind; never quarrelsome but needs patient and firm handling.

BULL TERRIER
UK and AKC Standards
No height or weight limits
Origin/history The Bull Terrier was bred to fight and is known as the gladiator of the canine race. Produced towards the latter part of the 19th century by English breeders who

crossed old fighting dogs, carrying Bulldog blood, with the more lively Terrier and Dalmatian. Although always ready for a dog fight he is benevolent towards humans.

Characteristics Well-knit muscular dog which should cover the ground smoothly and jauntily. Head distinctive, long, strong and deep; viewed from front should be egg-shaped. Ears small, triangular, stiffly erect. Eyes narrow, triangular, obliquely and deeply placed. Neck very muscular. Body well rounded with marked spring of rib and great depth from withers to brisket. Coat short and flat; skin should fit dog tightly. Colour, pure white or coloured with any one colour, brindle preferred, predominating. Tail short, set on low, carried horizontally.

Temperament Exceedingly friendly dog thriving on affection; ideal with children.

Drawbacks Requires firm handling.

BULL TERRIER, MINIATURE
UK Kennel Club Standards
Height Not exceeding 14in (35cm)
Weight Not exceeding 20lb (9kg)
No AKC Standards
Origin/history Similar in every respect to the Bull Terrier, except in size and weight.

CAIRN TERRIER (see page 182)
UK and AKC Standards
Weight 14lb (6.3kg)
Origin/history A true earth dog, the Cairn Terrier has belonged to the Highlands and Islands of Scotland since time immemorial. It seems likely that the Cairn and the West Highland White Terrier were originally one and the same dog – as proved by the pedigrees of Cairns bred at the turn of this century. In 1910 the English Kennel Club recognized the Cairn Terrier.

Characteristics Fearless and gay disposition. Skull broad in proportion to head, with strong but not too long or heavy jaw, and clear indentation between wide-spaced, dark hazel eyes. Ears small and pointed. Body compact with straight back and well-sprung deep ribs. Hindquarters strong. Coat double, the outer profuse, hard but not coarse, undercoat resembling fur. Colour, red, sandy, grey, brindle, or nearly black. Tail short, carried gaily.

Temperament Very gay, happy, active dog; excellent and adaptable companion.

Drawbacks None discernible.

DANDIE DINMONT TERRIER
UK and AKC Standards
Height 8–11in (20–28cm)
Weight 18–24lb (8–11kg)
Origin/history The Dandie Dinmont Terrier is an old Scottish Border breed made famous in Sir Walter Scott's novel *Guy Mannering* published in 1814. In this work the author relates the story of the (fictional) sporting farmer Dandie Dinmont and his terriers. The breed acquired his name and the first Dandie Club was formed in 1876.

Characteristics Long-bodied, short-legged Terrier with pendulous ears and long curved tail; differs from most other terriers in having gently flowing rather than straight outlines. Head strong and, though large, in proportion to dog's size. Ears set low and hanging close to head. Eyes large and dark. Neck very muscular. Forelegs short. Body long, strong and flexible with well-sprung and round ribs. Hind legs a little longer than fore ones. Coat important, hair about 2in (5cm) long; from skull to root of tail should be a mixture of hard and soft hair. Colour, pepper (grey shades) or mustard.

Temperament Very amenable, loves human company and makes a good companion and guard dog.

Drawbacks Regular coat care is necessary.

FOX TERRIER, SMOOTH (see page 184)
UK and AKC Standards
Weight 16–18lb (7.2–8kg)
15–17lb (6.8–7.7kg)
Origin/history The Fox Terrier was developed to hunt fox and badger, above and below ground. One of the best known of purebred dogs it reached the peak in popularity at the end of the 19th century. The English Fox Terrier Club was formed in 1876, the American Fox Terrier Club in 1885.

Characteristics The Fox Terrier should stand like a well-made hunter, covering a lot of ground, but with a short back. Skull flat, moderately narrow and gradually decreasing in width to dark, lively eyes. Ears V-shaped and small. Neck clean and muscular. Chest deep and not too broad. Back short, straight and strong. Coat flat and smooth, hard, dense and abundant. Colour, white should predominate; brindle, red or liver markings are objectionable. Tail set on high, carried gaily but not curved.

Temperament Gay, lively and active; very adaptable.

Drawbacks Can be quite sharp with other dogs.

FOX TERRIER, WIRE
UK and AKC Standards
Height Not exceeding 15½in (38cm)
Bitches slightly less
Origin/history As the Smooth Fox Terrier.

Characteristics Similar to the above except for coat. This is of dense, wiry texture, like coconut matting, the hair growing so closely together that when parted with the fingers the skin cannot be seen. Colour, white should predominate.

Temperament Extremely lively, tireless and devoted companion, mischievous but utterly dependable.

Drawbacks As Smooth Fox Terrier.

IRISH TERRIER (see page 182)
UK and AKC Standards
Height 18in (46cm)
Weight 27lb (12.3kg)
25lb (11.4kg)
Origin/history Established in his native Ireland since the 19th century, there is evidence to show that the Irish Terrier is one of the oldest of terrier breeds. It is thought that the English Black and Tan Terrier was used to bring a certain amount of refinement to his body; the result was first shown at Dublin in 1873. The Irish Terrier Club was formed in 1879.

Characteristics Known as the Red Devil he is a great sportsman. Active, lively, lithe and wiry appearance. Head long, skull flat and rather narrow between small V-shaped ears. Eyes small, dark and bright. Chest deep and muscular, neither full nor wide. Body moderately long. Quarters strong and muscular. Coat hard and wiry. Colour, whole-coloured, preferably bright red, red wheaten or yellow red. Tail docked, set on high, carried gaily.

Temperament Good-tempered with humans, but always ready to resent interference from other dogs. Devoted to their masters and family.

Drawbacks Aggressiveness with other dogs.

JACK RUSSELL TERRIER
Not yet accepted by any Kennel Club
Height up to 11in (28cm)
11–15in (28–38cm)
Origin/history The Reverend John Russell (1795–1883)

from Devonshire, England, and a Master of Fox hounds, built up a strain of Fox Terriers that ran with his hounds and were trained to go to ground and bolt a fox. Beloved and popular in Britain, this Terrier is not recognized anywhere as a distinct breed. The Jack Russell Terrier Club in England has produced a breed standard and hopes to obtain recognition from the Kennel Club.

Characteristics Head strong-boned with powerful jaws. Good strong cheek muscles. Ears small, V-shaped, dropping and carried close to head. Eyes almond-shaped. Straight topline with tail set high. Strong quarters. Coat smooth or broken, not woolly. Colour, basically white with black, tan or traditional hound markings.

Temperament Tough, brave, active and high-spirited. Makes a good family companion.

Drawbacks Can be aggressive with other dogs.

KERRY BLUE TERRIER
UK and AKC Standards
Height 18–19in (46–48cm)
 Bitches slightly less
Weight 33–37lb (15–17kg)
 Bitches slightly less

Origin/history Originated in Ireland and first known as the Irish Blue Terrier. The Bedlington and Bull Terrier probably played some part in its development. Classes for Kerry Blues first appeared at Crufts Dog Show in London in 1922 and proved highly successful. The American Kennel Club gave them Championship Show rating in 1924.

Characteristics Compact and powerful, showing the gracefulness and alert determination which define Terrier style. Flat skull with slight stop. Ears small to medium and V-shaped. Eyes small and dark. Short-coupled body with good depth of brisket and well-sprung ribs. Well-developed quarters. Coat soft and silky, wavy. Colour, any shade of blue, with or without black points. Tail set on high, carried gaily.

Temperament Fearless watchdog and excellent companion.

Drawbacks Coat requires regular trimming. Can be aggressive with other dogs.

LAKELAND TERRIER
UK and AKC Standards
Height 14½in (36cm)
Weight 17lb (7.7kg)
 15lb (6.8kg)

Origin/history One of the oldest working breeds of Terriers, originating in the English Lake District and known as the Patterdale Terrier. It is said that farmers used to hunt foxes in the mountains with the aid of a couple of hounds and tough Lakeland Terriers. The modern Lakeland was recognized by the Kennel Club in 1928.

Characteristics Elegant and workmanlike, with gay, fearless disposition. Skull flat and refined. Jaws powerful, muzzle broad but not too long. Eyes small, dark or hazel. Ears small, V-shaped and drooping. Reachy neck. Chest reasonably narrow. Back strong and moderately short. Coat dense and weather-resistant. Colour, black and tan, blue and tan, red, wheaten, red grizzle, liver, blue or black.

Temperament Bold, gay, friendly and self-confident.

Drawbacks Coat requires regular stripping.

MANCHESTER TERRIER
UK Kennel Club Standards
Height 16in (40cm)
 15in (38cm)
AKC Standards
Weight Not exceeding 12lb (5.4kg) – Toy Variety

Not exceeding 22lb (10kg), but above 12lb (5.4kg)
 This variety to be known as the Standard

Origin/history This Terrier goes back to the old hunting Terrier, possibly crossed with a Whippet; in contrast to most other British Terrier breeds it is a smooth-coated dog and more a companion than a working dog. In the 1870s the breed was popular at rat-catching contests and for rabbit coursing.

Characteristics Compact in appearance with good bone and free from any resemblance to the Whippet. Skull long, flat and narrow. Ears small, V-shaped, carried well above topline and hanging close to head. Eyes small and oblong, dark and sparkling. Body short with well-sprung ribs. Coat short and close, smooth and glossy. Colour, jet black with rich mahogany tan markings.

Temperament Faithful and intelligent.

Drawbacks A good ratter given the chance.

NORFOLK TERRIER – NORWICH TERRIER
(see pages 181 and 184)
UK and AKC Standards
Height 10in (25cm)

Origin/history The Norfolk Terrier was previously known as the Norwich Terrier and recognized as such in 1932, but in 1964 the English Kennel Club decided to separate the two breeds, the Norfolk Terrier becoming the breed with drop ears, the Norwich Terrier with erect ears. Both breeds have been known for many years; during the 19th century they were used successfully for ratting and rabbiting. In 1914 the first Norwich Terrier was taken to America and the breed was recognized by the American Kennel Club in 1936. In America they are registered as one breed: Norwich Terrier (prick ear) and Norwich Terrier (drop ear).

Characteristics Small, low and keen dog, compact and strong with short back, good substance and bone. Skull wide, muzzle strong. Short back, level topline, well-sprung ribs. Quarters well muscled. Coat hard, wiry and straight. Colour, all shades of red, red wheaten, black and tan, or grizzle.

Temperament A 'demon' for his small size; alert and fearless. Lovable and never quarrelsome.

Drawbacks Coat needs regular stripping.

SCOTTISH TERRIER
UK and AKC Standards
Height 10–11in (25–28cm)
Weight 19–23lb (8.6–10.4kg)

Origin/history Until the middle of the 19th century any dog that went to ground after fox in Scotland was called a Scottish Terrier, and this particular breed was known as the Broken-haired or Aberdeen Terrier. In 1897 it was registered as a separate breed at the English Kennel Club under the name of Scottish Terrier.

Characteristics Sturdy and thick-set, suggestive of great power and activity. Head long, cheek bones in proportion. Ears erect, fine textured. Eyes dark brown, almond-shaped. Well-rounded ribs which flatten to deep chest. Quarters powerful for the size of dog. Two coats: undercoat short, dense and soft; outer coat harsh, dense and wiry. Colour, black, wheaten or brindle.

Temperament Agile, active dog of good temperament. Makes excellent companion.

Drawbacks Coat requires regular attention.

SEALYHAM TERRIER
UK and AKC Standards
Height Not exceeding 12in (30cm)
Weight Not exceeding 20lb (9kg)
 18lb (8kg)

Origin/history The Sealyham derives its name from Sealyham, Haverfordwest, Wales. It was developed between 1850 and 1891 from breeds successful in quarrying fox and badger. First shown in Haverfordwest in 1903, and the Sealyham Terrier Club of Haverfordwest was formed in 1908. The breed was recognized by the AKC and the English Kennel Club in 1911, and in the same year Challenge Certificates were offered at the Great Joint Terrier Show in London.
Characteristics Balanced, active dog of great substance in a small frame. Skull slightly domed and wide between ears. Eyes round, dark. Neck fairly long. Body medium length and flexible with ribs well sprung. Chest broad and deep. Long, hard and wiry topcoat with weather-resistant undercoat. Colour, all white, or white with lemon, brown or badger pied markings on head and ears.
Temperament Alert and fearless but of friendly disposition.
Drawbacks Coat requires stripping and trimming.

SKYE TERRIER
UK and AKC Standards
Height 10in (25cm)
Weight 25lb (11.4kg)
Origin/history The Skye Terrier has changed little in the four centuries of existence. His home was the Island of Skye, off the northwest coast of Scotland, where tough, rough-haired earth dogs were used to bolt fox and badger.
Characteristics Short-legged Terrier with ears pricked or dropped. Head long with powerful jaws. Eyes hazel. Neck long and slightly crested. Body long and low with back level. Ribs well sprung. Tail well-feathered. Coat double, hard overcoat long and straight, flat; undercoat short, close, soft and woolly. Colour, dark or light grey, fawn, cream, black, with black points to nose and ears.
Temperament A one-man dog, distrustful, sometimes intolerant of strangers, but not vicious.
Drawbacks Coat needs care. A canny dog needing careful handling.

SOFT-COATED WHEATEN TERRIER
UK Kennel Club Standards
Height 18–19½in (46–49cm)
Weight 35–45lb (15.8–20.4kg)
No AKC Standards
Origin/history For more than 200 years, the Soft-Coated Wheaten Terrier, from Munster in Ireland, has been bred as a farm dog. Registered by the Irish Kennel Club as a distinct purebred Terrier in 1938 and accepted in 1943 by the English Kennel Club. First exhibited at Crufts Dog Show, London, in 1949.
Characteristics Medium sized, compact and upstanding. Head moderately long and profusely covered with coat falling forward over the bright, dark hazel eyes. Ears V-shaped and folded at skull level. Body compact with powerful short loins. Back strong and level. Thighs strong and muscular. Coat soft and silky, naturally waved or curly; curls should be large, light and loose. Dogs with overtrimmed or stylized coats are penalized. Colour, good clear wheaten; white and red coats are objectionable.
Temperament Good tempered and spirited, full of confidence. Delightful and intelligent companion.
Drawbacks Coat needs careful grooming.

STAFFORDSHIRE BULL TERRIER
UK and AKC Standards
Height 14–16in (35–40cm)
Weight 28–38lb (12.7–17.2kg)
       24–34lb (11–15.4kg)
Origin/history The Staffordshire Bull Terrier, first recog-nized by the English Kennel Club in 1935, was a product of the old Bulldog-Terrier cross. His cousin, the white Bull Terrier, had been shown for several decades previously. Bred as a fighting dog for baiting bulls and bears; in 1835 this was prohibited by law in England, and Staffordshires were used to fight one another until this, too, was outlawed.
Characteristics Smooth-coated dog of great strength, very muscular, active and agile. Head short and deep with pronounced cheek muscles. Close-coupled body, with level topline, wide front, deep brisket, rather light in loin. Quarters well muscled. Coat smooth, short and close to skin. Colour, red, fawn, white, black or blue, or any of these with white; any shade of brindle with white.
Temperament Tremendous courage, high intelligence and tenacity. Very affectionate with people he knows and particularly good with children.
Drawbacks Aggressive with other dogs and needs firm and careful handling.

WELSH TERRIER
UK and AKC Standards
Height Not exceeding 15½in (39cm)
Weight 20–21lb (9–9.5kg)
Origin/history The Welsh Terrier is an old breed, a descendant of the rough-coated black/tan Fox Terrier which greatly resembled a miniature Airedale. Used in his native Wales for hunting otter, fox and badger. The first show for Welsh Terriers was held at Pwllheli, North Wales in 1884.
Characteristics Small upstanding Terrier with V-shaped drop ears. Skull flat and rather wider between the ears than on the Wire Fox Terrier. Eyes small, dark and keen. Back short and well ribbed up, loin strong, chest of good depth and moderate width. Strong quarters. Coat wiry, hard, very close and abundant. Colour, preferably black and tan; or black grizzle and tan.
Temperament Gay, volatile disposition. Affectionate, obedient and easily controlled. Ideal as a house dog.
Drawbacks Coat requires trimming.

WEST HIGHLAND WHITE TERRIER (see page 182)
UK and AKC Standards
Height 11in (28cm)
Origin/history The West Highland White Terrier, said to come from Argyll in Scotland, was recognized by the English Kennel Club in 1907. It is thought to have been bred in the 1880s from a strain of cream-coloured and white Cairn Terriers, with selective breeding from the lightest-coloured specimens.
Characteristics Small and game Terrier rather full of his own importance. Skull slightly domed, the distance from occiput to eyes should be slightly greater than the length of foreface. Eyes widely spaced, as dark as possible. Back compact, level with broad and strong loins. Tail 5–6in (13–15cm) long, covered with hard hair and carried jauntily. Double coat, the outer hard about 2in (5cm) long and free from curl. Colour, pure white.
Temperament Bold and independent; affectionate, lively and gentle as a companion.
Drawbacks Coat needs regular tidying and grooming.

Utility Group

Known in the United States as the Non-Sporting Group, it encompasses those breeds which are perhaps best described as good companion dogs, of particular charm and character. They vary enormously in type, from the Spitz-type, such as the Chow Chow and the Japanese Spitz, to perky little Boston Terriers, spotted Dalmatians, and the popular Poodles. The group also includes three Tibetan breeds, the Schnauzers and last but not least the Bulldog. All different in body-shape and make-up, but all excellent family dogs. Fine specimens from this group have won top honours at shows all round the world; as recently as Crufts 1984, the Lhasa Apso was awarded Best Dog of the Year.

BOSTON TERRIER (see page 180)
UK Kennel Club Standards
Weight Not exceeding 25lb (11.4kg)
AKC Standards
Lightweight under 15lb (6.8kg)
Middleweight   15–20lb (6.8–9kg)
Heavyweight   20lb (9kg), not exceeding 25lb (11.4kg)
Origin/history Native to America, this breed is the result of a cross between the British Bulldog and a white English Terrier. The Boston Terrier Club of America was formed in 1891 and two years later the American Kennel Club accepted it as a purebred breed.
Characteristics Short headed, compactly built, medium height. Skull square, flat on top, free from wrinkles, cheeks flat. Ears erect, on back of skull. Eyes large, dark, set well apart. Deep body should appear short but not chunky, with good width of chest. Thighs strong and well muscled. Tail straight or screw. Coat short, smooth and shiny, fine texture. Colour, brindle with white markings.
Temperament Lively and highly intelligent dog suitable as a companion.
Drawbacks Whelping can be problematic.

BULLDOG
UK and AKC Standards
Weight 55lb (25kg)
       50lb (23kg)
Origin/history A descendant of the old bull-baiting dogs once used in England. Since this sport was abolished in 1838, the appearance of the Bulldog has greatly improved. The Buldog Club (England) was founded in 1864, and the breed was recognized by the English Kennel Club in 1875.
Characteristics Smooth-coated and thick-set, rather low in stature, but broad, powerful and compact. Head massive and large in proportion to overall size, with distinctive furrows and wrinkles, undershot and projecting lower jaw; large nose set squarely between wide-spaced eyes; small, thin ears set high. Body short and strong, very broad at shoulders and comparatively narrow at the loins. Fine textured coat, short, close and smooth. Colour, whole or smut.
Temperament Charming and good natured dog, excellent as a companion and a good protector if aroused.
Drawbacks None.

CHOW CHOW
UK and AKC Standards
Height 18in (46cm)
Origin/history As a breed, the Chow Chow is at least 2000 years old and one of the oldest recognizable types of dog. It belongs to the Spitz family and comes originally from China.
Characteristics Proud, dignified bearing, leonine in appearance, typified by the dense ruff round the head. Loyal but aloof, unique in the stilted gait and bluish-black tongue. Skull flat and broad with little stop. Ears small, thick and carried stiffly erect; placed well forward over dark almond-shaped eyes, and wide apart. Neck strong. Chest broad and deep. Tail set high and carried well over back. Coat abundant, dense, straight and manelike over neck and shoulder. Colour, solid black, red, blue, fawn, cream, or white.
Temperament Alert, intelligent and fearless. Self-assured and impatient of being restrained.
Drawbacks Sometimes aggressive and needs strict discipline.

DALMATIAN
UK and AKC Standards
Height 23–24in (58–61cm)
       22–23in (56–58cm)
Origin/history Although the breed is considered to have originated in Yugoslavia it has been bred and improved to its present standards mainly in England, where it was first shown in 1862. Used as a guard dog in Dalmatia it was also a popular stable dog and the aristocracy was fond of having it run with their horse-drawn carriages.
Characteristics Strong, muscular and active dog of good demeanour. Free from coarseness and capable of great endurance. Head moderately long with flat skull. Ears set on high tapering to rounded tips. Eyes well spaced, round and bright, colour in accordance with coat markings. Neck fairly long and nicely arched. Chest should not be too wide, but deep and capacious. Gait, great freedom of movement. Tail gradually tapering, carried with slight upward curve. Coat short, hard and dense. Ground colour pure white; black-spotted dogs should have dense black, clearly defined spots, and liver-spotted dogs liver-brown spots.
Temperament Good guard dog; excellent family companion distinguishing readily between friend and foe.
Drawbacks Requires regular exercise.

FRENCH BULLDOG (see page 183)
UK and AKC Standards
Weight UK   28lb (12.7kg)
            24lb (11kg)
Weight AKC 22–28lb (10–12.7kg)
Origin/history The French consider this to be one of their old native breeds while the English claim that it is descended from the British Bulldog – bred from the small specimens that occasionally cropped up in some litters. American breeders did much to improve the dog and certainly to preserve the bat ear which is a distinctive feature. The French Bulldog Club of America was the first club in the world devoted to the breed and held a show in 1898. In 1902 the French Bulldog Club of England was formed.
Characteristics Sound, active and intelligent, of compact build, medium or small sized. Head massive, square and broad. Ears, bat shaped, of medium size, carried upright. Eyes dark and round, set deep in skull. Neck powerful with loose skin at throat. Body short, cobby, muscular and well rounded; wide at shoulders and narrowing at loins. Coat of fine texture, smooth, short and close. Colours, brindle, pied and fawn.
Temperament Very good companion and watch dog. Dependable and sweet tempered. Alert and playful but not usually noisy.
Drawbacks None apparent.

JAPANESE SPITZ
UK Kennel Club Standards
Height 12–16in (30–40cm)
       10–14in (25–35cm)
No AKC Standards
Origin/history Most members of the Spitz family came from the Northern Hemisphere; the Japanese Spitz obviously

originates in Japan and resembles a miniature Samoyed.
Characteristics Bold and lively. Overall body firm, strong and flexible. Head medium size, without coarseness, moderately broad and slightly rounded. Sharply pointed muzzle, black lips and nose. Triangular-shaped ears, standing erect. Fore and hind quarters well proportioned and balanced. Chest broad and deep. Gait light, nimble and energetic. Bushy tail carried over back. Coat straight and stand-off over profuse undercoat, mane on neck and shoulder reaching down to brisket. Colour, pure white.
Temperament Lively and remarkably alert; very pleasing in attitude towards people. Enjoys barking.
Drawbacks Coat must be regularly groomed.

KEESHOND (see page 181)
UK and AKC Standards
Height 18in (46cm)
　　　 17in (43cm)
Origin/history The Keeshond is the Dutch National Breed and originally a barge and watch dog. During the general unrest preceding the French Revolution, Holland was divided into two camps; the Partisans of the Prince of Orange, whose mascot was a Pug, and the Patriots, led by one Kees de Gyselaer, who was a great dog lover and the owner of a little dog called Kees. This dog, a member of the Spitz family, became the symbol of the Patriots and gave the breed its name. It came to England around 1925.
Characteristics Short and compact body; alert carriage. Fox-like head with small pointed ears. Eyes dark with well-defined spectacles of lines round the eye areas. Quarters to show very little hock and not to be feathered below that joint. Well-feathered curling tail carried over back. Coat dense and harsh, thick ruff, and well-feathered, profuse trousers; undercoat soft, thick and light coloured. Colour, wolf, ash grey; all-black or all-white undesirable.
Temperament Alert and intelligent; ideal companion.
Drawbacks Regular grooming to maintain condition.

LHASA APSO (see page 180)
UK and AKC Standards
Height 10in (25cm)
　　　　Bitches slightly less
Origin/history The Lhasa Apso comes from Tibet where it is known as Abso Seng Kye – 'Bark Lion Sentinel Dog' – and was supposed to bring good luck. Introduced into England in 1928 and accepted in the American register in 1935.
Characteristics Well-balanced, solid dog, free and jaunty of movement. Head heavily furnished with good fall of hair over eyes, dark with good whiskers and beard. Length of body greater than height at withers; well ribbed up. Level topline. Well-developed quarters with good muscle. Tail set high and carried well over back. Top coat heavy, straight and hard over dense undercoat. Colour, golden, sandy, honey, dark grizzle, slate, smoke, parti-colour, black, white or brown.
Temperament Gay and assertive, rather wary of strangers. Makes a good companion.
Drawbacks Coat needs intense grooming.

POODLE (Standard, Miniature and Toy)
UK and AKC Standards
Height: Standard　　　15in (38cm) and over
　　　 Miniature UK　 15in (38cm)
　　　　　　　　　　　11in (28cm)
　　　 Miniature AKC　15in (38cm)
　　　　　　　　　　　10in (25cm)
　　　 Toy UK　　　　 11in (28cm) and under
　　　 Toy AKC　　　　10in (25cm) and under

Origin/history Both the French and the Germans stake their claims to this very old breed, which originated as a water retriever and at one time was popular as a circus dog. The Germans claim that it is descended from their Pudelpointer and the French from the Barbet. Its rise to popularity has been spectacular and, irrespective of size, the Poodle is characterized by its trim – known descriptively as the lion trim (in the United States as the Continental clip). First registered at the English Kennel Club in 1875, and at the American Kennel Club in 1887. In the US the Toy Poodle is classified in the Toy Group.
Characteristics Well-balanced and elegant dog carrying himself proudly. Head long and fine with slight peak at the back. Eyes almond-shaped and dark. Neck long and strong to carry head high and with dignity. Skin must fit tightly at throat. Chest deep and moderately wide. Tail set on high and carried at slight angle away from body. Coat profuse and dense, of harsh texture without knots or tangles. Colour, any solid.
Temperament Very active and intelligent. Excellent house dog and companion.
Drawbacks Coat does not moult, but mats and tangles easily; it needs intensive and regular grooming and frequent (professional) trimming to the accepted style.

SCHIPPERKE (see page 179)
UK and AKC Standards
Weight UK　 12–16lb (5.4–7.2kg)
Weight AKC　up to 18 lb (8kg)
Origin/history The Schipperke was used to guard canal boats in the Low Countries, and he was well named – translated the name means 'little captain'. Queen Maria Henrietta, wife of Leopold II of Belgium, acquired a Schipperke at a Brussels Show in 1885 and helped launch the breed on a fashionable career as a companion dog. The Schipperke Club of England was formed in 1890, and the Schipperke Club of America was restarted in 1929.
Characteristics Small cobby dog with sharp expression. Head foxy in type, skull not round but fairly broad, flat and with little stop. Ears small, carried stiffly erect. Eyes black. Chest broad and deep in brisket. Back short, straight and strong. Tail docked close. Coat abundant, dense and harsh, smooth on head, ears and legs, ruff-like and thick round neck, forming a mane and frill. Black is preferred, other whole colours permissible in UK, not US.
Temperament Intensely lively, merry and attractive family companion. Good guard.
Drawbacks None apparent.

SCHNAUZER (Standard and Miniature)
UK Kennel Club Standards
Both breeds listed in Utility Group
Height Standard　 19in (48cm)
　　　　　　　　 18in (46cm)
　　　 Miniature　 14in (35cm)
　　　　　　　　 13in (33cm)
AKC Standards
Height Standard　 18½–19½in (47–49cm)
　　　　　　　　 Listed in Working Group
　　　 Miniature　 12–14in (30–35cm)
　　　　　　　　 Listed in Terrier Group
Origin/history The Schnauzer is of German origin and is recognizable in 15th-century paintings. The Standard is the prototype of the Schnauzer family, probably derived from crossing the black Poodle and the wolf-grey Spitz with old German Pinscher stock. The Miniature Schnauzer is thought to have been derived from a selection of small specimens of the

Standards with Affenpinschers. Schnauzers were first exhibited in Germany in 1879 as Wire-haired Pinschers.

Characteristics Powerfully built and robust, almost square in outline. Head strong and elongated with powerful muzzle. Ears neat and V-shaped. Chest moderately broad, deep with visible strong breast bone. Tail docked, set on and carried high. Coat hard, short and wiry. Colour, all pepper and salt in even proportions, or pure black.

Temperament High spirits, reliability, strength, endurance and vigour. Expression keen and attitude alert. Attractive personality.

Drawbacks Coat needs regular attention.

SHIH TZU
UK Kennel Club Standards
Height not exceeding 10½in (26cm)
Weight 10–18lb (4.5–8kg)
AKC Standards (listed in Toy Group)
Height 9–10½in (23–26cm)
Weight 12–15lb (5.4–6.8kg)

Origin/history Shih Tzus have lived for many centuries in Tibet and were brought from there to the Chinese Court. In 1930 an English lady living in China imported the breed to England. In 1946 the English Kennel Club granted it a separate register, and numbers have gradually increased. First registered by the American Kennel Club in 1969.

Characteristics Bright, quick, full of fun and very arrogant. The English Standard emphasizes that he is neither a Terrier nor a Toy dog. Head broad and round, wide between large dark eyes with hair falling well over them. Body between withers and root of tail longer than height. Quarters short and muscular with ample bone. Tail set on high, heavily plumed and curled well over back. Coat long and dense, not curly, with good undercoat. All colours permissible, white blaze on forehead and white tip to the tail highly prized.

Temperament Very active, lively and alert, makes an amusing and devoted companion.

Drawbacks Coat must be regularly groomed.

TIBETAN SPANIEL
UK and AKC Standards
Height 10in (25cm)
Weight 9–15lb (4–6.8kg)

Origin/history For centuries the monks of Tibet trained the Tibetan Spaniel to turn prayer wheels by means of a small treadmill. It originated in Tibet and was reintroduced to England after their almost complete extinction during the Second World War. The Tibetan Spaniel Association in England was formed in 1958.

Characteristics Quick-moving, active and alert. Outline of well-balanced appearance, slightly longer in body than height at withers. Head small in proportion to body and proudly carried. Mouth ideally slightly undershot. Ears pendent and feathered. Eyes dark brown, set wide apart. Neck moderately short and covered with mane of long hair. Level back and good depth of body. Tail richly plumed and carried in gay curl over the back when moving. Double coat, silky in texture. All colours and mixture of colours allowed.

Temperament Gay and assertive, highly intelligent, aloof with strangers. Makes a good family pet.

Drawbacks None apparent.

TIBETAN TERRIER
UK and AKC Standards
Height 14–16in (35–40cm)
    Bitches slightly less.

Origin/history Originally used in Tibet for herding stray animals from the steep mountains. In spite of its name it is not a true Terrier, having never been used to go to ground. Explorers of Asia and Tibet knew these dogs as active companions of the nomadic tribes.

Characteristics Well-muscled, medium sized dog, in general appearance not unlike an Old English Sheepdog in miniature. Skull of medium length with marked stop in front of large dark eyes. Ears V-shaped, pendent and well feathered. Head well furnished with long hair. Lower jaw should carry small amount of beard. Compact and powerful body; length equal to height. Quarters slightly longer than forelegs and low set hocks. Tail set on high, feathered and carried in curl over back. Coat double: top coat profuse, fine but not silky or woolly; undercoat fine wool. Colour, white, golden, cream, grey or smoke, black, particolour and tricolour.

Temperament Alert, intelligent and game. Makes a good house dog, wary of strangers.

Drawbacks Coat must have regular attention.

Working Group

This is a large group consisting mainly of Guard and Working dogs, and Herding and Shepherd dogs; the AKC divides these dogs in Working and Herding Groups. Some of the breeds are definitely 'one-man' dogs and need careful handling to ensure that they are well-behaved and acceptable members of society. Properly trained any dog, irrespective of size, is an asset, but if it is allowed to take over the household it becomes a menace and danger, to itself and to all who come into contact with it. Dogs in the Working Group are of exceptional size and strength, and well schooled they make outstanding guard dogs, combining their work with loyalty and devotion to their master and household.

ALASKAN MALAMUTE
UK and AKC Standards
Height 25in (66cm)
Weight 23in (58cm)

Origin/history The Alaskan Malamute is one of the oldest Arctic sled dogs and was originally bred by the Eskimos of northwest Alaska. An Official Standard was issued by the American Kennel Club in 1927.

Characteristics Primarily a working sled dog hauling heavy freight in the Arctic; consequently heavily boned and power-fully built. Head broad and powerful. Ears erect. Eyes brown. Neck strong and moderately arched. Chest strong and deep. Back straight and gently sloping over croup. Hind legs broad and powerful. Tail moderately high set, carried over the back. Coat thick, outer coat with coarse guard hairs, undercoat dense. Colours range from light grey to black, or from gold through shades of red to liver, always with white on underbody, parts of legs, feet and part of face mask.

Temperament Affectionate and friendly, but not a one-man dog. Loyal and devoted companion, playful on invitation. Tends to be aggressive with other dogs.

Drawbacks Being large and strong, requires strict and careful handling.

ANATOLIAN SHEPHERD DOG
UK Kennel Club Standards
Height 29–32in (74–81cm)
28–31in (71–79cm)
Weight 110–141lb (50–64kg)
90–130lb (41–59kg)
No AKC Standards

Origin/history The Anatolian Shepherd Dog is also known as the Turkish Shepherd Guard Dog; the breed is very ancient, dating back some 3000 years, and has immense stamina and speed. It first came to England about 1965.

Characteristics Large, upstanding and powerfully built, with broad heavy head. Mature males have broader heads than females. Neck slightly arched, powerful and muscular. Slight dewlap. Chest deep to point of elbow, ribs well sprung. Body powerful and well muscled, never fat. Back short in proportion to leg length. Relaxed even gait. Coat short, dense, with thick undercoat. Colour, any shade of fawn; characteristic black mask varies in extent.

Temperament Steady and bold without undue aggression, naturally independent, very intelligent and trainable.

Drawbacks Unsuited for town life.

BELGIAN SHEPHERD DOG (Groenendael, Laekenois, Malinois, and Tervueren)
UK and AKC Standards
Height 24–26in (61–66cm)
22–24in (56–61cm)

Origin/history The Groenendael, Laekenois, Malinois and Tervueren all belong to the same family of Belgian Shepherd Dogs, the only difference being in the coat. They take their individual names from the Belgian village or town where they originated. In America they are simply known as Belgian Sheepdogs, and the Laekenois is not yet recognized.

Characteristics All four share the same overall dimensions, being well-proportioned dogs of hardy disposition and bred to withstand adverse weather. Head finely chiselled, long but not excessively so. Ears stiff and erect, set high and of proportionate length. Neck very supple. Body powerful without being bulky. Chest not very broad but deep and low. Ribs well sprung. Movement brisk and even.

Groenendael: outer coat long, straight and abundant; undercoat very dense. Colour, black.

Laekenois: coat rough, dry, untidy looking and not curly. Length about 2¼in (6cm). Colour reddish fawn with black shading.

Malinois: coat very short on head, exterior of ears and lower parts of legs, short on remainder of body, thicker round the neck, resembling ridge or collar. Colour, all shades of red and fawn, with black overlay.

Tervueren: outer coat long, straight and abundant; extremely dense. Colour, all shades of red, fawn, also grey with black overlay.

Temperament Very alert and attentive, of lively and enquiring attitude. Great potential as guard dogs. Should not be timid or aggressive.

Drawbacks Need careful training.

BERNESE MOUNTAIN DOG (see page 184)
UK and AKC Standards
Height 26–27in (66–69cm)
24–26in (61–66cm)

Origin/history The Bernese Mountain Dog is one of the four varieties of Swiss mountain dog introduced into Switzerland more than 2000 years ago by invading Roman soldiers. Originally used as haulage dogs, the breeds were almost allowed to die out, and not until 1907 were efforts made to rehabilitate them as family companions and watch dogs.

Characteristics Large, well-boned and strong working dog, active, alert and of striking colour. Strong flat skull with well-defined stop, strong straight muzzle. Ears V-shaped close to head. Eyes dark. Neck strong, muscular, of medium length. Body compact rather than long. Back firm and straight. Rump smoothly rounded. Quarters broad, strong and well muscled. Bushy tail reaching just below hock. Coat soft and silky, with bright natural sheen. Colour, jet black with distinctive rich reddish brown on cheeks, over eyes, on legs and chest; white blaze on head and white chest marking essential.

Temperament Intensely loyal to his own people, but does not readily make friends with strangers. Slow to mature.

Drawbacks None apparent.

BORDER COLLIE
UK Kennel Club Standards
Height 21in (53cm)
slightly less
No AKC Standards

Origin/history The Border Collie is one of the world's finest sheepdogs and has been used for centuries to herd sheep. It has only recently been recognized by the English Kennel Club. It is essentially a working rather than a show dog and sheepdog trials have been held since 1873.

Characteristics Well-proportioned, graceful dog, of perfect balance combined with sufficient substance to convey impression of endurance. Skull fairly broad, occiput not pronounced. Cheeks lean. Neck of good length. Ribs well sprung, chest deep and rather broad. Back broad and strong. Quarters broad and muscular. Gait free, smooth and tireless. Two varieties of coat: one moderately long, the other smooth; in both, top coat should be dense and undercoat short, soft and dense to give good weather resistance. Variety of colours permissible, but white should never predominate.

Temperament Should be neither nervous nor aggressive, but keen, alert, responsive and intelligent. Makes ideal companion and excels at agility trials.

Drawbacks Has very active mind and must not be allowed to get bored.

BOUVIER DES FLANDRES
UK and AKC Standards
Height $23\frac{1}{2}$–$27\frac{1}{2}$in (60–70cm)
$\quad\quad\quad$ $22\frac{3}{4}$–$25\frac{1}{2}$in (58–65cm)
Weight 77–88lb (35–40kg)
$\quad\quad\quad$ $59\frac{1}{2}$–77lb (27–35kg)

Origin/history The Bouvier is a descendant of Flemish Cattle Dogs and its French name means cowherd. First found in southwest Flanders and in northern France, where it was used for driving cattle, the breed is now employed in security work and as guard dogs. First shown in Brussels in 1910.

Characteristics General appearance is short-legged and cobby, of great strength without clumsiness. Proud upright bearing. Head appears big, prominent moustache and beard even more so. Ears set high. Eyes oval, brown. Neck strong, well muscled and thickening slightly towards shoulders. Body strong, deep, broad and compact with little tuck-up. Length of body and height about equal. Quarters very strong with pronounced muscle. Tail docked at about 4in (10cm). Coat coarse and wiry to the touch, dry and matt, about $2\frac{1}{2}$in (6cm) in length with rather unkempt look. Colour, usually fawn or grey, often brindled or shaded; black permitted, light washed-out shades undesirable.

Temperament Calm and sensible dog of lively appearance. Full of energy and very intelligent. Good guard dog.

Drawbacks Coat needs regular grooming, and dog should have plenty of exercise.

BOXER
UK and AKC Standards
Height UK $\quad$ 22–24in (56–61cm)
$\quad\quad\quad\quad\quad$ 21–23in (53–58cm)
Weight UK $\quad$ 66lb (29.9kg) approx.
$\quad\quad\quad\quad\quad$ 62lb (28.1kg) approx.
Height AKC $22\frac{1}{2}$–25in (57–64cm)
$\quad\quad\quad\quad\quad$ 21–$23\frac{1}{2}$in (53–60cm)

Origin/history The Boxer is a descendant from breeds of the Bulldog type, all of which go back to Molossus blood. It was developed in Germany towards the end of the last century and the Official Standard was first issued in Germany in 1905. The breed gained recognition as a guard dog in 1926.

Characteristics Medium sized, sturdy, smooth-haired dog, short square figure and strong limbs. Head imparts unique individual stamp and must be in perfect proportion to body. Muzzle deep, square, should be one-third the length of head. Ears small, thin, close to cheeks, not cropped in UK. Eyes dark. Neck strong, of ample length, not too thick or short. Length of body equal to height. Back short, straight, broad and very muscular. Quarters strongly muscled. Tail docked to not more than 2in (5cm). Coat short and shiny, lying smooth and tight to body. Colour, fawn, brindle and fawn in various shades, with or without white markings.

Temperament Shows great love and faithfulness to master and household. Alert and courageous. Good with children.

Drawbacks Due to inherent guarding instincts needs careful training as a youngster.

BRIARD
UK and AKC Standards
Height 23–27in (58–69cm)
$\quad\quad\quad$ 22–$25\frac{1}{2}$in (56–65cm)

Origin/history The Briard belongs to an ancient race of sheepdogs and originates in the Brie district of France. The breed was used primarily to guard and herd sheep, and during World War I as a war and Red Cross dog. An Official Standard, sponsored by the French club *Les Amis du Briard*, was approved in France in 1925 and amended in 1930.

Characteristics Of rugged appearance, supple, muscular and well proportioned. Muzzle square and very strong. Ears set on high. Moustache, beard and eyebrows typical of breed. Neck of good length. Back firm and level. Chest broad and well let down. Double dewclaws set low on the hind legs essential. Gait effortless. Tail well-feathered. Coat not less than 3in (8cm), slightly wavy and very dry, with fine dense undercoat. Colour, all black, or black with white hairs, all shades of fawn, darker ones preferred, slate grey.

Temperament Very intelligent, gay and lively, fearless.

Drawbacks Coat needs regular attention.

BULLMASTIFF
UK and AKC Standards
Height $\quad$ 25–27in (64–69cm)
$\quad\quad\quad\quad$ 24–26in (61–66cm)
Weight 110–130lb (50–59kg)
$\quad\quad\quad\quad$ 90–110lb (41–50kg)

Origin/history The Bullmastiff is the product of crossing the Bulldog with the Mastiff and has been known since 1860 as a guard and service dog. It did not gain recognition in England until 1924, when a Breed Club was formed and recognized by the English Kennel Club. The American Kennel Club recognized the breed in 1933.

Characteristics Powerfully built, symmetrical dog showing great strength but not cumbersome. Skull large and square, skin wrinkled. Ears V-shaped. Eyes dark or hazel. Neck well arched, of moderate length. Back short and straight, giving a compact carriage. Loins wide and muscular with fair depth of flank. Tail set high, tapering. Coat short and hard, giving weather protection. Colour, any shade of brindle, fawn or red, colour to be pure and clear.

Temperament High spirited and reliable. Good guard dog.

Drawbacks Needs firm handling when young. Plenty of exercise required.

COLLIE, BEARDED
UK and AKC Standards
Height 21–22in (53–56cm)
$\quad\quad\quad$ 20–21in (51–53cm)

Origin/history The origin of this breed is somewhat vague and largely unrecorded although it is known to have worked at cattle herding on the hills of Scotland for many years. Known at one time as the Scottish Bearded or Highland Collie and even earlier as the Hairy Mountain Dog. The breed was recognized by the English Kennel Club in 1959 and approved by the American Kennel Club in 1977.

Characteristics A lean and active dog, longer than it is high, with shaggy coat and beard. Head in proportion to size; broad skull, strong muzzle; ears medium size, set high, and drooping; eyes toning with colour of coat. Neck moderately long, muscular, and slightly arched. Back level, ribs well sprung but not barrelled. Quarters well muscled. Coat double, with soft, furry and close undercoat; outer coat flat, harsh, strong and shaggy. Colour, slate grey or reddish fawn, black, blue, and all shades of grey, brown and sandy, with or without white markings.

Temperament Dependable and alert, primarily a working dog; a bright intelligent expression is a distinctive feature.
Drawbacks Requires regular grooming and exercise.

COLLIE, ROUGH AND SMOOTH
UK and AKC Standards
Height UK   22–24in (56–61cm)
              20–22in (51–56cm)
Weight   45–65lb (20.4–29.5kg)
              40–55lb (18–20.4kg)
Height AKC 24–26in (61–66cm)
              22–24in (56–61cm)
Weight   60–75lb (27.2–34kg)
              50–65lb (22.7–29.5kg)
Origin/history It is thought that several breeds have been used in the make-up of Collies. All Collies originated in Scotland as robust sheepdogs, but modern types are more elegant in appearance. Coat is the only difference between the two breeds, but the Rough Collie is by far the more popular.
Characteristics Of greaty beauty, grace and perfect proportions to the whole. Head when viewed from the front or side bears a general resemblance to a well-blunted wedge. Ears highly expressive, at rest thrown back, on the alert brought forward, semi-erect with tips drooping. Eyes almond-shaped, sweet and gentle. Neck muscular and powerful, of fair length and well arched. Body a trifle long compared to height, back firm with slight rise over loins. Tail long with bone reaching at least to the hock. Coat of Rough Collie follows outline of dog, and very dense; outer coat straight and harsh, undercoat soft, furry and very close. Smooth Collie has short, flat top coat of harsh texture, very dense undercoat. The three recognized colours are sable and white, tricolour and blue merle.
Temperament Alert and active dogs of great intelligence. With the appearance of working dogs they still make faithful companions.
Drawbacks Rough Collies require regular grooming.

DOBERMANN
UK and AKC Standards
Height 27in (69cm)
      25½in (65cm)
Origin/history This is a manufactured German breed which took its name from Louis Dobermann, who aimed for a giant Terrier with a guard dog's aptitudes. By 1890 he had bred a satisfactory type of Dobermann, and Otto Galler further helped to improve the breed, adding Pinscher (German for Terrier) to the name. Since 1922, breeding in Germany has been very carefully controlled. The National Dobermann Club in Germany was formed in 1900.
Characteristics Of medium size, with well-set body, muscular and elegant. Proud carriage and bold, alert temperament. Head long, well filled under the eyes and clean cut. Ears cropped where permitted. Eyes almond-shaped. Neck fairly long. Body square. Back short and firm with topline slightly sloping from withers to croup. Belly fairly well tucked up. Gait free, balanced and vigorous. Tail docked short. Coat smooth and short, hard, thick and close lying. Colours, definite black brown or blue with rust red markings.
Temperament Highly intelligent; excellent watch dog, loyal and obedient to his master. Lively and vivacious.
Drawbacks Needs very careful handling when young; resents teasing.

GERMAN SHEPHERD DOG (ALSATIAN)
UK and AKC Standards
Height 24–26in (61–66cm)
      22–24in (56–61cm)

Origin/history The German Shepherd Dog is derived from old breeds of herding and farm dogs and was developed in Germany, where the first two specimens of the breed were exhibited at the Hanover Show in 1882. Probably no other breed has brought such a wide range of services to man: from war dogs they graduated to police and security work, guard dogs, and guides for the blind. Its high rating among dogs has been fostered in many countries by German Shepherd Clubs and, having been bred to a fine degree of excellence, this breed is now one of the most popular of the Working Group.
Characteristics Well proportioned with great suppleness of limb. Head long, lean and clean cut, broad at back of skull. Ears broad-based, pointed at tips. Eyes dark, almond-shaped. Neck strong, fairly long with plenty of muscle. Back broadish and straight. Belly shows waist without being tucked up. Good depth of chest. Quarters should show breadth and strength. Gait supple, smooth and long-reaching. Coat double, outer coat close, straight and lying flat, longer and thicker along neck; undercoat woolly. Colour, unimportant but all-white or near-white undesirable.
Temperament Distinguished by loyalty, courage and ability to learn. Alert to every sight and sound and with decided suspiciousness of strangers.
Drawbacks Needs careful obedience training when young to make him excellent companion and guard. Plenty of room and exercise essential.

GIANT SCHNAUZER
UK and AKC Standards
Height 25½–27½in (65–70cm)
      23–25½in (60–65cm)
Origin/history Originally from the Bavarian Highlands, the Giant Schnauzer was used by drovers to herd cattle. For many years known as the Munchener Dog, and in 1909 in Munich about 30 black dogs were shown as Russian Bear Schnauzers. The breed was classified as a working dog in Germany in 1925 and is perhaps less popular than its smaller relatives, the Standard and Miniature Schnauzers; all are Utility Dogs.
Characteristics Strong dog with broad deep chest, strong breast bone. Back strong, straight, ribs well sprung. Head rectangular and powerful with stubby moustache and whiskers. Ears cropped where permitted, otherwise dropping forward to temple. Coat hard and wiry. Colour, pepper and salt in even proportions, or pure black.
Temperament Combines high spirits with reliability, strength, endurance and vigour.
Drawbacks Requires correct and plenty of exercise; coat needs regular trimming.

GREAT DANE
UK and AKC Standards
Height (minimum) 30in (76cm)
                 28in (71cm)
Weight (minimum) 120lb (54kg)
                 100lb (45kg)
Origin/history The Great Dane, from Germany, is known there as the Deutsche Dogge or German Mastiff and has no particular connection with Denmark. Around the 17th century these dogs were used to hunt boar and stags, but the present-day Great Dane is more refined. In 1883 a breed club was formed in England and in 1889 the German Mastiff or Great Dane Club of America was formed in Chicago.
Characteristics Remarkable in size and very muscular, strongly though elegantly built. Head gives impression of great length and strength of jaw. Ears small and set high. Eyes dark, deeply set. Neck long, well arched, quite clean and free from loose skin. Body very deep, with ribs well sprung and

belly well drawn up. Back and loins strong. Tail thick, tapering. Coat short, dense and sleek. Colour, brindle, fawn, blue, black, harlequin.

Temperament Very proud, somewhat reserved and occasionally suspicious with strangers, but friendly, affectionate and gentle with friends.

Drawbacks Must have sufficient space for exercise, and comfortable living quarters.

HUNGARIAN KOMONDOR
UK and AKC Standards
Height   26–31½in (66–79cm)
          23½–27in (60–69cm)
Weight UK 110–135lb (50–61.2kg)
          80–110lb (36–50kg)

Origin/history The Komondor is the largest of the Hungarian herdsman's dogs, known as the king of them all and as an excellent guard. First mentioned in 1544 and in 1673 referred to by Amos Comernius as a guardian of cattle. The International Standard was adopted in 1954.

Characteristics Large muscular dog with plenty of bone and substance, powerful conformation. Head looks somewhat short in comparison to wide forehead. Ears small, set high. Eyes brown. Neck strong, moderately arched, no dewlap. Body broad, slightly longer than height. Chest deep, muscular. Back level. Rump broad, slightly sloping towards root of tail, which is thickly covered with hair and turns up at the tip. Gait light and easy. Coat consists of longer coarse outer coat and softer undercoat. Hair corded together giving a tassel-like appearance. Colour, always white.

Temperament Excellent guard dog, wary of strangers, courageous, faithful and devoted to his master, whom he will defend against any attack.

Drawbacks Needs very careful training to curb any aggressiveness. Coat requires frequent grooming.

HUNGARIAN PULI
UK and AKC Standards
Height   16–18in (40–46cm)
          14–16in (35–40cm)
Weight UK 28½–33lb (13–15kg)
          22–28¾lb (10–13kg)

Origin/history Probably the best-known Hungarian breed outside its own country, the Puli is thought to have arrived in Hungary from Asia in the 9th century. Used in his own country as a shepherd dog. The first standard was drawn up in Hungary in 1915 and revised in 1924 and 1955. The breed first came to the United States in 1930, to England about 1950.

Characteristics Medium sized, nimble and very sturdy. Head small and fine with slightly domed skull. Roof of mouth dark or variegated. Eyes large, brown and deep set. Withers should be slightly higher than the level of back, which should be of medium length. Loin short and broad, belly slightly tucked up. Ribs deep, broad and well sprung. Quarters strong and well muscled. Stride not far reaching and gallop short. Tail curled over back or drooping. Coat corded in long dense tassels. Colours, black, rusty black, apricot, and shades of grey and white.

Temperament Keen, alert and gay; very intelligent and amenable to advanced training.

Drawbacks Coat requires regular attention to keep it in good condition.

JAPANESE AKITA
No UK or AKC Standards
Height 25–27½in (64–70cm)
       23–25in (58–64cm)

Origin/history The Akita is the national breed of Japan. A member of the Spitz family it was originally bred for hunting bear and deer; today it is much valued as a guard and security dog.

Characteristics Well-built strong dog of elegant bearing. Broad head; skull rather flat, stop distinct. Small prick ears set high and carried erect, well forward over dark eyes. Short back, deep chest well rounded. Tail set on high, carried curled, straight or sideways, over rump; profusely covered with hair. Coat hard. Colour, red, white, wheaten, black, shades of grey, steel blue, black and tan, or brindle.

Temperament Excellent guard and watch dog.

Drawbacks None apparent.

MAREMMA SHEEPDOG
UK Kennel Club Standards
Height (minimum) 25½in (65cm)
                 23½in (60cm)
Weight   77–99lb (35–45kg)
                 66–88lb (30–40kg)
No AKC Standards

Origin/history The Maremma is known in his own country as *Cane de Pastore Maremmani* or *Abruzzes Maremma* and is the best known of the Italian sheepdogs. It was used to protect the sheep from bears, wolves and thieves. It is not unlike the Pyrenean Mountain Dog. The present line of Maremmas came to England in 1932 and in 1950 was recognized by the English Kennel Club.

Characteristics Majestic and sturdy, yet lively and intelligent, with aloof expression. Lithe and strongly built. Head triangular in shape. Nose black. Ears folded over to sides of head. Eyes dark brown. Neck strong, of medium length. Body strong, shoulders slightly above level of broad and straight back. Length of body slightly longer than the height. Movement free and active. Tail plume-like. Coat fits outline, long, plentiful and rather harsh. Colour, white; slight shading of ivory, pale orange or lemon permissible.

Temperament Bold and courageous without any trace of aggression.

Drawbacks Needs space and careful handling when young to ensure correct temperament.

MASTIFF
UK and AKC Standards
Height (minimum) 30in (76cm)
                 27½in (70cm)

Origin/history The Mastiff is recognized as the oldest British breed. It is thought to have originated in Asia and to have been brought to Britain in the 6th century BC. A ferocious fighter of bulls, bears and lions until animal baiting was abolished in Britain in 1835. The breed lost its popularity and almost became extinct during the Second World War. Only the efforts of the Old English Mastiff Club saved the breed by buying stock from America.

Characteristics Massive, powerful, symmetrical and well-knit frame. Head of square appearance when viewed from any angle. Skull broad, forehead flat but wrinkled when excited. Ears small and thin, lying close to head. Neck slightly arched and very muscular. Body well let down and deep between forelegs. Ribs well arched. Quarters broad, wide and muscular. Tail set high, wide at root, tapering. Coat short and close-lying. Colour, apricot, silver, fawn or dark fawn-brindle. Muzzle, ears and nose black.

Temperament A combination of grandeur and good nature, courage and docility.

Drawbacks A large dog needing suitable accommodation, and something to do.

NEWFOUNDLAND (see page 183)
UK and AKC Standards
Height 28in (71cm)
　　　26in (66cm)
Weight 140–150lb (63.5–68kg)
　　　110–120lb (50–54kg)

Origin/history There is no evidence to show how and when this dog arrived in Newfoundland. When England founded the first settlement there the breed was unknown. By 1732 there were large bear-like dogs on the island used in helping fishermen drag in their nets and in pulling their carts. The breed was first shown at Birmingham, England, in 1860, and the English Kennel Club recognized it in 1878.

Characteristics Of great strength and activity. Head broad and massive with occipital bone well developed. Ears small, triangular, close to head. Eyes dark brown, small. Strong neck. Body well ribbed with broad back. Chest deep and fairly broad. Quarters very strong. Tail broad and well feathered. Coat flat and dense, oily in texture and water-resistant. Colours, black, brown, white with black markings. Dogs with the latter markings are called Landseer Newfoundlands.

Temperament A water dog and, because of his exceptionally gentle and docile nature used for life saving.

Drawbacks Suitable roomy accommodation and regular grooming are necessary.

NORWEGIAN BUHUND
UK Kennel Club Standards
Height 17¾in (45cm)
　　　Bitches slightly less.
No AKC Standards

Origin/history The Buhund has been kept mainly as a farm dog in Norway for thousands of years, but was only officially recognized in 1943.

Characteristics Typical Spitz dog, small and lightly built, with short compact body. Head lean, rather broad between wedge-shaped ears. Body strong. Chest deep with good ribs. Back straight, good loins, strong couplings, slightly drawn up. Tail set on high, short, thick and hairy, tightly curled. Coat close and long, but smooth, and soft on head and front of limbs consisting of harsh top hair and soft woolly undercoat. Colour, wheaten, black, red, wolf-sable.

Temperament Fearless and brave; faithful guard dog.

Drawbacks None apparent.

OLD ENGLISH SHEEPDOG (see page 180)
UK and AKC Standards
Height 22in (56cm) and upwards
　　　Bitches slightly less

Origin/history Also known as Bobtail because of the short docked tail, the Old English Sheepdog is not particularly ancient, its existence spanning a mere few centuries. It was probably developed in the West Country of England. Originally a working sheepdog, and depicted as such by the English artist Gainsborough in 1771, he is now more popular as a lovable companion.

Characteristics Strong, compact dog of great symmetry. Free from legginess. Skull capacious and rather square, covered with hair. Ears small, carried flat. Eyes dark. A long narrow head is a bad fault. Body rather short and very compact, ribs well sprung and brisket deep. Loins stout and gently arched. Quarters round and muscular. Coat profuse, of hard texture, shaggy and free from curl. Colour, any shade of grey, grizzle, blue or blue merle, with or without white markings.

Temperament Reliable and carefree house dog; good guard.

Drawbacks Coat requires careful attention.

PYRENEAN MOUNTAIN DOG
UK and AKC Standards
Height (minimum) 28in (71cm)
　　　　　　26in (66cm)
Weight (minimum) 110lb (50kg)
　　　　　　90lb (41kg)

Origin/history The Pyrenean obviously comes from the Pyrenees, where he has been known for centuries as a natural guard and protector of shepherds and their flocks. Known in America as the Great Pyrenees and recognized by the American Kennel Club in 1933. The English Kennel Club recognized the breed in 1944.

Characteristics Of great size, substance and power. Head giving impression of strength with no sign of coarseness. Ears rounded, V-shaped, carried close to head. Eyes dark. Neck fairly short, thick and muscular. Chest broad and of sufficient depth to reach below elbows. Back of good length, broad, muscular, straight and level. Thighs must have great strength and be heavily muscled. Gait unhurried. Tail long. Undercoat profuse and composed of fine hairs. Outer coat coarser, thick and straight. Colour, white or mainly white with patches of badger, wolf-grey, or pale yellow.

Temperament Excellent guard dog, extremely loyal to his master and home.

Drawbacks A large sometimes boisterous dog needing adequate space. Coat requires regular grooming.

ROTTWEILER (see page 179)
UK and AKC Standards
Height 25–27in (64–69cm)
　　　23–25in (58–64cm)

Origin/history The Rottweiler is recognized as one of Germany's foremost working breeds, unexcelled as a guard dog and much used in police and security work. The name came from the town of Rottweil in Germany, and the breed is thought to be a combination of the descendants of Roman cattle dogs, Molossus dogs and the smaller Bullenbeisser dogs.

Characteristics Above average-sized, stalwart dog. Correctly proportioned, compact and powerful form permits of great strength and endurance. Head of medium length, skull broad between small pendent ears close to head. Eyes dark brown, almond-shaped. Cheeks well muscled but not prominent. Roomy chest, broad and deep with ribs well sprung. Back straight, strong and not too long. Well-muscled thighs. Gait conveys an impression of supple strength, endurance and purpose. Tail docked short. Coat of medium length, coarse and flat; undercoat should not show through outer coat. Colour, black with clearly defined tan markings.

Temperament Very bold and courageous. Exceedingly loyal and excellent guard if properly trained.

Drawbacks Needs careful training as a young dog to make the most of his assets.

ST BERNARD
UK and AKC Standards
Height UK　The taller the better
Height AKC (minimum) 27½in (70cm)
　　　　　　　25½in (65cm)

Origin/history The St Bernard, known as the good samaritan dog, has been associated with the Hospice du Grand Saint Bernard in the Swiss Alps for more than two centuries. As trained guide dogs, the breed has been responsible for rescuing people lost in the mountains. Dogs were first bred at the hospice between 1660 and 1670. The name St Bernard first came into use in England in 1865 and the first show was held in 1882. The American Saint Bernard Club, formed in 1888, was one of the first breed societies in the United States.

Characteristics Tall powerful dog with an expression of token benevolence. Head large and massive, circumference of skull being rather more than double the head from nose to occiput. Ears drooping close to head. Eyes dark, small and deep set. Neck lengthy, thick and muscular. Back broad and straight, ribs well rounded. Loins wide and very muscular. Chest wide and deep. Coat long or short-haired; in rough (long-haired) specimens dense and flat; in smooth (short-haired) types, close and hound-like, slightly feathered on thighs and tail. Colour, orange, mahogany brindle, red brindle, or white with body patches of any of these colours.
Temperament Makes an excellent guard dog and a loyal, docile and faithful companion.
Drawbacks His great size and weight necessitates substantial feeding, particularly as a youngster.

SAMOYED
UK and AKC Standards
Height UK   20–22in (51–56cm)
            18–20in (46–51cm)
Height AKC 21–23in (53–60cm)
            19–21in (48–53cm)
Origin/history One of the most handsome members of the Spitz family, this breed is named after the Siberian tribe for which it has worked for centuries as a sled and herding dog. The Samoyed has bred true through the ages and was introduced to England about 1900 by fur traders.
Characteristics Strong, active and graceful. Head powerful and wedge-shaped with broad flat skull. Ears erect, thick and triangular, slightly rounded at tips. Back medium in length, broad and very muscular. Chest broad and deep, ribs well sprung. Feet long, flattish and slightly spread out. Should move freely with a strong agile drive. Bushy tail carried over back when alert. Undercoat thick, close and soft with harsh hair growing through, forming outer coat. Colour, pure white, white and biscuit, cream.
Temperament Intelligent, alert, full of action but above all displaying affection towards all mankind. Delightful companion.
Drawbacks Coat needs regular grooming.

SHETLAND SHEEPDOG
UK and AKC Standards
Height UK   14½in (36cm)
            14in (35cm)
Height AKC 13–16in (33–40cm)
Origin/history This small sheepdog comes from the Shetland Islands off the north coast of Scotland. It was originally known as the Shetland Collie, but the name was changed when the Shetland Sheepdog Club was formed at Lerwick in 1908. A standard for the breed was recognized by this club in 1910. Admired for its abundant coat, mane and frill, for its regal bearing and its gentle nature.
Characteristics Alert and intelligent dog of considerable beauty. Refined head, its shape a long blunt wedge tapering from ear to nose. Ears semi-erect, tips dropping forward. Eyes almond-shaped. Neck muscular, well arched and of sufficient length to carry the head proudly. The body slightly longer than high. Chest deep, reaching to the elbow. Ribs well sprung. Back level. Tail set on low, slight upward sweep. Gait denotes speed and smoothness. Coat, double; outer coat long and straight, of harsh texture; undercoat short, soft and close. Colours, sable, tricolour, blue merle, with white markings; black and white, and black and tan also recognized.
Temperament Affectionate and responsive to his owner. May show reserve but never aggressiveness or nervousness.
Drawbacks Coat must have regular grooming.

SIBERIAN HUSKY
UK and AKC Standards
Height 21–23½in (53–60cm)
        20–22in (51–56cm)
Weight 45–60lb (20.4–27.2kg)
        35–50lb (15.8–23kg)
Origin/history The Siberian Husky originated in northeast Asia as a sled dog of great endurance. He had to be capable of travelling great distances and to meet the special needs of the Chukchi people – a Siberian Eskimo tribe herding reindeer. At the turn of the century sled dog-racing became popular in Alaska, and the first team of Siberian Huskies made its appearance in the All Alaska Sweepstakes Race of 1909.
Characteristics Medium sized, with moderate bone, easy and free of movement. Head finely chiselled, fox-like. Ears small, pricked, rounded at tips. Eyes brown, set obliquely. Neck medium length, arched and carried proudly erect. Back straight and strong, with level topline from withers to croup, of medium length. Thighs well muscled and powerful. Gait smooth and seemingly effortless. Tail well furred, round fox-brush shape, usually carried over back. Coat, double, medium in length, undercoat soft, dense and of sufficient length to support softer outer coat. Colour, any (including white) is allowed, and all markings.
Temperament Friendly and gentle, especially with children, but also alert and outgoing. Intelligence, tractability and eager disposition make him an agreeable companion and willing worker.
Drawbacks None apparent.

SWEDISH VALLHUND
UK Kennel Club Standards
Height 13in (33cm)
        12in (31cm)
No AKC Standards
Origin/history Distantly related to the Welsh Corgi, the Vallhund comes from Sweden, where it has long been established as a watch dog and herder. Accepted by the Swedish Kennel Club as a pure breed in 1943.
Characteristics Small powerful and low-to-ground dog with fairly long back. Head long and clean cut with almost flat skull and well-defined stop. Back level, well muscled with short strong loins. Chest long with good depth. Well-angulated hindlegs. Tail length at most 4in (10cm). Coat, medium length with harsh, close and well-fitting top coat, abundant, soft and woolly undercoat. Colours, steel grey, greyish/brown, greyish/yellow, reddish/yellow or reddish/brown, with darker hairs on back, neck and sides of body.
Temperament Watchful, alert and energetic dog making an excellent companion.
Drawbacks None discernible.

WELSH CORGI (CARDIGAN)
UK and AKC Standards
Height 12in (30cm)
Origin/history The Cardigan Corgi is thought to be the oldest of the two Corgi varieties, and one of the oldest breeds in Britain (*corgi* means dog in the Celtic tongue). For centuries the breed has been used by Welsh farmers as herders of cattle, and only comparatively recently have they become show dogs. In 1934 the English Kennel Club classified the Cardigan Corgi and the Pembroke Corgi as separate breeds.
Characteristics Sturdy mobile dog capable of endurance. Head foxy in shape and appearance. Ears prominent, rounded at tips and sloping slightly forward when alert. Eyes usually amber. Chest moderately broad with prominent breast bone. Body fairly long, strong, and with deep brisket, well-sprung

ribs and clearly defined waist. Level topline. Free and active gait. Tail long and bushy, set on and carried low. Coat short or medium, of hard texture; weatherproof with good undercoat. Colour, any, with or without white markings.
Temperament Alert, active and intelligent with steady temperament. Good guard dog and family pet.
Drawbacks None apparent.

WELSH CORGI (PEMBROKE)
UK and AKC Standards
Height   10–12in (25–30cm)
Weight UK   20–24lb (9–11kg)
             18–22lb (8–10kg)
       AKC   27lb (12.3kg) approx.
             25lb (11kg) approx.
Origin/history As implied by the name, the Pembroke Corgi comes from Pembrokeshire in Wales and is thought to have been brought to Britain by Flemish weavers about 1100. Pembroke and Cardigan Corgis were interbred until the breeds were given separate classification in 1934. The Pembroke Corgi is a great favourite of Queen Elizabeth II, a fact not unrelated to its popularity in Britain.
Characteristics Low set, strong and sturdily built; alert and active, giving an impression of substance and stamina in a small space. Head foxy in shape. Ears pricked and slightly pointed. Eyes hazel. Body of medium length, with well-sprung ribs, not short coupled. Level topline. Chest broad and deep. Quarters strong and flexible. Tail short, docked or preferably naturally non-existent. Coat of medium length, dense but not wiry. Colour, self-colours in red, sable, fawn, black and tan, or with white markings on legs, chest and neck.
Temperament Very agreeable companion; affectionate, intelligent and a good guard dog.
Drawbacks None apparent.

Toy Group

This consists of a wide variety of different breeds, ranging in weight from 2 lb (1 kg) upwards. All breeds in the group have special characteristics, but common to them all is a sense of their own importance, and great courage for their size. They make ideal companions, especially for the elderly and the infirm. Although small in stature they are big in heart and always on the alert to warn of intruders, sometimes persistently. Reared sensibly they are as healthy as their larger relatives.

AFFENPINSCHER
UK and AKC Standards
Height $9\frac{1}{2}$–11in (24–28cm)
Weight 7–8lb (3–3.6kg)
Origin/history The Affenpinscher, or Monkey Dog, was well known in Europe and especially Germany as far back as the 17th century. In the first registrations, made in 1879 in German Stud Books, the Affenpinscher was listed under two: Miniature Pinschers and Affenpinschers. At the Berlin Show in 1896 the two breeds were officially separated and the wire-haired variety kept the name Affenpinscher.
Characteristics Sturdily built, small dog with a monkey-like expression (Kennel Club Standards: he should carry himself with comic seriousness). Head fairly small with domed forehead. Eyes round, very dark and sparkling. Ears set high, upright ears preferred. Neck short and straight. Back short and straight, height about equal to length. Gait a tripping, prancing movement. Tail docked, set high. Coat rough and harsh, short and dense on part of body, shaggy and long on legs and a round face. Colour, black, dark grey and black with grey; rich tan or brown markings permissible.
Temperament Lively and self-confident. Loyal and loving family companion; a little suspicious with strangers.
Drawbacks None apparent.

AUSTRALIAN SILKY TERRIER
(US: SILKY TERRIER)
UK and AKC Standards
Height 9in (23cm)
Weight 8–10lb (3.5–4.5kg)
Origin/history Native of Australia, the Australian Silky Terrier was created by crossing the Australian Terrier with the Yorkshire Terrier. For many years known as the Sydney Silky, the breed became recognized in 1955 as the Australian Silky Terrier.
Characteristics Compact and moderately low set. Refined structure, but of sufficient substance to suggest hunting abilities with Terrier characteristics. Head strong. Powerful jaws. Ears small, set high, pinched or dropped. Level topline with well-sprung ribs. Chest of moderate depth. Thighs well developed. Coat fine and glossy, silky in texture, the parted silky hair giving a well-groomed appearance. Colour, blue and tan, or grey-blue and tan.
Temperament Typical Terrier, friendly yet forceful. An excellent family pet and companion, capable of killing small rodents.
Drawbacks None apparent.

BICHON FRISE
UK Kennel Club Standards
Height less than 12in (30cm)
AKC Standards not yet issued
Origin/history Uncertainty surrounds the origin of many of the French Toy breeds, of which the Bichon is one. The term bichon is often used in general to describe a group of small, usually white dogs. The breed is now recognized by both the English and the American Kennel Clubs.
Characteristics Gay, happy little dog. Head carriage, proud;

dark eyes alert and expressive, ears hanging close to head. Chest well developed with deep brisket. The floating ribs well rounded and not terminating abruptly. Loin broad. Thighs broad and well rounded. Tail carried raised and gracefully curled. Coat, fine and silky falling in soft corkscrew curls. Colour, pure white.

Temperament Active small dog, excellent companion.
Drawbacks None apparent.

CAVALIER KING CHARLES SPANIEL (see page 180)
UK Kennel Club Standards
Weight 12–18lb (5.4–8kg)
No AKC Standards
Origin/history The Cavalier is the descendant of the Toy Spaniels of the 16th, 17th and 18th centuries and then a great favourite with royalty and the noble families of Europe. King Charles II of England (1630–85) was very fond of these little dogs, hence their name. The Cavalier King Charles Spaniel Club was formed in 1928 and the breed registration accepted by the Kennel Club in 1945.
Characteristics Active, graceful and well-balanced dog. Head almost flat between high set, drooping ears, without dome. Stop shallow, about 1½in (4cm) in length from base of stop to tip. Eyes set well apart, large, dark. Short-coupled body with plenty of spring in rib. Back level. Length of tail in balance with body. Coat long, silky and free from curl. Colours, black and tan, ruby, blenheim, tricolour.
Temperament Charming, happy dog, sporting in character and loving companion.
Drawbacks None perceivable.

CHIHUAHUA (Long and Smooth Coat)
UK and AKC Standards
Weight up to 6lb (2.7kg) permissible, 2–4lb (1–2kg) preferred
Origin/history The world's smallest dog, the Chihuahua originated in Mexico; it was a popular pet as well as a religious symbol of the ancient Toltec tribes and later of the Aztecs. The Chihuahua was first registered in America in 1904. Breeding began in Britain about 1943 with stock imported from the United States; it is now one of the most popular of Toy breeds, the smooth-coated type gaining particular favour.
Characteristics Alert, swift moving and cheeky-looking little dog. Dainty and compact. Well-rounded apple-domed skull with lean jaws and cheeks. Ears large, set on at an angle of 45 degrees. Level back, slightly longer than the height at shoulder. Tail of medium length carried erect or looped over back. Coat the only distinguishing feature: smooth coat, soft texture, close and glossy; long coat, long and soft, flat or slightly wavy; feathering on feet and legs, pants on hind legs, large ruff on neck. Colour (both), any, solid or mixed.
Temperament Bright, very active and bold. Excellent family companions, quick to warn of approaching strangers.
Drawbacks None apparent.

CHINESE CRESTED DOG
UK Kennel Club Standards
Weight 7–12lb (3–5.4kg)
No AKC Standards
Origin/history The name of the Chinese Crested is derived from the mop of hair on the crown of the head. The body is hairless, hot to the touch and with a kind of reptilian look not usually associated with canines. Accepted on the register of the English Kennel Club.
Characteristics A small and graceful dog, medium to fine boned, smooth hairless body, with hair only on feet, head and tail. Skull slightly rounded, moderate stop. Ears large, upstanding, with or without ear fringe. Body medium to long.

Level back. Rump slightly rounded. Chest deep and fairly broad. Tail carried over back or looped, but not curled. Colour, any, plain or spotted.
Temperament Happy and active dog, devoted to its owner.
Drawbacks Can be wary of strangers.

ENGLISH TOY TERRIER (BLACK AND TAN)
UK Kennel Club Standards
Height 10–12in (25–30cm)
Weight 6–8lb (2.7–3.5kg)
AKC Standards
Weight up to 12lb (5.4kg)
Origin/history A miniature version of the Manchester Terrier and although a Toy dog has strong Terrier characteristics; it was required in the past to kill rats. The breed was first known in England as Toy Manchester Terrier, then Toy Black and Tans followed by Miniature Black and Tans. The English Kennel Club recognized them in 1962 as English Toy Terriers (Black and Tan). In America it is known as the Manchester Terrier (Toy).
Characteristics Well-balanced and elegant Toy with Terrier temperament. Head long and narrow with flat skull. Ears pointed, set on high and carried erect. Eyes very dark. Body compact, head and legs proportionate. Back very slightly curving from behind shoulder to loin. Chest narrow and deep. Tail moderately short, tapering to a point. Coat thick, close and smooth, glossy in appearance. Colour, jet black and mahogany tan, both clearly defined.
Temperament Must have the fearless Terrier temperament. Undemanding as a household pet.
Drawbacks None discernible.

GRIFFON BRUXELLOIS
UK and AKC Standards
Weight UK   5–11lb (2.3–5kg)
Weight AKC 8–12lb (3.5–5.4kg)
Origin/history This breed came from Belgium towards the end of the last century and is said to originate from the German Affenpinscher and Belgian street dogs used for ratting. By 1890 it had become extremely popular in Belgium, where the royal family bred Griffons. The Griffon Bruxellois Club was founded in England in 1898 and in the same year the English Kennel Club recognized the breed. In America the first Griffon was registered in 1910.
Characteristics Well-balanced square little dog, measuring the same from withers to tail as from withers to ground. Head large and rounded. Chin prominent and slightly undershot. Ears semi-erect, high set, the smaller the better. Eyes large, round and dark. Chest rather wide and deep. Short back, level topline. Feet small and catlike. Tail short, docked, carried high. Coat in the rough variety (Griffon Bruxellois) harsh, wiry and free from curl, preferably with an undercoat. In the smooth variety (Petit Brabançon) coat short and tight. Colour, clear red, black, or black and rich tan.
Temperament Although a Toy he is a tough little dog, with a happy, gay, extrovert nature. Delightful companion.
Drawbacks None discernible apart from early consistent training.

ITALIAN GREYHOUND (see page 184)
UK and AKC Standards
Weight UK 6–8lb (2.7–3.5kg) desirable, not exceeding 10lb (4.5kg)
Height AKC 13–15in (33–38cm)
Origin/history The Italian Greyhound has existed in its present form for more than 2000 years and was brought to England during the early years of the 17th century. It is the

smallest of the true Greyhounds and of exquisite elegance. First registered in America in 1886.

Characteristics A miniature Greyhound, slender in all proportions and of graceful elegance in shape, symmetry and action. Typical high-stepping movement. Skull long, flat and narrow. Ears delicate, rose-shaped and set well back. Eyes large and bright. Neck long and gracefully arched. Chest deep and narrow. Back curved and drooping at the quarters. Long hare-like feet. Skin fine and supple. Hair thin and satin glossy. Colour, all shades of fawn, white cream, blue, black and fawn, and white pied.

Temperament Excellent companion with lovely disposition.

Drawbacks None apparent.

JAPANESE CHIN (UK)
JAPANESE SPANIEL (US)
UK and AKC Standards
Weight UK   4–7lb (2–3kg)
Weight AKC Under and over 7lb (3kg), smaller weight
                        preferred

Origin/history The Japanese Chin or Spaniel is an ancient breed, probably originally from China, where it is depicted on old temples. Japanese Chin arrived in America from Japan before it came to England, in about 1860. First registered with the American Kennel Club in 1888.

Characteristics Lively little dog of stylish appearance and elegant carriage. Large head with broad skull, rounded in front. Important that white shows in the inner corner of the dark eyes, thus giving the Japanese Chin its characteristic quizzical look. Muzzle very short. Body square and compact, wide in chest, cobby in shape. Tail set on high on straight back, profusely feathered, closely curved or plumed over back. Coat profuse, long, soft and straight, of silky texture. Colour, black and white, or red and white.

Temperament Bright and alert companion.

Drawbacks None discernible.

KING CHARLES SPANIEL (UK)
ENGLISH TOY SPANIEL (US)
UK and AKC Standards
Weight UK   8–14lb (3.5–6.3kg)
Weight AKC 9–12lb (4–5.4kg)

Origin/history The King Charles Spaniel's history is shrouded in obscurity. The first written reference seems to have been about 1570 and again in 1587 after the execution of Mary, Queen of Scots, when a tiny spaniel of similar type was found hidden in her clothing and soaked with blood. In spite of the name, the dog beloved by King Charles II was probably closer in type to the Cavalier King Charles. Early in this century the King Charles enjoyed tremendous popularity but has declined in numbers in recent years.

Characteristics Small and compact, of refined outline. Chest wide and deep, legs short and straight, back short and level. Head massive skull compared with size of dog, well domed and full over the eyes. Nose black, short and upturned; long ears set on low, drooping close to cheeks. Eyes very large and dark. Tail well feathered, not carried over back. Coat long, silky and straight, slight wave allowed but not curly. Colour, blenheim, ruby, tricolour, and black and tan.

Temperament Affectionate, intelligent little dog, intensely loyal to his family. Makes an ideal companion.

Drawbacks None apparent.

LÖWCHEN
UK Kennel Club Standards
Weight US 8–9lb (3.5–4kg)
No AKC Standards

Origin/history A member of the Bichon family and originally from France, the Löwchen is sometimes referred to as the Little Lion Dog. The body coat is clipped in the traditional lion clip and the tail, also clipped, is topped with a plume, in typical poodle fashion. Kennel Club Challenge Certificates were granted in England in 1976.

Characteristics An active, well-balanced little dog. Fairly broad skull, flat between the ears, head carried proud and high. Jaws strong. Neck good length. Body short and well proportioned. Level topline. Ribs well sprung. Coat fairly long and wavy, but not curly. Clipped in traditional lion clip. Colour, any, self or a combination.

Temperament Highly intelligent and ideal companion.

Drawbacks Coat must be clipped.

MALTESE
UK and AKC Standards
Height UK   Not exceeding 10in (25cm)
Weight AKC Under 7lb (3kg)

Origin/history The breed comes from Malta, where it has been a great favourite since Antiquity. Thought to have been brought into England during the reign of Henry VIII (1509–1547). The breed arrived in America in 1875 and was first registered with the American Kennel Club in 1888 as a Maltese Terrier.

Characteristics Lively and alert. Balanced head with defined stop. Nose pure black. Ears small, V-shaped and set above topline of head. Eyes small and oblong, dark. Body short and close-coupled, with good rib spring and straight back. Quarters nicely angulated. Feet round, pads black. Tail well arched over back. Coat of good length, silky in texture and no woolly undercoat. Colour, pure white.

Temperament Sweet-natured, clean dog, affectionate and with a tremendous will to please.

Drawbacks Coat requires regular grooming.

MINIATURE PINSCHER (see page 182)
UK and AKC Standards
Height 10–12in (25–30cm)

Origin/history Germany is the native land of the Miniature Pinscher; it has been known there for several centuries and predates the Dobermann Pinscher by many years. The Miniature Pinscher Club of America was formed in 1929; its popularity rating in America exceeds that of Britain.

Characteristics Well-balanced, compact, short-coupled dog of elegant carriage. Precise high-stepping gait different to any other Toy dogs. Head elongated rather than short and round, narrow and without conspicuous cheek formation. Ears set on high and as small as possible. Eyes dark brown or black. Neck strong yet graceful. Topline straight, sloping slightly towards the rear. Belly moderately tucked up. Tail docked short. Coat smooth, hard and short. Colour, black, blue or chocolate with tan markings.

Temperament Very alert and intelligent. Valuable watch dog and loyal to his master and family.

Drawbacks None apparent.

PAPILLON (see page 182)
UK and AKC Standards
Height 8–11in (20–28cm)

Origin/history The Papillon is thought to have originated in Spain, although Italy and France helped develop its popularity. Papillon, French for 'butterfly', is an apt name for this little dog, whose ears, fringed and set obliquely on the head, resemble the wings of a butterfly. One variety has drop ears and is known as Phalène (moth).

Characteristics Dainty Toy dog with an elegant head, alert bearing and lively expression. Skull slightly rounded between large ears, fully erect or fully dropped; muzzle finely pointed. Eyes dark and round. Level topline. Body well formed, with well-sprung ribs, good length of loin, slightly arched belly. Feet fine and fairly long as in the hare. Tail long and well fringed, arched over back. Coat long, fine and silky, abundant without undercoat; profuse frill on chest, short and close on skull, muzzle and front part of legs. Colour, white with patches of any colour except liver.

Temperament Very happy and lovable companion. Alert and good watch dog.

Drawbacks None apparent.

PEKINGESE (see page 181)
UK and AKC Standards
Weight UK   not exceeding 11lb (5kg)
              not exceeding 12lb (5.4kg)
Weight AKC not exceeding 14lb (6.3kg)

Origin/history The Pekingese has a distinctive, slightly superior personality; in ancient times it was held sacred in China and reached its peak as a royal lap dog in the middle of the 19th century. Its history goes back to the Tang dynasty of the 8th century, but its first appearance in Britain was in 1860, when five of the royal dogs, found during the looting of the Imperial Palace in Peking, were brought back to Britain and one was presented to Queen Victoria.

Characteristics Small and thickset, with a carriage of great dignity and quality. Head massive, skull broad, wide and flat between ears. Eyes large, round and dark. Body short, with broad chest and well-sprung ribs, falling away lighter behind. Lion-like with distinct waist. Hind legs lighter, but firm and well shaped. Feet large and flat, not round; dignified rolling gait in front with close gait behind is typical. Coat long and straight, with profuse mane. Colour, all colours and markings permissible, except albino or liver.

Temperament Of great dignity and loyalty but at the same time stubborn and independent. Great character and splendid companion; very courageous.

Drawbacks Coat needs regular grooming.

POMERANIAN
UK and AKC Standards
Weight 4–4½lb (2–2.2kg)
          4½–5½lb (2.2–2.5kg)

Origin/history The Pomeranian is a member of the Spitz family which originally came from the Arctic Circle. It arrived in England about 1860 via Pomerania in northern Germany and was then a much larger dog than today; British breeders did much to bring the breed to its present standard of a perfect miniature sheepdog. The American Pomeranian Club held its first speciality show in 1911.

Characteristics Short-coupled well-knit dog. Head foxy in outline. Neck rather short. Back short, body compact, well ribbed up and rounded. Chest fairly deep but not too wide. Tail, profusely covered with long harsh, spreading hair, should be turned over back and carried flat and straight. Coat perfectly straight, harsh in texture, with soft fluffy undercoat. All whole colours admissible.

Temperament Very lively, intelligent and vivacious; suitable as pet and companion.

Drawbacks Coat must have regular grooming.

PUG (see page 179)
UK and AKC Standards
Weight 14–18lb (6.3–8kg)
Origin/history The Pug, like other short-faced dogs with curled tails, originated in China. It came in the middle of the 19th century to England via Holland, imported by traders from the Dutch East India Company. It soon became extremely popular in England and was the favoured pet of the ladies of the nobility. The breed was first registered by the American Kennel Club in 1885.

Characteristics Decidedly square and compact, often described as *multum in parvo*. Head large and massive, round but not apple-shaped. Muzzle short, blunt and square. Forehead deeply wrinkled. Eyes dark and very large. Body short and cobby, wide in chest and well ribbed. Tail curled as tightly as possible over hip; double curl is perfection. Coat, smooth, soft and glossy. Colour, silver, apricot, fawn, or black.

Temperament Intelligent, faithful and affectionate. Makes an excellent house dog.

Drawbacks None apparent.

YORKSHIRE TERRIER
UK and AKC Standards
Weight not exceeding 7lb (3kg)

Origin/history Bred and produced in England, the Yorkshire Terrier was not acknowledged by the English Kennel Club until 1886. It is now one of the most popular Toy dogs. It lays no claim to antiquity, but is probably a result of breeders in the north of England crossing the Maltese with local Terriers. The first dogs were too large, but eventually the breeders achieved their aim of producing a small dog in which the true Terrier type was inherent.

Characteristics Toy Terrier distinguished by long coat over well-proportioned body. Head rather small and flat. Ears small, V-shaped, erect. Eyes bright and dark. Body compact with good loin. Level on top of back. Tail cut to medium length. Coat moderately long and perfectly straight (not wavy), glossy and of fine silky texture, dark steel blue from back of skull to root of tail, hair on chest, legs, and fall on head rich bright tan.

Temperament Affectionate and lively; ideal as a companion and self-assured in spite of the diminutive size.

Drawbacks Coat needs careful and daily attention.

Rare Breeds

This fluctuating group covers pure breeds of all types, not necessarily rare in numbers or in their countries of origin, but rare because they do not often appear on national or international show benches and are therefore less widely known. Popularity ratings frequently affect the status of a particular breed; the original Irish Setter, for example, was chiefly red and white, but today that combination is so scarce as to warrant classification as a rare breed. Similarly, breeds which were formerly classed as rare, such as the Bichon Frise and the Swedish Vallhund, have steadily increased in popularity and are now listed in the Toy and the Working groups respectively.

AUSTRALIAN CATTLE DOG
No UK or AKC Standards
Australian National Kennel Council Standards
Height 18–20in (46–51cm)
17–19in (43–48cm)
Origin/history This dog was developed by Australian sheep farmers to meet their particular demands for tough and agile dogs to round up and herd range cattle. A black, bobtailed dog, known as the Smithfield, was crossed with the dingo around 1830. The progeny were red, bobtailed pups called Timmins Biters. Unlike the Smithfield these dogs were silent, but fierce in snapping at the animals' heels. Blue Merle Collies were imported from Scotland and used in the final make-up.
Characteristics Sturdy, compact, symmetrically built working dog. Skull broad. Cheeks muscular, but not coarse, underjaw strong. Ears pricked. Eyes dark. Neck of exceptional strength and very muscular. Length of body greater than height. Outer coat weather-resistant and moderately short, straight and of medium texture, with dense undercoat. Colour, blue, or blue mottled with or without other markings, or red speckle.
Temperament Tough courageous dog with implicit devotion to duty. Loyal, but distrustful of strangers.
Drawbacks Must be properly trained as a young dog.

AUSTRALIAN KELPIE
No UK or AKC Standards
Australian National Kennel Council Standards
Height 18–20in (46–51cm)
17–19in (43–48cm)
Origin/history The Australian Kelpie was developed by Australian sheep farmers from smooth-haired, prick-eared sheepdogs. In 1870 a pair of smooth-haired dogs, which were called Fox Collies, were brought out from Scotland and mated on board ship. The litter was whelped after arrival in Australia to start the Kelpie breed in Australia.
Characteristics Lithe, active dog of great quality. Head in proportion to size of body. Neck of fair length. Chest deep rather than wide, ribs well sprung, with firm level topline. Length of body greater than height. Outer coat moderately short, flat, straight and weather-resistant; undercoat short and dense. Colour, black, black and tan, red, red and tan, fawn, chocolate, and smoke blue.
Temperament Alert, eager and highly intelligent, mild, tractable disposition and inexhaustible energy. Intensely loyal and devoted to duty.
Drawbacks Because of its natural instinct and aptitude for work not really suitable as a companion dog.

CATALAN SHEEPDOG
No UK or AKC Standards
Height 18–20in (46–51cm)
17–19in (43–48cm)
Origin/history The Catalan Sheepdog originates in Spain and is a descendant of the Spanish Mastiff.
Characteristics Dark eyes, drop ears, covered in long hair, lying close to the head, generally cropped. Head broad and pear-shaped. Skull with prominent occiput. Neck short and muscular. Back moderately long and horizontal. Loins broad, short and slightly arched. Chest powerful and capacious with slight, sprung ribs. Tail of natural length or docked to about 4in (10cm). Two sets of dew-claws on back legs. Coat long, o f standing and slightly wavy. Colour, black and white, grey, russet or black, and white and tan.
Temperament Courageous and intelligent.
Drawbacks None discernible.

ESTRELA MOUNTAIN DOG
No UK or AKC Standards
Height 25½–28½ (65–72cm)
24½–27in (62–69cm)
Origin/history The Estrela is known in its native Portugal as the *Cão Serra da Estrela* and is one of the oldest breeds of the Iberian Peninsula.
Characteristics Sturdy well-built dog of Mastiff type, giving an impression of strength and vigour. Skull square and slightly concave. Stop not well marked. Muzzle straight and blunt. Ears small, triangular with rounded tips. Cropping permitted. Eyes oval, calm and gentle. Chest deep and broad. Belly slightly drawn up. Shoulders strong and supple. Quarters powerful with well-bent stifles. Coat strong, slightly rough, smooth or a little wavy resembling goat hair. Long-haired and smooth-haired varieties exist. Colour, red with black mask, grey, pied or any other colour. Black muzzle desirable.
Temperament Trustworthy guard dog.
Drawbacks Can be a little wary of strangers.

GLEN OF IMAAL TERRIER
No UK or AKC Standards
Height not exceeding 14in (35cm)
Origin/history Bred in County Wicklow, Ireland, this tough little Terrier is used to hunt fox and badger. Recognized by the Irish Kennel Club in 1933.
Characteristics Body long, with broad chest and well-sprung ribs. Eyes brown and intelligent. Legs short and strongly boned; front legs may be slightly bowed. Feet turned slightly outwards. Tail docked and carried high. Coat harsh, soft rather than wiry and moderately long. Colour, blue, blue and tan, or wheaten.
Temperament A daredevil; courageous dog. Obedient and very loyal to his owner.
Drawbacks None apparent.

HOVAWART
No UK or AKC Standards
Height 25–27in (64–69cm)
22–26in (56–66cm)
Origin/history The Hovawart is correctly a new breed given an old name, for the Hofwarth is mentioned in documents of the Middle Ages as a reliable watch dog. It was re-created by German breeders from farmers' dogs of the Hartz, Black Forest and other mountain regions and given official recognition in Germany in 1936.
Characteristics Medium sized, active dog. Head broad and domed. Skull equal in length to muzzle. Ears set on high, dropped. Cheeks narrow, jaws strong. Back firm, strong and straight. Chest deep and broad. Forelegs straight and powerful. Tail long and bushy, thick at root and tapering to tip; curly tail undesirable. Coat long, waved, lying flat without curls; undercoat soft and short. Colour, deep golden, black and gold, or black without white markings.

Temperament Highly intelligent; alert and easily trained guard and companion dog.
Drawbacks Needs adequate exercise and frequent grooming.

IRISH SETTER (Red and White)
No UK or AKC Standards
Irish Kennel Club Standards
Height not given.
Origin/history The Red and White Setter is the forerunner of the Irish Setter. Both originate in Ireland, and while the solid chestnut Red Setter has become synonymous with Irish Setter, the Red and White is rarely seen.
Characteristics Athletic dog of great power. Skull domed, not showing the occipital protuberance seen in Irish Setters. Muzzle fairly square. Neck moderately long, muscular but not too thick. Body strong and muscular with deep chest and well-sprung ribs. Quarters wide and powerful. Coat finely textured with good feathering; slight wave permissible. Colour clearly particolour, base colour being white with solid red patches.
Temperament Affectionate and happy gundog.
Drawbacks None apparent.

ITALIAN SPINONE
No UK or AKC Standards
Height 23–27½in (58–70cm)
22–24in (56–61cm)
Origin/history Originally from the Bresse area of France, this old breed became established in Piedmont in north Italy. It resembles a coarse-haired pointing griffon, whose origins are closely linked to European griffons. Popular as a gundog.
Characteristics Large, squarely built dog. Head long and somewhat rounded. Ears long and drooping. Skull oval with well-marked occiput and gradual stop. Neck strong and muscular. Height equal to length of body. Chest deep and convex. Quarters strong and well muscled. Tail docked. Coat, rough and lying close and slightly curly, 1½–2in (4–5cm) long; soft undercoat. Hair long over eyebrows, cheeks and jaws. Colour, pure white, or white with orange or brown markings.
Temperament Docile and friendly; good companion dog.
Drawbacks None apparent.

KUVASZ
No UK Kennel Club Standards
AKC Standards
Height 26in (66cm)
Bitches slightly less
Origin/history The Kuvasz, an ancient sheepdog of the Hungarian steppe, originally came from Tibet and was brought to Hungary by the Kurds centuries ago.
Characteristics Remarkable for its strength and activity combined with agility. Head in proportion to size of body. Skull broad and flat. Body well ribbed up with a fairly broad back, neck comparatively short, well set on sloping shoulders; strong muscular loins. Forelegs strong in bone. Quarters strong and well muscled. Chest deep and fairly broad. Coat thick, long on neck and croup, shorter and slightly wavy on sides. Colour, pure white.
Temperament Courageous and fearless as a protector; docile, faithful and devoted to his owner and family.
Drawbacks None apparent.

LEONBERGER
No UK or AKC Standards
Height 30in (76cm)
27in (69cm)
Origin/history The Leonberger owes his name to his creator, Heinrich Essig of Leonberg in Württemberg, Germany. He crossed a St Bernard with a Newfoundland and at a later stage possibly introduced Pyrenean Dog bloodlines. The official standard for the breed was not accepted until the early 1950s. More frequently seen in Europe than in Britain and America.
Characteristics Strong, muscular and well-proportioned frame. Head considerably smaller than the St Bernard and lacks the wrinkles. Around neck, which is free of dewlap, a collar of thick, long hair, differing distinctly from that on chest. Feet webbed. Tail long with good plume. Coat long, thick, soft and oily, with dense waterproof undercoat. Colour, fawn, reddish, with or without black (wolf-like) markings.
Temperament Intelligent and extremely loyal to his owner; wary of strangers.
Drawbacks Requires careful training as a young dog.

PORTUGUESE WATER DOG
No UK or AKC Standards
Height 20–23in (51–58cm)
Bitches slightly less
Origin/history In its native Portugal this breed is known as *Cão de Agua*. Evidence of its origin is inconclusive. Formerly used as a hunting dog and now a keen water dog along the coast of Portugal, and used by fishermen for retrieving lost tackle and guarding boats.
Characteristics Strong and well-muscled dog of pleasing appearance. Head massive but well proportioned. Hind skull well domed and occiput prominent. Ears heart-shaped, set on high, lying flat to head. Eyes round, black or brown. Short straight back with croup falling away slightly. Chest broad and deep with long well-sprung ribs. Belly slightly drawn up. Thighs strong, and very muscular. Tail thick at root and tapering to tip. Coat either long and slightly wavy, glossy and not very close, with wig-like top-knot, or short and flat, forming cylindrical locks, dull and very thick, covering head, ears and body evenly. Colour, black, black and white, or brown and white.
Temperament By nature aggressive, high-spirited, and intelligent; hardy and loving water. Trained properly makes an obedient and sharp guard dog.
Drawbacks Requires careful training as a youngster.

SHAR-PEI
UK and AKC Standards not yet issued
Height 18–22in (46–56cm)
Origin/history The breed comes from China and although it was valued there for more than 2000 years, by 1971 only a few specimens were known to exist. It is thought to have originated from the Chow, having the same type of bluish-black tongue. Now it seems likely to make a comeback in several parts of the world.
Characteristics Medium sized, with a wrinkled coat that seems far too big for its frame. Chest broad and deep, back short, loins short and broad. Topline level, with slight rise over loin. The abundant loose skin is a characteristic of the breed. Coat bristly, short and soft or long and soft. Colour, solid or shades of black, red, and fawn.
Temperament Sweet disposition and a good household guardian. In its homeland trained for dog fights, but will only fight if taught to do so from infancy.
Drawbacks The heavily wrinkled coat must be carefully tended to prevent sores.

GLOSSARY

Apple-headed Descriptive term for a high, domed and rounded skull; a characteristic in Chihuahua breeds.

Apron Frill of long hair on the underside of the neck and on the chest of certain breeds, notably Rough Collies.

Bat ears Used to describe erect ears, broad at the base and rounded in outline, resembling a bat. Characteristic of the French Bulldog, distinguishing this breed from the (English) Bulldog.

Beard Thick, long and bushy hair on the lower jaw of such dogs as the Griffon Bruxellois.

Bite Descriptive term defining formation of the jaw and position of the teeth.

Blanket Solid colour over back and sides and extending from the neck to tail; often characteristic of Beagles.

Blaze Narrow white facial marking running from nose to skull, between the eyes.

Blue merle Coat colour of blue and grey mixed with black.

Bobtail Of a non-existent or very short-cropped tail; the Old English Sheepdog is commonly known as 'Bobtail'.

Bone Term used to describe the appearance of leg bones: a well-boned dog has shapely, strong legs with good spring.

Bossy Of shoulder muscles which are too heavily developed in proportion to body, as in some French Bulldogs.

Breaking Applied to house-training of dogs in general, and particularly to the training of sporting and working dogs.

Breeching Colour of the hair at the back of thighs and rear part.

Breed standards Specifications compiled by national kennel clubs, detailing construction, form and coat of recognized breeds.

Brindle Describing a coat colour which is a texture of dark and light hairs, usually grey or brown.

Brisket That part of the body between the forelegs.

Broken Applied to coat colour and describing one broken up with white or another colour.

Brush Bushy, fox-like tail.

Butterfly nose Usually describes a black nose with pink spots, as in some Setters and Spaniels.

Caudal In anatomy, situated near the tail.

Cat-feet Rounded, compact feet as in Terriers; the opposite of splay-feet.

Challenge Certificate (C.C.) In Britain, an award made to best of breed at certain major dog shows.

Champion In Britain, an award made after winning three C.C.'s, under three separate judges, at shows of championship status. In the US, championship is awarded on points.

Chops The pendulous upper lips or jowls of deep-mouthed dogs like Bulldogs and Hounds.

Cobby Compact and short-bodied, with well-sprung ribs.

Collar White coat markings around the neck.

Couplings The length of the body between the last rib and the hip bones; a dog may be short or long-coupled.

Crest The arched part of the neck.

Crossbred A dog whose parents are of different, but pure breeds.

Croup The rump and hindquarters.

Culotte Long, feathery hair on the back of the thighs, as in the Pomeranian.

Cushion The thickening of the upper lips, characteristic of the Mastiff, Pekingese, etc.

Dew Claw Situated on the inside of the forelegs and usually removed shortly after birth to prevent the claws and nails from growing in. Retained in some mountain dogs and essential in the breed standards for the Briard.

Dewlap The loose, drooping skin under the chin and throat of, for example, the Bloodhound.

Dish-faced Descriptive term for a concave nasal bone, having the effect of setting the tip of the nose higher than the stop.

Docked Of tails which are cut short or to a determined length on quite young puppies.

Down-faced The opposite of dish-faced, the nose curving downwards from stop to tip.

Dorsal In anatomy, relating to the back of the dog.

Drop-eared Of pendent ears hanging close and flat to the face.

Ear-cropping This practice is illegal in Britain, though permitted in some other countries. An aesthetic operation, under anaesthesia, is performed on young dogs to shape the ears to conform with the shape of the skull.

Ethology The study of animal behaviour in relation to their natural environment.

Fall Descriptive term for long hair falling over the face and eyes.

Feathering Long fine hair fringes on the back of the legs, under the belly and on the ears, especially in Setters.

Flag The fringe of hair under the tail of Setters and Retrievers, shortest at the tip of the tail. Also applied to high tail carriage.

Flews Deep upper lips, drooping at the corners.

Fly-eared Applied to ears which fold or curl at the tips when they should stand erect; or *vice versa*.

Gay Of tail carried erect or curled forward over the back.

Hare-feet Of long, narrow feet, with the digits clearly separated.

Harlequin Descriptive term for patched coat coloration, as in the black and white pied Great Dane.

Haw The inner membrane of the lower eyelid, red and exposed in breeds such as the Bloodhound and the St Bernard.

Hock Joint in the hindleg, located below the stifle and roughly corresponding to the heel in man.

Inbreeding Mating of two closely related dogs, such as mother and son, father and daughter, sister and brother; the progeny will inherit known qualities, including possible defects. See also line breeding.

Interbreeding Mating of purebred dogs of different breeds, usually to transfer the desirable characteristics of one to the other.

Kiss marks Descriptive term for tan spots on the cheeks and eyebrows.

Leather The ear flap, especially on breeds with large and drooping ears.

Level Applied to a back which runs in a straight line, with no obvious sway; it does not necessarily imply a back line parallel to the ground. Also applied to the bite when upper and lower incisors meet perfectly.

Line breeding The mating of two pedigree dogs with common ancestors, less closely related than with direct offspring as in inbreeding.

Lion trim Known in the US as the Continental clip and describing the special coat presentation of show poodles. Originally used for retrieving ducks, poodles had their hindlegs shaved to facilitate swimming; later, pompons of hair were left as protection over bony protrusions, and on the tip of the tail.

Maiden Term applied to a bitch which has not been mated.

Mandible In anatomy, the lower jawbone.

Mask Facial shading on the muzzle and foreface, distinct in outline and differing sharply in colour.

Merle Genetic colour factor, relating to coat, usually blue-grey streaked with black, and common in Collies and Shetland Sheepdogs.

Muzzle The dog's face in front of the eyes. Also applied to a make-shift or ready-made arrangement of straps or wire used to restrain a dog from biting or barking.

Occiput The upper, rear part of the skull, often well-defined as in the Irish Setter.

Outbreeding Mating of dogs from the same breed, but with no common ancestors or relatives.

Overhang Applied to a fold of loose skin protruding from the skull on to the nose, notably in Pugs and Pekingeses.

Overshot Descriptive term for a jaw where the upper teeth protrude beyond the lower.

Pads The tough, horny cushions on the undersides of the toes.

Parti-coloured Applied to a coat with patches of two different colours in equal proportions.

Pastern That part of the foot, on the foreleg, between the carpus and the digits.

Peak The pointed tip of the occiput, pronounced in Bloodhounds.

Pedigree The authenticated record of the ancestry of a purebred dog.

Pencilling Dark lines demarcating the tan on the toes of such Terriers as the English and the Manchester Terrier.

Pied Of a coat having two colours, the patches being unequal, unlike parti-coloured.

Plume The long and soft hairs on the tails of such breeds as the Pekingese and the Pomeranian.

Point Term applied to colour markings on face, eyebrows, ears and legs.

Prick-eared Of ears carried erect, as in Chow Chows, German Shepherds and Welsh Corgis; often pointed at the tips.

Puppy In general, puppy describes a dog up to its first birthday when it is considered to have reached maturity (though large breeds remain at the puppy stage for up to two years). In show classes, a puppy must be at least six months old and not exceed twelve months.

Purebreeding Mating between dogs of the same breeds, both parents being the offspring of other purebreds.

Roached Of the curvature of the back, arched convexly as in the Italian Greyhound and the Whippet.

Roan Descriptive term for coat colour, in a fine, indistinguishible mixture of coloured and white hairs.

Rose-eared Applied to an ear which, though folded, twists back to expose the inside of the ear, as in the Bulldog.

Rudder Term sometimes applied to the tail of the Greyhound.

Ruff The apron or frill of long and thick hairs round the neck as in the Chow Chow.

Sable Of coat colour, describing black overlaid on gold or brown, as in Collies and Shetland Sheepdogs.

Saddle Solid black colour extending over the back of some breeds.

Screw Of a naturally short tail, twisted into a screw, as in some Boston Terriers.

Self-colour Of a coat with a single, whole colour, except for white or pale shading.

Sickle Of a tail carried in a semi-circle.

Splay-feet Applied to broad feet with spread-out toes, notably in sporting breeds used for water retrieving.

Stern Alternative term for tail, used especially with reference to Beagles and Foxhounds.

Stifle Joint between upper and lower thighs, corresponding roughly to the human knee joint.

Stop The indentation between the eyes where skull and nasal bone meet.

Topknot Profuse tuft of long fine hair on top of the head, as in the Dandie Dinmont Terrier.

Tricolour Of a coat, to describe three colours, more or less in equal proportions, and usually black, tan and white.

Tuck-up Descriptive term for shallow depth at the loins on deep-chested dogs like Greyhounds and Whippets.

Undershot Applied to a jaw where the lower teeth project beyond the upper.

Ventral In anatomy, pertaining to the abdomen.

Whiskers The beard on Fox Terriers, usually neat and long rather than bushy.

Withers The highest point of the back, between the shoulder blades; a dog's height is measured from the withers to the ground.

Wrinkle The puckered, loose skin folds on the face of Bloodhounds, St Bernards and Pugs.

CONTRIBUTORS

Editorial Adviser

Dr David Macdonald is Ernest Cooke Fellow in Animal Behaviour in the Department of Zoology, University of Oxford. He is particularly well-known for his research into mammals and has written several books and papers; his projects on foxes, cats, capybaras and mongooses have all been featured as television films. He is the editor of the two volume *Encyclopedia of Mammals*, published worldwide in 1984.

Contributors

Ronald S Anderson BVMS PhD MRCVS is Professor of Animal Husbandry at the Liverpool University Veterinary School. Sometime lecturer in veterinary physiology at Glasgow Veterinary School and for many years Head of Pedigree Petfoods, UK, Animal Studies Centre, he has contributed extensively to the field of companion animal nutrition and husbandry through numerous papers and lectures, in UK and abroad.

W F Butler BVSc PhD FRCVS is a veterinary surgeon who has spent twenty-five years as researcher and teacher in the Anatomy Department at the School of Veterinary Science in Bristol. He has written many articles for scientific journals, and spent a year in Iran, helping to establish a new Veterinary School in Shiraz.

Andrew Edney BA BVetMed MRCVS is a Past President of the British Small Animal Veterinary Association and veterinary adviser at Pedigree Petfoods, UK, Animal Studies Centre. He is sometime adviser on Companion Animal Affairs to the World Health Organization at Geneva, and Secretary of the World Small Animal Veterinary Association. He is a contributor, editor and author on the subjects of euthanasia, zoonoses, dog and cat husbandry, and clinical nutrition.

Peter Messent MA DPhil is Product Development Supervisor, Pet Keeping, for an American petfood manufacturer. Formerly Secretary of the Society of Companion Animal Studies, he has a special interest in the human-dog relationship. Author of *Understanding Dogs*, he has also contributed widely to scientific papers and books.

Terry McHaffie MBE for many years senior instructor at the RAF Police Dog School, is now an adviser to the Ministry of Defence on dogs and their training. He judges working trials and show dogs, regularly officiates abroad, and breeds champion dogs.

Valerie Riley BVSc MRCVS has worked for several years in mixed and small animal veterinary surgeries in various parts of Britain. She is now a lecturer in veterinary anatomy at Liverpool University. A member of the BASVA (British Small Animal Veterinary Association), she has a particular interest in radiology.

James Serpell BSc PhD is a zoologist based at the Sub-Department of Animal Behaviour, University of Cambridge. He has contributed extensively to books and scientific journals both in the UK and overseas.

M J R Stockman MRCVS is an experienced veterinary surgeon and head of a large animal hospital near London. A well-known dog breeder and show judge, he is a member of the Kennel Club's General Committee and chairs two of the Club's special committees.

Catherine Sutton is one of the foremost judges and dog breeders in the UK. Author of *Dog Shows and Show Dogs*, she exports Beagles to many parts of the world and is Chairman of the Judges' Sub Committee of the Kennel Club.

Malcolm Willis BSc PhD is senior lecturer in animal breeding and genetics, University of Newcastle, a member of the Kennel Club and on its Breed Standards Sub Committee. He has written several books and papers on canine genetics, has a special interest in German Shepherd Dogs and has judged them around the world.

Stephen Wright comes from a dog-breeding family and competed in obedience and breed trials before joining the Guide Dogs for the Blind Association in 1962, and is now their Education and Development Manager. He is also president of the British Whippet Racing Association.

Charles Wyant is a member of the Kennel Club and one of the best-known and widely respected trainers on the international scene. He has travelled all over the world as one of the Senior International Judges of Obedience Tests, and in 1980 judged at Crufts Dog Show.

USEFUL ADDRESSES

Fédération Cynologique Internationale
Rue Leopold II
14 B-6530 Thuin
Belgium

UNITED KINGDOM
The Kennel Club
1 Clarges Street
London W1Y 8AB

The Scottish Kennel Club
6B Forres Street
Edinburgh

British Veterinary Association
7 Mansfield Street
London W1M 0AT

EIRE
The Irish Kennel Club
23 Earlsfort Terrace
Dublin 2

EUROPE
Denmark
Dansk Kennelclub
Parkvej 1
Jersie Strand
2680 Solrød Strand

Finland
The Finnish Kennel Club
Suomen Kennellitto-Finska
Bulevardi 14A
Helsinki

France
Société Centrale Canine
215 Rue St Denis
75083 Paris
Cedex 02

Germany
Verband für das Deutsche Hundewesen (VDH)
Postfach 1390
46 Dortmund

Holland
Raad van Beheer op Kynologisch Gebied in Nederland
Emmalaan 16
Amsterdam

Italy
Ente Nazionale Della Cinofilia Italiana
Viale Premuda
21 Milan

Norway
Norsk Kennelclub
Teglverksgt 8
Postboks 6598
Rodelokka

Spain
Real Sociedad Central de Fomento de las Razas en España
Los Madrazo 20
Madrid

Sweden
Svenska Kennelclubben
Norrbyvägan 30
Box 11043
161 11 Bromma

Switzerland
Schweizerische Kynologische Gesellschaft
Falkenplatz 11
3012 Bern

NORTH AMERICA
The American Kennel Club (AKC)
51 Madison Avenue
New York NY 10010

The Canadian Kennel Club
2150 Bloor Street West
Toronto M6S 1M8
Ontario

AUSTRALIA & NEW ZEALAND
The Australian National Kennel Council
Royal Show Grounds
Ascot Vale
Victoria

New Zealand Kennel Club
Private Bag
Porirua

INDIA
Kennel Club of India
17 Mukathal St Purasawaltam
Madras 600 007

SOUTH AFRICA
Kennel Union of South Africa
6th Floor
Bree Castle
68 Bree Street
Cape Town 8001

ACKNOWLEDGMENTS

Artists' Acknowledgments
All drawings throughout this book were executed by
Andrew Macdonald
with the exception of the following:
Priscilla Barrett p62–74
Tony Lodge p30–31, 60–61, 90–91, 134–135, 176–177
Gary Martin p93–101
Sue Sharples p102–109

Photographic Acknowledgments
Anne Cumbers p180 top right, bottom right; p182 top left;
p183 bottom right; p184 top right
Joan Ludwig p181 bottom left; p182 bottom right
Maxwell Riddle p179 centre right
J. Ritter p180 top left; p181 centre left; p183 top right, centre
left
Anne Roslin-Williams p182 top right
Sally Anne Thompson p179 top right, centre left, bottom
left, bottom right; p180 bottom left; p181 top right, centre
right, bottom right; p182 centre right, bottom left; p183 centre
right, bottom left; p184 top left, centre right, bottom left,
bottom right
J R Trelease p180 centre left

The Publishers wish to thank the following people for their
help and advice in preparing illustrations and text:
Mr & Mrs M J R Stockman and their Keeshonds
Mrs Catherine Sutton
Mr Charles Wyant and his German Shepherd Dogs
Many people – and their dogs – provided help and models for
drawings and photographs. Thanks are due to:
Miss M P Ashbridge and *Lucy*; Miss P Aze and her many dogs;
Veronica Banfield; Sue Baker at Caywood Kennels, South
Newington; Mrs E Briggs; Sheila Cartwright, the Boxers and
the kennel maids at Tyegarth Kennels, Worplesdon near
Guildford; Dave Cavill; Mrs M A Collins; Gillian Darley and
Creeper; Mr E A Foster; Mr & Mrs Gissane and *Susie*; Mrs
Hamilton, Angela Dowell, the Cairns and *Benson* at
Oudenarde Kennels, Cricklade, Wiltshire; Mrs W Harris;
Mrs P P Landon-Harrisson and *Sam*; Alma Leeper and her
puppy *John*; Penny and Nikki McCann and *Benson*; Miss
Malin and her Beagle; Pamla Toler and *Trog*.

INDEX

Index

Index

Index

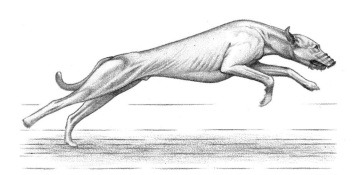

herman de vries

traces 2005

from top

kein anfang kein ende

'no beginning no end'

panta rhei [in greek characters]

'everything flows'

all in one one in all

steigerwald, northern bavaria

herman de vries and
susanne jacob de vries
in the forest near
Eschenau, northern Bavaria 1999.

herman de vries

chance and change

MEL GOODING

Thames & Hudson

This book is dedicated to Chris Humphries, Paul Nesbitt and Henry Nolte: friends who know that science and art are one.

Acknowledgements
Special thanks are due to Jill Hollis and Ian Cameron, whose knowledge, understanding and admiration of herman de vries have been critical to the making of this book. To herman and susanne de vries I owe every gratitude for their material and critical assistance, and to their marvellous generosity of spirit. All who care about the art of herman de vries are indebted to the work of Cees de Boer. Thanks, also, to Nadine Gomez-Passamar, Henry Nolte and Sarah Patterson.

Photographic credits
Falko Behr jacket front, 18 (bottom), 22, 23 (top left and bottom left), 28, 33, 38 (top), 44 (bottom), 73, 77, 84 (bottom); Jean Brasille/Espace de l'Art Concret, Mouans-Sartoux 21, 45, 112 (both), 113 (both), 114-115; Centre PasquART, Biel/Bienne 62-63; Eric Camoin 111; susanne jacob de vries 10, 16, 76, 96; Gert Elzinga 2; Jean-Denis Frater 135 (left), 136 (both), 137 (all), 140; Galerie Mueller-Roth 61, 97, (Christian Blei) 68, (Nikolaus Koliusis) 25; Mel Gooding 65; Catriona Grant 91; Graphische Sammlung Albertina, Vienna/Bridgeman Art Library 67; M. Hanslmeier 110; Jill Hollis 96 (top), 119 (top), 124 (top and bottom), 126 (bottom), 131, 132, 134; Studio Kauffelt 48; Kunsthalle Bremen 66; Andreas Lauble 68 (left); Joseph Marando 120 (all), 121 (all), 122 (all), 128, 129; Rudolf Mattes 85 (bottom); Heinz-Günther Mebusch 11; Roman Mensing 126 (top left, centre and right), 127 (left); Musée Condé, Chantilly/Bridgeman Art Library 80 (both); Musée de Digne (J. Marando) 116, 117 (all), 118 (top), 118-119 (bottom); Bob Negrijn/De Verbeelding 127 (right); Paul Nesbitt 7, 74 (left), 95; Peter Neumann jacket back, 92; David Paterson 70 (right); Gisela Pernau 98; Rijksmuseum Twenthe 37 (top); Friedrich Rosenstiel 50, 60; Bruno Schneyer 1 (top, centre and bottom), 13, 36, 100, 101, 108, 109, 135 (bottom), 138-139 (all). All other pictures come from the archive of herman de vries.

First published in Great Britain in 2006 by
Thames & Hudson Ltd, 181A High Holborn, London WC1V 7QX

Produced by Jill Hollis and Ian Cameron
Cameron & Hollis, PO Box 1, Moffat, Dumfriesshire DG10 9SU, Scotland

Set in Futura Light and Stone Sans by Cameron & Hollis, Moffat
Colour reproduction, printing and binding by Studio Fasoli, Verona

British Library Cataloguing-in-Publication Data
A catalogue record for this book is available from the British Library

ISBN-13: 978-0-500-09327-6
ISBN-10: 0-500-09327-X

Printed and bound in Italy

Endpapers
joy joy 2005 (detail)
crayon on paper
113.5 x 172.5 cm

contents

preface

the arrangement of this book

In 1970, with an epiphany on a Seychelles beach, the creative project of herman de vries arrived at an absolute clarity of purpose. His artistic philosophy was at last defined and its expressive means and materials identified. Thereafter de vries has made many different works in many different places, and the diversity of his art has much to do with the varieties of circumstance in which it has been made. It always entails the presentation of concrete actualities: found natural objects; photographic and other traces; words spoken and written, incised or printed; performances, actions and interventions in specific places; absence and presence, silence and inaction.

At the end of his frequent journeys and sojourns elsewhere, he returns to the house in Eschenau, the small village in Bavaria where he has lived and worked with his partner and close collaborator, susanne, since 1970. Not far away is the forest where he spends much of his creative time, and which he regards as a vast outdoor studio. Close to the village is *the meadow*, where he allows nature, unimpeded by anything more than the most tactful and sensitive of intrusions or interventions, to proceed in its own way, a living contrast and ecological-ethical reproach to the intensively cultivated and botanically impoverished agricultural land around it.

Any account of his work that reflects its true nature will acknowledge that its vitality and beauty is a function of particular circumstances of time and place, of topography, ecology and history, and of what de vries calls 'chance and change'. Its unity is a function of its intellectual coherence and its consistency of presentation; its diversity is that of its materials, and their relation to the place where they have been found. When de vries's early progress has been described, there is no story to tell of the artist's further development, no analysis to be made of changes in style: both approaches are irrelevant to the mature work.

A conventionally chronological treatment of de vries's life-work would not do justice to its singularity or its diversity, and this book is, therefore, arranged in another way. The prologue provides a summary of his work and ideas as a whole, distinguishing its philosophical purposes from those of other contemporary artists who also work in the landscape and use natural objects. Thereafter, the book is arranged in four parts, each subdivided for clarity of presentation.

The first chapter is an account of the artist's formations, traced in his childhood passions, in his professional work as an applied botanist, and in the dynamic interrelations of his scientific understanding and his philosophical intuitions. It covers his early artistic career within the ambit of contemporary conceptual and concrete art. This first part necessarily deals with many of the conceptual and creative issues that have remained at the heart of de vries's subsequent artistic project, which has maintained an absolute philosophical coherence. 'In my beginning is my end', wrote T.S. Eliot, whose imagination was fed by certain of the eastern spiritual sources – especially the Vedic – that have informed de vries's own poetics. Part 2 is concerned with de vries's creative life and work in Eschenau and nearby. Part 3 chronicles various important projects and activities undertaken since the early 1970s, with special attention given to the two major works, the *earth museum* and *natural relations*. Part 4 describes, as an exemplary project, his artistic interventions, over several years and continuing, in the small French spa town of Digne-les-Bains and its environs in Haute-Provence.

Each part is concerned with a distinct complex of objects, publications, actions and events, which, taken together as an ever-growing body of work, constitutes one of the most deeply interesting and significant artistic projects of our time. It is the more impressive and moving for its vital connection with the great collaborative work of all those scientists, ecologists, philosophers, poets and artists whose primary and urgent concern is the survival of the living world. They seek, collectively, an understanding of the proper place of the human within the natural, and of the ineluctable interdependence of all living things in the fragile biosphere we share.

a note on language and terms

de vries's use of English terms and phrases is sometimes idiosyncratic and inventive: e.g. 'manifest', 'identic', 'the seeings of my beings', 'objectivation', etc. In each case I have retained his own forms. Wherever he is quoted, I have maintained his own convention of using no capital letters, adopted early in his career to signify his rejection of conventional hierarchies in written language and by extension in life itself. Similarly, where a caption in its entirety has been supplied by de vries and therefore constitutes his title for a work, lower case letters have been used exclusively. In translated texts, by de vries and others, I have made silent emendations to aid sense or remove obvious solecisms.

Mel Gooding
Barnes, February 2005

herman de vries working in his garden,
Eschenau, northern Bavaria, 1998.

the poet in his poetry

The art of herman de vries takes place within the natural world, which includes human existence – human being – in all its manifestations. His rubber stamp *to be* succinctly acknowledges the fundamental fact of human existence as being itself in nature, taking Hamlet's anguished existential question and reducing it to pure infinitive verb, unlimited by any specific person, tense or negative contingency. (The Latin *infinitivus* means literally 'not limited'.) The work of de vries takes for granted the coexistence – or more precisely the existence of each *within* the other – of science, art and poetry, recognising that these activities all begin in being on the earth, in the apprehension of natural phenomena, and in our thoughts and feelings about them.

'No ideas but in things' wrote the American poet William Carlos Williams in a credo for the kind of literary modernism that rejected vague evocation, airy generalisation, rhetorical flourishes and sentimentality. Williams, Ezra Pound, T.S. Eliot, James Joyce and others in that line of modernism favoured the concrete image over the generalising symbol, and often incorporated in their work found texts and verbal fragments, but their work was by definition literary, a matter of linguistic representations, however concrete its various references to the world's objects, natural and man-made. de vries, however, as a visual artist, has taken the injunction literally: he does not *represent* the world in discursive descriptions, references and reflections; he *presents* not ideas, but the things themselves.

It is of course true that the presentation of any object in a particular context – in this case that of art – gives it possibilities of meaning determined by the context: an array of real leaves in a box frame, for example, whether ordered in a particular way or apparently random, is something very different from a litter of leaf-fall beneath a garden tree. To take the leaves from the garden and to preserve and present them as components in a work of art is to invite many possibilities of response, associations and diverse thoughts, feelings and ideas. And these will be in many (though not all) ways different from those invoked by the preservation and presentation of a sample in an herbarium, or in a botanical display in a natural history museum, where the arrangement has systematically demonstrative purposes. They are different again – more so, indeed – from a painted or drawn representation of leaves, however accurate, made for whatever purpose, scientific or artistic (among other things, say, to aid identification, or to symbolise abstract qualities). They are *the things themselves*, the actual leaves from the living, mortal tree.

In encountering an array of this kind by de vries we begin with the irreducible fact that a natural object has been taken from the phenomenal world – the world perceived by the senses – and transported, a natural 'readymade', into the context of art within culture. Such a work, among other things, constitutes a challenge to certain prevailing aesthetic-critical assumptions: on the one hand, to those that have to do with art as a tradition of *making*, historically validated by the critical appreciation of particular skills of technique or manipulation (drawing, painting, sculpture, hand-printmaking); on the other, to those that underpin the quintessentially modernist arts of assemblage or collage, practised most famously by such artists as Marcel Duchamp, Pablo Picasso, Georges Braque, Kurt Schwitters, Joseph Cornell, Arman and Robert Rauschenberg, which borrow a kind of syntax from the discursive (*a* added to *b* creates *c*). Even in the works by de vries that consist of several or many parts, such

to be 1974
postcard, printed on rice paper at the sangram press, kathmandu

8

as the *journals*, and the written word pieces, the array as presented by de vries denies both craft and discourse: every item is there for its own sake, is its own thing among other things.

Historically, in the case of collage and assemblage, the components have typically been objects taken from the material culture of the modern world, art fragments and quotations, or socio-cultural ephemera such as bits torn from newspapers or magazines, or tickets, or fragments of typography. de vries has broken new ground in the directness of his use of natural objects, and in his utterly minimal treatment, rearrangement and presentation of them. He has never limited himself purely to the use of natural objects, but his deployment of what might be called cultural detritus and of photography has always placed a particular emphasis on natural processes, an emphasis that locates it within the thematic ambit of his work as a whole.

The work of de vries differs, too, from that of those other artists of more recent years who have also used natural objects as the material media for a diversity of practices that in one way or another deal with the human relation to, or experience of, the natural world. These artists have made work by modifying, relocating or rearranging such things as stones, trees, plants, flowers, petals, leaves, water, earth, etc., sometimes *in situ* (where they have been found), sometimes back in the studio or gallery where such materials are used in the making of sculptural objects or installations. Other artists have systematically undertaken creative excursions into the landscape (near or far, ordered or wild) to register a presence and to carry back information that is then ordered to provide the basis for wall-drawings, wall-paintings or mural or printed texts which serve as records or analogues of actions and passages, or for photographic presentations; in addition to photographs, such information might also include lists of locations and notes on actions, events and objects, the names of natural objects, records of weather conditions, place names, records of topographical dimension and distance, citations of starting points and destinations, etc.

The diverse works of such artists − Sjoerd Buisman, Susan Derges, Chris Drury, Ian Hamilton Finlay, Hamish Fulton, Andy Goldsworthy, Richard Long and David Nash, among others − nevertheless have much in common. Such art is almost always characterised by the use of geometric and sacramental signs and symbols that have histories of currency and recurrence across human cultures such that we refer to them as 'universal' − the line, the wave, the circle, the spiral, the labyrinth, the sphere, the hand-print, the wheel, etc. Or else it figures symbolic objects that have widespread phenomenological resonances, usually to do with the human experience of safety or survival, of celebration or commemoration. In this category of signifying objects, there are cairns, columns and other simple monuments, gardens, shelters, huts, aedicules and temples, boats and sails, baskets and boxes. By and large, though not entirely, de vries eschews both kinds of symbolism. He resorts instead to modes of presentation which are determined by a predilection for absolute clarity. These displays identify objects as being at once representative and unique, and provoke a poetic apprehension of the un-mediated beauty of the objects as such.

Photography has been necessary to much of the artistic activity of those artists just mentioned, who are often described as 'working in the landscape': it provides vivid records of selected natural objects, whether simply observed (Fulton), or modified or re-arranged (Long, Goldsworthy, Buisman), and of evanescent natural processes (Derges). Photography has also been essential to the documentation, gallery presentation and publication of artistic inter-ventions, often ephemeral, in landscape settings, works often secret or remote, or otherwise inaccessible to the art public (Drury, Long). de vries has himself used photography extensively, but, characteristically, for purposes that differ radically from those of an aestheticising record or artistic documentation. His photographs emphasise, rather, their factual existence as object-traces of unique moments in time, whose significance is inseparable from that moment-of-being

the poet in his poetry 1972
schöntal, steigerwald, northern bavaria

in the world. The circumstance might be that of the ever-changing chance conjunction of windswept pine-needles on a wooden floor, or of the never-to-be-repeated light on objects seen from any window; the being might be that of the artist himself – *the poet in his poetry* – or that of moving water or of fleeting clouds.

In the early years of his artistic career de vries worked and thought his way towards his distinctive vision of art and the world with a remarkable economy and coherence, carefully defining and developing the methodologies by which it might be realised. During those years – from 1953 (when he first became an artist) to the mid-1960s – he thought deeply about the conceptual and philosophical implications of his previous work as a scientific researcher. And it was during his association with the various activities that are now referred to as *art informel* and conceptual art (in Amsterdam he exhibited with '0 (zero or nul)', co-editing and publishing early issues of the magazine *revue nul = 0*), that he came to a key realisation: personal feelings and idiosyncratic reactions, expressed as such through technique and style or intellectual proposition, were not interesting as art. His work during this period was thus a radical clearing of the ground, a reduction of his creative project to its essence. For de vries from this time on it was not the personal expression of the poet that mattered so much as the poetic reality of the world, which wrote itself through the poet. In his poem-mantra 'my poetry is the world', 'the poet' stands for the human.

It had also become apparent to him that art might be logically understood as a phenomenon on the same plane as nature itself. Buddhism and Tao on the one hand, and his highly personal reading of Wittgenstein's *Tractatus* on the other, were crucial to this development. 'true philosophy is immediate actual,' he wrote in 1976. 'so any communication of it can go from and to the actuality of it, which is not symbols. so, liberated of thinking with symbols, philosophy is life and actuality.' The paragraphs which follow repeat this formula, substituting for 'true philosophy', respectively, 'true art', 'true life', 'true actuality' and 'true communication'. The text relates closely to de vries's succinctly complete statement of his being in the world; of the world being in him:

my poetry is the world
i write it every day
i rewrite it every day
i see it every day
i read it every day
i eat it every day
i sleep it every day

the world is my chance
it changes me every day
my chance is my poetry

statement, im löchla, wonfurt 1986

The Löchla is a pond near Wonfurt, northern Bavaria.

Any proper critical engagement with the world of herman de vries must begin with an understanding of the centrality to his life and art of this vivid sense of the 'immediate actual', and an appreciation of his view of nature as a process of which he is an integral part. It is a process that de vries identifies as consciousness itself: 'when i said "nature is art" ', he wrote in 1998, 'i could do this because i see nature as a conscious process which is experienced through the senses and experiences itself through our senses (and those of other beings).' It is not a mystical sense of identity that de vries is speaking of here, but one which comprehends his life as a human being in the society of human beings. He continues: 'therein [i.e. within that experience of nature through the senses] my identity – which is what I communicate – always [involves] being aware of my social function.' Identity might be defined here as what is communicated by the being in question: it is for a human as for a plant, an animal or an insect, or, indeed, as for a leaf, a wing or a shell. Like every other species of thing on earth we are at once similar and different: 'different and identic'.

Identity – like intelligence, like knowing – is something shared. The intelligence of the world is communicated through its phenomena; that communication through things and between things is consciousness itself. 'the world we live in is a revelation that can be "read", experienced. everything we experience or are able to experience is significant for itself and for everything. we can find this significance everywhere around us.' It is the purpose of de vries's art to make this consciousness manifest: '[art] for me has to do with the formulation of consciousness or with the process of becoming conscious. this consciousness i see happening around me in nature and i show what i have seen happening, what i have seen being.'

From his earliest beginnings as an artist de vries has conceived of art, in common with science, as a revelation of reality through the 'immediate actual', a means to the raising of consciousness: 'the spectator completes the work by absorbing its information. The social function is thus the participation in a consciousness-raising process.' In a long conversation with the artist Piero Manzoni, in 1962, de vries discovered that they shared a similar view of the social purpose of art, which they defined as 'deconditioning': the liberation of the imagination from habitual responses to things, from conventional modes of seeing, thought and feeling.

It was this conviction that led de vries to pursue a lifelong study of mind-moving (a term he prefers to 'psychedelic') substances. It had become clear to de vries that the vast repository of precious knowledge about the healing and hallucinogenic properties of plants, accumulated in diverse cultures through the millennia, is in grave danger of being lost forever. The use of mind-moving substances, often deemed sacred, is understood by de vries to be but part of a broader set of dynamic interrelations between human culture and the vegetable world, within which the life-enhancing, palliative and curative properties of plants and their derivatives are integral to the well-being, in every sense of that term, of humanity. These natural relations are threatened, to the detriment of animal, human and plant life alike, by the loss of an active interdependence in which there is a proper reverence for all living things, and respect for the life-sustaining elements of earth, water, air and fire.

natural relations (1989), the climax of this study, was the outcome of extensive fieldwork, of innumerable consultations and conversations with experts, savants, holy men, market traders and amateur investigators over many years of travel to India and Africa, and of intensive researches in the literatures of botany, ethnobotany, pharmacology, philology, religion and folklore. *natural relations*, a complex multi-part work, consists of collections and arrays of plant and substance specimens, a temporary glasshouse herbarium of living plants, and a beautiful, astonishingly capacious encyclopaedic catalogue of information.

The 'deconditioning' which frees the mind and the imagination is also, for de vries, a freeing of the spirit from its entrapment in limiting assumptions about the reality of the world as we see it. These assumptions derive from a failure of the sympathetic imagination, which has its intellectual origins in Cartesian dualism. In a statement of December 1994/January 1995 entitled 'physics and metaphysics are one', de vries writes 'everything we know is in the world, is the world.' This adapts and elaborates the great proposition that opens Wittgenstein's *Tractatus*: 'The world is everything that is the case.' de vries's statement develops his version of the proposition in terms of our down-to-earth, everyday experience of the 'immediate actual': 'the metaphysical and physical are one in the world, in us, in me. to experience what we call metaphysics, we need our own physical universe: the body and its processes. we are not without experience. we are these experiences.' de vries is aware, of course, that his title contains a memory of another Wittgenstein proposition – 'Ethics and aesthetics are one' – and that the truth of that axiom is implicit in his own formulations.

The experience of reality, conceived in these terms, must begin in the continuous encounter with those things with which we coexist. It is the function of contemplation, meditation, art and science, to raise this consciousness to the highest levels possible. In thus being, we enter into our inheritance as creatures on and of the earth: it is a matter of something more than seeing and knowing. 'one needs experience. the most importance experience we call joy... i cannot and do not want to limit experience to the senses. to be able, however, to recognise, we need this physical universe, which first made this experience possible. the *wonder* remains.' The art of herman de vries offers particular and specific experiences of the marvellous diversity and beautiful order of nature, a nature which comprehends the human social world. It reminds us – induces us 'to recognise' – that knowing begins in revelation, may develop through explanation – 'within our conditions and the conditions of meanings (meanings are also part of the world)' – but must end in wonder and in joy.

belladonna 1999

The plant is surrounded by
its common names
indicating its properties in
various European languages.

scientist into artist

this lonesome leaf's a study
never finished, since
we aren't sure what *one*
of anything is.

Mark Doty
(on a watercolour of a croton leaf
by the poet Elizabeth Bishop)

1. the young naturalist

'Let nature be thy teacher' William Wordsworth

herman de vries began his professional life as a natural scientist, and in his work as an artist there have persisted certain procedures that significantly resemble methods used in empirical scientific research, especially in the field of taxonomy. The impulses behind this artistic activity and those that animate the work of the scientist are very close. Both artist and scientist are engaged in the revelation of a reality that is greater than the sum of specific actualities, both aim to find an order in apparent disorder, to see beyond the random event to explicable causalities. And scientists, in thus seeking knowledge, are never far from wonder: the discovery of underlying patterns in things, the revelation of elegant hidden structures and relationships, the formulation of fruitful hypotheses or powerful theories; all of these bring pleasures and satisfactions that are aesthetic as well as intellectual.

Encouraged by his parents and a sympathetic elder sister, herman displayed as a very young child a remarkable capacity for wonder at natural phenomena, and experienced an unusual intensity of pleasure in natural objects and events. These sympathies shaped him emotionally and intellectually, and in them can be traced the origins of his philosophy. 'when i was about four years old my mother used to take me for walks in my pushchair... even at that age i knew the parks well and individual trees to which i was very attracted. if one was suddenly felled, it pained me deeply and i would collect wood chippings from each tree, keeping them separate and knowing which each one was.'

From an early age he and his sister belonged to a local natural history society, which instilled in him a lifelong passion for walking, looking, collecting and identification. School,

Left to right:
herman de vries outside his parents' summer home, c.1934.

The kind of landscape which first inspired dreams of 'no society'.

herman de vries in the countryside as a twelve-year-old.

de vries has said, was like a prison to him; as with the schoolboy in William Blake's poem 'it drove all joys away', and he chafed at institutional authority and social hierarchies.

> as a child I had a deep mystic feeling for nature. sometimes in a quiet spot in the dunes on the dutch coast i undressed myself and pressed my body to the earth or fell into a light trance by looking at the sea and the endless incoming waves. once i read a book on the hopi indians from the local library and discovered their holy number was six: the four directions, earth and sky. it became so important to me that i ordered almost everything in life after this number.

The world is experienced by the child with a directness, a sharpness and sweetness of savour, and a unity of apprehension that it is hard, though not impossible, for the adult to recapture. When as adults we attempt to regain, if only momentarily, that unforced unity of self and world – that state of Blakean 'joy and innocence' – it is quickly clouded, compromised by a knowledge that comes from its contrary condition, 'experience'. The components of this knowledge are codified in a language that necessarily brings into play distinctions between the subject and the object of subjective regard: '...this is what language does' says de vries; 'language is "you and me", "we and them", "here and there", whereas in effect, it is all part of the same, it is one. but language is a human instrument of great power, like the words of sorcery. It gives us the means to communicate what we are doing, what is around us, and gives us a grip on reality and great social power. but we also pay for it in the loss of unity.' He adds, wryly: 'but still I am talking!'

de vries has maintained a preternatural ability, it seems, to maintain a childlike immediacy of relation to natural things. He takes a simple delight in what the world presents to him – as something to be seen, touched, smelt, heard, tasted, eaten, drunk, smoked – at the same time as having the surest grasp, a wholly professional comprehension, of both the taxonomic classification and the ecological interdependence of plants. 'ever since i was a little boy, when i was five years old i already knew the names of most common plants – except grasses – around our town near the dunes of north holland. my parents stimulated my interest very much, and later they bought me a picture book so that i could identify plants for myself.' That qualification – 'except grasses' – is a token of both honesty and exactitude of recall. Many years later he returned to the area of his childhood with his partner in life and art, susanne: 'we went to the dunes where i remembered beautiful valleys in which grew *parnassia* and wintergreen and creeping willow, but we were prevented from going further by a fence, and when i looked over this fence there, in the valley of my youth, stood the first dutch atomic power station...'

There can be no return to the Eden of childhood, but the adult is never beyond the possibility of a vision regained. de vries has written that although his studies in horticulture and agriculture and his field work as a biologist brought him into constant contact with nature, 'the relationship in those times was never so intensively connected as in childhood.' It was in his

Left to right:
The 'grote ganzenveld' – a valley in the dunes in northern Holland known as 'the great goose field'.

herman de vries with his mother, sister and father in the Veluwe – a large area of heathland in central Holland.

Dune formation near Schoorl created by the wind and known as 'de ijsbeer' – the polar bear, 1930s.

work as a scientist during those years that he gathered the impressions he needed as an artist. In 1992, in the Royal Botanic Garden, Edinburgh, one of the foremost institutions for the study of plant taxonomy in the world, de vries gave a reading-performance, *remember gustav theodor fechner*.

The occasion was his major exhibition at Inverleith House, the gallery in the Botanic Garden; in the performance, English translations of the texts by Fechner were read by Paul Nesbitt, the curator of the exhibition. The readings comprised two passages from *The Soul of Plants* by the nineteenth-century German physicist and naturalist, which were later to be published in a pamphlet by de vries's eschenau summer press. The first, declaimed on a lawn close by a flowerbed in the garden outside the gallery, is a moving description of an apprehension of natural beauty which clearly expresses for de vries something of his own freshness and clarity of vision:

> I remember very well my impression when, after many years of being afflicted with an eye ailment, I could look, without a bandage over my eyes, from my dark room out into the flowering garden. Its breathtaking beauty seemed far beyond any human endeavour; every blossom shone with exceptional clarity, as if illuminating the very light of day. The whole garden seemed to radiate, as if not I but nature had been transformed, and I thought: one has only to open one's eyes for mother nature to appear young and fresh again each day. Yes, it is difficult to believe how renewed and lively nature seems to the one who sees her with fresh sight.

The further significance of the text – emphasised by the scientific setting of its reading – lies in its registering of the passionate aesthetic engagement of a scientist with the objects of his study. It is a kind of allegory of the human encounter with radiant natural objects. In the second passage, read by the artist by the waterlily pool in the Tropical Aquatic House, the scientist gives poetic expression to his identification with the living organism, and to his animistic intuition of the vibrancy of its sense of being:

> Once on a hot summer's day, I stood by a pond and gazed at its waterlilies; their shiny leaves spreading out over the water; their open blossoms drinking up the sunshine. The singular beauty of this flower bathed in sunlight and immersed in water made me wonder if perhaps it could actually feel something of the sun's radiance and the water's liquid coolness. How exceptional this flower would be, I thought, if it could feel such things. And why, I asked myself, should it not? For it seemed to me that nature would not have created such a splendid being, so painstakingly beautiful, for it to be seen only as an inanimate object, idly observed, since thousands of waterlilies fade away without anyone ever having seen them. On the contrary, the thought occurred to me that nature created the waterlily so that it could gather the utmost enjoyment and benefit from bathing in brilliant sunshine and cool water, and feel this down to its innermost part.
>
> Under these circumstances how delightful the flower's existence appears.

In the light of these passages, the title of the performance – *remember gustav theodor fechner* – may be seen to be both commemorative and admonitory: we should honour Fechner for his intellectual and scientific achievements (which included contributions to experimental psychology and aesthetics), and also, in our daily interaction with natural things, bear in mind the exemplary vitality of his empathy with the flowers.

remember gustav theodor fechner 1992
reading-performance at the royal botanic garden, edinburgh, with paul nesbitt

de vries had wanted to leave school early and travel, but his father was opposed to the idea, and in 1949, at eighteen years of age, he enrolled at the National School of Horticulture at Hoorn, where his special area of study was, perhaps not surprisingly, arboriculture. After a year spent as an agricultural labourer in France, he returned to Holland in 1952 to become a research worker at the Institute for Research in Plant Pathology at Wageningen. Later, from 1961 to 1968, he was at the Institute for Applied Biological Research in Nature at Arnhem. de vries was thus actively engaged in scientific research as an applied biologist for over sixteen years.

It was a profession that allowed him ample time for the solitary contemplation of natural processes and for philosophical reflection, and it is not too much to say that during this period the central preoccupations of the mature artist were formulated and clarified. He remembers, while working at Arnhem, carrying Buddhist texts with him to read as he rested for lunch in the branches of a tree, and making clandestine visits during working hours to the nearby Kröller-Müller Museum at Otterlo where he was able to study classic works of constructivism and De Stijl. It was as early as 1953, when he was in his early twenties, that de vries first defined himself as an artist.

At Wageningen he studied the factors in the population growth of rats and mice in order to devise ways of preventing their depredations on agricultural plants; in the pine woods and sandy heathlands around the research station at Arnhem he was studying determinant factors in the population variation, over time and in different locations, of caterpillars of the moth *Bupalus piniaria* (known in England and Scotland as the Bordered White), a pest of the Scots Pine (*Pinus sylvestris*). This latter research also entailed the study, with statistical calculations, of the apparently random distribution and succession of pine seedlings, young and mature trees. A prerequisite for objective research in each of these instances was the creation of random conditions to allow for the isolation, identification and distribution of causal factors.

To generate such conditions in the experimental situation de vries used the random number charts from a standard text, *Statistical Tables for Biological, Agricultural and Medical Research*, by Ronald A. Fisher and Frank Yates (1953). In one experiment, different numbers of caterpillars were isolated with different food plants in jam jars, which were coded with coloured dots and arranged systematically in a grid. There were nine series in all, relating to the variables of food type provided and the number of caterpillars in the jar: looking at these arrays, which represented an objectively random distribution, de vries discerned a pattern, or the possibility of one. He came to see that this arrangement was itself a way of presenting reality, of bringing into material visibility what was, in the scientific discourse prevailing at the Institute, a mathematical (statistical) abstraction. What he was contemplating, however, was not something abstract, it was, in his words, 'reality as a documentation of itself': the distribution of the caterpillars in their marked jars was a model, accurate in its randomness, of their distribution in the pine woods.

These modellings of natural circumstance that formed so significant a part of his scientific research had a profound effect on de vries the artist. In his own words, he became obsessed with 'models of the world' and with visual demonstrations of its reality, a reality which must by definition comprehend order and chaos, regularity and randomness, similarity and difference. It would take him many years of travel, artistic experiment and intellectual work, and successive revelations of different kinds, to come to the extreme simplicity of the marvellous presentations that constitute his major work. But it was in his work at the Institute that he effected a paradigm shift in his approach to the world: from a consideration of models of reality whose origins were conceptual, 'formed through thought' (*wirklichkeitsmodelle von gedachter form*) to reality considered as 'a document of itself' (*wirklichkeit als dokument von sich selber*). Recognising this, de vries was to draw a distinction crucial to the definition of his creative project: his art was not conceptual, it was *concrete*.

Research experiment into the population dynamics of caterpillars in pine woods – the random array of coloured markers identifying the specimens gave de vries the idea of applying programmed randomness in art.
Institute of Applied Biological Research in Nature, Arnhem, The Netherlands, 1962.

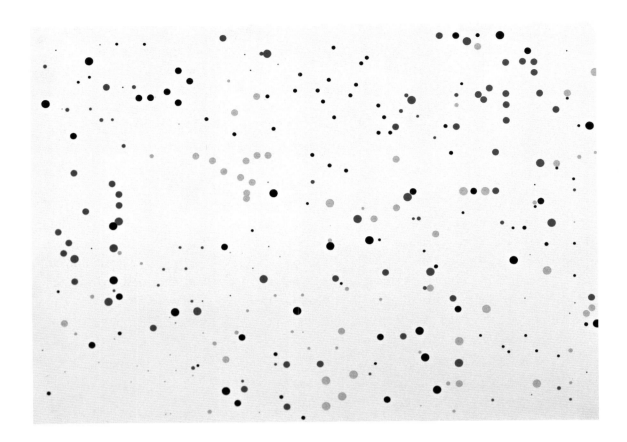

random colour dot fields 1974
ink on paper
73 x 102 cm

random colour dots in a random grid 1975
ink on paper
73 x 102 cm

During this prolonged period of scientific research and philosophical reflection, with its experimental emphasis on the random aspects of natural reality, de vries was becoming increasingly active as an experimental artist whose work was closely related to – and in some ways paralleled – that of his scientific studies. Much of his artistic work derived from his study of randomness and of the workings of apparent chance that determined aspects of the distribution, at any one time, of natural objects, mineral deposits, plant and animal life.

For many years de vries demonstrated these ideas in randomly determined, but objectively structured, non-figurative images and objects. These presentations were variously drawn, painted, printed, collaged, constructed or assembled. His works in this field can now be seen as his principal contribution to formal 'concrete art', as commonly understood since the publication of Theo van Doesburg's *Art Concret* manifesto in 1930, and in Max Bill's similarly succinct and influential *Concrete Art* of 1936, which was revised and widely republished in 1949, not long before de vries set out on his dual career as scientist and artist. Bill had written: 'Abstract ideas that previously existed only in the mind are made visible in a concrete form.'

The 'concrete' works – drawings, paintings and sculptures – of de vries were, though in a sense certainly not anticipated by van Doesburg in the words of his manifesto, 'entirely conceived and formed by the mind before [their] execution', and they received 'nothing from nature's given forms, or from sensuality, or sentimentality'. Extending van Doesburg's strictures by introducing the paradox of a programmed randomness, they were also 'entirely constructed from purely plastic elements', and fulfilled his prescription that [their] construction... as well as [their] elements, must be simple and visually controllable.' In de vries's 'random objectivations' the 'control' was, of course, that provided by his arbitrary resort to statistical tables rather than by any pre-visualisation or by the application of the rules of geometry. Van Doesburg had introduced the idea of a programmed work uninflected by subjective feeling and expression, objectively structured and predictable in its forms. de vries's created a programme for the generation of forms and relations that were perfectly 'objective' and rule-governed but entirely *unpredictable*, and capable of infinite variations. They were perfect diagrammatic analogies of natural diversity.

This phase of de vries's work came to a climax, though not to an end, in the early 1970s, with two significant summarising publications. The first was the handsome *random objectivations* of 1972 (Edizione Amodulo, Milanino sul Garda, Italy), which featured ninety-nine diagrams, a number that almost always implies an infinite number of further possibilities, which were generated, interestingly enough, by procedures using table XXXIII in Fisher and Yates, the first page of which he reproduced as an appendix. In 1973, with the publication by the Waßermann Galerie in Munich of *chance-fields/chance-felder*, came the definitive projection, this time in geometric terms, of a mathematical 'topology of randomness' (*see* pages 34 and 35). From around 1970, de vries, having resigned from his employment in scientific research, was working as an artist in the expanded field beyond the studio, and had begun in earnest the creation of what he has called 'the real works', incorporating natural objects, photographic records of events, actions in time and space at specific sites, and words.

2. concrete concepts: the early work and its philosophy

This is to anticipate: we must now return to the artistic research which de vries began to undertake in the early 'fifties and continued through the 'sixties and into the early 'seventies: a process, as we shall see, of progressive clarification of aesthetic-critical ends and means, and of intellectual development towards the deep imaginative simplicity of his mature philosophy. Through these years de vries was engaged, sometimes at the level of personal experiment, sometimes as part of an organised movement, with various tendencies in the art of the time. Intellectually and spiritually consolidating his own distinctive philosophical position, he was also defining, by both assimilating and rejecting formal possibilities, his creative *modus* as a professional artist.

During this time (as ever after) he was reading widely in eastern philosophy and mystical-spiritual writings. In the original texts of Tao and Zen and contemporary expositions of them by D.T. Suzuki and Alan Watts among others, and in Vedanta and the Upanishads of Hinduism, interpreted by Pratyagatmananda Saraswati and Aldous Huxley, de vries found not only enlightening insights and ideas, but practical ways of being with and knowing nature. What these eastern systems (or non-systems) of thought and practice have in common is a profound respect for the physical processes of nature as revelatory. It was an attitude that confirmed de vries in his instinctive tendency to an intuitive, or ecstatic, apprehension of nature, and to a non-dogmatic belief in the essential unity of existence.

Both Buddhism (in its various manifestations) and the Vedantic school of Hinduism encourage what William Wordsworth memorably described as 'a wise passiveness'. This is an openness-to-experience that eschews the actively strenuous intellectual effort of the analytic rationalist to understand things objectively. Wordsworth, whose poetry may be seen as the fountainhead of a specifically *western*, romantic strain of unitary thought and feeling, expresses beautifully this idea of unaffected apprehension:

> Nor less I deem that there are powers
> Which of themselves our minds impress
> That we can feed this mind of ours
> In a wise passiveness.

There is in this something akin to what John Keats, the principal poet of the next romantic generation, called 'negative capability': 'that is, when a man is capable of being in uncertainties, mysteries, doubts, without any irritable reaching after fact and reason'.

'Be unaffected' advised Lao-Tzu in the classic text of Taoism. The Chinese written character he uses here refers to the untouched background of unbleached silk in a landscape painting. Another translation of the same passage makes explicit the reference to art: 'Exhibit the untouched and cherish the uncarved block'. We might interpret this as 'do not favour the active figure against the passive ground'. In life, as in art, we should feel the presence – the condition of being in the present – which Wordsworth described:

drawing on paper 1955
65 x 50 cm

> A motion and a spirit, that impels
> All thinking things, all objects of all thought,
> and rolls through all things.

In a note written in December 1970 de vries remarked: 'what the artist sees – observes – belongs just as much to his concept as what he makes.' The artist, who is simply a representative human being, is to be regarded as part of nature, indistinguishable from it. Seeing is being, a creative interaction with the world: to see is, in itself, to create, to be an artist, *to be.*

It should not be surprising that a young artist starting out in the early 1950s, unburdened by the dubious benefits of an academic art training, should first set out to practice what many of the most talented contemporary artists and critics thought to be the most exciting and radical art making of the time. For the young de vries, the expressive informal abstraction of *tachisme* (characterised by the haphazard distribution of dabs, blobs and strokes of colour) offered possibilities of a non-figurative mode that was not a style but a way of working. It allowed him personal freedom from the constraints of the essentially academic, cubist-inspired abstract styles that first emanated from post-war Paris and were influential all over Europe. These might be characterised as either reductively formalist or decoratively abstract; in either case an art of intention and design. *Tachisme* or *art autre* or *art informel*, on the other hand, was dedicated to the chance discovery of the automatic image. It also encouraged the idea of the

d'une forêt brulée/from a burned forest 1991
charcoal from the forest of Mas Boeuf, Bras (Var)
260 x 330 x 170 cm

*pierres trouvées à côté du chemin de saint-vallier
de thiey à la chapelle de saint jean/stones found
on the edge of the road leading to saint-vallier de
thiey near la chapelle de saint jean* 1991
189 x 294 cm

espace de l'art concret, mouans-sartoux, france

brushstroke as expressive of unconscious impulses beyond the reach of logical processes and mere technical artifice.

It would have appealed to the youthful artist experiencing his first encounters with the Tao and Zen that the unpremeditated paint stroke (the basic unit of *tachisme*) or the gestural mark or incision could be thought of as having something of the truthful spontaneity inscribed in the calligraphic or expressive stroke of Japanese and Chinese ink-brush painting. Zen painting was in itself conceived as a work of nature mediated through the artist whose patient preparation was simply that of awareness and readiness. 'The constructive powers of the human mind', wrote Alan Watts, the most widely read western advocate of Zen, 'are no more artificial than the formative processes of plants or bees, so that from the standpoint of Zen it is no contradiction to say that artistic technique is discipline in spontaneity and spontaneity in discipline. [...] when you paint it is the brush, ink, and paper which determine the result as much as your own hand.'

It follows from this that the disciplined and watchful eye may find already existing objects and events as revelatory as any created by the artist. For such objects are not made by artistic will and intention but by the hazards of chance and change, and the artistic act of creation consists in their discovery. Between 1956 and 1959 de vries 'created' a number of *collages trouvés* whose beauty increases with the effects of time as it modifies them and distances them from their source. They are to be distinguished from the cubist and the surrealist forms of classical modernist collage, both of which were constrained by what might be described as syntactic or logical structures. In both those forms of collage, new meaning is generated by adding one thing to another to produce an implicit connection. In cubist collage this was a bringing together of familiar objects (represented by drawing or paint, or by fragments of 'reality' – wallpaper, veneer, newspaper, etc.) which had multiple implications, to do with perception, art and life. In surrealist collage (and montage) it was the juxtaposition of objects and images from categorically different fields of meaning that created a super-reality and engendered the appropriate shock. Both types of collage depended on a logic of connection/disconnection.

As an artist de vries was interested in neither procedure. He was, however, an admirer of the *merz* works of Kurt Schwitters, the first collages that lacked those formal, or 'logical', structures. Many (but by no means all) of Schwitters's collages incorporated items of cultural detritus – bus tickets, bits of newspaper, used postal stamps, rags, etc.- into arbitrary structures, whose coherence is to be discovered after the act of creation: they have a kind of inevitable objectness. The a-logical nature of Schwitterian collage appealed to de vries, who could see that the operations of chance – in both the finding of random materials and in the somewhat random processes of his gluing them together – had resulted in an object that had an irrefutable reality in the world. What made the object what it was could only be described retrospectively, in relation to the actuality of the object itself.

de vries was aware, too, of the related Duchampian concept of the readymade: that an object, arbitrarily removed from the field of its intended utility and meaning and placed deliberately in the context of art, might acquire the new status of *art-object*, and be invested with a multiplicity of potential meanings. The artistic act consists in the choice of the object, its naming and designation. Thus the notorious urinal is transfigured: perfectly white, empty of meaning, it becomes, in Suzuki's (perfectly apt) phrase, 'a fountain of infinite possibilities'. Marcel Duchamp famously denied any aesthetic intent in his choice, indeed he selected his readymade objects with a vaunted 'visual indifference', a state which might be compared to the 'emptiness of mind' required by the Zen swordsman or archer. At the moment of effective action the artist is untrammelled by inhibiting consciousness. In his selection of natural objects for presentation de vries abides by this approach: how could one leaf of a particular kind, or one plant of a species, or one clump of turf be 'more beautiful' than another? The effect of both Duchamp's and de vries's 'indifference' is, of course, to direct our attention to the potential beauty of *any* object or action.

de vries at this period created a number of 'found works', each with its own particular interest. In *collage trouvé* (1959), for instance, he preserved a discoloured filter paper from a laboratory experiment, containing traces of plant extract: seen against a dark background this abject object assumes the grandeur of a cosmic image, its stains and tears like the dark marks on the surface of the moon. A second *collage trouvé* of 1959 which includes leaves and foil anticipates (unconsciously) the many later works de vries created by the laying down and framed preservation of a bed of leaves found on the forest floor, or of bits of discarded 'rubbish' found in wild places.

The signature piece of this series is *what is rubbish?* (1956), which asks directly the question they all pose implicitly. A tattered *collage trouvé* of layered sheets torn from a much fly-posted wall, it is a fragment of the urban world redeemed by art. Rubbish has been defined as 'displaced matter': like the designation 'weed' it is not a description of a thing so much as an expression of an attitude towards it ('a weed is a plant growing in the wrong place'). Change the context, change the meaning. The question posed by *what is rubbish?* is both

Above:
collage trouvé 1956
fragment of posters taken from a wall in Paris
49.8 x 20.5 cm

Opposite, top left:
what is rubbish? – collage trouvé 1956
fragment from a wall of posters
15 x 12 cm

Opposite, below:
collage trouvé 1959
filter paper with plant remains
35 x 20.7 cm

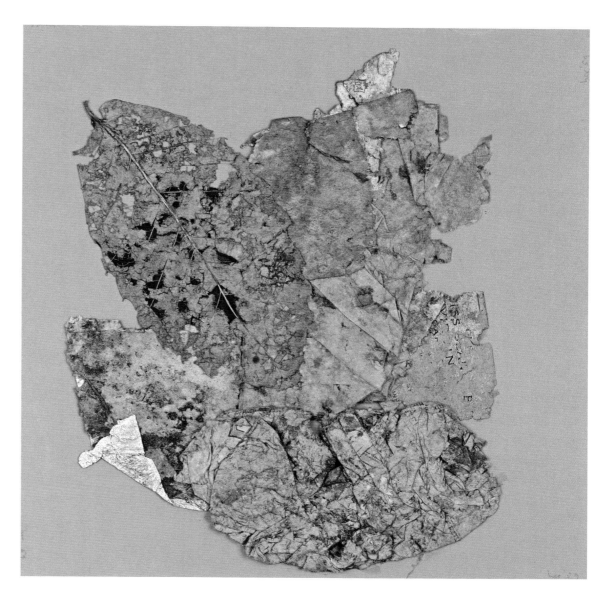

Right:
collage trouvé 1959
leaves, paper and silver foil
24.8 x 24.8 cm

direct and rhetorical, both a general question and a challenge specific to the work itself. It recalls, in reverse, the essential Duchampian question, 'what is art?'

We may be tempted here to think, briefly, of Mimmo Rotella's torn-poster works of the same period (of which de vries, as it happens, was unaware), but there is a significant difference: whereas Rotella's *décollages* sought to look like 'art', de vries's *collage trouvé* is happy to come into its own, and look like nothing but itself. In Rotella's work, the referential elements – remnant images and names from the popular culture advertised and promoted by the posters – have a social and political poignancy intensified by their defacement and fragmentation. In *what is rubbish?* the object is itself the subject of the work: it is itself a trace of the transformations its material elements have undergone. It has reverted thereby from the world of social signifying to the indifferent materiality of the processes by which all things, of whatever worth and grade, are 'degraded' to 'rubbish' in the cycle of nature.

A great deal of de vries's earliest work – each painting, brush drawing, assemblage or ready-made collage – is philosophically exemplary in this way. Each is scrupulously precise in its representation of a particular creative position *vis-à-vis* media, materials and expression. It is as if de vries found it necessary to adopt a succession of conceptual-creative modes, to work through them for himself, to enter into a way of thinking-through-material that would enable him to find himself as an artist. de vries thus became an artist by *being* one. The intuitive procedures of action or inaction by which an abstract thought discovers its concrete expression in direct physical presentations or simple indications (what in Zen is called 'direct pointing') became habitual to de vries's creative practice. By such means, he realised, the abstract is displaced, or abrogated, by the concrete. This explains the poetic or gnomic nature of de vries's statements about art and nature, his insistence that those words are part of his work as an artist, and that his theory is not separable from his practice, nor his art from his life.

Such an insistence does not register a dismissal by de vries of analytic or theoretical discourse so much as a Wittgensteinian awareness of its limitations. What gives his philosophical position its authority is precisely, and perhaps paradoxically, his history as an experimental applied scientist. de vries declared the inner connection-contradiction of his art to his scientific work in a work of 1960, *manifest of castrated reality*. This took the form of a physical action performed on a manifestation of analytic activity. de vries took a paper published by the journal *Mammalia* in which he had written up his research into the distribution of small mammals, removed its covers, turned them inside out and refastened them with the new title typed on what had been the blank *verso*.

de vries was perfectly aware of the utility of research of the kind contained in the journal and was to continue to make his living from such work for several more years. But he knew that its meticulous attention to purely statistical minutiae, its synthesising of analytic evidence, were aspects of a larger process of generalisation and theorising. In distancing the researcher from the living reality of the creatures in the field, it denatured concrete actualities, with all their complexities of action and reaction, transmission and feedback, into purely abstract data. Mice and rats breathe, feed and breed, and they multiply at different rates in different places and circumstances; but each creature is subtly distinct from all others of the same species. Statistics translate this living reality of difference to reductive mathematical equivalence. This was the sterile 'reality' manifested by the statistical tables and the research conclusions of the academic paper.

The *manifest of castrated reality* (as its title suggests) is a making plain, a demonstration, rather than an art-work: it is gestural rather than aesthetic. In the same year, 1960, de vries made another book-work, *wit is overdaad/white is superabundance*, closely related, by way of contrast, to *manifest*. Unlike the re-packaged scientific journal, which was replete with printed matter – figures, maps, analysis, diagrams, data, information – this publication was, apart from a simple text on the first page (to be exact, the cover *verso*) absolutely empty. The text is as follows:

> wit / wit is overdaad / blanc est superabondance / white is superabundance /
> weiss ist übermässig / wit / wit / wit is overdaad

In western culture, the book, comprising a sequence of printed pages, is still a primary mode of intellectual and cultural transmission. A white page is a *tabula rasa*, a nothingness, a negation of the page inscribed with matter; a book of white pages is a negation of the book as a container of information of whatever kind. Its silent presentation of nothing (but its own whiteness, which is of course *something*) is in direct contrast to the publication of a discursive synthesis of facts and ideas into useful information: it is an abrogation of the ego of analytic intelligence. It is an object without utility, but not without purpose: its purpose is, in fact, to raise doubt about purposes, and questions about utility. It signifies no contradiction that de vries has an impressive library of his own creating, and that the book as information-carrier featured as a central element in a major work, *natural relations* (1989). For what is contained in the encyclo-paedic *natural relations* (the book) is implicit in the emptiness of *white is superabundance*.

The whiteness of the book's pages is an image of the silence out of which sound – that of music or of speech – may emerge but without which they could not exist: it is an image of origins. Looked at in the light of Zen, *white is superabundance* presents images of the emptiness which, according to Suzuki, 'is in truth no less than the concreteness of reality itself': 'emptiness is the fountain of infinite possibilities.' The Tao 'emptiness of mind' is the precondition of *satori* – the state of enlightenment. In w*hite is superabundance*, whiteness is the image of potential, an image of the void from which all things, with all their complexities of structure and relation, emanate. White is without expression, it is like a mirror into which you may look and see nothing reflected. The publication of *wit is overdaad* and the repeated statement it contained was not a repudiation of science-as-knowledge; it was a direct riposte (in the robust and homely tradition of Zen teaching) to the arrogance of the western scientific mind.

In 1959 de vries made his first white painting. But as early as 1956 he had begun to make white-on-white paper collages, and we have seen how, in 1960, in the manifesto publication of *white is superabundance*, by way of its antithetical relation to the discursive matter of the printed page, he had arrived at the definitive presentation of whiteness as a *tabula rasa*, an image of emptiness. For de vries the blankness of the white and monochrome paintings, however, is linked in particular to his growing interest at the time in the dialectics of Mahayana Buddhism. There he found the dynamic opposition of *nirvana/samsara* in which the emptiness, or the void, of liberation from 'the round of being', is set against the world of forms, of living and dying, and the one is discovered to comprehend the other: *nirvana* is *samsara*. This relates closely to the Mahayana formulation: 'Form is not different from emptiness; emptiness is not different from form. Form is precisely emptiness; emptiness is precisely form.'

monochrome painting 1958
emulsion paint on hardboard
96 x 104.5 cm

Looking at de vries's first monochrome paintings, which he had meant to signify nothing, to be devoid of intention and expression, and therefore of meaning, he realised they were not void, but objects in the world of forms, not empty but *white*, or *grey* or *black.* In those in which there was some agitation of surface, there were further complications, even the suggestions of the psychological aspects of making and authorship, from which he had tried to free himself as an artist. They enacted the Mahayana opposition in that they were, in the Upanishadic phrase, *neti, neti*: 'not this, not that'. They possessed the quality of *tathata*, which may be translated as 'suchness' or 'thusness', or, as de vries puts it, 'just this'. This directness of visual apprehension, in which the act of indication replaces verbalisation, is, as Alan Watts describes it, '[of] the world *just* as it is, unscreened and undivided by the symbols and definitions of thought. It points to the concrete and actual as distinct from the abstract and conceptual.' Paintings of nothing, the monochromes were neither 'abstract' nor 'conceptual' art; they were things, concrete and actual.

The teachings of Zen, Vedanta and Mahayana – patterns of insights and actions that are neither intellectual nor intuitive, neither conceptual nor affective – went deep into the living practice of de vries, and shaped a central desideratum of his work: that art as such is neither here nor there, and is inseparable from life, being but an aspect (as science is another) of the means by which reality is revealed to the seeker. This in no way, he considered, invalidates the findings of artists, the best of whom are among the most assiduous researchers. In the years around the turn of the decade – 1960 – de vries reached a point of understanding that resulted from the making of the white and monochrome paintings: they had effectively set him free from common assumptions about the importance of the artist as the specially gifted, specially trained author of his works.

In the journal *Art International* in early 1959, Pierre Restany had written of the artist Jean Fautrier in terms that throw some light on what was seen by a major critic as the potential significance of *art informel*. It gives a clue to the radical nature of de vries's own rejection of painting, including paintings as extreme as his own monochromes. Restany's words reflect also something of the terms within which new programmes and new procedures were being sought for art, expressing ideas which de vries would have found deeply interesting: 'In creating his synthetic spatiality Fautrier has annihilated the classic notion of Form... Matter, line, colour operate on an equal footing. *No hierarchy of values, no dominant preference at the base of this original spatiality...* [my emphasis] The notion of Form always appears as a product of a system radically contrary to this... Form is born precisely from the strict dependence of pictorial means, from the superiority of line over colour, from the total submission of the paint substance to the graphic contour.' Restany saw the elimination of form and 'the liberation of colour, of matter and of line' as an intermediate step towards a greater artistic expression beyond the traditions of figure and ground. de vries saw *art informel* as the last step towards the final liberation of art from the limitations of psychological and emotional personal expression.

Such thoroughgoing radicalism, usually seen as heralding the final end of art as such, had its provenance in certain aspects of high modernism. For Dutch artists in the middle years of the twentieth century, above all, the luminously idealist theory and practice of Piet Mondrian was an inescapable presence in this respect. For Mondrian, whose psychology and ideas derive essentially from the Calvinist predisposition to the ordering and the control of external nature, art was a philosophical and spiritual activity central to the higher development of human nature. He saw an abstract plastic art (and the modernist architectural environment of the future) as the means to escape from the tragic contingency of nature, from a state of disharmony to a condition of spiritual and psychic equilibrium beyond art.

In Mondrian's seminal tract, *Natural Reality and Abstract Reality An Essay in Trialogue Form* (1920), the conversation between three friends takes place, significantly, while they are 'strolling from the country to the city'. Speaking of 'the capricious in nature', the 'naturalistic painter' exclaims: 'The fantastic is beautiful!' 'Beautiful but tragic', replies the 'abstract-real' painter (Mondrian himself); 'if you follow nature you will only in small measures abolish the tragic in your art. Naturalistic painting can make us *feel* the harmony that transcends the tragic, but it does not express equilibrated [and purely abstract] *relationships* exclusively.' Finally, he states the logical conclusion: as 'the tragic, the lyric, and the sentimental' is left behind 'the individual [matures] into the universal: the new man can live only in the sphere of the universal... The new era is a higher stage of the one, single life force... Man grows beyond nature...'

In his first editorial for the new *revue nul=0*, which he founded in Amsterdam with Henk Peeters and Armando, de vries gives expression to ideas that are surprising in their Mondrian-like absolutism, especially in the light of his subsequent thinking and practice, and its profound opposition to Mondrian's elevation of the abstract over the concrete, the ideal over the material. The editorial is a limpid statement of the position de vries had arrived at by 1961, and marks a crucial moment in his career. It articulates emphatically his repudiation of the singularity of personal expression in art. True to its intention (and its historical provenance) it is more of a philosophical declaration than a statement of merely artistic aims:

> the change which began in the informal works has had its outcome in a new concept. objective, namely, personal feelings are eliminated [from the work] as far as is possible. the normative is no part of the outcome. stupidity: art no longer requires expression through the operation of skilled technique or the working of the intellect because now it can be made by anyone. it can be said that at this point art ceases to be.
>
> expression is no longer what is visible. it is internalised and hermetically sealed.
>
> zero: everything is unity, everything happens at once. there are no contraries.
> zero is not a starting point, it is a plane of existence.

de vries's 'stupidity' in this passage relates to the Zen idea of the *no-mind*: the unconscious in its most receptive state, which can respond to and encompass consciousness as a dynamic component of its own unknowing and yet be unmoved by the inhibiting exercise of the ego. It is best expressed in a famous letter by Takuan, the great Zen master, on the art of swordsmanship. de vries appended a free translation of a fragment of this text to his editorial statement. Here it is in the translation of Suzuki (it is an article of Mahayana Buddhism that everyone is a potential buddha):

> [Prajna is possessed by all Buddhas and also by all sentient beings. It is transcendental wisdom flowing through the relativity of things] and it remains immovable, though this does not mean the immovability of such objects as a piece of rock or wood. It is the mind itself endowed with infinite [mobility]: it moves forward and backward, to the left and to the right, to every one of the ten quarters, and knows no hindrances in any direction. Prajna unmovable is this mind capable of infinite movements. [When the highest stage is reached in studying Buddhism] a man turns into a kind of simpleton who knows nothing of Buddha, nothing of his teaching, and is devoid of all learning or scholarly acquisitions... intellectual calculations are lost sight of and a state of no-mind-ness (*mushin*) or of no-thought-ness prevails.

For de vries this is at once an expansion of the *zero* concept – 'everything is unity, everything happens at once. there are no oppositions. zero ... is a plane of existence' – and a clear indication

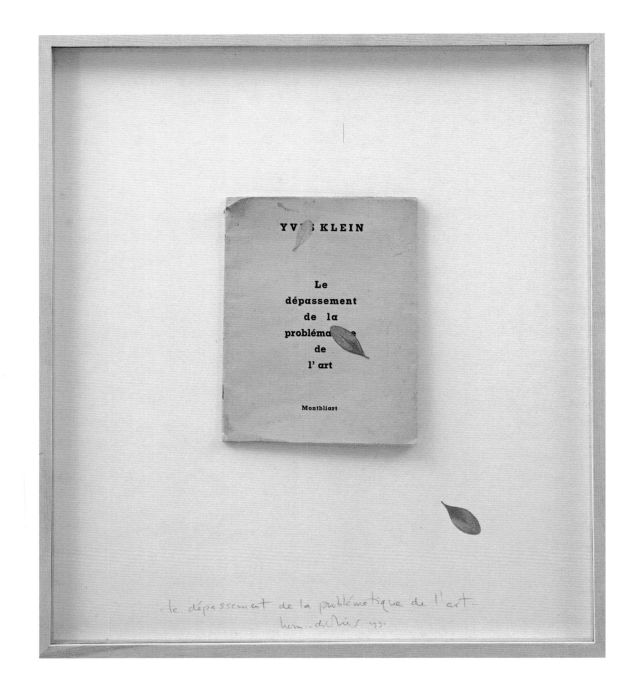

le dépassement de la problématique de l'art/beyond the problematic of art 1990
56 x 50 cm

of an important source of his thinking. His participation in the Amsterdam-based '0 (zero or nul)' movement at this time was indicative of other important sources, and also of his active consciousness of a flow of ideas and practices in the art of that historical moment that were profoundly connected to his own. de vries was well aware that the Dutch group's title corresponded closely to that of the Düsseldorf 'ZERO' group, whose leading member, Günther Uecker, was deeply concerned with whiteness, light and immateriality as components of art. (de vries was later to exhibit with 'ZERO'.)

It was de vries himself who provided the title for the magazine: *revue nul=0.* It was not the first time in European art that the idea of zero as 'a plane of existence', a space that goes in every direction, had been invoked by artists seeking a new beginning, a clearing away of 'expressive' bourgeois aesthetics. Kasimir Malevich had first revealed his 'Suprematist' paintings, including the astonishing monochrome *Black Square,* to the world at the famous *'Last Exhibition of Futurist Pictures' 0.10 (Zero.Ten)* in St Petersburg in 1915. In the manifesto to accompany *0.10* Malevich had written: 'I have transformed myself into the zero of form and fished myself out of the rubbishy slough of Academic art. I have destroyed the circle of the horizon and escaped from the circle of objects, the horizon ring that has imprisoned the artist and the forms of nature. The square is not a subconscious form. It is the creation of intuitive reason.'

The closeness of this to aspects of the texts of both Takuan and de vries requires no emphasis. In December 1957, amid great excitement among artists and curators, more than a dozen of the so-called 'Berlin' paintings by Malevich – the largest group of Suprematist works seen in the West since the Berlin exhibition of 1927 from which they had been preserved – went on display at the Stedelijk Museum in Amsterdam. Among them were, significantly, several of the Russian master's late Suprematist paintings, including at least three of the 'white on white' works, in which painted forms appear to dematerialise into empty space. This was a body of work no artist in Amsterdam could avoid or ignore. At this potent moment in European post-war artistic history, Malevich joined Mondrian as a seminal presence in Dutch art.

A powerful influence on the Düsseldorf 'ZERO' group was Yves Klein (Uecker's brother-in-law) whose monochrome canvases had first been seen in Paris in 1956 and Italy and Germany in 1957, and it was during this time that Klein's ideas, profound, mischievous and mystical, had wide currency among the European avant garde. Piero Manzoni, whom de vries met in Amsterdam in 1962, had been closely associated with Klein since the latter's Milan *exposition* in 1957. Klein had studied judo in Japan, and was deeply aware of its base in Zen thought and practice. Manzoni, who showed a number of his monochrome *Achromes* with '0 (zero or nul)' at the Stedelijk in March 1962, had written in 1960: 'Infinity is rigorously monochrome, or, better still, it has no colour [...] In total space form, colour and dimensions have no meaning... pure material becomes pure energy. The obstacles of space and slavery to subjective weaknesses are annihilated: all the problems of art criticism are overcome.' Here too, then, was another flow of thought and connections of deep significance to de vries as he first placed himself at the centre of 0 (nul) group and then, gradually, established himself as independent of all art 'movements'. He was making himself independent, especially, of the idea of 'art' as psychologically, intellectually or emotively expressive, personal and special. Art, he had come to realise, is a mode of *being*.

Klein's 1959 book of essays *Le Dépassement de la problématique de l'art* [Beyond the Problematic of Art] contains a key text concerning the abnegation of the ego in the true pursuit of art-as-being: 'I propose [that artists] go beyond art itself and work individually for the return to real life, where thinking man is no longer the centre of the universe but the universe is the centre of man [...] We will know the force of attraction toward the higher realms, towards space, toward nowhere and everywhere both at once.' In his 1990 work, also ironically entitled *le dépassement de la problématique de l'art*, de vries framed his own copy of Klein's book on which he had allowed three leaves to fall from a plant on his desk, fixing them where they landed. In Japanese and Chinese art the image of a fall of leaves is elegiac, a sign of time passing, and thereby of the vanity of human wishes: for all the ebullient and beautiful rhetoric of Klein, it is nature itself which goes beyond 'the problematic of art', beyond art itself, and is itself at the periphery and the centre of things, beyond thought and outside action.

3. random objectivations and other works from 1960 to 1975

In the publication *random objectivations* (1972), de vries helpfully reproduced one of the pages (119) in Fisher and Yates's *Statistical Tables for Biological, Agricultural and Medical Research* that he had used as the basis for the many works he created from the procedure of plotting random points on a given plane, each of which bears the generic title. The procedure itself he had described in detail in an article in the second issue of *revue nul=0* in April 1963, which also gives a summary of the various works that de vries had undertaken in the previous four years in which he had used random methods of composition. It is worth quoting the article in full:

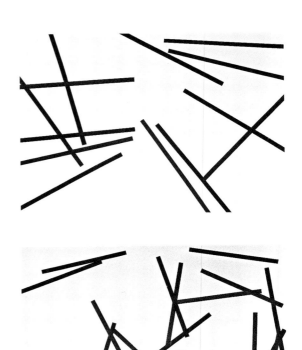

random objectivations 1966
collage
each 50 x 70 cm

> objectivation is important as a part of my occupation with 'visual information'. 'visual information' is here used in the sense of hans sleutelaar (3) who thought the term more appropriate to the new conception than the term 'art'. as an extreme consequence of objectivation i tried to eliminate the personal – not the human! – element in my compositions by way of the random method.
>
> the word random here implies the purely haphazard treatment of the experimental material. therefore it is desirable to ensure that the events in question are sufficiently random by using some special technique (1).
>
> the true meaning of randomness has profound philosophical aspects, but there is no reason to go into these here.
>
> various sources of random numbers are available, but the most convenient is table XXXIII in fisher and yates (2). the first six pages of the table contain 15.000 numbers arranged in pairs. these numbers have been generated so as to be an effectively random or haphazard series of digits. without embarking on any detailed logical analysis, we can loosely define what we mean by "random" in this context as follows. each of the digits 0, 1, 2, ... 8, 9 ought to appear in a long series with approximately equal frequencies; so would all possible pairs 00, 01, 02, ... 99, and all possible triplets, etc. in fact any specific pattern of digits ought to appear with approximately its calculable chance of occurrence. the tables have been tested to make sure they have these properties.
>
> carrying out my compositions called 'random objectivations', i started reading the numbers from a haphazardly chosen point of the table, and gave a 'value' to each digit. value here means: a colour, gluing a square or leaving it out, etc. in this way i obtained results which were acceptable for the spectator and gave the impression that they were intended as art. i would like to point out that all compositions are of equal quality if they are sufficiently large i.e. made with more than 20 or 30 numbers.
>
> the 'random objectivations' I started in 1962. other things i am doing are white collages (first in 1958, continued in 1960); white paintings (since 1959); reflecting objects and surfaces, made with glass granules (since 1960); objects in the forms of blocks and columns, mostly of wood painted white; and also of such materials as glass and steel (since 1960); white books (1961 and 1962). objectivations is an important element common to all these activities. the choice of the depersonalised act is as important as the creative act itself.
>
> notes:
> (1) n.t.j.bailey – 1959 – statistical methods in biology.
> (2) r.a.fisher and f.yates – 1953 – statistical tables for biological, agricultural and medical research
> (3) hans sleutalaar – 1962 – at the vernissage of the exhibition 'anno 62', art centre 'het venster' rotterdam.

In writing of 'visual information', de vries was resorting to a term that emphasised the objective nature of the works generated by the random procedures he had employed. By 'objective' here, I mean both the negative quality of what might be called 'inexpressiveness', and the

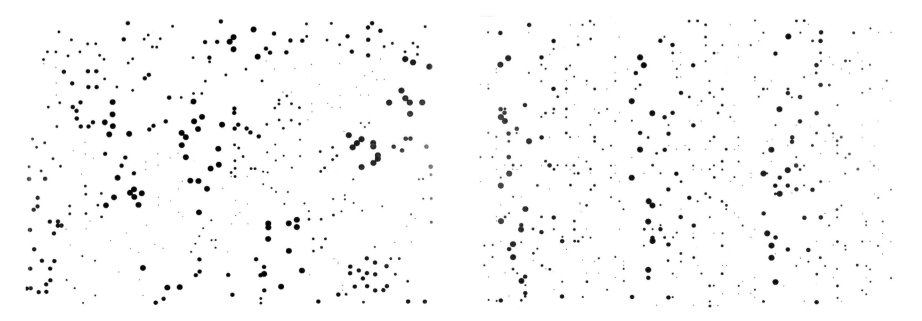

random objectivation 1972
drawing, ink on paper
73 x 102 cm

Below
random objectivations both 1973
drawings, ink on paper
both 73 x 102 cm

positive quality of 'suchness' – of their being objectively what they are and nothing else, and referring to nothing else. These works may be regarded as works of art for they are indeed endlessly various and fascinating, and elegant in the sense attached to that term by mathematicians describing a perfectly economical and balanced equation. They could not be but as they are, and, if we choose to do so, we may find their address to the mind abstractly beautiful.

We may, fortuitously, find them beautiful in other affective ways, of course: the configuration of elements across a plane may resemble a constellation of stars, or a scatter of dandelion seeds, or we may find visually exciting the play of unpredictable random black or colour points across the perfect order of an invisible grid. Every one of these random objectivations was made by using an arbitrarily determined procedure and resort to the random

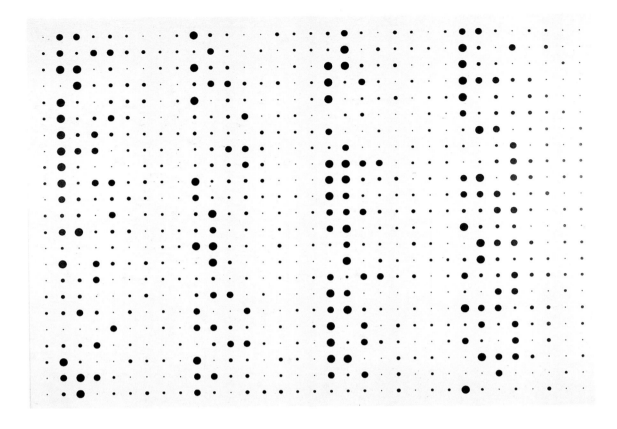

random dot grid field 1973
drawing, ink on paper
73 x 102 cm

tables in Fisher and Yates. The *random dots in space* works of the early 1970s may thus look at first glance like a spatter of inkspots, but each dot (in reality a disc of black ink whose size is exactly determined by stencil) is carefully plotted on a series of random crossing points, set against the co-ordinates of the sheet edges, in what de vries calls 'an irregular weaving'. That a real and random spatter of blots might look like this, is, in the final order of things, no coincidence at all, any more than that the stars in the universe are where they are (or were) merely by cosmic accident.

> ... i obtained results which were acceptable to the spectator and gave the impression that they were intended as art.' They may give that impression, but they carried no such intention, of course: in fact, they were as devoid of the normal intentionality of art as their making was an avoidance of the technical skills that are traditionally considered to be central to artistic creation, the characteristically personal deployment of which is the signature of "style". The "visual information" they contained was nothing more nor less than the purely objective facts that were the unpredictable outcome of the random method. The human element which de vries admitted to be present was that of the choice of method, and of the materials.

The human element was present, in fact, above all in the philosophical position implicit in the various art actions and their diverse outcomes, and this was the creative energy that gave them meaning and interest. 'the true meaning of randomness has profound philosophical aspects, but there is no reason to go into these here.' 'No reason', because it is in the nature of art that it is not discursive, and it is in the nature of de vries's philosophy that it is not susceptible to analytical disquisition. It depends, rather, upon demonstration and indication: the revelation of the true relations of things in reality (relations often unseen, unsuspected and unexpected) by direct pointing, by the array, by the repositioning of found objects and by other demonstrative procedures. Each of the potentially infinite number of *random objectivations* is at once specific to its constraints and a demonstration of the principle of randomness. For

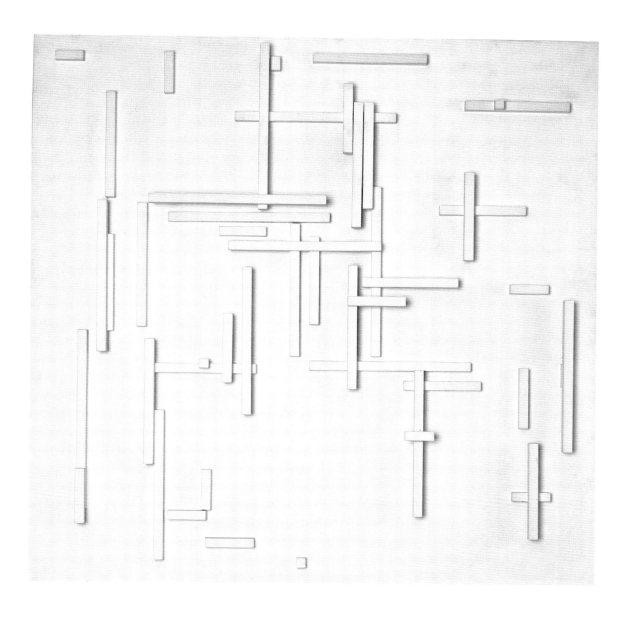

random objectivation 1965
120 x 120 cm
wooden sticks, wooden board, white paint

de vries, its value as a philosophical proposition lies both in its specific realisation and in its possibilities of generic multiplicity.

The 'profound philosophical aspects' which de vries declined to explain in his text in *revue nul=0* were succinctly outlined by the Danish art historian Troels Andersen in a publication, *panel 13 information*, produced in Copenhagen to accompany de vries's exhibition there in early 1969. Andersen, who in the previous year had edited a comprehensive collection of Malevich's writings, and in 1970 was to publish, in Amsterdam, the definitive *catalogue raisonné* of Malevich's Berlin exhibition, including those paintings in the Stedelijk, was critically well-equipped to comment on the philosophical content of de vries's work of the previous ten years. He was steeped in Malevichian thought, at the centre of which was a concept profoundly relevant to a consideration of de vries's project: that the work of art is a visible and material manifestation of invisible energies, physical, metaphysical and spiritual. Adopting the convention then common (among concrete poets and artists) of using no capital letters, Andersen wrote:

> the use of random structures reveals a precise concept of the visual world and of visual experience. any sensory experience is determined by relations between factors; for communication these factors can be substituted by any symbols. the

33

simplest visual symbols are black and white, line and square, representing different qualities, extensions, etc. the visual experience can be rendered as soon as relations between two or more factors are indicated. The interrelations between the factors will, if their number is larger than a handful, be so complex that no choice can be made, no preference is possible a priori. *By accepting this fact one is led to accept that a random distribution of the given factors can be as valid as any intuitive or logical method. it includes all possibilities of distribution created by such methods and is therefore of a more general order* (not necessarily also a higher order). simultaneously, in the visual arts, work has been carried out on two levels. the work of art has been exposed to a confrontation with the objective world on the level of material construction, and the principles according to which visual experiences are formalised have been brought into correspondence with the philosophical interpretation of the objective world. the former process is illustrated in the objets trouvés and counter-reliefs, the second in the non-objective works corresponding to axiomatic geometry in their attempt to clarify our mode of thought and insight. the random structures [de vries's 'objectivations'] are a consequence of the latter concept and carry it on to a point where it is possible that it will again be able to infiltrate our thinking on other levels. *defining the totality of an artefact as consisting of certain [given] relations and accepting your ignorance of the majority [of those that obtain] you come closer to reality.* [my emphases]

Andersen, in what is a densely compressed text, makes clear that what he values in de vries's work is its rigorous demonstration that the world as perceived – the phenomenal world in all its manifestations – is subject to the universal law of randomness; that what may seem 'natural' or 'logical' is subsumed under a condition of actuality that is beyond the order we may be trying, intellectually, to impose. What is controlled by any ordering of our own invention is what comes into our logical understanding or what offers evidence to our senses; what remains outside our rationally comprehended 'knowledge' or is beyond our senses is nevertheless a bigger part of reality with a coherence that we obviously cannot comprehend. In this, Andersen puts his finger on a central insight of de vries's, and one which is close to that expressed in the final proposition of Wittgenstein's *Tractatus* – 'Whereof one cannot speak, thereof one must be silent' – which may refer to both the physical facts of the world and to metaphysical realities beyond ordinary comprehension.

'Being silent' – in de vries's case, refusing to elaborate a philosophical position in critically rationalist, discursive terms – should not be taken to intimate that he (any more than Wittgenstein) considers that certain aspects of 'reality' are beyond all demonstration; indeed (and this is true of de vries's work as a whole and not simply of the *random objectivations*) every work is just such a demonstration. Each one of the *random objectivations* is, precisely, giving an instance of the reality that lies behind it; it is a demonstrative *illustration* (a means to throwing light on something): taking many together (and bearing in mind that the series is potentially infinite) we are presented with a glimpse of the beauty that informs things and determines their infinite diversity. You, the spectator, are presented with *figures* – diagrammatic geometric images – as immediate material actualisations of dynamic energy and as images of an order the majority of whose determinant relations you do not know: thus, 'you come closer to reality.' As de vries was to write in 1976, in a text begun in Frankfurt and completed in Mumbai:

true philosophy is immediate actual.
so, any communication of it can go from and to the actuality of it, which is not symbols. so, liberated of thinking with symbols, philosophy is life and actuality.

5 chances out of a range of
442.032.795.979.776
(with the use of a cm structure and 3 elements)

5 chancen aus einem bereich von
442.032.795.979.776
(mit dem gebrauch einer cm struktur und 3 elementen)

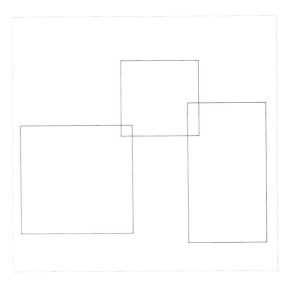

Pages from the book *chance-fields/chance-felder, an essay on the topology of randomness* 1973

5 chances out of a range of
6.579.329.566.975.974.127.670.720.595.328.889.430.137.295.077.376
(with the use of a cm. structure and 10 elements)

5 chancen aus einem bereich von
6.579.329.566.975.974.127.670.720.595.328.889.430.137.295.077.376
(mit dem gebrauch einer cm struktur und 10 elementen)

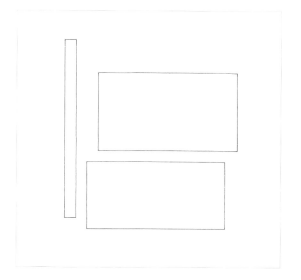

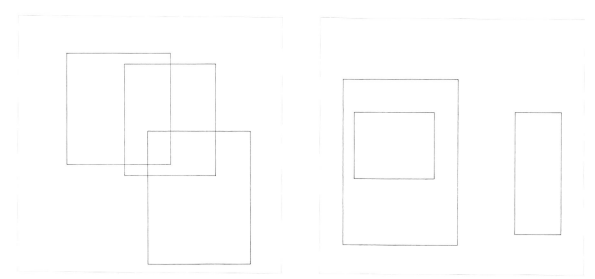

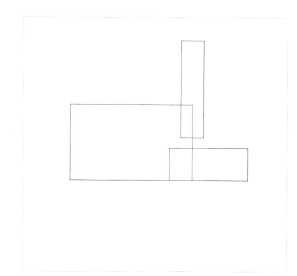

true art is immediate actual. so, any communication of it can go from and to the actuality of it, which is not symbols. so, liberated of thinking with symbols, art is life and actuality.

true actuality is immediate actual. so, any communication of it can go from and to the actuality of it, which is not symbols. so, liberated of thinking with symbols, actuality is life and actuality.

By adopting random procedures de vries demonstrates that out of randomness comes a multitude of possible immediate actualities, each of which is also an intimation of an order: the *random objectivations* are figures that, for Andersen, 'correspond' to those of 'axiomatic geometry', and that will 'clarify our mode of thought and insight'. The idea implied here of randomness as constituting in itself an order of complexity is neatly summarised by the mathematician, A.M. Born, as quoted by de vries in a text of 1968 (*fragmentarische argumente*): 'in his long pursuit of order in nature, the scientist has turned a corner. he is now after order and disorder without prejudice, having discovered that complexity usually involves both.' de vries the artist-poet is truly Wallace Stevens's 'connoisseur of chaos', who proposes:

A. A violent order is disorder; and
B. A great disorder is an order. These
Two things are one. (Pages of illustrations.)

The introductory note to de vries's *chance-fields/chance felder, an essay on the topology of randomness* (1973), lightly hints at its essentially philosophical purpose:

look back, any place, any time, to actuality, when you have read chance-fields.

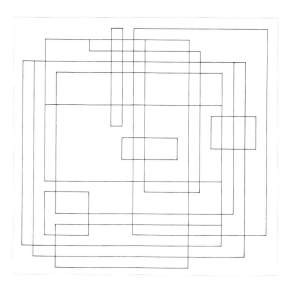

What has the appearance of a book of geometric figures, an exercise in mathematical abstraction, is in fact a proposition about the nature of our everyday reality in the phenomenal world. de vries had been familiar with Wittgenstein's *Tractatus* since 1965, and proposition 5,634 had long been a key text for him:

Everything we see could be otherwise.
Everything we can describe at all could also be otherwise.
There is no order of things a priori.

The *random objectivations* are, in a profound sense, formal visual extensions of these propositions of Wittgenstein, just as the many later works, presenting natural objects or traces of natural process in various ways, are concrete demonstrations of them.

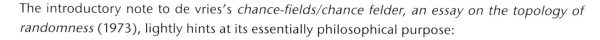

chance-fields presents five sets of five geometrical figures, each one composed of five random configurations of rectangles in outline, of random dimensions in centimetres (the chosen elements) distributed on the white field of the page. The first set deploys 1 rectangular element, the second, 2 such elements, the third, 3, the fourth, 5 and the fifth, 10 such elements. Complexity increases necessarily with each successive set, as the number of elements increases and their given relations multiply exponentially: the first set thus presents '5 chances out of a range of [a mere] 76,176' such chances; the final set presents '5 chances out of a range of 6,579,329,566,975,974,127,670,720,595,328,889,430,137,295,077,376' [an astonishing, and literally inconceivable number]. The 'pages of illustrations' that comprise *chance fields/ chance felder* provide a perfect example of Andersen's 'visual experience' that allows 'no choice to be made, no preference [to be] possible a priori' and demonstrate the fact that 'a random distribution ... includes all possibilities of distribution... and is therefore of a more general order' than those created by 'intuitive or logical' methods.

The three-dimensional structures, reliefs, objects and sculptures that de vries made during

white blocks and *columns* 1961 (second from left) and 1963
wood, white paint with quartz sand
left to right: 51 x 5 x 5 cm; 81 x 15.5 x 6 cm; height 71.5 cm; height 48 cm; 70 x 6 x 6 cm

random objectivation 1970
coloured cardboard collage
100 x 100 cm

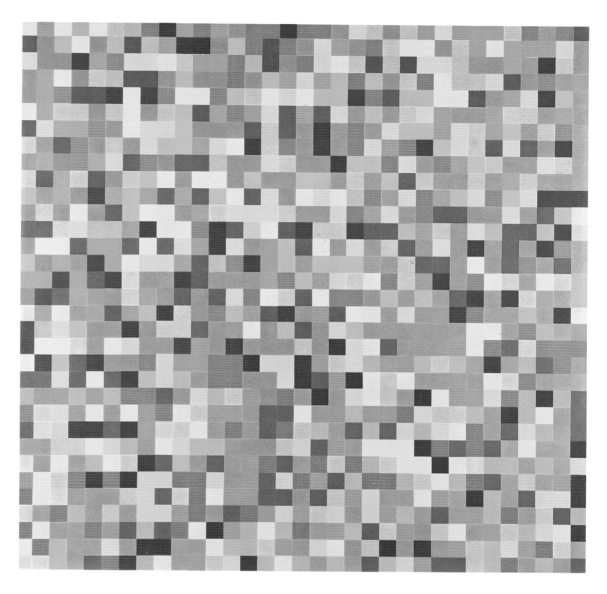

assembled block 1961
wood, white paint with quartz sand
height 41 cm

this period are all in accord with the general principle that they could be otherwise than what they are: they offer no ground for preference. All are painted white, and carry into the three-dimensional world the whiteness that was so important a feature not only of *white is super-abundance*, where it signified both absence *and* superabundance − the void *and* the chaos of infinite potentiality − but also as the 'field of chances' in the diagrammatic planar *objectivations*. After forty years or more their poignancy as historical objects is intensified, ironically, by the anonymous neutrality of their material presence, the whiteness of their surfaces, whose im-personal purpose in both aspects was precisely intended to achieve the elimination of affect, but which now speak of their creation, in acts of personal intention, in a period of idealistically revived avant-garde-ism. They have become poignant relics of late modernism.

History has many ways of modifying the impact and meaning of objects. (Consider Marcel Duchamp's provocatively propositional *Fountain*, whose secondary career as *affective* object began only after the publication of Alfred Stieglitz's moody and shadowy photograph of it.) On the occasion of the first exhibition of *assembled block* (1961) a bystander asked the question: 'mr de vries, where is the expression?' to which the artist replied: 'in the glue'. This was a double-edged joke: we see now that the decision to 'compose' the block (which entailed the glue) was indeed less impersonal than it seemed at the time. The random colour configurations of *random objectivation* − collage (1970) have a beauty of form and colour

relations that is inescapably connected, we see now, at the deepest level, but coming from the opposite direction, so to speak, to that of the 'concrete abstractions' of Richard Lohse. Far from being random in their construction, Lohse's paintings are demonstrations of perfectly predictable relations in what the Swiss artist, with whom de vries had discussions in the 1970s, described as a 'structured field'.

The artistic enactment of the random principle in the three-dimensional world was most immediately obvious in the sculptures which consist of a blind scattering (different in every manifestation) of wooden cubes and blocks, and in works of randomly plotted arrangements such as *zufallsstapelung* (1975), dating from the same year as a seminal work of de vries – *one, two and three hours under my apple tree* – which demonstrates the principle of randomness as it obtains in the natural domain. By this time, de vries had settled in the village of Eschenau in northern Bavaria and had already embarked on his work with natural processes and natural objects, which has been central to his project ever since. *four stems*, made as early as 1960, in certain obvious respects anticipates this later body of work, but it is very much a 'modified readymade' in that the natural objects of the title, randomly chosen with none of them having any quality more special than any of the others, have been tied together and painted white. Nature has become art here in more ways than one: *four stems* is a sculpture.

zufallsstapelung/random stack 1975
six lengths of wood randomly dropped
each 11x 11 x 120 cm

herman de vries working on *one, two and three hours under my apple tree* 31.10.1975

38

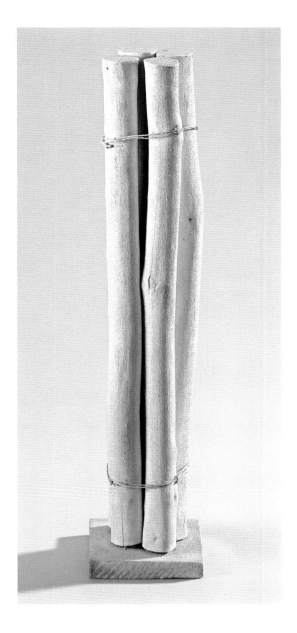

four stems 1960
wood, wire, white paint and sand
70 x 70 x 15 cm

one, two and three hours under my apple tree 1975
each 86 x 118 cm

In September 1965, in the Stedelijk Museum in Amsterdam, a large *random spatial structure* was created which took the concept of random objectivity into the domain of the architectural. This was constructed by museum staff according to a manual provided by the artist. This gave the positions of the hanging panels in relation to two linear co-ordinates (aligned with two sides of a square drawn on the floor, which was removed when the structure was completed), with random heights for the hang of the panels, and with the direction of their placement being determined in relation to the two walls of the space in which there were windows. 'personally', wrote de vries afterwards, ' i saw only the object completely finished, 35 minutes before the opening of the exhibition. by then, any personal encroachments on my part were no longer possible, nor needed either.'

Nine months later, de vries sent from Arnhem a letter to the Destruction in Art Symposium (DIAS), organised by Gustav Metzger at the Roundhouse in London, which throws further light on these various manifestations of white 'concrete' art created by random procedures: 'dear sirs, as an explication of my "white panel" (1960) in which i eliminated all composition and so all personal participation of me as an "artist", so that the spectator is free ("information is information", wiener), i send you an abstract of 6 pages of my book "wit" ("white"), published in 1962. (the original text of the book consists of 200 pages, with an introduction of 1 page of the same character [!] by the poet j.c. van schagen.). i hope you can have a use of it.' There followed six perfectly empty white pages. These might well be regarded as 'elucidations', in the sense proposed by proposition and comments 4.112 in *Tractatus*:

> The objective of philosophy is the logical clarification of thoughts.
> Philosophy is not a theory but an activity.
> A philosophical work consists essentially of elucidations.

de vries's engagement with Wittgenstein's *Tractatus* concerned not so much the rigorous progression of its logical argumentation, through its sequence of propositions and comments, as those particular propositions and comments whose ideas concerned him directly in relation to his own being in the actual world and his project as an artist (for de vries, the same thing). Wittgenstein's classic treatise has continued to be an indispensable source, regarded by de vries in a manner similar to that he might adopt in his reading of the great and sometimes gnomic texts of the Buddhist and Zen masters.

There is much in *Tractatus*, besides the famous final Proposition 7, that gives clear indication of Wittgenstein's own sense of the limitations of purely logical discourse as a means to the understanding of the problems of life. de vries would certainly have noted that Wittgenstein's 'Preface' emphasises these limitations, in a language that has at times the ring to it of the distinctly modest and paradoxical sagacity of Zen:

This book will perhaps only be understood by those who have themselves already thought the thoughts which are expressed in it – or similar thoughts. [...] its whole meaning could be summed up somewhat as follows: What can be said can be said clearly; and whereof one cannot speak thereof one must be silent.

The book will, therefore, draw a limit to thinking, or rather – not to thinking but to the expression of thoughts; for, in order to draw a limit to thinking we should have to be able to think both sides of this limit (we should therefore have to think what cannot be thought).

The limit can, therefore, only be drawn in language and what lies on the other side of the limit will be simply nonsense.

[...] the *truth* of the thoughts communicated here seems to me unassailable and definitive. I am, therefore, of the opinion that the problems have in essential been solved. And if I am not mistaken in this, then the value of this work secondly consists in the fact that it shows how little has been done when these problems have been solved.

random spatial structure (detail) 1965
stedelijkmuseum, amsterdam
polystyrene sheets
each 100 x 100 x 5 cm

de vries began his study of *Tractatus* in earnest in 1967, when he had taken a solitary contemplative retreat in the estuarine area of Biesbosch in western Holland in order to re-think his approach to his professional life. He has playfully used its text in several ways as the basis for works which either amplify or take issue with certain of its propositions. The first of his Wittgenstein concrete poems in 1967 took the letters of the first proposition, 'Die Welt ist alles, was der Fall ist' (the world is everything that is the case), and of proposition 1.2 'Die Welt zerfällt in Tatsachen' (the world divides into facts) and deployed them across a sheet using the random procedures that determined the scale and distribution of elements in the *random objectivations* to determine their scale and placement.

These concrete poems have a visual poetry that relates wittily and with great graphic ele-gance to the simultaneous clarity and mystery of the original statements. What is verbal becomes visual, accessible to the senses: the case is altered by a new addition to everything that has previously constituted the world; the facts of a proposition are fragmented in the way proposed within it. But what we are contemplating is something concrete not something abstract: a sheet of paper with pigmented marks – letter-forms – in a certain configuration; it is a thing. Each is thus a visual refutation of the second proposition of *Tractatus* 1.1: 'The world is the totality of facts, not of things.'

In *the wittgenstein papers* (1975), after raising brief but pointed questions of three propositions (5.634, 5.4733 and 6.5), de vries takes two further propositions and brusquely interrogates their assumptions:

die welt ist alles was der fall ist/the world is everything that is the case 1967
letter press typography
33.5 x 24 cm

The object is simple. (2.02)

Hand-written above the type-written proposition is de vries's question: 'what is the object?' Above his question is a photograph of flowing stream water: in what sense is the moment of flow an object? How simple, how complex is it? The next proposition follows immediately in *Tractatus*:

Every statement about complexes can be analysed into a statement about their constituent parts, and into those propositions which completely describe the complexes. (2.0201)

de vries's hand-written response is: 'completely describe the complexes?' Above this rhetorical question is a second photograph of flowing stream water, taken three seconds later than the first:

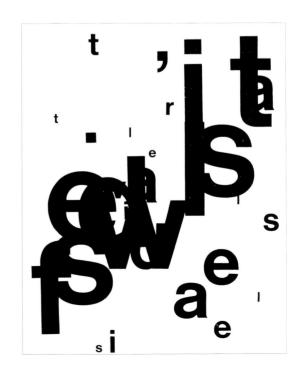

split-seconds of an endlessly changing complexity. The third page has as its text the famous final comment on the sixth set of propositions, the penultimate paragraph of *Tractatus:*

> My propositions are elucidatory in this way: he who understands me finally recognises them as senseless, when he has climbed out through them, on them, over them. (He must, so to speak throw away the ladder, after he has climbed up on it.) He must surmount these propositions; then he sees the world rightly.

Above this on a bare page, the hand-written phrase 'surmount these propositions' is roughly scored through with a single line, a graphic cancellation that enacts the injunction.

The body of work made by de vries between 1955 and the early 'seventies constitutes an extraordinarily rigorous intellectual, philosophical and spiritual preparation for the life-work of his subsequent career as an artist. From some time in the mid-'sixties de vries underwent a period of personal and professional crisis, a journey of contemplation, self-redefinition and renewed dedication to his vocation as an artist. In 1968 he resigned his post at the research institute at Arnhem, and within a year he had left his home and family and begun the first of many journeys to other parts of the world – to India, Africa, Scotland, the Middle East, the Seychelles, the Canary Islands.

In 1970 on the beach at Mahé in the Seychelles de vries picked up two handfuls of broken white coral, and observed, as if it were a revelation, that every piece was created by the same process, and yet that each was utterly distinct from the other: what was the same was different. From the same beach de vries took twenty-four seashells of the same species, and arranged them in a small cabinet frame in a three-line grid. 'what is the case, the fact, is the existence of atomic facts' wrote Wittgenstein in *Tractatus,* Proposition 2. A fact is an abstract classification: that the shells presented in the work are of a given species of mollusc is a taxonomic fact. As shells, however, they are irreducibly *things*, and every one is different from every other. *collected mahé, seychelles (august 1970)* presents us not with facts but with the actuality of twenty-four unique seashells. It is the first of what de vries has called 'the real works', and it inaugurates an extraordinary and sustained artistic-philosophical project of great significance and like no other in the art of our time.

collected mahé, seychelles (august 1970)
seashells
dimensions variable

at eschenau

1. the house: life and art

'... our house is our corner of the world... it is our first universe, a real cosmos in every sense of the word.' (Gaston Bachelard)

In 1970, en route to Ireland to look for somewhere suitable to settle, herman de vries visited by chance the agricultural hamlet of Eschenau in northern Bavaria, close to the edge of the great forest of the Steigerwald. Eschenau is an unremarkable place: a handsome church stands on a knoll overlooking the village, which measures the hours by its bell, and there is a small and comfortable family inn, with a number of farmhouses centred around it. The beer it serves is no longer brewed in the village, though traces of the hops that once flavoured it can be found living wild on such local trees and hedges as have been spared the chain saws and mechanical diggers of modern agriculture. Like the other small towns and villages of the region, Eschenau is quiet, neat and, perhaps, *too* well-kept. It is certainly not picturesque. Unless you had business here it is unlikely that you would stop the car. Its inhabitants are, by and large, devout and hard-working farmers, traditional in their social values, discreet and respectable.

It was the quiet anonymity of the village, and its proximity to the forest, that appealed to de vries: here was a place that would provide few social distractions, where he would be able to work undisturbed. In 1970, de vries came to live in Eschenau and was joined there in 1971 by his partner and close collaborator, susanne; the house where they now live and work has been their home and base of creative operations since 1990. They are on friendly terms with

the effects of the hailstorm of the end of july on our apple tree 1978
each 22 x 16 cm

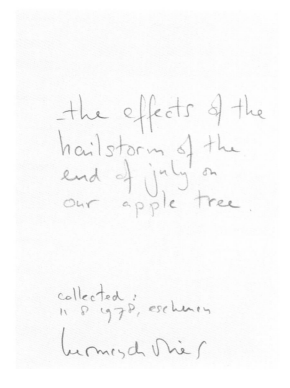

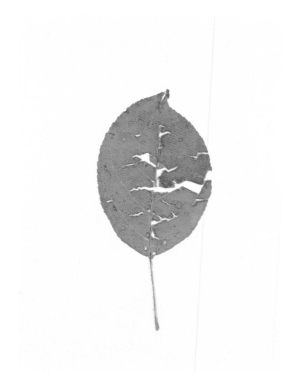

the local people, but have little contact with them, and they do not attend the church, which is the social hub of the village. de vries came here from Arnhem, a city of over a hundred thousand, and it was his express intention to escape from city life, and from the controls and constraints of the art scene in Arnhem and in Holland as a whole: 'the dutch art scene was very close-knit and there was a kind of control, a kind of scene control and I wanted to be outside it. it felt good to be away from thinking about art like other people do and to just direct myself towards the work i was doing.'

What de vries sought at Eschenau was complete independence; after moving there he refused to take further part in any organised movement or group activity. ' i stopped reading art reviews. i didn't want all these ideas of others and influences. i still had contacts. i made exhibitions sometimes and met other people, other artists. but i wanted to be independent. and distance from the centres of art allowed me to follow my own way... nature is our primary reality. our human environment, our human life-space in cities and factories and city streets and traffic is a secondary reality for me. all these things are derived from nature and follow certain laws of nature, but i wanted to be in the primary reality. the big forests I found here, with little streams here and there and small meadows...'

As we have seen, by 1970 de vries had set his course towards the 'real works', although he continued to work on the *random objectivations*, moving towards the definitive published presentations of them in 1972 and 1973. This shift in the nature of his formal 'making' derived from a contemporaneous philosophical development at the heart of de vries's thinking:

> chance & change, i wrote in my notebook on 4 july 1970, in teheran, on my way
> from arnhem to bombay and the seychelles, to buy there with friends an island, to
> live there. the island is not bought. chance and change − change and chance.

So it was that chance and change, change and chance brought de vries to Eschenau that year, rather than to an Indian Ocean island or a cottage in Ireland. In 1974 he published a note recounting the epiphany − in 1970 − from which his new conception of the dynamics of natural reality was to develop:

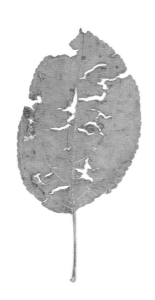
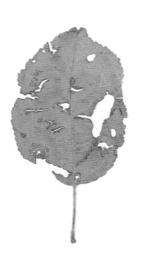

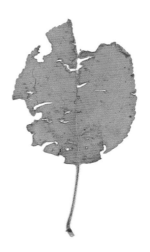

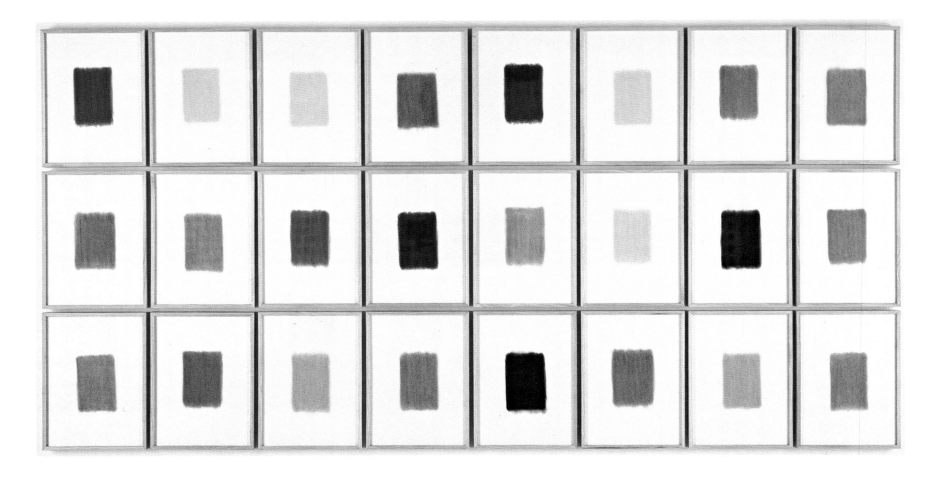

sitting in the train from arnhem to frankfurt i look outside over the snow-covered fields. dark earth clods form a regular but nowhere identical pattern. ponies move over a snowy field, constantly changing their relations to each other. at the edge of the far platform at emmerich station there is visible an irregular wavy line where the melted snow has penetrated the concrete. it starts to snow again and the wind blows the wet flakes on to the platform under the awning, where they remain as white dots for a moment and then become dark spots. a long train of waggons laden with coal passes in front of the platform, a load of energy bound for holland. a crow comes, lands on the platform edge and flies away immediately. chance and change situations out of a complicated chance and change structure, some observed situations from an infinite series: any time, any place, anything. fields and drawings, trees and sculptures, sculptures and fields: there are no contradictions. chance is anywhere, as conditions determine.

aschen von eschenauer sonnende feuer/ashes from fires lit in eschenau for the summer solstice
2001

earth museum at Eschenau (detail)
begun 1979

It is characteristic of his way of thinking that de vries should remember so exactly the particular circumstances of his insight; and that the insight should itself be reduced to a piece of Zen-like word-play, potent of implication: 'chance and change'.

He does not separate a moment of thought or revelation from the contingency of its occurrence, and neither does he elaborate it discursively. This embeddedness of thought in material circumstance, in a specific time and place, reflects a deep and longstanding conviction: 'abstraction', wrote de vries in his notebook in 1957, during the period in which he was making monochrome paintings and *collages trouvés*, 'has value for me only when it contributes to our relation to the world in which we live (or can live).' This is an Heideggerian insight: the abstraction of ideas from the flow of sensory experience – in thought, language or art – as a vital component of the material and imaginative complexity of human existence. Meditating on Hölderlin's lines – 'Full of merit, yet poetically, man/Dwells on this earth' – Martin Heidegger sees the state of being – of 'dwelling on the earth' – as itself poetic, a continuous creative making of the self, within a world constantly renewing its own earthly reality.

The house at Eschenau stands detached, at the corner of a track that goes into a farmyard, and overlooks a crossroads. The house is a world in itself, a personal and professional universe. It is, first of all, a home in which daily domestic life is reduced to great simplicity. The food and drink enjoyed here is of a kind that continuously reinforces a sense of human interdependence with the natural world as the direct provider of the necessities of a life of well-being and peace of spirit. The life lived in this house is by no means that of a monastic austerity: there is good local wine, bread and cheese, vegetables and fruit, and delicious home-made cake; good tea and infusions concocted of herbs and spices from both the locality and brought home from travels to places far away. There is good light from windows that face in different directions, and to look out of any window is to be immediately aware of the seasonal changes, of the nearby birch trees coming into leaf and catkin or changing into autumn gold, and of the chance conjunctions of clouds and birds against the sky, of winter's early dark and summer's bright mornings: constant visible evidence of the natural cycles of the day and of the year.

from earth 1991

from an installation at L'Espace de l'art concret, Mouans-Sartoux, France

The house at Eschenau is, of course, a workplace, an archive, and a complex studio in every sense of that term: a place of creative work, of practical activity, of intellectual study and research. There is a great library of books and publications on every aspect of botany – historical, folkloric, taxonomic, geographic, pharmacological – and plant use. There are also books and journals on the other passions and interests that have fuelled de vries's single-minded programme of creative research and imaginative discovery: natural history, art, eastern philosophies, natural medicine, psychopharmacology (the study of 'mind-moving', hallucinogenic and psychedelic drugs), anarchist politics, etc. There is the archive of books, pamphlets, catalogues, magazines and documents that are the inevitable deposits of a history of exhibitions and actions, relevant publications by museums, galleries, independent publishers, and of publications by de vries's own eschenau summer press and temporary travelling press, and the bilwis-verlag eschenau.

A whole room is occupied by the *earth museum*, with its collection of over 7,000 earth samples from all over the world, and its huge archive of earth-rubbings taken from them. In another room there are, carefully stacked, the numerous framed works that comprise the *eschenau journal* (2002) and other individual and serial-works, each composed of actual objects taken directly from the world, presented in their actuality, items drawn from the infinite and unending primary reality, assimilated into art, arrayed for contemplation. In a workroom are a huge pile of newspapers, and boxes of fragments, samples, shells, and other natural objects, all awaiting their arrangement and transformation into new works.

Talking to de vries at Eschenau, the artist-editor William Furlong observed: 'Looking around the house with you I have seen earth samples, leaves, twigs, which are indexed almost as if they are an inventory of artist's materials in a highly organised, even scientific manner. It seems to suggest the way in which a scientist or a botanist or archivist or researcher works rather than the methodology of an artist. Your initial training in horticulture and botany seems significant here.' de vries agreed: 'my scientific background gave me insights into working in a disciplined way, and i still make use of this because of wanting my own standpoint to be at the zero and in this way to allow freedom to the spectator... i am collecting and presenting and using my knowledge of scientific methodology to give me the opportunity to follow this very simple aim: to do only what is necessary to present the work, without any personal additions.' Furlong's remark, a moment later – 'This house feels as though it is animated by intense curiosity' – captures precisely the dynamic vitality that gives the house at Eschenau its unique quality, that of a scientific-artistic, philosophical research station, situated, as it happens, at Eschenau. In Wittgenstein's memorable words: 'a point in space is an argument place.' (*Tractatus*, Proposition 2.0131)

2. chance and change: the world as art

'the world is my chance
it changes me every day
my chance is my poetry'

herman de vries

Behind what goes on at the house at Eschenau there is, of course, a great deal more than an intense scientific curiosity, although the creative animation felt by Furlong certainly has its source in a passionate interrogative engagement with the living world. 'it is not only what an artist is doing, making or thinking that are part of his concept, but also what he perceives, what he takes up into himself. he is connected to the world by his senses: his eyes, his sense of taste and his ears. it's not just the environment, it's his life space and he is connected to his life space

from under the willow tree 1984
73 x 102 cm

all the time, not least by his breathing. he takes air in, he lets it out, he takes it in, he lets it out, like everybody else.' There is a vital trace here of the thinking of Jacob von Uexküll, the early twentieth-century Estonian German biologist and ecological theorist, whose writings de vries first read some time after finding himself at Eschenau.

Uexküll was a polymath biologist, one of whose principal contributions to scientific discourse was to emphasise the importance to our understanding of behaviour in organisms of the subjective perception of the environment proper to any species of living thing. (We may here indeed 'remember gustav theodor fechner'!) There is, therefore, not one perceived universe but a myriad; every consciousness within every relationship is shaped by these differences of apprehension. And the meaning of any object will be determined for every subject by its entirely subjective usage of the materials the world offers for its existence and survival.

This emphasis, in the scientific contemplation of the natural world, on ontogenetic factors – aspects of individual development – is in keeping with the line of biology that stems from Uexküll's great teacher, the Estonian Karl Ernst von Baer, who opposed it to the phylogenetic evolutionary focus – a concentrations on species and genus – of his rival, Charles Darwin. Its appeal to de vries lies in its attention to the particularity of the organism, and to the uniqueness of the individual consciousness, even when this is a generic function, which it is, of course, in humans as much as in other beings.

For de vries, what seemed also especially significant was Uexküll's assertion that physics and metaphysics are continuous, and his belief, which finds an echo in de vries's words, 'that biologists should not be afraid of metaphysics: life [itself] may be a metaphysical process.' Metaphysics in this context relates closely to de vries's sense of the world as essentially *poetic*: as being itself in a constant condition of the kind of creativity referred to as *poiesis* by the ancient Greeks, a state of 'making' and being made, revealing itself as constantly new and original. This idea, of nature as its own author, derives from a famous exchange between Diotima and Socrates in the *Symposium*, made much of by Heidegger, which extends the idea of the 'poetic' from the utterance of man to the unceasing self-disclosure of nature: 'You'll agree', observes Diotima, 'that there is more than one kind of poetry (*poiesis*) in the true sense of the word – that is to say, calling something into existence that was not there before...' This is precisely what de vries means when he repeats 'my poetry is the world': his existence is embedded in the world, and becomes visible and palpable only in relation to it. 'the world we live in', de vries has written, 'is a revelation that can be "read", experienced. everything we experience and are able to experience is significant for itself and for everything.'

Addressing himself directly to Furlong's remark ('This house feels as though it is animated by intense curiosity'), de vries's immediate response was, significantly, more emphatic on the aesthetic aspects of his response to things than on the quality of his (scientific) 'curiosity': 'yes, when i look around i realise i live in the midst of a perfect wonder. what surrounds me is intensely beautiful. but i do not have to talk about beauty, i can show what i have been seeing, keeping as close as possible to the real facts.' Notwithstanding the lack, understandable in a conversational exchange, of Wittgensteinian exactitude with regard to the word 'facts', what de vries refers to here is the strategy of presenting actuality, the collection and display of the natural object itself: the abnegation of theoretical and taxonomic approaches to reality in exchange for the presenting of 'real works'.

He is also referring to the shift, already mentioned, made during the early years of his residence at Eschenau, from the abstract-concrete experiments with randomness to the demonstration of chance and change in the actuality of natural processes as they create the infinite variety of configurations, complexities and species-forms. Each natural object possesses – like the coral fragments and the shells collected on the Mahé beach – the quality of 'suchness': each one is 'just this', what it is, and not something other. 'so i came to realise that nothing is the same', says de vries of that moment when he saw that every shell, though of the same species, had a different black and white pattern: 'every chance of a realisation in our primary reality is a new chance, nature never, never repeats itself. you can pick a thousand leaves from one tree and when you come to compare them you won't find two the same. they can be similar but they are different, they have a kind of programme of their own and it works out always in an individual way ... even two leaves beside each other on the same twig are not the same.'

de vries came to realise that the principle of randomness does not sufficiently account for this apparently infinite variation in natural phenomena. Works such as *one, two and three hours beneath my apple tree* (1975), *under the birch* (1982) and *beneath the maples beside the spring* (1992), in which he has fixed the leaves as they have fallen in a seemingly random configuration, have made visible, says de vries, 'that which people do not see any more. but [they're] also about randomness in nature, as well ... randomness and chance. in the beginning i said when a leaf falls from a tree there are many factors making the leaf at a certain moment fall on a certain point, and this togetherness [of factors] i called randomness.

unter der birke/under the birch 1982
50 x 70 cm

but later i saw that everything is *causal*, and "randomness" in fact expresses our inability to grasp the complexity of all these causes.' (from a conversation with Paul Nesbitt, Royal Botanic Garden Edinburgh, 1991).

This realisation of de vries's, tantamount to an admission that we cannot know why certain aspects of objects and events in nature are as they are, but that they are in principle ultimately explicable, is close to sentiments expressed in a notable passage from *Walden* by Henry David Thoreau: 'If we knew all the laws of Nature, we should need only one fact, or the description of one phenomenon, to infer all the particular results at that point. Now we know only a few laws, and our results are vitiated, not, of course, by any confusion or irregularity in Nature, but by our ignorance of essential elements in the calculation. Our notions of law and harmony are commonly confined to those instances which we detect; but the harmony which results from a far greater number of seemingly conflicting, but really concurring, laws, which we have not detected, is still more wonderful.'

'The universe is harmonic,' wrote the American essayist Guy Davenport (b.1927), 'or it wouldn't work.' But it is true that we do not yet, and probably never can know, all the laws that determine that harmony, and that we are confronted daily by what appears random and chaotic. It may be true that the second law of thermodynamics is the ultimate explanatory law, and that in the sphere of biology natural selection is unlikely to be surpassed as the governing principle of evolution, but some informal observations of Wittgenstein's are pertinent: 'Hegel seems to me to be always wanting to say that things which look different are really the same. Whereas my interest is in showing that that things which look the same are really different.' 'His concern', writes his biographer, Ray Monk, 'was to stress life's irreducible variety.' Walking in the Dublin Zoological Gardens, where he was fascinated and enlivened by the wonderful diversity of plant and animal species, Wittgenstein remarked that a single scheme such as Darwin's could not be right, it had not 'the necessary multiplicity'. He would have known, of course, that Darwin himself agreed. The final sentence of the Introduction to *The Origin of Species* reads `... I am convinced that Natural Selection has been the main but not exclusive means of modification.'

chance and change situation (1972) is one of the earliest photo-works with this title: it features a scatter of pine-needles strewn by the wind over a plank floor dappled by sunlight and shade. The complex disposition of the needles and the momentary variegation of light and shade are subject to immediate change, depending upon the chance occurrence of the next puff of breeze and the next moment's reconfiguration of light and shadow. Change creates at all times chance possibilities: every field – such as this floor – is a field of chances; chance creates at any moment in time possibilities of change. 'change is everywhere. nothing remains the same', said de vries in a 2004 interview. 'every manifestation is a new one. every moment is new. nothing is stable: the process is durable. douglas huebler [the American conceptual artist] called this "duration". i call it "change". duration and change are the same as "fact". change brings chance. without changes no chances. things can be different but can still be identical, an embodiment of world as fact, as happening.' This is not a banal observation of the mutability of things; it is a proposition of principle. 'Fact' here denotes abstract process, it equates to the term as it is used in Wittgenstein's *Tractatus*: 'The sign through which we express the thought I call the propositional sign. And the proposition is the propositional sign in its projective relation to the world... the propositional sign is a fact.' (Propositions 3.12 and 3.14)

'chance and change' is, then, de vries's dynamic version of the evolutionary principle, accounting at once for the development of species and species variation. In this sense, works such as *72 x erophila verna* (1994) and *148 x salix elaeagnos* (1993) may be regarded as demonstrations of chance fields, for every specimen in each of the arrays – identified as of identical

chance and change situation 1972
pinus sylvestris – fallen pine needles

species (and in the case of the *Salix* leaves, coming from the same tree) – is different from every other, and the differences have been wrought by subtle 'changes' in their immediate situations, in what de vries calls 'a complicated chance and change structure'. 'chance and change' works through millennia to originate and develop species, within a single generation to create morphological and behavioural diversity, and within the single life of an organism to determine its most minute transformations. The principle also accounts for every moment's difference from every other: the opposition of the moment of stillness to the timeless flow; the cloud now billowing, now dispersing, the ripple and wave now visible, now taken up into the next turbulent surge: stasis/ kinesis unending!

'chance and change' at once comprehends the principle of randomness, which obsessed de vries as a scientist and an artist for so many years, and transcends it. For it is both more complete and at a higher level of generality: it is more elegantly explanatory and more deeply poetic. I mean 'poetic' in the sense defined above: 'bringing forth' into existence and visibility, Socrates's 'calling something into existence that was not there before'. Heidegger elaborates this: '*Physis*, also, the arising of something from out of itself, is a bringing forth, *poiesis*.

72 x erophila verna 1994
73 x 102 cm

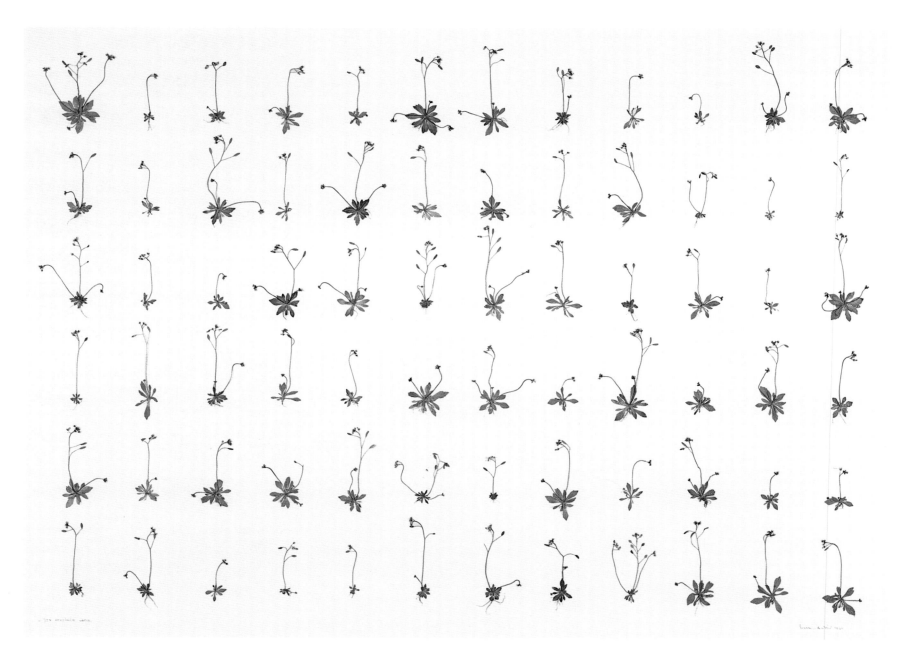

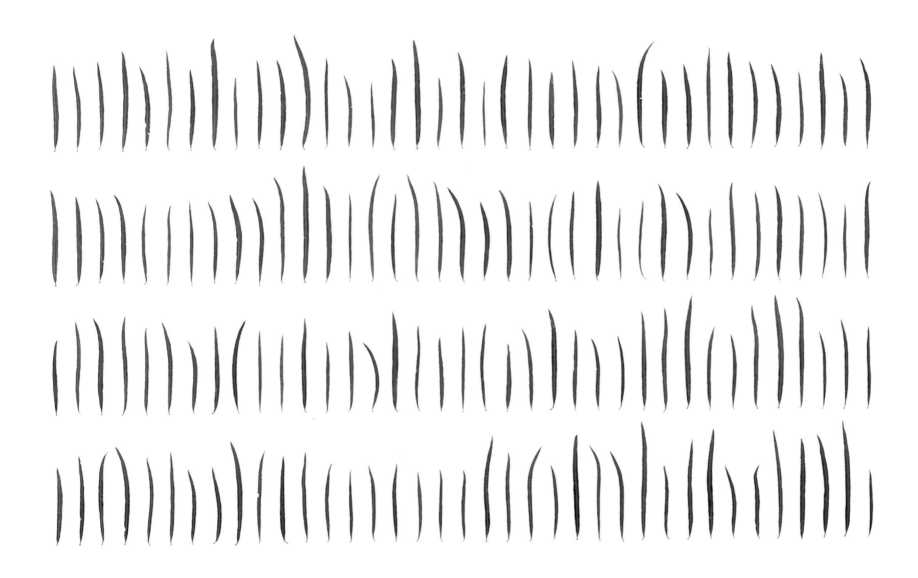

148 x salix elaeagnos 1993
76 x 104 cm

Physis is indeed *poiesis* in the highest sense.' What manifests itself by means of physical being – i.e. the material natural world in all its immediacy and potential - is a poetic becoming, 'e.g. the bursting of a blossom into bloom, in itself (*en beautoi*).' We are reminded by this strange neologism, and its definition by Heidegger as 'itselfness', of de vries's expostulation, already quoted above: 'what surrounds me is intensely beautiful. but i do not have to talk about beauty, i can show what i have been seeing, keeping as close as possible to the real facts.' His work is to allow the 'itselfness' – the 'suchness' – of the shell, the fern, the stem, the leaf, the clod of grass, the cloud, the rabbit dropping, the leaf-mould on the forest floor, to come into visibility, to 'irrupt' into our consciousness.

At the level of our everyday human existence, every moment of perception is the apprehension of a chance field, every moment is a part of 'a chance and change structure': a principle that for de vries has evolutionary, phenomenal and circumstantial implications is thereby assimilated to the existential. It describes both an objective and a subjective reality. In the many series of photo-works entitled by de vries *a random sample of the seeings of my beings* (1972-75) – *see* page 86 – this existential working of the principle is simply demonstrated in photographic traces of events on de vries's travels with susanne and in the closely linked photographic arrays entitled *random samples of my visual chances.*

What is seen is part of being, as is what is received by any of the senses; in the 'real works' we are presented with objects that have in their prior turn presented themselves to the artist. In this sense they are at once objective – the things themselves configured, framed and arrayed – a trace, and also a record of that subjective encounter, in the way of a *souvenir*, and their presentation is a kind of evocation. And now they enter the viewer's presence, become a seeing of his being, a sampling of his visual chances. Their operation at this level of personal experience is one of the aspects that gives the various mixed-media *journals* of time and place their power and poignancy, for, as their titles imply, they act as a kind of record, a necessarily subjective gathering of materials, a collection of events.

3. the eschenau journal and other real works: nature and art

'pick up a stem of grass and the whole world comes with it' (Zen saying)

A personal journal is a record, but it is by its very nature subjective and partial. When it is intended for publication, its purpose is to record a process or a progress in time, in a particular place or on a particular journey, and to use the events as the basis for reflection and speculation. Henry Thoreau's *Walden, or Life in the Woods* (1854), may stand here as a classic example of the genre, and one with a particular resonance in any discussion of de vries's own work at Eschenau. It is worth noting that the Latin *diurnalis* (daily) is the root both of 'journal' and of 'journey' (originally the distance travelled in a day): 'journal' thus encapsulates the idea of movement through time and space. de vries has made several *journals*, usually in the course of a journey or a visit to a specific place or area, each of them having in common the ordered bringing together of a series of framed 'entries' of materials gathered in the period of the journey or stay.

The heterogeneity of the materials reflects always the diversity both of the artist's experience and of the landscape in which they have been gathered. They may include plant forms, animal traces, mineral objects and human artefacts: leaves, twigs, seeds, stems, pieces of bark etc., lichens, fungus, shells, feathers, stones, earth and ash rubbings, fragments of 'rubbish', text works, photographs. They demonstrate, by implication, unity in diversity by means of the visual order of their presentation in grid-like arrays. Each 'entry' may seem to be a fragment of reality: put together they present an image that implies both a thrilling chaos and a beautiful order in things. The visual ordering accords with the underlying principle that in every part of complex reality there is both the natural disposition to form and order and the impulse to entropy.

The most comprehensive of these serial part-works is the *eschenauer journal* of 2002, which comprises one hundred and seventy-three entries made in the course of the one year. (The year is a common temporal limitation in published nature journals, for the annual cycle has an exemplary unity.) Although the individual pieces are undated, de vries has numbered the entries in chronological order, and each consists of a framed work of A4 dimensions, as if to emphasise the analogy with a written journal. They may be hung in any order, any such configuration being necessarily arbitrary, but in exhibitions de vries has twice arranged them in vertical columns of four beginning with number one at top left. This does not essentially affect the anti-didactic character of the work, its lack of any intent to show the effects on objects of a particular period of time. For what obtains in the natural world is at any moment simultaneous: 'to be all ways to be' in de vries own gnomic phrase. The ravages visited by a winter frost on a fallen leaf; the tough fragility of butterfly wings (collected from under a buddleia tree around which birds have probably attacked the insects); the conditions of decay that have made possible on a fallen tree the growth of the stag's horn fungus: all are present, in the present, 'here and everywhere'.

eschenauer journal 2002
42 out of 173 entries, dated as marked

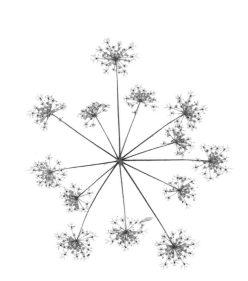

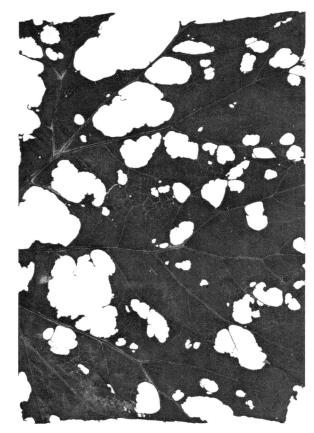

- eschenauer journal -
jannar - dezember 2002

herman de vries
&
susanne jacob-de vries
mitarbeit: marien reigner

title page with view of eschenau from the forest 2002

forest floor: beech with dead fern leaf 04.02.02

heracleum sphondylium 18.07.02

quaking grass 05.06.02

petasites hybridus 22.05.02

rye 05.06.02

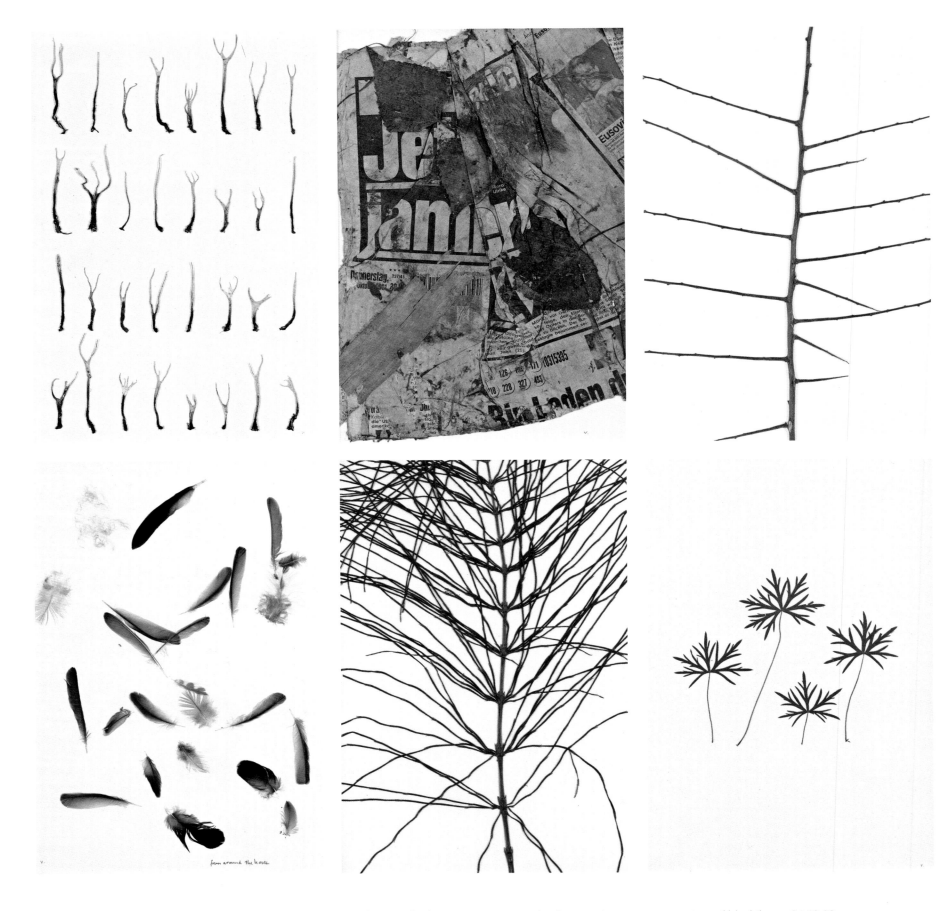

xylaria fungus 12.02

feathers collected outside my home and then dropped randomly onto paper 08.09.02

artefact: crushed newspaper among dead vegetation 14.02.02

equisetum sp. 27.06.02

young stem of blackthorn 24.12.02

geranium colombinum 06.02

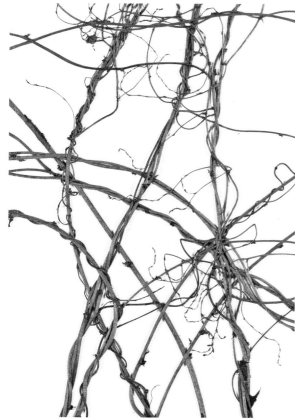

earth rubbings from around eschenau 2002

field names from the landscape around eschenau 2002

acer pseudoplatanus with fungus that typically grows on it and beech leaves from the previous year 29.12.02

fallopia dumetorum (polygonaceae) 29.12.02

fallen leaves of acer platanoides 06.11.02

peucedanum sp. 21.06.02

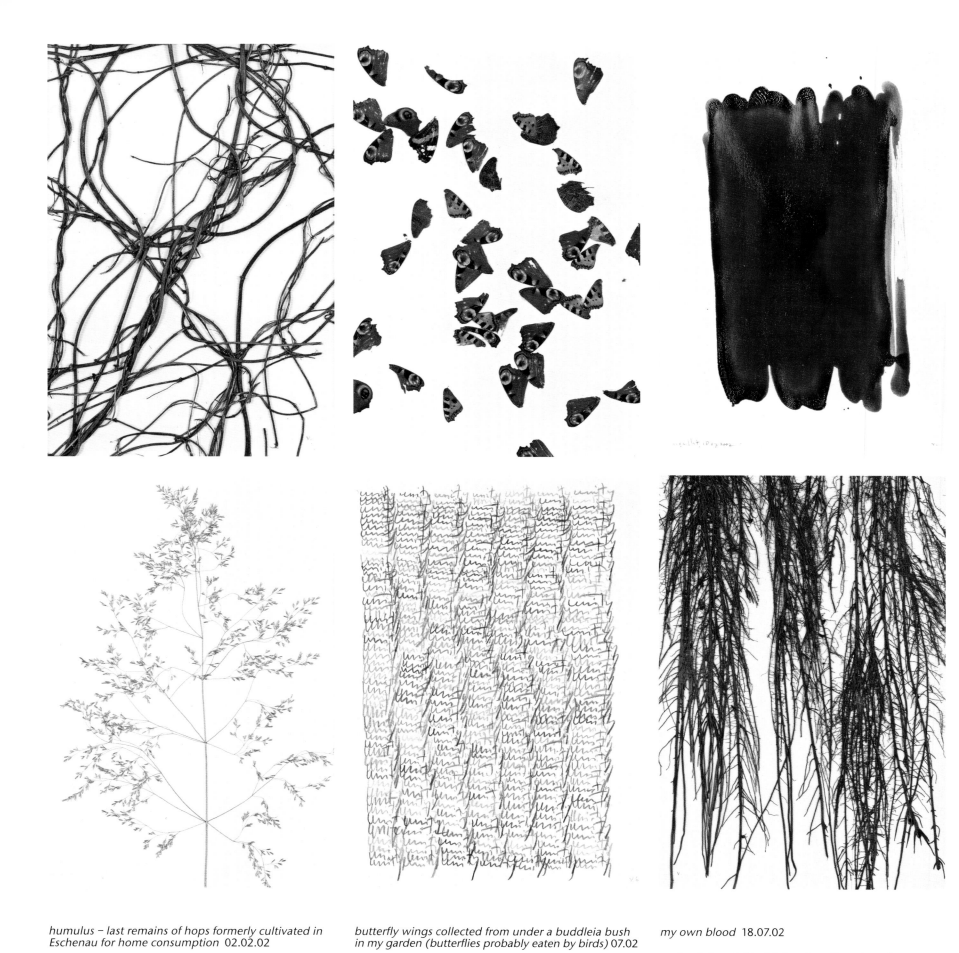

humulus – last remains of hops formerly cultivated in Eschenau for home consumption 02.02.02

grass 18.7.02

butterfly wings collected from under a buddleia bush in my garden (butterflies probably eaten by birds) 07.02

unity 2002

my own blood 18.07.02

roots of alnus (alder) taken from the edge of a stream 01.10.02

fragment of forest floor with fur from the breasts of boxing hares 26.03.02

bupleurum falcata 26.08.02

sanguisorba officinalis 22.07.02

dead grass lying flat on ground after snow with the feathers of a bird killed by a bird of prey 05.02.02

mainly euonymus alata (spindle tree) leaves 14.10.02

carex/sedge 02.06.02

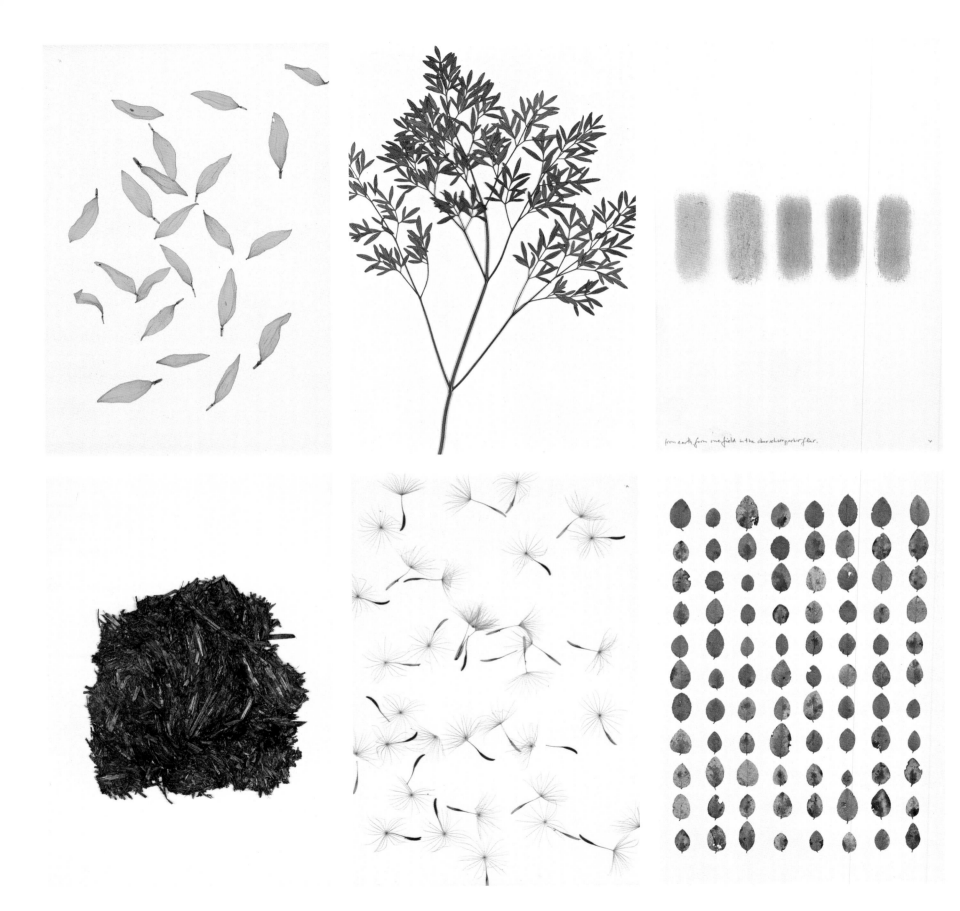

sunflower petals (plants grown as crop) 15.07.02

cow dung flattened by tractors and cars on a track through fields 07.09.02

peucedanum sp. 22.05.02

seeds of tragopogon pratensis 17.06.02

earth rubbings: five earths 09.02

vaccinium myrtillus 10.02

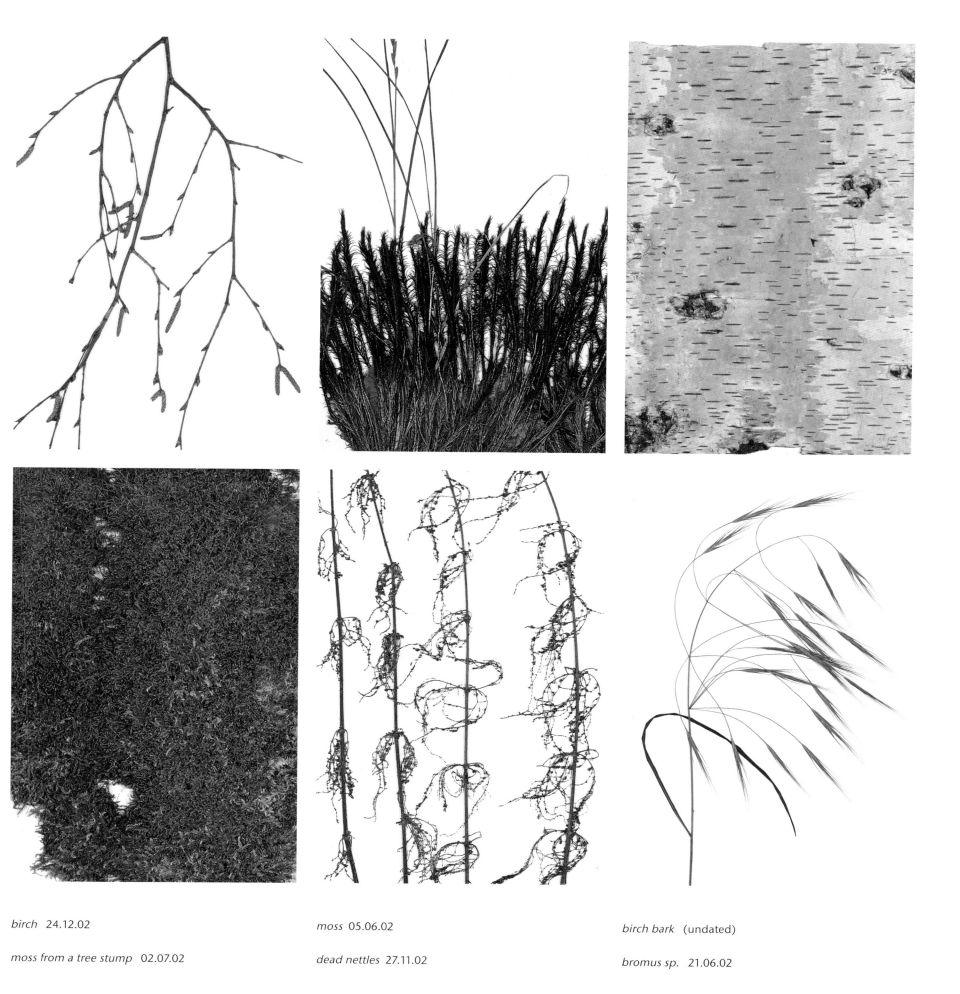

birch 24.12.02

moss 05.06.02

birch bark (undated)

moss from a tree stump 02.07.02

dead nettles 27.11.02

bromus sp. 21.06.02

The *eschenauer journal* has the special significance of being made from materials and events in the immediate environs of the house and the village. It has in this something of the quality of a manifesto or a testament. For herman and susanne de vries, Eschenau has become a centre of the living world, as any point on the surface of the earth might be. Chance made it so for them. But there was a degree of deliberation in this choice of habitat, and in this respect their presence there has a rationale that is comparable to that of Thoreau when he settled for his sojourn at Walden: 'I wish to meet the facts of life' he wrote in the journal on which *Walden* is based, ' – the vital facts, which were the phenomena or actuality the Gods meant to show us – face to face. So I came down here.' In *Walden* he writes: 'I went to the woods because I wished to live deliberately, to front only the essential facts of life, and see if I could not learn what it had to teach, and not, when I came to die, discover that I had not lived. I did not wish to live what was not life, living is so dear.'

In another passage of Thoreau's great and exemplary work there is a description of those phenomena and actualities that immediately brings to mind the 'vital facts' around Eschenau, with its great forest close to hand: 'My house was on the side of a hill immediately on the edge of the larger wood ... in my front yard grew the strawberry, blackberry, and life-everlasting, johnswort and goldenrod, shrub-oaks and sand cherry, blueberry and ground-nut. Near the

from our garden 1987
123 x 182 cm

die zweige der bäume/twigs from the trees 2003
147 x 243 cm overall

end of May, the sand-cherry (*Cerasus pumila*), adorned the sides of the path with its delicate flowers arranged in umbels cylindrically about its short stems which last, in the fall, weighed down with good sized and handsome cherries, fell over in wreaths like rays on every side. I tasted them out of compliment to Nature, though they were scarcely palatable.'

In its exactitude of visual presentation, its accuracy of description and identification, its plenitude of reference and example, and the intensity of its relation to the actuality of experience ('I tasted them out of compliment to Nature...'), Thoreau's record here seems close to the presentations of the *eschenauer journal*. 'when there are apples on the trees,' said de vries to Furlong about the meadow at Eschenau, 'we eat the apples; when there are nuts on the trees we collect them, but if the animals eat the nuts, that's okay. we have cherry trees and also wild cherries – mostly the fruit is eaten by birds...' *from our garden* (1987) is a perfect equivalent in 'real' terms to Thoreau's vivid and exact verbal description of the plants in his front yard. de vries describes the making of the work: 'around our house is only a small garden. many plants grow there of many species and all kinds of insects abound around and between. but the richness of it is only seen by her or him who can see. i collected from all the species in this little garden one leaf and mounted them on the surface of paper. a multitude of forms became visible...'

Thoreau's words, his naming and description of the individual plants are, of course, abstract: we must imagine the plants, aided by his words, by memory, and perhaps by such illustrations as we may find. de vries presents the things themselves, actual, still subject to physical change,

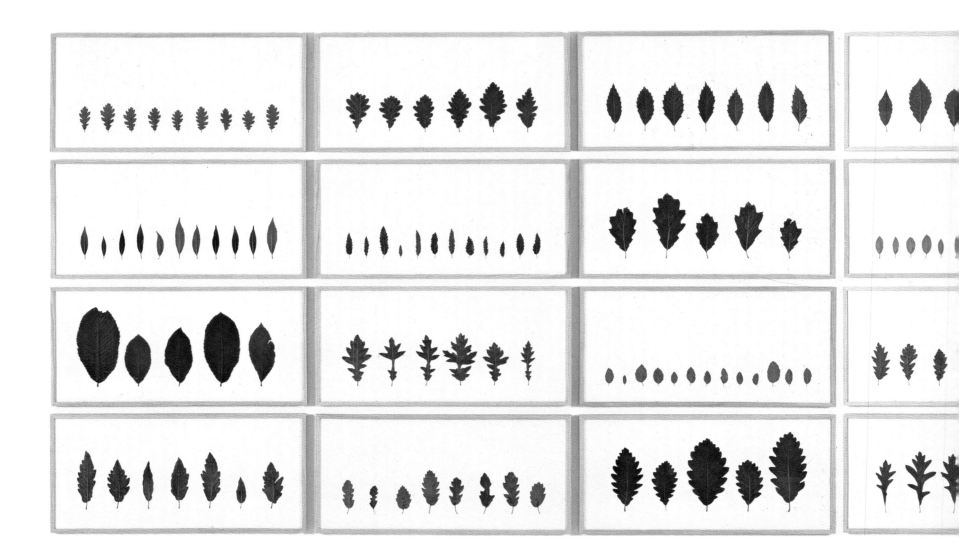

to the discoloration that comes as the plant dries. Thoreau is descriptive, poetic, reflective and discursive: those aspects of expression, articulated through language, are absent from the de vries's presentations. Any reflection must thus be that of the spectator confronted by the work, contemplating this portion of 'actuality'. It is, without question, a constrained actuality: these objects have been selected, collected, mounted, framed, placed in juxtaposition with other things in galleries and rooms. They are not scientific samples, and their purpose within the culture into which they have been transported is not that of science, whether 'pure' or 'applied'. (As we shall see, de vries is, in fact, deeply concerned with the multifarious purposes to which human beings put the plants with which, alongside other creatures, we share the biosphere.)

In providing 'not ideas about the thing but the thing itself' (the title, incidentally, of a poem by Wallace Stevens), de vries is meeting his self-imposed restriction 'to present the work, without any personal additions.' But he is an artist, and even when he uses the grid to place items in an array, either within a single work – examples (on pages 50 and 51) are *72 x erophila verna* (1994), or *148 x salix elaeagnos* (1993) – or in serial works such as *quercus* (1992) or *die zweige der bäume* (2003), it is not for scientific purposes. It is, rather, to eliminate aesthetic subjectivity: 'the grid is not determined by my aesthetic thoughts and feelings, it is determined by the shape of the biggest leaf. in this way, every [object in the array] occupies the same-sized space so that you can compare the leaves ranged together.' By eliminating, as an artist, the exercise of subjective feelings he leaves the spectator free to exercise his own aesthetic. de vries, however, has no doubt of the power of the objects themselves, thus

quercus 1992
oak leaves collected in the royal botanic garden, edinburgh
each 36 x 75 cm

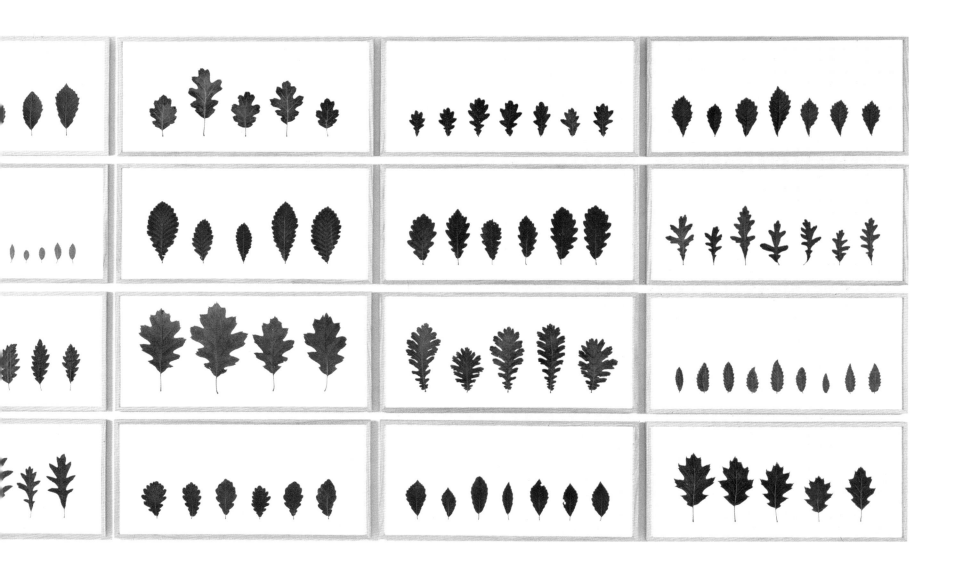

presented, to move the spirit of anyone who encounters them, including the artist himself: 'this [array of objects] does not exclude their beauty. i love their beauty. i feel the poetry of the things i work with, and i cannot explain it, but do not have to add myself to this.'

Where the scientist works systematically, both in practical terms of collection and presentation for analysis, and in the theoretical regard to the materials of his discipline, de vries as an artist feels free to work in arbitrary ways, according to a methodology that lacks the determination of utility or documentation. But the acts of observation and collection that go into the making of a journal must be kept up on a regular basis. de vries, in fact, spends up to five hours of any day outside the house, whenever that is possible. He may walk the local fields and footpaths, examining, where they have survived, the local hedgerows and trees, he may spend time in his meadow, or he may drive deep into the Steigerwald, along restricted forest trails for which he has a special permit to travel, or to meditate, in its oldest part, the ancient Kleinengelein (Little Angel wood).

From any of these excursions he may bring back to the house materials for a work such as the *eschenauer journal* or the *kleinengelein* suite. Sometimes he finds things spontaneously, as they catch his eye; sometimes he travels to find something specific. His collecting, he says, is determined not by system but by 'the poetry of the moment', by his 'visual chances' in the field. ' i have seen much more poetry than this but this is what i have taken.' Anything might be considered to be as significant as anything else: 'naturally, [the artist] has to pick up the leaf – and the whole world goes with it – or he can leave it on the ground. it depends on his state

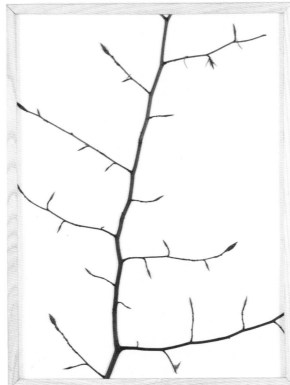

title page of journal with photograph of view inside
the forest

beech twig in early spring

bracken

young beech leaves

earth rubbing

beech bark

64

journal vom alten buchenwald, kleinengelein –
steigerwald/journal from the ancient beech wood,
kleinengelein, in the steigerwald 2002
six of a total fifteen entries

of awareness. As far as i'm concerned, i'm just a mediator.' de vries works to no rule, but his training as a biologist informs his observation at every turn; he knows how to look at nature in a systematic way, and his knowledge of plant forms, of taxonomy and nomenclature, and of plant distribution, are inscribed into his 'reading' of the landscape. Things are collected from this known world, brought back, and in the weeks after, when a work has been determined in daily discussions with susanne, the mounting of the objects and their transmogrification into works of art begins. Out of this continuous collaboration in life and art between herman and susanne an astonishing body of work has been brought into existence.

What cannot be eliminated from our consideration is the consistent formal grace and beauty of the presentations. It would be anathema to herman and susanne de vries, both of whom play a part in the technical production of the works, to ascribe this quality to the exercise of taste, and, as we have seen, de vries is emphatic in his denial of subjectivity in their making. But, ironically, the very grid which imparts equality of standing for every element brings an aesthetically (as well as a morally) pleasing formal order to their array. This applies as much to works such as the *eschenauer journal*, where the individual works (which de vries calls 'parts', because each one is 'a part of nature') are displayed in a grid formation, as to those in which many individual objects are displayed within a single frame. And where the grid is not the informing principle, as for example in those works which present a random scatter of elements or a single object ('a part') as found, then the framing itself introduces an aesthetic parameter (as well as a formal perimeter). This formal grace is something added, a consequence of both the original choice of items and of the intuitive choices that have gone into their arrangement. Nature becomes art through *the practice* of art.

Nature becomes art. This simple formulation is problematic, though de vries has a cunningly simple way of avoiding the problem: 'art is not definable. every definition is a limitation. but for me it has to do with consciousness, or with the process of becoming conscious. this consciousness i see happening around me in nature and i show what i have seen happening, what i have seen being.' (Eschenau, 1992) A later statement can be read as a complicating elaboration of this, whereby the idea of nature as itself a mode of consciousness is assimilated to a social consciousness conceived as having a collective human aspect, deriving from *aesthesis* (reception through the senses): 'when i said that "nature is art [...] i could say that because i see nature as a conscious process which is experienced through the senses. therein [lies] my identity, which is what I communicate: my constant awareness of my *social* function.' (June 1998)

In addition to its revelatory nature, art, then, for de vries, has a social, and thereby, an implicitly political function. This latter passage come from the short statement in which he recalled the 1962 Amsterdam conversations with Manzoni in which they established that they shared the view that art has as its purpose what they termed 'deconditioning'. There is in this passage from 1998 a telling partial definition of the social purpose of art which relates closely to the work that de vries has made and continues to make from materials collected in the environs of Eschenau, especially such serial works as the *eschenauer journal*: 'the artwork as document/witness of a process of consciousness, which can also be immediately communicated. The spectator completes the work by absorbing *information*. The social function is thus the participation [of artist and spectator] in a collective consciousness-raising process.' de vries's reversion here to the early 1970s catchword 'information' is indicative of the persistence in his thought of certain key ideas, especially those concerning the artwork's autonomy of its author, and the importance of art as an information-sharing process. There is a complex coherence of intellectual connection and continuity between the early abstract work, much of which may be considered as within the ambit of 'conceptual art' (remember the relation to Duchamp), and the later 'real works' featuring found natural objects.

herman de vries in the Kleinengelein, an ancient area of beech forest in the Steigerwald, northern Bavaria, 2004.

4. das grosse rasenstück: art and nature

What might the 'information' in a de vries 'real work' consist of? Clearly it has something to do with reality, but 'reality' has many definitions. The problem of the presentation, and *re*presentation, of reality has a long and interesting history in the art of nature. And it is inevitably intertwined with the history of scientific approaches to the natural world, especially insofar as drawn and painted representations of species have been crucial as keys to taxonomic differentiation and as guides to identification. But it is especially significant, particularly with regard to de vries's claim for his work that it is imparting useful, if not scientific, information about natural reality, that the first precisely accurate modern depiction of plants is the work of artists rather than of scientists. For artists are concerned first of all with the actuality of sensory experience: every great representation of a natural object might be regarded as an act of 'direct pointing', whatever may be the intention of the picture as a whole. We respond with a profound delight – the joy of recognition – to such 'actuality' in painting.

Among the earliest and most truly accurate (and most beautiful) representations of the botanical actuality of shrubs and flowers are in mid-fifteenth century drawings by Pisanello, Jacopo Bellini and Leonardo da Vinci, and in details of Flemish painting by artists such as Jan and Hubert van Eyck and Hugo van der Goes. It is in that period that the truly naturalistic rendering of plant life, based on careful observation and study of the real thing, began in modern European art and science. Such drawings were often made from the life as studies for details in paintings, mostly devotional. This was certainly the case with Albrecht Dürer, whose marvellous watercolour study of *Irises* (1503), held by the Kunsthalle, Bremen, was carefully utilised in the painting of the London National Gallery *Madonna with the Iris*, executed by his workshop in 1508. It is to Dürer, certainly, that we look, also, for the first accurately observed study of plants in a natural ecological community (it might best be described as a habitat fragment): this was the famous *Das Grosse Rasenstück* (*The Great Piece of Turf*), completed in 1503.

Dürer's miraculous watercolour depicts with astonishing exactitude a clump of plants characteristic of a damp meadow edge. There are rough meadow grasses, plantain (*Plantago major*), dandelion (*Taraxacum officinale*) in the stage between flowering and fruiting, fool's watercress (*Apium nodiflorum*) and yarrow (*Achillea millefolium*). The painting is clearly made from the life, the clump lifted from its meadow habitat, and viewed at eye-level, as if placed on a studio table or shelf, its background the plain vellum of the support. (In this respect of presentation it greatly resembles those works of de vries that share its title, and other such 'real works' in which a naturally occurring group of plants is arbitrarily lifted from the earth, or from a pond, and framed.) As a study it was, like *Irises*, used as a reference in the workshop painting of the *Madonna with the Iris*, but it is clearly made by an artist who has a passionate love of the natural world, a fascination for the diversity of the plant forms, their subtleties of colour (it is a virtuoso exercise in tonalities of green) and the complex intricacies of their ecological inter-relationships. It is as remarkable for its regard to humble weeds as in its celebration of the (for Dürer, divine) beauty to be found in such commonplace circumstances. His precision is an aspect of exemplary attention, and of a meditative composition of the eye and spirit.

Speaking of his own version in relation to Dürer's masterpiece, de vries exclaimed; 'but mine is more real!' He was, of course, speaking truly, but his own version is no more a simple botanical or herbarium specimen than is Dürer's, and is susceptible of as many 'readings' as that early masterpiece of complex naturalism to which it explicitly pays homage. Both works are informed by love and reverence for the natural world, both are manifestations of wonder

Irises c.1503
by Albrecht Dürer
watercolour on paper

Das Grosse Rasenstück/The Great Piece of Turf 1503
by Albrecht Dürer
watercolour and bodycolour on vellum

at the beauty, diversity and complexity of the commonest plants of the field. Both are in their different ways symbolic, even as they appear to present nothing more than a piece of reality, a humble natural fact. Although both seem to project an objective reality that places them in certain respects within the domain of scientific investigation, they are both without doubt works of art.

But there is an interesting paradox here, a paradox which takes us directly to the problematic heart of de vries's project, and which raises the most crucial critical questions about what we mean when we speak of 'the real'. Dürer's wonderful painting depicts its common field plants with the exactitude of observation that makes it possible not only to identify the species and name the plants (as I have done above) but, also, if we so wanted, to use it as a guide to identify other specimens of the same species. The other watercolour drawings by Dürer or from his workshop, especially *Irises* and *Lily-of-the-Valley and Bugle* (c.1503-04), in their isolation of the plants depicted from any ground or other plants, are even more schematic: they have something of the *representative* qualities of botanical and herbal illustrations, whose purpose is indeed simply to enable identification and impart information about a plant's properties and uses.

Each of de vries's own *rasenstücke* is likewise a group of meadow plants found (literally so) growing together, and framed and named in such a way as to deliberately remind us of its famous predecessor. de vries's *rasenstücke* present us with unique examples and to identify them − to name them − we would require precisely the kind of skilled identificatory *depiction* that we first find, in the modern era, in the drawings of Pisanello, Leonardo and, of course, Dürer himself. For such *r*epresentations have behind them the force of an *idea*, the idea of the species, which is logically related to the idea of the genus, and which is a mental construct, an abstraction, a 'fact', not a thing. (That Linnaean taxonomy was not invented until later does not affect this.) Herein lies the paradox: no ideas but in things! But things acquire the identity that makes them concrete to the mind, makes them knowable, only through the abstractions of words and classifications. It is, necessarily, a paradox that de vries, the scientist-artist, is certainly aware of and must live with. It provides him with a playful freedom.

The idea of species depends upon observation, description and generalisation, and identification is made possible by drawn or written descriptions which provide the basis for comparison. That which makes a particular specimen of a plant what it is, is that which transcends its particularity. As the art historian Joseph Koerner has pointed out, Dürer himself actually wrote of art as being concerned with difference rather than likeness. Of Dürer's detailed drawings of the human form he writes: 'The canon of human proportions established by his method does not represent ideal types, [Dürer] argues, because perfect beauty can neither be attained or known. Rather, it provides a gathering of diverse but internally consistent types, of calibrated forms of difference (*unterschyd*), that are permissible, because visibly plausible, within the construction of the body.'

In a passage that prefigures de vries's own statement about 'giving freedom to the spectator', Dürer wrote, 'I wish to set free for everyone all the various things I've described −

rasenstück − phalaris arundinacea 1998
198 x 69 cm

das grosse rasenstück 1979
96 x 149 cm

Opposite, above: *das grosse rasenstück* 2003 all three 185 x 246 cm; and below, de vries securing boards around the reeds *in situ*.

which I've also myself varied – so that, if one so desires, one can leave nothing be as it is shown here.' In a passage that touches directly on Dürer's own conception of *poiesis*, Koerner continues: 'An image is never the perfect likeness of a thing [... the artist] actively seeks out difference, making things reflective of the diversity of things and instancing his own unique, inborn genius by producing (in Dürer's phrase) a "new creation"...' Given that it not only describes a particular clump but also contains information about 'diverse, but internally consistent, types', it might be said of Dürer's 'great piece of turf' that in the sense of offering a painting of real things which allow other (necessarily varying) things to be identified, it is actually 'more real' than de vries's, for all the actuality of the latter!

In Ian Hamilton Finlay's garden at Stonypath in Lanarkshire, by a garden pool, there is a small stone block inscribed with Dürer's famous AD monogram. The actual clod in which the stone is set is of course but one of an infinite number of possible clods – of such possible *chance and change situations* – but what gives it its *representative* reality is the accuracy and truth to observation of Dürer's extraordinary creation, its essential reality. Hence the appropriateness

rasenstück – molinia caerulea 1999
144 x 103 cm

Das Grosse Rasenstück/The Great Piece of Turf
by Ian Hamilton Finlay
1975
stone inscribed with Albrecht Dürer's monogram

of the monument, and of its placement. As its etymology tells us, a 'monument' is a reminder, an act of remembering: if you seek a monument to Dürer, Hamilton Finlay's simple stone seems to say, look around you; every clod is a monument to the great Bavarian artist's love of and respect for nature.

Incidentally, Dürer's picturing of the great clod and de vries's presentations demand a similar kind of optical attention. The eye must move its centre of focus to take in the visual actuality

parts 1998
Top left: *carex sp., from a location between wonfurt and steinsfeld, collected 24.07.98;*
top right: *juncus effusus, from schäferholz, collected 21.7.98;*
bottom left: *unidentified;*
all three 21 x 29.7 cm;
bottom right: *herman de vries preparing a similar, larger piece in September 1998.*

of any one of the detailed features of the clod, all of which are represented with an identical clarity. In the Dürer, its exactitude of depiction of every detail at every point in the picture demands a play of the eye equivalent to that when it engages with the visual actuality of the world: it can focus at any one moment on only one area, and what is peripheral is blurred. Precisely the same thing happens when we look at de vries's clumps (and indeed all the other 'real works'), for every part is there in its actuality of presence. Perspective and vagueness, the illusionistic tricks of realism in painting that suggest distance and emphasise significance, are absent from both, neither has a 'background': in both, what we view is the thing itself, and in neither does any element have a significance beyond any other. The eye must isolate for itself the object of its particular attention.

Visual apprehension consists in an active processing of the reality found in nature and in art; it is a subjective answering to that complex of sense experiences. The purpose of art, according to de vries, is, then, that 'raising of [collective] consciousness' that comes from the subjective 'completing' of the work in 'absorbing [the] information' it carries. We may return to that problematic formulation once more by way of another poem by Wallace Stevens, in which he speaks of a bouquet of roses:

...too much as they are
To be anything else in the sunlight of the room,

Too much as they are to be changed by metaphor,
Too actual, things that in being real
Make any imaginings of them lesser things.

And yet this effect is a consequence of the way
We feel and, therefore, is not real, except
In our sense of it...

Our sense of these things changes and they change,
Not as in metaphor, but in our sense
Of them. So sense exceeds all metaphor...

It is like a flow of meanings with no speech
And of as many meanings as of men.

That 'flow of meanings with no speech' is what, in the final words of Stevens's poem, puts our experience of the actual 'beyond the rhetorician's touch'. It is a purpose of de vries's real works to demonstrate that there are indeed relations between things, and between us and things, that are beyond taxonomic analysis and the scientific demand for comparative identification. In our comprehension of the world, the perception of particularity and difference is as crucial as the recognition of identity and likeness.

5. the meadow and the forest: nature, politics and the ecopoetic

A tree ascended there. Oh pure transcendence!
Oh Orpheus sings! Oh tall tree in the ear!
And all things hushed. Yet even in that silence
a new beginning, beckoning, change appeared.

Rainer Maria Rilke

Not far from the house at Eschenau is *the meadow/die wiese*, a 4000 square metre patch of land purchased by de vries in 1986. A narrow rectangle of uneven ground with rough meadow grasses, mixed shrubs and young trees, it extends into acres of gently undulating arable land from its upper boundary with the edge of a small forest which rises behind it. This is itself but a remnant of the great forest that once covered this area. Once there were many more small meadows around the village, between the forested lands, but the economies of scale deter-mining the farming of the local land, here as in so many other parts of Western Europe, have led to the grubbing out of hedgerows, copses and small orchards, and of the many wild shrubs and trees of all kinds that they sustained in the varied landscape and open countryside in previous times. *the meadow* was at the time of its purchase simply a demarcated plot con-tinuous with and indistinguishable from the denatured landscape around it.

The agricultural land for miles around Eschenau is now characterless and uniform, the countryside of this part of Bavaria having been subjected, in the universal manner of modern agribusiness, to a reductive regime of highly managed, high-yield, cash-crop production. The large bare fields that surround *the meadow* are heavily fertilised and treated with pesticides, enabling the farmers to harvest at least three separate cuts of a monocultural commercial hay in the course of the year. de vries observes with some asperity: 'the land [around] ... is [liquid] manured and fertilised. it's a strange word, 'fertilised', because fertility is something different

Opposite:
the meadow/die wiese 1987, 1994, 2001

in het bos stand een eik/in the wood stood an oak
1991
Charcoal gathered in the Steigerwald.
178 x 122 cm

from what you achieve with artificial or chemical manure.' The grasses in de vries's *meadow* are cut once a year, and the land is not treated, and 'in becoming poorer it [becomes] richer in plants' as the taller grasses are mown and cannot succeed and eliminate the less robust meadow flowers and herbs. This is part of the process that de vries has called 'decultivation for renaturalisation'.

Protective hedges have been grown and the area planted with fruit and nut trees. In living memory there were as many as seven thousand fruit trees spread across the local landscape, cherries, apples, pears, plums, as well as walnuts and hazels, which were harvested by the farming families and set in winter stores, or used for the autumn stocks of jams, pickles and preserves. Now there are perhaps a thousand or eleven hundred commercially cultivated in the area. It is not only the land use and its physical aspect that have changed; it is the pattern of human relations to the land and to its living forms in their seasons that has also been irrevocably altered: the impoverishment is not only natural but social and cultural. In a poem entitled 'from the shortness of the moment' (1984), de vries expresses his own keen sense of loss:

> it is my love of these trees
> it is a personal relation to these trees,
> it is their resilience and their resistance
> that gives them their forms,
> it is the scent of their blossom
> and my joy each time i see hawthorns blossoming
> and my gratitude each autumn
> when i pick their berries
> which help to regulate my heart-rhythms
> and give me strength,
> it is this combining of strength and beauty that causes my bewilderment
> when once again beside the road
> i see one hawthorn less
> (now let them all remain!)

herman de vries in *the meadow/die wiese* 1992

View from inside *the meadow/die wiese*, looking across agricultural land towards Eschenau, 1993.

An entry in the *eschenauer journal* records, in de vries's hand, individual field names in the locality taken from old maps and the memories of an old farmer (*the meadow* was called *köhlerin* – denoting a female charcoal burner – indicating its origins as a cleared woodland plot). The only other text piece in the entire journal repeats the one word *unity* in many colours, recalling the natural unity that existed in the diversity of the old landscape, in which no field was the same as any other. It also comments, by implication, on the agronomic unification of the land-space in which every field now looks the same as every other, and their names and identities and the subtle differences they signified, are forgotten in a single-minded reduction to an impoverished utility. de vries insists that unity in diversity persists, whether or not it is recognised or respected.

the meadow itself is mown once a year in July after the flowering and seeding of the summer, as is necessary to keep the land open for next year's growth of wild flowers, diverse grasses and herbs. This accords with the ancient (and ecologically sound) historical pattern of annual seasonal mowing or cropping of meadow grasses (sometimes done by releasing sheep or cattle to graze the pasture) and thus conforms with the initial aim of de vries to 'reconstruct' a micro-version of the landscape as it was before the clearance of the land, the removal of hedgerow field-boundaries and the destruction of the bio-diversity that existed before the mechanisation and economic 'rationalisation' of modern farming. Now, in spring and summer, as in successive years the chemically enriched land becomes 'poorer', and the pesticidal deposits leach away, the meadow becomes receptive to the wild flowers that once grew in profusion in the hayfields around Eschenau. In the early years of their making of *the meadow*, herman and susanne gathered the seeds of many of these flowers from path edges and embankments close to the forest edges, margins where the older, wilder plant life had maintained a tenuous hold.

To walk with de vries into *the meadow* is to enter another kind of life space, and to attain an insight into other possibilities of relation between the human and the natural, possibilities that recognise human being as itself part of nature and not separate from it. This state of human being on the earth comprehends all that comes with it, including the use of the land and of natural resources in what is, properly, termed agriculture: 'the cultivation of the field'. It includes also the complex pattern of mysteries and understandings that constitutes the great human artefact of science. Science plays its useful part in the improvement of the conditions of human living, but it can be employed also to exploit and destroy when its revelations of the complexities of natural interconnectedness and interdependence are ignored.

And at the heart of this human being is the celebration of that being itself, manifest in the Orphean singing of poetry, music and art: 'my poetry is the world'. This is the deeper meaning of *the meadow:* it is itself a work of art, an Orphean song, the manifestation of *poiesis*. 'When there is poetry/it is Orpheus singing', wrote Rilke. de vries is clear about this. Asked by the present writer if he had kept an inventory of the plants that grow in *the meadow* he replied: 'i could have done it, of course ... but i didn't want to have too scientific an approach, it should be more like a poem than a scientific work.'

the meadow is enclosed by a barrier of small trees and shrubs, several kinds of cultivated hazel, hawthorn, the impenetrable blackthorn (whose white blossoms before the leafing of early spring are an especial joy), rowan, medlar, dog rose (*Rosa canina*), which were among the earliest plantings made after its acquisition. This was to bring seclusion and protection from the wind. Among other trees and shrubs growing in the meadow are hornbeam, silver birch, dogwood (the Cornelian Cherry, *Cornus mas*, valued for its small yellow flowers in late winter and very early spring), cherries, pear, a silver maple from North America, Antarctic beech (*Nothofagus antarctica*, specially grown to provide a harvest of its little autumn leaves for a work), willows, aspens (spreading from the forest border) and balsam poplar (whose buds are enjoyed in a health-giving infusion by de vries). de vries is generously careless of the geographical origins of his meadow trees, and the planting is haphazard and ungoverned by rules. The pleasure principle governs rather than any purist or scientific conservationist ethic. Dog roses, for example, were planted early on in a circle to provide a secluded bower for quiet contemplation or for sheltered picnics surrounded by sweet-smelling flowers.

the meadow is a peaceable kingdom, shared with the birds and beasts that are attracted

herman de vries working on *16dm² – an essay* in a hillside meadow near his home in 1974. (*See* page 78 for a description of this work.)

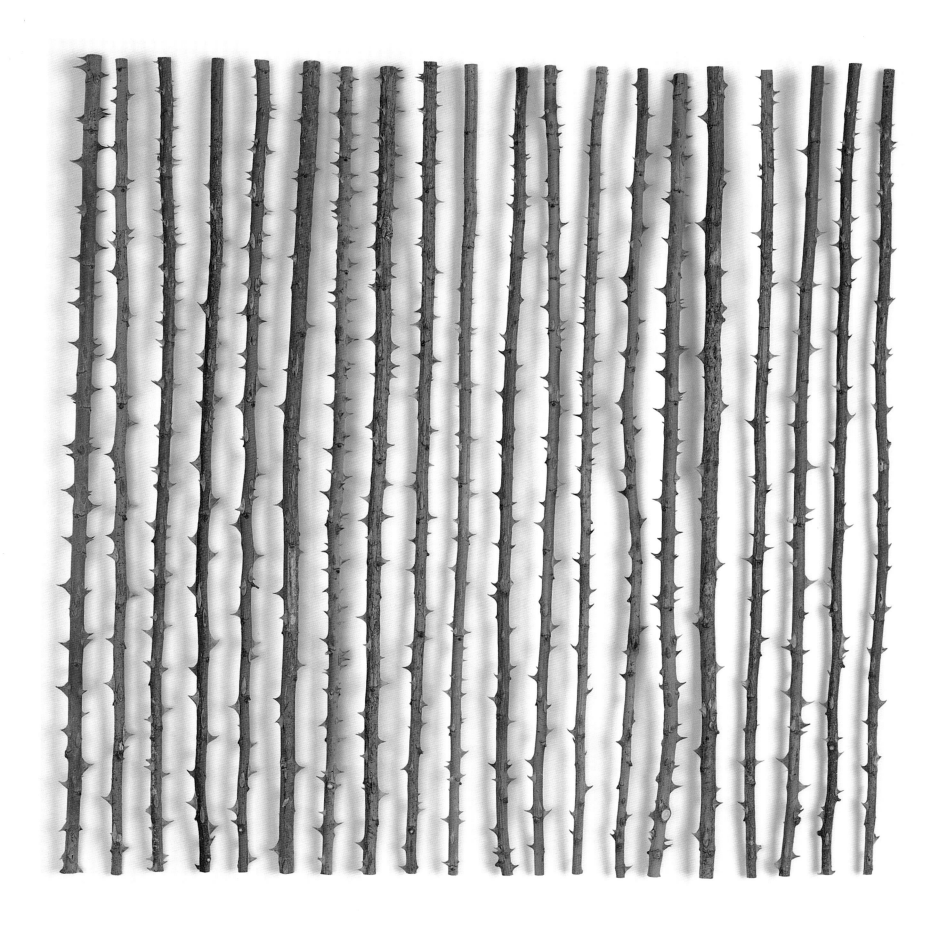

rosa canina 1994
80 x 76 cm

by its seasonal harvests of buds, fruits, berries and nuts, by its richness of insect life and by the peace and quiet that affords them security. Edible dormice eat the green hazelnuts, and by the time they are ripe de vries is lucky to be left with a handful; voles, red squirrels and field mice also enjoy the nuts. Moles burrow below the ground, and in recent years wild boar have come down from the woods to forage and dig for cockchafer grubs. In the ground thus turned and opened susanne has planted the wild seeds gathered for the meadow. For the birds, the trees and shrubs provide cover for nesting; in the grass there are beetles and grasshoppers. In spring and summer there are butterflies. Diversity is further increased by the clearing of the small stream at the bottom of *the meadow*, and frogs and dragonflies have joined the Orphean gathering.

In the spring there are the flowers of primroses and wood anemones, in the summer columbine (*Aquilegia vulgaris*, once a common meadow flower in the area), scabious, agrimony, avens, valerian, mugwort, flag iris, comfrey, hops, clovers, cranes-bills and deadly nightshade (*Atropa belladonna*) abound. de vries quotes a naturalist's aphorism, 'everything is everywhere': when conditions occur that allow for the settlement and growth of a species, in time its seeds will find their way there to take advantage. Scarcity is a condition of circumstance: 'rare species', wrote the social biologist Chr. G. van Leeuwen, are indicators of rare circumstances.' *the meadow* is an image of potential; its plenitude is exemplary.

Two works, in particular, demonstrate that plenitude, which is not only of what may grow and multiply within the meadow itself, but of what that process of growth and development might mean for the human visitor. The first, *16 dm² – an essay*, was begun in 1974 and finally completed in 1979. This was, of course, before *the meadow* was created, but its import can be carried over into the latter work, which may itself be seen as a 'habitat fragment' writ large. For, like *das grosse rasenstück*, *16 dm²* takes a living clump of herbage, in this case sixteen square decimetres (each side measuring forty centimetres) and subjects it to close scrutiny of a kind that has something in common with a scientific examination. Where the 'great clod' is seen whole, as a synthesis of growth and flowering, *16 dm²* is the outcome of an analytic process, which considers separately each and every plant as a thing in itself, an individual 'part' of the whole.

The square in question was measured out by de vries in the manner of a botanist's quadrat (a metre-square piece of ground sectioned off by stakes to be studied as a biotope, which may be used to study its population of plants, or scraped clear to demonstrate generational succession and change); then, with the utmost exactitude and careful recording on a grid plan of the plot, each plant was removed from the ground, dried and mounted on a separate page of a large volume, in the manner of the herbariums in the great botanical collections. In contrast to the purposive ordering of the herbarium, de vries refused to identify by species or arrange in any systematic manner the individual plants, or to count the recurrence of species, each being placed in the book in the order in which it was removed from the ground. Any resort to scientific nomenclature was regarded by de vries as a concession to the classificatory impulse, a move towards abstraction and the imposition of intellectual order and control.

The pages of the book were simply marked with the position on the grid at which the plant was found growing. In this way the volume becomes a record without a key, and is precisely an example of what de vries terms 'reality as a document of itself', hence its subtitle, *an essay*. The square was marked off on a hillside meadow then relatively untouched by modern hay-farming methods, in sight of the house at Eschenau, and its revealed botanical richness is typical of the farmland as it was, a richness now being demonstrated by the less than twenty years of diverse growth in *the meadow*. From 1600 square centimetres de vries removed an astonishing 473 plants; each occupies its own page in the book. Since making *16 dm²*, de vries has, in later works, changed his mind about the usefulness of species identi-

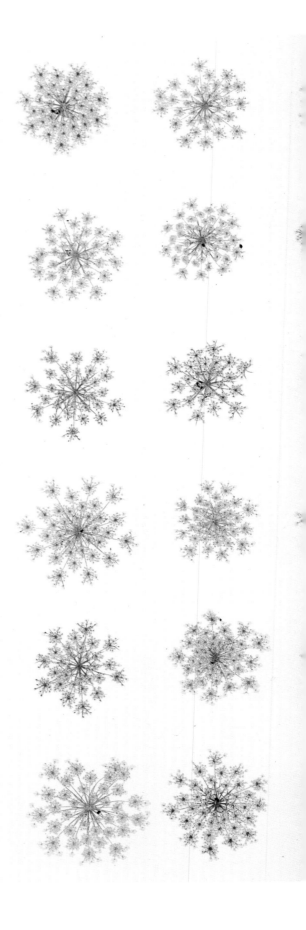

64 x daucus carota 2001
73 x 102 cm

Les Très Riches Heures du Duc de Berry
by the Limbourg brothers (fl.1400-1416).
Left: November – feeding acorns to the pigs;
right: December – hunting wild boar.

fication, believing now that to name the species in the real works is to increase possibilities of communication: to identify the species does not destroy the unique actuality of the specimen.

If *16 dm²* is concerned with potentialities in space, the second work to be considered in the context of *the meadow* at Eschenau is, as its title implies, concerned with the use of precious time. *les très riches heures de herman de vries* (1981) was inspired, conceptually, by the beautiful *Très Riches Heures du Duc de Berry.* The Limbourg brothers' supreme masterpiece of the *genre* (created between 1411 and 1416 and containing 131 exquisite miniatures) conformed to the conventional form of the book of hours, being a prayer book in which the canonical hours (*horae*), the Little Office of the Virgin, a calendar of months with appropriate zodiac maps and signs, etc., were elaborately illuminated and illustrated for the delectation of the very rich patron who commissioned it. In the innovative realism of the early fifteenth-century International Gothic, the calendar miniatures vividly depict, with much lively detail, the Duke's extensive domains, in which his powerful chateaux rule over productive agricultural landscapes of farms, vineyards, pastures and hunting forests, and over his feudal subjects at their seasonal labours.

de vries's *heures* are, conversely, those of a single summer day spent by the artist – the experiencing subject – in the woods near Eschenau: the work consists of 131 black and white photographs taken of whatever detail of the life around him has caught his attention, a fall of sunlight through leaves, grass stems, a single leaf half-eaten by insects, foliage, the bark of a tree. Without regard to any order of devotions or any systematic relation to the passing of the hours, every exposure catches a trace of the actual light of the day on the reality of a single moment. The picturesque and idealised celebration of ordered hegemony and toiling servitude within a religious context is replaced by the haphazard ceremony of being and of what befalls. What is courtly, complicated and richly wrought is re-figured as democratic, simple and immediate. *the meadow*, so small in compass, so unproductive and marginal a terrain as seen

Opposite:
les très riches heures de herman de vries
1981
Fifteen from a total of 131 black and white photographs taken by the artist over four hours at a single spot one summer's day near Eschenau, northern Bavaria.

by the modern farmer, is an image of another aspect of man's estate, that of his place in the living, growing world experienced as a vital complexity of interdependencies. It is a place set aside for meditation and recreation.

There is in this contrast so subtly proposed by de vries's evocation of the *Très Riches Heures*, a deeper political implication. The picturesque, as the word implies, entails the viewing of the world as a picture, its ordering to a preconceived idea or ideal. It implies the separation of the subjective eye from the objective world as seen, and the primacy of the eye and mind over the secondary reality of the world as seen by an eye that is informed by particular ethical and ideological preconceptions. It depicts what it desires to project. The Limbourgs were commissioned to represent the Duke's lands as the very picture of social and political harmony and prosperity in an age of brutal warfare and political turmoil. Each calendar image is, then, in the words of art historians Hugh Honour and John Fleming, 'a view not only *of* but, as it were, *from* the castle, both literally and metaphorically looking down on the peasants.' That this pre-ordained order of things is to be regarded as fixed and universal is indicated by the canopy of stars and the zodiac signs in the lunettes above each calendar image: it is the heavenly constellations that determine what obtains below them on earth.

de vries's conversion of the 'hours' from the objectively ordained ordering of the ritualistic *horae* of the devotional day, within the calendric turn of the seasons, to the subjective *zufall* ('what befalls') experience of what occurs in real time, events shaped by chance, change and circumstance, is profoundly witty. de vries's 'hours' consist of moments experienced in the subjective here and now, with the world as a presence manifest in minute particulars. (Significantly, there is only one border in the whole of the Duke's prayer book in which the depiction of individual flowers is naturalistically detailed.) In de vries's own *très riches heures* it is the broader view, the general prospect, the landscape as an ideal, that are absent. Reality, to paraphrase Flaubert, is in the detail.

the meadow, as a work, similarly fails to conform to any preconceived notion of beauty or order; it is a piece of the world, what de vries calls a *terrain vague* (*see* pages 125-126), not a garden planted and landscaped for the eye. It is not art but nature: 'i hate art in nature!' is the title of a de vries text: 'nature is sufficient unto itself... what we can still find around ourselves of nature (i speak of being aware, not of possessing) requires no human intervention. it is itself...' Later, he wrote: 'when i said "nature is art" (adding: "but it doesn't need this label"), i could do this because i see nature as a conscious process which is experienced through the senses...' – which is to say, not through the eye alone. 'The world is round around the round being', wrote Gaston Bachelard. That 'roundness of the world' is experienced through all the senses, as simultaneous light, space, temperature, atmosphere and texture, it is our complex element, it is where we live. *the meadow* is a microcosm of that complex all-around-us reality.

The natural succession of plant life-forms, in which the stronger overwhelm the weaker, until their own success is modified by other circumstances (fire, the grazing of animals, the increase of shade at ground level, etc.) is the primary ecological feature of any unregulated stretch of terrain. In the meadow this progression is held in check by the very particular human intervention I have described and discussed. In the fullness of time, it is de vries's intent that the meadow plot will be allowed to revert completely to the natural cycle, and what is now a beginning, still less than twenty years in development, will ultimately climax in forest, and this little spur of land will become an admonitory natural extension to the artist's beloved Steigerwald.

For the Duc de Berry, the forest is a private domain for the husbandry of swine and the cruel hunting of wild boar (see *November* and *December* in the calendar); for the modern logging industry the natural forest is an industrial resource to be ruthlessly exploited; for the modern tourist industry small fragments of native forests may be preserved to provide a brief taste of

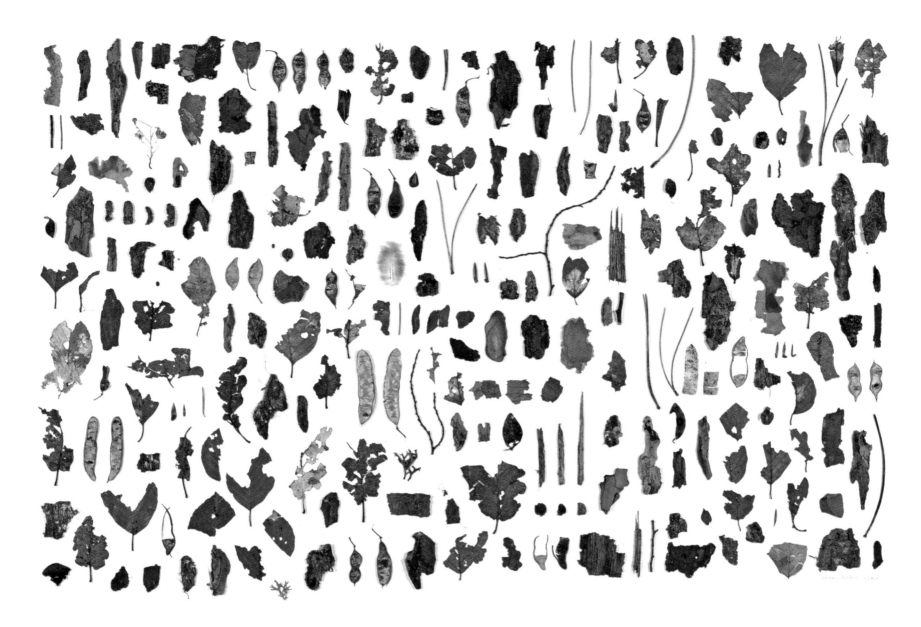

from the forest floor 1997-98
50 x 70 cm

an illusory 'wilderness'. While it is true that some vestiges of the once extensive European forests are carefully managed and conserved, we are living through the period of their continuing destruction and diminution. A viable future for the human world depends upon the most radical ecological intervention in the conservation of the last remaining forests in both hemispheres, and for that to happen there must be a drastic change of heart and re-direction of political will.

For de vries, the great forest that is part of his studio, and which provides him with so much natural material for his work of discovery and revelation, has the beauty and balance of any mature and irreplaceable biotope. For de vries its unabated interest is intensified by the fact that it has been a home for myriad living creatures, including those of human kind, providing shelter and sustenance. In this it is like all the other forests that breathe to sustain the earth, and whose biology is of a richness never likely to be fully known or understood. The forest is nature, and man is part of nature. In much of European history and myth the forest has been seen as the dark site of strangeness and the unknown as well as a place for religious experience; for de vries it is a welcoming place for the spiritual contemplation and empathetic study of natural processes and the objects they shape. And the forest, for all its physical splendour and wonder-provoking grandeur, is itself part of a never-ending cycle of events, itself subject to constant modification and change.

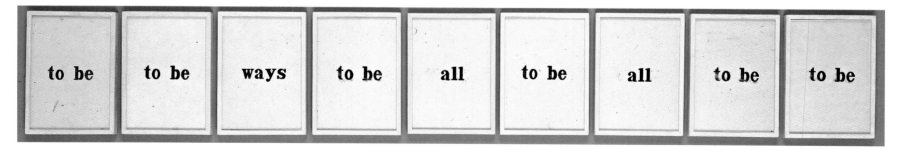

If that change of heart of which I spoke is to come about there must be a raising of consciousness and a collective political effort. For de vries, it is the intention of his work to contribute to this process, for he is an artist who will not propagandise or engage directly in the politics of the environment or in the academic and polemical discourses of ecology. He works not through declarative rhetoric, but by creating and enhancing awareness by means of a demonstrative *ecopoetic*: through the exemplary enactment of being-in-the-world, and through the wordless presentation of the objects of nature itself. Language may, of course, be employed in the process of consciousness-raising, and, as we have seen, de vries is a master of the brief philosophical statement, of the gentle provocation, and, above all, of the simple mantra whose repetition may shift the mind from the critical-discursive to the contemplative-ecstatic:

4 pages from a total of 15 in the *eschenau sutra* (2000), published by the Musée de Beaux Arts, Lausanne, in 2002.

to be all ways to be 1974
printed on rice paper, at the sangram press, kathmandu
each frame 21.2 x 15.1 cm

to be all ways to be all ways to be to be to be to be all ways

eschenau sutra, published by the Musée de Beaux Arts, Lausanne, in 2002, contains, among others, the following familiar word repetitions, each presented on its own page, reproducing the artist's distinctive graphite or colour crayon orthography:

in the studio 1977
steigerwald

> all all all all all all all all all all all all all all all all all all all all all all all all all
> this this this this this this this this this this this this this this this this this this
> you me you me you me you me you me you me you me you me you me you
> is is is is is is is is is is is is is is is is is is is is is is is is is is is is is is is is
> part part part part part part part part part part part part part part part part
> different different different different different different different different
> identic identic identic identic identic identic identic identic identic identic
> one all one all one all one all one all one all one all one all one all one all one

The awareness that de vries seeks to inculcate demands not only thought and action but requires also the 'wise passiveness' of 'no-thought' (*mushin*) and inactivity:

> went into the wood to think something, but forgot to think and didn't find it necessary to draw any conclusions from this. (1975)

journeys and projects

1. 'the seeings of my beings'

'here and everywhere' (herman de vries)

In January 1975, while visiting Luang-Prabang, in Laos, de vries published, and put up at various points in the town, a poster which advertised the whole of the town as an exhibition of itself: *exposition complète de luang-prabang*. As the poster indicated, this was an example of '*poésie actuelle*' – 'actual poetry': the town constituted, or was in the continuous act of constituting itself, as a work of art, it was, like everything else, in the condition of *poiesis*, a perpetual becoming. The poster declared that this *exposition* comprehended all the aspects of the townscape and all the objects, living and inanimate, of the region, and that it was open for all, every day for all time.

It was, of course, 'a part of reality' as a document of itself, something to be seen and walked through, experienced in all its aspects, nothing excluded. The exhibition of Luang-Prabang treated the entire town, in a manner of speaking, as a 'readymade', a found object whose re-nomination as an 'exhibition' redirected and changed the intensity of attention paid to it by taking it out of the world of politico-geographical administration and placing it within the magical domain of art.

In 1976 de vries created the *catalogue incomplet d'exposition complète de luang-prabang: a random sample of my visual chances, 18.1.1975*. This contains a copy of the poster with thirty-five black-and-white photographs taken on the day in question, each of a view, selected at random, of something, somewhere in the town. The sample of the visual chances is random in that the selection is taken from an infinite number of possible photographic opportunities, each itself related to a similarly infinite number of visual opportunities, the 'visual chances' of the title. Hence the necessarily incomplete nature of the catalogue, which is in any case something quite different from a 'documentation' in the manner of those orthodox conceptual art presentations that offer a textual and photographic record, or the poignant archaeological relics, of an art action or an event. The Luang-Prabang catalogue, it might be said, replicates (or enacts, or imitates) the relation of the experiencing subject to the inexhaustible, unending source of his experience: the world itself. As an art work, the catalogue is itself also a demonstration of the ancillary relation of art to the primary reality – the *poésie actuelle* – of nature and its objects (Luang-Prabang being here properly regarded as a part of nature).

The *exposition* of Luang-Prabang was an elaborated version of a particular type of work that de vries had begun to make at least two years earlier. This was the use of photography to document the randomness of a great deal of the subjective experience of seeing. The act of seeing – if that is an appropriate phrase for something that happens to us as much as something we do – is ineluctably private: no one else can see through our eyes. Even a shared sighting, of an object or an event looked at simultaneously with someone close by, is actually made up of two quite distinct views, and every such individual view is informed and shaped by a unique personal history of seeing and looking. 'The eye is part of the mind' (as Leo Steinberg expressed it), and 'thus nature presents every... person with a unique and unrepeated facet of appearance.

Poster for *the complete exhibition of luang-prabang* 1975
30.6 x 24.8 cm

EXPOSITION COMPLETE

de

luang - prabang

comprenant tous les éléments de paysage de ville et tous les objets, vivants et morts de la région de

luang - prabang

l'exposition est ouverte tous les jours, par tous les temps à continuer partout et par tous.

18 of 35 photographs comprising the *catalogue incomplet d'exposition complète de luang prabang: a random sample of my visual chances,* 18.1.1975

And the Ineluctable Modality of the Visible ... is a myth that evaporates between any two works of representation.' We make the world ours as we move through it, busily editing out much that presents itself to the potential of seeing.

The act of seeing, then, consists largely in selecting that to which we will pay attention, that upon which we will focus, out of the largely unseen flux of the visible. But to place exclusive emphasis on the active agency of our seeing is to falsify visual experience. For a

great deal of what we see, and what we look at (the act of attention that may or may not follow on from seeing) is not so much selected as found by chance; it places itself, so to speak, within sight, it presents itself to our eyes. This constant renewal of the visible world, to which our response is anything but passive, is one of the wonders of our existence, a source of constant surprise and delight. By placing the actuality of *seeing* within the reality of *being*, de vries asserts the complexly dynamic interaction of consciousness with the primary reality of the world.

The *exposition complète* was intended to awaken consciousness to the undeniable truth that anything and everything, here and everywhere, is interesting enough to warrant attention. de vries demonstrates this in practice in the series of photoworks entitled *the seeings of my beings* (begun in 1973 and sporadically returned to over the next three years), each one itself consisting of a random sample of such 'seeings'. In this respect *the seeings of my beings* are like the 'visual chances' taken in Luang-Prabang. For it was by chance and change that de vries found himself in that particular Laotian town, and anywhere could have served as well for the purposes of the work, which is in itself simply exemplary. Similarly, the locations chosen for his series of *seeings* – Eschenau, Senegal, Morocco, Kathmandu – have in themselves no special significance. Wherever de vries found himself he might make such works.

a random sample of the seeings of my beings, kathmandu 1974
this page, above left and right: 11.12.1974, 10h38; below left and right: 12.12.1974, 13h17.
opposite, above left and right: 13.12.1974, 12h21; centre left and right: 15.12.1974 8h30; below left and right: 17.12.1974 14h23.

Each pair of photographs shows a) herman de vries and b) the object of his gaze.

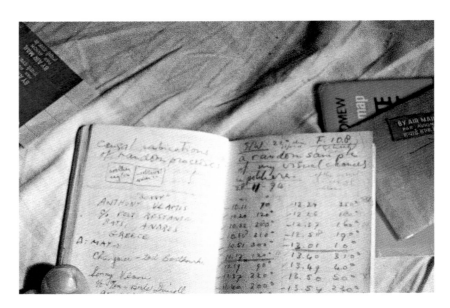

The photographs that make up the various series are, in terms of function, exactly opposite to holiday snapshots, whose deliberate purpose is the capturing of personally significant moments, persons and objects, just as they also differ from those photographs taken of picturesque views, or of natural or cultural topographies, or of objects, buildings, streets etc. of historical, artistic or personal interest. What is more, they have no artistic quality, are in no way posed or composed. As photographs having no burden of emotive or informational intent, they are categorically distinct, that is to say, from almost any common, culturally sanctioned or useful kind of photography. They thus fulfil the terms of the proposition-text:

every

thing

is

all

ways

significant

for

all

The makings of the series of *the seeings of my beings* were governed by strict protocols that ensured randomness and purposefully eliminated any ascription of special personal significance to any particular moment on a journey or any particular subject for the camera. A typical protocol would determine the date and the time of the taking of a photograph (the camera was often held and operated by susanne). At a specified moment the first photograph – of herman, his *being* at that precise moment – would be taken. Handed the camera, he would then take the second photograph, of what was in front of his eyes – his *seeing* – at that moment (*see* previous spread).

It is a paradox, not without a certain humour, that only an elaborate protocol of such a kind could determine randomness. In this respect, as we can see, the procedure is directly analogous to that which created the particular, specific and entirely unpredictable configurations of the *random objectivations* of the same period. *the seeings of my beings* constituted, then, an important means by which de vries took his art from the abstraction of the graphic plane into the experienced reality of the concrete world. What is most significant about these works is the pure inconsequentiality of the recorded occasion: de vries might be working at a table, anywhere, walking along any street, standing on any balcony, looking into any cupboard, or looking out of any window.

A work closely related in concept, and also made in the turning-point year of 1973, is actually entitled *look out of any window*. This consists of a pamphlet, published by international artists cooperation (i.a.c.), Friedrichsfehn, which contains thirteen photographs of views taken from different windows, each recording some different circumstance of view: a different 'chance and change situation'; the work is completed by a title page, a text and a colophon. de vries's text takes as its title the injunction that opens the song 'Box of Rain' by Grateful Dead and quotes extensively from the song.

In 1979, for a group exhibition at the Groninger Museum in Groningen, Holland, de vries made looking out of the window itself the substance of the work he contributed. A simple wall plaque of the kind commonly used in museums and exhibitions to identify a work was attached to the wall by the window: *blik op de a en het pottebakkersrijge – look out and see potters street*. Here it is the mundane and unspectacular street outside that is brought into sharp focus, as if the window were a kind of lens to sharpen and enhance the reality, the 'actual poetry' of the everyday world.

photographs taken at three-second intervals of water in a small stream at glen shieldaig, close to loch dughaill, scotland 1986

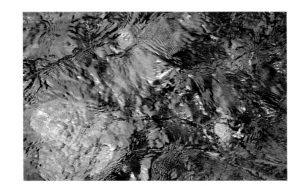

108 livres de fleurs de lavande/108 pounds of
lavender flowers 1998
inverleith house, royal botanic garden, edinburgh

There is in this a historical reference, appropriate to its placement in a museum, to the framed view of the city or the street, or of the ordinary working landscape, in Dutch seventeenth-century painting, whose masters – Jan Vermeer, Pieter de Hooch, Meindert Hobbema – were similarly concerned with the poetry that resides in quotidian actuality. To invoke such art is simultaneously to allude ironically to the later traditions in European painting of the picturesque and the sublime, which in their different ways dramatise, sentimentalise or falsify the actual. But even the modest and truthful realism of Dutch painting cannot compete with the marvellous unpredictability of looking out of a real window, in real time, to see the sun shining, maybe, or the rain raining, or a bird winging through the suburban air.

> How do you know but ev'ry bird that cuts the airy way,
> Is an immense world of delight, closed by your senses five?
>
> William Blake

In his many journeys to other places in the world, however exotic or remote those places may seem to be, it is what de vries prosaically calls the 'facts' that make their way into the journals that he creates as a documentation and a record. As with *the seeings of my beings*, it is what singles itself out from the infinite diversity of possibilities that is caught in the frames of the journals, which are composed of random samples thus encountered in whatever place the artist finds himself at a given moment. How could any plant, blade of grass, leaf, shell, rabbit dropping or earth specimen be more significant than any other? Every natural object is like Blake's 'ev'ry bird' – 'an immense world of delight'. 'If the doors of perception were cleansed' wrote Blake elsewhere, thinking of the 'clos'd senses five', 'every thing would appear to man as it is, infinite.' For de vries, the opening of the senses – sight, hearing, touch, taste and smell – and the consequent expansion of consciousness are primary purposes of art.

The significance of the senses other than that of sight is emphasised in a conversation recorded with Paul Nesbitt at the Royal Botanic Garden, Edinburgh, while de vries was preparing for his exhibition there in 1992: 'perhaps the most direct connection to our environment is our sense of smell (i prefer to use the word life-space rather than environment, because for me it has the sense of us being part of it more). when we were in the rock garden and the

rosa damascena – 108 pounds of rose petals 2003
cistercian abbey, bebenhausen, germany

peat house, i smelled the juices from the small-leaved species of *ledum* and *rhododendron*. every species smelled different, and you can with some experience identify many plants from their smell. we have no words to describe this, and it's nice to do something that we don't need words for. our nose has perhaps the most direct connection to our environment of all our organs.' At Inverleith House in 1992, de vries dramatically demonstrated his point with *108 livres de fleurs de lavande*, a work made at Mouans-Sartoux the previous year, whose perfume permeated the beautiful house. Elsewhere, he has made similar scented floor works, such as *rosa damascena* – 108 pounds of rose petals in 1984 and 2003 and *hopfen* (hops) in 2001.

For his installation *human life* (1989) de vries brought back from the market in Kathmandu thirty-six food samples – rice, peas and pulses, aromatic spices, etc. – and set them out in terra-cotta bowls in a grid-array, adding to them three further bowls, containing earth and water, the necessities of all living things, and cannabis, an example of the 'mind-moving' plant substances that have always aided human contemplation of the mystery of life itself. In *documents of a stream* (1976-1981), de vries recalls sound-works, such as *water, the music of sound* (1977):

diary of a visit to
pashupatinath

january-february 1989

herman de vries

with some additional facts from
kirtipur, patan, nagarkot, sajrabarahi, kathmandu/pokhara.

diary of a visit to pashupatinath
january-february 1989
10 out of 44 entries

title page

thevetia neriifolia

ficus religiosa

aerial roots of ficus religiosa

adhatoda vasica

skeleton of an epiphytic fern

cannabis indica from a field near patan

ancient and much worshipped stone figure of ganesha

earth rubbings

unidentified leaves

Behind herman de vries,
from earth: nepal and india 1992
100 x 140 cm;
in front of him,
human life 1989
a complete sample of cereals and beans from the
bazaar of kathmandu with, closest to him, dishes
containing water, earth and hemp seeds

'once i made a recording of water... it contains the sounds of rain, the sounds of the sea on the west coast of ireland, and the sounds of six little waterfalls from a brook here in the forest [steigerwald]. and every waterfall had its own sound, its own individuality. and still it is the same stream... and still it is the same water...' To the seeings of our beings, then, we might add those other bodily senses by which we establish our reality in the unstoppable all-around-us 'round world' of our phenomenological experience, not forgetting that with every step we take we touch the earth.

On the title page to his *diary of a visit to pashupatinath, january-february 1989* de vries appends a further note:*with some additional facts from kirtipur, patan, nagarkot, vajra bahini, kathmandu and pokhara.* This elaboration serves both to make for accuracy of record and to enact in the procession of names the progression of his journey. But by his simple description of the entries in the *journal* as 'facts' – they include, as do all the *journals*, plant specimens, fronds and single leaves, earth rubbings, photographs of natural objects and cultural artefacts – de vries is subverting the Wittgensteinian distinction so baldly stated in *Tractatus* 1.1: 'The world is the totality of facts, not of things.' Things, for de vries, *are* facts, and *contra* Wittgenstein (*Tractatus* 1.2), 'the world' does not 'divide into facts' but is composed of *things.* They may fall into generic categories but the things here present in the *journals* are of a specific place, collected at a particular time: Mouans-Sartoux (1991), Leros and Patmos (1996), l'Île Sainte Marguerite (9th April 1997), Gomera (2000), Eschenau (2002), etc.

Of course, the many entries in the many *journals* constitute an ever-growing conglomeration of singular reminders: 'everything' de vries remarked to Nesbitt, 'represents always something.' To commemorate, make memory possible, and to communicate something to others of the flow of an individual experience, are the principal motives for making a diary. de vries also conceives of the artist as the journeyman rememberer for the tribe (as we shall see, to keep alive memories of important things is the very purpose of his great documentary work, *natural relations*, which I discuss in the final section of this chapter). Travelling in Scotland for the first time in 1985 (when he made his first journal, *Scottish Diary*) de vries noted on the maps the names of many forests. 'but when i visited these places, i found not forest, but moorland, or grazing land. [the great caledonian forest that covered the biggest part of scotland was almost completely destroyed for timber, and in the first place to make charcoal for smelting iron ore. this happened after the occupation of scotland by the english.] realising the impoverishment of this landscape, i studied all the topographical maps and made the text of a book, *in memory of the scottish forests*, containing the names of all those lost forests. but with a book you don't get back a forest.' Those absent forests can no longer be walked in, experienced by the sentient being: they remain only in word-traces on maps. At Inverleith House, the moving litany of their names was inscribed on the gallery wall in charcoal – a trace of wood transformed by fire – carrying in this case a particular poignancy. It was a temporary monument to lost local things, itself soon to be erased.

2. from earth

The *earth museum* in the house at Eschenau holds over seven thousand samples of earth, gathered by de vries or sent to him from all over the world. Begun in 1983, it is a unique collection; it is extensive and diverse, and although it has no scientific purpose it constitutes a compendium in which every type of earth (limestone, sandstone, peat, volcanic, marl, ash, etc., etc.) is represented, and which visibly demonstrates the endless variety, beauty and subtlety of the colours of earth. Each specimen is dried into a powder-like consistency,

Above:
from earth: las tierras de las rosas de la gomera
1990
120 x 180 cm

Opposite, above:
herman de vries with the *earth catalogue*,
Eschenau, 2004

Opposite, below:
herman de vries collecting earth on the island of
El Hierro, Canary Islands.

securely bagged, boxed and labelled with its date of collection and its place of origin; each is represented in the *earth catalogue* by a rubbing made by hand on paper, identified by source, and carefully kept in identical Solander boxes. Thus the first and last of things – 'a handful of dust' – is given its due, and each sample is held in common with every other, none preferred to any other.

In *The Ninth Duino Elegy,* Rainer Maria Rilke speaks of

> ... the traveller [who] returns from the mountain slopes into the valley,
> [who] brings, not a handful of earth, unsayable to others, but instead
> some word he has gained, some pure word, the yellow and blue gentian.

Rilke elevates the word over the object, in the romantic/modernist belief that reality is discovered and mediated through language (and art), that the thing experienced – the handful of earth, the yellow and blue gentian – is transcended by the word, which, once uttered, creates meaning, induces intensity of feeling, and bestows grace:

> Perhaps we are *here* in order to say: house
> bridge, fountain, gate, pitcher, fruit-tree, window ...
> but to *say* them, you must understand,
> oh to say them *more* intensely than the Things themselves
> ever dreamed of existing.'

The philosophical idealism that lies behind this is, for de vries, as he would put it, 'a metaphysics without the physics'. On the contrary, he would assert that 'the things themselves' – *les choses mêmes* – speak themselves, have a reality that is concrete. A specimen of earth is not a represented concept, it presents itself as mineral material, its history and its nature are, to use the *mot juste*, manifest in every handful. Crushed to a powder, reduced to its basic mineral 'suchness', rubbed down with the tips of the fingers into a simple rectangle of colour, the earth itself is transformed not into the sayable abstraction of the word, but into a material sign of its self-ness. It is an important aspect of the work that it declares the method of its making, that its unconcealing is unconcealed. It enters thus the domain of art, but an art that speaks of the irreducible actuality of the thing itself.

All of the *journals* that de vries has made on his travels and sojourns – in India, south-east Asia, North Africa, the Seychelles, the Canaries, Provence, the Greek islands, Scotland – have included rubbings of the local earth. (He has, also, of course, made many rubbings of earth collected in the vicinity of Eschenau.) Often, returning from a journey, or in preparation for an exhibition, he creates works that belong to the generic series *from earth*, presenting rubbings sometimes as a single rectangular image-object, more often in grid-arrays of various magnitudes. In certain exhibitions (the 2001 *exposition* at Digne, for example), the presentation of *from earth* (usually with a sub-title that indicates the origins of the samples) becomes a central element, sometimes involving a floor-based grid arrangement or a carpet of earth. In his *library of earth colours*, each of seven volumes (issued over several years by the Paris-based Lydia Megert Editions) consists of ten sheets or more with individual earth rubbings of a particular colour range – brown, grey, yellow, lilac etc. *from earth* continues to be of central importance to de vries's artistic-philosophical project.

It is tempting to think of the typical *from earth* array as a form of implied or abstract landscape art, in which the pigments that create the images are drawn from the very countryside whose name is given as sub-title. This might especially be so in a case such as the work shown at Digne-les-Bains (Haute Provence) entitled *de la terre, pays de cézanne* (2001). Such an inference is not justified by reference to either the technique or the presentation of the rubbed earth works. In the manner of their making de vries adopts a formulaic procedure, its simplicity consistent with everything else he does as an artist; it involves rubbing the sample with his fingers into a finely absorbent paper in an invariable up-and-down motion to create a distinctly vertical roughly square or rectangular image. This portrait format militates forcibly against a reading of the colour rectangle as a simplified landscape, with foreground, recession and horizon.

The presentation of the earth samples in grid configuration also in itself clearly precludes topographical allusion, and has, moreover, in these works, political implications. Historically speaking, European landscape painting has often been ideologically inflected in such ways as to be expressive of aspects of a specifically national political and social vision of the native land. The 'view' of the land taken in much, especially academic, landscape painting has also, incidentally, tended to perpetuate a one-way spectatorial prospect of the land. It is a view that can be traced to the Cartesian dualism (discussed earlier) that has provided the philosophical underpinning of both the Enlightenment and modern exploitation of the natural world. In *from earth*, de vries is concerned above all to dissociate himself from both kinds of ideological perspective, and to find an art form that registers ecological concern, love and wonder.

Intensely aware of the bitter European conflicts of his own lifetime, de vries knows too of the dark and mystical significance invested in the absurd idea of national earth. The commonest rallying cry in the many wars of the twentieth century has been to extend or defend the soil of the fatherland (or motherland), irrationally identifying the earth itself with family, tribe and nation. His collection and presentation of earth samples from everywhere under the sun, in a

herman de vries and susanne jacob de vries on the road to Tagaluche, Gomera, Canary Islands.

polska ziemia/polish earth 1991

this installation, Ulm 1998

erde/earth – baracke 15, kz, buchenwald 1995

Earth taken from the site of Barrack 15, Buchenwald concentration camp, Germany.

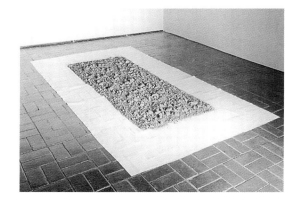

curatorial system that denies hierarchical classification, and in formations of display that privilege none, repudiates in practice and by implication such pernicious notions of national identity and ownership.

In certain cases, de vries has directly invoked particular historical events. In his exhibition at Erfurt in 1995 he created a temporary enclosed space, its walls made of white cotton fabric; within it, on the tiled floor, lay a white rectangular sheet with the shape and dimensions of a grave. On this was laid a rectangle of earth brought from the site of Barrack 15 of Buchenwald concentration camp, where medical experiments had been undertaken on prisoners. For de vries the poignancy of the action was intensified by the fact that Buchenwald is located in the beech woods between Erfurt and Weimar where Goethe, the supreme German exemplar of scientific and artistic humanism, had often walked. de vries personally returned the earth to its original site, keeping as a memento a mother-of-pearl shirt button he found in it. In *polish earth* (1991), earth samples from Polish cities are displayed in a grid on the floor of the gallery with their collection sites identified on the wall by their Polish place names, irrespective of the historical shifts of the national boundaries, and the changing political status (and therefore names) of those regions and cities that became by turn Polish, German, Soviet, etc. It is of course not only to these more overtly commemorative or contentious works that de vries referred when he responded to an observation from the present writer: 'oh yes! there is a lot of politics in my work!'

Each individual colour rectangle in *from earth* (whether presented singly or in multiples) is in fact a soft-edged cloud of colour-texture, an indefinite image with indistinct boundaries. We are thus confronted not by an analogy for the demarcation of the land, the arbitrary mapping of human territories, but by a neutral sign for the elemental substance. The geographical sub-

from earth: la vimonderie, normandy
1997
73 x 102 cm

titles, denoting the sites of collection, may refer to political entities – a city, a region, a state – but what we see carries no evidence, betrays no hint, of historical circumstance. What we see is a specific example of generic *earth*, a universal phenomenon, the very element which gives the planet its name, and which, with the fire and gas that forged its mineral character, is akin to the physical substance of countless other planets in the universe. Against the poignancies of the historical-geographical, and the divisive portioning out of the earth's surface, it asserts the absolute of timeless actual.

Questions of classification apply here as elsewhere in de vries's work. For the geologist, the earth scientist, the agronomist, the distinctions between the samples we see are definable and definitive: generic earth is classified into specific soils, each with distinct chemical properties and the particular values that derive from them. de vries is well aware of this, but his project is not concerned with those scientific aspects, being more epistemological and political in nature. The differences between the samples, in the *earth museum* and in the visual arrays, are of no particular significance beyond their demonstration of the ineluctability of difference: in the *earth museum* and in the other *from earth* works, it is only the naming of their origins that signifies difference. This purely circumstantial geographical identification provides the

von acht brandstellen/from eight bonfire sites 1991
76 x 104 cm

Ash from the remains of eight bonfires around
Eschenau.

only systematic order to the collection. Take the labels away and every sample is, for all the distinction and nuance of its colour and texture, merely earth. Each, however, is different.

There is a wonder in this nuanced diversity. It is emphasised in the ordering of the presentations, which have the poetic, or musical, virtues of colour variation and tonal change within a rhythmic formal structure of regular intervals. It is present also, by implication, in the references to their many different places of origin. Cees de Boer, the most sympathetic and perceptive interpreter of de vries's work, has written memorably of these aspects of the earth works, linking their formal repetitive music to the structures of Vedic and Buddhist meditation: 'when all the titles of de vries's earth rubbings are strung together, it articulates the mantra which his earth museum silently sings to itself. when we consider that this earth museum is a fragment of the whole earth, then this mantra is in turn taken up in the never-ending mantra which the earth herself sings, spinning her journey through the universe like a prayer wheel.' This catches well the implicit oppositions in *from earth* between the specific and the general, the local versus the universal, the thing versus the sign, the concrete versus the abstract, the down-to-earth versus the stellar and transcendent.

3. natural relations

'in memory of what has been forgotten' (herman de vries)

In 1989 herman de vries published *natural relations: eine skizze* (*a sketch*). The title is not without a gentle irony, for this 'sketch' is a hardcover volume of 797 crowded pages, the exhaustive summation of many years research in the library, in the field and in the market-places of the world. Into this capacious portmanteau of a book de vries packed an extraordinary body of information and knowledge concerning the medicinal and psychedelic – 'mind-moving' – properties of plants and their pharmacological derivatives. *natural relations* draws upon extensive sources in anthropology, philology, botany, ethnobotany, mycology, phytochemistry, folklore, herbal history, pharmacology; on information supplied by shamans, herbalists, holy men and shopkeepers in the markets of India and North Africa; and on the artist's own ex-perience, and that of others, of the effects on body and mind of herbs, plant derivatives and other substances.

It is 'a sketch' because the totality of the knowledge that has been known, so much of which has been in any case forgotten or lost, can never be assembled or described, and every attempt to summarise such knowledge – from oral accounts, from literature, from folklore, from scientific investigation – can be nothing more than a brief adumbration. 'experience and know-ledge which has been collected over thousands of years', wrote de vries in the introductory essay, 'has been thoughtlessly lost. natural relations have to a great extent disappeared. although the materials I have collected may seem to be of some magnitude, they are nevertheless merely fragments.' The ignorant and arrogant zeal of Christian missionaries contributed in no small way to the loss of precious unitary knowledge wherever they spread the Word and promoted the dualistic values of enlightenment: 'these natural relations at once constituted religion and philosophy and were a guide to practical life. "superstition" was the name given to what was not understood or what appeared to challenge the introduced religion, which itself was based not on the actualities of experience but on pure belief.'

It was not, of course, only in the colonies of the Americas, Africa and Asia that the patterns of accumulated wisdom, and the specialised knowledge of plants and their healing and visionary properties, were destroyed, but in European societies also. de vries traces in religious arrogance, and in the contemptuous rationalistic mistrust of both common custom and arcane knowledge, the tragic 'disintegration of the original nature of man' and the con-sequent breakdown of his harmonious relations to the natural world. The spiritual and cultural basis of these 'natural relations' was replaced by the rigid doctrine of original sin on the one hand, and a narrowly prejudiced scientism on the other, often in an unholy ideological alliance. All over Europe during the sixteenth and seventeenth centuries, the witch hunt – 'the first anti-drugs movement, [which] resulted in the horrible deaths of hundreds of thousands of people' – was a component of the cruel and near-universal suppression of surviving pre- and non-Christian customs and knowledge.

There can be no proper understanding of de vries's complex/simple artistic philosophy that does not take account of the centrality to his vision of the cultural significance of the old wisdom of 'natural relations'. At its heart is a desire to reinstate and elaborate the forgotten knowledge and understanding of the vegetable kingdom, from subterranean fungus to great forests, as the home of our human terrestrial life, the provider of all we need to survive, the vital shelter and source of our well-being on earth. The revival of this ancient lore can only be enhanced by the findings of the modern natural sciences: 'within the coherent, self-regulating system of nature, the existence of so many diverse vegetable substances is no accident, for they have functions within the system, not only for the plants themselves, but even more for the

With Omar Gaye in Dakar, Senegal, collecting ethno-botanical information for *natural relations*, 1985.

other organisms within this complex system, which [theodor] schwenk appropriately described as "the sensible chaos" '.

de vries's many-faceted understanding of these things, grounded as it is in his history as a professional scientist, and also in his personal experience of mind-moving plant and mushroom derivatives and of psychedelic drugs, including LSD, is the mainspring of a deeper politics than that described as 'environmentalism'. For as well as its conscientious concern for material and recreational utility, it comprehends a loving consideration of all the other living things that share this life space, and a consciousness of the spiritual and metaphysical aspects of human

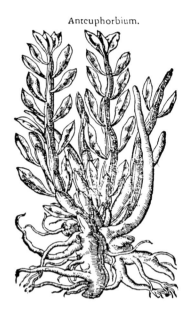

ma 229. --- battata uschi ("pomme de terre de loup")
muster: wurzelstücke
"mit zwiebeln (am besten wilde zwiebel) kochen und
essen gegen magenschmerzen" (=bauchschmerzen?).

ma 232. *senecio anteuphorbium* sbardo
      compositae
muster: sukkulente stengelteile
gesammelt im feld.

Anteuphorbium.

<u>tabernaemontanus</u> (1731), gibt eine deutliche abbildung,
(hier reproduziert) und teilt mit:
"das anteuphorbium wird auch von <u>dodonaeus</u> an bemeldtem
ort ("lybia") beschrieben / das es viel runde grüne
stengel habe / welches blätter sich den portulacen ver-
gleichen / haben auch ein dicke grosse wurtzel mit viel
nebenwurzeln."
"von diesem kraut schreibt <u>dodonaeus</u>, dass es viel saffts
bey sich habe / welcher gar nicht scharff sey / sondern
etwas schleimig und kalt / und werde von den einwohnern
wider die grosse hitz und schärffe des *euphorbii*
gebraucht."

74

"entire plant used against burns often occuring due to
the caustic latex from the cactus-like euphorbias common
in sw-morocco, where the plant grows. resinous sap
prescribed as a calmative; internally for stamachache
and enteritis () strong sedative for all pains including
abdominal, dorsal, burns." (<u>boulos</u>)

"le latex de cette plante est employé en frictions dans
les rhumatismes. il intervient également dans les soins
des plaies et blessures en qualité d'hémostatique. intus
et extra le latex est utilisé comme sédatif de toutes
les douleurs: abdominales, dorsales, brûlures etc.

le miel butiné sur ses fleurs, âcre et un peut amer, est
considéré comme un bon fortifiant." (<u>bellahdar</u>)

ma 242. *ocimum tereticaule* habak
      labiatae
muster: blütenstände mit samen
dt.: basilikum
"zum aussähen in blechdose oder topf".
"in wasser zum gesicht waschen".
man sieht diese pflanze oft, gepflanzt in blechdosen in
fensteröffnungen von kleinen restaurants, zur abwehr von
fliegen, aber auch manchmal auf den dächern der häuser
(zauberabwehr?).

restaurant auf dem souk von inezgane.

ma 243. *amomum grana paradisi* l gusa saharouia
      zingiberaceae
muster: samen
dt.: paradieskörner

75

life − of those things 'of which we cannot speak'. In *natural relations* he quotes the anthropologist Gerardo Reichel-Dalmatoff on the beliefs of the Tukanoan Indians of the Colombian Amazon: 'there is no religion in terms of prayers or sacrifice. the spiritual life of man consists in acquiring discipline in what concerns food, sex and social interrelations because it is always nature that is the model, even for the supernatural. tukanoan thought operates on the principle of analogy: man is central and nature is an analogy of man ... [of] the human body.'

For de vries the triply beneficent properties of plants for the individual organism − nutritional, healing, consciousness-enhancing − serve identical purposes in the general sphere of social existence. They do far more than serve human material and aesthetic purposes, they are a necessary part of a complete system, the ecology of life on earth. In his first editorial for *integration*, de vries's interdisciplinary learned journal devoted to 'mind-moving plants and culture', published from Eschenau through the early 1990s, de vries wrote:

a basic difference between the western culture and the so-called primitive cultures
is that our culture is primarily and basically a commercial one. everything is exploit-
able and will be judged after its chances for profit. (the plants of the gods became

Pages from *natural relations: eine skizze*, published by the Verlag für Moderne Kunst, Nürnberg, 1989.

104

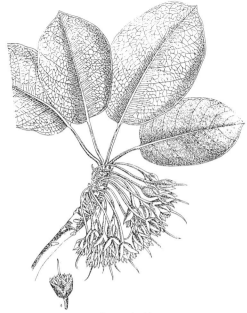

madhuca indica

some food before anything else. so bhaghavan gave him twenty-
five sacks of rice and twelve sacks of lentils. he ate it all
and said, "this is nothing; give me more." then they gave him
twelve sacks of gram. when he had eaten that also, he said to
bhagavan, "old uncle, you've given me nothing to drink."
"you must go and find some liquor," said bhagavan.
"what is that?" asked bhimsen.
"go and see," said bhagavan.
bhimsen went to the forest and searched and searched. after
a long time he came to a mahua tree. the tree was hollow and
that hollow was full of liquor. all round on the branches
were sitting birds who had been drinking it - haril, phadki,
parrots, crows, maina, every kind of bird. they were all
nodding their heads. "why are they nodding their heads like
that?" thought bhimsen. he climbed the tree to see and there
the hollow was full of liquor. bhimsen dipped his hand in and
sucked it.
"this is liquor! this is liquor!" he shouted, and began to
drink. when he had had a bellyful his head began to nod also.
he sat down with the birds and they all nodded their heads
together.
then he filled twelve gourds full of the liqour and brought
it back for bhagavan to drink. they sat down, bhagavan and
the wind and the crow, and they drank the liquor out of leaf-
-cups. then when their heads were nodding, bhimsen got up and
walked round the earth.

416

Destillationsapparat der Bhil.

1. Hãndluñ — Tontopf mit Mahuwa-Fruchtwasser
2. Babari — Kleiner Verdämpfer
3. Nãl — Bambus-(Überlauf) Rohr
4. Guñiyo — Kupfernes Auffanggefäß
5. Khado — Kühlwasser

für "heilige bäume" siehe weiter unter coll.nr. 1189
(butea frondosa)

417

consumer goods.) for our dealing with psychoactive substances this has been
disastrous... there has to be found a way out of this hysterical drug paranoia!

The purpose of *integration*, of which six substantial numbers were issued between 1991 and
1995, was to bring together scientific, historical and cultural perspectives to a field of study
generally neglected in the academy. The journal, so named, was a continuation of the total
creative project of *natural relations*; its editorial programme had been effectively defined in
the 1989 introduction to the book:

> these 'natural relations' include virtually everything within the environment of
> our life on earth – the air we breathe, the water we drink and in which we bathe,
> the food we eat, the electromagnetic fields which surround us, the earth on which
> we walk. it is the plants we ingest that connect us, however, to our life-space,
> because of the substances they contain that sustain and regulate our organism
> [...] what was once life-space is now [merely] 'environment'.
>
> 'the world does not divide into facts, it is a self-regulating unit! In this sense i
> would conceive of my work as also political.

händler in der nähe des pashupatinath-tempelkomplexes, nepal, die rudraksha rosenkränze an hindu pilger und besucher ver-kaufen.

zerbrochene betelnüsse auf dem markt in alt-delhi. (*areca catechu*).

mango- und pipalblätter sowie orange *tagetes* blüten über der tür eines geschäftes in patan, nepal. eine magisch-religiöse handlung "zum schutz und für viel glück." mango-blätter fehlen auch nie bei hindu-heiratsritualen. sie deuten auf fruchtbar-keitsvorstellungen hin.

pan, *piper betle*, blätter auf dem markt in alt-delhi.

'*coacervavi omne quod inveni*' – 'I made a heap of all I could find': the words of the eighth-century historian Nennius, introducing his *Historia Brittonum*, might well apply to the making of *natural relations: eine skizze*. Nennius compiled his record, from many sources, to ensure that valuable materials from the past 'might not be trodden underfoot' and such precious infor-mation and such precious information 'be like smoke dissipated'. Such strenuous, single-handed compilation of natural history, natural philosophy, information and legend has a long history, beginning, appropriately perhaps, with the *Natural History* of Pliny the Elder. It includes such works as Robert Burton's *Anatomy of Melancholy* and *De Amboinsche Rarieteitkamer* (*The Am-bonese Curiosity Cabinet*) compiled by the amazing German naturalist Georg Eberhard Rumpf (Rumphius), known as the 'Indian Pliny', which was published in Amsterdam in 1705, three years after its blind author had died. Even this 400-page encyclopaedia, recording and investigating the marine life and rock types in the coastal waters of Ambon, is modest compared to Rumphius's greatest work, the exhaustive *Herbarium Amboinense* (*Ambonese Herbal*), which was finally published between 1741 and 1750. This, in over 1600 folio pages, fully described over twelve hundred plants from the small Dutch East Indian island, whose principal crop for the Dutch East India Company was the nutmeg. The many illustrated Herbals of the fifteenth

Pages from *natural relations: eine skizze*, 1989.

Top left: traders outside the pashupatinath temple complex, nepal, selling rudraksha garlands to visitors and pilgrims;
top right: cracked betel nuts (*areca catechu*) in a market in old delhi;
bottom left: mango and pipal leaves and the orange flowers of *tagetes* hanging over the door of a business selling objects 'for protection and for great luck'. mango leaves are also used in hindu marriage ceremonies to signify or enhance fertility;
bottom right: *piper betle* – pan leaves in the market in old delhi.

der frauenmarkt in dakar, marche de la gare. hier mit
pflanzlichen duftstoffen im angebot. vorne tontöpfe zum ver-
räuchern von tsuray, harz.

strassenhändler mit amuletten. rundum tüten mit pflanzen-
substanzen womit die amulette gefüllt werden.

marktstand mit aphrodisiaka, dakar.

markt in der nähe von dakar mit bündeln kinkelibah, *combretum
micranthum*.

Top left: marché de la gare – the women's market in dakar, with fragrant plants for sale. In the foreground are clay pots used for smoking tsuray, harz;
top right: street traders selling amulets, surrounded by bags of plant substances with which the amulets are filled;
bottom left: market stall with parts of plants believed to have aphrodisiac qualities, dakar;
bottom right: bundles of kinkelibah – *combretum micranthum* in a market near dakar.

and sixteenth centuries, drawings and descriptions from which de vries reproduces in his compendium, together with many quotations from them, were clearly also a source and an inspiration for *natural relations*.

Such volumes were often, like the prototypical Pliny, more than merely scientific. They were poetic in texture, steeped in esoteric lore, fanciful and speculative, receptive to odd fragments of information; they passed on reports from travellers, recounted personal anecdotes. This suggests quite another way of looking at the extraordinary achievement of *natural relations*, the book. It is to see it as a compendious poem, an eclectic rhapsody. Viewed thus, it takes its place in the diverse body of modernist writings – from James Joyce through Ezra Pound, David Jones and William Carlos Williams to Günter Grass and W.G. Sebald – which turned its back on self-contained unity of form in favour of the encyclopaedic gathering together and presentation of heterogeneous materials. Such works might contain fictional and discursive prose, rhetoric and poetry in several languages; aspects of folklore and myth; information drawn from sources scientific, historical, anthropological, botanical and pharmacological; quotations; digressions; photographs and illustrations, typographical experiments, graphics. In its incorporation of found texts, quotations, fragments from other books and other cultures, and in its delight in language,

and in the naming of things, *natural relations* may be said to share the poetics of that modernism: 'no ideas but in things!'

After a discursive introduction, the work is held together, in fact, by the extensive 'catalogue', a directory of almost two thousand plants (the last entry is 2031, but some numbers are missing from certain of the sections) that are known to have medicinal or 'mind-moving' properties. The catalogue is divided into sections relating to the geographical sources of specimens – Morocco, Eschenau, Delhi, Senegal – and of information about them. The plants and their derivatives are the real 'things' whose names and physical qualities are the very object of the monumental effort to remember and record. This extensive listing is itself a kind of litany, a roll call, and, as the epigraph of the book suggests, a memorial: '*zum gedächtnis dem, was vergessen ist* – in memory of what is forgotten'. Among other things, *natural relations* is an elegy to the innumerable plants whose healing and sacred virtues have been lost to human use, and a lament for a lost wisdom.

The total project centred on *natural relations* culminated in the publication of the book by the Karl Ernst Osthaus-Museum in Hagen, to accompany an exhibition and the installation there of

natural relations: part of *eschenau collection*
1985

the locked paradise. This consisted of a greenhouse, placed in the gallery, containing living specimens, collected by de vries, of twenty-one 'mind-moving' plants, including various species of thorn-apple (*Datura*), *Cannabis indica*, poppy, morning glory, tobacco, peyotl, tea, coffee, and others. Of the most significant plants in the defining category, only that of the coca was absent, its inclusion forbidden by the Federal authorities. The work was both a celebration of the beauty and value of the plants, and a warning that the loss of their properly integrated uses, sacred and medicinal, was a sign of man's increasing alienation from his own biosphere, and of the individual from his 'life-space'.

The crowded glass *cabinet*, a kind of garden into which the spectator could look, but whose door was officially sealed against entry, presented an image of a green Eden, like a miniature and special version of the botanical garden glasshouses that inspired Henri Rousseau's visions of paradise. Its vegetable inhabitants, moreover, could be acknowledged as companions of man in an ancient natural history of beneficial interrelations. Now this Paradise may be lost. Those living connections are disrupted, and modern man is estranged from the green world around him. From being within that Edenic life space, he has become a spectator of it,

109

natural relations: the locked paradise 1989
with mind moving (psychedelic) plants
karl ernst osthaus-museum, hagen, germany

viewing it 'as through a glass darkly'. Man's acquisition and elevation of one kind of scientific knowledge has entailed the loss of another in which poetry and science are as one.

In a memorable work, de vries demonstrated that this disconnection from natural relations is not, and never can be, complete. In *i am what i am. flora incorporata*, a book published in 1988, the artist listed on individual pages the names of the 461 plants that he could recall having ingested in his life, whether as seed, shoot, leaf, fruit, juice or substance, in whatever way – eating, drinking, smoking – and for whatever purpose – nourishment, healing, stimulus or consciousness-altering. 'the names of the plants which contributed ... the most to my being conscious are placed at the beginning: *cannabis indica, psylocybe* spec., *papaver somniferum, peganum harmala, withania somnifera, atropa belladonna, hyoscyamus* spec., *datura* spec., *lophophora williamsii.* they are the holy herbs of peoples and civilisations, more spiritually connected to their life-space than our bourgeois-industrialised barbarity can be, where these plants are degraded to the level of consumption only, as is everything else. our bodies have special receptors for their messages, receptors that are degenerating, and thus the message of unity will be lost.'

In the text introducing this litany of honoured names, this remembrance of those things that have made him what he is, herman de vries has written what amounts to an eloquent and succinct manifesto of his life's work, a statement of the nature of his being in the world:

> *i am what i am* is a document of my unity with my life space. in fact, it shows that we cannot separate 'me' and my life-space. i use 'life-space' instead of en-vironment because 'life-space' shows connection, unity, identity. 'environment' is a general word. it signifies what is around us. it can be everywhere. life-space is here, where I am. environment is around men, it is centred on man... men and environment are separated. life-space signifies the space we live in, live with, live from its space we move in, are in, where we eat, from which we eat, wherein i breathe, from which i drink. it is to what my excrement returns. it's the space of my cyclic participation. here i plant my maize, here i buy eggs, here i collect nettles, elder berries, hawthorn, which i need for the continuation of my life. by them i live, with them i live, from them i have life. what i take into me is what i am. my life space is my identity: 'i am what i am'.

digne: a point in space

'digne became quickly part of my life, it settled itself in my heart for it is real poetry that i found here as almost nowhere else.' (herman de vries 2003)

1. honouring dr honnorat: collecting, naming and culture

At the Musée Gassendi at Digne-les-Bains (Haute Provence), in 2001, herman de vries created *le cabinet de botanique en l'honneur du docteur honnorat*, a remarkable permanent installation in tribute to an outstanding naturalist who was the town's physician in the early years of the nineteenth century. It was not unusual throughout Europe during that period for professional men – lawyers, doctors, clergymen – to take a keen interest in the folklore and natural history of their native region, indeed a great deal of the most important groundwork of specimen collection, identification and factual description of biological and geological phenomena was undertaken by keen amateurs. Their findings were published in local guides and manuals, and formed the basis of hundreds of scientifically invaluable local museum collections.

Following the universal adoption at the end of the eighteenth century of the Linnaean system of classification and binomial nomenclature, the following century was to become the golden age of natural history collections, and of systematic identification and classification. Among even the most gifted of the great company of amateur scientific naturalists, Simon-Jude Honnorat was an exceptional polymath: he was a botanist, geologist, palaeontologist and entomologist of extraordinary ability, commitment and energy, and in addition to meeting the demands of his everyday medical work in the town, his assiduous collecting of rock types, biological specimens and fossils, and his scientific work of identification and classification, he also compiled the first Provençal/French dictionary, which was published in 1846-48. This was a work of great etymological importance, for Provençal was already a language in decline.

Something very interesting was already well under way when de vries was first invited to visit Digne with a view to creating work in the region around the town and to make an exhibition and a publication. The invitation came from the museum director, Nadine Gomez-Passamar, on behalf of CAIRN (Centre d'Art Informel de Recherche sur la Nature), a vital agency pioneering creative collaboration between the Museum and the Réserve Géologique de Haute-Provence, centred on the promotion of contemporary art as a means to deepen public understanding of the natural world as a whole, and of the ecological richness of the region itself. CAIRN, under the direction of Gomez-Passamar, whose understanding of de vries's life-project is profoundly sympathetic, was in this respect a perfect organisation within which the artist could develop a new and coherent complex of works responding to an environment that is in so many ways different from that of Eschenau. In terms of both its informing ideas and its practical programme there was a close correspondence with de vries's own personal philosophy and practice, and susanne and herman have continued to work creatively with Gomez-Passamar and CAIRN.

de vries made his first visit to Digne in April 1999. He began at once to explore the mountains and valleys of the Réserve Géologique, collecting earth samples and prospecting sites for possible works. It was on this visit that he was surprised and delighted to learn of Dr Honnorat's close connection with the town and of his scientific researches in the region, for he

herman de vries and susanne jacob de vries collecting plant specimens at Faillefeu, Haute-Provence, France, May 2000.

had already encountered the philological work of the good doctor some years earlier during his first sojourn in Provence. This was when, in 1991, de vries had been a guest of the Espace de l'Art Concret at the Château de Mouans at Mouans-Sartoux in the hills behind Cannes. Here was held his first one-man show in France, *terre, vie et poésie*, for which he prepared a journal, and a number of works using materials from the surrounding area.

In addition to the *journal de mouans-sartoux* (1991), these included (also in 1991) *le témoin* (*the witness*) and *le lierre par lui-même* (*the ivy by itself*), the former the untreated trunk of an old olive tree placed on a low stone plinth, the latter a framed ivy plant growing on a wall. ('Exhibit the untouched and cherish the uncarved block.') Both neatly encapsulate key ideas. *the witness* is both that which has seen time pass, and that which stands as a record of its own being, a witness-informant to the processes of its own formation and deformation, a part of the world that is a document of itself, literally a piece of information. The ivy's *self-portrait* is likewise itself: its realisation as an art work conterminous with its realisation as a work of nature. The photograph of the work is but a trace of the work itself, a piece of information. And unlike a painted portrait this is an image that changed, as its subject changed, with time: like de vries's *rasenstücke*, it is 'more real' than a painting of the natural object would be (the photograph is the record of a moment – a 'seeing of its being'). The *journal de mouans-sartoux* contains ferns and fungi, earth rubbings, photographs and other materials, and rubbings of local earth. de vries included in his exhibition an array of stone fragments collected from the roadside near a local chapel devoted to St John, and a collection of the bagged earth samples. As always, these 'real works' are images of themselves.

As we have seen, it is habitual for de vries to comprehend within his imaginings of a given site the human histories inscribed in the landscape and in the natural objects that compose it. Imagining is an active mental and intuitive engagement with the world: 'what the artist sees – observes – belongs just as much to his concept as what he does.' Human presence in the work begins with that of the artist himself, for the works derive from the 'seeings of his being', but what is seen – 'witnessed' – is the outcome of human agency (or neglect of action) as much as of natural processes: it is the product of millennia of creative interaction between man and the rest of nature. *le témoin* is an ancient olive tree from an olive grove that had been rooted out nearby, the ivy was growing on the château wall, the perfume carpet made for the exhibition at Mouans-Sartoux was of the cultivated lavender flowers of Provence (*see* page 91). Agronomy and science go hand in hand with technology and art in the human relation to the natural aspect of the world that is not human but within which the human takes its natural place.

Language is one of the keys to the mediation of that ineluctable relation of the human to extra-human nature, and, since Descartes, language has become the central focus of the modern endeavour, intellectual and artistic, to define the human project. The challenge de vries makes to the assumptions underlying that concentration on language have great philosophical subtlety and force; his originality lies in the beauty and diversity of his demonstrations that language has its limitations. In choosing the title *les chose mêmes/the things themselves* – for his exhibition at Digne (a title borrowed from an essay by the French writer Anne Moeglin-Delcroix), de vries was, in effect, rehearsing a familiar point of argument, which he had elaborated many years earlier in his playful interrogations of certain propositions in the *Tractatus* of Wittgenstein (*the wittgenstein papers/fragmentary arguments*, 1975). It is that things speak themselves: 'this line of thought is still guiding me now. i have nothing to say: it is all here.'

At another level, it might be said that de vries is actually deeply complicit with Wittgenstein, being always aware of the famous final Proposition 7. 'Whereof one cannot speak, thereof one must be silent.' In his *The Brown Book*, responding to the idea that music conveys 'feelings', Wittgenstein expostulated: 'music conveys to us *itself*!' This follows closely on an anecdote

Top
le témoin/the witness 1991
olive trunk

Bottom
le lierre par lui-même/the ivy by itself 1991
ivy plant growing on wall with frame

both espace de l'art concret, mouans-sartoux

and an observation that de vries would undoubtedly find deeply sympathetic: 'A friend and I once looked at beds of pansies. Each bed showed a different kind... Speaking about them my friend said "What a variety of colour patterns, and each says something". And this was just what I myself wished to say. [...] If one asked what the colour pattern of a pansy said, the right answer would have seemed to be that it said itself.'

In the opening remarks of *Philosophical Investigations*, Wittgenstein writes, almost as an aside, of the relationship between language and actions: 'Explanations come to an end somewhere'. The *Investigations* opens, famously, with a quotation from the *Confessions* in which St Augustine, whom Wittgenstein greatly admired, asserts that language begins – or consists – in the act of pointing at and naming objects. It is 'a primitive idea', Wittgenstein remarks, 'of the way language functions', and it proposes, moreover, 'the idea of a language more primitive than ours'. de vries would share with Wittgenstein an awareness of the limitation of the Augustinian model, recognising that it is inadequate to the extraordinary sophistication of a great deal of human utterance, but he knows also (as does Wittgenstein) that it contains a truth about the uses of such a simple language embedded in action. Explaining the rules by which certain kinds of linguistic meaning are generated does not help us with other kinds of (non-linguistic) meaning. The work of de vries begins where explanations come to an end, and things 'say themselves'.

Whatever else may be true of language, Augustine is absolutely right to emphasise that the process of naming and of pointing is, from the outset, central to the human interaction with

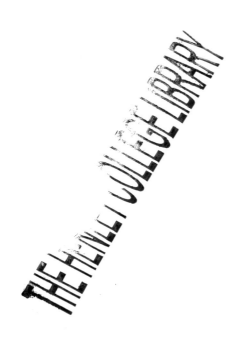

lou camp provençau/provençal field 1991
crayon on paper
123 x 155 cm

things and with other people in their reaction to things: 'When they (my elders) named some object, and accordingly moved towards something, I saw this and I grasped that the thing was called by the sound they uttered when they meant to point it out.' That simple gesture, and the act of naming, once elaborated, is productive of human culture in general, and in its specific features definitive of any culture in particular. This is the implication of one of the key works made by de vries at Mouans-Sartoux: *lou camp provençau* (1991) – provençal field – which consists of over a thousand Provençal wild plant names, written out by de vries in horizontal lines of various shades of green crayon.

These names were collected by de vries from a reprint of Honnorat's indispensable *Dictionnaire* (1846-48) and from the later dictionary (1879-86) compiled by Frédéric Mistral. Donated by the artist, *lou camp provençau* hangs now in the *le cabinet de botanique en l'honneur du docteur honnorat* in the museum at Digne. Closest attention to it is paid most usually by local visitors over the age of sixty, who may remember some of the dialect names even now as the language dies in common parlance, and the names might be forgotten forever. Their roll-call graces this monument to the language of the place, and to the people who used it in their everyday lives as they walked and worked in field and forest, and knew the virtues and uses – domestic, culinary, medicinal and magical – of the plants to which they gave their native names; like de vries's great book, *natural relations* (*see* pages 102-108), it is a work 'in memory of what has been forgotten'. The visual effect is, both optically and figuratively, of a green field, in the latter sense as if each name were a plant itself growing in the field.

le cabinet de botanique en l'honneur du docteur honnorat/the botanical cabinet in honour of doctor honnorat 2000
musée gassendi, digne-les-bains, france

It is not surprising that Honnorat the philologist would know and show an interest in the local plant names, for he was a tireless collector of the plants themselves, creating as comprehensive an herbarium of regional species as has ever existed. His herbarium is thought to have contained thousands of specimens. Many of these were collected in the heavily wooded mountainous area of Faillefeu, in the hills above the upper valley of the river Bléone, and he presented a special two-volume herbarium to the landowner of the area who had facilitated his botanising there. This was a stroke of good fortune, for Honnorat's entire collections of geological and botanical specimens were thrown away, unwanted and unsaleable, when his son, who worked in textiles in Flanders, came, after his father's death, to clear out the doctor's house in Digne. These two beautiful volumes of c.1804, almost all that remains of Honnorat's botanic collections, are the centrepiece of the *cabinet*, occupying a glass case in the middle of the room, with each week a new page turned.

At de vries's request, the floor of the narrow oblong room is made of local early nineteenth-century tiles, discovered recently when repairs were undertaken in the museum, and the walls are panelled to dado height with walnut, the wood used locally over centuries in the manufacture of vernacular furniture. Above this, on the two longer walls, there are arranged 111 of de vries's own botanical 'real works' of various dimensions, framed in walnut, and in free configurations that deliberately deny the paradigmatic ordering of nineteenth-century museum presentations. This informal array is of specimens collected by herman and susanne in the woods and valleys of Faillefeu, with Honnorat in mind. They are plant self-portraits, each plant 'saying itself', each at once a document, and an image, of itself: nature has become art, and their irregular configuration signals their status as distinct from that of the scientifically systematic herbarium of which the two volumes in the room were a part.

The installation is perfectly completed by a contemporary portrait of Dr. Honnorat brought into the light after long exile in the museum storerooms. He is pictured, gravely handsome, seated at his work table, quill pen in hand, working on the introduction to his *Dictionnaire Provençal-Français*. Behind him on a shelf, as attributes, are piled three stout volumes: Linnaeus,

Portrait of Simon-Jude Honnorat (1783-1852)
by Jean François Hyacinthe Jules Laure
oil on canvas, 1828

Two pages from Honnorat's *Herbarium*, c.1804, of which the two surviving volumes are displayed at the Musée Gassendi, Digne-les-Bains.

Hippocrates and Jean de La Fontaine. Each is emblematic of some aspect of the doctor's activities, the scientific, the medical and the literary-folkloric. It is a portrait of a many-sided man. The ensemble, thus completed, implicitly celebrates not only the natural history of the region, but also the language of the *pays*, and the tragically lost achievement of Honnorat himself. In the *cabinet*, de vries reminds us of the inescapable nexus of historical, cultural and linguistic circumstance, and of their diverse and particular interactions in the mediations of nature through science and art. In honouring Dr Honnorat, de vries, as an artist, honours the engagement of disinterested science with the natural world and its objects.

At his exhibition at the CAIRN gallery in Digne in May, 2001, de vries also presented the *journal de digne* (2001), comprising forty-five individual pieces, identically framed and displayed in a grid formation, of diverse materials collected on the visits to the area in November 1999 and May 2000. The entries in the *journal* are wonderfully rich and various: two text works which record, respectively, local place and field names and the names of *ravins* (narrow valleys through which streams flow) from the region of the Réserve Géologique; a triple photograph of the flowing water of the Bléone, its frames taken at three-second intervals; plants, leaves, lichens; rabbit droppings, snail shells; found objects – fragmented *artefacts* – and shards of pottery and tiles found at Vieil Esclangon and other sites of human settlement; earth samples from the region; and a final, valedictory entry of grey ashes. The landscape, its rivers and ravines, its mountains and passes, its roads and settlements; traces of all the aspects of nature, mineral, vegetal, animal, including those of human presence (and transience), are given their due acknowledgement in this gathering of evidences, this song book of the earth of Haute Provence.

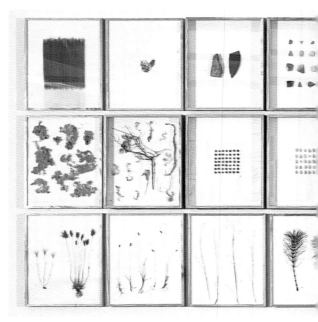

This page, top:
les choses mêmes/the things themselves 2001
exhibition at the CAIRN gallery, Digne-les-Bains,

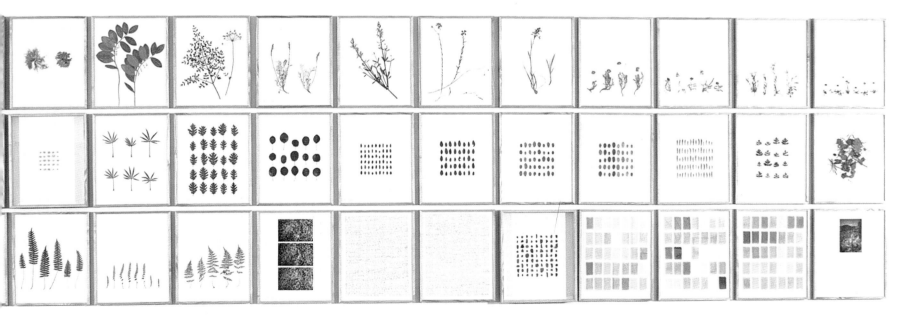

Haute-Provence, including *les terres d'autour de digne* − twenty-eight earth rubbings from around Digne, 2001, each 70 x 50 cm,

marnes noires (floor installation) and plants collected by de vries for *le cabinet de botanique en l'honneur du docteur honnorat.*

Above: marnes noires in the valley of the river Bès.

Below: *le journal de digne* 2000

119

Extract from *le journal de digne*, 2000 – 18 of 45 frames, each 35 x 25 cm.

polypodium vulgare, roche-rousse 4.11.99

ravins/ravines 2000

laserpitium gallicum, saint-benoît 27.5.00

polygonatum officinalis, saint-jean 22.5.00

stipa pennata, la robine-sur-galabre 21.05.00

les terres/earths 2000

120

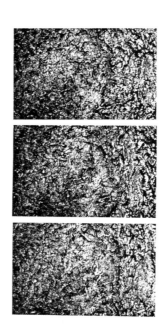

linum campanulatum, les dourbes, saint-benoît
28.05.00

cendres/ashes 2000

artefact: barrême la tuillière 3.11.99

astragalus monspessulanus, haute vallée du galabre
21.5.00

eaux de bléone/bléone waters 2000
photographs taken at three-second intervals

helleborus foetidus, la tuillière 9.11.99

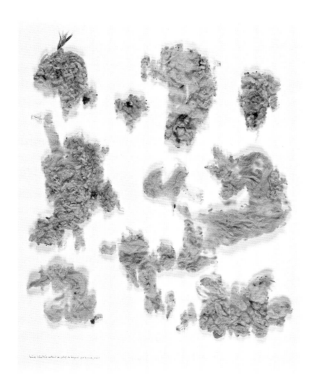

laines de beynes/wool from beynes 2000
collected by emma passamar

crataegus oxyacanthe, barrême la tuillière 26.5.00

lieux/places 2000

quercus pubescens, les dourbes 29.5.00

quercus ilex 26.5.00

cotinus coggyria, saint-lyons 3.11.99

The earth itself provided the material of two other major pieces in the 2001 *exposition*. The first was a huge grey-black carpet of *marnes noires*, a characteristic soil appearing in the valleys of the Bès and the Bléone, limestone earth with an admixture of at least 40% marl, its darkness of colour determined by the quantities of the latter. This brought the earth itself and its rich mineral smell into the museum, creating an image of primal chaos emanating the dark radiance of potentiality. It was particularly appropriate in an exhibition created out of a collaboration with a major geological reserve that its centrepiece should be a presentation of earth itself: 'the thing itself', transformed into art merely by the act of its selection, re-location and temporary configuration. Its work done, effected by its grandly elemental physical presence, it would be returned to the land to which it belongs.

Rubbings of *marnes noires*, of various gradations of tone, also featured in the great wall array in the same room of *les terres d'autour de Digne/earths from around Digne* (2001), together with samples of the pale whites and greys of *marnes blanches*, in which the limestone soil contains mixtures of gypsum, and of other brown, yellow and gold earths. In a note for the publication, which recalls his remarks concerning Dürer's *Das Grosse Rasenstück*, de vries invokes the memory of the greatest artist of the Provençal landscape: 'cézanne painted his impressions of the landscape. i have collected the earth of the countryside. their colours are more real than those of the paintings, they are the true colours.' An array of twenty-eight of these earth rubbings is now held permanently in the museum: an 'earthscape' homage to their region, a documentation of an ever-present reality, which surprises the local people into realising the vibrancy and variety of the 'true colours' of the earth beneath their feet.

2. a walk in the sacred wood: a sanctuary, a well, a place to stand

'...but a stone is something and not nothing, and so is a fly, and so is everything else.' (Pierre Gassendi)

de vries made his second visit to Digne in November 1999, and began to collect plants for the projected *cabinet* for Honnorat. He had determined from his first visit that as part of his commission from CAIRN he would create a *sanctuaire* in the Réserve Géologique (the sanctuarium was commissioned by the French Republic through the Ministry of Culture and curated by CAIRN). On this visit he began to prospect sites to the north of the town in the wooded mountains above where the river Bès runs fast through a spectacular narrow valley, and found what he was looking for at Roche-Rousse. Here, high above the valley road, were the remains of a ruined farming hamlet that took its name from the distinctive reddening of the limestone rock faces in the locality.

Here in times past men had lived and worked; now the place is deserted, and nature has reclaimed its ground. 'all changes. change brings chance. change, *c'est la vie*. without change, no chance. nature gives and takes.' For a while in the last century (the area was acquired by the nation in 1904), the foresters had used what remained of the limestone buildings built into an overhanging rock for shelter and for protection from the wind. The site perfectly suited de vries's purposes, for its present loneliness and desuetude were a poignant reminder of the vanity of human wishes, of the truth that 'all things shall pass', and that human purposes and their necessary habitation find their place as natural within the natural cycle. Roche-Rousse, having this history, spoke eloquently for de vries of contingency and eternal return, ideas that connected his work there to the heart of the Buddhist and Vedic philosophies that had nurtured his own thought.

The *sanctuaire* at Roche-Rousse was the third *sanctuarium* that de vries had made. The first (1993) is situated on a grassy knoll of unused ground at a busy road junction in Stuttgart, the rich city of Mercedes and the motor car, and consists of a circular enclosure of pointed steel stakes, each resembling a Roman spear with a gold spearhead. In this protected space the ground is safe from the city maintenance department whose task it is to tidy up and destroy 'weeds'. Such plants and wild flowers as will colonise the little sanctuary will be left in peace, such trees as will seed themselves there will grow to the height that natural circumstances will determine. What happens in this untouchable little domain is visible to all who cross the road and care to look; to those speeding by it will be as insignificant as any other piece of waste ground glimpsed from a car window. It is a tiny nature sanctuary, an exemplary demarcation and protection of what de vries calls *terrain vague*.

In a 1999 text with that title, de vries has summarised one important aspect of the philosophy that underlies his concept of the *sanctuarium*; a sanctuary not for humans to escape to but within which nature itself, untroubled by human intervention might renew itself, and in doing so – visibly – present the reality and the image of its cycles and successions. The text presents a vision of the modern city that is continuous in certain respects with that of the mechanised farmland of Eschenau and the deserted hamlet of Roche-Rousse:

Opposite, above and below:
le sanctuaire de la nature de roche-rousse
digne-les-bains, haute-provence, france
inaugurated october 2003

sanctuarium 1993
stuttgart, germany
diameter 11 metres, height 2.85 metres
photographed 2003

to many, *terrain vague* means uncultivated/wasteland, empty lot, fallow, disorder, which must be done away with quickly, but the *terrain vague* shows the viewer who can see, who wants to see, something else: it is a niche, which nature swallows in its own way with a succession of life forms. i always admire the wonderful world revealed on unsupervised property at the edge of the city or between buildings. first come the so-called weeds, pioneers that revitalise the land destroyed by humans, which make the land inhabitable for many living creatures. the process lasts for years, and if nobody interferes, after a period of successive plant communities, the area would become a forest: forest – the most complicated living community that once almost completely covered our earth.

a park: a culturally impoverished nature: imagine the possible, enriching experiences that might exist if nature were allowed to develop freely here. one aspect of my utopia. 'the wild park' and *terrains vagues* everywhere, too, protected from destruction; park services are limited to removing the coca-cola and beer bottles that have been thrown away. wild boars plough up the park ground. the beauty of blossoming thistles ... new life would grow on left-over rubble, blackbirds and nightingales sing evenings and mornings, butterflies and wild bees are there, we hear frogs and toads croaking from the damp ruins of cellars. *freedom* has returned. the scent of flowering elderberry bushes penetrates houses through open windows, inviting us to realism: the television is tuned off, superfluous.

terrain vague is the future of cities; new worlds of experience, which guide our consciousness to a different order, away from the chaos of planning. the *terrains vagues* are the *avant-garde* of nature.

de vries's second *sanctuarium*, built for the second decennial Skulptur Projekte in Münster, in northern Germany, in 1997, is a perfectly circular brick wall with no entrance to the inner sanctum, which is visible through four oval oculi, piercing the wall at eye-level at the cardinal points, the directions of the winds. Writing in the catalogue for the Projekte of this work de vries emphasised the specifically spiritual dimension crucial to the concept of the *sanctuarium*: '[the word] comes from the latin *sanctus*: "sacred, holy, venerable", "inviolable, untouchable, exalted"...; *sancio*: "to sanctify, i.e. to make inviolable through religious consecration...' The ground in the *sanctuarium* is not, then, merely protected against human interference, a haven for nature itself (as in the English term 'wild-life sanctuary'), but a holy ground, a place to be revered.

This re-introduction of an idea of natural sanctity and reverence for all kinds of life, utterly free of all convention or dogma, is central to de vries's whole artistic and philosophical project. Its sources may be found in all human cultures, and it finds secular expression in quotations de vries makes from Wittgenstein: 'what is mystical is not how the world is, but that it is'. (*Tractatus*, Proposition 6.44) 'the unspeakable does exist, it shows itself, it is the mystical'. (Proposition 6.522) The wall, being perfectly circular, is without beginning, without end, an image of everything and of nothing. Inscribed in gold in the sandstone crown above each of the oculi is a Sanskrit text from the Isá-Upanishad: 'this is perfect, that is perfect, perfect comes from perfect, take perfect from perfect, what remains is perfect.' On looking into the interior of the *sanctuarium* de vries suggests that the viewer contemplates another text: 'physics and metaphysics are one.'

The *sanctuaire* at Roche-Rousse encloses with gold-tipped pointed railings the crumbling ruins of the farm, at one point passing through an original masonry wall, preventing any further access to them, allowing them time to complete their ruin without human intervention, and protecting the plants that will grow without disturbance within the palisade. What distinguishes this *sanctuarium* from other works in this genre (if that term may be considered appropriate) is the richness and complexity of its natural, historical and artistic context. For it constitutes the central thematic statement within the total *ensemble* of works and actions centred on Digne, a body of work that has a complex intellectual, spiritual and aesthetic co-herence. It might be seen as providing material for what Joseph Beuys called 'social sculpture', by which he meant the structured thought, discussion and actions in everyday life of political and cultural ideas embodied in art objects and actions. 'Sculptures', wrote Beuys, 'are not an end product themselves but focal points around which ideas are built and transmitted.'

'Social sculpture' clearly relates to those earlier modernist efforts to extend art into life and to collapse the distinction between them. What de vries has created at Digne is, in this view, a continuous work that contains many disparate components, with a structural – i.e. sculptural – unity of purpose. Among a multiplicity of mental and sensational aspects, its components

sanctuarium 1997
münster, germany

Circular brick wall, 3 metres high and 0.4 metres thick; diameter 14 metres; sandstone coping engraved with Sanskrit text coated with gold leaf.

'by 2001, 32 plant species had been recorded within the enclosure, including *acer campestre*, *aesculus hippocastanum*, *corylus avellana*, *rosa sp.*' hdv

Iron railings topped with gold leaf – detail of *le sanctuaire de la nature de roche-rousse*.

Above right:
sanctuarium 2001
buitendijks, zeewolde, the netherlands

'earth wall 2.80 metres high planted with *rosa canina*, intended to grow to a thick covering. the opening in the west side of the wall is filled with gold-tipped railings.' hdv

include the steep walking necessary to reach the sacred wood around Roche-Rousse and the ruined village of Vieil Esclangon, contemplation of the physical and intellectual legacy of Dr Honnorat, the complex encounter with the 'real works' in the museum, and meditation and reverie in the landscape. The individual physical constituents of the ensemble maintain their separate identities within this unity: each plays a part in the general programme of intellectual proposition, affective provocation and spiritual consciousness-raising. Such a work, moreover, assimilates into its capacious form elements of critical discourse. This essay on de vries's work at Digne is a critical and descriptive component of the 'sculpture', as is *les choses mêmes/the things themselves*), the publication that de vries conceived for his exposition at Digne in 2001. For the work comprehends the subjective responses of its viewers, the conversation and writings it generates, and the statements of its progenitor.

de vries has declared the forest woodland around the sanctuary *le bois sacré* (the sacred wood) – and its boundary is marked on each of the five pathway approaches to the site itself by steel stakes sharpened like spears, with gold tips. Each of these emblems of protection has inscribed on its shaft the word *silence*. As the visitor approaches the sanctuary, they induce a sense of ceremony, occasion and solemnity appropriate to the place and its meditative purpose. In an essay for *les choses mêmes*, de vries writes of the idea and history of the sacred wood: in ancient times, and still in certain parts of the world, humankind inhabited and was nurtured by the living forest, the 'final stage of all vegetal evolution, of all successions of growth'. Allowed to maintain its natural equilibrium, the forest would last for thousands of years: 'the forest furnished men with all they needed – fruit, wild game, honey, medicinal plants, materials for construction etc. it provided also psychedelic plants which gave man access to a more profound [spiritual] knowledge, leading to the condition of ecstasy ... the title "sacred" ensured, in many lands, a guarantee of respect for nature.'

le sanctuaire de la nature de roche-rousse was inaugurated in October 2003, at a ceremony in the heart of *le bois sacré* to which de vries, unable at the time to make the climb, was airlifted by helicopter. In attendance were Nadine Gomez-Passamar and the CAIRN staff, local people, and one of the two hermits who live and study in solitude at a ruin nearby, close to the deserted village of Nicolas. The valleys echoed to the ringing sound of a conch blown by the artist in celebration of the dedication, and he read an address in French:

> silence gives us the opportunity to experience a new kind of sensibility, it gives us another, better, opportunity for contemplation: experience itself. language is a formidable resource, but it creates *divisions* in the unity of our existence: between you and me, between here and there, between man and tree, between tree and forest. In silence division disappears, solitude gives us the chance to experience unity ... union ... yoga (from the the word *yuj, to unite*) ... the sacredness of nature,

Two of the five pathway entrances to *le bois sacré/the sacred wood* at Roche-Rousse.

here and everywhere (but always here) gives us a chance to know this unity, because the idea of sacredness offers us a way to a change in our attitude – and chance and change always go together. in the nature sanctuary of roche-rousse there is a ruined house. inside it are a rose tree, a bush, plants, a tree, lizards, birds passing through, butterflies... here people lived, ate, worked, loved (i hope) and departed. now nature has reclaimed this space, and we see how we are part of this process, of the sacredness we can rediscover here here here here.

In modern western societies this sacramental mystery of the forest, or of natural objects in general, is something largely lost: the very idea of the sacredness of nature seems forgotten; we live in a time and in places 'where nothing is sacred'. But on his travels, especially in Nepal in 1989, de vries visited and documented sacred woods and holy trees still venerated by Hindus and Buddhists, and in his essay he relates these to historical examples in Europe, to contemporary Amerindian beliefs and rituals in the Amazon forests, and to the beliefs of the ancient Greeks and Romans. He quotes Pliny's *Natural History*: 'for us, the shining statues of gold and ivory inspire us to veneration less than the sacred groves and the silence that belongs to them.'

Writing of the Christian repudiation of such pagan sacredness, de vries cites as their sanction that most influential of texts, verse 28 of the first chapter of Genesis: 'And God said, be fruitful and multiply, and replenish the earth, and subdue it; and have dominion over the fish of the sea, and over the fowl of the air, and over every living thing that moveth upon the earth...' In Düsseldorf, on the green by the river, close to the Kunstakademie (art school) where Joseph Beuys had taught until he was dismissed in 1972, de vries encircled a young oak tree with a protective fence of gold-tipped lances, inscribed in gold letters: *wynfrith me caesit – herman me recreavit* (*wynfrith felled me – herman recreated me*). This living monument recalls the zealous destruction of many ancient sacred oaks by Wynfrith (St Boniface), the early Christian missionary to the Low Countries and Germany, and commemorates de vries's re-dedication of the holy oak, traditionally in pagan Europe the most sacred of trees. His Düsseldorf oak thus takes its place thematically with Beuys's great project of the 1980s, *7 Thousand Oaks*, which sought to encourage the replanting of oaks and their re-dedication within modern culture as living symbols of a re-sanctified natural creativity.

wynfrith me caesit – herman me recreavit/ wynfrith felled me – herman recreated me 2002
reuterkaserne, düsseldorf, germany

To reach the sanctuary at the old settlement of Roche-Rousse high up above the Bès requires a rugged and demanding walk up through the woods from the road, a discipline that is itself preparatory to the meditation appropriate to the *sanctuarium*. Not far from the sanctuary on a boulder close by the path de vries has set a simple carved inscription in gold: *ambulo ergo sum*. By this point on the steep pathway to Roche-Rousse, the sense of self as embedded in the physical experience of the body may well be especially acute, and serve to confirm the truth of the observation at its simplest level. But of course the proposition will be recognised immediately as a contrary riposte to the most famous dictum of René Descartes. 'I walk therefore I am' is often attributed to the scientist and philosopher, Pierre Gassendi, who was born in the tiny hamlet of La Grau near Digne in 1592. In fact the statement occurs as a provocative and sarcastic reduction by Descartes himself of Gassendi's *Objection* to the 'Cogito' principal in the *Objections and Replies* appended to *Meditations on First Philosophy*, first published by Descartes in 1641.

Gassendi had countered the 'cogito ergo sum' argument (I think therefore I am), as re-stated in the *Second Meditation*, by first paraphrasing Descartes's own formulation: 'I am, I exist, is true each time you pronounce it, or that you mentally conceive it.' He continues: 'But I don't see that you needed all this mechanism, when you had other grounds for being sure, and it was true, that you existed. You might have inferred that from any other activity, since our natural light informs us that whatever acts also exists.' This down-to-earth response to Descartes's agonistic mentalism was powerfully and dismissively repudiated in Descartes's reply: 'When you say I could have inferred the same conclusion from any of my other actions, you wander far from the truth, because there is none of my activities of which I am wholly certain (in the sense of having metaphysical certitude, which alone is here involved), save thinking alone. For example you have no right to make the inference: I walk therefore I am, except insofar as our awareness of walking is a thought [...] from the fact that I think that I walk I can very well infer the existence of the mind that so thinks, but not that of the body which walks. So it is in all other cases.'

Opposite
ambulo ergo sum – 'i walk therefore i am' 2000
sanctuaire de la nature de roche-rousse
réserve géologique de haute-provence

Against the mechanistic dualism of Descartes, Gassendi adduces the truth of an empirical 'common sense', the experience of everyday actuality. The sharp edge of Gassendi's objections and the sometimes acerbic brusqueness of Descartes's responses to them are indicative of a gulf between two thinkers whose approaches to reality are fundamentally at odds. (In his *Objection*, Gassendi addresses the great philosopher playfully as 'O Mind'; in his *Reply*, Descartes sarcastically responds to his antagonist as 'O Flesh'.) Descartes is the supreme advocate of the deductive, the natural philosopher of absolute doubt, bent on the rigorous testing of knowledge by the reduction of enquiry to first principles. Gassendi is committed to the assiduous gathering of facts and their investigation by inductive observation, sceptically arranging them to create an undogmatic picture of how the world might be. (The exchange ended their friendship for many years.)

La Grau, near Digne, where Pierre Gassendi was born in 1592.

It delighted de vries to discover that so sympathetic a figure as Gassendi should have close connections with Digne and have been born within the area of the Réserve Géologique. (Indeed, Gassendi has his own room in the museum at Digne.) For the significance of the great Provençal philosopher-scientist is not the immediate cogency or otherwise of his *Objections* to the *Second Meditation* but his humane scepticism and his passion for nature. A vastly and variously learned European intellectual, Gassendi always returned to his beloved native valley after his many academic sojourns in Flanders, Paris and elsewhere in France. He stands for a feet-on-the-ground materialism, and an insistence on *being* as corporeal, for a conception of phenomenal nature as experienced through subjective engagement and empirical observation rather than as apprehended *a priori*, its reality validated through logic.

There is a deeper point to de vries's lapidary inscription of *ambulo ergo sum* in the middle of the sacred wood. Descartes's 'cogito ergo sum', and the dualism it predicates, in which mind and body are conceived as separate, and the mind placed in ascendance over the body and all other material creation, is the clarion call of the Enlightenment. Its original formulation in Part 4 of *Discourse on the Method* is followed by its elaboration in the final two sections. Descartes demonstrates that birds and beasts (and, by extension, butterflies and other insects, not to mention plants) are but natural automatons without mind or soul, and asserts the dominion of man over all animal, vegetable and mineral creation, which awaits its more successful exploitation by man as a consequence of new sciences and more effective technologies:

> For they [the laws of physics, in this case] caused me to see that it is possible to attain knowledge which is very useful in life, and that, instead of that speculative philosophy which is taught in the schools, we may find a practical philosophy by means of which, knowing the force and action of fire, water, air, the stars, heavens and all the other bodies that environ us, as distinctly as we know the different crafts of our artisans, we can in the same way employ them in all those uses to which they are adapted, and thus render ourselves the masters and possessors of nature... [new arts and crafts will] enable us to enjoy without any trouble the fruits of the earth and all the good things to be found there...

This language of use and employment, of mastery and possession, has not only accompanied the vast improvements in the material lot of much of humankind, but also justifies the systematic despoliation of the planet and the destruction of natural resources. It conceives of the natural world as *other*, a place to which man has come, seen and conquered: '... finally I should deal with man because he is the spectator of all.' This division opposes the objective observer of a world essentially separate from the surveying subject to the subject *being within* nature. The eye is conceived as a window between the primary reality of the mind and the secondary reality of the external world. It is precisely this image that links Cartesian dualism to the exploitative distancing of man from nature that characterises the Picturesque, with its emphasis on the processes of composing 'the prospect'.

Descartes's use of the term 'environ' is also significant, for it anticipates the widespread use of the term 'environmentalism' to describe that type of conservation that, for all its well-meaning intentions, and its many small political victories, nevertheless perpetuates a spectatorial view of the world that separates the humans who are at its centre from those phenomena in the animal, vegetable and mineral kingdoms that surround them, and persists in a division of the world as given into designated territories, with regions for development that allow for the preservation of marginal 'wilderness'. By appropriating 'ambulo ergo sum', de vries affirms the subjectivism of what has come to be termed 'deep ecology' in which the phenomenological has precedence over the analytical-mental. The seeing of the walker is 'the seeing of his being', he is part of the natural environment, not the master of all he surveys.

High on a green alp across the narrow valley from Roche-Rousse are the ruins of the deserted village of Vieil Esclangon, once a small, remote farming hamlet, now reduced to nothing more than an uneven turf clearing with a scatter of crumbling limestone masonry and broken terra-cotta tiles. The countryside hereabouts was depopulated in the last years of the nineteenth century and the first decades of the twentieth, as young men left behind the harshness and poverty of mountain life to find less arduous and better paid work in the expanding cities of Nice and Marseilles, or were called away to die on the flat northern battlefields of Flanders. 'but life [at vieil esclangon] continued in another way,' de vries has written in a note on his work at Digne. 'shrubs, trees, weeds have taken over, birds are singing, butterflies fly everywhere, and only the remains of walls, a rare fruit tree and the fountain remember the lives of the people in this place. at the bottom of the fountain cistern are now written some words in gold that you can read through the water that flows through it: *siáu dins tot çõ que viu* – 'i am in all that is living.'

The text chosen by de vries to be thus inscribed, in typeface Futura, in the native language of Haute-Provence, speaks of the elemental importance of the water that makes life possible

and flows through all living things. The modest cistern itself, sheltered by the most substantial ruin, that of the village wash house, is fed by the spring that once supplied the village, newly-tapped and connected by a simple copper pipe. Here, to complement the sacred wood on the mountainside opposite, de vries has in effect created a holy well: two ancient traditions revivified. Water is an ancient symbol for life itself, for renewal and refreshment. On the lip of the cistern is a cup, and those who climb the steep wooded gully from the road are rewarded by a grassy meadow, high skies, a mountain panorama of astounding beauty, and a draught of cold fresh water. For de vries, the ruins of the ancient village, now reclaimed by nature, the landscape once marred and scarred by usage now healed and covered with green vegetation, are traces and signs of a recurring natural process that assimilates man to its cyclic pattern.

The non-assertive presence of being within the landscape is something de vries continues to celebrate in works commissioned by CAIRN in the country around Digne. His most recent ones – *traces* – are interventions of the most tactful kind, consisting of small texts and signs 'engraved in gold in rocks and stones, indicating a philosophy that is related to the natural process but so modest that you can easily overlook them: they should have no impact on the landscape and nature that is of such great beauty that art can easily be a disturbance. further, there have been places in the region that have been sacred forests in ancient times, places of a human relationship that i think worth indicating and recalling.' The inscription of these subtle and inobtrusive texts and signs, most of which have recurred over the years in de vries's statements and writings, in the *journals* and in many of the publications of the eschenau summer press and temporary travelling press, is thus an act of homage at once to nature and to the culture of human interaction with the natural world over the millenia.

Recently de vries has created *traces* of the same kind in the woods and quarries around Eschenau, thus making an invisible bond between the spirit of his home landscape and that of the other landscape of his heart, in Haute Provence. In the sacred woods, and the ruins, rocks and quarries in either place, the observant walker may chance upon *ambulo ergo sum*, or the Sanskrit saying that adorns the capping of the circular *sanctuarium* at Münster. On rock faces in both the Steigerwald and the Réserve Géologique de vries has placed the mysterious

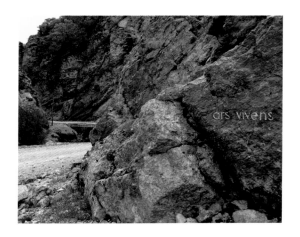

traces 2005
ars vivens – 'living art'
a quotation from Giordano Bruno (1548-1600)
clues de feissal, réserve géologique de haute-provence

traces 2005
ambulo ergo sum – 'i walk therefore i am'
steigerwald, northern bavaria

gnomic Latin inscription discovered at various locations across the Roman empire, including Herculaneum and Pompeii, and sometimes referred to as the satorquadrat. It can be read left to right, right to left, top to bottom and bottom to top and may be interpreted to mean (by the implication of its palindromic form) 'what goes round comes round'. de vries's own reading is 'the sower (or originator)/no work/keeps/the work/going round', working from his assumption that the cryptic 'arepo' is merely 'opera' rendered backwards and thus signifies 'no-work' – analogous to the Tao principle of *wu-wei* (non-action) or the the Zen *mushin* (no thought).

Elsewhere there may be found the sign for infinity, the ourobouros (the circular symbol of a snake eating its own tail), the Hindu sign for *om*, and other characteristic de vries texts and quotations: *chance and change*; *to be to be*; *veritas existentiae* ('the truth of existence' – a quotation from Gassendi); *natura numquam errat* ('nature never makes a mistake' – a quotation from the Italian philosopher, Giordano Bruno, 1548-1600); *ars vivens* ('the art of living'); *was wieso vonwo wohin* in the Steigerwald, and *quoi pourquoi d'où vers où* in the Réserve Géologique ('what why whence whither').

In certain places in the Réserve Géologique, and in the forests of Faillefeu and the Steigerwald, de vries has placed on stones and rocks, or on the masonry of certain buildings, a small engraved dot of gold. Each of these constitutes a virtually invisible point on the surface of the earth, its positioning random or, rather, intuitively arbitrary, having no topographical or historical significance beyond its presence as a marker of de vries's respect and love for the terrain. Gold, which is the crucial constituent of the *traces* made around Digne and Eschenau, is used for its

Above:
traces 2005
sator arepo tenet opera rotas
vieil esclangon, réserve géologique de haute-provence

Opposite, below, and this page:
traces 2005
quoi pourquoi d'où vers où – 'what why
whence whither'
les portes d'entrages, réserve géologique de
haute-provence

intrinsic beauty as a pure mineral element, for its ancient sacramental significance, and as a reminder of its usage as an index of value in its broadest sense in the cultores of both East and West. Each gold dot might also be seen as making an axis point at the junction of the sacred six dimensions by which the Hopi Indians defined a human being's presence on the earth – the four directions of the wind, down into the earth, up into the sky – an idea that has haunted de vries since childhood. 'everything, everything represents the continuum,' he wrote in a sketch-book in 1990, 'in which we ourselves are a point – a continuum point, the continuum itself.'

The small gold points are quite specifically related by de vries to Proposition 2.0131 in *Tractatus*: 'A spatial object must lie in infinite space. (A point in space is an argument place.)' In this, however, they represent not arguments of the kind propounded by men in favour of their mastery and possession of the finite and measurable earth, but rather the material actuality of space itself, and its infinite reach in every dimension, including that of the imagination. They are not of the nature of the professional surveyor's point of distance, the mark made to demarcate a territorial boundary, or the limit of a measuring chain, but speak in gold of the earth's own claim to be heard and respected. Encountered in their settings, embedded in the material, surrounded by grass and trees, open to the sky, and near the flow of water, these points in infinite space invite reverie, contemplation or meditation. Such a point might be anywhere or nowhere; seen or unseen, its 'argument' is a note in a song of the earth that has no beginning and no end.

In a publication celebrating the reopening of the Musée Gassendi and the CAIRN project at Digne and in the Réserve Géologique, de vries wrote of his deep connection to the area in which he has made some of his finest work: 'i love this country, the valley of the bès, the sound of streaming water in the many deep ravines, the empty bed of the bléone that can be roaring when the stream swells and the stones are rolled by the power of so much water, flowers blooming in spring, the forests with their dense underbrush, the smell of vegetation, thyme everywhere, the sight of a white mountain, a country road that is still unmetalled, the thrilling possibility of meeting a wolf... digne became quickly part of my life, it settled itself in my heart for it is real poetry that i found here as almost nowhere else.'

traces 2005
Top left: sanskrit text – 'this is perfect, that is perfect, perfect comes from perfect, take perfect from perfect and perfect remains'; top centre: *es war einmal* – 'once upon a time'; right: *veritas existentiae* – 'the truth of existence'; below: *natura numquam*

errat – 'nature never makes a mistake'
steigerwald, northern bavaria

Overleaf: *traces: point of view* 2005
clues de feissal, réserve géologique de haute-
provence

notes and references

herman de vries has written and published in Dutch, English, German and French; most texts exist, sometimes in slightly varying forms, in more than one of these languages. This can make for difficulties of citation. For bibliographies see *to be: texte – textarbeiten – textbilder* (Cantz, Stuttgart 1995) and *herman de vries* (The Netherlands Foundation for Fine Arts, Design and Architecture, Amsterdam 1998). The definitive source for information on works published by de vries himself, including those of the eschenau summer press and the temporary travelling press, is the recently published *herman de vries les livres et les publications*, the catalogue raisonnée of books and publications, with texts (in French, German and English) by de vries, anne mœglin-delcroix and didier mathieu (centre des livres d'artistes, saint-yrieix-la-perche 2005).

Prologue

Quotations from Ludwig Wittgenstein's *Tractatus Logico-Philosophicus* throughout this book are from the original translation into English (Routledge and Kegan Paul, London 1922).

p.8 'Say it, no ideas but in things' first occurred in William Carlos Williams's early poem 'Paterson' (1927) and reappeared in the first part of his classic long poem *Paterson* (1946-51).

p.9 For a discussion of the work of Buisman, Derges, Drury *et al* see 'Listening to the Music', my introductory essay to *Song of the Earth: European Artists and the Landscape* (Thames and Hudson, London 2003, and, titled *Artists Land Nature,* Harry N. Abrams, New York 2003).

p.11 'my poetry is the world' was written by de vries in 1972 'on a walk in our vast forests'. See *to be* (Cantz, Stuttgart 1995), a collection of texts in German, Dutch and English.

'when I said "nature is art"...': in *herman de vries*, published by The Netherlands Foundation for Fine Arts on the occasion of the award to de vries of the Oeuvreprijs (hereinafter referred to as *Oeuvreprijs*) p.55.

'the world we live in is a revelation...' (1992): see *to be* p.156.

p.12 'physics and metaphysics are one' (1994-95): for both German and English text, see *Oeuvreprijs* p. 55.

Scientist into Artist

1 the young naturalist

p.14 Mark Doty's poem is from *Source* (Jonathan Cape, London 2002).

The epigraph and the later quotations from William Wordsworth in this section are from 'Expostulation and Reply' and 'The Tables Turned: An Evening Scene on the Same Subject' first published in *Lyrical Ballads* 1798.

p.14 'when i was about four years old......': from the German in *aus der wirklichkeit* (Stadthaus Ulm, 1998) p.103.

p.15 William Blake's 'The Schoolboy' is from *Songs of Innocence and Experience*: 'But to go to school in a summer morn, / O! it drives all joy away; / Under a cruel

eye outworn, / The little ones spend the day / In sighing and dismay.'

'as a child i had a deep mystic feeling for nature...': from *to be* p.159.

'this is what language does...'; 'ever since i was a little boy...': from *herman de vries*, exhibition publication, Royal Botanic Garden, Edinburgh (1992).

p.16 remember gustav theodor fechner eschenau summer press and temporary travelling press publication 33 (Eschenau 1992) *see* Wordsworth, 'Lines Written in Early Spring' (1898): 'Through primrose tufts, in that green bower, / The periwinkle trailed its wreaths; / And 'tis my faith that every flower / Enjoys the air it breathes.'

Theo van Doesburg's 'Art Concret' manifesto is reproduced in *The Tradition of Constructivism* ed. Stephen Bann (Thames and Hudson, London 1974), and Max Bill's 'Concrete Art' in *Theories and Documents of Contemporary Art* ed. Kristine Stiles and Peter Selz (University of California, Berkeley and Los Angeles, California 1996).

2 concrete concepts: the early work and its philosophy

p.20 Wordsworth, again from 'Expostulation and Reply' as above.

for John Keats on 'negative capability', see letter to George and Thomas Keats, December 1817.

'Be unaffected': Lao Tzu as translated in Alan Watts, *The Way of Zen* (Thames and Hudson, London 1957) p.21.

'A motion and a spirit...': Wordsworth, 'Tintern Abbey' (*Lyrical Ballads* 1798).

'what the artist sees...': de vries, note written December 23/24 1970, quoted in *Oeuvreprijs* p.31.

p.22 'the notorious urinal': Marcel Duchamp's *Fountain* (1917).

All quotations from D.T. Suzuki are from his influential study, *Zen and Japanese Culture* (Routledge and Kegan Paul, London 1950).

'In western culture, the book...': *see* de vries: 'a book is a book is a book... the form is perfect and there is not much that can be changed we can fill it with signs of our ideas or conceptions and we can empty it of all ideas and conceptions the book remains a book...' (in the catalogue to the exhibition *het boek en de kunstenaar*, Stadsgalerij, Heerlen, The Netherlands, 1988.)

p.25 Mahayana Buddhism is the subject of Chapter 3 of Alan W. Watts's *The Way of Zen* (1957).

p.26 Pierre Restany's article on Fautrier appeared in *Art International*, Vol. III/1-2 1959.

p.27 Piet Mondrian is quoted from his 1920 essay, *Natural Reality and Abstract Reality: An Essay in Trialogue Form* (George Braziller, New York 1995).

p.27 Takuan's letter is translated in Suzuki p.95.

p.29 'Infinity is rigorously monochrome...': Piero Manzoni is quoted from his 1960 essay 'Free Dimension' (first published in *Azimuth* No.2, Milan) English version in *Piero Manzoni: Paintings, reliefs and objects*, exhibition catalogue, Tate Gallery, London (1974). In the essay,

Manzoni writes of his white 'achromes': 'A white that is not a polar landscape, not a material in evolution or a beautiful material, not a sensation or a symbol or anything else: just a white surface and nothing else ... a surface that simply is: to be (to be complete and become pure).'

Yves Klein's *Le Dépassement de la problématique de l'art* was published by Editions de Montbliart (La Louvière, Belgium 1959).

3 random objectivations and other works from 1960 to 1975

p.29 random objectivations was published in an edition of 1000 by edizioni amodulo (Milanino sul Garda 1972).

p.30 The text of the *revue nul=0* 'random objectivations' is reprinted in *to be* p.29.

pp.34-35 'true philosophy is immediate actual' is reproduced in *Oeuvreprijs* p.56 and in *to be* p.91.

p.35 fragmentarische argumente can be found, in German, in *to be* p.54.

Wallace Stevens is quoted from 'Connoisseur of Chaos' in *Collected Poems* (Faber and Faber, London 1955).

chance-fields/chance-felder, an essay on the topology of randomness/chance-felder, ein essay über die topologie des zufalls was published in an edition of 1000 by edition'e in association with the Waßerman Galerie (Munich 1973).

p.37 Alfred Stieglitz's photograph of Duchamp's *Fountain* appeared in *The Blind Man No.2* in May 1917.

p.38 'The pictorial field is a structured field': from Richard Lohse's statement 'Lines of Development (1943-1972)' reprinted in *Theories and Documents of Contemporary Art* ed. Stiles and Selz (1996), as above.

At Eschenau

1 the house: life and art

p.42 Gaston Bachelard is quoted from *The Poetics of Space* (1958) trans. Maria Jolas (Beacon Press, Boston 1969).

p.43 'the dutch art scene was very close-knit...'; 'i stopped reading art reviews...': from interview with William Furlong, Eschenau, April 1999, in *Song of the Earth*.

pp.43-44 'chance & change...'; 'sitting on the train...': *to be* p. 72; published in English, May 1974, in leaflet for exhibition at Lucy Milton Gallery, London.

p.44 'abstraction has value...': *to be* p. 22 (from a notebook, 15 April, 1957).

p.45 Martin Heidegger is quoted from his essay '...Poetically Man Dwells...' in *Poetry, Language, Thought* trans. Albert Hofstadter (Harper and Row, New York 1971).

2 chance and change: the world as art

p.46 'it is not only what an artist is doing...'; 'biologists should not be afraid...': interview in *Song of the Earth*.

p.48 Plato's *Symposium* is quoted from *The Collected Dialogues* ed. Edith Hamilton and Huntington Cairns (Princeton University Press, Princeton, New Jersey 1961).

'the world we live in...': *to be* p.156.

'so i came to realise...': interview in *Song of the Earth*.

pp.48-49 The conversation with Paul Nesbitt is recorded in *herman de vries* (Edinburgh 1992).

p.49 'If we only knew...': Henry David Thoreau's observation is from the chapter of *Walden* entitled 'The Pond in Winter'.

'The universe is harmonic...': from Guy Davenport, 'The Critic as Artist', in *Every Force Evolves a Form* (North Point Press, San Francisco 1987).

Wittgenstein on Hegel and Darwin is quoted from Ray Monk's *Ludwig Wittgenstein: The Duty of Genius* (Jonathan Cape, London 1990).

'change is everywhere...': from an interview with John K. Grande in Art Nature Dialogues: Interviews with Environmental Artists (White University of New York, New York 2004).

p.50 '*Physis*, also, the arising of something...' is from Heidegger, 'The Question Concerning Technology' in *Basic Writings* trans. William Lovitt, ed. David Farrell Krell (Harper San Francisco, San Francisco 1977).

3 the eschenau journal and other real work: nature and art

p.52 Thoreau is quoted from the *Walden* chapters entitled 'Where I Lived and What I Lived For' and 'Sounds'.

p.61 'around our house...': *to be* p.156.

p.62 'to present the work... the grid is not determined... this [array of objects]': interview in *Song of the Earth*.

p.63 'naturally, [the artist] has to pick up the leaf...': from *Oeuvreprijs* p.49.

p.65 'art is not definable...': *to be* p.158.

'when i said...': *Oeuvreprijs* p.55

4 das grosse rasenstück: art and nature

p.66 'Among the earliest and most accurate...': for an account of the beginnings of botanical naturalism see 'The Rebirth of Naturalism' in William Blunt, *The Art of Botanical Illustration* (Collins, London 1950).

'but mine is more real!': from 'from white to perfect, herman de vries – the real works' by Paul Nesbitt, in *herman de vries*, catalogue to exhibition at Städtische Sammlungen, Schweinfurt, Städtische Galerie, Würzburg, galerie d+c mueller roth, Stuttgart 1993.

For an illustrated account of the use of botanical studies in Dürer's studio *see Dürer and the Virgin in the Garden* by Susan Foister (National Gallery, London 2004), published to accompany the exhibition of that title at the National Gallery, London.

p.68 Joseph Koerner's essay 'Albrecht Dürer: A Sixteenth-Century *Influenza*' is in *Albrecht Dürer and his Legacy: The Graphic Work of a Renaissance Artist* by Giulia Bartrum (British Museum Press, London 2002), published to accompany an exhibition at The British Museum.

p.72 Wallace Stevens is quoted from 'Bouquet of Roses in Sunlight' in *Collected Poems*.

5 the meadow and the forest: nature, politics and the ecopoetic

p.72 Rainer Maria Rilke is quoted from 'The Sonnets to Orpheus (1,1) in *The Selected Poetry of Rainer Maria Rilke* trans. Stephen Mitchell (Pan Books, London 1987).

'the land [around]...': from interview in *Song of the Earth*.

'decultivation for renaturalisation': from a conversation

with the author, Spring, 2003.

p.74 'from the shortness of the moment': *to be* p.98. Title in English, text in German (translated by Jill Hollis and Mel Gooding).

p.76 'When there is poetry...': from Rilke, 'Sonnets to Orpheus' (1,5).

p.82 Hugh Honour and John Fleming are quoted from *A World History of Art* (Macmillan, London and Basingstoke 1982).

'i hate art in nature!': *to be* p.178 (German text). The text ends, 'natur *ist* kunst': 'nature *is* art.'

'The world is round...' from Gaston Bachelard from *The Poetics of Space* (1958) as above.

p.85 'went into the wood...': 'a fruitful walk' in English in *Oeuvreprijs* p.31; in Dutch and German, in *to be* p.80.

Journeys and Projects

1 'the seeings of my beings'

p.86 Leo Steinberg's essay 'The Eye is a Part of the Mind' was first published in *Partisan Review* Vol.XX no.2, and reprinted in *Reflections on Art* ed. Suzanne K. Langer (The John Hopkins Press, New York 1958).

p.90 For a description, in German, of the procedures for 'the seeings of my beings', and a sample protocol, see *to be* pp. 82-84.

p.91 Blake's couplet is from *The Marriage of Heaven and Hell* (c.1793).

p.92 for 'documents of a stream' and see *herman de vries* (Royal Botanic Garden, Edinburgh 1992).

2 from earth

p.97 Rilke's Ninth Duino Elegy is quoted from *The Selected Poetry* trans. Stephen Mitchell (London 1987).

p.99 For de vries's own description of the Buchenwald 'from earth' work at Erfurt and the 'from polish earth' see interview in *Song of the Earth*.

For Cees de Boer's essay see *herman de vries from earth – von der erde*, catalogue to exhibition at Städtische Galerie am Markt, Schwabisch Hall, Nov.1997-Jan.1998.

3 natural relations

p.102 herman de vries *natural relations eine skizze* published by Karl Ernst Osthaus Museum in Hagen in association with verlag für moderne kunst (Nuremburg 1989).

'[the] disintegration of the original nature of man'; 'the first anti-drugs movement' etc.: English quotations from *natural relations* are from *Oeuvreprijs* pp.45-47. The introduction is reprinted, in German, in *to be* pp.105-129.

p.104 *integration*, 'the journal for mind-moving plants and culture', was edited, from Eschenau, by w. bauer, m. hanslmeier, l.e. luna, j. ott (nos.4-6), and h.de vries, between 1991 and 1995. Six numbers were published (in five volumes; nos 2 & 3 being combined in one).

p.106 '*coarcervavi omne quod inveni*' is quoted by David Jones in his 'Preface to the Anathemata', in which he draws an analogy between his own creative method of 'gathering together' diverse materials and that of Nennius.

An English version of Rumphius's *The Ambonese Curiosity Cabinet*, trans. and ed. by E.M. Beekman, was published by Yale University Press (New Haven and London 1999).

p.107 'modernist writings': e.g. Joyce's *Ulysses*, Pound's *Cantos*, Jones's *The Anathemata*, Williams's *Paterson*,

Grass's *The Flounder*, Sebald's *The Rings of Saturn*, etc. re. 'no ideas but in things!': *see* in *Paterson 1*: 'of this, make it of *this*, this/ this, this, this, this...'

i am what i am – flora incorporata: *to be* p.142.

At Digne-les-Bains: A Point in Space

p.111 'digne became quickly part of my life...': from 'this is perfect that is perfect', an essay in *nouvelles curiosités/new curiosities*, publication of Musée Gassendi (Digne 2003), edited by Nadine Gomez-Passamar.

1 honouring dr. honnorat: collecting, naming and culture

p.112 'what the artist sees...': *Oeuvreprijs* p.31.

'*les choses mêmes*': *préface* by Anne Mœglin-Delcroix to *herman de vries*, published by Galerie Aline Vidal, Anthèse, France, 2000.

'this line of thought...': *to be* p.158

Wittgenstein is quoted from 'The Brown Book (II)' p.178 in *The Blue and Brown Books* and from *Philosophical Investigations* (both Blackwell, Oxford 1958).

p.123 'cézanne painted his impressions...': from *les choses mêmes*, published by Musée Gassendi, Digne, to accompany de vries's exhibition there in 2003.

2 a walk in the sacred wood: a sanctuary, a well, a place to stand

p.123 '...but a stone is something...': from Pierre Gassendi's 'Objections' to the 'Second Meditation', from René Descartes's *Meditations on First Philosophy* trans. John Cottingham (University of Cambridge Press, Cambridge 1986) Other quotations from Gassendi's 'Objections', and Descartes's 'Replies', are from this edition.

p.124 de vries's essay *terrain vague* (1999) was published in *No Art = No City! Urban Utopias in Contemporary Art*, the catalogue to an exhibition at Städtische Galerie, Bremen, 2003.

Skulptur. Projekte in Münster 1997 [Sculpture. Projects in Münster 1997] ed. Klaus Bussman, Kasper König and Florian Matzner (Munster 1997) was published to accompany the third decennial public sculpture exhibition in the city.

p.127 The address, written and read by de vries in French, is quoted from his typescript, translated by Jill Hollis.

p.130 'Sculptures are not an end product...': from *Cencrastus*, issue 80 Spring 2005, ('Joseph Beuys in Scotland'); see also Beuys's definition: 'SOCIAL SCULPTURE - how we mould and shape the world in which we live: sculpture as an evolutionary process; everyone is an artist.' Note that the old watchword – 'unity in diversity' – was adopted as a motto by Beuys.

Quotations from part 4 of *Discourse on the Method* are from *Descartes Key Philosophical Writings* trans. Elizabeth S. Haldane and G.R.T. Ross, ed. Enrique Chavez-Arviz (Wordsworth Editions, Ware, Hertfordshire 1997).

p.133 'but life [at vieil esclangon] continued...'; 'engraved in rocks and stones...': from 'this is perfect that is perfect' (nouvelles *curiosités*, 2003).

p.138 'i love this country...': from 'this is perfect that is perfect' (*nouvelles curiosités*).

index